AMERICA, AMÉRICA

AMERICA, AMÉRICA

A New History of the New World

Greg Grandin

PENGUIN PRESS NEW YORK 2025

PENGUIN PRESS
An imprint of Penguin Random House LLC
1745 Broadway, New York, NY 10019
penguinrandomhouse.com

PP colophon is a registered trademark of Penguin Random House LLC.

Illustration credits appear on page 715.

Designed by Alexis Farabaugh

LIBRARY OF CONGRESS CATALOGING-IN-PUBLICATION DATA
Names: Grandin, Greg, 1962– author.
Title: America, América : a new history of the New World / Greg Grandin.
Description: New York : Penguin Press, 2025. |
Includes bibliographical references and index.
Identifiers: LCCN 2024041617 (print) | LCCN 2024041618 (ebook) |
ISBN 9780593831250 (hardcover) | ISBN 9780593831267 (ebook)
Subjects: LCSH: America—History. | Spain—Colonies—America—History. |
Great Britain—Colonies—America—History. |
Latin America—History—Wars of Independence, 1806-1830. |
United States—History—Revolution, 1775-1783. |
United States—Relations—Latin America. |
Latin America—Relations—United States.
Classification: LCC E18 .G74 2025 (print) | LCC E18 (ebook) |
DDC 970—dc23/eng/20250122
LC record available at https://lccn.loc.gov/2024041617
LC ebook record available at https://lccn.loc.gov/2024041618

Printed in Canada
1 3 5 7 9 10 8 6 4 2

The authorized representative in the EU for product safety and compliance is
Penguin Random House Ireland, Morrison Chambers, 32 Nassau Street,
Dublin D02 YH68, Ireland. https://eu-contact.penguin.ie

For Eleanor and Manu, and for Diane, much missed

"I can see America seated on liberty's throne, wielding justice's scepter, crowned with glory, revealing to the Old World the majesty of the New."

SIMÓN BOLÍVAR, 1819

"Can we, the Republics of the New World, help the Old World to avert the catastrophe which impends? Yes, I am confident that we can. . . . We offer hope for peace and a more abundant life to the peoples of the whole world."

FRANKLIN DELANO ROOSEVELT, 1936

CONTENTS

PART VI

TOWARD A WORLD DOCTRINE

PART VII

LABORATORY OF
THE WORLD

PART VIII

THE KILLING OF
JORGE ELIÉCER GAITÁN

On the Utility of Magpies

T he traveler sat silently in Quaker meetings for hours during the day and visited brothels at night. In Philadelphia, he watched a raucous crowd welcome the arrival of George Washington, with men, women, and children as ecstatic as if "the redeemer had entered Jerusalem." General Washington, the Venezuelan Francisco de Miranda wrote in his journal, was magnificent in his bearing and grace. He embodied virtue, and focused all the New World's desires for independence into a single flame—a flame, Miranda said, that belonged to all America.[1]

Miranda, as a colonel in the Royal Spanish Army, had already fought on the side of the North American rebel colonists during the bloody siege of Pensacola. He would later go on to defend the French Revolution and lead one of Spanish America's first independence movements. Now, in the middle of 1783, he was beginning a yearlong tour of the new United States. Miranda wanted to see how the world's first modern republic fared. He spoke with tradesmen, farmers, and Revolutionary War veterans. In New York's Hudson Valley, he waxed lyrical about the sweet "grasses of the field" and mistakenly assumed the Catskills were North America's highest point. He dined in gentry estates even as he noticed much hardship amid the wealth. Many of New York's Dutch-speaking farmers couldn't afford shoes, while the well-off, men and women alike, adorned themselves with silks, perfumes, pomades, and powders. The money spent on such "vanity," he noted, would cover a year's interest on the new country's war debt. New York's politicians and preachers professed abolition, Miranda noted, yet slavery still existed in the state. "The number of Negroes is large."

In Boston, he was introduced to Phillis Wheatley, a formerly enslaved West African woman who had won her freedom and became a celebrated poet only to die penniless. Miranda cited Wheatley as proof that all humans, regardless of color or sex, were rational beings. Miranda's family in Caracas owned slaves, as did Miranda himself. They lugged around his famous library, many bundles of papers and an ever growing number of books. While in Philadelphia, he purchased the indenture of a Scottish boy who had arrived in port on a ship carrying over three hundred shackled Africans. But Miranda would soon embrace the abolitionist cause, as part of a broader belief that all the subjugated peoples of the Americas should be liberated, including Native Americans. When the New World was finally free, Miranda suggested, it might be called *Columbia*, with the English-language *u* instead of the Spanish *o* (as in Colombia), a spelling he picked up from Wheatley's ode to Washington: "Celestial choir! enthron'd in realms of light, Columbia's scenes of glorious toils I write."[2]

The Venezuelan thought both Native Americans and women were more oppressed in the new English-speaking republic than in colonial Spanish America. In the United States, the wives of revolutionary leaders were forced into a "monastic seclusion, and such submission to their husbands as I have never seen." Boston's General John Sullivan, who gained fame pacifying the British-allied Iroquois, kept "his wife and numerous children completely segregated from society and without giving the latter formal education." Miranda, his journal pages full of detailed sexual encounters, was appalled when a Shelter Island parson refused to baptize a baby conceived prior to wedlock.[3]

In New Haven, Yale's president, Ezra Stiles, gave him a tour of the university. Miranda sat in on a Hebrew lesson, which he enjoyed, and was pleased that Optics and Algebra were taught "simply and naturally." He was shocked, though, that the university offered no modern-language instruction, a bad omen for educating modern citizens, thought Miranda (who spoke English, French, and Italian, and read Greek and Latin). Nor was he impressed by Yale's library: "nothing special." He read Cotton Mather's history of New England as "curious evidence of fanaticism." And kept himself busy in Sunday New England with a pack of playing cards and flute practice, which violated strict Sabbath restrictions. No kite flying either. Stiles, in his own journal, called Miranda a "flaming son of liberty."[4]

Miranda took in the full variety of the new republic. He was welcomed everywhere he went, though he was often mistakenly introduced as a Mexican. Most men were polite but also, he thought, "unsocial," or *huraño*, that is, aloof and disinterested in the wider world.

Some of the people he met did ask questions about Spain's American empire. Others proved stubbornly ignorant. In Providence, Miranda visited the estate of Esek Hopkins, who had commanded the rebel navy during the Revolution. Miranda made mention of Mexico City and was surprised to hear Commodore Hopkins respond by saying that there was no such place. A century earlier, New England Puritans had been entranced by Mexico City, the command center of New World popery, with its wide cobbled streets, many horses, and fine carriages. Now, when Miranda tried to correct Hopkins, the Commodore refused to believe him. "Very vulgar," Miranda wrote in his journal of the encounter. He found most of the university presidents he met to be equally provincial and pedantic.

Miranda admired the United States, its dynamism, and early steam power. He liked the psalm singing of Methodists and the organ playing of Episcopalians but was taken aback at how strictly religious most people were. He thought river baptisms absurd, that they indicated a stubborn literal-mindedness. There was too much pulpit "braying" of hatred directed at Jews, Catholics, and Muslims. Miranda singled out one parson for praise, James "Redemption" Murray, who preached that there was no such thing as damnation. "Salvation was universal," Murray said, which Miranda found refreshing compared to Catholic and Protestant brimstone.

Miranda was catching the first notes of the Second Great Awakening, a religious revival movement that went in many directions. There was the harshness Miranda criticized, but also a passion for political reform, for making the United States a vital, healthy, democratic, and energetic nation.

He was repulsed by the return of Cotton-Matherism, but compelled by the energy, by the expectation, the scent of something new on the morning wind. And he shared with many of the leading figures in the Awakening the conviction that America, which for him meant all of America, was history's redeemer.[5]

One gets a sense from Miranda's diary that he hoped the new United States would overcome the problems he recorded: poverty, slavery, the subordination of women, a tendency toward antisociability, and an occasional flash of unflattering self-regard. The diary also makes clear that Miranda wasn't sure that it could.

South America will be to North America," declared the *North American Review* early in the 1800s, "what Asia and Africa are to Europe."[6]

Not quite.

Europe's liberal capitalist powers—Great Britain, France, and the Netherlands—would rule over culturally and religiously distinct peoples in Africa, Asia, and the Middle East. British travelers to India made much of the impenetrability of Hinduism, with its jumble of noises, colors, deities. "There is no dignity," said E. M. Forster after entering a temple to witness a celebration of the birth of Krishna, "no taste," in what Indians call ritual. Only chaos. Forster was overcome by India's mulligatawny metaphysics, the barrage of chants, ecstatic dancing, and indecipherable music. "I am very much muddled in my own mind about it," he wrote. Forster worked the experience into his novel *A Passage to India*, writing that nothing the worshippers did seemed "dramatically correct" to the non-Hindu observer. It was, he thought, a jumble, a "frustration of reason and form."[7]

There was no frustration, not of reason nor form, when English and Spanish Europeans, Protestants and Catholics, engaged with one another in the New World. Miranda saw the differences separating Boston and Caracas society, but they didn't muddle his mind. An indifferent Catholic, he didn't like Protestant braying. But as a Christian, he understood the theology of the brayer.

The republican insurgents who broke from Great Britain defined their system of liberties against what became known as the Black Legend, a compound of negative stereotypes that held the Catholic Spanish Empire to be especially cruel and corrupt. The Legend, though, was legible, emerging from Europe's political rivalries and religious schisms, its scientific revolutions, renaissances, and enlightenments.

When on one Sunday in 1774, future presidents George Washington and John Adams wandered into Philadelphia's new Catholic Cathedral, they appreciated the priest's sermon on the duty of parents to care for the spiritual and temporal well-being of their children. Adams, though, in a letter posted to his wife, Abigail, said that he was dismayed at the servility of the congregants, as they fingered their beads, crossed themselves with holy water, and chanted Latin incantations. A painting of "our Savior" in his "agonies," blood streaming from his wounds, appalled him. So did the Church's dominion over the senses: "Everything which can lay hold of the eye, ear, and imagination"—organ music, Latin prayers, stained glass, velvet and gold cloth covering the pulpit, the lace of priests' vestments, candles, crucifixes, and statues of the saints—combine to "bewitch the simple and ignorant." "I wonder how," he wrote to Abigail, "Luther ever broke the spell."[8]

The freethinker Adams's contempt for Catholic superstition mirrored the freethinker Miranda's for Protestant fanaticism, and later, when Adams searched for some way to describe Francisco Miranda's revolutionary enthusiasms, he reached for a satire that all literate people in the Americas, of a certain class, had read, either in its original Spanish or its many English translation editions: Miguel de Cervantes's *Don Quixote.* The Venezuelan, Adams said, was "as delirious as his immortal countryman, the ancient hero of La Mancha."[9]

There was an intimacy to such disdain, with both disdainer and disdained living in the same ideological village, sharing the same Savior, the same republican patois, reading each other's books. Adams might have thought Miranda, and other Spanish Americans of his generation, foolish. But they were not inscrutable. They were not the incomprehensibles Forster found in Krishna's temple. American insurgents, whether they spoke English or Spanish, inherited a set of common assumptions related to the dominance of Christianity and the fight against monarchism. They were mostly all republicans. Some were loosely deists, in one fashion or another, and most were Freemasons, some more anticlerical than others. And they all believed that the right to govern required the consent of the governed, even if that consent needed to be overseen by a caste of elites schooled in the virtues of civic republicanism.

The men who would topple the Spanish Empire in the Americas felt they had a kindred spirit with their English-speaking counterparts. They looked to the North American revolution for inspiration, hoping that once Spain was thrown off they might replicate its system of liberties, representative government, and equality under the law. In any case, they shared a faith in the redeeming power of the New World, that America was more an ideal than a place.

Simón Bolívar and Thomas Jefferson could at times sound as if they had fallen into a cataleptic trance as they prophesized the future. "It is impossible not to look forward to distant times," Jefferson wrote, when the United States will "cover the whole Northern, if not the Southern continent with a people speaking the same language, governed in similar forms." Bolívar imagined himself flying "across the years" to a moment when America had united the world under a system of rational laws, with the Isthmus of Panama a planetary capital, binding north and south, linking east and west. Greece and Rome had its laws and philosophies, but, really, asked Bolívar, what was "the Isthmus of Corinth compared with that of Panama?" Miranda conspired with Alexander Hamilton to liberate all South America, believing their escapades would "save the whole world, which is oscillating on the brink of an abyss."

And yet. When Jefferson and Adams used the word *America*, they were referring to the United States. When Bolívar, Miranda, and other Spanish American republicans used the word *America*, they meant *all* the Americas. "Our dear Country America, from the North to the South," Miranda wrote Hamilton.

W̱ho is an *American*? And what is *America*? These questions go back a long way. "I that am an American," affirmed Cotton Mather in the early 1700s. In 1821, the radical Catholic priest Servando Teresa de Mier—born in northern Mexico to a family that traced its lineage back centuries to the first dukes of Granada—also thought himself an *American*. Having escaped the dungeons of the Inquisition, Mier had set up a printing house in Philadelphia to publish books banned by Spain. He complained, in a letter he sent to a revolutionary compatriot, about the way English speakers used the word *America*. There were two problems, actually. The first was the constant equation of Spanish American with South America. Mier was tired of pointing out to his English-speaking acquaintances that *North* America was also *Spanish* America—that there were more Spanish speakers in Mexico (which at that point ran well into what is today the United States' Southwest) than in all South America.[10]

The second problem was that each European empire used the word *America* to refer only to their colonial or former colonial possessions. Great Britain called the United States America, Spain called its colonies America, Portugal referred to Brazil as America, France and the Dutch did the same for their Caribbean islands. It is as if, Father Mier said, "there is no other America other than the one they dominate." "A thousand errors," he said, lamenting how America was fractured by such usage. All the New World is America.

Confusion was natural. America, for Anglo settlers before their revolution, was *both* the entire New World *and* their sliver of that world—*both* their narrow dominion of a thin slip of land between the Alleghenies and the sea *and* all the land west of those mountains. In 1777, the Articles of Confederation named the new country the United States of America, but also referred to it as just America. Europeans liked to point out that the "United States" wasn't really a "proper name" but rather an adjective attached to a generic noun.

Washington Irving agreed. Irving wanted "an appellation" of his own to ensure that he wasn't confused with a Mexican who by rights could also call himself an American. He wanted a name that would identify him as "of the Anglo-Saxon race which founded this Anglo-Saxon empire in the wilderness." He suggested *Appalachian* or *Alleghanian*. The New England social activist Orestes Brownson thought such ideas rubbish. The "name of the country is America," he wrote in 1865, "that of the people is Americans.

Speak of Americans simply and nobody understands you to mean the people of Canada, Mexico, Brazil, Peru, Chile, Paraguay, but everybody understands you to mean the people of the United States."[11]

Brownson was right at least about royal Canadians, who tended not to call themselves *Americans* to distinguish themselves from their English-speaking republican neighbors. But Mexicans, Brazilians, Peruvians, Chileans, and Paraguayans all thought themselves Americans, as did the Venezuelan Francisco de Miranda. *Nosotros los Americanos*—We, the Americans—was how early Mexican nationalists called themselves. *Somos da América e queremos ser americanos*, said Brazil's republican leaders, who wanted to overthrow their monarch: We are from America and want to be Americans.[12]

Proprietary claims to *America* became politicized over time, serving as stand-ins for struggles about more substantive issues. "We've lost the right to call ourselves Americans," the Uruguayan Eduardo Galeano wrote in 1971. "Today, for the rest of the world, America means nothing but the United States. We inhabit at best a Sub-America, a second-class America of confused identity." "We are *more* American," goes a song by the Mexican *norteño* band Los Tigres de Norte "than the sons of the Anglo-Saxons." Los Tigres are a favorite of migrant and borderland workers, suggesting the matter is not just a concern of literate elites.

In 1943, the diplomatic historian Samuel Flagg Bemis struggled to decide what adjective he should use to refer to the United States, reluctantly settling on *American*. It sounds better, Bemis wrote, than "the less euphonious adjective United States." Latin Americans will occasionally refer to the United States as *América del Norte*, but generally use *Estados Unidos* and *estadounidense*, which in Spanish with all its rolling vowels is euphonious, mellifluent even.[13]

I've written this book not to fuss over names but rather to explore the New World's long history of ideological and ethical contestation. Philosophers use the phrase *immanent critique* to describe a form of dissent in which challengers don't dismiss the legitimacy of their rivals' worldview but rather accuse them of not living up to their own stated ideals. It's a useful method for considering the Western Hemisphere, for Latin America gave the United States what other empires, be they formal or informal, lacked: its own magpie, an irrepressible critic. Over the course of two centuries, when Latin American politicians, activists, intellectuals, priests, poets, and balladeers—all the many men and women who came after Miranda—judged the United States, they did so from a shared first premise: America was a redeemer continent, and its historical mission was to strengthen the ideal of human equality.

One can't fully understand the history of English-speaking North America without also understanding the history of Spanish- and Portuguese-speaking America. And by that history, I mean all of it: from the Spanish Conquest and Puritan settlement to the founding of the United States, from Indian Removal and Manifest Destiny to the taking of the West, from chattel slavery, abolition, and the Civil War to the rise of a nation of extraordinary power—from the First World War to the Second, from the Monroe Doctrine to the League of Nations and the United Nations and beyond. And the reverse is true. You can't tell the story of the South without the North.

But *America, América* is more than a history of the Western Hemisphere. It's a history of the modern world, an inquiry into how centuries of American bloodshed and diplomacy didn't just shape the political identities of the United States and Latin America but also gave rise to global governance—the liberal international order that today, many believe, is in terminal crisis.

The book starts with the Conquest. The astonishing brutality that Spain, in the first decades of the 1500s, visited on the people of the New World shocked the Catholic realm—Europe's realm—leading to a reformation *within* Catholicism, a dissent as consequential as Luther's. The Catholic Church claimed to be universal, the agent of human history and bearer of *humanitas*, all the world's wisdom. And what had that wisdom wrought? Carnage unprecedented. The slaughter, which inaugurated what scholars place among the greatest mortality events in human history, forced theologians to consider Catholic claims to universalism with new attention. Many of these clerics wound up defending Spanish rule, not so much dehumanizing America's native peoples as refusing to admit they were human at all. Those who died by the Spanish lance, or by European diseases, were of a lesser kind than those people who lived in Europe—defective, not touched by the divine, but rising from the muck and mire. Their dispossession and enslavement were allowed.[14]

Others dissented—first among them Father Bartolomé de las Casas—realizing that what had previously been called universal was but provincial, that Europe was just a farrago of fiefdoms whose princes and priests knew nothing about the fullness of the world, nothing of its hitherto undisclosed millions. The dissent of these theologians and jurists has rung down the centuries. Protestant England paid attention to the interminable Spanish debates, to the Catholic friars who insisted on the humanity of the New World's people, and wondered if they might secure their settlements, in Jamestown and Plymouth, on more defensible principles. They couldn't. They opted for evasion.[15]

Then came the Age of Revolutions, when the New World broke free from the Old. The United States did so first—a republic alone, as many of its leaders imagined, an "Anglo-Saxon empire in the wilderness." Spanish American nations, in contrast, came into being collectively, an assemblage of republics, an already constituted league of nations. They *had* to learn to live together if they were to survive. And they largely did so, with their intellectuals, lawyers, and statesmen elaborating a unique body of international law: doctrines, precedents, and protocols geared not toward regulating but outlawing war, not adjudicating conquests but ending conquest altogether.

But how to contain the United States? The hemisphere's first republic seemed more a force of nature than a political entity. More than one of its founders said they could see no limits to its growth, that once they drove the natives beyond the stony mountains they'd soon fill both North and South America with Saxons. What to do with a kinetic nation that believed itself to be as universal as Christianity, as embodying the marching spirit of world history?

What Spanish and Portuguese Americans did was update the criticisms aimed earlier at Spain during the Conquest and directed them at the United States. In so doing they sparked a revolution in international law.

The triumph of liberal multilateralism after the Allied victory in World

War II (especially the nullification of the right of conquest, the prohibition of aggressive war, and the recognition of the sovereign equality of all nations) is often narrated as a transatlantic story, a fortuitous evolution of ideas. Concepts in their infancy during the seventeenth and eighteenth centuries grew stronger in the nineteenth, matured in the twentieth century's cataclysmic wars, and then found their moment in a series of meetings in the last years of World War II: Moscow, Tehran, Dumbarton Oaks, Yalta—onward to the establishment of the United Nations in San Francisco in 1945 and the UN's ratification of the Universal Declaration of Human Rights in 1948.

Most scholars ignore, or pass quickly over, Latin America when considering the founding of the League of Nations, and then the United Nations. It's a curious indifference, for the English-speaking statesmen involved in founding global governance, along with those who laid prior groundwork for such an effort—Woodrow Wilson, Andrew Carnegie, Nelson Rockefeller, Henry Wallace, Sumner Welles, and Winston Churchill, among others—openly and repeatedly held up the New World as what the whole world should look like. Wilson often said that Latin America was the model for what he had hoped to accomplish in Paris. FDR told Stalin that Pan-Americanism would be a good template for a postfascist Eastern Europe.[16]

America, América argues that the New World's magpie rivalry, its immanent critique, played a vital role in the creation of the modern world, shaping its economics, politics, and moralities. The Protestant settlers who colonized, followed by the republicans who revolutionized, North America looked to Spanish America not as an alien other but as a competitor, a contender in an epic struggle to define a set of nominally shared but actually contested ideals: Christianity, freedom, law, sovereignty, property, equality, liberalism, democracy, and, above all, the very meaning of America.

America for America," said Washington's leaders as they tried to fashion their relationship to the hemisphere's new nations in a way that was, as the *North American Review* suggested, something like London's to India.

"America for humanity," Latin Americans answered back.

PART I

TO BEGIN IN WONDER
THE SPANISH

Bartolomé de las Casas

1.

Leaves of Grass

Philosophy begins in wonder, Socrates said. It matures, Hegel added, in terror, on the "slaughter bench" of history. So it was with the arrival of the Spanish in the New World.[1]

Wonder there was when Christendom realized there existed another half a world, filled with *rarezas*, rarities, curious plants and animals but above all people, many more and many more different kinds than lived in all of Europe. Even before Copernicus, Europe was awakening to the idea that the Earth wasn't the center of existence, and that the universe contained, Giordano Bruno would soon reckon, "innumerable suns" and "infinite earths that equally revolve around these suns."[2]

Scholars intuited a link between the celestial and earthly multitudes. There was one heavenly realm, containing an incalculable number of stars. There was one earthly estate, now known to contain many more millions of people than previously imagined. The realization that the earth was not the center of divine creation was as unsettling as the knowledge that Europe wasn't the center of the world.

What did this multiplication mean for the idea of Catholic holism, for the story of Genesis when God at Creation called into being first Adam, then Eve, who together produced a single *linaje*, or lineage, of descendants with a shared, if gory, history?

When reconciled with the Catholic premise of celestial unity, the diversity of the New World's peoples could support the ideal of equality. Time spent in the Caribbean, Mexico, and Central America convinced the Dominican priest Bartolomé de las Casas that the ancient philosophers and theologians who had argued that there existed categories of inferior humans, people born to be "natural slaves," were wrong. As it turned out, Las Casas wrote, the ancients didn't "know very much" about the world. The Dominican would continue to cite the sages when it suited his purpose, but for him, now, truth was to be found not in Aristotle but in America—and the most important truth was that humans everywhere were fundamentally the same. All were made in God's image. Their differences—skin color, hair texture, cultural practices, and religious beliefs—reflected the vast variety of the infinite divine.

And differences in appearance had nothing to do with human essence, which for Las Casas was everywhere the same. Every Indian he had met in the New World, he said, possessed both free will and the ability to reason. That alone made them human. They could remember the past, imagine the future, estimate probabilities, and could see, hear, feel, smell, and taste. They were born, matured, grew old, and became ill, and when they died their families grieved, as humans did everywhere. When happy, they laughed. When sad, they cried. They took delight in the good and despised the bad. From this, Las Casas issued a famous declaration: *Todo linaje de los hombres es uno*—All humanity is one.[3]

At the same time, the New World's conquerors mocked the idea of humanity's oneness, laying the foundation for race supremacy. Spanish settlers and colonists legitimated cruel killing on an unprecedented scale, forcing the New World's inhabitants to labor in mines, fields, and waters, to extract the riches of America—gold, silver, pearls, dyes, and soon sugar and tobacco—that Europe would use to gild its empires, muster its armies, fund its wars, build its cathedrals, and pay for more voyages of conquest and enslavement. Never mind what priests like Las Casas were saying. Theologians were known to say one thing and its opposite. Indians were little better than apes put on earth to serve man. To dominate them was just. To work them to death no more a sin than to butcher a hog.

An Infinity of People

The people of the New World were "found." Then they were lost. Not immediately and not completely, but enough so that a group of Dominican and Franciscan priests wrote their superiors in Spain in 1517 wanting to know where they went. "Where are they, oh most illustrious fathers?" What happened to the men and women who upon Columbus's arrival two decades earlier were so many that they were like "leaves of grass?"[4]

Demographers today aren't sure what the size of America's population was before the arrival of the Spanish. Most estimates fall between fifty and one hundred million inhabitants. The Spanish couldn't say. They knew that the Indies (the name *América* was in use for the New World in the early 1500s but not widely adopted until a little later) were densely populated with wildly varied peoples. They ranged from the elysian Taino, who seemed to have lived lush and well-nourished lives on the islands of the Caribbean; to the hierarchically organized, ostentatious, and scientific Aztec and Inka Empires in Mexico and Peru. Columbus thought the island of Hispaniola—Spain's first Caribbean colony, from where Hernando Cortés would soon lead his assault on Mexico—was "paradise," but a populated paradise, completely "cultivated like the countryside around Cordoba." He estimated that the island was home to over a million souls. Las Casas, who was seventeen years old when he arrived in the Caribbean on April 15, 1502, thought that number too low. "An infinity of people" lived in the new lands, he later wrote. The New World was "filled with people, like a hive of bees."

"It was," he said, "as if God had placed all, or the majority, of the entire human race in these countries."[5]

Later, European romantics would use the word *sublime* to describe the sensation evoked by confrontation with the grandeur and terror of nature, its existential enormity. And there's some of this feeling in the letters and chronicles left by Spanish warriors. As the Conquest proceeded, as Cortés began his march through Mexico, they wrote of their exploits climbing high peaks equal to the Alps, navigating great river systems, and trekking through dense forests. The volcano Popocatépetl rained fire and ice, bursting, Cortés wrote King Charles, with "so much force and noise it seemed as if the whole Sierra was crumbling to the ground."

Yet it wasn't nature that bedazzled the Spaniards as much as the "great city" of Tenochtitlán sitting below the volcano. "As large as Seville," Cortés wrote, and more populated than London, with "many wide and handsome streets," fine noble houses, engineered canals, and a complex hydroponic agricultural system. Further south, it wasn't volcanic eruptions that shivered European souls. It was Mapuche warriors overspread across a vast Andean valley mustered to defend their land. They "shook the world around them," one conquistador wrote, "with sudden dread."[6]

There were so many people.

Then they began to die. The consensus is that the population was cut by between 85 to 95 percent within a century and a half. The Spanish Conquest, driven forward at a relentless pace by the consolidating Kingdom of Castile, inaugurated what the demographers Alexander Koch, Chris Brierley, Mark Maslin, and Simon Lewis call history's "largest human mortality event in proportion to the global population," a drop of upwards of fifty-six million people by 1600. "The greatest genocide in human history," wrote Tzvetan Todorov in the 1980s.[7]

The first wave of death was brought by Conquistador terror.

All the World Knows

Bartolomé de las Casas's transformation into a critic of the Conquest didn't happen until after the Conquest had made him rich. As a young boy growing up in Seville—he was born in 1484—Bartolomé had witnessed the glory heaped on Columbus upon his return from his first cross-Atlantic voyage and heard the stories of islands filled with gold, spices, and potential slaves. His merchant father, Pedro, and uncles Francisco and Juan were part of Columbus's crew, and Pedro used the wealth he acquired from sailing to pay for his son's education. Bartolomé became a "good Latinist" and began studying to become a priest. When Las Casas first landed in Hispaniola (today divided by Haiti in the west and the Dominican Republic in the east), his head was already crowned with a friar's tonsure. He worked with his father, who had given up sailing to settle on the island as a merchant. Las Casas continued his religious studies and, in 1507, traveled to Rome for his ordination.

He was gone for two years, returning to the Caribbean in 1509, and in his later writings was circumspect about his own service to the Conquest. He accompanied at least one incursion into Hispaniola's western lands, provisioning troops with supplies but also perhaps lending a hand to put down Indians with sword and harquebus. Christopher Columbus's son Diego Colón, Hispaniola's governor, granted him an *encomienda*, or consignment of Indian laborers, on the north coast of the island in the Cibao Valley.[8]

The term *encomienda* refers to a kind of slavery, but *indios encomendados,* or commended Indians, weren't considered private property, or chattel. Rather, they were formally something like wards, members of an existing village or community, who, in exchange for labor, were to receive instruction in Christian doctrine from their overlords, their guardian *encomenderos.* The *encomienda* was important, but it was just one of many coerced labor systems. There was out-and-out enslavement, of Native Americans and Africans; there were onerous tribute demands and a labor corvée called the *repartimiento.* The "Conquest brought about so many forms of Indian servitude," wrote one historian in the early 1900s, "that it is very difficult to master the nature of them all, and to follow them into all their minute details."[9]

Las Casas's conversion was slow in coming, and can be dated to 1512, when he accompanied Captain Pánfilo de Narváez on an expedition to pacify Cuba. He went as a priest, and was horrified as the campaign turned into, as one historian writes, "an odyssey of pillage and plunder, of death and destruction." Massacre followed massacre, until Narváez's men arrived at the last unconquered village, Caonao. There, the soldiers were greeted at dawn by thousands of kneeling Indians, who bowed their heads as Narváez's mounted men took their place in the plaza. The tension Las Casas sets up, as he later reflected on the day's events, between motion and stillness is stunning. The Indians kneel quietly. The horses tower over them. All is quiet except for the shuffle of hooves, as the mounts shift the weight of their riders and their heavy armor. No provocation on the part of the town's inhabitants interrupts the tense calm. Then, suddenly, a soldier unsheathes his sword and starts slashing at those kneeling below him. The rest of Narváez's men join in, killing men, women, children, the sick and the old. They use lances to disembowel victims.[10]

Narváez himself, Las Casas writes, sat calm amid the chaos "as if he were made of marble."*

One villager, his intestines spilling out of his stomach, fell into Las Casas arms. The dichotomy in Las Casas's narration is now birth and death, being and nothingness: Las Casas baptized the man and performed last rites in the same breath. After the slaughter was over and the killers had moved on, Las Casas stayed behind to tend to the injured. He cleaned bandages, cauterized wounds, and tried to find some rational explanation for the carnage. He couldn't. The Spanish assault on Cuba, he said, was "a human disaster without precedent: the land, covered in bodies."[11]

Still, though, he remained silent and accepted a second *encomienda* for his service on Narváez's campaign. This one, on the southern coast of Cuba, was made up of inhabitants from the village of Canarreo, which sat on the banks of the Arimao River. Las Casas lived there as a merchant priest, in a large, comfortable house built by his Indians. He said Mass in a small chapel and became wealthy. He couldn't, though, shake off the feeling that he was living in sin, violating the commandment not to steal.

Then, in preparation for a sermon to preach on Pentecostal Sunday in 1514, Las Casas, now thirty years old, came upon this sentence from Ecclesiastes: "To take a fellow-man's livelihood is to kill him, to deprive a worker of his wages is to shed blood." No scales fell from his eyes, no repulsion at witnessing babies being torn apart by dogs awakened his consciousness. Rather, he simply reflected quietly on these words from Ecclesiastes and then made a decision to change his life. He abandoned his *encomiendas*, gave away his riches, and began a life of mendicant poverty and humanist advocacy.

---

* How intentional was this imagery? Was it a critique of the kind of history statues teach, which glorifies warriors while rarely making mention of their victims? In the early 1900s, Washington's National Mall was home to a statue of Pánfilo de Narváez, which faced a monument to another Indian killer, Andrew Jackson. The statues were placed next to each other in tribute to the role Narváez and Jackson played, at different historical moments, in conquering Florida.

Shortly after Las Casas's conversion, a smallpox epidemic swept through Hispaniola, killing, within a few months, nearly a quarter of the island's population. Settlers mounted more expeditions to capture more slaves from other Caribbean islands and from villages along Venezuela's coast. Africans were now being brought in to replace disappearing Taino, to pan rivers, dig mines, herd cows, and cut cane. As the population dwindled, Spanish cruelty increased.

"So many massacres, so many burnings, so many bereavements, and, finally, such an ocean of evil," wrote Las Casas. The priest's denunciations of violence against the New World's darker people perfected a polemical style based not on revelation or appeals to authority but the power of personal witness. More than a century before the French philosopher René Descartes would posit the thinking, self-aware man as the essence of the modern ego, Las Casas gave us the seeing man, mindful not only of his own existence but of the agony of others: "*Y yo lo vi*"—I saw all this, I saw it with my own eyes.

"All the world knows," Las Casas said.[12]

All the world knew largely because Las Casas had told them. Las Casas's famous account of the Conquest, *Brevísima Relación de la Destrucción de las Indias* (*A Brief History of the Destruction of the Indies*), written in 1542 and first published in Seville a decade later, with the word *destrucción* a play on *instrucción. Instruction* being what Catholics were supposed to be providing the inhabitants of America. The book was quickly translated into English, French, German, Dutch, and Italian and widely distributed, especially throughout Protestant Europe. John Milton's nephew published it as *Tears of the Indians* in Cromwellian London, one of at least thirty-seven editions printed in England between the late 1500s and the middle of the 1600s.[13]

Las Casas lived during the middle of one of the most violent periods of human history: a three-centuries-long crisis that roiled Europe and the Mediterranean world. Famines, pestilence, crusades, and war. Wars that lasted a hundred years, wars between Lutherans and Catholics and between Christians and Muslims, the siege of Constantinople, Mitteleuropa's peasant rebellions, the lowland's revolt against Spain, England's conquest of Ireland. Combined, these upheavals turned "the whole of Europe into a bloodbath." Mass murder of unarmed communities was commonplace. Unbelievers, heretics, and infidels were burned at the stake, and mutilated body parts of the enemy were catapulted into besieged cities.[14]

Still, Las Casas maintained that what the Spanish were doing in the New World was worse.

Las Casas filled page after page with extreme colonial gore. Torture, mutilations, massacres. Spanish conquistadores raped women at will. They broiled captives alive and then fed their corpses to dogs. They chopped off the hands of Indians and then told them to deliver the "letter" (that is, the severed body part) to compatriots hiding in the mountains as a message to surrender or face worse. In Mexico, the Spanish wrapped native priests in straw and then burned them to death. "Boar-hounds" tore children apart. Conquistadores used their swords as spits to roast babies as their mothers watched. They tossed infants into rivers, laughing as they guessed how many times they would bob up for air before drowning.

"The Spanish came like starving wolves, tigers, and lions, and for four decades have done nothing other than commit outrages, slay, afflict, torment, and destroy," Las Casas wrote.

A New World and a new kind of mass murder carried out with a new kind of animal cruelty: of a quality "never before seen," said Las Casas, "nor heard of, nor read of."

Las Casas denounced but couldn't make sense of the creation of a slave system that provided food and wealth to the Spanish but also eliminated the labor needed to produce food and wealth. "Gold unlike fruit," wrote Las Casas with the dark sarcasm that runs through his prose, "lies underground and does not grow on trees, and therefore is not easily picked." Indians had to dig for it. And the Spanish forced them to dig until they died, faster than the priests could bury them.[15]

Clearly, not all infants were killed for sport by the Spanish or fed to their dogs to give them the taste for human flesh. Yet that such horrors did take place reveals an indifference, not just to life but to the reproduction of life. In Hispaniola, the Spanish put Taino men to mine gold and women to grow food. Segregated, and worked so hard for so long, the enslaved couldn't reproduce.

Women who did carry pregnancies to term had no milk to keep newborns alive. Women forced abortions rather than bring children into a world that had gone so horrifyingly wrong. "They will not rear children," the early chronicler of the Conquest Pietro Martire wrote. European travelers to Hispaniola in the 1500s produced a series of drawings and engravings depicting the many techniques Indians would use to kill their children and themselves, which included hanging, clubbing to death, throwing oneself or one's children from cliffs or into rivers, rather than accept the Conquest. The toxic juice of manioc and the poisonous smoke of herbs were other methods. The killings and suicides were often committed collectively, a last act of mournful solidarity.[16]

By the time the Spanish moved into Mexico and the Andes, most of the population of the greater Caribbean was gone and the islands were turned into what Las Casas called *deserts*, suggesting that the land was once populated but had been emptied, or *deserted*. There were more cows than people on Hispaniola, brought across the Atlantic from Europe and Africa, large free-range herds that destroyed corn and squash lands, contributing to widespread hunger. In Mexico and South America, cattle would likewise facilitate the elimination of Native Americans and the establishment of sprawling Spanish haciendas.[17]

The second wave of death was brought by microbes, which launched epidemics that lashed again and again the peoples of the Caribbean, Mexico, and the Andes—already ravaged by war, wracked by drought, and compelled to labor beyond capacity. The worst was a hemorrhagic fever with multiple, cascading symptoms, which Mexicans called *cocoliztli*, the Nahuatl word for *pestilence*. Spanish and Aztec doctors couldn't figure out the basis of the illness, which scientists now believe was caused by a salmonella bacterium brought from Europe. The century after the arrival of the Spanish saw at least thirteen serious outbreaks, the worst being in 1520, 1545, and 1576. The shepherding of survivors into concentrated *reducciones*, or *pueblos*, accelerated the rate of contagion.

Between fifteen and thirty million people lived in Mexico in early 1519, when Hernando Cortés and his army of five hundred men arrived to begin his assault on the Aztec Empire. By 1600—eighty-one years, the length of a long life—only about two million remained.[18]

2.

There Is Only One World

In 1493, with Spain barely a presence in Hispaniola much less the greater Caribbean, the pope announced a "donation" that gave King Ferdinand and Queen Isabella all the New World's "islands and mainlands," both those discovered and those yet to be discovered. The king of Portugal, himself presiding over an ambitious, seafaring empire, objected. A round of diplomacy between the two Iberian monarchies led, a year later, to the Treaty of Tordesillas. The treaty, with the Vatican's approval, drew a line on a map of the world running north and south. Lisbon got what was east of the line, including much of what today is Brazil. Spain took most of the rest of the hemisphere. The split focused Spain's expansionist energies on the Americas, and eventually the Philippines in the Pacific, while pointing Lisbon south, toward the coast of Africa, where Portugal would dominate the slave trade. The settlement was to "continue in force and remain firm, stable, valid forever and ever."

France, equally Catholic and equally imperially ambitious, wasn't happy to be cut out of the spoils. When Spain demanded the return of half a ton of gold, six hundred pounds of pearls, and three jaguars delivered to Paris by an Italian privateer, King Francis I of France told his Spanish counterpart that he'd like to "see the clause in Adam's will that excludes me from a share in the world."* The sun shines as much on France, Francis said, as it does on Spain.[1]

Others, too, wanted their part, including soon-to-be-Protestant England, the Dutch, and the bankers of Germany. No European power, apart from Spain and Portugal, accepted the legitimacy of Tordesillas's boundary line, its nonsensical nature made obvious as navigators started circling the globe. Once it became clear that one could wind up east of the line by sailing west, it was impossible to say where Spain's Vatican-granted sovereignty ended and Portugal's began.

Discovery, and Other Doctrines

A New World and a new kind of mass murder carried out with a new kind of animal cruelty needed a new morality.[2]

The fast transformation of what we now call Spain from the Iberian Peninsula's multilingual and fractious Catholic fiefdoms into an empire larger than anything Caesar could have dreamt of raised questions—questions

---

* France had success colonizing large parts of North America and the Caribbean but failed to make significant inroads in South America. In the 1550s, France did sponsor a colony on an island off the coast of Brazil. The enterprise was utopian, comprised of an ecumenical mix of Catholics and Calvinists. The Calvinists meant to proselytize. But little missionary work took place, for their unyielding, punitive doctrine of predestination, in which people were already either damned or chosen, made it hard to know what to do with the local Tupinambá, who anyway didn't seem interested in learning about Christ. For their part, the French Catholics had little but disdain for the natives, whom they described as lacking in "courtesy and humanity." Later, Claude Lévi-Strauss would write about the episode: "What a film it would make! A handful of Frenchmen, isolated on an unknown continent—an unknown planet could hardly have been stranger—where Nature and mankind were alike unfamiliar to them." Having given up trying to preach to the Tupinambá, the Catholics and Calvinists "soon began to try to convert one another." Where they should have been working to keep themselves alive, they spent week after week debating ritual and theology: How should one interpret the Last Supper? Should water be mixed with wine for the Consecration? What was the nature of the Eucharist? Here, the New World staged a ludicrous solipsism, with Christians too busy rehearsing schismatic arguments to notice the Native Americans dying from the diseases they carried from Europe. Instead, they taught salty phrases to local parrots. The colony eventually collapsed, overrun by the Portuguese, and the survivors returned to France with their parrots.

that couldn't be easily answered by jurists and priests born into a world they were told was all, only to learn it was but a part. There existed no law in the medieval Catholic canon capable of processing the enormity, territorially and psychically, of the New World, much less one that could justify Spanish and Portuguese claims to its possession. Papal edicts and the Tordesillas treaty cited the old Roman doctrine of discovery, which held that merely to find heretofore unknown lands conferred sovereignty. "With each day that we drift our empire grows larger," sighs Don Fernando de Guzmán, in Werner Herzog's *Aguirre, the Wrath of God*, as his raft floats listlessly down the Amazon.

Spanish and Portuguese soldiers found it easy to pass through any bit of the vast Americas and claim it for their monarchs. More difficult was to establish control, not to mention the impossibility of keeping other European powers out. Spain claimed as its own most of the New World's mainland and islands and declared not just the Caribbean but the Pacific to be "closed seas," off-limits to the merchant ships of other European nations.

The main question, the one that would obsess Spanish theologians, philosophers, jurists, and clerics like Las Casas was this: By what right did Spain wage cruel war on the New World's inhabitants? The reasons Spain gave for driving Islam off the Iberian Peninsula provided no helpful answers. That long struggle, starting in 718 and ending in 1492, was valid on the grounds that Iberia, before the arrival of Islam, had been populated by Christian Visigoths. So, Catholic war against Al-Andalus was, legally, not a conquest but a *reconquest* of lost Christian territory: *La Reconquista*. The fact that Muslims lived in a world that knew of Christ and yet they still rejected him bolstered arguments that Spain's fight against Islam was righteous, since waging war against infidels, in canon law, was just. Such arguments could not be made about the New World—that is, if it really was "new."

Some scholars contested the premise that the Indies were heretofore unknown. A miner in Panama had reportedly found a coin minted with the name and profile of Caesar Augustus, which fueled the idea that the Romans had traded with the New World. If Rome had earlier "discovered" America, then the Spanish monarchs, understanding themselves heirs to

Caesar's empire, could claim a right to rule. And if *jus belli*—the law of war—granted Rome the right to wage war and seize territory at will, then Spain, said defenders of the Conquest, had that right as well. Spanish bards wrote odes comparing the conquistadores to centurions. Painters depicted Spanish kings garlanded with Roman laurels and decked out in Roman armor. Cortés, Mexico's conqueror, was compared to many rulers, among them Caesar.[3]

Historical analogies could only go so far in one direction before crossing paths with analogies traveling the other way, opposing the Conquest. Las Casas was especially adept at picking apart the myth that Spain was heir to Rome. He pointed out that since the Romans had brutally conquered Iberia centuries before Christ was born, a more precise analogy would equate Native Americans with the Spanish. Both were victims of imperial tyranny.

Some theologians placed the curse of Ham on the heads of New World peoples, linking the Amazon to Africa, and the New World's peoples to Ethiopians. The Jesuits said they found Saint Thomas's footprints on a rock in Bahia, and others believed that Saint Bartholomew, after preaching in India, had traveled to the Indies. "God sent the Holy Apostles to all parts of the world," said the Dominican friar Diego Durán in his *Historia de las Indias de Nueva España*, and, anyway, if Indians were God's children, as many insist, then God would not have "left them without a preacher of the Gospel." The point being that the New World's people did "know" Christ and must have, at some point, rejected him, making them infidels and legally conquerable.[4]

Also popular was the idea that the peoples of the New World were descendants of the lost tribes of Israelites. Or, perhaps, of Jewish exiles from Rome, evidence of which was the finely wrought golden jewelry found in the Yucatán. "We can almost positively affirm," wrote Father Durán, that Mexicans "are Jews and Hebrews." Almost positively. Fernando de Montesinos spent years in Peru producing five dense manuscript volumes reading New World history through the book of Revelation, arguing, among other things, that the Andes were the site of King Solomon's fabled mines. The Spanish destruction of the Inka Empire, then, wasn't so much a conquest as a rediscovery and reestablishment of Israel of old. Since, according to

Christian esoterica, a new Jerusalem had to be raised and Jews converted to Christ before the Apocalypse could begin, the Conquest was a necessary step in the fulfillment of prophecy, and thus legal.[5]

Half Man, Half Monkey

Clashing analogies and end-time theology aside, most influential theologians accepted, or soon did, the fact that the New World was new. Las Casas reported that the people of Seville poured out to see Columbus upon his return from his first voyage across the Atlantic, for news had already come that he had "discovered another world." He was the first, Las Casas writes, to "open the gates of the Ocean Sea." Francisco López de Gómara, among Spain's most influential chroniclers, would write to the Holy Roman Emperor to say that the Conquest was "the greatest event since creation of the world" except for "the crucifixion of he who created the world." History's Trinity was complete: Creation, Christ's Crucifixion, Conquest.[6]

We might speak of "two worlds," old and new, as the Peruvian Garcilaso de la Vega, the illegitimate son of a Spanish conqueror and Inka noblewoman, would say later, but "there is only one world." And one world required—for the unifying Catholic kingdoms of Castile and Aragon (the core of an aborning empire that claimed to represent universal Christian history)— one law. By the 1500s, Catholic theologians had mashed together Roman doctrine, the writings of ancient philosophers, the teaching of the saints, including Thomas Aquinas and Augustine, and papal and royal edicts to create a legal system that had evolved over the centuries. Yet suddenly Spain was in possession, or claimed to be, of an incalculably large land mass, home to an "infinity" of souls who had lived for untold centuries beyond the horizon of Catholic authority. Their existence revealed canon law to be provincial, its claim to universalism a sham.

Who were these people living, thriving even, outside the Catholic realm? Where did they come from? Were they sons and daughters of Adam and Eve? Did they descend from one of the eight people who came off Noah's ark after God's Great Flood? If so, how were they separated from the rest of humanity? If they weren't children of Adam and Eve, did they carry the burden of original sin?

Three kinds of people could be legitimately enslaved according to existing Catholic doctrine. One: infidels or idolators. Two: prisoners taken in a just war. Three: a whole class of people understood as "natural slaves." This last grouping was a category derived from Aristotle, as Catholic theologians interpreted the Greek philosopher, made up of beings closer to beasts than humans, lacking reason and incapable of forming political communities. In Seville, Salamanca, and other Spanish centers of learning, theologians and philosophers debated whether any of these categories could be applied to the people of the New World. Meanwhile, back in the Caribbean, far from Spain's debating halls, conquerors and colonists didn't wait for Aristotelian authorization. Columbus happily admitted, in a 1493 letter to Spain, that "in these islands I have so far found no human monstrosities, as many expected, but on the contrary the whole population is very well formed." Yet he still captured hundreds of Taino and sent them back to Spain to distribute as slave booty to his loyalists and to pay off his debts, while the men who stayed on the islands took thousands of Indians as their slaves.[7]

Father Juan José de la Cruz y Moya, who later ministered in Mexico, described a sharp-edged rank-and-file racism that took hold during the Conquest's early days, a conviction that the "first Americans" were created without a touch of divinity but rather emerged from "the putrefaction of the earth." According to Father de la Cruz, many believed that "*indios americanos* weren't true men with rational souls but rather a monstrous third species of animal, falling between man and monkey and created by God to serve humans." Settlers spread the lie that "Indians weren't true humans but savages," that "there was no more sin in killing them than in killing a field animal."* Father de la Cruz condemned such ideas as heresy. The only thing "monstrous" about the New World was "the cruelty and greed that the bastard Spanish brought to this land."[8]

---

* Bartolomé de las Casas spent the second half of his life arguing against the idea that Indians weren't human. But oh, he said, how he "wished to God the Spanish did treat Indians like they treat their beasts. If they did, there wouldn't be so many corpses, so much death."

Conquistadores encountered fierce resistance in some places. In response, supporters of the Conquest came to loathe Indians as perverse, as the Devil's barbarous minions, "destitute of all humanity." Satan was angry that he was losing the New World, went one popular explanation for Indian opposition to Spanish rule, so he "drew a line" across which it was difficult to teach "Catholic truths." The earliest chronicles of the Conquest describe lands inhabited by rebellious Indians—in northern Mexico, southern Chile, or the Amazonian slopes of the Andes—as populated by monsters and giants, proof of which were the enormous bones that the Spanish said they found, including a skull big enough to bake bread in. Grotesquerie created the impression of wickedness, cutting against Christian hope that the New World was a land of innocence. Columbus was wrong. There were monsters. And monsters could naturally be enslaved.[9]

The New World was big, its rivers broad, jungles dense, deserts unfathomable. How could there not be giants? Red-haired, one-eyed, and humpbacked, Spanish chroniclers reported all kinds. Amerigo Vespucci saw them himself. They chased him off Curaçao for trying to kidnap two women to give as gifts to King Ferdinand. One account sounds like the inspiration for Roald Dahl's *The BFG*: eight leagues from Guadalajara there lived twenty-seven "lazy and gluttonous" giants, thirty-five feet high, whose hideous voices echo for miles. They carried clubs and supped every night on "four grilled children."[10]

When Bartolomé de las Casas's father, Pedro, returned to Spain from one of Columbus's voyages, he brought with him a young Taino slave named, in Spanish at least, Juanico, whom he presented to his son as a gift. Bartolomé kept Juanico as a companion while he studied to enter the priesthood. Queen Isabella, though, abrogated Columbus's authority to hand out the New World's inhabitants. "By what right," she asked in 1495, "does the Admiral give my *vassals* to anyone?" The queen ordered the return of Juanico and hundreds of other enslaved Taino to Hispaniola and nixed Columbus's plan to set Hispaniola up as a slave export port: "Until we know whether we can sell them or not."[11]

"Until we know whether we can sell them or not." In Isabella's doubt was a universe of political theory, encompassing all the questions related to seizing the New World, with all its new people, by force. When it came to the status of Amerindians, the taking of their land, their reduction to forced labor, and their subjugation to the Spanish Crown, the royal court decided, undecided, reconsidered, and then decided something else.

Eventually, in 1503, a learned commission answered the queen's query, sort of: No. The people of the New World could not be sold. Indians hadn't had a chance to reject Christ, so they weren't infidels. And they were clearly fully human, in possession of rational minds and divine souls. They couldn't be enslaved—unless, that its, they were captured in a "just war."

The debate over the justness of the entirety of the uppercase Conquest would go on for decades. In the meantime, Spanish settlers took it for granted that all the lesser campaigns, the backwater massacres and dawn raids, were justified, especially if the immediate cause of any given skirmish could be blamed on indigenous incitement. Captives taken in these campaigns could be enslaved.

This was around the time Las Casas first sailed to Hispaniola. He went on a ship that was part of a large fleet carrying thousands of Spanish settlers, administrators, priests, and would-be conquerors (including Francisco Pizarro, who, along with his brothers Hernando, Juan, and Gonzalo, would go on to defeat the Inka Empire and rule the Pacific side of the northern Andes). As the armada approached the island, a messenger came aboard the lead vessel to report that Spanish troops had just pacified a large rebellious village. The news flew from ship to ship, and cheers went up among Las Casas's fellow settlers, happy that a fresh supply of "prisoners of a just war" would be available for them to enslave.

Shortly after Las Casas's arrival, Isabella granted permission to the Spanish governor of Hispaniola to capture and enslave the refugee survivors of a Spanish massacre of over seven hundred residents in the town of Xaragua, or Jaragua. The slaughter was deemed "just" because the town's residents had fought back. Indians who fled in canoes to the island of El Guanabo were hunted down. Captured, some were shipped across the Atlantic and sold in Castile, while others were put into service on the island.

"One was given to me," Las Casas later wrote.[12]

3.

Ego Vox

On December 21, 1511, the Dominican priest Antonio de Montesinos—
eight years before Cortés's drive into Mexico, six before Luther nailed
his theses to the door of Wittenberg's church—walked to the pulpit
of Hispaniola's thatched cathedral and told the island's notable Spanish residents, among them Columbus's son, Governor Diego Colón, that they were
damned. Expect perdition, he said, for turning Hispaniola and its surrounding islands into death camps. Montesinos called his sermon "Ego Vox Cla-
mantis in Deserto": I am the voice crying in the desert, or, as it is usually
translated, *wilderness.* The priest meant the phrase not as a metaphor for
New World nature but rather for the wasteland of Spanish morality.

The Dominican offered hellfire, though not the kind associated with later
Puritan jeremiads. In those New England sermons, many preached in the middle of a long North Atlantic winter, English settlers focused obsessively on
individual sins, which helped them make sense of the hardships they faced.
Diseases, droughts, storms, wars, malformed fetuses, crop failures, massacres,
and financial troubles were all understood as proof of God's displeasure. The
solipsism was intense. Indigenous peoples played only bit parts in the stories
Puritans told of themselves, important only to the degree they provided clues
to help decipher God's judgment. Except for a few moralists, Indians remained
shadow dancers, flickering around the fringes of the Puritan imagination.

Not so for Hispaniola's Dominicans. Indians weren't hidden in the wings of Spanish Catholicism, offstage as plot devices to keep the story of the pilgrims' progress moving forward. For Montesinos, Indians were the main thing, central to the great debate over the justness of dominion and possession, conquest and enslavement.

The Divine Whisper

The sins Montesinos condemned weren't spiritual failings. Today, we would call them social and structural violence. What Montesinos and Las Casas described as "slavery" was in fact a dizzying array of mechanisms that wrenched labor and tribute out of Indians.

The *encomienda* was just one such institution, with *encomenderos* living like lords, forcing their Indians to dig faster for gold, plant more land for food, cut more cane, shovel more salt, dive deeper for pearls. "Hardly had the Indian pearl fishermen come out of the water with a supply of oysters," Las Casas wrote, "when their masters forced them to dive again without allowing them time to recruit their strength and draw breath." If they lingered too long on the surface, foremen would use the lash to force them back down. Spanish "greed was insatiable," wrote one royal official, the work murderous. "Out of every hundred Indians who go" to work the gold fields, which often were far, far from their homes, "only seventy come back." On their long marches, workers were forced to drink from stagnant *jagüeyes*, ponds filled with infested water, which led to more sickness, more death. Bodies were twisted, brains deprived of oxygen from deep dives, backs broken from their burdens.[1]

The Dominicans, including Montesinos, had landed in Santo Domingo, the capital port city of Hispaniola, in 1510, to establish their order and build a monastery. The first large consignment of hundreds of Africans as slaves had come that year, as epidemics, famine, and labor demands continued taking their toll on the island's original residents. After a decade and a half of Spanish rule, what Columbus had called paradise was pandemonium, a scene that shocked the senses of the Dominicans upon their arrival and contributed to the harshness of their condemnation. Montesinos was to deliver the verdict, but his sermon was collectively edited and approved by his fellow clerics, and their repudiation of settler rule was unanimous and total.[2]

Las Casas was there for the sermon, not as an ally of the Dominicans but as an accused, as an *encomendero*. "For a good while," he later described the event, "Montesinos spoke in such pungent and terrible terms that it made the congregant's flesh shudder." Here's his transcription of Montesinos's sermon:

> I am the voice of Christ in the desert of this island. Open your hearts and your senses, all of you, for this voice will speak new things harshly, and will be frightening. . . . This voice says that you are living in deadly sin for the atrocities you tyrannically impose on these innocent people. Tell me, what right have you to enslave them? What authority did you use to make war against them who lived at peace in their own lands, killing them cruelly with methods never before heard of? How can you oppress them and not care to feed or cure them, and work them to death to satisfy your greed? . . . Aren't they men? Have they no rational soul? Aren't you obliged to love them as you love yourselves? Don't you understand? How can you live in such a lethargic dream?[3]

Montesinos then told the congregants that they were as certain to fall into the abyss as were the Turks. Their abuse of Amerindians was no less a sin than that of a pagan who had a chance to convert to Christ but refused.

Disbelief among the congregants turned to anger, murmurs to indignation. Montesinos finished his lecture and left the pulpit with his head high and returned home to eat a lunch of cabbage soup. The Dominicans hoped the sermon would lead to settler reflection and contrition. But, as Las Casas dryly noted, the congregants didn't spend the rest of the day quietly reading Thomas à Kempis's *De la imitación de Cristo y menosprecio del mundo*. Kempis was a favorite of Catholic renunciants, a Dutch priest who wrote that property was slavery and true freedom could only be attended through a "disposal" of the self.

Rather, they marched to Governor Colón's house to condemn the Dominicans and their "new and novel" doctrines. The crowd then moved on to the Dominican monastery to demand a retraction. Colón, who had joined the crowd, pleaded with the priests to consider the hardships he and his men had in conquering the island and "subjugating the pagans." Montesinos's sermon, he said, disrespected what they had achieved.

The friars tried to answer these concerns, yet they might as well have been speaking Taino. Their words, according to Las Casas, were morally unintelligible to the settlers. "Blessed are the ears that gladly receive the pulses of the Divine whisper," Kempis had said. To understand, much less accept, Montesinos's injunction would "mean that they couldn't have their Indians, they couldn't terrorize them." Their "greed wouldn't be satisfied, and all their sighs of desire would be denied."

Montesinos, Las Casas, and other Catholic critics of settler abuse are often called "reformist," in that they sought to ameliorate the worst abuses of colonialism. They remained loyal to the monarchy and supported Spanish rule as a providential mission to spread Catholicism. Yet even limited reform—better wages and limits on work requirements—would have ended Spanish colonialism as it existed. Christopher Columbus himself, in the earliest days of Spain's Atlantic expansion, was clear that work, especially coerced work, was what created colonial value: "The Indians of Hispaniola were and are the greatest wealth of the island, because they are the ones who dig, and harvest, and collect the bread and other supplies, and gather the gold from the mines, and do all the work of men and beasts alike." Without them, the conqueror of Peru, Francisco Pizarro, later wrote in reference to Indian laborers, "this kingdom is naught."[4]

Colonial settlement—the planting of fields, the mining of minerals, the moving of rocks, the chiseling of stone, the building of houses—required enormous toil. The Spanish wouldn't do the work. "There are no Spaniards here who will work for anyone," one priest wrote the Crown. Instead, they grafted themselves onto island life—onto either Indian communities that already existed or new ones created by concentrating rebels and refugees into controllable villages—and then forced their inhabitants to do the work needed to extend the realm. They didn't care what the system was called.

The words *encomienda* and *esclavitud* were often used interchangeably. Spanish colonists weren't committed to a particular definition of "slavery," or much concerned with what Church law had to say about it unless such law threatened their control over labor. Call Indians "free" if you want, say they are the queen's vassals and even God's children. As long as they did the work.[5]

"God is in heaven, the King is far away, and I rule here" was a popular settler expression. What mattered was that no third party—not Crown officials, not the Church, and especially not Montesinos and his fanatical Dominicans—stand between them and their Indians.

Eventually the crowd in front of the Dominican convent dispersed, believing they had secured a promise that Montesinos would retract his slanders in his next sermon. They misunderstood the pulse of the divine whisper. The following Sunday, Montesinos walked to the pulpit, his head again high. This time, he began his remarks with a quotation from Job: "*Repetam scientiam meam á principio, et sermones meos sine mendatio esse probabo.*"

"I will start from the beginning and will prove my sermon is correct."

We and You and All

Many of the lawyers and theologians who surrounded the Crown during the first decades of the 1500s were war-hardened traditionalists, having come of age during the final, triumphal years of the Reconquest. They supported the Conquest and sought to validate it within the terms of existing canon law. The solution they came up with to criticisms like those preached by Montesinos was to require conquistadores to read out loud a treatise, either in Latin or Spanish, "to those not yet subject to our lord the king" before launching an attack.

In 1513, two years after Montesinos's sermon, Juan López de Palacios Rubios, a Castilian expert on canon law, drafted what became known as *el Requerimiento*. The Requirement—or the Demand—crams five thousand years of Catholic world history into one very long paragraph. The document makes no mention of Christ but rather affirms that God, after making heaven and earth, anointed Saint Peter the first pope, "lord and superior of all the men in the world." The text then relates how one of Peter's papal heirs "donated" the islands and mainland of the New World to the Spanish monarchy. The person reading aloud the thousand-word document, usually a scribe or a notary, finished by saying that there existed papers, such as the Treaty of Tordesillas, proving the truths just narrated. They could be, if the listeners so wished, made available for review: "You can see them if you so desire."[6]

The Requirement is easy to mock as the last gasp of a dying worldview. A close look at its text, though, reveals a stealth modernist sensibility, one that, even as it insists on the singular authority of the Catholic Church, accepts the necessity of recognizing and living with pluralism.

El Requerimiento upheld the unity of creation, of "one man and one woman from whom we and you and all the men of the world were and are descendants." The phrase *we and you and all* was meant to include the inhabitants of the New World as descendants of Adam and Eve. Then, after having affirmed the common origin of humanity, the manifesto went on to explain its fracturing and dispersal across the globe as resulting from the "multitude" that issued forth from Adam and Eve: "It was necessary that some men should go one way and some another, and that they should be divided into many kingdoms and provinces, for in one alone they could not be sustained." Diversity was *necessary*, since the earth, though bountiful, couldn't support a surging population in a single religious community. Palacios described a world comprised of major religious differences yet integrated by politics, placing Christians alongside, not above, Muslims, Jews, Gentiles, and "other sects." The "requirement," or "demand," was not that the people of the New World convert. The document expressly says that faith is a free decision. Conquistadores wouldn't compel anyone to become Christians. All that was required was that the audience recognize Spanish monarchs as their sovereigns.

The script's nuance, however, mattered little. What mattered was its performance, its offering of a choice that wasn't a choice at all. To accept Spain's rule would bring many "benefits," including, so the text said, freedom from servitude. To refuse, the text explained, would visit utter destruction:

> With the aid of God, we will enter your land against you with force and
> will make war in every place and by every means we can and are able,
> and we will then subject you to the yoke and authority of the Church and
> Their Highnesses. We will take you and your wives and children and
> make them slaves, and as such we will sell them, and will dispose of you
> and them as Their Highnesses order. And we will take your property
> and will do to you all the harm and evil we can.

The text of the Requirement cut against the idea, popular among settlers, that Indians were a race apart, perhaps not even human. But the violence it sanctioned confirmed the notion that the New World peoples were lesser beings.

The historian Lewis Hanke writes that conquistadores recited the text "to trees and empty huts when no Indians were to be found. Captains muttered its theological phrases into their beards on the edge of sleeping Indian settlements, or even a league away before starting the formal attack, and at times some leather-lunged Spanish notary hurled its sonorous phrases after the Indians as they fled into the mountains." Captains would have scribes read it in camp to his men to the beat of drums, and ship commanders would sometimes have "the document read from the deck as they approached an island, and at night would send out enslaving expeditions." Soldiers would march into a vacant village—its people having fled upon the Spanish advance—and a scribe would recite the Requirement to the wind, after which soldiers and their mastiffs were let loose to hunt the refugees down. Those who were captured were bound together in coffles, their necks tied one to another with thick rope. After reading the Requirement to them, their abductors would march them off into slavery. Frustrated that Indians seemed not to understand, the notary Gonzalo Fernández de Oviedo suggested to his captain that they hold off further recitations "until we have one of these Indians in a cage," and we can teach him the meaning of the text.[7]

Some Native Americans tried to engage with the content of the Requirement. Somewhere along the Sinú River Valley (in northwestern Colombia), the leaders of one community responded thoughtfully to the document, after one Captain Martín Fernández de Enciso had an interpreter read it in the local language. "The part about there being one God who rules heaven and earth sounds good and seems right," one of the community's leaders reportedly said. He thought less of "that part that says the Pope is the master of the whole universe serving as God's agent, and that he gave the earth to the King of Castile. . . . The Pope must have been drunk when he did this, since the earth isn't his to give." As for the king, the Sinú Indians decided that he must have been "a little crazy" when he accepted the pope's donation, since he can't possess "something that belonged to others." Apparently impressed by this response, Fernández de Enciso left the community in peace. Soon, though, another group of conquistadores returned. "A brief orgy of grave looting by the Spaniards followed," reads one account of how the Sinú Valley was pacified, "after which they almost forgot the area; for its gold had come from elsewhere and few Indians remained to be exploited as a labor force."[8]

El Requerimiento wasn't written only for Native Americans. The warrant's rote reading generated cynicism among the troops, and cynicism is a useful animator when it comes to killing. A disenchanted world in which legal formalism is used not to restrain but to unleash is easier to despoil.

The royal court continued to argue over the criteria for just enslavement. In 1526, a council of jurists upheld the legitimacy of the Requirement, yet ordered that its text be simplified, so that it could more easily be understood by Indians. By this point, though, the text did little but undermine Spanish legitimacy.[9] Protestants, who were gathering strength in northern Europe, didn't recognize the Vatican's authority. They read the popish document as proof that Spain had no credible title whatsoever to the New World.*

In the Indies, most Church hierarchs and clergy, many of them living off the labor of commended Indians, didn't doubt the justness of the Conquest. Yet Montesinos wasn't alone in the wilderness. A moral schism was growing,

---

* Walter Raleigh, one of the pirates knighted by Queen Elizabeth as a reward for raiding Spain's American possessions, suggested that the English write up a "counter-requerimiento," based on the information found in Las Casas.

one that paralleled Luther's break from the Vatican but remained within the jurisdiction of the Catholic Church.*

Hispaniola's Dominican convent became a cell of opposition, its priests comparing the island's settlers to the ancient Pharaohs. The Christian settlers "go through the land like rabid wolves in the midst of gentle lambs," their "filthy passions have broken and destroyed the land," read one of a series of letters the Dominican convent sent to Church regents in Spain. The few thousand Indians left on Hispaniola were "broken and weakened, living in agony," the clerics reported. Survivors look more like "painted corpses than living beings." The capricious cruelty of the Spanish knew no bounds, with settlers grabbing swaddled babies out of the arms of Indian women to feed their hungry dogs.[10]

As the indigenous population collapsed, Spanish vessels fanned out across the Caribbean from Hispaniola, their crews desperate for new slaves. So many captive Indians died on their return voyages, wrote the Dominicans, that their bodies, having been tossed overboard, served as buoy markers for other ships approaching Hispaniola.[11]

Las Casas had given up his *encomiendas* and slaves in 1514. Now he joined the Dominican opposition and soon became its incandescent center—a "candle that lights the world," as a friend described him.[12]

---

* As to Montesinos, he apparently was murdered by agents of the Welser brothers, prominent Bavarian bankers who helped finance the Conquest. The Welsers had already been invested in the sugar and slave trade when Spain's King Charles, to pay off a debt, gave them a good portion of Venezuela to settle, mine, and enslave. The German colony was under the command of a mercenary named Ambrosius Ehinger, who earned a reputation for cruelty equal to any Spanish conquistador. Las Casas, in describing the "inhumanity" of the "Germans," rhymed *animales* and *alemanes*. The pun doesn't work in English, but Las Casas asked if the perpetrators of such cruelties were "animal tyrants, or German tyrants." King Charles sent Father Montesinos to Venezuela to impose some order on the settlement. The details are vague, but Welser agents, finding Montesinos tiresome, poisoned him in 1540.

4.

Goodbye Aristotle

L as Casas formally entered the Dominican order in 1522. He went into scholarly seclusion for several years, immersing himself in law, Scripture, and philosophy before reappearing in public life, more formidable than ever. He wrote treatise after treatise, in an outpouring of intense yet often playful prose arguing against the legitimacy of settler rule. His advocacy was scattershot, at once appealing to decency, tugging at the conscience of Crown officials to act mercifully, at other times using Canon Law and Christian Doctrine to prove that the Conquest was theft on a planetary scale. Throughout the 1530s, he traveled to Venezuela, Guatemala, Nicaragua, and Mexico, seeing firsthand how the terror he witnessed on the islands had spread over the mainland.

Las Casas challenged *encomienda* power on every front he could organize. He traveled often to Spain, waiting months to gain audiences with court officials. Drawing on an unshakable certainty of purpose, he insinuated himself into the cloistered center of Spanish imperial power, where a relatively small contingent of priests and lawyers set the rules for a growing empire that would soon cross the Pacific and encompass the Philippines. He eventually gained the king's ear. By this point, Charles was both the king of Spain and the Holy Roman emperor, having taken both thrones in 1519, shortly after Luther launched the Protestant Reformation. As king he was Charles I, as emperor, he was Charles V.

Over the course of two days in 1540, Charles and his counselors listened to Las Casas read from his *Larguísima Relación*—a very long account of the destruction of the Indies (from which he would excerpt his yet-to-be-published *Brevísima Relación*). One moment Las Casas was a gnomic monk bent over reams of Latin text. The next, he commanded the room, speaking extemporaneously, his eyes burning as spittle shot from his mouth. Las Casas knew his intensity provoked strong reactions. "God gave me this ability," he once said, "to use words to float the good to heaven and sink the bad to hell." The friar possessed a strangely numinous pull, his passion for the wretched transfixing those around him.

Recitations of horrific abuses were followed by dense scholastic arguments. Las Casas cited Cicero to insist that New World people were free not because they possessed individual rights, in the modern sense, but because they were *gente*, individuals who came together to live socially—*"gentes para vivir socialmente,"* as Las Casas wrote. They were equal to Spaniards and could not be considered "natural slaves." There were too many of them for Aristotle's criteria to apply.

The notion that there existed a category of people on earth who were bestial monsters, "errors of nature," *required*, as Las Casas, ever the logician, put it, that such creatures exist in limited numbers. Las Casas continued to believe that the Indies were home to most of the world's population. It was inconceivable, he said, that God would create so many people as an inferior class. "Only someone who despises God and was an enemy of nature," Las Casas said, "would dare to write that the great mass of people who lived on the other side of the ocean were barbarians, savages, lacking reason." As he moved through his argument he introduced a Latin refrain, repeated each time he came to a point: ¡*Valeat Aristóteles!*—Goodbye Aristotle![1]

More than a few of Charles's advisers thought there was something odd, perverse even, about the hold the Dominican had on their king. They dismissed Las Casas, along with other critics, as "hysterical mystics" who wrote in a "state of absolute delirium." They saw Christ in the filthiest Indian, Christ's Crucifixion in every epidemic. Las Casas's followers took every complaint they heard from Indians in confession, no matter how fantastical, as the gospel truth. Many of the Dominican's critics, including other clerics, were absentee *encomenderos*. They didn't want to know the details of how their foremen got them their gold and silver.

Groping in the Darkness

Spain was the first empire in modern history to have actively publicized its colonial atrocities. The Franciscan Toribio de Benavente Motolinía couldn't understand why the Crown would allow the "printing of such a thing," referring to the *Brevísima Relación*. Perhaps, Father Benavente wondered, God wanted the book published to give good men a chance to answer Las Casas's lies. Answer they did. Yet even when they were directly refuting Las Casas, or just writing their own odes to conquistador glory, the ghastly scenes they described were hardly exculpatory.[2]

Printers in Seville, Madrid, Valencia, Toledo, and other cities stamped out sheet after sheet of carnage: mass hangings, drowned babies, torched towns. They rolled out pages defending such horrors. Sometimes force was needed to save souls, to bring guests to "the banquet table of eternity."

Common soldiers wrote, or paid others to write, their stories of mayhem. A good tale might bring land, an administrative job, recognition of title, or a larger allotment of Indians. The reading public was eager for news of the New World's strange peoples. Strangeness and violence went hand in hand, for descriptions of the first—especially of cannibalism—legitimated the latter. "They eat each other, like demons," reported an early history of Mexico; "public butcher shops sold cuts of human meat as if they came from a cow or sheep." The most well-known account of cannibalism appears in a history written by the veteran Bernal Díaz del Castillo to support his request for financial compensation. Díaz even provided a recipe: "They planned to kill us and eat our flesh, and already had the pots ready with salt, garlic and tomatoes."³ "We killed many of them, and others we burned alive," wrote Díaz matter-of-factly of his would-be devourers.*

Even official reports were stuffed with descriptions of horror. Martín García Óñez de Loyola, Chile's royal governor (probably the nephew of Saint Ignatius of Loyola), wrote to the king of the mutilations meted out by the Spanish on the Mapuche, in their long war for control of Araucanía, a region in southern Chile. The Spanish had turned Araucanía into a post-apocalyptic landscape filled with the walking near-dead: a "multitude of lame and maimed Indians, without hands, or with only one hand, blind, their noses cut off, earless." Others were castrated, branded, and sold as slaves. Some had their tendons cut. They couldn't run away, yet, hobbled, neither could they work.⁴

"Our cruelty," Óñez said, "incites and animates them to die rather than surrender." The Mapuche think the unthinkable, the governor continued, that all people are the same under heaven's eaves. Heliocentrism, the idea popularized by Copernicus, that the earth wasn't the center of the universe, nurtured the idea of equality: Doesn't the same sun that warms Europe, they asked, also warm us?

Gonzalo Fernández de Oviedo, the notary who suggested putting Indians in cages to teach them the Requirement, wrote one of the first histories of the Conquest, justifying Spanish rule while introducing readers to the strangeness of the New World. The first European to draw a pineapple, Oviedo feared that he had barely touched the "marrow" of the New World's "great and innumerable secrets, which remain to be discovered."

"Shameless nonsense," Las Casas thought. There was only one secret to be discovered, one thing to marvel at: "the massacres of innocent people."

"Silence all talk of other wonders of the world," he begged. The Dominican unwaveringly resisted exoticizing the Indies. No pearls and pineapples for Las Casas, unless he was describing the coerced labor required to snatch such items from the sea or the land. What was unfathomable was the devas-

---

* A whiff of the familiar. London burned its heretics, the last in 1612, within smelling distance of Smithfield Market's slaughterhouse and meat stalls, perhaps explaining the English-reading public's fascination with the New World's "cannibal butcher shops."

tation wrought by Spain. There was no explanation for it, it was *unknowable*. Histories of the Conquest were mostly lies, exercises in "dry sterility" that couldn't "penetrate into the reason of men." Historians were writing fables, "groping in the darkness" of their own prejudices.[5]

So vast was the scale of cruelty that even Las Casas, who repeatedly affirmed that he witnessed firsthand the atrocities he wrote about, doubted, as time passed, his own memory. Were Christians capable of such horror? "My eyes saw all these things," he wrote, "so strange to human nature, and I almost fear telling them, not believing myself thinking perhaps they were a nightmare."[6]

The terror assaulted the senses. The smell of burning flesh and disemboweled viscera, the sound of the sizzle of the firebrand and the cleaver on bone, wailing orphans and sobbing parents, the sight of pus-covered rags wrapped around suppurating skin forced a range of emotions on witnesses: anger, despair, sorrow, rage, repulsion, helplessness. It is too much to write, as an early biographer of Las Casas did, that because of Jeremiahs like Las Casas "the Spanish national conscience recognized the obligation" it had toward its New World vassals. Spain wasn't a nation but rather a patchwork of fiefdoms transforming into an empire. And nations don't have consciences.

But the Catholic Church did have to defend itself as a magisterium of mercy, charity, and love. Its priests were shepherds tending to sheep. Most royal officials kept filing reports saying the sheep were doing fine. Las Casas and others like him kept posting anguished letters to Spain reporting that the sheep were being slaughtered at an incalculable rate.

A half century into the Conquest there still existed no legal consensus that easily justified the ongoing wars. The Crown found it impossible to translate whatever wisdom might be gleaned from all these deliberations— much less all the published accounts—into policy. When it tried to enact laws mitigating abuses, *encomenderos* balked and forced Spain to retract them. The wheel kept spinning. Nothing could help authorities adjudicate opposing unreconcilable opinions concerning the nature of indigenous peoples. All they could do was sit for another lecture, read another treatise, hold yet another council, issue another edict, listen to another debate.

By Nature Just

On one side of the question were the brutalists, scholars like Gonzalo Fernández de Oviedo and Juan Ginés de Sepúlveda who defended papal authority and the belief that some humans were "natural slaves." They weren't so crass as to say, as the frontline conquistadores said, that Indians were animals or monsters. They agreed with Las Casas that such a belief was heresy. But they argued for gradations, and Indians were lesser humans. For them, the conquest of the New World was fundamentally just, as was the idea that the pope and Spanish monarchs held both spiritual and temporal sovereignty over all the world's people, Catholics as well as heathens.

They described war, evangelization, and resource extraction as three parts of the same mission. Oviedo wrote that Indians were naturally indolent, living among such abundance—within easy reach of those pineapples he painted—that no wage could tempt them to work. They receded into the forest rather than establish lasting contact with the Spanish. So evangelization by necessity required coercion. And though they weren't animals, many of them lived like animals: "the great majority of them naked, barbarous, and without laws and all subject to tyrants, and more distressing, to the tyranny of the Devil." They indulge in "abominable vices" and commit "sins against nature, and in many parts eating one another and sacrificing to the Devil and to their idols many children, men and women."[7]

"Crimes against nature," Sepúlveda said, legitimated their subjugation.[8]

Sepúlveda was hailed by popes, cardinals, inquisitors, and consultants to kings as one of Spain's preeminent humanists, meaning a scholar-theologian who engaged with the wisdom and languages of the ancients. Having earned his reputation by translating Aristotle's works into Latin and the New Testament into Spanish, he was implacable in his defense of the hard edge of the Spanish Empire, the edge that was sharpened in total war against Muslims, Jews, and Native Americans. He believed that the inhabitants of the New World had to be pacified to prepare the way for Christ's Second Coming.

That Sepúlveda, chaplain to the emperor, is considered an exemplary Renaissance humanist gives a sense of how violent, paranoiac, and apocalyptic humanism was in the early 1500s.[9]

Sepúlveda never visited America, though his arguments were appreciated by its new rulers. Settlers in Mexico City sent him "some jewels and clothing from this land to the value of 200 pesos" in appreciation of his defense of their interests. At a banquet in Barcelona, Cortés personally briefed Sepúlveda on one of his largest massacres, in the city of Cholula, home to over four hundred "mosques," as Cortés called temples to the god Quetzalcoatl. There, Cortés's men killed upwards of seven thousand residents and plundered the city for days. Survivors crawled under the rising mountain of corpses to hide. When they could no longer bear the stench, they crawled out. The Spanish, waiting, "hewed them to death."

Cortés called such killings "chastisements," a warning intended to radiate terror throughout the countryside and keep the people in "awe" of their new overlords.

Sepúlveda cited conquistador tales of Indian barbarism to argue that the Conquest was just, and then conquistadores cited Sepúlveda as expert opinion that the Conquest was just.

They "bedazzled the world," Las Casas said.[10]

Sepúlveda understood that Spain's dominance of world politics depended on Indian labor: America's silver and gold paid for the empire's many wars, against the Ottomans in the east and low-country Calvinists to the north. And so he, along with other influential Catholic theologians, made a series of reinforcing arguments in favor of the *encomienda* system and natural slavery. "The man rules over the woman, the adult over the child, the father over his children," Sepúlveda wrote, as the king ruled over his subjects and a master over his slaves. Such a worldview justified both *encomienda* bondage and chattel enslavement of Africans. Sepúlveda also rejected Las Casas's dismissal of Aristotle, citing stories of paganism, cannibalism, sodomy, rudeness, and savagery to argue that Indians might be humans, but they weren't innocent humans. All humanity may be one, but not all humans were equal.[11]

Spain was the vanguard of the Catholic Counter-Reformation, a bastion of reaction that was carrying out, through the office of the Inquisition, a purification, and Sepúlveda's defense of the Conquest was bound up in this movement. To question the legitimacy of Spain in America was to question the legitimacy of Catholicism in Europe, to throw open the door to Luther and Calvin. It was a savage world, Sepúlveda argued, one that could only be organized around an economy of coerced trade, forced labor, and constant war.

Sepúlveda's most important argument in favor of natural slavery held that Native Americans couldn't organize themselves into a true civilized society founded on property. The ability to possess was among the first questions that concerned Columbus. "I have not been able to learn if they hold private property," he wrote just after making landfall in the Caribbean on his first voyage; "It seemed to me to be that they all took a share in whatever anyone had." The Aztecs "consider themselves the most civilized people," Sepúlveda wrote, yet they have "established their commonwealth in such a manner that no one individually owns anything."

For Sepúlveda, indigenous peoples in the New World could not possess, they could only be possessed.

True Dominion

On the other side of the question were the moral revolutionaries, the clerics and jurists who humanized humanism. In the late 1540s, the Conquest seemed like it might go on forever. The Spanish fought long campaigns in the south, in Patagonia against the Mapuche, and, north of Mexico City, against the Chichimec, who were blocking access to valuable silver mines. The pacification of the Philippines and Florida was still to come. Amid this interminable war, there emerged successive generations of Spanish thinkers whose combined body of work anticipated liberalism, socialism, pacifism, and internationalism.

There were the Franciscans, who came to Hispaniola on Columbus's second voyage and were among the first to condemn the enslavement of the island's natives. There was Montesinos and his fellow Dominicans. There was Las Casas, absolute and inescapable, present either in body or spirit at what seemed all the key moments of the formation of the Spanish Empire.

And in Spain, there was the law professor Francisco de Vitoria, like Las Casas also a Dominican.

Six years old when Columbus made landfall, Vitoria was educated in Paris at the Sorbonne and came to be considered among the greatest legal theorists, an intellectual heir to Aquinas himself. He was scholastic to the core. To accept the first premise of whatever relentless argument he was making meant accepting his whole claim. After graduation, Vitoria returned to Spain to take up a professorship at the University of Salamanca, where he was also affiliated with the city's monastery, the Convento de San Esteban, a cradle of critical theory and dissent.

Vitoria was Las Casas's temperamental opposite, recessive, more comfortable debating theory and arguing logic than reciting facts. He wanted a "more humane theology, a more intelligible theology." Vitoria spoke cautiously in public, using the "cold language of reason." In private, he was disgusted with the "utter impiety and tyranny" of the conquistadores, as he wrote to a friend in 1534.[12]

Vitoria thought that the solution to the problem of sovereignty in the Indies might also be the solution to the crisis of legitimacy in Europe—to the spread of Lutheranism, which was making it impossible to justify the rule by Vatican dispensation; and to the spread of capitalism, and the creation of new secular interest groups, including powerful banking houses. In 1532, the Pizarro brothers conquered Peru and ruled as if Spain, much less the Vatican, mattered not one bit. Two years later, Henry VIII announced that England would form its own church and not be subject to the dictates of the pope.

The Christian world was losing its focal point; papal power was in eclipse.

Vitoria grasped for a theory that might help stem the desegregation, an answer to Protestant radical theologians who argued that "dominion was dependent upon God's grace." Such a position taken to its extreme would bring chaos: every man guided by his inner light, a million monarchs, an endless revolution of the self. Applied to nations and empires, the result would be perpetual war.

Palacios's Requirement had begun to recognize the world's diversity, the necessary coexistence of different peoples: Catholics, Protestants, Moors, Gentiles, Jews, and other sects. But his solution—a stubborn insistence on the legitimacy of the Papal Donation—was untenable. A new law was required based on universal rules that applied to all, that could incorporate the familiar people of the Old World and the *rarezas*, the oddities, of the New. Vitoria composed such a law, justified not by revealed authority, nor power politics, but by the idea that "all human beings" formed "one community," and all the world's nations formed "in a sense a commonwealth." This "natural law" was created by God but couldn't be altered by God, and bound all people regardless of their faith.

Vitoria never published a book or treatise. Yet his breakthrough lectures on *jus gentium*, the law of nations, or law of peoples, were recorded by his Salamanca students and published after his death in 1557 as *Relectiones Theologicae*, which taken together were so rigorous, so generative of disciples, they gave rise to a series of premises that formed the foundation of modern international law:

- Reason and not divine revelation was the foundation of the law of nations, which opened the door to political pluralism, to accepting both Protestants and pagans as potentially sovereign.

- Indians were human beings, possessors of their own lives and property.

- Just cause was needed to wage war, to take captives, and to confiscate property.

- Spain had a right to evangelize, but neither the objective of civilizing nor conversion provided just cause for war.

- Nor could accusations of cannibalism, "pederasty, buggery with animals, or lesbianism."*

---

* Las Casas said that cannibalism couldn't justify war since the most ferocious cannibal was the *encomienda*, which consumed the bodies of its victims in unimaginable numbers. The *encomienda* allowed the settlers, Las Casas wrote, to drink the "blood and eat the bodies" of its victims.

"Every country is full of sinners," Vitoria said. If vice justified conquest, then international politics would consist of nothing other than permanent warfare. "Kingdoms could be exchanged"—or to use more modern terms, regimes would be changed—"every day."[13]

In response to theologians like Sepúlveda, Vitoria insisted that Indians had and exercised the right of property. Prior to the arrival of Spain, "the barbarians undoubtedly possessed as true a dominion, both public and private, as any Christian. They could not be robbed of their property, either as private citizens or as princes, on the grounds that they were not true masters."

Vitoria was one of the earliest Catholic jurists to argue that the pope's "donation" of the New World to Spain, and the division of the Indies between Spain and Portugal, was illegitimate. "When the Spanish first sailed to the land of the barbarians," they "carried with them no right at all to occupy their countries." Neither the Catholic monarch nor the pope, he said, had temporal power over the whole world. Refusal by the peoples of the Americas to recognize Catholic authority justified nothing: not war, not seizure of their goods and lands, and not the deposing of leaders. Indians were rational beings who both had and enjoyed the right of possession and lived in clearly recognizable complex societies with their own rulers.*

Vitoria insisted that only a systematic, rational law of peoples—*jus gentium*—could organize a fractured world.[14]

Among his greatest challenges to the legitimacy of the Conquest was his rejection of the doctrine of discovery. Since "the barbarians were true owners, both from the public and the private standpoint" of the New World, the

---

* Vitoria raised doubts about the legality of the Conquest, yet he didn't seek to nullify the right to conquest; he believed that conquest in a just war was legitimate. And he laid out several criteria that might allow a war to be considered just. He suggested that a just war might be waged to free oppressed people, as Cortés helped free Tlaxcala from oppressive Aztec rule. He also argued that a just war might be waged to defend basic rights, including the right of free trade on open seas; the right of all people, including the Spanish, to travel, to engage in commerce, communicate, and preach; and the right to use the things that make up humanity's commons, including water, fish, birds, and, conveniently, precious metals. Vitoria here previewed later "free trade" arguments, foreshadowing future wars waged to open markets and gain access to resources. In the decades following Vitoria's lectures, Spanish officials in the Americas increasingly cited indigenous obstruction of highways and communication as justification for pacifying and enslaving uncooperative Native Americans.

so-called right of discovery gives "no support to the seizure of the aborigines any more than had it been they who had discovered us."

Had it been they who had discovered us. Here, Vitoria cracks open the door to ridicule, to a darkly humorous *reductio ad absurdum* humor that used the premises of Catholic universalism to undermine Catholic prerogative. To legitimate the barbarism of the conquistadores by invoking the barbarism of the Indians, as someone like Sepúlveda would do, was itself a joke, a cruel one. The Mapuche understood the irony. In southern Chile, they forced their Spanish prisoners to dress like Indians, while they donned Spanish clothing. Would-be lords became "subjects and slaves, obeying the Indians as their master and the Indians gave orders like superiors." There are different accounts of how the Mapuche executed the Spanish captain Pedro de Valdivia. One describes Valdivia's mouth being forced open and molten gold poured in, a tribute to the unquenchable Spanish thirst for the metal. Another version has the Mapuche leader Caupolicán dress in the dead conquistador's armor: a green and purple tunic, trimmed with silver and gold thread, a strong breastplate and a steel headpiece topped by an emerald.[15]

Kitted out as his enemy, Caupolicán announced, sounding a little like Vitoria, that he would soon "invade Spain and subject the great, invincible King Charles to Araucana dominance."[16]

The Spanish Crown struggled to find a worldview that could organize the power it was fast accumulating, that could justify the blood it was spilling and mediate the extremes of Las Casas and Vitoria on one hand and Sepúlveda on the other. Charles and his counselors would have liked to silence the critics. The king-emperor sent a letter to the prior of Vitoria's Salamanca monastery, the Convento de San Esteban, complaining of priests and professors who were questioning the "authority of our Holy Father in these realms." Charles's tone was reproachful, and he ordered the prefect to shut down all such discussions, sermons, and commentaries and confiscate related printed matter.[17]

Yet there was no turning back. The printing press made criticism hard to contain.

5.

New Laws

fter nearly three decades of advocacy, Las Casas had achieved a significant number of ineffective successes. He won almost every battle. But little changed.

He had Spanish settlers banned from entering Verapaz in Guatemala, a
region meant to showcase the Dominican model of peaceful conversion.
The Spanish kept entering.

In 1535, Las Casas wrote to King Charles's wife, the empress-regent Isabella, asking her majesty to stop the Germans in Venezuela from exporting
indigenous slaves to Hispaniola. Isabella ordered the enslaved Indians be
returned to their homes. They weren't returned to their homes.

That same year, Las Casas successfully petitioned the Crown to condemn
two slave-raiding expeditions to the Spanish mainland from Hispaniola,
one financed by a member of Charles's court, the other by a Genoese sugar
merchant. Spain ordered the slaves sent back to Venezuela. The slaves
weren't sent back to Venezuela. They were distributed among Hispaniola
families as "servants." Also in 1535, Las Casas denounced the pacification
campaign under way in the province of Nicaragua. The Crown ordered it
halted. The campaign continued. Las Casas wrote to Pope Paul III arguing
for the humanity of Indians, and the Vatican, influenced by the Dominican's arguments, affirmed the humanity of Indians. They were "true men"

said the Vatican in 1537, in the papal bull titled *Sublimis Deus*. God might have been sublime, but Spanish settlers continued to disregard the humanity of Indians.[1]

So it went. Some success came in 1542. Las Casas was in Spain, in Seville, still lobbying royal officials and church superiors, waiting for yet another audience with the king while working on what would become *Brevísima Relación de la Destrucción de las Indias*. His determination paid off, as King Charles agreed to a sweeping set of regulations, known as the New Laws, meant to prevent settlers from becoming a landed aristocratic class. *Las Leyes Nuevas* declared Indians to be free subjects of the Crown, prohibited the creation of new *encomiendas*, and mandated the dissolution of existing ones upon the death of the *encomenderos*. The idea that this was a root-and-branch revolution in colonial policy was reinforced when King Charles named Las Casas bishop of Chiapas, an elevation to a rank of considerable power within the Catholic hierarchy.

In April 1544, accompanied by a contingent of forty-three Dominican friars and priests, Las Casas left Spain on the *San Salvador*, the lead ship in a convoy of twenty-six merchant vessels carrying the largest congregation yet of religious people sent to the New World—Las Casas at the head of his own holy battalion. The priests set sail in "glory," one of Las Casas's traveling companions wrote in his diary, "singing liturgies and other songs." Chiapas's new bishop, many in the mission believed, had been invested by the king with "powers and provisions" to transform colonial rule, to subordinate settler life to ecclesiastical authority.

Las Casas was going "to free the slaves."[2]

The Protector of Indian Dogs

The voyage was hair-raising, the ships battered by storms. Nine of Las Casas's handpicked clerics drowned. In Hispaniola, settlers blockaded the Dominican monastery where he and his close advisers stayed and refused to provision the compound with food and other necessities.

Las Casas resumed his journey to Chiapas, and Hispaniola's Spaniards were happy to have him off the island. At the Mexican port of Veracruz, what was left of Las Casas's entourage split up, as clerics headed in different directions to their assigned posts. Those who accompanied Father Las Casas to Chiapas went by foot and mule, passing through villages that were just then raising simple adobe churches, with carvings in their facade preserving bits of pre-Conquest iconography of vines, animals, sacred Ceiba trees, and even glyphs and symbols representing Aztec deities, including the god of flowers. Many are still in existence. After traveling three hundred miles, the pilgrims reached Chiapas's capital city, Ciudad Real, sitting nearly seven thousand feet above sea level. They received a cold welcome from the city's Spanish settlers—along with reports that the New Laws were everywhere under threat.[3]

In Peru, *encomenderos*, in reaction to the New Laws, declared themselves independent, in a revolt led by conquistador Gonzalo Pizarro, who had the king's viceroy beheaded. It took two years, but royalist troops finally captured and executed Pizarro, restoring royal rule. The uprising shook Spain, which depended on Peru's silver. In Mexico, Crown officials simply refused to enforce the New Laws, while Mexico's archbishop, once a defender of indigenous rights but worn down by years of fighting with settlers, wrote a letter asking the king to suspend the reforms. Royal officers in the province of Guatemala didn't enforce them either. There, a group of *encomenderos*, shocked that they wouldn't be able to bequeath their Indians to their sons, sent a letter to the king condemning whom they supposed was the laws' author: Las Casas, "a friar unread in law, unholy, envious, vainglorious, unquiet, not free from cupidity, and, above all else, trouble maker."[4]

In Chiapas, Las Casas tried to claim the power to defend Native Americans absolutely and without limits. Indians, Las Casas said, deserved full rights, equal to the Spanish in God's common *"universo orbe."* Yet he was set upon by the settlers, who, due to their small numbers, lived in fear of Ciudad Real's growing, increasingly defiant Maya population. Spanish protesters surrounded Las Casas's rectory. They yelled insults, calling him a "protector of Indian dogs," and held up copies of Vatican edicts that gave the Americas to Spain and Portugal. Spain's colonists clearly understood the threat dissident jurists and theologians represented to their interests. For them, *el*

Requerimiento was still the last word. Las Casas's deacon disobeyed his orders and the town's sheriff refused to protect the bishop. At one point, Las Casas escaped a violent mob by taking refuge in the Indian part of town. There he was treated warmly.

Elsewhere, in Nicaragua and southern Mexico, priests who tried to enforce the New Laws were targeted. Some were killed, others imprisoned. Las Casas soon understood that rather than giving him a command center to supervise the enforcement of the New Laws, his Church superiors had seated him on the top of a remote mountain, besieged by enemies, unprotected and far from centers of colonial power. He decided to give up his post and return to Spain, never again to set foot in the New World. By now, the most important provisions of the New Laws had been revoked, and what was left of the legislation was, in many places, ignored.[5]

Once back in Spain, Las Casas watched the same pattern of unenforceable policy victories play out. He convinced Charles that *encomenderos* who didn't provide for religious instruction should be obligated to pay reparations to their commended Indians. *Encomenderos* paid no mind to this obligation. In 1548, the Crown issued a law freeing most Indian slaves. They remained slaves, the names of their owners fire-branded on their foreheads.

The Dominican lobbied Charles to halt the Conquest until the political status of Native Americans could be decided once and for all. Charles agreed. The Conquest continued. The king's advisers suggested that the Crown stop using the word *conquest*. Instead, they said, let's call Spain's advances across the Americas and the Pacific "discoveries."

Whatever the word used, fighting continued. The Philippines and Florida were incorporated into the realm. The Spanish continued their war on the unvanquished peoples in southern Chile and northern Mexico. Hernando de Soto's expedition into North America's southwest reaped only a single string of pearls as booty but left behind a trail of "sadism and violence that included murder, rape, maiming, and enslavement."[6]

Charles was the "world emperor," the ruler of Holy Rome, king of Spain, and sovereign of the New World, the Pacific, much of middle Europe, and enclaves of northern Africa. He was enormously powerful—and yet no one of consequence in the empire would heed his will, at least when it came to the enslavement and killing of Indians.

Unable either to stop the violence, or silence criticism of the violence, the royal court had little choice but, in 1550, to convene yet another debate, in Valladolid's Colegio de San Gregorio, between the two priests most associated with slavery and liberty.

Juan Ginés de Sepúlveda defended the idea of natural slavery and spoke in favor of keeping Amerindians enslaved. Bartolomé de las Casas argued otherwise. Las Casas by then was in his midseventies, but he still had the power to transfix. Reading from a massive manuscript, the priest spoke with the same facial expressions, eye rolls, and playful use of Latin that had captivated an earlier royal audience. Scholars hold this "dispute" up as a highlight in the history of ethical thought. Really, it was hardly different from the case that Las Casas had long been making, including in his 1540 debate. After each man—Sepúlveda and Las Casas—had had their turn, the royal jury began its deliberations, which went on for years without coming to a firm decision as to who had won.

"Great disputes took place among famous jurists, canonists, and theologians," wrote Oviedo, "yet no good came to the land or the Indians."[7]

Rules and Advice

Frustrated, Las Casas rethought his tactics. Along with his companion of twenty-five years, Father Rodrigo de Andrada, Las Casas established residency in various Spanish monasteries.* First in Valladolid's Dominican Colegio de San Gregorio and, after 1561, in Madrid's Nuestra Señora de Atocha, the couple turned their monastery cells into the "general headquarters" of an "ideological war." Las Casas led seminars on indigenous rights, and though effectively barred from returning to the Americas, continued to

---

* Not much is known of Las Casas and Andrada's relationship, except that their friends nicknamed them Elijah and Enoch, after the only two men mentioned in the Bible who ascend to Heaven alive.

live, emotionally, in the New World, continued to witness its history with what one Spanish historian calls his inner eyes.[8]

With the Caribbean destroyed and Mexico largely pacified, Las Casas focused his attention on Peru. Unlike in Mexico, where Cortés, with indigenous allies who had suffered under Aztec rule, had quickly established effective Spanish authority, Spain's hold on the Andes was tenuous. Upstart settlers competed with royal officials for power. Spanish authorities also had to deal with still living Inka royal elites, including one who had fled with a large contingent of followers to the Andean piedmont and established an insurgent rump Inka Empire.

During the last decade of his life, Las Casas had given up lobbying for change within the councils of state and instead focused on radicalizing Catholic doctrine, publishing at least eight theological treatises insisting that true faith was irreconcilable with conquest and slavery. One controversial passage argued that "all the things that have been done so far in the Indies, upon the arrival of the Spanish in each province, such as the subjection and bondage of the inhabitants, have been a violation of natural law and human law, as well as divine law." The entire Conquest "is unjust, iniquitous, tyrannical, and worthy of the fires of hell. Thus, the Conquest is null, invalid, devoid of value, illegal, and therefore not a penny of tribute was taken justly." Settlers, he said, "are obligated to make complete restitution" to the people they dispossessed. Sepúlveda referred this passage to the Inquisition, calling it heresy.[9]

Las Casas turned to confession to advance emancipation. He got the idea of using the Holy Sacrament of Penance as an ideological weapon from when *he* was denied, prior to his conversion and renunciation of his *encomiendas*, absolution from a Dominican priest. After his debate with Sepúlveda, Las Casas decided to sharpen the strategy, writing a series of "rules and advice" books for priests, on how to properly hear confession.[10]

The act of telling one's sins to another man—as opposed to just praying silently to God—represents the intercessional essence of Catholicism: the Church as an institution that mediates social and spiritual life, that represents God to man and man to God. In Christianity's early centuries, before the sacrament was standardized into the private practice we know today, confessions were public events. They generally took place once a year on a day set aside for reconciliation. Gathered neighbors might or might not overhear the confession. Most sins were understood not as individual offenses against individual victims but as acts that harmed the whole community. Even theft and adultery were treated as collective violations since they tore at the social fabric, creating distrust, anger, and cycles of vengeance. The public performance of absolution on the part of the priest thus was an important element in the ritual of communal healing.[11]

The fight against Lutheranism and Calvinism elevated the importance of confession. Reforms enacted by the Council of Trent in the middle of the 1500s led to a reimagining of the sacrament, investing in the confessor the symbolic power of "judge," charged with probing the inner thoughts of the penitent. The legal imagery was reinforced in the 1560s with the introduction of the confessional booth, which gave the priest his own small courtroom. The anonymity of the booth detached the sacrament from its communitarian origins and reinforced the individualizing thrust of the time, the idea of sin and forgiveness as a private matter between man and maker. Increasingly, penitents were confessing not just sins of commission but sins of intent and desire, vices such as lust and envy.[12]

Las Casas wasn't interested in digging deeper into the interior of man's mind and soul. The bishop went in the other direction. Contrition for him, especially one's final confession, was the furthest thing from a private, psychological matter. In his various treatises on the subject, he pushed for atonement to be maintained as a collective ritual—one focused not on the small grievances of rural life but on the empire's greatest crimes against humanity.

Medieval wills of penitents who broke the Eighth Commandment, the prohibition against stealing, often contained codicils detailing how restitution, or reparations, would be made to victims, either by attestants or by their heirs. Failure to make reparations was considered a mortal sin. There was nothing controversial or exceptional about this practice, until Las Casas—taking advantage of the Counter-Reformation's empowerment of the confessor—applied it to the Conquest. He intended his "rules and advice" to do what the New Laws had failed to do, what the Crown had failed to do: break *encomienda* power.

The Conquest, Las Casas said, was one large act of theft, and theft was a sin. A penitent was to ask forgiveness not just from God but from his commended Indians and slaves: "For the injury he did to them in making them slaves, usurping their liberty." Then he was to grant them "irrevocable freedom, without any limitation or condition."

Las Casas instructed priests to interrogate the penitent's personal history: "Did you participate in conquests?" "Did you enrich yourself?" The person seeking penitence would be expected to provide a detailed description of his participation in "the wars against Indians" and "declare if all that he possesses comes from Indians." One of Las Casas's confessional guides defined the Conquest as a collective crime, akin to what lawyers today call conspiracy or racketeering, and that the crime wasn't limited to the riches one person took from Indians but all the riches that everyone took. Las Casas's treatises listed "an astonishing variety of guilty Spaniards" required to pay restitution: aging conquistadores, *encomenderos*, slavers, and mine owners. Merchants were to pay reparations to Indians for selling weapons and other goods that aided *encomenderos* in exploiting Indians: "arquebuses, gunpowder, crossbows, lances, and swords." Horse ranchers were guilty too. "Horses" were "the worst" weapon, Las Casas said, never having forgotten witnessing their use in the Cuban campaign. Penitents were to make restitution not just for the evils they committed, but for "all the evils and harms that others did [or] with whom they collaborated . . . every one of them is obligated *in solidum*"—that is, in joint liability.[13]

Confessors, too, needed to be on guard. Leniency would implicate them in the penitent's crimes. The confessor "must tremble" in fear. No empathy was permitted. Interrogate the conquerors and settlers to the depths of their souls. Do not "oblige" where they need not be "obliged."[14]

Local priests sympathetic to Las Casas's vision wrote their own guidelines, some more stringent in their insistence on reparations. In Mexico, royal authorities had just finished burning Las Casas's writings when a new shipload of his confessional guides arrived, causing, according to a priest hostile to Las Casas's perpetual agitation, "no little uproar and scandal." The guides accused "conquerors and *encomenderos* and merchants of being tyrant-thieves, rapists, kidnappers, predators." The guidebooks declared all tribute taken from Indians had been taken "unjustly and tyrannically."[15]

Las Casas had never visited Peru, yet his influence was felt. Indigenous leaders were aware of his advocacy and repeated many of his arguments, as did priests and clerics. In 1560, Lima's Dominican archbishop, Jerónimo de Loayza y González, a student of Vitoria, issued "instructions for the confessors of conquistadores," based on Las Casas's template, throwing the highlands into a moral crisis. Many original conquistadores, old and widowed, were coming to the end of their lives and had to figure out what to do with their estates. Las Casas's insistence that the Conquest was something for which one had to make amends had penetrated the minds of aging settlers. One survey of last testaments drafted in Peru during the 1550s and 1560s reveals that it had become common for dying conquistadores to confess their complicity in the Conquest and to offer some form of "restitution."[16]

Nicolás de Ribera, *el Viejo*, the elder, a captain in Pizarro's conquering troop, presided over a *casa poblada*, a bustling house filled with family members, slaves, and servants, with Lima's notables coming and going. As Ribera entered old age he drafted a will, along with a series of addendums. Read as a whole, they reveal Las Casas's stamp. Ribera confessed to having shared in the looted gold and silver of the original Conquest, along with "*otros despojos*"—other dispossessions, such as a large *encomienda* he had been given in the Ica Valley, about 160 miles south of Lima. Ribera also confessed to having "mistreated" Indians by taking more tribute from them than merited. After consulting with "theologians and learned men," Ribera calculated that he owed the Indians of his *encomienda* fourteen thousand pesos. "I took advantage of them," he said, and intended to make amends. Ribera had the "will" to "satisfy any and all Indians to whom I am bound."[17]

Coming from a highly respected elder conquistador who didn't participate in any of the various settler rebellions against Spanish rule, Ribera's deathbed contrition carried weight, as one historian wrote, calling "into question the legality of the conquest."[18]

Then there was Captain Mansio Serra de Leguizamón. The captain took Las Casas's admonitions to heart as he approached his death in 1589. Sixteen when he joined Pizarro at the sacking of Cajamarca, Serra used his will to denounce the Conquest: "We found these realms in such order that there was not a thief, nor a vicious man, nor an adulteress, nor were there prostitutes, nor were there immoral people, each being content and honest in their labor. And that their lands, forests, mines, pastures and dwellings and produce were regulated in such a manner that each person possessed his own property without any other seizing or occupying it." Captain Serra addressed the king directly: "I wish Your Catholic Majesty to understand the motive that moves me to make this statement is the peace of my conscience and because of the guilt I share. For we have destroyed by our evil behavior such a government as was enjoyed by these natives." Serra also confessed that he received fifty thousand pesos of gold from indigenous tribute, and though he couldn't afford to pay it back, "it is what I owe them."[19]

Such dramatic acts of remorse were rare, however. Priests, especially empathetic ones, had created a powerful cultural image: *un indio triste*, a sad Indian, a miserable Indian, stripped of property, his prince dispossessed of dominion, his community robbed of labor, land, and goods. Las Casas used it as a political weapon in his relentless effort to free Native Americans from settler rule. But the caricature was easily transformed into a pitiful image of abjection, remedied not through a rollback of the Conquest but through Christian charity, mercy, and good works. In the end, Ribera didn't distribute his lands among his laborers, nor did he free his commended Indians. Those he left to his son, Alonso de Ribera. Instead, to make up for the crime of the Conquest, Ribera left money to establish a twenty-five-bed hospital to treat poor Indian men and women. Other orthodox clerics also assured their penitents that the obligation of restitution would be fulfilled by leaving a donation to Church institutions. These donations wound up bolstering the institutions of Spanish rule, the hospitals and other benevolent associations that tended to the empire's wretched.[20]

Elderly conquerors could also invoke the legal concept of "good faith," arguing that since they didn't, at the time, know that the Conquest was a crime, they weren't guilty of sin. A typical clause ran: "I swear and declare that from when I first entered this land until the war was won, I always operated in Good Faith, believing that the war waged against the Natives of the country was just because it was waged by . . . a Christian King, as if it was a war against the Turk or Moors." And there was, as Vitoria had once written, "no lack" of complicit priests, "even within the Dominican order," willing to "salve their consciences, and even to praise their deeds and butchery and pillage."[21]

Far away in Spain, Las Casas damned "good faith" defenses. "Invincible ignorance," he said, would be required for settlers not to know that what they were doing was wrong. They must have been reading, he said, an amended version of the Ten Commandments, one which allows killing and theft.

"Not one Spanish Conquistador," Las Casas said, dropping the sarcasm, "has good faith."[22]

Europe's sudden, brutal contact with the New World opened a breach in legal and moral thought. There was no law, no philosophy, no faith that could justify what true humanists like Montesinos and Las Casas had witnessed in the Indies.

Out of a splintered Christendom, as Luther's Reformation gained ground in northern Europe, the Conquest generation of Dominicans, along with their Franciscan, Jesuit, and Capuchin allies, helped create a new ethics of universalism, a step toward what the psychologist Sam McFarland has called the "slow creation of humanity." Early in his missionary life, in 1517, Las Casas had infamously proposed importing Africans to free Indians from the demands of the Spanish for their labor. Yet he soon considered the enslavement of Africans as illegitimate as the enslavement of Native Americans. He "repented," as he put it, for making the proposal as he watched slavery mutate into something infinitely crueler than what had been called slavery in his Sevillian childhood. He condemned the Portuguese for using the cover of the war against Islam to expand the trade, amazed at the capacity of Portuguese historians to glorify "heinous" slave raiding on the coast of Africa "as great sacrifices made in the service of God." Even Vitoria thought African slavery justified, since it was better to be a Christian slave than live free in Africa. Las Casas, though, as early as the 1520s, had rejected all excuses for depriving Africans of their freedom.[23]

Erasmus, Thomas Moore, and other Christians were, at the time of Las Casas's most active period, elaborating a new humanism. But it was Las Casas, and only Las Casas, who hitched the Catholic Church's prophetic, communitarian tradition that promised deliverance to political action. And such action: he witnessed, he wrote, he preached, he lobbied, he theorized, he consoled, he condemned, and he conspired. Las Casas stood against the unfathomable brutalities of the Spanish Conquest of the New World, advancing a moralism that, no matter how much he appealed to the laws of medieval Catholicism, pointed toward a modern ethics of equality. In this, he was a kind of Adam.[24]

6.

Bartolomé's Many Ghosts

On July 17, 1556, Bartolomé de las Casas lay dying in Madrid's Atocha Convent, surrounded by friends and followers. He had been given last rites, confessing that his greatest sin was that he didn't do enough to defend the people of the New World. Las Casas held his deathbed candle tight—his *candela de la agonía*—and said he was ready, that he was certain in the righteousness of his cause. And then he was gone. He was eighty-two.[1]

Las Casas remained active until this last moment, achieving his most tangible policy victory shortly before he passed. From his monastery battlements he had, even as he pushed his confessional strategy, built a network of allies in the high Andes of like-minded priests, friars, and Inka leaders. Together, they strategized how to respond to a serious threat: a proposal made by a group of *encomenderos* to Madrid to let them buy their *encomiendas* outright.[2]

The monarchy didn't want to privatize *encomiendas*, which would have transformed Crown lands into something close to private property and turned commended laborers into formal slaves. But King Charles had bequeathed an indebted, war-wracked empire to his son Philip, who felt he had no choice but to accept the proposal. In Peru, alarmed leaders of the Quechua—the largest indigenous group within the Inka Empire, and also a catchall term for all former Inka subjects—began convening emergency juntas throughout the highlands to fight the sale, landing on a strategy of granting Las Casas, along with his local collaborator, Father Domingo de Santo Tomás, power of attorney to make a counteroffer. The Inka leaders would buy the *encomiendas* themselves, topping the settlers' bid by one hundred thousand ducats. Father Santo Tomás, the head of Lima's Dominican order and a university professor, dispatched priests and friars to gather indigenous opinions on the proposed sale of *encomiendas* to settlers. The most common Quechua response to these queries: *Never!* Priests reported growing discontent, including refusals to meet required labor demand and tribute and the stirring of an Inka millenarian movement.[3]

Negotiations went on for years. *Encomenderos* kept raising their bid. Quechua Indians kept matching the offers and becoming more forceful in their dissent. Echoing Las Casas's position, they wanted to end the *encomienda* system, to bring about a "full restitution of lands and property, usurped by the Spaniards, and the payment of rewards and liberties for services they had rendered the king." The *encomenderos* kept pushing to buy their Indians. Las Casas, now in his seventies and heading a Catholic-Inka vanguard, pushed back. The Crown needed the money. Yet, constantly reminded by Las Casas of the turmoil that would be unleashed if settlers ruled Peru, the royal court finally gave up on the idea.[4]

It was a rare, substantial victory in a long life of symbolic intellectual and moral triumphs that had brought little "good to the Indian." Las Casas by this point had driven himself to the edge of modern political thought: legitimacy derives from the consent of the governed, he wrote in one of his last treatises, and nations have the right to self-determination. He didn't, as did Vitoria, question the Papal Donation. He remained a Catholic monarchist who submitted to the authority of the successors to Saint Peter. But he did say that the consent of the original inhabitants of the New World was required for such a donation to be legal. "The people, naturally and historically," he wrote, "are antecedent to kings." The contradiction is obvious. If the power of king and pope come from God, and God is absolute, how can consent be required?[5]

That conundrum notwithstanding, Las Casas's position was clear:

Spain's king, he wrote, is obligated under the pain of hellfire to restore the "power and authority" of the Inka throne.

Related or not, upon Las Casas's death, a messianic indigenous movement spread throughout much of the highlands, in areas that Santo Tomás and Las Casas had helped organize and especially in Dominican parishes. Participants, either falling into intense trances or breaking out in wild dances, said that the old Inka earth spirits, angry at the spread of Christianity, had entered their human bodies. Spanish witnesses reported Indians rolling on the ground and walking "like fools" who had "lost their senses."[6]

The movement was repressed. Royal officials blamed the frenzied dancing on Las Casas and his Dominicans, who tolerated and even encouraged Native Americans to keep their pre-Conquest rituals alive. Or maybe, some historians have argued, royal officials exaggerated the threat of the enraptured, in order to crack down on the Dominicans. In any case, now that Las Casas was dead, the push to bury his memory was under way.

The Viceroy Arrives

The Crown went on the offensive. The Andes were to be brought to heel.

Francisco de Toledo's appointment in 1569 as Peru's viceroy was part of the broader campaign to consolidate royal control: over the troublesome mendicant orders; over settler mayhem; over the countryside; over both the insurgent Inka Empire and the more remote Guaraní; over whirling indigenous mystics, along with the equally provocative dancing of enslaved Africans; over the large number of women who were arriving in Lima and other Peruvian cities; over the labor system, which was falling apart as a result of high mortality rates and *encomendero* abuse; over taxes and the budget. And over the Pacific: English pirates blessed by Queen Elizabeth were about to start rounding South America and sacking coastal cities in Chile and Peru.

Toledo carried out many of these objectives with alacrity, though he nearly died from malaria on an expedition to pacify the Guaraní. The new viceroy tamed the *encomenderos*, establishing a centralized system of tribute, taxation, and labor conscription to ensure that most of the wealth extracted from the Indians went to Spain and not into settlers' purses. He balanced the books, and put strict limits on dances held by both Indians and Africans, looking to prevent festivities from fusing into one large, racially mixed bacchanal. Then he set out to destroy the Inka rebels. Spanish officials had been treating the rump Inka Empire as quasi-sovereign, regularly sending ambassadors to negotiate various issues. But Toledo used the killing of two Spanish envoys on route to the provisional Inka capital as a pretext to launch an assault on the rebel holdouts and execute Túpac Amaru, the last insurgent emperor.[7]

Also on Toledo's agenda was to confront the religious orders, especially the Franciscan and Dominican allies of restless Quechua leaders. Toledo arrived in Peru with an "unbridled" hatred of Las Casas. The "harm" wrought by the "Bishop of Chiapas," he said, was unparalleled. Toledo wrote to the king that the Andean clergy influenced by the Dominican acted with more arrogance than did the settlers. These "*señores* believe themselves absolute lords of the spiritual realm, and barely recognize any authority at all in the temporal realm."

Toledo ended the autonomy of the friars, limited their influence in the university, and had Las Casas's books confiscated and withdrawn from circulation. A similar crackdown took place in Mexico and in Spain. A few allies and ideological heirs of Las Casas were burned to death.[8]

Destroying his books and executing his followers was just part of the clampdown. The man himself had to be discredited. Rumors spread that there had been something demonic about Las Casas. His "carnal" passion was shocking. Las Casas was less a priest than an "instrument of demons," responsible for "all the doubt respecting the legitimacy of the conquest," wrote one anonymous critic. Kings treated him as if he were an "apostle," but, his critics said now, he was likely a follower of Satan.[9]

It was well past time to give up the idea of restitution or reparations, Toledo argued. There was no going back to what was. Later, in the 1700s, Spain's Royal Academy of History committed to keeping Juan Ginés de Sepúlveda's works in circulation, calling him the sixteenth century's "most distinguished learned man." Las Casas's pages, meanwhile, sat in the archives.[10]

Toledo's campaign was effective, to a degree. Las Casas might have been discredited in Spanish society, but his memory lingered among the Quechua leaders whom he had worked with from afar. In their petitions for redress, they cited Las Casas the way Las Casas would cite Aquinas, as *the* authority. Fifty years after the Dominican's passing, in 1615, the Quechua intellectual Felipe Guaman Poma de Ayala published a political treatise that directly drew on Las Casas's later radical ideas regarding indigenous sovereignty, especially the priest's insistence that Spain should "abandon altogether its rule over the Andes." Other followers of Las Casas, both Dominicans and Quechua leaders, took a more apocalyptic turn, predicting that God would soon visit ruin on Spain as retribution for its treatment of Native Americans.[11]

The Dominicans Have Deceived Us

Toledo's economic and political reforms helped stabilize royal authority, as did his campaign to discipline the mendicant orders. One of his first acts upon arrival in Lima was to establish an office of the Inquisition—not to stamp out Indian magic but to eradicate heresy, which in Peru in the 1570s increasingly expressed itself as a fusion of Las Casas–influenced emancipation and apocalyptic mysticism. Priest after priest fell to Toledo's Inquisition, interrogated, imprisoned, tortured, exiled, and a few, burned at the stake.[12]

Toledo's crackdown forced oppositional energy to find new outlets. Aroused apocalyptics, some of them drawn to gnostic mysticism, filled the void left by the defeat of Las Casas's political program, sublimating the horror of the Conquest into carnal pain and pleasure.[13]

Consider the exorcism of María Pizarro, which lasted many long years and corresponded to the viceroy's campaign to establish royal authority. María, the daughter of Martín, who was a conquistador cousin of the Pizarro brothers, was one of the highland's many *beatas revelanderas*, blessed prophets, women whose trances, fits, and ecstasies foretold all sorts of marvelous and terrible things for the Americas. María might have suffered from schizophrenia, but her seizures were said to be visions. She gained a cult following of erotic mystics, men and women who used sex, or had sex forced on them, as a way of reaching the divine. Among María's disciples were influential Dominicans, including admirers of the deceased Las Casas.

María's two exorcists were directly linked to Las Casas's failed political project. In Spain, Dominican father Francisco de la Cruz had studied under Francisco de Vitoria and Las Casas. He left Europe to escape the Counter-Reformation's suffocating orthodoxy but found little relief in Lima. The freedoms of the imperial hinterlands—its dissenting priests, dancing Indians, and cataleptic prophets—confused him. Father de la Cruz didn't become a nonbeliever. He didn't know what to believe. He even wrote directly to King Philip to say that, when it came to the sacrament of confession and how to apply it to dying conquistadores and *encomenderos*, he did "not know what to do."[14]

María's was Father de la Cruz's first exorcism, which he performed alongside the Jesuit Luis López. As might be expected, the ritual mixed hysteria, lust, doubt, guilt, and politics. The exorcists described María's body as "fantastical," able to assume the shape of demons. She gave off the smell of tropical fruit.* Before long, María turned the tables. The admittedly confused Father de la Cruz, along with Father López, had come to believe that the devil had left María, and now an angel, perhaps the Archangel Gabriel or Saint Dionysius, spoke through her. De la Cruz joined her cult, and took as lovers four sisters who were also followers of María. One of the siblings, Leonor Valenzuela, gave birth to de la Cruz's son, Gabrielico.[15]

De la Cruz listened to María when she told him to give up his sympathies for Las Casas's ideals and Vitoria's political theories. The priest now insisted that the enslavement of Africans was just, as was the Conquest, and that *encomiendas* should be held in perpetuity. "The Dominicans have deceived us," the angel, speaking through María, told the exorcist.[16]

María died in confinement in December 1573. The Inquisition arrested Father de la Cruz. Subjected to six years of torture, the disgraced priest elaborated what he said was a New Testament, a rambling *American* testament. His delusional declarations clearly signaled a rejection of Las Casas's

---

* "The whole enigma of the tropics," Gabriel García Márquez once said, "can be reduced to the smell of a rotten guava."

politics. Yet they hardly added up to a defense of the existing Spanish Empire. Conquistador men claimed all sorts of brutal and illicit liberties. Now, Father de la Cruz, speaking in the name of María, claimed the right to do the same, to travel along the carnal, sensuous road to salvation. Christians should make a world "as the flesh wants."

The fallen priest insisted that he had been called on by God and chosen by María to preach *la nueva cristiandad indiana*: a new Indian Christianity. His son, Gabrielico, was a new John the Baptist, who would prepare the way for the savior's return, which would take place in Peru. America, De la Cruz predicted, would break with Spain, and the pope would move his seat from Rome to the New World. America would be the future site of the world's redemption.*

María's other exorcist, the Jesuit Luis López, didn't join her cult. He remained loyal to Las Casas's political vision, believing in Indian emancipation and in the illegitimacy of the Conquest. He too was arrested, for arguing that Father de la Cruz wasn't a heretic but rather suffered from a psychological illness. Inquisitors found some of Las Casas's writings in Father López's possessions, as well as a notebook with an outline of an essay arguing that the Conquest was illegitimate.[17]

The Inquisition burned de la Cruz at the stake for heresy and exiled López for life from the New World.[18]

Tricks and Hexes

Viceroy Toledo had as little patience for dancing and fornicating mystics as he did for Las Casas's causes. To rein in the ecstatics and emancipationists, Toledo promoted Catholic orthodoxy. The viceroy, with the help of conservative Jesuits, sponsored a clerical conference—the Tercer Concilio

---

* At some point, the young Gabrielico started telling people that he was the son of God and Mary. Others accused him of being the Antichrist, to which the child answered by saying that the Antichrist would be born of a priest and a nun, and his mother was not a nun. Toledo shipped the boy off to Panama and placed him with a Spanish family.

Limense—with the goal of standardizing and stabilizing Christian doctrine. The clerics singled out women as the cause of their problems.

An "over-abundance of women" afflicted the Andes, the viceroy complained to King Philip. A significant number of Spanish women had arrived in Peru following the original Conquest and, Toledo lamented, "more are born here every hour." Toledo and other officials, along with priests, accused women of dressing licentiously and, among the wealthy, extravagantly. *Encomendero* wives were becoming conspicuous, a symbol of settler excess. But women were also accused of dressing *too* modestly, of using veils and cloaks to hide their true selves.

The famous *tapadas limeñas* moved through public life completely veiled, with only one eye showing, a vexing mix of burlesque and provocation. Before Toledo's arrival, efforts to ban the style were met with a women's strike: "Domestic anarchy loomed. Women refused to tend to their houses, servants dallied, cooking was bland, and children couldn't find their mother to hug them and wipe their noses. . . . Everything was upside down."[19]

Women resisted Toledo's renewed efforts to ban the *saya y manto*, as the skirt and cloak that made up the attire was called. The fashion would transfix visitors to Lima for centuries. Some saw Islam: "They could be taken for those phantoms of invisible women that travelers to the Orient find in Constantinople and all the Muslim cities," wrote a French traveler. Others glimpsed Indian sorcery in the "one sinister eye peering" out of the veil. Another observer thought Africa lay behind the "treacherous" shawls, which made it impossible "to guess the color of the skin" and might conceal "an African, black as the night" and "flat-nosed as death." Wealthy and poor women alike adopted the dress, adding to the uncertainty. The cloak "afforded women only advantages" and "men only discomforts."[20]

Women also got in the way of Toledo's efforts to take control of the *encomienda* system. He wanted conquistadores to die without heirs, making their commended Indians available for a state-run forced labor draft. But widowers rushed to marry young *doncellas* to prevent the dissolution of estates. Toledo charged that young wives of old men were aborting their fetuses, drinking certain herbs to prevent conception, or even committing infanticide to ensure that they, and not a male child, would inherit the wealth. Women, the viceroy said, used "tricks and hexes" to marry aging conquistadores. Pedro de Portocarrero was eighty years old when he married his Indian servant an hour before he died, so as to legally recognize a seven-month-old baby the servant said was his. The viceroy thought it physically impossible that Portocarrero was the baby's father.[21]

The old conquistador was "*in articulo mortis,*" on the verge of death.

Angel Beings

In Mexico City, royal officials burned all the copies of Las Casas's writings they could find in the main plaza, keeping watch until the pyre had died down to be sure there was nothing left but ashes. Still, there were those who carried on his advocacy, though in quieter ways, trying to stop the abuses of forced labor demands and tending to the ill as the rate of epidemics accelerated and the population started to die off in massive numbers.

The Franciscan friar Gerónimo de Mendieta arrived in Mexico in the mid-1500s at the age of twenty and spent most of his life in a monastery in Xochimilco, an independent city in the Aztec Empire (now part of Mexico City). He did most of his pastoral work, political advocacy, and writing after the death of Las Casas, and the two men differed in important ways. Whatever the nature of Las Casas's faith, his advocacy was worldly, steeped in Roman and ecclesiastical jurisprudence. Mendieta was a mystic, though of a gentler tradition than that at work in Peru, one associated with Saint Francis of Assisi (1181–1226), the patron saint of animals. The priest learned Nahuatl so quickly he thought it a "miracle," akin to the Holy Spirit descending on the biblical apostles to give them the power to preach to polyglot peoples.[22]

The Reformation in Europe was irreversible by this point, with Protestants calling on the Catholic Church to denounce its worldly corruptions and return to its earlier simplicity. For Mendieta, however, the New World's common people were already simple *genus angelicum*, angel beings, "an isolated fragment of the human race that had retained the primordial innocence, simplicity, and purity that Adam and Eve had known in the Garden of Eden."[23] Indians instinctively lived the values Christ preached on the Mount.

Mendieta was a utopian upon his arrival in Mexico. The pure souls of the common people, freed from their sacrificial Aztec overlords, made the New World the ideal place to fulfill the Franciscan ideal of "self-emptying," as gleaned from Paul's Letter to the Philippians, where Christ "emptied himself," taking the "form of a humble slave." America, Mendieta also hoped, was the place where history would be redeemed, where the Catholic Church could return to its earlier primitive values.[24]

The Spanish Catholic Empire in the Americas was anything but a community of self-emptying poverty. It was an exploitation machine. Some conservative theologians tried to argue that slavery harmonized with Franciscan ethics, which urged Christians to choose to give up the things of this world. Mendieta, though, said it meant one thing to embrace poverty freely and willingly when plenty was an option. It meant another altogether to be born into a society that produced hunger and was ruled by a class that profited from that hunger.

For Mendieta, having access to basic material necessities—to food, clothing, shelter, and health care—was essential for the virtuous community the Church claimed it wanted to create among the natives. Food first, then ethics, as the German playwright Bertolt Brecht later said.

Mendieta's life spanned exactly the "greatest mortality event" in history. He was born in 1525, arrived in Mexico in 1556, and died there in 1604. And he lived at the reaper's focal point: Mexico's great central valley. Measles, smallpox, typhoid, and other diseases attacked a population already made vulnerable by malnutrition and chronic drought. Bodies became covered in pox. Corpses piled up. The stench in towns hit by disease was overwhelming.

Mendieta struggled to reconcile the misery that surrounded him with the mysticism that inspired him. To be a Christian mystic, says the Chilean theologian Segundo Galilea, is to see all, to take in all, the past, present, and future, creation and destruction, the self and others, all in an instance, through Christ. Las Casas saw all through the original Conquest, and the terrors Spain first imposed on Indians. A generation later, Mendieta saw all through their disappearance. As he watched wave after wave of disease take countless souls, Mendieta still believed that forced labor was the greater killer: "the worst and most harmful pestilence of all."[25]

Gold first, then death. Mendieta's long, long fight against forced labor was second only to Las Casas's. And like Las Casas, he took the diversity of the New World as confirmation of universal equality: "We are all descended from Adam and Eve," he wrote to King Phillip II, and equal in the eyes of God.[26]

Mendieta damned those who tried to explain away pestilence as punishment divine, as God's "secret judgment" leveled against indigenous peoples for failing to fully accept Christ, for having returned to old ways, to idolatry, sodomy, and bestiality. The Franciscan turned that argument on its head. The Lord was calling Indians home to punish the Spanish for their greed and inhumanity. God was visiting the worst punishment that could be visited on a settler: he was cutting off their labor supply, their source of wealth and status.

As Mexico's indigenous population fell, the imperial mood turned dark, and Mendieta's earlier utopianism—the idea that mendicants like him would build an Indian Church as a counter to Luther's schism—gave way to a grim realization that the Age of Mammon reigned. Nothing could diminish Spanish avarice.

Two million people died in 1582 from a *cocoliztli* surge. Prophesies abounded that soon the hemisphere would be emptied out. "There would be no one left." One friar speculated that future generations might not even know that the skin of Indians was a different color than that of the Spanish. Some thought the epidemics a blessing, making the continent's land available for the settlers' taking. At least those interminable debates concerning property and sovereignty would be rendered moot.

But, Mendieta asked, who would do the work? Who "will grow the wheat when the Indians are gone?"[27]

Las Casas's vision of an emancipated Christian commonwealth did not take hold in Spanish America. Neither did Vitoria's rule-based global order, nor de la Cruz's utopia of the flesh, nor Mendieta's return to the primitive church. Rather, it was the success of programs like Toledo's that would become the model for Spanish dominion: an expansive state in which coerced labor was rationalized and the Church was under Crown control, its doctrine justifying (not questioning) imperial rule.

Still, Las Casas's universalism, his belief that humankind, despite its staggering diversity, reflected the unity of God's Creation, lingered on in everyday practices and belief.

Spain is responsible for many imperial "horrors," Octavio Paz wrote half a century ago in *The Labyrinth of Solitude*. Yet compared to later English settlement in North America, "at least it did not commit the gravest of all: that of denying a place, even at the foot of the social scale, to the people who composed it. There were classes, castes and slaves, but there were no pariahs, no person lacking a fixed social condition and a legal, moral and religious status." Even the Devil had his place.

Jews, Muslims, Lutherans, and women like María would argue otherwise, and no one should underestimate the coercion used by the Spanish to maintain their empire. But Paz's point, I think, does contain an essential truth: that royal Catholicism in America organized itself not by suppressing but administrating difference, by placing Indians, the people colonists came close to exterminating, at the center of things, theologically, economically, legally, and bureaucratically. An orrery of courts and royal offices held the realm together administratively, backed up by an ever-enlarging legal code: *el derecho indiano*, the Law of the Indies. The courts were biased, as one can imagine, but, over time, came to enjoy significant legitimacy in poor, rural indigenous villages. Even the poorest plebes had access to some form of legal redress.[28]

This creation of "universal order" out of chaos, Paz wrote, was extraordinary. Colonial poetry, law, philosophy, histories and historians, baroque art and architecture, all things, "even fantastic fruits and profane dreams were harmonized within an order as rigorous as it was ample."

"Profane dreams" is one way to talk about the rape, sex, concubinage, and marriage that produced potentially infinite permutations of race, status, class, and gender. The original colonial system was meant to include only two distinct castes: *españoles* and *Indígenas*. That Aristotelian symmetry broke down straightaway, creating an ever bigger racial lexicon, which included categories such as: *creole, mestizo, pardo, moreno, negro de color, mulato, amarillo, trigueño, negro, jabao, indio, cholo, prieto, zambo, quinterón, tentenelaire, tercerón, cuarterón, negro libre, negro pardo, negro ladino, negro bozal, negro criollo, mestizo blanco*, among many others. In the Philippines, the Spanish added more, including *sangley, mestizo de sangley, chino*, and *mestizo de Bombay*. A list of 103 such categories compiled in the 1770s, identified 16 that were used only in the province of Guatemala.[29]

As America's population, starting around the end of the 1600s, began to stabilize and, eventually, grow, royal officials struggled to keep pace with who was called what. One eighteenth-century Mexican scribe tried to clarify the terms as he knew them:

1. Spaniard and Indian beget mestizo

2. Mestizo and Spanish woman beget castizo

3. Castiza woman and Spaniard beget Spaniard

4. Spanish woman and Negro beget mulatto

5. Spaniard and mulata woman beget morisco

6. Morisca woman and Spaniard beget albino

7. Spaniard and albina beget torno atrás

8. Indian and torna atrás beget lobo

9. Lobo and Indian woman beget zambaigo

10. Zambaigo and Indian woman beget cambujo

11. Cambujo and mulata beget albarazado

12. Albarazado and mulata beget barcino

13. Barcino and mulata beget coyote

14. Coyote woman and Indian beget chamiso

15. Chamisa woman and mestizo beget coyote mestizo

The scribe had a sense of humor. *Torno atrás*, number 7 on the list, the too-white child of a Spanish man and an albino woman, means, in English, "a step backward." Number 15 was the offspring of a "coyote mestizo" and a mulata, which the scribe called "*ahí te estás*." And there you have it.[30]

There you didn't have it, for the lists kept growing. The scribe seemed to be composing some kind of "Celestial Emporium of Benevolent Knowledge," a fantastical classification system based on pure whimsy: *tento en el aire* (tempted in the air), *lunarejo* (polka dot), *rayado* (striped), and so on. The category *no te entiendo* (I do not understand you) must have meant that the compiler had reached the limits of his imagination, and you were unclassifiable.

Edward Gibbon, in his six-volume *The History of the Decline and Fall of the Roman Empire*, described ancient Rome filling up with people from all the earth's corners, "as subjects and strangers from every part of the world" brought their beliefs, customs, languages into the imperial capital. "All the gods of mankind" were represented, all stood side by side on their own pedestal.

The Spanish Empire created such variety from within. Terror-bred wonder created a magical beast of an empire, one founded on high, hectoring claims of Catholic universalism—*all humanity is one!*—even as it presided over a vast, racialized system of coerced labor.

It couldn't last. As categories divided and divided again down the generations, Spanish Catholicism's ability to harmonize diversity within universalism gave way to the inevitable collapse into meaninglessness: *no te entiendo*.

Until then, though.

PART II

EMPTY HOUSES
THE ENGLISH

Vacuum domicilium

7.

Empty Houses

The Spanish came, and death followed. When the English came, death took point.

On November 11, 1620, the *Mayflower*, after sixty-six days at sea, made landfall at a peninsula sticking out into the Atlantic like a fishhook, later named Cape Cod. The ship's voyagers arrived in the wake of an epidemic that had raged through the homelands of the Wampanoag, Pokanoket, Abenaki, and other peoples of what is now southeastern Massachusetts. The historian Neal Salisbury describes the Puritans' landing site as a "vast disaster zone, comparable to those left by modern wars and other large-scale catastrophes." "Not one in ten among them left alive," wrote Cotton Mather, a few decades after the *Mayflower*'s arrival. Medical historians and archaeologists agree with Mather's numbers, estimating that 90 percent of Wampanoag had perished in an epidemic. Scholars give the same estimate, *90 percent*, whether they are discussing Hispaniola alone, the greater Caribbean, all of America, or specific regions, like the North Atlantic coast. In the case of the Wampanoag, a starting population of between twenty and twenty-five thousand means that approximately eighteen thousand people had died or fled in a short period, just prior to the coming of the settlers.[1]

Europeans who had sailed this coast six years earlier thought the place an Eden, a land of such abundance and health that they could scarcely believe their eyes. In 1614, Captain John Smith, the founder of Jamestown, called it, as Columbus did Hispaniola, "paradise." Smith recorded fields of planted corn, gardens overflowing with mulberries, tended to by "great troupes of well proportioned people." The land was "wooded to the brink of the sea," except for the bits trimmed back for towns and farming fields, populated by pines, junipers, sassafras, and oaks, their nutritious acorns covering the ground. Smith counted about forty well-organized villages, their houses made of bent saplings and matted floors. "Here are many rising hills," he wrote, "and on their tops and descents are many corne fields and delightful groves." Other Europeans likewise saw a land of precolonial plenty. Squash, pumpkins, tobacco, corn, bean, berries and other fruit, all planted in culti-vated fields. Beavers were everywhere. Clams, eels, and lobsters packed the coastal mudflats and inlets. Whales cavorted in the bay, under the largest flocks of "fowl we ever saw."[2]

The plague came in 1616. By the time the *Mayflower* dropped anchor and its people established Plymouth Colony four years later, most of the vil-lages had been abandoned, their houses empty. "I passed along the coast where I found some ancient [indigenous] plantations not long since popu-lous, now utterly void," wrote Captain Thomas Dermer.

"All dead," said his indigenous guide.[3]

Rat Fever

The worst of the disease spared the Narragansett. But the coastal Abenaki were gone, along with most of the Pokanoket on the eastern and northern shores. The epidemic struck with such fury that the sick couldn't "bury one another and their skulls and bones were found in many places laying still above the ground," wrote William Bradford, Plymouth's first governor. It was, Bradford said, a "very sad spectacle to behold." Skeletons lay on aban-doned paths, their bones picked by carrion birds. There was evidence that the stricken had grown too weak to gather wood to make fires, so they burned their bowls, trays, bows, and arrows. "Many of them did rott above ground for want of burial."[4]

"This mortality was not ended," wrote one of the early Pilgrims, as the dying continued after the arrival of *Mayflower* settlers. The English, who were apparently immune to the virus or bacteria, compared its symptoms to diseases they had known in Europe: smallpox, measles, yellow fever, influenza, chicken pox, typhus, or the bubonic plague. "A sorer disease cannot befall them, they fear it more than the plague," wrote Branford; "For want of bedding and linen and other helps they fall into a lamentable condition as they lie on their hard mats," the pox oozing, "the skin cleaving by reason thereof to the mats they lie on. When they turn them, a whole side will flay off at once. . . . And then being very sore, what with cold and other distempers, they die like rotten sheep." Symptoms included headache, nosebleed, fever, jaundice, skin sores, and dysentery.[5]

The bacteria might have been introduced by Thomas Hunt, who captained a ship in the 1614 expedition led by John Smith. Smith had returned to England, leaving Hunt in charge. Hunt took advantage of Smith's absence to organize a raiding party to capture twenty Wampanoag and Nauset peoples and sell them in Spain as slaves. Hunt's men, according to one account, "spread the disease to the Wampanoags, nearly wiping out their population by the 1620s, just about the time the Pilgrims came to America." Other possible sources of the disease were French traders, Basque whalers, Portuguese fishers, and Spanish sailors.[6]

Medical historians today think the epidemic was leptospirosis, also known as rat fever, caused by the bacteria *Leptospira*, introduced into the local environment by ship rodents. The animals contaminated the water, soil, and food stocks, and infested other animals, like moles, deer, and dogs. Native Americans who walked in bare feet were susceptible to infection. Ships dumped their rat-urine infected ballast stones at the mouth of tidal rivers, and the bacteria might have spread through the coastal wetlands and ponds, sources of drinking water and food. Roger Williams, a Puritan minister, wrote that he was impressed by the "naked hardned feet" of the Wampanoags, that could cut paths in the "most stony and rockie places." Not hardened enough to keep out the bacteria.[7]

New Golgotha

The voyagers of the *Mayflower* arrived hungry, cold, and sick. It took months to decide where to settle, as the ship skirted the coast and landing parties explored the terrain. There is no evidence that *Mayflower* voyagers resorted to survival cannibalism—as did the earlier Europeans at Jamestown in the winter of 1609, eating the dead and drinking the blood of the dying. But advance scouts did dig up Indian graves with their hands looking for buried corn. They found some, which they brought back to the ship. A few noticed, judging from their writings, that they had landed in a place of terrible suffering. They looted the abandoned houses they came upon. "Some of the best things we took away with us, and left the houses standing still as they were." Among the items taken were bowls, trays, dishes, earthen pots, food, oil, acorns, dried fish, baskets made of crab shells, and "sundry other of their household stuff."[8]

They found more corn. And more skeletons. Thomas Morton, who arrived two years after the *Mayflower*, saw the horror:

> For in a place where many inhabited, there hath been but one left alive, to tell what became of the rest, the living being (as it seems) not able to bury the dead, they were left for the Crowes, Kites and vermin to prey upon. And the bones and skulls upon the severall places of their habitations, made such a spectacle after my coming into those partes . . . it seemed to mee a new found Golgotha.[9]

Massachusetts wasn't a New England but a New Golgotha, the Aramaic word for *skull*, and the name of the hill outside Jerusalem's walls, where the city crucified its condemned, including Christ. "Vast and empty chaos," as another Puritan described the scene.

In late December, the settlers decided to squat in an abandoned village nestled between two hills. The *Mayflower* dropped anchor in what would be called Plymouth Bay. Voyagers rushed off their ship, Cotton Mather wrote later, like Noah's family rushing off the Ark. They had "a whole world before them to be peopled."[10]

The site seemed defendable. Settlers placed their cannon on one of two high hills, overlooking a stretch of cleared pineland, which provided a line of sight. The deserted town had been called Patuxet, as the colonists would learn when an indigenous visitor told them of the "extraordinary plague" that had killed all. "Indeed we find none to hinder our possession," wrote a settler agreeing with the visitor.

Labor was a necessity in settler life, and it would be a few years yet before the Europeans could press Indians into slavery or servitude. Twenty of the *Mayflower*'s 102 passengers were themselves indentured servants attached either to specific families or to the Virginia Company, which had funded the journey. Some of the fields looked as if they had been prepared to welcome the settlers: the previous residents of the land had just completed their harvest work before dying or fleeing. Still, there was much to do. Brush had to be cleared, trees cut, stumps removed, soil fertilized. Eventually, the indigenous huts would be dismantled. Their branches would be used for kindling as soon as a rude sawmill and kiln could be set up and planked houses built.

The ground was frozen in winter, and the English had to depend on the goodwill of surviving Indians to live through the first months of 1621. The plague had "abated" Wampanoag courage, making them, as a settler named Robert Cushman put it, "a people affrighted." They dealt on supplicating terms with the Europeans. Still, the settlers were vigilant. More than fifty original voyagers, many of them servants, died from scurvy, hunger, and exposure before the winter had ended. Some corpses were dragged into the forest and propped up against trees, left to freeze in place with rifles at the ready as if they were sentinels. Diggers waited for the sun to set to hack through frozen earth to conduct "secret night burials," out of sight from "lurking savages." Settlers then planted the graves with corn to hide the graves.[11]

European colonists didn't, at this early moment, intentionally spread disease.* They did use fear of disease as leverage. A rumor spread among the remaining Wampanoag that the English carried the plague with them and

---

* Native Americans believed that Europeans knowingly infected them. In the early 1630s, Captain John Oldham traveled through the upper Connecticut River Valley and every Narragansett village he passed through became infected with smallpox—resulting in hundreds of deaths—though Oldman and his men remained healthy. The Narragansett thought the dis-

had buried it in an underground vault. There was indeed a vault. But it was filled with a different kind of death-dealer: barrels of gunpowder. When an indigenous visitor pointed at the broken-up ground, which clearly had *something* buried underneath, one Puritan responded that that was where they kept the plague.[12]

It Pleased God

The empty villages that the Puritans encountered in North America allowed them to avoid the doubt that vexed their Catholic forerunners, at least for a time.

As the years went by, the descendants of the "first comers" talked more and more about the plague that foreshadowed the *Mayflower*'s arrival, and the reason they did so was clear: to justify the taking of indigenous land. Gone were the early descriptions, by Captain Smith and others, of a well-populated and well-gardened paradise. Now, preachers and scholars looking back at the settlement's early days stressed the continent's emptiness.

Commentary in sermons, memoirs, and histories, most of it produced after 1630, was of one mind: God cleared the land to prepare for the arrival of his people. Psalm 78:49–50 was a favorite: "He cast upon them the fierceness of his anger, indignation and wrath, and vexation by the sending out of evil angels. He made a way to his anger: he spared not their soul from death, but gave their life to the pestilence."

Examples of such thought among the first eminent Puritans and their descendants are abundant. Just some, of many, examples:

> **John Winthrop:** "God hath consumed the natives with a miraculous plague, whereby the greater part of the country is left voide of inhabitants."

---

ease was intentionally "sent" by the English. Later, during the 1763 siege of Fort Pitt, British forces distributed blankets thought to be infected with smallpox to their indigenous enemies.

Edward Winslow: "An extraordinary plague, and there is neither man, woman, nor child remaining."

Edward Johnson: "A three years' plague, about twelve or sixteen years past, swept away most of the inhabitants all along the sea-coast, and in some places utterly consumed man, woman, and child, so that there is no person left to lay claim to the soil which they possessed."

Thomas George: "The Lord sent his avenging Angel & swept the most part away."

William Bradford: "It pleased God to visit these Indians with a great sickness."

Nathaniel Morton: "Thus God made way for his people, by re-moving the heathen and planting them in the land."[13]

The English spoke of a "miraculous plague," an "extraordinary plague," a "three-years plague." Even King James I celebrated, in the charter he granted to the Plymouth Company, the "wonderful plague." Wrought by "God's visitation," the epidemic led to "utter destruction, devastation, and depopulation" of the Wampanoag.

Whatever the epidemic was called, those who survived the disease to witness the arrival of the *Mayflower* and the establishment of Plymouth-on-Patuxet continued to die from hunger, sickness, weakness, and war. There were few left to "hinder" the English's claim to the land. "There was no one," a Puritan historian later put it, "to dispute their right of possession." When a "quarrel" started between Salem settlers and neighboring Indians "about their bounds of land," Edward Johnson relates, the "Lord put an end this quarrel also, by smiting the Indians with a sore Disease, even the small Pox; of which the great numbers of them died." Even the "Winters piercing cold" could not stay "the strength of this hot Disease."[14]

"They waste, they moulder away, they disappear," left to decompose in the ground as God's fertilizer, nourishment for Puritan soil.

The contrast I'm drawing should be clear. The Spanish encounter with colonial death, the catastrophe heralded by the arrival of Ferdinand and Isabella's conquistadores, their mastiffs and horses, provoked a near century-long process of obsessive moral introspection. Few doubted the Conquest's righteousness. But, confronted with cruelty supreme, a significant number of clergy on the front lines and jurists and theologians in Spain led a revolution in legal and ethical thought: an acknowledgment, at least as official policy if not practice, that Native Americans were humans, all humans were equal, and no one was born a "natural slave." The Spanish Crown and most of its court lawyers—even before Las Casas starting to describe the density of the Americas as "infinite" and "incalculable"—knew their conquest was a conquest of people living in society.

Plymouth's settlers experienced something different. They came on their ships thinking of the ancients, imagining themselves the new Adam, the new Noah, the new Moses, leading the chosen into an empty—or empty enough—Canaan.

God Having of One Blood

Eventually, the Puritans moved beyond first impressions of a vacant, pestilent land. Their successors developed a more coherent set of legal principles justifying dispossession, at first in reaction to a protest led by Roger Williams.

The oft written-about Williams—one of the founders of Rhode Island as a sanctuary state—was a tolerant Puritan. He had curiosity about the wider world, and empathy that eluded many of his fellow divines, who often seemed incapable of seeing beyond the perimeter of their own souls and psyches. Roger and his wife, Mary, arrived in New England in early 1631. Having established themselves among some of the original settlers, Williams chafed under Puritan conformity and began spending time with the Wampanoags.

Living with the Wampanoags, learning their language, gave Williams an appreciation of indigenous humanity equal to that of Las Casas: "Nature knows no difference between Europe and Americans in blood, birth, bodies, etc. God having of one blood made all mankind," he wrote. He had no doubt that the natives were, like the English, rational social beings, not children of wild nature. They "love society," wrote Williams, who compared the Wampanoags to ancient Athenians since they took great "delight in newes." They wanted to know what was going on in the world.[15]

Williams spent three years conversing with the Wampanoag, who peppered the Puritan with questions about Europe. They told Williams stories of the plague, their suffering, how they fled their homes, left their dead, and abandoned their fields. He listened as they explained how they measured the "bounds of their lands" in a precise way, confirming for Williams that the Wampanoag had a well-developed understanding of property. He watched as they used fire to clear undergrowth in a sustainable manner that didn't despoil the land, nor lead to the cutting down of ever more trees for larger fields.* Eventually, Williams could no longer deny the truth: the *Mayflower* and subsequent settlers had built their New Canaan on stolen land.

When Williams took these concerns to town elders, they asked him to write up his ideas in a "treatise." He did, laying out a three-point argument. First, the king was blasphemous, acting in the "spirit of the devil" when he claimed sovereignty in the New World. Second, the Wampanoag had clear title to their land, including the land they had to flee because of the plague.

---

* According to Williams, the Wampanoags had a sophisticated understanding of the cause of European migration. They often asked Williams, "Why come the English hither?" And then gave their own answer. Because Europe must be short of trees. "After having burnt up the wood in one place," Englishmen had to move on "to follow the wood; and so to remove to a fresh place for the woods sake." The Wampanoags linked expansion to unsustainable resource extraction, specifically to wood used as fuel to supply energy, light, and heat, as well as the need for boards to build bigger ships and finer houses. The Wampanoags were right; London, one of the largest cities in Europe, was running out of firewood, according to the economic historian John Nef. The shortage precipitated both the increased use of coal and the search for new woodlands, a search that reached across the Atlantic. In America, settlers looked at the dense forest with some ambivalence. Firewood from trees would bring warmth but required work to cut. And where there were trees, there were Indians. The English "have an unconquerable aversion to trees," said one observer, "and whenever a settlement is made, they cut away all before them without mercy; not one is spared," not even to provide shade for the farmhouse. The Wampanoag were prescient: between 1650 and 1850 half of the northeastern forest would be gone.

Third, settlers' claims of possession to land, be they based on the king's grant or the fact that the land was empty when they arrived, were null.

Williams already had a reputation for possessing too questioning a spirit. Now, his treatise shocked the Puritan elite, who demanded that Williams appear before an emergency assembly. Williams, a man of ethics and determination, couldn't muster the resolve to withstand the fury his questioning of property rights unleashed. Unlike Montesinos, Williams retracted his accusations. The elders apparently had asked him to write up his heresies only for the satisfaction of ordering him to burn them, which he, recorded one observer, "very submissively" did.

Williams would continue his dissent against Puritan intolerance, eventually leaving the community to establish a new, more open-minded colony. But never again would he make indigenous dispossession the centerpiece of his dissent.

Nobody's Thing

Williams seemed penitent. Still, Governor John Winthrop, famous for preaching his City on a Hill sermon a few years earlier, responded with a detailed refutation, writing a lengthy defense of "our title to what we possess." Winthrop agreed with Williams's opening premise: America was not the king's to give. But he disagreed with the rest.[16]

Upon arrival in the New World, he wrote, the English acquired land in one of two ways. Both, Winthrop insisted, were legal. The first was through purchase, and indeed there exist records of English settlers buying property from Native Americans, especially as the colony grew beyond its original boundaries. The second method was decisive and entailed the ability to "subdue" land as *vacuum domicilium*, a Latin term meaning empty place, or empty house. Lawyers, philosophers, and theologians around this time had been using other venerable Latinate concepts to refer to unpossessed land, including *terra nullius*, nobody's thing, or *feria bestia*, a wild thing of nature. But *vacuum domicilium* wasn't yet part of the legal lexicon.

Winthrop didn't coin the term. Theologians occasionally used *vacuum domicilium* to refer to a corpse, its soul having left the body. It's an uncomfortable metaphor, that *vacuum domicilium* could be used to refer not just to abandoned property but also to a soulless corpse, suggesting that European settlers were spirits possessing another's body.

Winthrop, though, was among the first to use it as a legal term, and to use it forcefully to counter the view that he and his fellow settlers were trespassers and thieves: "*Vacuum domicilium* gives us a sufficient title against all men," he wrote, the Latin providing heft to a term, *empty houses*, that it didn't possess in English. Winthrop wanted to leave no doubt that his city had legal title to its hill: "They had taken up that place as *vacuum domicilium*, and so had continued, without interruption or claim of any of the natives."[17]

In the years to come, *vacuum domicilium* became a term much cited by English and Dutch settlers alike. The phrase, and the idea behind it, worked its way into sermons. John Cotton, a prominent Puritan cleric, said that the first English settlers "had planted themselves in a *vacuum domicilium*," using that term here to suggest not just a plot of land but perhaps all New England. Cotton insisted that settlers had a right to land anywhere on God's earth even if it was "not altogether void of inhabitants, yet void in that place where they reside." "Where there is a vacant place," the reverend continued, "there is liberty for the Sons of Adam or Noah to come and inhabit, though they neither buy it, nor ask their leaves." The ideal that unused, voided, or wasted land was open for settlement became part of settler common sense, seamlessly mixed into the unfolding drama of Christian history. Didn't the Lord lead the Israelites into Canaan? Moses to the Promised Land? "Why may not Christians have liberty to go and dwell" in "waste lands and woods," asked Winthrop, "as lawfully as Abraham did among the Sodomites?"[18]

The ancient patriarchs were always on the move, wrote Robert Cushman, one of the organizers of the *Mayflower* voyage, leaving crowded settlements for parts of the earth that were "more roomy, where the land lay idle and waste." Cushman was underscoring the argument that even if people lived on the land but didn't use it, didn't cultivate it, then it was available for the taking. "It is lawful," he wrote, "to take a land which none useth, and make use of it."[19]

Vacuum domicilium was soon cited in courts, with jurists affixing other Latin words for extra gravitas: *Vacuum domicilium cedit occupant,* or, "an empty house yields to the occupier." Winthrop and Cotton implicitly used the phrase to describe land and homes vacated because of pestilence, but it was also applied to property left behind by people fleeing wars and massacres. By the end of the nineteenth century, *vacuum domicilium* found a place in law books, used to explain, post facto, how Indians lost their land. One late nineteenth-century textbook identified "*vacuum domicilium*" as a doctrine that rendered "the right of the aboriginal nomads to the possession of the soil" into a "mere passive right" that could be "ignored."[20]

The assertion that Wampanoag, Narragansetts, Pequots, and other indigenous groups didn't "improve," or "claim," land flew in the face of evidence to the contrary. They did farm the land, proof of which were the abandoned fields the *Mayflower* settlers appropriated as their own. As in all worldviews, there were caveats. Settlers often did recognize Indians as owners of their land. Indians, as property owners, could even, at times, expect protection under the colonial legal system. Still, it became common for Puritans to proclaim that Amerindians kept the world as God made it, leaving it unenclosed, available to "first takers."

"If therefore any sonne of Adam come and finde a place empty," wrote John Cotton, "he hath liberty to come, and fill, and subdue the earth there."[21]

Governor Winthrop, after he had countered Williams's arguments, declared that all that really mattered in the end was God's pleasure. And his pleasure was made clear in the ongoing disappearance of the land's original inhabitants:

"If God were not pleased with our inheriting these parts, why did he drive out the natives before us? And why dothe he still make roome for us, by diminishing them as we increase?"[22]

8.

Irish Tactics

L ong before any hungry Puritan had stumbled upon an empty Wampanoag house, England had declared itself an empire. "This realm of England is an Empire," Henry VIII decreed in 1533. He was speaking aspirationally. England at this point was but one part of a quarrelsome archipelago. London had annexed Wales, but Scotland was a rival sovereign nation equal in power, and Ireland remained rebellious. There was, though, pressure to push outward, as many English felt their island rather small. The beginning of merchant and agricultural capitalism created ambitions— needs, demands, and hungers: for wealth, raw materials, new markets, and new investment opportunities, none of which could be satisfied within the bounds of the kingdom of England. The enclosure of common lands was under way, forcing more and more rural folk into cities. In 1500, London had a population of fifty thousand people, less than a third of that of Mexico City. By Queen Elizabeth's coronation in 1559, that number had more than doubled. Fifty years later, a quarter of a million people were jammed into its miasmic rookeries, cramped neighborhoods with narrow, winding streets and squalid tenements. Politicians and clerics urged the Crown to find someplace to send surplus peoples, like those indentured servants who would later be sent to Plymouth, and not to leave the greater Atlantic World in the hands of the papists.

Elsewhere in Europe, in Brittany, Languedoc, and the Black Forest, among other places, fledgling nation states and empires were putting down the wild men of their marchlands with impressive brutality. "Murderous, thieving hordes," was Luther's description of rural rebels in Upper Swabia. So before London could fully move outward it first committed to establishing authority over its own hinterlands, to populating Catholic lands in Ireland with Welsh and English Protestants.

The military campaign was horrifying, with English troops setting themselves on the Irish as if their opponents were less than humans, their lives worth little. Such terror prompted few qualms, neither among England's establishment Anglican priests or dissident Puritan divines, nothing of the moral unease that so unsettled friars like Las Casas, Montesinos, and Mendieta.

Heddes of the Dedde

London's effort to establish control over all Ireland kept pace just behind the Spanish Conquest of the New World. In 1521, the year Cortés captured Tenochtitlán, Henry VIII's court began to make plans to subdue Gaelic rebels. England's full-on military campaign in Ulster began in the early 1530s, as Pizarro was starting his assault on the Andes. In 1541, a year after Spanish conquerors began their trek through North America, Henry VIII declared himself king of Ireland. In 1557, with Spain taking control of the Philippines, Sir Henry Radcliffe, commander of the Crown's forces in the Irish Midlands, ordered his men "to plague, punish and prosecute with sword and fire and other warlike manners all Irishmen and their countries." Sir Humphrey Gilbert first offered a queen's pardon to targeted towns. The besieged had a minute to think over their decision, after which Gilbert "never after gave them another chance, but exterminated them all, male and female, young and old." No prisoners meant no wasted time and men left guarding prisoners. Troops could move quickly on to the next town.

Massacre followed massacre in Ireland, as it did in the Americas: in Munster, Rathlin Island, Connacht, and other places. In the early 1580s,

Father Mendieta was worrying about the loss of Mexico's native population. The English at that moment were pursuing the "extirpation" of "the entire race of Burkes," a particularly rebellious clan. When men fled their towns, royal troops did what Spanish conquistadores did. They set houses on fire and killed all left behind—women, children, and the elderly—to provide an "example with terror," like Cortés's "chastisements." Both in Ireland and Mexico, the point was illustrative: "to strike terror into the hearts of these unhappy creatures." After one slaughter, Sir Gilbert had the heads cut off the corpses and taken to his camp, where they were laid side by side on the path leading to his tent. Irish petitioners had to "passe through a line of heddes," causing "greater terror to the people, when they sawe the heddes of the dedde fathers, brothers, children, kinsfolk and friends lye on the ground before their faces."[1]

"Plague and famine stalked together," wrote one Irish poet, as they did in the Americas. Two great hungers swept through Ireland during these wars (1582–83 in Munster and 1602–1603 in Ulster), the result of a deliberate policy to starve the Irish into submission by, as Lord Grey, who oversaw the queen's troops, put it, "burning their corn, spoiling their harvest and killing or driving their cattle." Denied planting and pastureland, villagers starved under the English stranglehold.[2]

These starvations were not the great potato famines that came centuries later. Walter Raleigh, one of Queen Elizabeth's sea-dog pirates, had brought potatoes, a strain he found in Virginia, to Ireland in 1589 and planted them in his County Cork estate. They wouldn't be adopted as a field crop for decades, though the root vegetable quickly gained repute among Europeans as an aphrodisiac. "Let the sky rain potatoes," Shakespeare has Falstaff say in *The Merry Wives of Windsor* in 1602, "let there come a tempest of provocation."

Rather, these early famines were caused by royal troops destroying tillage crops, like wheat and barley, and confiscating livestock.

Cannibalism, that great obsession that Europeans used to justify slaughter in America and enslavement in Africa, was manufactured as a military tactic by the English in Ireland. "A million swords will not do them so much harm as one winter's famine," wrote Sir Arthur Chichester in 1600, as his troops left the land "desolate and waste." The Irish would, said Edmund Spenser, a poet and avid propagandist of English colonization in Ireland, "quickly consume themselves, and devour one another." Formerly "stout and obstinate rebels," Spenser wrote, "came creeping forth" from their hiding places "upon their hands, for their legs could not bear them. They looked anatomies of death, they spoke like ghosts, crying out of their graves; they did eat of the carrions, happy where they could find them, yea, and one another soon after, in so much as the very carcasses they spared not to scrape out of their graves."[3] The passage could have come from the pen of Las Casas, except Spenser, Grey's secretary, approved of the tactic: "Ireland is a diseased portion of the State, it must first be cured and reformed."*

Chichester himself reported seeing "three small children—the least not above ten years old—feeding off the flesh of their starved mother." Bodies piled up in ditches, the mouths of the dead stained green from last meals of nettles and docks. The induced famine was so bad that there were reports, perhaps rumors meant to confirm the bestiality that justified the war, that old women were lighting fires to attract children with their warmth, only to capture and "devour them." Hundreds of thousands of Irish lost their lives.[4]

This campaign, which lasted for more than a century, took place as the English were increasingly comparing themselves to the Spanish. As early as 1583, Sir George Peckham, an investor in English expansion, endorsed the methods of the Spanish conquistadores and recommended reading Spanish authors to understand the nature of the challenges that would confront the English when they finally made the leap across the Atlantic.

The Spanish Conquest, Peckham said, had "awakened" Europe out of its "dreams."[5]

---

* In his notes on Ireland's pacification, Karl Marx described Spenser as "Die Elizabeths Arschkissende Poet"—Queen Elizabeth's ass-kissing poet. Regarding the potato, there's a legend that the potato arrived not at County Cork with Raleigh but when Spanish galleons from the failed 1588 Armada broke up on the sea rocks near Connemara cliffs, with hundreds of potatoes washing up on shore.

Be Like the Spanish

The comparisons took place in a dissonant, cross-purposed way. The English were reading Spanish authors like Oviedo, whose *Historia General de las Indias* had been translated and published in London in 1555, to accommodate themselves to the new severity of war. The English also borrowed Spanish justifications of the Conquest to explain why they had to put down the Irish, sounding like Sepúlveda when they invoked Gaelic barbarism, listing cannibalism, incest, and the Irish people's supposed inability to form political communities as just cause to wage their war. They live, wrote one war promoter, in "waste wild places." And at least one royal official cited, approvingly, Spain's removal of Muslims from Iberia to legitimize England's expulsion of Catholics from Ulster.[6]

The English also confirmed their own goodness by reading Las Casas on Spanish badness. Las Casas's *Brevísima Relación* had been translated into English many times throughout the sixteenth and seventeenth centuries. As relentless as a modern slasher film, with its descriptions of Spanish hounds ripping a "little sweet babie" to shreds, the book helped give rise to what scholars later called the Black Legend. Against Spanish avariciousness and excess, England saw itself as moderate. Against Catholic decadence and superstition, Protestants were modern and rational. Cruel Spain. Just England.

Yet the English also read Las Casas to rouse themselves to violence against the Irish. The Puritan translation of *A Brief History* urged Cromwell to avenge the "twenty millions of the souls of the slaughter'd Indians" destroyed by "Popish Cruelties." The logic went that since the Catholic Irish were allied with Catholic Spain, they were as responsible for the destruction of the Indies as were Cortés and Pizarro.

As she neared her death in 1603, Elizabeth ruled an Ireland of "corpses and ashes." *Hibernia Pacata*. Ireland Pacified. It wasn't. The English war to uproot the Catholic religion and the Irish language from Ireland would last many more decades.

The Irish campaign was a prelude to empire. Even as the fighting in Ireland continued, London started making forays across the Atlantic and down the African coast. By the early 1600s, London financiers were investing more capital in Atlantic piracy than in any other enterprise. The money men said they were interested in cloth and tobacco. They really wanted slaves, whose resale as contraband brought the highest profit.* Jamestown was founded in 1607 and Plymouth in 1620.[7]

The establishment of North American settlements added a new, confusing dimension to England's comparisons with Spain. The references pushed against themselves: The English were and weren't the Spanish. The Irish were and weren't Native Americans. Some of the most vicious Irish haters imagined the English flying across the Atlantic on a humanitarian mission saving noble innocent Indians from the Spanish. "The people of America crye out to us," wrote Richard Hakluyt, an English historian and ceaseless promoter of colonialism, "to come and helpe them." There was "no doubt" that were the queen to take the "firme of America," all the "natural people there with all humanitie, curtesie, and freedoms" will place themselves under her authority and "revolte cleane from the Spaniarde."[8]

England would free Indians from the Spanish. England would also conquer the Indians like the Spanish. Walter Raleigh presumed that England, if it could gain a toehold, would follow the Spanish model. The Spanish endured many "miseries" in the New World, Raleigh wrote, yet they "persisted in their enterprises with invincible constancy," expanding the Spanish realm to such a degree that their success has "buried the remembrances of all dangers passed."[9]

"More rich and beautiful cities, more temples adorned with golden Images, more sepulchers filled with treasure" awaited the English in America, thought Raleigh. He believed that the English conquest would come to possess cities more "shining" than anything found by Cortés in Mexico or Pizarro in Peru. Elizabeth's would-be colonialists in the late 1500s wanted

---

* In 1618, Robert Rich, the Second Earl of Warwick and a member of the Virginia Company, worked with Virginians to outfit a privateer "to rove in West Indian waters and to prey upon Spanish commerce" looking for gold, silver, and enslaved Africans. The ship, the *White Lion*, waylaid the Portuguese *San Juan Bautista* off the Mexican coast near Veracruz and confiscated its human cargo, bringing "20 and odd" Africans to Hampton, Virginia, in the fall of 1619—this being the founding event of the 1619 Project.

desperately to emulate not just Spain's crusading spirit but its scientific knowledge, which was far more advanced than England's, especially when it came to maritime techniques. Spain had a school staffed by retired seamen teaching the practical arts of sailing, and sponsored a sailors' guild, with graduates obtaining the grades of gromet, mariner, master, and pilot. The English navy was always eager to get copies of Spanish geographies, navigation textbooks, and maps. Hakluyt, influential in stirring the queen's interest in colonial expansion, drew heavily on Spanish chronicles for basic information.[10]

When Captain John Smith and his men invaded the Powhatan homeland—comprising roughly tidewater Virginia and the Chesapeake's Eastern Shore—to establish Jamestown, he was "armed in part with expectations based on their readings and misreading of Spanish American colonization." They thought they'd find a large, complex society that they could exploit for tribute and labor. "The preference for Spanish models," writes historian April Lee Hatfield, "helps explain the Virginia Company's failure to establish a colony that could feed itself." Replicating the Spanish practice of relying on "plunder and Indian tribute for food" was the likely source of "Virginia officials' belief that they, too, could neglect the issue of food production." The English had already failed in their first attempt at a settlement, a decade earlier at Roanoke, relying unsuccessfully on the Powhatan for sustenance. Yet the allure of the Spanish example proved more powerful than this firsthand experience.[11]

Captain Smith styled himself on Cortés. The "worthy" Cortés, Smith wrote, managed with "scarce three hundred Spaniards . . . to conquer the great City of Mexico, where thousands of Savages dwelled in strong houses." Smith spent time looking for gold and silver mines (including one reportedly rich deposit of gold he was told existed on Martha's Vineyard) and Indians "to work in chains." The English should learn from the Spanish, Smith wrote later, and force "the treacherous and rebellious Infidels to do all manner of drudgery work and slavery for them, themselves living like soldiers upon the fruits of their labors." Smith's motto on his coat of arms, adorned with the profiles of three "Turks," had a Cortesian ring to it: *vincere est vivere*—to conquer is to live. Later, and further north, the arch-antipapist

Cotton Mather admitted he admired "the remarkable zeal of the Romish missionaries, encompassing sea and land to make proselytes."[12]

Drive on, Smith urged, into "the unknown parts of this unknown world." Be like the Spanish and make a New World.

A Wicked Race

The idea that the English would imitate the Spanish to save the natives from the Spanish didn't last long. At Jamestown, the colonists went looking for a people who would pay them tribute and work in the mines they hoped to find. Instead, they were forced to live off Powhatan handouts. This dependence grew antagonistic.

Resentment led to killings led to massacres. In 1610, London had dispatched Thomas West, the notably titled "Baron Lord de la Warr" (from which the place-name Delaware derives), as Virginia governor and captain general. West had fought in Ireland during a grizzly period of that campaign and introduced "Irish tactics" in the war against the Powhatans. Reinforced with more English veterans from Ireland, the Jamestown colonists "took the offence against their nearest Indian neighbors in a brutal and atrocity-ridden four-year war" that was "reminiscent of campaigns in Ulster."[13]

The interleaves of terror during these transatlantic wars are intricate and puzzling to trace. Tactics used by the Spanish against Native Americans, which many in Spain imagined were modeled on Roman wars against barbarians, became the model for English pacification and colonization of the Irish. In turn, the English extended that model across the Atlantic in their early wars against Native Americans. The Powhatans, like other indigenous peoples along the Atlantic seacoast, had been accustomed to fighting small-scale, ritualistic wars. Desperate upon realizing that settlers had an inexhaustible source of reinforcements, in fear that they would soon lose their homeland, the Powhatan began to imitate the English and adopt "Irish tactics" of their own, climaxing in a March 1622 raiding party that killed about a third of Jamestown's population. England responded with a retaliatory campaign against the Powhatan confederacy that was led by a military detachment with long experience fighting in Ulster. As the English torched Powhattan food sources to induce famines and applied other tactics worked out in Ireland, little distinction separated "wyld" Irish from "wyld" Indians. Such methods would become standard English procedure in all the many Indian wars to come, up and down the Atlantic Coast.[14]

There was one thing that the English didn't share with the Spanish: misgivings. Few churchmen or jurists thought the terror unleashed in Ireland (or the Chesapeake) merited remorse, much less a revision of the rules of war. Books were written on the Irish campaigns. They were justifications, not mortifications. Most writers wanted to prove the inferiority of the Irish, not trouble the soul. There was no first-principle debate over the morality of mass murder. "How godly a deed it is to overthrow so wicked a race the world may judge: for my part I think there cannot be a greater sacrifice to God," a lieutenant to Queen Elizabeth wrote in 1573, about driving the Irish into the mountains to freeze and starve. If the Tudors and Stuarts, their lords and high churchman, hated the Irish, the Puritan divines who supported Oliver Cromwell hated them more, especially the pastoral or bog Irish who lived far from the city of Dublin. Cromwell, after coming to power as Lord Protector in 1653, intensified the killing. His soldiers set Catholic priests alight with kindling made from broken-up church pews. "God damn me, God confound me; I burn, I burn," one engulfed cleric yelled out, wrote Cromwell in his report to Parliament.[15]

When it came to the Irish, England was a country filled with Sepúlvedas and very few Las Casases, despite the latter's popularity with the English-reading public.*

---

* Puritans and other Protestant dissenters might be compared with mystics like Mendieta and other activist priests and friars in that they hoped to establish a purer church, except that Catholics mystics looked for rejuvenation through the radical recognition of the humanity of indigenous pagans. Puritans, notably, had no issue slaughtering their pagans, Ireland's Catholics. An exception to this would be William Penn, the founder of tolerant Pennsylvania, whose Protestant father was granted a large Catholic estate in Cork County, Ireland. Young William converted to Quakerism. Life in Ireland as the son of a Protestant overlord apparently had a great influence on his expanding consciousness. Quakers did come to renounce violence. But, for most, this renunciation was not a reaction to the suffering of the Catholic Irish or an insistence on the equality of all people. Rather, it was a matter of personal ethics.

Scales of Creatures

Why did Spain's Conquest of the New World spark an existential reckoning with the morality of war and the humanity of its victims, while the English remained untroubled about the righteousness of the Irish campaign?[16]

Maybe, considering Catholicism's continental dominance, Protestant leaders of a dissident and besieged movement didn't want to question the authority of the English monarchy, their only real European toehold— though no such concerns stopped Puritans from relentlessly heckling the monarchy on all sorts of other matters. Likewise, the ferocity of Catholic repression against Protestants (French Catholics murdered thousands of Huguenots in 1572's Saint Bartholomew's Day Massacre; in 1554, when Queen Mary briefly reconverted England back to Catholicism, she burned to death scores of Protestants in the infamous Smithfield Market fires) might have hardened anti-Catholic sentiment and created a hunger for revenge. Also, Ireland, as a backdoor for a possible Spanish or French invasion, was for England a national security issue: a status that, then as now, tends to mute moral concerns.

In any case, it was around this time, as colonialism in the New World and Ireland advanced and the chattel enslavement of Africans began to increase, that what is called race and racism became politically vital ways of thinking about the world. The word *barbarian* had long been used by Europeans to describe the rude inhabitants at the margins of their polis. The Gaelic Irish, an early English writer said, are a "wild and inhospitable people. They live on beasts only *and* live like beasts." They are, he continued "a barbarous people." As English repression against the Irish grew more monstrous, the bestial imagery used to justify killing grew more grotesque. No moral doubt diluted the rhetoric of dehumanization.[17]

This escalation of terror and its legitimating rhetoric corresponded to an intellectual movement in Oxford, Cambridge, and Edinburgh to define what exactly it meant to be Anglo-Saxon. Scholars committed themselves to categorizing peoples, a research project that William Petty, an English economist, physician, and philosopher writing in the late 1600s, understood as establishing the "scales of creatures." That was the title of Petty's book, which, though unpublished, circulated widely among London's Royal Society intelligentsia. Petty (who helped organize the distribution of Irish Catholic lands to Protestant conquerors) used new scientific and anthropological concepts to spruce up the old medieval categories of *savage* and *barbarian*. Humans were divided "into several species, some of which were considered to be closer to animals."[18]

Mass murder and enslavement led Las Casas to believe that all humans shared a common lineage. English intellectuals took a different lesson from the killing. Many of the most influential among them embraced the idea of intractable racial divisions, of ever sharper lines marking unbridgeable differences—differences that some argued proved the theory of polygenesis, the idea that people shared not a common lineage but rather were of distinct origins. Perhaps they even comprised distinct species.[19]

The New World had burst into the European imagination at a time when the scientific method was on the rise and Christianity in flux, leading to all sorts of new speculations about the history of humanity. Awareness of America scrambled accepted geological knowledge, contributing to the idea that the world was far older than the Bible had suggested. Maybe America was older than Europe. If so, perhaps its peoples could trace their first ancestor back to a time before Adam. In 1512 (the year Michelangelo finished his Creation frescoes on the ceiling of the Sistine Chapel, with Adam about to be touched by God Divine), Pope Julius II had ruled that Amerindians were heirs to Adam and Eve. Yet—after the establishment of the slave trade, the expansion of European empires, the proliferation of wars of conquest, and the growing reliance on the world's peoples of color to deliver the world's treasures to Europe—what Julius thought mattered little.

The evolution of racism didn't require belief in polygenesis (an idea considered heretical by Catholic and Protestant theologians alike). All of humanity might very well have descended from Adam. Yet over time, the differences that emerged—related to slippery criteria including belief, custom, dress, language, social organization, planting techniques, and so on—deepened divisions among conquerors and those who could be conquered;

among slavers and those who could be enslaved; torturers and those who could be tortured; possessors and those who could be dispossessed; colonizers and those who could be colonized; humans and those not fully human.

Skin color soon become one determining criterion.* Until then, though, there were many categories to choose from: Nordic, Goth, Germanic, Caucasian, Jewish, Mongol, Negro, Ethiopian, Asiatic, Teuton, Slav, Hindu, and, of course, Gaelic Irish. And many qualities to pick from to define one's race: "Furious fanaticism; a love of war and disorder; a hatred for order and patient industry; no accumulative habits; restless, treacherous, uncertain: look at Ireland," wrote the Scottish physician Robert Knox. "The source of all evil lies in the race, the Celtic race of Ireland."[20]

The English were superior, English professors agreed, for many reasons but especially because they were the historical agents of natural liberty. The myth, as it evolved in the 1600s, rooted the origins of this liberty deep in the German forest, brought forth by Teutonic or Saxon woodsmen who crossed the channel to the British Isle. Many of the same characteristics cherished in the Saxons were damned when found among the Irish: their independence, and their refusal to be mastered. Yet the Irish weren't seen as heritage peoples, torchbearers of a simpler, freer time. Rather, the new ideologues of Anglo-Saxonism, in their savage war to take Ireland, isolated the

---

* Spain in the 1500s and 1600s had its share of polygenesist or "preadamite" (before Adam) thinkers. Yet however easy it is to dismiss Catholic universalism as ineffectual hypocrisy, it did dilute the kind of pariah racism being advanced by Anglo-Saxon theorists. Francisco López de Gómara, who supported the Conquest and aggrandized Cortés, assigned no moral value to skin color. On the contrary, the diversity of hues was a sign of God's glory: "Color," he wrote in 1553, is "one of the marvelous things that God useth in the composition of man . . . beholding one to be white and another black, being colors utterly contrary. Some likewise to be yellow, which is between black and white . . . And how from white they got to yellow . . . to brown and red; and to black, by ash colour, and murrey (mulberry) somewhat lighter than black, and tawny like unto the west Indians, which are altogether in general either purple, or tawny like unto sodden quinces, or the color of chestnuts or olives." Be they the shade of a sodden quince or a dusky chestnut, "we be all born of Adam and Eve." "His Divine Majesty hath done this," López de Gómara thought, "to declare his omnipotence and wisdom in such diversities of colors."

Irish as "all evil" and targeted them for extermination if possible, or at least removal. "The race must be forced from the soil."

Flood Ireland with Saxons—and solve the Irish problem.[21]

The love of Saxons and reviling of the Irish might seem sentiments based on differences without much distinction. Yet this fledgling art of "pariah-craft" came into its own when transplanted to North America—where settlers dispossessed Indians and enslaved Africans on a scale heretofore unimaginable.

9.

Lost in the World's Debate

I n 1607, as John Smith and other settlers were sailing into the Chesapeake, members of the Virginia Company met to consider whether they should compose "some form of writing" that could legitimate their effort to set down a colony in Virginia. Several of the Company's officers had been paying close attention to the debates in Spain among Catholics regarding the legitimacy of the Conquest and the legality of slavery. They had identified two distinct schools of thought. The first was defended by what the English called "perfect Spaniards," those who continued to insist that Pope Alexander's "donation" provided all the justification the Spanish Crown needed to take and rule the Indies. They were of no concern to English Protestants, who didn't recognize papal authority.

The second, though, known as the Salamanca School—those theologians and jurists generally associated with the University of Salamanca— had to be taken seriously. They were scholars like Francisco de Vitoria, who argued from reason, not revelation, and priests like Las Casas, who not only called into question Spain's claims to New World dominion but raised doubt whether conquest settlement in the Americas could ever be justified.

Vitoria, and after him the Jesuits Luis de Molina and Francisco Suárez, had narrowed to a sliver the criteria that could deem a war justified. Molina argued almost to the point of pacificism. It would be, he suggested near the end of the 1500s, impossible to be a good Christian and a good soldier. Wars executed for glory and gold, or to suppress pagans and sinners, were unjust, according to Molina. Preemptive strikes were illegal. Molina's massive treatise *On Justice and Rights* can be read as one of the founding documents on what is now called "social justice." For his part, Suárez argued for a generous understanding of social obligation and mutualism. He imagined a harmonization between the rights of individuals, nations, and humanity. The "human race" is held together by sociality, a "certain unity," not only a "species unity" but a "moral unity" based on the values of love and mercy that "extends to all, even to strangers." An acknowledgment of the social nature of existence would help all obtain a "better mode of life."[1]

For the would-be English colonists of the Virginia Company, the Salamanca School's rejection of Aristotle's concept of "natural slaves" was the most daunting challenge. They agreed that invoking the need to enslave "natural people" was the "worst way" to justify settlement. Yet they grasped the problem: natural slavery may be the *worst way* to legitimate settlement, but (once limits were placed on war and conquest) it might be the *only way* to legitimate settlement. Once that concept was off the table—once it has been established that all people were morally equal—there was no sound basis on which to legalize colonialism.

The dispute in Spain went on with "much intricacy, perplexity, and replication." Each advance in moral reasoning (starting with the fact that Native Americans were human, part of a common family, and had rights, including the right to govern their territory and possess property) undercut all possible rationalizations for their dispossession. Half a century of "indeterminable" arguments resulted, company officials noted, in little that could legitimate settlement. Catholic theologians couldn't justify anything their empire did: establish authority, take land, enslave people, and wage war.

The Virginia Company opted to avoid the question altogether. Why draw attention to the issue? If the public started questioning the morality of settlement, if the Virginia Company was forced to morally "defend our title," then the English wouldn't just have to be "comparatively" as good as the Spanish. They would have to "absolutely" good in their dealings with native people. They couldn't just violate the rights of Indians less than did the Spanish—they wouldn't be able to violate those rights at all.

It would be better, the Company decided, "to abstain" from making any positive declaration and merely defend itself as needed.[2]

The promise of bringing Christ to the heathen offered an evergreen fall-back pretext. "Cry the name of Jesus among the infidels," said John Dee, who in the 1580s had organized a voyage in search of the Northwest Passage. The moral paradox, though, remained inescapable. The Spanish take from Indians the "pearls of the earth," and "sell to them the pearls of heaven." The officials of the Virginia Company asked: Are we to do the same? Free their souls but enslave their bodies? Protestant clerics associated with the Company would have liked to align their plans for America with an emerging universalism, a universalism attached not to a specific religion or a revealed truth but to the logic of rights and reason. They found such an alignment impossible. And so, in contrast to the Spanish who wouldn't stop arguing about "the nature of the Indian," the English said nothing. Rather than admit ethical problems, the Virginia Company invoked its right to remain silent.

"Let the divines of Salamanca," the Company later wrote, "discuss that question how the possessor of the west Indies first destroyed, and then instructed."[3]

As Cited by Vitoria

The silence couldn't last. The Virginia Company eventually had to publicly claim a right to settle in the Americas. Violence, inescapable from colonial settlement, made such justification inevitable.

By the early 1600s, many English jurists and clerics accepted that Indians lived in civil society and enjoyed the right of possession. "As cited by Vitoria" was a common footnote to English treatises and pamphlets, including one by Reverend Samuel Purchas, a strong supporter of the Virginia Company who nonetheless argued, at first, that Amerindians could not be dispossessed. To take from them what is theirs would be, Purchas said, as wrong as any one item on a long roster of perversities: "filthy Sodomites, sleepers, ignorant beasts, disciples of Cham . . . clouds without water, corrupt trees twice dead, raging wars, wandering stars . . . wells without water, clouds carried about without a tempest." The Reverend William Crashaw kept his Spanish law books, including the complete works of Vitoria and his followers, in a library above his chapel. "We will take nothing from the Savages by power nor pillage, by craft nor violence, neither goods, lands nor liberty, much less life," Crashaw said, sounding like Vitoria.[4]

Vitoria did allow that the violation of the natural right of Europeans to travel and trade might justify war and conquest, though he didn't elaborate on the point, nor did he extend the premise to justify the Spanish Conquest. Rather, it was the English promoters of colonialism associated with the Virginia Company who made that leap. The Company clearly planned to do more than travel and trade. It meant to settle, claim land, and secure political dominion over those settlements. And so, as the historian Andrew Fitzmaurice put it, they walked through a door left open by Vitoria. One company pamphlet cited the University of Salamanca and paraphrased Vitoria, saying it would preach Christ "by discoverie, and trade." And as relations with the Powhatans deteriorated, the Virginia Company and its allies began to argue that war and dispossession was justified because Native Americans were preventing "community betwixt man and man."

Then, in March 1622, the Powhatans raided Jamestown and killed hundreds of its residents, and whatever checks Vitoria and the Salamanca School placed on the Virginia Company fell away.

"A flood, a flood of blood" had washed over Jamestown, the Reverend John Donne preached to the members of the Virginia Company after the massacre. Donne told his audience that with patience the colony would prosper in America as the world prospered after God's great flood. Edward Waterhouse, a member of the company's council, thought the Powhatans' massacre of settlers "beneficial" since it would untie English "hands which before were tied with gentlenesse and fair usage." The colonists were "now set at liberty by the treacherous violence of the Savages." Self-defense gave the English the right to "invade the Country, and destroy them who sought to destroy us." Settlers had until then taken for themselves only the "waste" of Indian land. Now, however, all their land would be taken as a spoil of war. There was another benefit to understanding American settlement as a perpetual war: it justified, Waterhouse said, forcing Indians into "servitude and drudgery."[5]

Earlier, Reverend Purchas had cited Vitoria on indigenous property rights to liken settler dispossession to a perversion of nature. Now, he made Sepúlveda sound like Las Casas. The reverend called on the English to spill Powhatan blood "in showers" and said the "dispersed bones" and "carkasses" of the victims would give the English an eternal claim to the land. They cry from the grave: "this our earth is truly English, and therefore this Land is justly yours O English."[6]

Within just two decades, the Company went from not wanting to make any grand claims justifying its presence in America to shouting that it would take all.

The World's Debate

"Tawny Spain lost in the world's debate," Shakespeare has the King of Navarre say in *Love's Labour's Lost*. And in modern histories of the consolidation of international law, Spain often does go missing. Samuel Johnson, though, a conservative critic of colonial pillage, appreciated Spain's contribution to modern morality. "I love the university of Salamanca," Johnson wrote about a century after the Virginia Company debate. "When the Spaniards were in doubt as to the lawfulness of their conquering America, the university of Salamanca gave it as their opinion that it was not lawful."[7]

Other northern European legal philosophers, however, did not love the Salamanca School. But they recognized its authority. The implications of Spanish jurists such as Vitoria and Molina, if extended to their conclusion, would have indeed made conquest, colonialism, dispossession, slavery, war, and exploitation "not lawful." And so for intellectuals invested—either emotionally or in some cases financially—in expanding English (or Dutch or Swedish) power, a work-around was needed. They walked a fine line, wanting to use the arguments of Spanish jurists to limit, or undermine, Spain's claim on the New World, without limiting or undermining London's (and Amsterdam's and Stockholm's) right to make similar claims.

Alberico Gentili, the Regius Professor of Civil Law at Oxford, was a tutor to Queen Elizabeth. His active period was in the late 1500s and early 1600s, close to the golden age of Spain's colonial theorists. He cited the "learned Vitoria" for insisting that religion could no longer justify war, a position credited with laying the groundwork for the Peace of Westphalia, which ended Europe's religious wars by recognizing that Catholicism, Lutheranism, and Calvinism were, from a diplomatic standpoint, equally valid religions. The Vatican objected strongly. Such an appeasement to heresy would remain "null, void, invalid, iniquitous, unjust, damnable, reprobate, inane, empty of meaning and effect for all time." Protestant purists also condemned the peace settlement. But the Old World needed stability. A flood of American silver into Europe had led to a great transformation in agriculture, manufacturing, trade, and finance. The spread of commerce and accumulation of fortunes created new centers of power and private interest, enterprises that included German banking houses, the East India Company, the West India Company, the London Merchant Adventurers, and the Royal African Company, among many others. The Christian ideal that the sacred should reign over the secular was giving way. Vitoria's vision of a "law of nations" was applied, in the face of these corrosive forces, in the hope of holding things together.[8]

Gentili, however, broke with Vitoria over the question of Amerindians. The "cause of the Spaniards is just," he said, when they waged war against people who practiced bestiality and other vile acts. "Such sins are contrary to human nature" and justified violent repression. Gentili even flirted with a crude form of polygenesis as a warrant for war and conquest. It was righteous, he said, to conquer people who "have the human form, but in reality, they are beasts."

Hugo Grotius, who was born in the western Netherlands and wrote in the early 1600s, appreciated Vitoria but complained of the absolutism of his followers, of "Molina and others," and the obstacles they placed in the way of waging war. He disputed Molina's argument that violations of natural law could only be punished by local civil authorities. In other words, under

Molina's rule, no European power could legitimately wage war under the pretext of protecting Native Americans from their own rulers or from other Native Americans. Grotius, in contrast, said that not only did European empires have the right to punish violations of natural law, but so could private-trading companies such as the Dutch East India Company. Grotius here was defending Dutch imperialism in Asia.[9]

Heralded as the founder of international law, Grotius advanced a generous array of rights for European nations to punish, wage war, and appropriate land. Europe's storied protoliberal legal theorists didn't want to end conquest but regulate how it was executed.[10]

Then there was John Locke.

All the World Was (Spanish) America

The first sentence of John Locke's *Two Treatises of Government* is clean to the bone:

"In the beginning all the world was America."

At once sweeping and terse, the phrase introduces readers to divine creation and then quickly moves them into a secular world ruled by law. Locke's rhetorical strategy wasn't new. By 1689, when *Two Treatises* appeared, it was common to start an argument about society by invoking what things were like before society. *America*, for Locke, was time out of mind, a clean slate, an open field, a place that existed prior to politics and money. It was fantasia, a pristine baseline from which Locke could theorize about human nature, the origins of property, the fundamentals of natural rights, civil society, and the foundation of legitimate government.[11]

In the beginning all the world was Spanish America would have been a less felicitous yet more appropriate opener, for Locke drew heavily from the work of Spanish jurists to make his most well-known arguments. For instance, Locke's famous section on the social contract—where he argues that the consent of individuals vested with natural rights is required to organize civil society and invest governments with legitimacy—tracks point by point a passage written by the Jesuit Juan de Mariana a hundred years earlier, in a book published in 1599 titled *De Rege et Regis Institutione.**

Locke knew of Mariana's book but didn't cite the priest in his *Two Treatises.* He did acknowledge the work of another Spanish Jesuit, José de Acosta, whose *Historia Natural y Moral de las Indias* appeared in Spain in 1590 and was soon translated into English and other European languages. (Acosta, coincidently, was Father de la Cruz's inquisitor and helped Viceroy Toledo in his campaign to establish Catholic orthodoxy in Peru.)[12]

Acosta's wildly popular *Historia Natural* was a study of the different kinds of societies that existed in the New World, its arguments helping English and European philosophers like Locke bypass Vitoria's prohibition against conquest and dispossession. What set Acosta apart from other Conquest chroniclers was that he didn't posit an either-or, this-or-that opposition between savagery and civilization. Rather, the traveling Jesuit offered a secular evolutionary account of the transition between primitive and complex societies. He identified human history as passing through definable stages. First: simple societies which mostly hunt and gather, and which have neither leader nor religion. Second: close-to-the-land settled communities that were governed loosely by elders. Third: a kingdom or empire that exercises dominion and is organized around a clear political hierarchy and religion. According to Acosta, America was home to all three. Societies like the Inka and Aztecs had reached the highest levels of civilization. Other societies were perhaps moving toward more complexity but their mode of life still fell within one of the first two stages.[13]

This was just the schema European political theorists needed to skirt the formidable absolutism of Salamanca humanism. Father Acosta was especially valuable in loosening the tight proscriptions jurists like Vitoria and Molina placed on war and the doctrine of discovery: since New World

---

* At times, Locke uses Mariana's exact phrases, translated into English. For instance: Locke wrote that the government may "not raise taxes on the property of the people without the consent of the people." A century earlier, Mariana wrote: "*no puede imponer nuevos tributos sin que preceda el consentimiento formal del pueblo.*"

"barbarians" had exercised the right of possession, Vitoria taught, there was nothing in America to be "discovered."

Not quite, Acosta countered. The Jesuit agreed that *much* of the New World was possessed. But not all of it. There existed empires, yes, that exercised dominion and possessed extensive landed property. But America also contained large, empty swaths of territory thinly populated by people living in the simplest of ways. Propagandists for English colonialism had already begun citing Acosta, carrying his books on their ships, including those that sailed into Jamestown. The Jesuit's classification scheme was used to justify taking Chesapeake land, with settlers arguing there was little difference between the Powhatan, who lived and hunted on the land, and "brute beasts."

Acosta used what today we would call sociology and anthropology to update, and render respectable, the old medieval spectrum separating the barbaric from the civilized. After the Powhatan massacre of 1622, Reverend Samuel Purchas stopped footnoting Vitoria and started citing Acosta. Acosta's schema allowed Purchas to declare that most of the land north of the Aztec realm was "thinly inhabited, and indeed in great part not at all." Acosta's social evolutionism laid the foundation to justify coming dispossession.

Locke read "Josephus de Acosta" closely. He agreed with the Jesuit's "great conjecture" that large parts of the New World were pristine, inhabited not by the storied Aztecs or the cultured Inka but by artless peoples whose simplicity offered a window back in time to what Europe was like before written records and political society. In the beginning, all was America. Not Tenochtitlán or Cuzco, those wondrous cities that bewitched Cortés and Pizarro. Not what Tenochtitlán became—the densely populated Mexico City, the great metropolis of the Catholic Spanish Empire. But *America*, empty and unclaimed.

Vitoria lectured that Indians could, and did, possess property because they had reason. Acosta said: True, *some* of them did. But many didn't possess the land over which they rambled. That qualification was enough to breathe life into an idea as old as Rome, that waste land was free to the "first taker," and that *terra nullius*—unused or underused land—justified the dispossession of inferior tribes or barbarians by their superiors.[14]

Locke also used Acosta to put forth a more materialist theory of property than that advanced by the Spanish scholastics. The right to property, for Locke, wasn't based on the medieval obsession with people's capacity to reason and constancy of mind. Rather, labor was what created property. "Every man has a property in his own person," Locke wrote. "The labour of his body, and the work of his hands, we may say, are properly his." Whatever he removes from nature and mixes with his labor is made "his property."

Earlier, Alberico Gentili, Elizabeth's counselor, considered the taking of unused land akin to a biblical or military commandment. "The seizure of vacant places is regarded as a law of nature," Gentili said. Even if that land belonged to others, power "abhors a vacuum" and empty lands "will fall to the lot of those who take them."[15]

Locke smooths out this argument. He puts forth a gentler, yeoman-like idea that unworked land was up for grabs. Locke does state unequivocally that Indians have the right to possession and that such a right, if exercised and title established, should be defended. But he drew from Acosta to argue that many Amerindians didn't make use of this right. They didn't work nature. They didn't dig wells. They didn't build cider houses, put up fences, or boil acorns. They didn't add value to nature's bounty. For Locke, the legitimacy of government was based on the ability to protect the activated right of possession. This meant that those simple communities, whose people Acosta said roved and ranged and enjoyed nature's plenty, couldn't claim sovereignty, since they didn't mix their labor into that bounty and create value.

The historian Andrew Fitzmaurice argues that John Locke, along with other promoters of British colonialism, completely reversed "the moral force" of the Salamanca School's defense of indigenous rights, with an assist from Acosta. Acosta gave the English a way to continue to condemn the Spanish Conquest of the advanced Aztecs in Mexico and the Inka in the Andes, while claiming their own move into North America was something else entirely.

The reach of Acosta's influence is impressive. He was cited by both the learned in Europe and the Puritans in New England. The Swiss-German jurist Emer de Vattel used the wiggle room provided by the Jesuit's anthropology to relativize different kinds of conquest: "The conquest of the Empires of Peru and Mexico *was* a notorious usurpation," Vattel said in the late 1770s, in contrast to the English settlement of North America, where Natives "ranged" rather than settled. Those colonies have been "extremely lawful."[16]

First there was medieval law, with all its theocratic, confusing, and deductive validations of war, theft, and slavery, based on tattered tomes of royal decrees; revealed papal truths; dire prophesies of world's end; magical ideas about the power inherent in papal donations and the "right of discovery"; the convoluted writings of ancient philosophers and saints; and fantastical notions about a race of "natural slaves." In the 1500s, came Vitoria, Las Casas, and their followers, who, shocked by the Conquest, provided the foundation of rational thought that made it difficult to justify domination in all its many forms.[17]

Then, in the 1600s and 1700s, modern colonialism's intelligentsia buffed all the old medieval arguments into a shiny new language meant *not* to end war, slavery, and dispossession, but to make those activities viable in a plural world of multiple empires and religions and secularizing financial interests. The idea that there existed a continuum from savagery to civilization, which rested heavily on Acosta's ethnography, was how modernism dressed up its medievalism. Locke's labor theory of value offered a modern way of determining the distinction between "primitive" and "civilized" peoples, of judging where a society stood on the ladder of progress better than did all the old obsessions of cannibalism, sodomy, lesbianism, and paganism: Does a society have laws protecting the right of property? Does it continually strive to mix labor with nature? Does it create wealth? Does it improve itself?

Yet English colonists, as their settlements multiplied, didn't need Locke or any other European writer to tell them that what they were doing was right. They saw it with their own eyes. "This remote, rocky, barren, bushy, wild-woody wilderness," wrote Edward Johnson in the middle of the 1600s, "a receptacle for lions, wolves, bears, foxes, raccoons, bags, beavers, otters, and all kind of wild creatures, a place that never afforded the natives better than the flesh of a few wild creatures and parched Indian corn inched out with chestnuts and bitter acorns, now through the mercy of Christ become a second England for fertileness in so short a space that it is indeed the wonder of the world."[18]

The social history of settlement created its own intellectual history, a common stock of common sense that legitimated expansion, no matter the theories of Oxford dons. Settlers often dealt with Native Americans as equals, or near equals, as circumstances demanded. They bought land from them and, at times, respected deeds, honored property lines, and signed treaties. Colonial courts, on a case-by-case basis, might recognize indigenous property rights, even to land left "unimproved" or unfenced.[19]

Yet as the settler frontier radiated west, north, and south, and as indigenous society retreated and wars and massacres sundered what early comity might have existed between colonizer and colonized, there soon emerged a consensus that Spanish America was for the English to take.

10.

The Western Design

The Great Puritan Migration wasn't meant to go just to New England. In 1629, Robert Rich financed an expedition to establish a Puritan colony on a small volcanic island off the coast of Nicaragua. Providence, as the settlement was called, became not a camp of saints but a nest of English privateers and slave smugglers. Spanish forces soon broke up the outpost, finding 350 settlers and 600 enslaved Africans (a number that might have been inflated, to plump up the insurance claims of English investors). The English around this time were also expanding into the eastern jungle lowlands of Guatemala, Honduras, and Nicaragua, and consolidating plantation colonies in Bermuda and the Bahamas.

Then, in 1655, Oliver Cromwell—who came to power two years earlier, during England's republican interregnum, following the English Civil War and execution of King Charles—sent a squadron of ships to take the Caribbean, including Hispaniola, from the Spanish. Cromwell was ambitious. His plan, which he called the Western Design, was to establish an island base, and then launch an assault on the Spanish Main to break the Catholic hold on the New World. It was the first time a European nation dispatched a military fleet across the Atlantic to attack another European power.

One of Cromwell's advisers, General John Lambert, thought the assault rash. London would do better, he thought, using its finances at home to calm a restive people. Cromwell answered by saying that there was no distinction between foreign war and domestic policy. God, he said, wants us to advance the "work that we may do in the world as well as at home."

"Providence," Cromwell said, "seemed to lead us hither."[1]

What Is the Lord Doing?

Prior to his decision to try to take Hispaniola, Cromwell had looked for guidance. In 1651, he wrote to Boston's Reverend John Cotton. "What is the Lord doing? What prophesies are now fulfilling?" Cromwell asked.[2]

Cotton, the Cambridge-trained grandfather of the better-known Cotton Mather, had been an esteemed Puritan reformer in England, a humanist, a gentle interpreter of the Gospel. As minister of Saint Botolph's Church in Lincolnshire, he was, due to his renown, the closest thing the Puritan world had to a bishop. But he felt squeezed. The Anglican establishment believed him to be a nonconformist, a separatist who wanted to establish a church free of the government. Strict Puritans, meanwhile, thought his preaching too liberal. Cotton agreed with Puritan conservatives that mercy was decided by God. But he thought that decision—whether God damned or saved any given individual—depended on how they saved their life. England had grown too commercial for him, too cutthroat, and he urged his congregants to sail to New England if they could. As he bid farewell in 1630 to a large group of voyagers on Southampton's pier, including John Winthrop, Cotton spoke nostalgically of how things used to be, before competition had taken hold of daily life. "Tradesman no longer live one by another," he said, but now "eat up one another."

Soon after, Cotton learned he was being called by Anglican authorities to answer charges that he was a separatist. Rather than waiting for the warrant, Cotton shed his church garments and went underground, hiding until he could escape to America. "Fly to your safety," his friends told him, which he and his wife did, sailing to Boston in 1633. They were soon followed by his most faithful congregants and mentees, including Anne Hutchinson and her family.

In America, Cotton regained his prestige, becoming one of the city's most influential magistrates and religious leaders. Back home, in England, many of his congregants were reprobates, and ministers could only go so far in preaching mercy. In Boston, though, the goodly filled his pews, and he felt a greater liberty to emphasize God's compassion, the belief that people had some say over whether they were saved or not. Boston witnessed more conversions in just a few months after Cotton's arrival than it had all the previous year.

Yet worry quickly set in. His fellow Puritan divines were chronically distraught. Much ink has been spilled on the "Puritan ordeal," on identifying the emotional and ideological sources of the self-doubt that overcame New England spiritual life, the jeremiad, the hectoring sermon, that blamed believers of having gone, somehow, wrong.

Puritans who migrated to America imagined themselves founding a purer community than the one left behind in Europe. They wanted a commune of faith that wasn't subordinated to the political state, wasn't corrupted by base institutions, subverted by court intrigues, or confused by false doctrines. Such desire would be hard enough to satisfy in a place of comfort. In cold, remote New England, surrounded by increasingly hostile Native Americans, it was impossible. Winters were long, nights dark, the ground hard. Epidemics no longer spared settlers but took all, flames consumed homes and their inhabitants on a regular basis, ships wrecked, crops failed, wolves attacked, mothers and children died at birth. Danger was everywhere, always present. Apart from sabbath psalms and spirituals, the main entertainment was public hangings, mostly of pirates and Native Americans.

The saints set many traps for themselves in their simultaneous freeing and repressing of the self, their preaching that "sanctification"—the living of a self-controlled, sin-free life—was thought of as sign that one's salvation was already predetermined. Saintly behavior was an outward sign that one was chosen, cultivating self-righteousness that easily manifested as intolerance. Yet could the unchosen act saintly? Could the chosen reverse God's original determination by not acting saintly? Such uncertainty gave rise to a policing instinct, leading to serial campaigns to root out apostates. And since Puritans were so interior, so self-obsessed, they believed that certain thoughts and desires were as sinful as actual behavior. Surveillance of the inner life of one's neighbor couldn't but spread suspicion and paranoia.[3]

Roger Williams was among the first to be banished, after which the chosen set on Cotton's mentee, Anne Hutchinson. Hutchinson preached an expanded version of Cotton's merciful doctrine and, given Cotton's personal association with Hutchinson, many understood that the attack against her was also an attack against him. Cotton at first maneuvered to defend Hutchinson. Yet the space for Cotton's kind of reform Puritanism had narrowed, leading him to publicly denounce Hutchinson. The betrayal weighed on him privately. Publicly, though, he gloated upon learning she had miscarried after being cast out of Boston. Cotton, along with the colony's governor, John Winthrop, became obsessed with learning the shape and nature of the discharge, described by a doctor as a combination of wind and water. Cotton had turned a dear friend into a pariah, preaching that Hutchinson's "unnatural birth" was punishment for her belief that "all was Christ in us."[4]

Heretics within, enemies without. The two-year-long Hutchinson affair overlapped with the Pequot War, which transformed Boston into an armed garrison and its militia into mass murderers. In May 1637, a detachment led by captains John Mason and John Underhill committed the last bloody massacre of that war in Mystic, Connecticut. The captains burned hundreds of people they found huddled in a roundhouse, mostly women, children, and the elderly, since warrior-age men were out on an expedition.

"It was a fearful sight to see them frying in the fryer and the streams of blood quenching the same, and horrible was the stink and scent," wrote Governor Bradford.[5]

Survivors were marched through Boston in shackles, since the city's leaders had, as the war progressed, legalized the enslavement of captives taken in a "just war." Boston was fast becoming a key North Atlantic slave port, a source of indigenous captives for planters in the Bahamas, Bermuda, and other English plantation islands.

The commune of the faithful seemed to be in a state of perpetual unraveling. Many of the indentured servants sent by the Massachusetts Bay Company to do the hard "wilderness-worke" of cutting down trees and planting fields fled nearly as soon as they arrived. Some of them set up makeshift communities scattered "along the coast" after stealing company supplies. Others escaped to live among the Wampanoag and other indigenous communities. To "become like an Indian" was a Puritan sin. Yet many poor settlers were happy to adopt the "sordid spirits of the neighbouring Indians" if it meant escaping indenture.[6]

By the 1630s, regulations put in place to limit individual gain and nurture a commonweal—the keeping of common pasture and planting lands, the creation of a communal store of grains, limits on the right to own property, and controls on how much merchants could charge for their wares in order to maintain a "just price"—had come undone. Hardship wasn't as equally distributed as it had been earlier in the settlement. Poverty became entrenched, wealth became more ostentatious, and class position became generational, passed down from parents to children. The economic competition and exploitation that Cotton had fled from in England had followed him to the New World.

Piety intensified, and what Andrew Delbanco calls a "rekindled millenarianism" turned men like Cotton away from reform and toward obsessive readings of Revelation to make sense of world events. Many came to believe that the solution to schisms *within* the community lay *outside* the community, in taking action to help accelerate the end-time. If they couldn't create a decent, Christlike community they could at least prepare the way for Christ himself. There existed many debates, many disagreements, of what, exactly, needed to be done to hasten the Second Coming. But all agreed on one thing: the Spanish Catholic hold on America would have to be broken.[7]

Reverend Cotton already had an accelerationist vision of history. Delbanco says he built his New World ministry by cultivating a psychological expectation among congregants that a return to a Golden Age of Christianity was imminent, that in the flash of a moment, the sanctified would be liberated from history and coddled in divine timelessness. "When this veil shall be removed," he preached, "then shall you see the stars of heaven." Cotton believed the apocalypse was coming soon and urged New England to get right with Christ or risk being "cast into outer darkness." When the storm comes, "Indians and Jews and Pagans" will be left "gaping after salvation," having realized that their religions were "but so many refuges of lies."[8]

It wasn't only eschatology that led Puritans to look outward. Demography did as well. New England was getting crowded. Twenty thousand settlers had arrived in the 1630s alone. The English spread out fast from Plymouth and Salem, and soon had settled all around the bay, in Dorchester, Roxbury, Watertown, Newtown (Cambridge), Charlestown, and Boston. Settler families were growing, and many had hoped that Cromwell's assault on the Spanish would open new areas to settle.

One settler complained to Cromwell that Puritans were trapped between the sea and a "rocky rude desert." Take the Caribbean, he urged the Lord Protector, since in New England "all convenient places for accommodation on the sea coast" are "already possessed and planted."[9]

Preachers used their sermons to tell congregants to prepare themselves for a second great migration, this time to Mexico and Hispaniola.

Dry Up the Euphrates

So when Cromwell wrote asking what he should do, Reverend Cotton had an answer: take America from the Spaniards, the New Englander wrote the Protector, and prophecy will be fulfilled: the Euphrates would surely "dry up."

The reference to the Mesopotamian river is in Revelation 16:12: "And the Sixth Angel poured out his vial upon the great river Euphrates, and the water thereof was dried up, that the way of the kings of the east might be prepared." That verse was popular among preachers close to Cotton, used to mean any historical event that might portend that the end of the world was nigh. Cotton told Cromwell that he now believed the passage referred to the Caribbean, that its drying up would signal the beginning of the Second Coming and that Cromwell would be crowned one of the kings of the east. "There is a power in true religion," Cotton had preached in an earlier sermon, that could vanquish the "King of Spain, and of the rest of the Catholic princes."[10]

New England's Puritans represented but one vanguard in the rush to war with Spain, men driven by a religious fire. In England proper, the aristocratic and merchant elite were motivated by more earthly desires. Before Cromwell, those elites had been split between those who favored stability and peace (a position understood to be "pro-Spanish") and those who wanted to break open the Spanish Empire, to gain access to its trade routes, markets, and resources. By the second half of the 1600s, the more aggressive anti-Spanish imperialists had gained the upper hand. Nearly all bankers, merchants, and investors understood prosperity to be dependent on expansion. The Dutch were ahead of the English in establishing trade routes, in the Caribbean and down to Brazil, and London financiers didn't want to be cut out. They also wanted a bigger part of the growing and lucrative transatlantic slave trade. It was time for London to force the Spanish to make room.

John Cotton died in 1652, before the launch of Cromwell's Western Design. The Lord Protector had put two veterans of the Irish campaign in charge: General Robert Venables and Admiral William Penn. Venables had led the 1649 siege of Drogheda, on the east coast of Ireland, which ended with a horrific massacre and most of the surviving Irish shipped off to Barbados. Penn's fleet had blockaded Irish ports, a service for which he was given estate lands in County Cork that had been owned by the Catholic McCarthy clan.

Cromwell imagined his Western Design as a gravitational force, pulling the faithful into the fight as news spread of victory. A few New England Puritans did join the campaign, though most of Cromwell's conscripts were picked up from elsewhere in the English Atlantic. They were, according to one witness, mostly "hectors, and knights of the blade, with common cheats, thieves, cutpurses, and such like lewd persons." "Slothful and thievish servants likewise" also signed up "to avoid the punishment of the law."[11]

Cromwell's battleships arrived at Hispaniola having maintained an element of surprise. And still they were turned back almost immediately. The island's forces were hurriedly mustered by John Murphy Fitzgerald, an Irishman known by his Spanish name Captain Juan Morfa. Morfa had switched his loyalties from England to Spain years earlier. Now, he led a spirited defense of the island where Columbus and his men had rampaged, Montesinos preached, and Las Casas converted. Cromwell had been led to believe that the island was his for the taking. Thomas Gage, a former Catholic priest turned Puritan with years of experience living in Spanish America, had told Cromwell that the people of the Americas were desperate to throw off their Catholic yoke.

"Proclaim liberty to Mullatoes, Negros, and Indians," Gage said, and they would gladly "joyne" you "against the Spanish." Cromwell trusted Gage. He told Venables that most of the people on Hispaniola were "Indians, who will submit to you," because they hate their Spanish lords.[12]

Gage was mistaken. Morfa's ragtag militia made up of "Whites, Negroes, and Indians" forced Venables and Penn to retreat. The demography of the island had changed since Montesinos's sermon. Over the course of more than a century, decimated Native Americans had been replaced by enslaved Africans. But, importantly, with Spain focused on extracting resources from the mainland, a looser peasant economy with less onerous tribute and labor demands had taken shape on Hispaniola. Cromwell's forces were surprised to see "negros and molatos" fighting with "great confidence." Maybe some of the retreating English, splashing through the waves to get back to their ships yelled "Freedom for all who join us." Yet none of Hispaniola's defenders defected, and for good reason.[13]

The English in the Caribbean could hardly claim to be better than the Spanish. They were raiders, slavers, and kidnappers—not the bearers of liberty's banners.

Natural to Mankind

The English failed to take Hispaniola, much less move on the Spanish Main. They did take and hold Jamaica, which allowed England to expand its involvement in African slavery.

Known as the Protector's Darling for the rest of Cromwell's rule, Jamaica was transformed into a contraband slave bazaar. Spain tried to keep a tight hold on its colonial economy, granting a limited number of companies or nations the exclusive right to trade certain commodities. Slavery was an especially prized monopoly, which the Portuguese had long held. Now, the taking of Jamaica gave the English a base to engage in contraband, selling captured Africans to Spanish buyers and undercutting the price offered by Spanish-sanctioned slave merchants. The English continued to grab bigger parts of the slave trade. In the mid-1660s, an English raiding expedition occupied nearly all the Dutch slave ports off the Gold Coast of Africa before swinging across the Atlantic and taking, also from the Dutch, New Amsterdam, an island in the mouth of the Hudson River. The raiders renamed the island New York, after the Duke of York, one of England's leading investors in the slave trade. The Dutch were already supplying the isle with "as many blacks as it possibly can." The English supplied more.[14]

The English had been capturing Africans and selling them in large numbers since the 1560s, and few of their philosophers and theorists of political or economic freedom were interested in challenging the institution the way, say, Las Casas or Vitoria confronted the Conquest. Adam Smith thought slavery intractable. In recent years, Smith's reputation as a moral thinker has grown, and he's no longer considered as celebratory of emerging commercial society as previously portrayed. But his questioning mind wasn't up to challenging bondage. "Slavery takes place in all societies at their beginning, and proceeds from that tyrannic disposition," which is a quality of all humans, Smith wrote. "It is indeed almost impossible" that slavery "should ever be totally or generally abolished." "Love of domination and tyrannizing" was inherent to the human condition.[15]

Some of the philosophers of freedom in the English-speaking world, like John Locke, were financially invested in the slave trade. David Hume brokered his financial patron's purchase of a slave plantation in the West Indies. Centuries after Las Casas forcefully insisted that all humanity, regardless of color, was one, Hume in 1753 was promoting racial polygenesis: "I am apt to suspect the negroes and in general all other species of men (for there are four or five different kinds) to be naturally inferior to the whites. There never was a civilized nation of any other complexion than white."[16]

The horrors of chattel slavery were well and widely known to the public by the mid-1600s. Influential Spanish priests had been denouncing the slave trade for nearly a century—for them, the enslavement of Africans was just one part of the larger savagery created by the Conquest, impossible to separate from the stealing of Indian land or indigenous bondage. In contrast, Locke, Smith, and Hume—tribunes of tolerance, skepticism, human sympathy, and freedom—had little to say on the topic. At best they threw up their hands, helpless. At worst they wrote laws regulating slavery, reaped profits off its trade, and dealt in dehumanizing theories that justified the institution's existence.

This wasn't just hypocrisy. Rather, it reflected the centrality of slavery in underwriting liberty. The extraction of the world's resources—the coin, food, and commodities needed to keep up the growth rate of an expanding world economy—produced the wealth that allowed more and more Europeans and European settlers to enjoy more freedom. Slavery (not the old feudal-servant slavery of Las Casas's Mediterranean childhood, but a new system in which humans as property provided the labor for large-scale debt-capitalized, export-oriented plantations) was as essential to the emergence of bourgeois order as was the right of commerce and communication and the freedom of the seas.

After the failure of Cromwell's Western Design, London began lobbying to win the monopoly, called the *asiento*, to supply captive Africans to Spanish America. In 1713, Spain finally granted London the monopoly. A torchlight parade passed through the streets of the city celebrating the news. "Happy days had, it seemed, come again!"[17]

England's Royal African Company, which administered the *asiento*, was capitalized by the highest level of English society, including by members of the royal family, and the queen herself. And Spain's grant of the slave *asiento* to London in turn expanded other kinds of commerce. The Atlantic Ocean economy boomed, and England was at the center of it. Between the failed Western Design of 1655 and Parliament's abolition of the Atlantic slave trade in 1807, English ships took over three million enslaved people from Africa.[18]

How We Thrive

By the middle of the 1630s, it had become common for settlers to enslave Native Americans. In New England, the first significant group of slaves were Pequot prisoners of war, whom the Puritans described as "cannibal negroes," blurring the line between enslaved Indians and enslaved Africans. The enslavement of their indigenous neighbors sparked, according to the historian Margaret Ellen Newell, "little moral, legal, or political debate among" Puritan moralists. In fact, John Cotton, so concerned with so many different matters, wrote the legislation legalizing the Pequot enslavement. To the degree that slavery was discussed among religious and political leaders, it was in terms of utility, of the need to secure labor to compensate for runaway indentured servants, or of the money that could be made selling enslaved Indians to Barbados, the Bahamas, or Jamaica.[19]

Colonial law was largely silent on the details, but indigenous slaves were understood to be property. John Bacon, a "lawyer of a large practice," willed that his slave Dinah should be sold and the proceeds used to buy Bibles for all his grandchildren. Cotton Mather brought a "Spanish Indian" slave as a gift to give his father. A vibrant indigenous slave market developed. Masters looking to sell their slaves regularly placed ads in newspapers: "An Indian woman who is a very good cook, and can wash, iron and sew"; "A likely Indian wench about nineteen years of age fit for any business in town or country"; "An Indian woman . . . fit for all manner of household work either in town or country, can sew, wash, brew, bake, spin and milk cows"; "A lusty Carolina Indian woman fit for any daily service." Governor Winthrop wrote in his 1639 will that he would leave Governor's Island and "also my Indians thereon" to his son, Adam. The "Indians thereon" were taken in the Pequot War, branded by Winthrop as his property.[20]

By the mid-1600s, African slavery was well established throughout Spanish America and the Caribbean, as well as along the North American coast. By 1644, Puritans were sailing directly to the east coast of Africa, to Cape Verde, looking to buy "whatsoever negars, or goods, gold, or silver." Enslaved Africans began arriving in New England ports with frequency. Planters in the English Caribbean were around this time transitioning from tobacco to sugar, a shift that led to a greater demand for slaves. New England serviced this expanding sugar-slave economy, either trading directly with the English Caribbean, or triangularly, via ports in England or Africa. Plymouth and surrounding colonies sent out textiles, dried fish, fur, wool, and rum. Ships came back from England with manufactured items and, from the Caribbean, with consignments of enslaved people. As towns like Duxbury built shipyards, New England began to supply the Atlantic slave trade with slave ships, and parts for those ships.[21]

Even as African chattel slavery spread, the enslavement of Indians continued. The Mystic Massacre had defeated the Pequot. An end to hostilities reduced the possibilities of collectively enslaving prisoners of war. This resulted in Puritans kidnapping men from groups that had been friendly, or allied, with the English, including the Narragansetts, Nipmucks, and Wampanoags. When pressed about the legality of their actions, slave raiders simply invoked the principle of "just war," making up some pretext that they had been attacked. Indians could also be reduced to slavery for committing common crimes. In 1678, in Barnstable, "certain Indians" named Canootus, Symon, and Joel were found guilty of theft, and sentenced "to be perpetual slaves."[22]

For a short period after the Pequot War, settlers felt penned in by peace. In 1645, Emanuel Downing, John Winthrop's brother-in-law, desperate for labor, urged that Puritans launch a war against the Narragansetts to acquire more slaves. "I do not see how we can thrive until we get a stock of slaves sufficient to do all our business," Downing said, complaining about the "great wages" demanded by European servants. Downing thought it best to trade Indian slaves to Caribbean islands for African slaves, who were unfamiliar with the territory and thus unlikely to run away.

For the sake of our "children's children," he wrote: if we want to "see this great continent filled with people," we need more slaves.[23]

Downing needn't have worried. Slaves there'd be. Cromwell's failure to take the Caribbean increased pressure on New England's frontier. English settlement spread out, leading to new confrontations with indigenous communities, to new wars, and to new opportunities to grab slaves. The longest and most bloody, King Philip's War (1675–1678), concluded with the utter destruction of Wampanoag coastal society. Colonists killed or captured nearly half of the area's indigenous population. Hundreds of enemy Wampanoag were executed. Many were turned into slaves. Slaves were given to veterans for their service. Others were distributed to towns to compensate for financial losses. The enslavement of the defeated Wampanoags became a war spectacle. Captives were marched into Boston "tied neck to neck, like galley slaves," or some other port, and put on ships to be sold abroad. Revenue from their sale was used, writes Jill Lepore, to refill "coffers emptied by wartime expenses."[24]

Eventually, colonies did begin to recognize slavery in their written legal codes: Massachusetts was the first, followed by Connecticut in 1650, Virginia in 1661, and New York and New Jersey in 1664. Massachusetts's 1641 "Body of Liberties" officially legislated, and defined, slavery: "That there shall never be any Bond-slavery, Villenage or Captivity amongst us, unless it be lawful Captives taken in just Wars, and such strangers as willingly sell themselves or are sold to us." Later, the word *stranger* was struck from the statute, which meant that now colonists could buy and sell people who weren't strangers, including the children of slaves who lived in the community. In 1670, Massachusetts amended its "Body of Liberties" again, making it even clearer that children born to an enslaved mother were also slaves.[25]

Raids north into Maine and Nova Scotia netted Acadian and Mi'kmaq slaves. And subsequent wars—Pontiac's Rebellion, the War of Jenkins' Ear—brought fresh supplies. Soon, though, the business of importing enslaved Africans supplanted indigenous slavery, funded by investors such as Sir Robert Rich, who kitted out privateers to intercept Africans being brought to Spanish America, rerouting them to English colonies.

In August 1676, Metacom—King Philip's Wampanoag name—was, in retreat, captured and killed in a swamp. His Puritan vanquishers refused him burial. May he "lie unburied and rot above the ground," said one of his executioners, for having "caused many a Englishman's body to lie unburied." Metacom's body was quartered, its four parts hung from trees. His head was sent to Plymouth, whose residents were about to celebrate a wartime Thanksgiving in gratitude to God for turning the course of the war in their favor. The Almighty "delivered Philip into their hands a few day before their intended Thanksgiving," wrote Increase Mather. "Thus did God break the head of that Leviathan and gave it to be meat to the people inhabiting the wilderness, and brought it to the Town of Plymouth the very day of their solemn Festival." Metacom's head remained mounted on a pike on the palisade of Plymouth's fort for two decades.[26]

At some point, after carrion birds had picked off the skull's flesh and its ligaments turned brittle, John Cotton's grandson, Cotton Mather, made a pilgrimage to Plymouth from Boston and broke off Metacom's jawbone. The act was a ritualization of a scene from the book of Job, when God asks the Bible's famous man of misfortune if he has the power to subdue the Leviathan:

> Canst thou put an hook into his nose? or bore his jaw through with a thorn?

Job couldn't. But by breaking Metacom's jawbone, Cotton Mather was showing that he could subdue the beast—and proudly so, imposing a compact of perpetual slavery: "Will he make a covenant with thee?" The verse in Job continues: "Wilt thou take him for a servant forever?"[27]

Metacom's wife and children had already been shipped to the Caribbean as slaves.

11.

Opening the Mexican Fountain

S hould not Christians have more mercy and compassion?" "Why should you be so furious?" "Did you have to kill them all?"

These were some of the questions asked of John Underhill, who led the pyro-genocide of the Pequots at Mystic. Did you have to burn the women and children? Captain Underhill referred such inquiries to David's war against the Philistines, when God helped the Israelites smite their enemies: he "harrows them, and saws them, and puts them to the sword." Scripture requires, Underhill said, that "women and children must perish with their parents." "We had sufficient light from the word of God for our proceedings."[1]

Philip Vincent, who also fought in the Pequot War, realized upon seeing native organs spill out after a body was split open by a lance that there was no physical difference between Indians and Europeans. "Their outsides say they are men," Vincent said. Their spilled-out insides said the same thing. We are all the "sons of Adam," the "same matter, the same mold." Such insights didn't accumulate into a larger morality, as when that disemboweled Indian fell into Las Casas's arms.[2]

John Eliot was one Puritan to take the call to convert Indians seriously, one of the few. He set up "praying towns" to shelter Native Americans from English encroachments and give them time to study the Gospel, convert, and assimilate at their own pace. He condemned "the terror of selling away such Indians unto the Islands for perpetual slaves." Yet unlike Las Casas, Eliot wasn't part of a broader phalanx of religious and legal humanists. His was a voice in the wilderness.

I That Am an American

Daily settler life remained hard and precarious well into the late 1600s. Still, the world, including New England's world, was growing richer. Money was inspiriting. It was also corrupting. The economist Albert Hirschman has said that one of the great contributions of the American Revolution was to recalibrate the meaning of *ambition*, transforming the trait from a vice akin to greed into a virtue. By the second half of the 1600s, it was hard to tell the difference between "a covetous worldling" and "an honest thrifty Christian" grown rich.[3]

Every Sunday, sermons summed up New England's many failings: a decay of godliness; insubordination to authority; too much pride-taking in apparel, which was especially notable among servants and the poorer classes; failure to observe the Sabbath; sinful hearts; greed; speculation; drinking; too little "publick spirit"; and too much "laying out of Hair"—women not wearing their hair in a bun under a tight coif. Self-adornment mocked the idea that the commonweal should be organized around something more transcendental than the individual pursuit of wealth and status. And those periwigs! Like Lima's cloaked women, New England's wigged men might be hiding their true essence, creating a divide between what was on the surface and what lay underneath. The call of the wild, of frontier freedom, was also a vice that needed to be controlled. Settlers were moving out of the community and away from the control of ministers. They wanted what Spanish *encomenderos* wanted: more elbow room.

What was cause and what was effect? Were the many tribulations settlers suffered caused by God's disapproval of his people's actions, or were they proof that divine disapproval was predestined, no matter their actions? Indians helped Puritans answer these questions. Vitoria's scholasticism was abstract. Las Casas can be accused of paternalism. Yet a decency ran through their writings, an understanding that real humans underwrote their new humanism. Puritans, in contrast, took Indians more as portents than people. Indians could be either an instrument of God's will or an obstacle to the fulfillment of God's will.

As the seasons wore on, American Puritans intensified their end-time mania. Several English theologians, most influentially Joseph Mede, argued that the New World, far from being the place to which Jesus would return, was Hell, the worldly estate of Satan where the Lord of Darkness was rallying his Catholic and Indian minions against Christ in history's last battle. Mede cited the theory of José de Acosta, the Jesuit who influenced John Locke and other European philosophers, that Amerindians crossed an ice bridge from the Old World to populate the New. Christian apocalypticism was nothing if not tactile in its historicism, in its depiction of the forces of good and evil evolving in real historical time, in real historical places. Writing to a friend in 1634, Mede translated Acosta's account of migration into the Western Hemisphere as a satanic military history, in which the Devil, unable to gain footing in the Old World, tempts migrants to cross the ice bridge to form a colony in the New World.

"And where did the Devil ever reign more absolutely and without control, since mankind fell first under his clutches?" Mede asked and answered: "The Mexican Kingdom." Puritan engagement with Mede widened the imaginative frontier, populating the continent with a diverse cast of phantasmagoric characters, of demons made flesh in Native Americans.[4]

Reverend Increase Mather wavered on what role America would play in the apocalypse. His son, Cotton, rejected the idea that the Devil reigned in the New World, yet still borrowed from Mede to blame Puritan vulnerability to witchcraft on the Devil's influence among Indians. Mather shared a general settler hatred of Native Americans. He called them "God's apes," and if not that, then "rattlesnakes." And "the most unexceptional piece of Justice in the world" was to kill snakes. And Mather, like Mede, believed that the "Indians which came from far to settle about Mexico, were in their Progress to that Settlement, under a Conduct of the Devil, very strangely

Emulating what the Blessed God gave to Israel in the Wilderness." Indians were the Chosen People, chosen not by God but by the Devil.

Still, despite the presence of Satan in America and his influence over Native Americans, America itself, Mather insisted, was not lost. If God did choose the continent to be the site of the final battle, Indians, Mather wrote, might even be pulled from the Devil's thrall and saved.[5] "I that am an *American*," declared Mather in defense of his homeland, perhaps the first English speaker to identify as such—and here using the adjective to refer to all America.

In the meantime, the first Americans bore a heavy burden. It wasn't easy for them to have the fate of the world hang on either their conversion or elimination.

To This Mexican Valley

Like his friend Cotton Mather, Samuel Sewall defended America against those who saw it as lost to Satan. Sewall was a second-generation Puritan settler and third-generation merchant, a prominent and respected saint: an honest Christian grown rich, the owner of a warehouse, on Merchants Row, near the swing bridge that led to Boston's Long Wharf.

These two worlds, spiritual and commercial, existed easily within him. When he died in 1730, he was, as the historian Bernard Bailyn put it, "neither sunk in a convulsion of brooding introspection" nor "uplifted in grim rectitude." "Men stood in awe of Cotton Mather, and children must have run from him," one historian wrote, "but neither awe nor fear threw their shadow across Sewall's path." He was, Bailyn said, a pleasant soul. In spring, Sewall was glad to hear the first "swallows flying together and *chippering* very rapturously." When fall came, he took delight in flicking caterpillars off apple trees.[6]

Sewall did think about sin, quietly in his diary and correspondences, and how sin was subverting the promise of the New World. He read weather patterns as signs, which he recorded in his diary. A "duckish dark" night during a "blody-coulour'd Eclipse of the Moon," one entry noted, was a bad omen, signaling the birth of a tongueless child who counted six fingers on one hand and four on the other. "We have had many sudden deaths of late." The morning following an eclipse in late 1675 brought "fair" and "exceedingly benign" weather. Sewall, though, sensed something sinister in the breeze, something "metaphoric, dismal, dark, and portentous, some prodigie appearing in every corner of the skies."[7]

He was right. That eclipse had tracked the escalation of King Philip's War and seemed to herald a series of tragedies: tortured Englishmen, captive women, sieges, massacres, razed villages, famines, plagues, and, once the fortunes of war turned in favor of the English, Indians slaughtered en masse. Sewall's diary followed the course of the war: "News of the 18 Indians kill'ed, and one taken," reads one entry.[8]

Quakers walked the streets of Boston urging all to repent. Sewall "never before saw" such death. Not all of it was directly connected to the fighting. Except, for Sewall, everything was connected. Unexpected storms capsized boats; the bodies of the drowned pulled out of the sea were laid side by side and included eight young children. Old men "drowned in flegm." The war, another divine said, was a "universal deluge," equal to that of Noah's flood.[9]

In 1692, Sewall presided over the Salem witch trials. Along with other Puritan judges, he had sent over a dozen people, mostly young women, to their deaths. However shadowless Sewall's soul might have appeared to others, these executions weighed on him. He soon came to repent of his role condemning his neighbors to the flames. Out of the nine witch trial judges, he was the only one to ask for forgiveness. Others, including some who gave testimony or accused neighbors, recanted. They mostly blamed "external manipulation" as the cause of their sin. In contrast, Sewall wrote an apology that was read out loud at Sunday sermon, where he took the "Blame & Shame of it" completely on himself.

Sewall's growing disquiet led him to public action and proposals for reform. On January 1, 1700, Sewall welcomed the new century by publishing a broadside calling on his brethren "to set the Indian free." Then in June, he printed one of New England's earliest antislavery pamphlets, *The Selling of*

Joseph. The wrongness of "fetching Negros from Guinea" had long been on his mind, he said. "All men," he wrote, "have equal right unto liberty."*

As a public Puritan, Sewall might have wanted reform and Christian charity to be shown to captive Africans. As a private merchant, less so. Sewall continued until the end of his life to buy captive Africans brought to port, selling them from his warehouse on Merchants Row. "A Very likely young Negro Wench that can do any Household Work to be Sold, inquire of Mr. Samuel Sewall" was one of at least fourteen similar advertisements he ran after publishing *The Selling of Joseph.* Sewall seemed comfortable denouncing slavery even as he traded slaves. Evidently Professor Bailyn was right: the spiritual and commercial world existed easily within Sewall.

In any case, it was around the time of his public apology for his role in the witch trials and his call to free Indians and Africans that he published his masterwork of Christian esoterica, *Phaenomena Quaedam Apocalyptica ad Aspectum Novi Orbis Configurata,* which made the case that Mexico would be the seat of the New Jerusalem.[10]

The Mexican metropolis, founded around the time that his great-great-great-grandfather was born, nestled high up in the Sierra Madres, in the center of the New World, was the unofficial capital of Spain's American empire. Descriptions of the city fired the imagination. For Mede, it was Satan's great garrison. For others less concerned with eschatology, it was a place of splendor. For those who wanted to drive Catholic Spain out of the New World, it was a prize to be taken. "All America should be converted, Mexico overcome," one Reverend Lee preached in 1686, according to an entry in Sewall's diary.[11]

The Catholic-turned-Puritan Thomas Gage provided wonderous descriptions of Mexico City. Unlike the settlers of frigid, militarized New England, Mexico City residents, Gage wrote, lived open to the world, with

---

* Sewall's *The Selling of Joseph* expressed the common belief that white and Black would not mix well in a single society, based on the "disparity in their Conditions, Colour, & Hair." "They can never embody with us," but would "remain in our Body Politick as a kind of extravasate Blood." *Extravasate* is a striking word, a metaphor drawn from medicine referring to blood that seeps out of its proper channel into surrounding tissue, often to form a tumor.

"neither gate, wall, bulwark, platform, tower, armory, ammunition, or ord-nance" for defense. Joseph Mede believed the city to be the Devil's general headquarters. Thomas Gage described it as an American Venice, its floating gardens a wonder, its thick-walled houses and multitude of horse-drawn coaches an object of envy, one of the world's "greatest" and "richest" me-tropolises.

New Englanders paid close attention to news from Mexico and other Spanish American centers, wondering what reports of earthquakes might portend, or rumors of revolts. They prayed that every rumor carried by sail-ors of revolution or disaster, anything that might dislodge Spanish rule, was true.[12]

Sewall had become convinced that Mexico would be the site of Christ's Second Coming. He forcefully countered Mede's opinion that the New World was damned, instead insisting that America would be the scene of Christ's great victory. In his schema, Indians were the descendants of Jews (because according to one reading of the Song of Solomon, Jews during end-times would be gathered in a garden of nuts, and Mexicans, according to Sewall, ate a lot of nuts). America, he said, still with Mede on his mind, "was not a place of damnation."[13] Europe's Jews would migrate to the Americas and join with their lost brethren, and Mexico's New Jerusalem, he wrote, will "wonderfully dilate, and invigorate Christianity in the several Quarters of the World; in Asia, in Africa, in Europe, and in America."

Like the imprisoned Father de la Cruz in Peru a few decades earlier, Sewall was declaring that America would be the future seat of the returned savior, and in the process he put forth a generous, sweeping vision of the New World as humanity's redeemer. "Shout, Sing triumphantly," Sewall ec-statically wrote, "O America! America! America!"[14]

"Christ shall come to this Mexican Valley."

A Little Fire May Kindle

As the early years of the 1700s moved forward, Sewall remained certain that Mexico was the future, the seat of Christ's coming earthly reign, where everything "amiss is to be thorowly Reformed." The time "is very nigh, if not come."

Sewall celebrated the migration that led to the founding of the Aztec Empire in Mexico's central valley, which he described as the "heart of the Americas." The good news for Europeans, Sewall said, was that Mexico was centrally located. Once Christ came and established his throne in the New Mexican Jerusalem, it would be easier for Londoners to get to Mexico City than to the Middle East.

Whatever his spiritual yearnings, the merchant in Sewall knew the economic value that breaking up the Spanish Empire would bring, not only to traders like him but to England. Sewall was sure that the pope was the Antichrist, and that God would strike him hardest in the place where he got his riches: America, and, more precisely, Mexico City.[15]

Mather had his doubts. He completely rejected Mede's insistence that America was damned, but he wasn't sure he agreed with Sewall that the path to salvation lay through Mexico. Sewall did at least convince him that it was worth trying to convert Catholics in the Caribbean and Mexico. By 1702, both men were studying Spanish, maybe with the help of one of Mather's Spanish Indian slaves. Mather claimed that by studying just a few minutes every day he had learned enough of the language within two weeks to translate verses of the Puritan gospel into Spanish. "I have been much engaged," he wrote, "both in public and private supplications, that the Lord would open a way, for the Access of His glorious Gospel into the vast Regions of Spanish America." They both raised money in London to print "ten thousand copies in fair octavo" of a catechism, Mather's *La Fe del Cristiano en 24 Artículos de la Institución de Cristo* in order to carry out, figuratively speaking, the "bombing of Santa Domingo, Havana, Porto Rico, and Mexico itself."[16]

"A little fire may Kindle," Mather said.[17]

On the night of February 18, 1702, Sewall spotted a comet in the sky. It got him wondering. Just the day before, Increase Mather had preached from Revelations 22:16 about a "bright and morning star," part of a series of sermons that emphasized the possibility of Puritan revival. Mather didn't speak specifically of Spain, or Spanish America, but he did say that the "falling of Stars from Heaven is a frequent expression denoting the downfall of Princes."[18]

And if Mexico was to be reformed, Catholic princes would have to fall. Sewall discussed the comet with a neighbor, Timothy Clark, and after some calculation, they believed it was on route to strike "just upon Mexico," which would undoubtedly spark a "revolution." "How great a thing it would be."

"I have long pray'd for Mexico," Sewall wrote in his diary, "that God would open the Mexican Fountain."

In Mexico City, the royal astronomer, Luis Gómez Solano, caught sight of the same comet on February 26, 1702. Gómez calculated its size, location, speed, and trajectory, describing its shape as a "burning lance."

"Knowing what it is," he wrote in a short summation of the comet, "can save us from panicked fears." The Mexican astronomer went on to describe different kinds of moving heavenly bodies and the shapes they can take: pyramids, candles, jumping goats, flying stars, dragons that spit flames. Gómez mentioned talk of a comet with "two human heads" that appeared in the sky upon the first arrival of the conquistadores, which greatly impressed the Indians. Many of them had died. But, Gómez wrote, many also lived to "enjoy the splendor of our Holy Catholic Faith." His point was that it is difficult to interpret the meanings of comets. Good could come from bad. When assessing "natural things," one should look at them with "one eye like Heraclitus, and another eye like Democritus," that is, both empirically and speculatively.

Other Mexican observers reported that the comet witnessed by Sewall and Gómez looked like a palm tree. In North America, Pierre-Charles Le Sueur, a French explorer traveling along the Mississippi River near Louisiana, described a "bright star with a tail."[19]

Gómez wondered if the passing of the comet might lead to a bad harvest or drought. He didn't, though, make mention of any hope that it would strike Boston.

PART III

AMERICAN REVOLUTIONS

EARTHQUAKE AT CARACCAS

A state of perpetual undulation

12.

Three Kings

It was Catholic Spain that would help Sewall's Massachusetts, along with twelve other colonies, break free of Great Britain. And then Madrid, with eyes wide open to the danger it had helped conjure, immediately moved to contain America's first republic.

With stunning speed, the independence of North America's British colonies brought a new, dynamic actor on the Atlantic stage, led by politicians and intellectuals with enormous self-regard and considerable ambitions. Spain was caught unaware by the certainty with which diplomats like Benjamin Franklin and John Jay pressed their nation's interest, even though more than a few Cassandras had warned Madrid that the latent power of the United States was nothing to trifle with, that by helping British rebels separate from London they would be unleashing troubles hard to contain.

A Great Upheaval

Spain's assistance to George Washington was critical. Washington's troops were desperate, hungry. The Continental Congress was short on money. As New England's leaves turned and the temperature dipped, Washington pleaded: "If the Spaniards would but join," he wrote to an ally in October

1778. With another long winter coming, the commander of the insurgent forces hoped to be better prepared than he had been the year before at Valley Forge.[1]

He would be. Benjamin Franklin, fresh from signing the Declaration of Independence, entered secret talks with the Spanish court seeking support for the rebels. Spain responded by sending two envoys to Philadelphia to manage the distribution of its aid, supplying the Continental Army with blankets, boots, gunpowder, and other necessities. Then, on June 21, 1779, Madrid declared war on London. Washington had been waiting for such a declaration. "Spain has at length taken a decisive part," he told one of his generals. "The House of Bourbon will not fail" in "establishing the Independence of America."[2]

Spain's decision to enter the war on behalf of the insurgents had to do with family obligations. The Bourbon king of France, Louis XVI, pressed the Bourbon king of Spain, Charles III, to support the "Revolution of the North Americans," in the hope that it would allow Paris to reclaim territory lost to London in 1762 at the end of the Seven Years' War. Louis wanted to take back French Canada and a few Caribbean islands.

Charles had his own reasons to try to weaken Great Britain. He ruled over an empire that was in evident decline, having recently lost, due to European wars and dynastic rivalries, the Spanish Netherlands and the kingdoms of Naples and Sardinia. Madrid wanted to hold on to its New World possessions, but the English were pushing into the Yucatán, the islands off Honduras, and the dense forests of Central America in search of tall hardwood trees to supply their naval repair shipyard in Jamaica. English smugglers and privateers moved up and down the coast of South America, undercutting Spanish merchants and avoiding royal taxes, and roved the waters of the Caribbean and Atlantic, confiscating Spanish cargo. A war against Great Britain might give Spain, with France on its side, a chance to establish firmer control over its sprawling territories in North America west of the Mississippi. Maybe Madrid could take back Jamaica, which had been lost to Cromwell and whose capital city, Kingston, generated more wealth for Great Britain than did Boston.

Spain knew the danger of going to war in support of North American republicans. The conflict could escalate out of control. Peru remained a tinderbox, having just put down a massive indigenous uprising led by a Jesuit-educated heir to the Inka throne, Túpac Amaru II. Royal officials had the rebel leader tortured, drawn, quartered, and beheaded. But Spanish authority had been badly challenged. A world war might spark more unrest, in the Andes or elsewhere in the empire. To settle the North American conflict, Spanish diplomats tried to negotiate a peaceful end to the revolution. Madrid's court proposed "the independence of the United States" as part of a "general peace" between European powers. England's King George rejected the idea out of hand.[3]

And so Spain joined France, escalating a provincial rebellion into an imperial world war: Charles and Louis against George. Over the next few years, thousands of Spanish troops fought on multiple fronts against Great Britain, in the Caribbean, and up the Mississippi, taking British forts as far north as Lake Michigan. Spain also occupied Mobile and Pensacola.

The historian Brian DeLay writes that London most certainly would have retained control of its American colonies had France and Spain not decided to enter the war on the side of the republicans and supply them with arms. Because of strict regulation of the arms trade, British colonists had nowhere near the weapons needed to defeat the British. Europe manufactured the most advanced weapons and artillery, keeping London's soldiers well-provisioned while Washington's men worked with ancient muskets, used for hunting rabbits, left over from the Seven Years' War. Now France and Spain gave the rebels the up-to-date weapons that allowed for their unexpected victory at Saratoga in late 1777.[4]

Madrid's agile troop maneuvers also forced Great Britain to disperse its strength. Central America doesn't usually come to mind when considering the American Revolution, even though the Battle of Nicaragua was critical. Spanish troops fought a long jungle campaign in that country's Atlantic lowlands against the British, cutting off an important supply of hardboards and masts London needed to repair damaged war ships. Meanwhile, Spain's dominance of the Mississippi Valley prevented King George's army from pressing in on the coastal rebels from the west. Likewise, the Royal Navy had to defend Great Britain's Caribbean holdings from French and Spanish troops. This meant there were fewer British ships available to lay siege to rebel ports and harbors. London's forces were spread out, defending not just Jamaica and other sugar islands but Gibraltar and trading forts on the Indian Ocean.

The French get the credit for, in 1781, sailing nearly every ship in Louis's fleet out of Saint-Domingue, today known as Haiti, to rout Sir Thomas Graves's armada in the Chesapeake, harrowing the British along the Atlantic coast until Lord Cornwallis surrendered to the rebels at Yorktown.* "The blow," writes one military historian, was "perhaps the heaviest that has ever fallen on the British Army."[5]

That blow was paid for by Spanish gold and silver. All parts of Spanish colonial society showed enthusiasm for North America's rebel cause, an ominous sign for the ongoing viability of the Spanish Empire. Free people of color volunteered to fight the British, helping to take Mobile and Pensacola. Legend has it that *las damas de la Havana* sold their jewelry and donated the money to the insurgents. Much of this fundraising was organized by Francisco de Miranda, then a young officer based in Cuba.[6]

Apart from the geopolitical concerns and familial obligations that led Spain's king to support the North American rebels, many Spanish royalists thought Great Britain an abomination that had to be punished. It represented more than simply Christian heresy. The island kingdom now symbolized the kind of commercialism that degraded God's earthly realm, making its people grubbier, more materialistic. "Evil must come to England," wrote Francisco de Saavedra, a royal official stationed in Cuba who helped coordinate assistance to the rebels, in his diary in 1780: "the amplitude of its dominion, the enormity of its commerce and the corrupting luxury of its wealth is incompatible with patriotism and public virtue."

Punishing another imperial power entailed a risk, Saavedra knew. "We can't begin to imagine," he wrote, "what great upheaval the North American revolution will produce in the future for the masses of the human lineage." The British surrender at Yorktown did more than defeat royal rule in

---

* France had gained control of Saint-Domingue—the western half of Hispaniola—in the middle of the 1600s (a claim formalized in 1697) and quickly turned the colony into one of the most lucrative sugar-slave colonies in the world. The eastern half of Hispaniola came to be called Santo Domingo and remained under Spanish control.

English-speaking North America. It ended monarchal timelessness, thrusting both the New and the Old World into the slipstream of secular, republican history, stirring a sense of expectation, of anticipation.[7]

Manifest Decadence

It is hard to say how large, in the annals of great-power diplomacy, was Spain's error in supporting the revolutionaries.

Marcos Marrero Valenzuela was among the first to urge Madrid to reconsider its support of the English rebels. Marrero was the son of the administrator of the Real Compañía Mercantil de la Habana, a merchant house that held the once rich monopoly on trade between Havana and Cádiz in Spain. His family knew the sting of imperial decline. Economic competition with Holland, France, Portugal, and Great Britain, brought about by faster, bigger ships, better navigational technology, the liberalizing of trade, including the slave trade, and the opening of ports had ruined many a royally chartered merchant house. By the time Marrero issued his warning, Havana's Real Compañía had ceased operations.

Marrero's long 1778 letter to the Council of the Indies—the office of the Spanish monarchy that presided over its empire—said that Great Britain's troubles could be traced back to its earlier triumph over Spain and France in the Seven Years' War. In victory were the seeds of defeat. By weakening its imperial rivals in North America, London removed a "solid and effective bulwark," Marrero said, that was "containing" its colonial subjects on the Eastern Seaboard. Marrero pointed out that it was not North America's first inhabitants—not the Iroquois, Hurons, or other Amerindians with valid claims to the land—who were demanding independence. If that was the case, there would have been little to worry about since Indians tended to live within their boundaries and work their land intensively.

That Marrero might even consider such a possibility—that the original claimants to the land, the people conquered by Europeans, might demand independence and sovereignty—gives a sense of how alive the question of rightful dominion still was for the Spanish, centuries after the Conquest.

Marrero was fully aware that the so-called American Revolution was what today would be called a settler-colonial revolution.

And those settlers, Marrero warned, were inherently expansionist and would immediately threaten Spanish holdings west of the Mississippi.

Marrero also stressed the importance of the Americas to greater Europe's sense of identity. By this point in the late 1770s, there was no shortage of imperial propagandists arguing that the New World was the source of English and Spanish wealth and power. Marrero agreed. But he went beyond declaring that any single nation wouldn't have prospered were it not for their American colonies. He said Europe *as* Europe would cease to exist if it gave up colonial exploitation. "Europe cannot maintain its current power unless it has the whole of America entirely in its dependence," he wrote. "Since its discovery, the riches provided by that part of the world has sparked a prodigious expansion of Europe's agriculture, arts, industry, commerce, and navigation." Marrero went on to say, "The wealth that circulates from these activities adds value to *all* of Europe's products and services."[8]

Wealth—gold, silver, and profits from sugar—has "multiplied in such a great excess that it has transformed" European identity, creating a "truly oriental pomp" worthy of the Ottomans or the Mughals. State revenue was so dependent on colonial extraction that all of Europe would suffer a "manifest decadence" were the "springs of America's wealth" to dry up. Do not permit "republican sovereignty" to take root in the New World, he warned. The issue was more important than mere revenue. The moral unity of Europe represented by its common adhesion to the glories of royalism was at stake. The monarchies of Europe needed to realize, irrespective of Christian schism, their shared interest. They needed to band together and ensure the "subordination of the whole of America."[9]

Us and Them

Another prophet who foresaw the United States' ascent as signaling Spanish decline was Pedro Pablo Abarca de Bolea y Ximénez de Urrea, better known as Conde de Aranda, or Count Aranda. Aranda was high Aragonese aristocracy. Trained for the priesthood, he instead entered a different kind of cler-isy: the royal diplomatic corp.[10]

Aranda served as Spain's chief diplomat for negotiations, which began in Paris in late 1782, called to formally end hostilities between London and the North American rebels. London had recognized its defeat. But the terms of the colonies' break with Great Britain had to be worked out, in talks that would include all the belligerents. Matters of great importance to Madrid and France had to be settled: determining the new nation's borders; settling what parts of North America and the Caribbean belonged to France and what to Spain; and deciding the fate of Native North Americans, those who supported the insurgents and those who fought alongside the British. The negotiations produced the Treaty of Paris, signed on September 3, 1783, which resolved some of these matters and, most importantly, affirmed royal Europe's recognition of the legitimacy and independence of the New World's first republic: the United States of America.

Aranda arrived at those negotiations hoping to secure for Spain most of the Mississippi Valley, much of the Caribbean, and West and East Florida. In the first plenary meeting, the count produced a map of North America and asked the U.S. delegate John Jay where he imagined his new republic's western boundary ran. Jay knew what he wanted. Without a second's hesita-tion, he traced a line down the Mississippi, then east across a good part of Florida to the Atlantic.

This would be the first of many reenactments, in the decades to come, of the original drawing of the Tordesillas line: the pulling out of a sketchy map, the tracing of a line with a finger, the partitioning of the earth as if it were cake.

Aranda was prepared for Jay's bold demand and countered with a pro-posal of turning the Mississippi Valley—the great watershed that reaches from the crest of the Allegheny Mountains in the east to the Rocky Moun-tains in the west—into a buffer zone made up of Native Americans, includ-ing many indigenous nations that had long-standing trading and political ties with Spain, Great Britain, and France. As such, Aranda suggested that the border of the new United States run just west of the Alleghenies—an offer he knew that Jay and his fellow delegates, including Benjamin Franklin, wouldn't accept. Franklin was alert to the danger of Aranda's proposal. Spain's goal, he wrote in a private correspondence, "to coop us up within the Allegheny Mountains is now manifested."[11]

Aranda was willing to settle on a border a bit further west. Yet neither Jay nor Franklin would accept anything short of the Mississippi River as the new nation's border. Aranda balked. He insisted that the rebel-colonists had no basis for such ambition: they had won the war, but not overwhelmingly so, and not without the guns and other supplies paid for by France and Spain. Aranda's French counterparts recommended that the count keep pushing for the creation of a "barrier" nation of Indians. Aranda was hoping to reinforce a policy that had long been in place informally, used by London, Paris, and Madrid to check Anglo settlement.

The count asked Jay an obvious question: By "what right" does the new United States presume to take "territories which manifestly belong to free and independent nations of Indians?" Jay responded sharply. That's a matter to be settled between "us and them," he said. It was neither Paris's nor Madrid's nor London's business. Jay then mordantly turned Aranda's question around, bringing up the Spanish Conquest. "His Catholic majesty had had no doubts of his right to the sovereignty" of the New World when he claimed it for Spain, Jay said.

Doubts there were aplenty, but Jay's point was made: Republicans held that popular consent bestowed authority; monarchists said the right to rule came from God. Yet here was John Jay saying that when it came to Indians, power was power. It was all the same—the Spanish Conquest and, centuries later, America's first republican revolution.

The United States had won its revolution, and no one was going to deny "the magnitude of the prize," as George Washington put it in a letter written exactly at the time Jay and Franklin were negotiating in Paris their new nation's borders. No matter where the diplomats lay the line, the "citizens of America," Washington said, were "sole Lords and Proprietors of a vast Tract of Continent." *America* here for Washington meant the United States, what it was and what it would become. Years even before the revolution broke out, speculators, including Washington and Franklin, had grabbed considerable Indian land in the Ohio Valley and settlers mustered their numbers to advance through the Lehigh and Shenandoah valleys, onward past Appalachia, taking the fertile land of Native Americans.[12]

Mostly, though, rather than push back against Aranda, the United States delegation simply turned away. Franklin and Jay sidelined France and Spain and began independent talks with Great Britain. It was a nimble move on the part of U.S. delegates. United with Paris and Madrid against London on the battlefield, the United States, now at the negotiating table, switched sides and joined the United Kingdom to isolate their former Bourbon allies.

Earlier, London had encouraged Madrid to push the idea of a buffer zone, which it saw as a continuation of its prerevolutionary effort to keep settlers and speculators east of the Alleghenies. Now, though, British negotiators dropped that demand and agreed to a quick peace. They let Jay have the entire eastern Mississippi Valley, up to the river itself. Aranda had been cut out and boxed in. Not wanting to be left out of the still-to-be negotiated fate of Florida and the Caribbean, the count had little choice but to accept the Mississippi as the United States' western border.

In the end, the Treaty of Paris affirmed Spain's possession of East and West Florida, New Orleans, and northern Mexico—that is, most of the continent west of the Mississippi, including California, roughly below what is today the United States–Canada border. London kept Canada, including French Quebec. France retained its Caribbean possessions, the most important of which was Saint-Domingue. London claimed no territory south of Canada, yet British merchants, working with indigenous allies, kept busy in the Mississippi Valley fur trade and in the Pacific Northwest.

The Treaty of Paris left Spain the only European power standing between the United States and the Pacific, a fact that rattled awake Madrid's royal court. The enormity of the risk involved in supporting the rebels had been realized. The Marquis de Castejón, who sat on the king's council, warned that the treaty would bring ruin:

Spain is about to be left alone, face to face with one other power in the whole of North America—a power which has assumed a national name, which is very formidable on account of the size of its population and the ratio of increase thereof, and which is ready for war even when there is no war. I think that we should be the last country in all Europe to recognize *any* sovereign and independent state in North America.

Castejón worried over the bond that existed between Great Britain and its former colonies, one that no revolution, no differences in political theory, could tear asunder. What eventually became known as a "special relation-ship" was already, in the side negotiations over the Mississippi, taking shape, a shared worldview that would survive commercial rivalries and even a future war. Great Britain and North America would eventually act as "one nation," Castejón warned, with "one character and one religion, and would so form their treaties and compacts as to obtain what they both desire." The threat of an Anglo-dominated Atlantic trade, ruled by an emboldened republic in league with a European Protestant kingdom, had fast come into view.

Mexico, the Marquis predicted, would soon be "lost."[13]

Decline and Fall

After negotiations had concluded and the treaty signed, Count Aranda wrote King Charles a lengthy, confidential report: "The independence of the English colonies is recognized, which for me is a cause of pain and fear." "Spain is exposed," the diplomat said, its territories in North America, pro-tected only by a few settlers and a handful of forts and missions. Madrid had gone to war against London because of a *pacto de familia*, family obliga-tions, a war that was "completely against our interests," Aranda said. It would have been better to let Great Britain and its colonies destroy one an-other.

The United States was "born a pygmy," but it would soon become "a gi-ant, the colossus of the hemisphere," spurred on by access to cheap land and benefiting from an influx of farmers and artisans. The United States' first "step" will be to "grab the Floridas and dominate the Gulf of Mexico," Aranda predicted. Then it will set its sights on Mexico.

Edward Gibbon had, by now, completed the first three volumes of his six-volume *The History of the Decline and Fall of the Roman Empire.* Banned by the Inquisition, Gibbon's masterwork wouldn't be published in Spanish until the 1840s. Yet extracts circulated in "many secret and select retreats." Francisco de Miranda had read part of it in Havana. Aranda knew Gibbon personally. If he hadn't read the book, either in English or French, he knew its arguments, and like many European intellectuals, felt the decline of Spain inevitable. "History over the centuries had provided many lessons in support of this indisputable principle," one official who shared Aranda's concerns noted, of the tendency of empires to enter their senescence at the height of their glory. The Romans were "kings of the universe," at their maximum grandeur, when their decline started.[14]

Aranda's advice to the king on how to avoid Rome's fate was radical: give it all up—all of it, Mexico, Peru, and the rest of the Spanish Main. Keep Cuba and Puerto Rico, Aranda said, but turn the rest of the vicegerencies into their own kingdoms under the rule of Bourbon princes: The king of Mexico. The king of Peru. And the king of Costa Firme (Colombia and Venezuela). All loyal, all paying tribute to the king of Spain, who would take the title of emperor. Others had similar ideas, suggesting adding the Philippines, Chile, and Buenos Aires to the list, creating a commonwealth of kingdoms. Such proposals were put forth in the hope of responding to two problems.[15]

The first related to the growing restlessness among the *criollos*, Spaniards who had been born in America. They complained endlessly about the Spanish Spaniards, who lorded over them. Nothing but pure accidents of birth, having been pushed out of their mother's womb in Seville rather than Caracas, gave Spanish-born merchants significant privileges and immunities. If Madrid were to allow its American realms their own monarchs, with their own locally rooted status hierarchies, such complaints would end.

The second had to do with the empire's defense. Distinct kingdoms would organize themselves into more effective, more agile political sovereignties. Each would have its own tax system, own military, own aristocratic elite, court, and crown. Especially important in Aranda's mind was that the kingdom of Mexico would be able to maintain a stable presence in the territories west of the Mississippi. Combined, the Catholic kingdoms of the

Americas would join a commercial and defensive alliance with Catholic Spain and France. No power, on either side of the Atlantic, would be greater. This was Spain's main chance to create a "force sufficient to block the aggrandizement of the American colonies"—and to reverse the rise of Anglo supremacy.

Having just signed the treaty recognizing the independence of the United States of America, Aranda said this was the only way to contain the United States of America.[16]

The count's scheme would not only help create a world alliance of Catholic monarchies but allow the proposed American kingdoms to establish a new kind of legitimacy, one that stressed not conquest but continuities with the Inka and Aztec nobility. Centuries had passed since the first round of post-Conquest chronicles, which emphasized the savagery of "bestial Indians." Now, during the last decades of Spanish rule, intellectuals started writing histories that emphasized the grandeur of the pre-Conquest Indian nobility. The New World prior to the arrival of the Spanish, as one earlier chronicler put it, wasn't "out of the reach of memory," in the sense that it had no written history. On the contrary, there were volumes of documents written in logograms or pictograms, especially in Mexico and Central America. Some of these sources were retranscribed, still in native language but using the Roman alphabet. Scholars used these documentary sources to create a *criollo* history, an *American* history that claimed a mystical, or cultural, kinship with pre-Colombian royalty. These writings solved the problem of sovereignty raised by the Conquest by skirting the Conquest, by finding affinities with royal lineages that ruled the hemisphere before the arrival of Columbus, Cortés, and the Pizarros. In the late 1770s, the keepers of Spain's royal peerage recognized a new aristocratic title, the Duke of Moctezuma, held by the descendants of the Aztec ruler to this day.[17]

Gone were the demonologies, the riffs on Revelation that had the plumed Aztec god Quetzalcoatl as Satan, or Satan's adjunct. Now, historians like the Jesuit Francisco Javier Clavijero wrote favorably of "Ancient" Mexico and its people, rejecting the view that pre-American arts and sciences were inferior, or degraded knockoffs of Old World originals. Aztec pyramids were not imitations of Egyptian pyramids. America before the arrival of the Spanish had its own splendid history, its own advances in science and astronomy.[18]

America was original, Clavijero said. It was itself. And in some things better than Europe. What Spain found in Mexico, he wrote, was "greatly superior to that which the Phoenicians and Carthaginians found in our Spain, and the Romans in Gaul and Great Britain."

These histories weren't popular among young republicans. The libraries of soon-to-be independence leaders were filled with Europeans: Voltaire, Rousseau, Pufendorf, Diderot, Grotius, Vitoria, Suárez, Soto, Molina, and, naturally, Las Casas. Rather, efforts to establish a link between Aztec and Inka royals and Spanish nobility appealed to the constituency Aranda imagined as the foundation of his three-kingdom proposal: Spaniards born in America who identified as American and who wanted more elbow room, more freedom to manufacture and trade as they wished.

Saavedra, the royal officer stationed in Havana who worked to win the revolution for the North Americans, shared in the spirit of Aranda's plan, saying that the success of the Protestant rebels had radically changed the situation in America. It was crucial that the Crown "make variations in the system." It must stop thinking of its colonies as mere "warehouses" for Spanish merchants and start treating them as an integral part of the Spanish nation.[19]

Aranda's proposal might have charmed the decorative Hapsburgs, who would have liked the idea of Catholic kingdoms stretched out across the world like a string of pearls. But it didn't appeal to the more-to-the-point Bourbons, who had scoured much of the Baroque out of colonial legal codes and customs ("The Court is not splendid," complained an English traveler passing through Spanish society to Gibbon in 1792). The Bourbons were more secular, more repressive, and more commercial. "Where the Habsburgs used priests," the historian David Brading once observed, "the Bourbons employed soldiers." And a ramped-up Inquisition.[20]

Still, something had to be done.

The prophets of decline were right about the contagion of the United States' insurrectionary fervor. The Atlantic World would soon be aflame, with revolutionary and counterrevolutionary wars in France (1789) and Haiti (1791).

Spain held its colonies together until 1810, but barely. Riots and revolts broke out across the empire as emancipatory ideas spread. In 1794, Santiago Felipe Puglia published *El desengaño del hombre*. Or *Man Undeceived*, a rousing manifesto calling on Spanish Americans to break from Madrid. A follower of Rousseau and Paine, Puglia, a Spanish subject whose mother was Italian and father Swiss, had worked as a merchant in Cádiz before moving to Philadelphia to teach Spanish and operate a printing press. Hoping to raise money to pay for paper and ink for a five-hundred-copy print run of his seditious tract, Puglia stood on street corners in Philadelphia asking passersby for donations. Thomas Jefferson and Alexander Hamilton subscribed. The plan was to have *El desengaño* distributed throughout Spanish America via Philadelphia's extensive merchant fleet. But a captain of a Spanish brig docked in Philadelphia got hold of the book and passed it on to royal authorities. Madrid's ambassador demanded that the United States close Puglia's press and turn the heretic over to Spain. The United States let Puglia be, but the Inquisition excommunicated him and banned his book, publishing a condemnation to be nailed to church doors in Mexico and elsewhere.

Puglia, the Inquisition's broadside read, was the kind of heretical writer "expected to appear just before Judgment Day." His crimes weren't only doctrinal. They were literary. His inquisitors didn't like his prose. Man undeceived was man disenchanted. Puglia, the judges said, took "sublime" themes and ground them into a "coarse and vulgar writing style" that reflected coarse and vulgar times. The spirit of the world was losing its filigree, politics its divinity.[21]

"This century," Puglia's royal Catholic critics complained, "has produced monsters."[22]

13.

Come the Crows

Spain tried many strategies, many of them confusing and contradictory, to defend its border—nearly three thousand miles long—from a nation that pushed hard against it. In their letters, reports, and proposals, Spanish authorities often conveyed a sense that those efforts might be all for naught, that there wasn't much they could do to contain the United States. Manuel Godoy, minister to the Spanish king, shrugged his shoulders upon receiving, in 1797, a request for reinforcements to stop an attempted incursion into Louisiana led by William Blount, a Revolutionary War veteran and land speculator who had claimed millions of acres in the Mississippi Valley. *No es posible poner puertas al campo*: it's useless to try to put doors up in a field, Godoy said. It was a common Spanish expression, indicating resignation of all sorts. Here, Godoy meant it literally. No structure, no physical bulwark like a wall, no shock of troops could stop the United States from breaking through.[1]

The following year, when Alexander Hamilton and other "war hawks" were plotting to seize Spanish Louisiana and Florida, Spain's response was much the same. What to do? Cuban officials told their counterparts in New Orleans they had no troops to spare. Godoy advised his diplomats and border officers to try *reciprocidad y maña*. Conciliation and guile.[2]

Two Hens, a Cock, and a Suckling Pig

Still, for two decades following the Treaty of Paris, signed in September 1783, Spain did put into place various strategies of containment, some of them far from cautious.

Madrid thought it might win the allegiance of some of the settlers who were pouring over the mountains westward, and thus create a backstop to United States expansion. Spain offered land at no cost to European home-steaders willing to cross the Mississippi, along with an "axe, a hoe, a scythe or sickle, a spade, two hens, a cock, and a suckling pig." In exchange, the newcomers were to swear an oath of loyalty to the Spanish king. The pio-neers might also receive a barrel of cob corn, a shotgun, and an extra hoe for each child old enough to work the fields. Arcadians from the eastern colo-nies were among the first to arrive. They were already Catholic, so no reli-gious instruction was needed. Protestant settlers who took Spain up on its offer weren't required to convert. But Spanish officials did employ a battery of Irish Catholic priests to preach the gospel in English in case they wanted to.[3]

There was still plenty of easy land to take from Native Americans *east* of the Mississippi, so Spain's effort to attract colonists went slowly at first. But the adoption of a policy of gradual emancipation in Canada, combined with growing abolitionist agitation within the United States, spurred an exodus of Anglo slave-owning families across the Mississippi. Spain let settlers know they could import their "slaves, stock, provisions, household and farming utensils without paying duty." The more slaves a family had, the more land it got.[4]

Andrew Jackson took Spain up on its offer. In Spanish Natchez on July 15, 1789, just after the ratification of the new United States Constitution, Jackson, a Presbyterian, placed his hand on a Roman Catholic Bible and pledged his loyalty to the king of Spain. He had no plans to live in Natchez— Jackson was based in Nashville. But the up-and-coming twenty-two-year-old, who already had extensive property holdings and commercial interests in the Mississippi bottom, was a slave trader. And so in exchange for swear-ing loyalty to Spain, he received "absolute freedom" in moving merchandise, including enslaved peoples, from Spanish Caribbean ports to Nashville. Jackson wasn't the only Westerner who wanted to throw in with Madrid, as backland Kentucky and Tennessee settlers hatched various plots to deliver their territories to the Spanish Crown. Like Jackson, they wanted to expand their area of liberty and thought Spain best able to help them do so. Such schemes all failed, but they made clear that loyalty to the new United States wasn't a powerful enough force to slow settlers down.

As to Spain, it was playing a dangerous game encouraging Anglo settlers to homestead in its territory—as dangerous as its original support for the Revolution. The military officer in charge of northern Mexico was against the policy, believing it would backfire and would give the United States a cat's paw to undermine Spanish rule. He described Anglo-Saxons as "crows who want to pick out our eyes."[5]

Nomadic Like Arabs

Florida's Spanish governor Vicente Manuel de Zéspedes kept track of Anglo plots and maneuvers. Zéspedes updated Spain on the ceaseless incursion of white settlers from Georgia into land belonging to Creek Indians, which lay along Spanish West Florida's Oconee River. Georgia officials, over Spanish objections, claimed the river was part of the new United States.[6]

Zéspedes also explained the term *cracker* to his superiors. The phrase was already common in English; Shakespeare used it in *King John* to refer to a braggart. Zéspedes defined it as referring to certain kinds of frontiersmen hostile to "all civil control." He described Anglo settlers as "nomadic like Arabs and distinguished from savages only in their color, language, and the superiority of their depraved cunning and unworthiness." They often feigned a British accent when dealing with Indians since Indians trusted Great Britain more than the United States. Once the Indian was being had for whatever he was being had for, the accent dropped. Crackers moved into Florida not to submit to Spanish authority but "to escape all legal authority," complained Zéspedes.[7]

The Spanish governor was a keen observer of how the domestic politics of the new United States drove expansion. There were, he reported to Spain, two parties in the United States: the Democratic-Republicans (or, the Jeffersonians) and the Federalists (or, the Hamiltonians). "These two parties rarely agree on anything," Zéspedes said. Except one thing: "their desire to seize the western territory." Jefferson himself had said in 1786 that the United States *had* to grow to "drown" political "divisions."

But Democratic-Republicans and Federalists had different visions regarding the western lands. The first organized their political party around settler, slaver, and speculator constituents who wanted to expand the country territorially toward the west. The second were less eager to cater to the crackers, to let the crows fly. The Hamiltonians weren't against expansion—far from it. They were committed to a grand nation. But they wanted controlled expansion, and an extension of the central government's power over new territories. They were more willing to recognize the autonomy of Native Americans, like the Creeks. The Federalist John Jay came close, in 1787, to signing a treaty with Spain that would have closed the Mississippi completely to the United States for twenty-five years, hoping the "west would lose much of its attractiveness," and the nation's energies would be oriented toward the port cities of the Atlantic. Slowing settler expansion would create a cohesive nation with a strong manufacturing base. Hamilton wanted *national* capitalism. He wanted banks to finance industry and stop wasting their capital in land speculation and slave trading.[8]

Yet settler anger at efforts to pen them in was so sharp it shocked Hamilton and others into dropping the idea of closing the Mississippi. It became understood that one of the few things that held the sprawling United States together was the promise of more sprawl.[9]

Settlers came up with one scheme after another to weaken Spanish rule and grab western territory. In 1785, Georgia tried to create the county of Bourbon out of Spanish-governed Natchez, selling large tracts of land to Anglo real estate speculators. Ten years later, settlers who had recently moved into West Florida rose in rebellion and declared themselves free of Spanish rule. That revolt was squashed, but the list of similar escapades is long: mercenary campaigns supported by eastern and tidewater financiers to "liberate" Louisiana, Central America, Cuba, and parts of Mexico. Andrew Jackson joined with Aaron Burr to invade Mexico.[10]

An especially attractive piece of Mexico was briefly called Las Nuevas Philippinas—a series of well-water, red-dirt fertile valleys nestled between the Coahuila mountains in the south and the Ouachita hills in the north that today is known as East Texas. The region enticed the denizens of what the historian Robert May calls "Manifest Destiny's underworld," a shadowy demimonde of arms dealers, mercenaries, adventurers, contrabandists, Indian killers, killer Indians (including unvanquished Comanches and Wichitas), slave catchers, French Creole Jacobins, and South American revolutionaries. Some came into Mexico over land, along the Camino Real that connected New Orleans to Mexico City. Or through the Cumberland Gap and down the Mississippi and then west, through the towns of Natchez, Natchitoches, and Nacogdoches. Others arrived by sea, landing along the pirate coast of Galveston, outfitted by Anglo merchants who hoped to gin up a war that would provide a pretext to annex Cuba and West Florida.[11]

Sanctuary States

Identities and allegiances were fluid over the long border separating the United States and Spanish Mexico, and so were the laws of humanity. Spain, even as it was telling settlers, "Come and bring your slaves," was also telling slaves, "Come, free yourself from your slavers."

Spain had long used the promise of emancipation as a geopolitical weapon. In October 1687, the first slave fugitives from Carolina—two unnamed women, a three-year-old child, and eight men: Conano, Jesse, Jacque, Gran Domingo, Cambo, Mingo, Dicque, and Robi—arrived in Spanish Florida and were given wage employment by the Spanish governor. When an English sergeant major showed up to retrieve them, the governor refused to turn them over. Madrid followed up with an edict that gave "liberty to all." Florida continued to serve as a sanctuary state for fugitive slaves. When one Captain Caleb Davis tried to recover slaves who had sought refuge at the Spanish fort at Saint Augustine, "the blacks laughed at him."[12]

Sanctuary was a geopolitical power play. It also was, for many, a Christian ideal, integral to the legitimacy of Spanish rule in the Spanish Caribbean and mainland, even as the Spanish themselves continued slaving. The historian Ada Ferrer writes that "enslaved people in Jamaica often stole canoes and other vessels in order to make quick sea journeys to freedom" to Cuba. Others paddled to Trinidad, Puerto Rico, or the mainland. Spain extended its asylum policy west of the Mississippi, as it did throughout the whole of the Spanish Empire.[13]

The paradox is notable. Spain was as constant in support of slavery as it was in support of sanctuary. Madrid held a position not unlike Adam Smith's: Slavery was an evil, a violation of natural law and reason. But as an established historical institution, it would be difficult if not impossible to extirpate. The demands of imperial security reconciled opposites. Starting in the last decades of the 1700s and continuing through 1816, Spanish troops in Northern Mexico captured thousands of "indios enemigos"—mostly Apache and Comanche warriors—and exiled them to Cuba as slaves. At the same time, the Crown repeatedly affirmed the humanity of slaves in terms that echoed Las Casas. Any enslaved person from another polity who entered the Spanish realm was made free, protected from being handed back to his or her master. Asylum seekers would be considered "vassals" of the monarchy and eligible for whatever employment they could find, as affirmed by a 1789 royal edict. When word spread of this order, enslaved people began fleeing the United States, crossing the Mississippi into Spanish Mexico. United States slavers complained that Spanish officials were using "every means to reduce, weaken and ruin the adjoining Country belonging to the Americans," including encouraging "the desertion of slaves."[14]

Spanish officials also signed treaties of friendship with the Mississippi Valley's indigenous nations, among others, the Muscogee, Cherokee, Choctaw, and Chickasaw, trying to create, on the ground, the buffer that John Jay denied them in Paris. U.S. presidents from George Washington forward accused Spain of "intriguing" with Indians, of arming them to harass U.S. settlements. "We are encompassed on all sides with avowed enemies and insidious friends," complained Washington to Jefferson, even as settlers poured down from the mountains into the valley, pushing Indians west.[15]

The Negroes of Natchitoches

Madrid eventually decided that the territory west of the Mississippi River was more trouble than it could handle. It was costly to guard such a long border with the United States, too expensive to maintain a river fleet of galliots and bombardiers. British traders, still a powerful presence in the Mississippi Valley, meddled in local politics. French colonists resisted Spanish authority.* The radicalism of the French and Haitian revolutions was spilling into Louisiana. In 1795, in Natchitoches, a local priest had organized a group called the Revenants, which ran rough over the settlement, chanting revolutionary slogans and singing revolutionary songs—apparently in opposition to the Spanish policy of encouraging Anglo settlement. *Revenant* comes from an old French word that means "the returned," referring, in myth, to reanimated corpses, an echo of the terrors then unfolding in Haiti. New Orleans likewise was feared to be a hotbed of Black Jacobinism, confirmed by the discovery, also in 1795, of a slave conspiracy to set fire to plantations.

And so Spain, in 1802, gave it up, turning New Orleans and greater Louisiana over to France. In compensation, the Spanish monarchy received Etruria, an Italian kingdom of about a million people. Tuscan hills were much preferable to Mississippi mosquitos.[16]

Spain's new border now ran out of the Gulf of Mexico up the Sabine River (today, the border separating Louisiana and Texas) to the lower Rockies, and then to Canada. Spain now had its barrier against Anglo advancement: The territory ceded to France was enormous, 828,000 square miles large, certainly large enough, Spanish officials thought, to buffer the threat posed by the United States. Let Paris deal with the restless Anglo-Saxons.

But Spain couldn't get away. A year later, Paris sold most of the land it had just received from Madrid to the United States: Thomas Jefferson's

---

* The Spanish conqueror Alonso Álvarez had claimed the Mississippi Delta region for Spain in 1519, but in the centuries to come the river became the heart of the French Empire in the Americas, linking French Canada to the French Caribbean. France, though, as it was about to lose the Seven Years' War, ceded Louisiana to Spain in 1762.

famed Louisiana Purchase. Once again, Spain's empire shared a border with the United States. Once again, Anglo mercenaries plotted to take Mexico.

In 1807, President Jefferson took note of the popularity of Aaron Burr's plan to seize part of Mexico, floating the idea of officializing a similar paramilitary operation to his secretary of state, James Madison. If the United States were to declare war on Spain, Jefferson wrote, they'd not only win the Floridas but "a Mexican army will flock to our standard, and rich pabulum will be offered to our privateers in the plunder of their commerce and coasts. Probably Cuba would add itself to our confederation."[17]

In response, the Spanish general commander of Mexico's northern provinces, Nemesio de Salcedo, drew up a defense plan. The world—France, Haiti and the Caribbean, central Mexico—was engulfed in seditionary flames. Yet Salcedo remained steadfast in guaranteeing sanctuary to escaped slaves.* He refused all formal demands from Anglo planters for their return and policed the border to prevent slave bounty hunters from entering. Royal officials and churchmen were put in charge of settling asylum seekers. According to one report, all of Nacogdoches refugee slaves had by 1808 found wage employment.[18]

Spanish officials explicitly contrasted what they considered the humanity of their slave system to the fast-expanding cotton plantation regime in the United States. Spanish America had its sugar fields in, among other places, Cuba, Venezuela, Mexico, and Peru, where foremen worked enslaved peoples to their death. Elsewhere, though, the labor relations that fell under the rubric of slavery were more varied, including smaller-scale agricultural work and urban craft production. In some places, slaves worked for pay, giving part of their wages to their owners. Enslaved people in Spanish America had recourse to the legal system and could expect fair treatment, at least at times. They could own guns and had property rights.[19]

The terrain between Natchitoches (now part of the United States, due to the Louisiana Purchase) and Nacogdoches (still in part of the Spanish Em-

---

* In the Caribbean, however, Spain, after the breakout of the Haitian Revolution in 1793, had backed away from accepting refugees and supplied its allies, the French, with dogs to hunt insurgents.

pire) was a swampy and dangerous no-man's-land stalked by highwaymen and bounty hunters. For runaway families of color, the route could be treacherous. Enslaved peoples escaped in groups across the Sabine River to Nacogdoches. Not all made it. The historian Alice Baumgartner writes of a case in 1805 when several captured fugitives were tied down and whipped outside of Natchitoches, "their wrists and ankles bound, their limbs splayed." They were making for Mexico, one of them said, to "obtain freedom, which everyone said was a sweet thing." Others caught and returned to the United States often had an *R*, for *runaway*, branded on their forehead.[20]

Spain's refusal to return escaped slaves was, for Anglo slavers at least, an act of diplomatic defiance that violated the ideals on which the United States was founded: the sanctity of property, including human property. Spain (and later republican Mexico) refused nearly every such request. "The Negroes of Natchitoches seem determined to avoid proper obedience to their masters," complained one slaver to Spanish officials. "The protection afforded in the Province of Texas to fugitive slaves," the U.S. governor of New Orleans complained in 1808, is intolerable.*

The American Revolution filled northern Spanish America with refugees. Large numbers of displaced and dispossessed indigenous peoples, some traveling in families, others in tribal remnants, poured into Mexico. Harassed by settlers; their hunting grounds fenced in; their planting lands taken; their numbers thinned by war, massacres, drought, and disease, Indians formed a growing exodus west. "Vagabonds," was how one slave trader and land speculator described the "Delawares, Shawnese, Miamis, Chicasaws, Cherokees, and Piorias" who had fled the United States to New Madrid, when that Mississippi River town had been governed by Spain. Then, when New Madrid passed to the United States as part of the Louisiana Purchase, the vagabonds were on the move again. Cherokees, Choctaws,

---

* Later in 1837, after white settlers broke Texas from Mexico to create an independent, slave-owning republic, escaping slaves had to flee further south for sanctuary. The Mexican city of Matamoros, across the Rio Grande, became a refuge, home to a growing community of Black farmers, blacksmiths, and carpenters. Mexico, the *San Antonio Ledger* wrote, was the escaped slave's "utopia for political rights, and his Paradise for happiness."

Chickasaws, and members of many other indigenous groups tried to stay
west of a border that seem to pursue them, like a reaper.[21]

The new leaders of the United States looked west and saw nothing but
promise. It didn't take long after the Louisiana Purchase for the lower Mississippi Valley to be transformed, not into an anarchic settlers' utopia, but a
dense network of highly capitalized slave plantations integrated into the national and Atlantic economy. The 1803 report sent by Jefferson to Congress,
"Description of Louisiana," made clear the vitality: the region's fast-growing
slave population had produced "20,000 bales of cotton . . . increasing,"
"45,000 casks of sugar . . . increasing," and 80,000 gallons of "molasses . . .
increasing."[22]

Increase, Lord, increase.

There was no doubt the United States would reach the Pacific: chattel
slavery was a powerful engine of expansion. Settlers led the way, and wealthier land speculators and plantation slavers came on their heels. The demand
for cotton grew. As the fertility of the Atlantic South's soil weakened due to
overplanting, Alabama's and Mississippi's humus-rich bottomlands beck-
oned. According to frontier historians Martin Ridge and Ray Allen Billington, slaver-planters, not yeoman settlers, were the country's true pioneers, at
least in the South as far west as Texas. Wagon caravans loaded with family
and stock headed west following "patterns common to all frontiersmen save
for one difference: much of their labor was performed by slaves." Slaves did
much of the work, including, as one settler wrote, "building as many negro
houses as will answer present purposes."[23]

Indians were cleared off the land. Then family households, many with
slaves, cleared the land. Then rich slavers purchased the new fields, combin-
ing various lots into large plantations. As "the forests rang with the sound of
axes, and a pall of smoke from burning logs hazed the air," speculators "who
watched the rush" cheered. The price of land soared, which favored well-
connected planters, since they had access to loans and credit, often advanced
by Northern banks. The United States moved across the continent with impressive speed. "They had forests to cut down," Washington Irving cuttingly

COME THE CROWS | 155

wrote in 1809 of the settler's busy life, "underwood to grub up, marshes to drain, and savages to exterminate."

In Spanish America, the last run of Bourbon monarchs did what they could to meet the challenge, taking steps to insert their colonies into the vibrant Atlantic economy in the hope they could keep pace with the United States. They liberalized the slave trade—freer trade meant freer trade of human beings—and encouraged the settlement of upper Mexico. Yet the empire couldn't generate the propulsive force equal to that powering the United States westward.

Too many factors limited slavery's usefulness as a motor of Spanish consolidation. The sanctuary policy the Crown used to check the United States made it difficult to fully commit to the kind of plantation chattel slavery pursued by Anglo settlers. In remote areas, Spain relied on missionaries to maintain colonial authority (which necessarily restricted royal authority, since priests and friars put the interests of the Church above those of the Crown, not to mention above those of slavers). Royal troops pursued and battled unconquered Apache and Comanche, yet Spanish officials were not inclined to fight another exterminating war against Native Americans to free up land. The fearsome Comanche had consolidated their unrivaled authority over an immense territory—which the Spanish called *Comancheria*—in the heart of Mexico's northern territory, ensuring that Spain wouldn't get to Colorado's gold, silver, and copper before Anglos did. Even if there existed momentum to use chattel slavery as a driver of expansion and state building, clerics would have stood in their way. Spain's potent strand of Catholic abolitionism, dating back centuries to Las Casas, wouldn't tolerate the hundred lashes on the back that defined the United States slave system.[24]

And so Mexico's leaders looked north, at the same land coveted by Anglo investors, and sighed. *Reciprocidad y maña*, after all.

14.

Grand Strategies

O f all the founders of the United States of America, Alexander Hamilton was the one most fired up by Francisco de Miranda's plan to mount a joint expedition, led by the U.S. and Great Britain, to break Spanish America away from Spain. "I wish it much to be undertaken," he wrote Miranda in 1797. Hamilton and Miranda met in New York City during the Venezuelan's earlier tour of the United States, where they designed, according to Miranda, "a project for the liberty and independence of the entire Spanish-American Continent." The two men stayed in touch and, as the French Revolution radicalized and Napoleon came to power, continued to plot the end of Bourbon rule in the Americas. "I consider him as an intriguing adventurer," Hamilton later wrote of Miranda.[1]

Together, Miranda and Hamilton would "revolutionize" Spanish America. And who better to lead the effort than George Washington? There was an eloquence to Miranda's idea, the Liberator of the United States extending the revolution to become the *Liberador* of the hemisphere, "not merely the father of the United States but of the United Empires of America."[2]

Miranda sent John Adams, then the second president of the United States, a lengthy proposal, along with a heavy trunk filled with plans, maps, and supplementary writings, which plotted out the "absolute independence of the whole Continent of the New World." Miranda's allies urged Adams to read the material.[3]

Venezuela and Venezuelans have long vexed the leaders of the United States, starting with Miranda's vexation of Adams. Adams thought Miranda's schemes, especially his idea of creating a "magnificent confederation" of all Spanish America, were fantastical. "The people of South America are the most ignorant, the most bigoted, the most superstitious of all the Roman Catholics in Christendom," wrote Adams. Miranda's dreams are as "absurd as similar plans would be to establish democracies among the birds, beasts and fishes," and his proposed expedition as viable as flying to the "moon in a car drawn by geese."[4]

Adams pushed back against entreaties that he support Miranda. The need to constantly rebalance foreign policy as relations shifted between Great Britain, Spain, and France led Adams to shy away from promoting Spanish American independence, much less launching an invasion to spark a revolution. To "revolutionize" Spanish America, Adams thought, would simply mean to universalize the terrors of the French Revolution or, worse, the slave insurrection in Haiti. He was no "lover of revolutions," having lived through them not just in the United States but in Holland and France. Adams had no desire to replicate "these eruptions of volcanoes, these *tremblements de terre.*"

Still, Miranda, for Adams, was hard to get a handle on. The Venezuelan appeared to have the support of men of substance, not just Hamilton but his ambassador to the United Kingdom, Rufus King, and other members of his administration. London's prime minister, William Pitt, and all Great Britain's intellectuals and abolitionists, including Jeremy Bentham, the abolitionist William Wilberforce, and James Mill (John Stuart Mill's father), likewise supported the Venezuelan. Miranda seemed a one-man cross between a library and printing press, judging from the amount of material he sent to Adams, including drafts for a New World constitution, a proposal to restore the Inka crown as a symbol of unity, and a plan to build a canal in Panama open to all the world's nations to use. Miranda produced "as many folios" as Voltaire, Adams said. "What was to be done with these papers?"

The real question that confounded Adams was: "Who and what is Miranda?"[5]

Francisco de Miranda

Sebastián Francisco de Miranda y Rodríguez de Espinoza was a Spaniard born into a wealthy family in Caracas in 1750, the first of ten siblings, only four of whom survived childhood. He purchased an officer's position in Spain's royal army, rising in its ranks through many tours of duty that gave him a sense of the empire's reach, its awesome strengths and points of weakness. This last included the growing discontent of many of its subjects: an intelligentsia suffocated by Catholic scholasticism and inquisitional censorship, merchant elites who wanted more free trade, peasant communities squeezed by too much free trade, and enslaved peoples pressed by demands that they cut more cane and dig for more silver to raise revenue to pay for Spain's many wars.

One of those wars was in North Africa, where Miranda, in 1775, helped defeat the forces of Mohammed ben Abdallah. The tenacity of Muslim resistance to Spanish rule sparked Miranda's anticolonial sympathies. Moroccans did not want to be governed by a foreign power any more than did many in his own Venezuelan generation, including Miranda's friend Juan Vicente Bolívar (father of Simón Bolívar), who saw no reason why Spaniards born in Spain should have it over Spaniards born in America.

When Miranda's Morocco campaign ended, he returned to Madrid and purchased a Quran to learn more about Islam. By this point, he had collected over a thousand books, including works by Rousseau, Burke, Locke, Swift, Shakespeare, and Las Casas. His enslaved porters lugged the pile from one bivouac to another, including to Cuba, where he raised money for the North American rebels to fund their fight against the British at Yorktown. He then deployed to Florida, where he fought the British at the Battle of Pensacola.

Soon, Miranda's freethinking ran afoul of his superiors, eventually leading him to slip out of Spain's jurisdiction, first to take his tour of the United

States, then onward to London, Scandinavia, Russia, and finally France, to see its revolution firsthand.[6]

Miranda was in Paris by March 1792. Prussia and Austria had just declared war on seditious France, and King Louis XVI was soon to be deposed. Jacques-Pierre Brissot, a leader of the moderate Girondist faction, approached Miranda shortly after his arrival and asked him to consider taking the governorship of Haiti, which was then in the second year of its own revolution. Brissot was a founding member of the abolitionist Société des Amis des Noirs, and he hoped that Miranda might use Haiti as a launching pad and harness the "agitation" in the French Caribbean to spur the emancipation of all Spanish America. Loss of America would, in turn, bankrupt the Bourbon dynasty and end the Austrian-led royalist siege of France. Brissot promised Miranda an army of twelve thousand French regular soldiers, to be joined, once Miranda arrived in Haiti, by another "ten to fifteen thousand brave mulattoes." Miranda, who by this time had embraced the cause of abolition and emancipated his own enslaved servants, would be "the idol of the people of colour." He would be the liberator of America.[7]

Miranda considered the proposal. It was ambitious. "Grand and magnificent," Miranda thought: the harnessing of one revolution, in Haiti, to spark another in Spanish America to save the revolution in France, and then, after the collapse of the House of Bourbon, to spread republicanism to Spain. Thomas Paine, soon to be appointed Washington's envoy to France, supported the plan. But a lack of on-the-ground intelligence from Haiti worried the Venezuelan.*

Miranda instead opted to defend France, joining the revolutionary army to fight the Austrians. He won praise for his audacity. At Valmy, just as it seemed that French troops would be overrun, Miranda mounted a large steed and, with sword in hand, galloped across the battlefield ordering his

---

* The Jacobin Jean-Baptiste Victor Hugues led a toned-down version of this plan, kindling slave uprisings on the small British plantation islands of Dominica, Saint Martin, Saint Vincent, Grenada, and Saint Lucia. The British kept control of all the islands except Saint Lucia. There, in 1794, Hugues helped organize escaped slaves who had taken refuge in the island's thick rainforests into a *L'Armée Française dans le Bois*—The French Army of the Woods—which drove white planters off the island. The British didn't regain control of Saint Lucia until 1803.

men to sing "La Marseillaise." The battle turned and the Prussians were driven back. Johann Wolfgang von Goethe, who observed this scene from the Prussian side of the battlefield, understood immediately its meaning. "On this day," he said, "begins a new era in the history of the world." But after a string of equally stirring victories, Miranda was blamed for a consequential defeat at the battle of Maastricht. This loss occurred in the spring of 1793, just after the beheading of Louis and his wife, Marie Antoinette.

Military setbacks combined with an antirevolutionary peasant rebellion in the Vendée drove the Jacobins to target the Girondists, who were condemned as too moderate in the face of the growing threat. The Jacobins arrested the Girondist-associated Miranda in August 1793, and he was thrown into Paris's La Force prison. Day after day, as guards came to take one or more of his cellmates to the guillotine, the Venezuelan waited his turn. Thomas Paine testified on Miranda's behalf, which might have kept Miranda alive but didn't get him out of La Force. Jean-Paul Marat himself, among the most radical of the Jacobins, was behind Miranda's persecution. Marat, though, would soon himself be assassinated, followed by the fall of the Jacobins. Miranda was freed in January 1795. Paine later said that the day Miranda was put on trial was the day he "abandoned hope for the French Revolution."[8]

Upon leaving prison, Miranda was offered a position in the new post-terror government. He declined, fearful of the extremism and violence that had befallen the Revolution. "Two great examples lie before our eyes: the American and the French Revolution," he wrote in a letter to a Venezuelan friend. "Let us discreetly imitate the first; let us most carefully avoid the disastrous effects of the second."[9]

Miranda even thought James Monroe, who took over from Paine as the United States envoy to France, too accommodating to the radicals. In a letter to Hamilton, Miranda warned of Monroe: "*Il est devenu un Marat tout a fait*"—He's become a total Marat. Soon, Monroe's name would be forever associated with a defining foreign policy doctrine. Miranda didn't really think the Tidewater-gentry, slaveholding future president a Jacobin. Yet like Thomas Jefferson, Monroe tended to be more sympathetic to the French than to the British. Overly so, thought Miranda, having just escaped the blade.[10]

"God grant that Monroe does less harm to the New World," Miranda wrote Hamilton, "than Marat did to France."[11]

Perfect for Revolution

Miranda stayed for a time in France, where he worked with a group of Spanish American revolutionaries to draft a proposal to present to Great Britain: in exchange for a fleet of ships, the would-be insurgents offered to pay off England's national debt with the mineral wealth they expected to capture in a liberated Spanish America. Miranda and his entourage then traveled to London to pitch the proposal to the British government, including to the prime minister, William Pitt.[12]

Pitt and his ministers encouraged Miranda, as did military officers, including General Cornwallis. Miranda, as a former officer in the Spanish army, possessed intelligence they found useful—"all sorts of books and numerous charts and maps," a trove of strategic intelligence.

Miranda in London lived at 27 Grafton Street (now 58 Grafton Way, halfway between Regent's Park and the British Library), which became general headquarters for anyone with an interest in Spanish American independence. He struck up friendships with several leading British intellectuals, such as Bentham, Wilberforce, and Mill. Miranda was exceptional in his vigor and contacts. Yet he was but one in a far-flung European network of writers, intellectuals, military men, politicians, and merchants who plotted the emancipation of Spanish America. Insurgent energy flowed through Freemason lodges (including one established by Miranda himself in London) and printing houses, which published books, pamphlets, gazettes, and weeklies highlighting Spanish cruelty or forecasting the glories of a free America. Even as Miranda was presenting his proposal to Pitt and corresponding with Hamilton, back in Venezuela a group of radicals was conspiring to establish a republic and abolish slavery, to break free of the "solitude and silence" imposed by theocratic rule and shout to the world that America was free. That plot was put down.[13]

The last years of the 1700s had witnessed a "rediscovery" of Las Casas. As Spain's hold on the Americas weakened, printers in Puebla, Bogotá, Mexico City, London, and Philadelphia, among other cities, rushed out new additions of *Brief History* or published excerpts from his post-1550s writings. Las Casas's political theories of consent and his polemics on Spanish cruelty had an impact on revolutionary leaders, including on Miranda and a young Bolívar. One revolutionary intellectual called for an enormous statue of Las Casas to be raised in Panama, so that all the New World's nations would live up to the principles of love and justice taught by the "father of the oppressed," the "hero of humanity." Simón Bolívar proposed founding a new capital city on the border of a united Colombia and Venezuela and calling it Las Casas.[14]

The radical Mexican Dominican priest Servando Teresa de Mier, in exile in Philadelphia, told a friend that once while saying Mass in Mexico he read, in lieu of the Gospel, a selection from Las Casas. Before he was finished, the congregation was ready "to take up arms." Las Casas, Mier said, "is perfect for revolution." Like other rebels, Mier invoked Las Casas to argue that not just enslaved Africans but all the New World's subordinated peoples needed to be liberated. Others began to refer to Las Casas as an "apostle," not only a "defender of Indians" but a "defender of Americans."[15]

Philosophers such as Mill and Bentham, partisans of Miranda, thought that breaking America free of Spain would give them a chance to test their theories. Bentham was certain he could create a utilitarian utopia in a free Spanish America, a society organized around the principle of achieving the greatest happiness for the greatest number of people. The philosopher tried for years to emigrate to Mexico and flirted with participating in a failed scheme, organized by Aaron Burr in 1804 (while Burr served as vice president to Thomas Jefferson), to occupy Spanish territory west of the Mississippi.[16]

Centuries of extreme exploitation had solidified entrenched inequality in Spanish America, ritualized by displays of extreme servility—by bowed heads, elaborate gestures of obedience, and avoidance of eye contact. Bentham thought that all that was needed was a good rule book to set the continent straight.

Brink of the Abyss

By the late 1700s, Miranda had reason to expect that his multinational plan to liberate Spanish America might work. He counted on the sympathies of two of the most powerful men on either side of the Atlantic, William Pitt and Alexander Hamilton. Hamilton had written to Miranda saying that their plan couldn't fail: "a fleet of Great Britain, an Army of the United States" would be unbeatable.

For Hamilton, at this point an officer in the U.S. Army's high command, Napoleon Bonaparte's seizure of power in Paris in 1799 and the beginning of the Napoleonic Wars added to the urgency of the plan. Napoleon's goal was a "universal empire," Hamilton warned. The best way to prevent that from happening would be to detach "America from Spain" and deny him the "riches of Mexico and Peru." Hence his enthusiasm for Miranda, who kept assuring Hamilton that he had Pitt's support.[17]

Hamilton was essentially working a back channel to organize a covert operation not authorized by the cautious Adams. "Are we yet ready for this undertaking? Not quite. But we ripen fast, and it may, I think, be rapidly brought to maturity," he wrote to Rufus King, who as U.S. envoy to London served as Hamilton's go-between with Miranda.[18]

Hamilton and Miranda corresponded cryptically, with Hamilton dictating letters to his six-year-old son so that they wouldn't be in his handwriting. Hamilton wanted to lead the mission himself, in partnership with George Washington. Washington would be the figurehead leader of the continental army of liberation, but the practical command of operations, he told King, "would very naturally fall upon Me." Hamilton lusted after martial glory, so much so that Jefferson began to refer to him as "our Napoleon." Miranda agreed to Hamilton's vision. The Venezuelan knew how to flatter. "Continue always," he wrote to his coconspirator, "to be the benefactor of the human race."

"We will save the whole world, which is oscillating on the brink of an abyss."[19]

This phase of Miranda's intrigues ended on July 11, 1804, when Aaron Burr shot Hamilton in a duel in Weehawken, New Jersey. Hamilton died the next day. Miranda was devastated, his anguish compounded by a growing realization that however much Pitt might have wanted to reduce the power of Spain, and maybe establish in Spanish America the same colonial relation Great Britain maintained in India, no fleet would be forthcoming. Pitt was as leery of Miranda as was Adams.

On June 13, 1805, Miranda wrote his last letter to Pitt to express his disappointment. He then made plans to return to the United States and make his case directly to Adam's successor, President Thomas Jefferson.

Piece by Piece

Jefferson was sympathetic to Miranda. Dreamers both. Jefferson had by now concluded that Spain's continued long-term existence on the North American continent, and in the hemisphere, was unviable.

Yet Jefferson wasn't sure about the timing of Miranda's scheme. Spain was a key player on the Atlantic chessboard and should be engaged with care. He didn't want to "press too soon on the Spaniards" but rather wait until enough Anglo settlers had moved into their territory so that the United States could "gain" Spanish America "piece by piece." Jefferson viewed Spain's power in the Americas as European diplomats did the Ottoman Empire: wait for its disintegration and then sweep in and capture the fragments. Jefferson wasn't as hostile to France as Hamilton, having brought to a successful conclusion the purchase of Louisiana. He didn't feel compelled, as Hamilton did, to free Spanish America as part of a grand strategy to contain Napoleon. Maybe a grander strategy would be to leave what was left of the west in Spanish control, for now.

Speaking of the Caribbean and what remained of Spanish North America, Jefferson said: "Those countries cannot be in better hands"—*better* for the United States since Spain's authority was waning, though slowly enough to give the United States a chance to orchestrate a controlled transfer of sovereignty.[20] Mexico would probably be the first to fall. "We ask but one month to be in possession of the City of Mexico," Jefferson wrote to an aide. Samuel Sewall's dream might have a chance yet. Then Cuba and the Floridas.[21]

Still, the possibility that Spanish America might claim independence, and either form one large confederation, as Miranda proposed, or break up into a concert of smaller republics, was perhaps the stickiest diplomatic and legal challenge for the North American nation. Jefferson's revolution had, by the early 1800s, proved triumphant, its Constitution ratified, its presidential system working. Subsequent revolutions in France and Haiti legitimated its precedent, even as the radicalization of those revolutions—their descent into regicide and race war—threatened to discredit all movements toward greater liberty. Monarchists could point to the guillotine in France or the machete in Haiti and say: see, that's where republicanism leads. Where would men like Miranda lead Spanish America?

Miranda arrived in New York City in November 1805 and took up residence in Mrs. Avery's boardinghouse, 7 State Street, on the Battery. He began meeting with government officials and coconspirators, rekindling friendships made decades earlier during his first tour of the United States. He eventually traveled to Washington, where he met often with high officials in Jefferson's administration, including Secretary of State James Madison and Vice President George Clinton. Over dinner, Jefferson, his daughter, and Miranda spent the evening talking of "our beloved Colombia." Jefferson's library held over sixty volumes on Spanish America, mostly geographies and histories of the region. He still complained that his knowledge of the place was spotty. The Spanish Empire, especially, was "almost locked up from the knowledge of man hitherto"—practically a hermit kingdom despite the prodigious number of books its printers published and its ship captains' eagerness to gossip.[22]

So Jefferson was happy to converse with Miranda. Their meetings nourished in Jefferson the seed of Pan-Americanism, or the "Western Hemisphere Idea," the notion that the world was politically and ethically divided into two hemispheres, and that the Americas had a "separate system of interests" from Europe.[23]

Jefferson told Miranda that perhaps he was "born too early to see the splendor of the new world" to come. But it would come: Spanish America was moving "toward its complete independence," the president said.[24] There still was mercenary interest in Spanish America, including Burr's. "Mexico glitters in our eyes," wrote one of Burr's supporters. Miranda knew about Burr's intrigues but kept away. He considered the killer of his closest ally "detestable" and "Mephistophelian."[25]

Miranda later claimed that both Madison and Jefferson, while unwilling to formally sponsor an expedition to strike at the South American mainland, gave him a "wink" and told him to go ahead. They wouldn't disapprove of his raising funds and recruits from private sources.[26]

M iranda's plans were dramatically reduced. Instead of a fifteen-ship flotilla and an army of tens of thousands of soldiers, he began to recruit a small contingent of men and raise a modest sum of money from New York merchants and slave traders invested in Caribbean, Mexican, and South American trade. The value of U.S. trade with Cuba was growing. A "free" Cuba, under U.S. tutelage, if not formal possession, would prove even more lucrative. Samuel Ogden, a wealthy merchant, gave his two-hundred-ton sloop, the *Leander*, to Miranda to launch his campaign. John Jacob Astor either donated or sold two hundred "horsemen's swords" to the enterprise.[27]

Miranda's recruits came from all classes, and included Bowery butchers, printers, coopers, and cobblers. John Adams's grandson, much to the former president's distress, signed on as Miranda's aide-de-camp. Some joined for the promised pay and had no idea what they were getting themselves into. Others were looking for glory, or excitement. The United States had just fought a sensational revolution, and freeing Spanish America gave men who fought in that revolution (or their sons and grandsons, who experienced the excitement secondhand) a chance to maintain the sensation, to hold the boredom and burdens of postrevolutionary life at bay.

The Dubliner father of the man who later would coin the phrase Manifest Destiny, Thomas O'Sullivan, joined. James Fenimore Cooper wanted to sign up. He had, according to the historian Alan Taylor, "longed to be a

Latin American revolutionary." Cooper rushed to New York Harbor but the *Leander* had already set sail, on February 2, 1806. Miranda dropped anchor off Staten Island, where it had been arranged that the ship would be loaded with its war matériel: Astor's sabers, muskets, blunderbusses, carbines, dozens of cannons, 2 petards, 440 cutlasses, flints, 65,000 cartridges, 1,586 pounds of ball, and tons of lead. The ship also carried a printing press and thousands of sheets of broadside paper. Once the cargo was secure, the *Leander* made way for the Caribbean.[28]

The expedition failed. Miranda did set foot in Venezuela after a thirty-year absence. But nearly all his men were immediately captured by Spanish troops. Ten were hung, their corpses decapitated, their heads put on pikes for public display. Others were sentenced to hard labor in Puerto Rico or Cartagena. Miranda escaped and made his way back to London.[29]

15.

The Ambiguity
in Which We Live

Miranda had struck too soon. In 1808, two years after the failed *Leander* expedition, Napoleon invaded Portugal and Spain, dethroning the Bourbon monarchs of their empires and sending Iberian politics into a tailspin.

As French troops marched on Lisbon, the British Royal Navy took charge of evacuating the city's aristocracy. In a torrential downpour, His Majesty's sailors boarded the Portuguese king and his family, nobles, bureaucrats, slaves, servants, pets, furniture, and jewelry boxes onto ships. Escaping the Old World, they set sail for the New, re-creating Lisbon's court in Brazil as a "tropical Versailles." The exiled royals served as the driving agents of an odd sort of bloodless independence: Brazil would gain its freedom as a monarchy, not a republic, and would remain so until the 1880s.[1]

Spain's King Charles considered doing the same, to flee to somewhere in Spanish America. But Napoleon's troops captured him before he could make his move. Imprisoned, Charles abdicated to his son, Ferdinand VII, who was kept under house arrest in France. Napoleon installed his brother, Joseph, on the Spanish throne. Joseph's power was limited. An insurgent regency court established itself in the port city of Cádiz, symbolically recognizing Ferdinand but in effect claiming to be the "sole representative of

Spanish sovereignty," not just of besieged peninsula Spain but of the entire Spanish Empire.

News of these developments eventually reached America, setting off a chain reaction.

"Juntas" sprang up throughout the New World realm, mostly in urban centers like Caracas, Quito, Buenos Aires, Montevideo, Valparaíso, and Bogotá. They were supposedly meant to defend the legitimacy of Ferdinand. They instead became launching pads for revolution. Venezuela was among the first to rebel. On April 19, 1810, Maundy Thursday of Holy Week, a day marking Christ's betrayal by Judas on the eve of his Friday Crucifixion, Caracas insurgents deposed Spain's captain-general and ordered the expulsion of most royal representatives.[2]

The prompt to break from Spain was led from above, politically, by *criollos*, or creoles—Spaniards born in the Americas—and well-off *pardos*, free merchants of color. Neither would tolerate being treated as second- and third-class citizens any longer. But the fire for independence came from below, from the great mass of the truly oppressed and dispossessed. For their part, Caracas's tight-knit clan of white Spanish aristocratic families, known as *mantuanos*—so called since only the city's wealthy women were permitted to wear the *manto*, or shawl—largely opposed independence or remained silent, with some notable exceptions, such as Bolívar's family.*

Imperial collapse came in waves, as the forces of destruction lashed at the colonial edifice from opposing directions. The largest insurgent armies were mustered in Mexico in the north, Colombia and Venezuela on the Caribbean plains, and Buenos Aires and Chile in the south. Fighting rolled across Spanish America for more than a decade, drawing in peasants, slaves, artisans, some on the side of the rebels, others in defense of the Crown. Diverse class and caste coalitions each advanced their own idea of what they thought freedom would mean.

---

* Unlike the *tapadas limeñas* in Lima, who used the shawl to confuse matters, *caraqueñas* abided by a 1571 law prohibiting *esclavas, indias, mestizas,* and *mulatas* from using adornment as status camouflage.

Toward Independence

In Venezuela, the path to declaring a complete break with Spain was, to use a word often associated with Spanish culture and law, baroque.

After ousting its Spanish officials in April 1810, Caracas established a "Supreme Junta to Preserve the Rights of Ferdinand VII." Yet where, exactly, sovereignty lay was confusing, to put it mildly. The Junta's name was for display—it cared little about Ferdinand's rights. And it largely ignored the authority of the Cortes de Cádiz, the insurgent body that established itself in opposition to Napoleonic rule (even though the Cortes had some support in Venezuela as throughout Spanish America, since it was putting forth an appealing set of liberal reforms long demanded by colonists). For his part, Napoleon had sympathizers in Spanish America. Some Spanish Americans saw the French emperor as the Enlightenment's "world-soul," the bearer of universal law, a rationalizer whose armies would muck out the Bourbon dynasty's private "slave pen," as one historian called Spanish and Portuguese America.

So by early 1810, at least five claimants vied for legitimacy in Venezuela: the Junta; the Cortes; Joseph (as proxy for his brother Napoleon); Charles (who hoped that followers would reject his abdication); and Charles's son, Ferdinand. Then there was the Catholic Church, the foundation of the colony's moral unity, whose hierarchs considered themselves a power unto themselves. Also claiming authority were the many revolutionary "societies" sprouting up, modeled on Samuel Adams's Sons of Liberty and the Jacobin Club of revolutionary France.

The "ambiguity in which we live," as a Venezuelan patriot called the situation.

Francisco de Miranda had retreated to his Grafton Street house in London after his failed *Leander* expedition. There, he had waged a relentless "paper assault," mobilizing his friends James Mill and Jeremy Bentham, among others, to write on behalf of Spanish American freedom, with many of their essays translated and published in Venezuela.[3]

One of the leaders of the insurgents, Simón Bolívar, sailed to London in late 1810 and convinced the sixty-year-old Miranda to come home with him and join the fight. They made an inspiring duo embodying a sense that the struggle for freedom was now multigenerational. Miranda was acclaimed in Venezuela as the "precursor" of independence and renowned for his military skill. The twenty-seven-year-old Bolívar was less than half Miranda's age, yet his family's wealth and status, and his single-minded commitment to achieve a complete break with Spain, had lifted him quickly in the ranks of Caracas's revolutionaries. His full name was Simón José Antonio de la Santísima Trinidad Bolívar Palacios Ponte y Blanco, the fourth and last child of a family that could trace its American roots back centuries. Bartolomé de las Casas was still alive when the first Bolívar, also named Simón, arrived in Hispaniola in the early 1560s. Over the years, the family became among the richest, not just in Venezuela but all Spanish America. Simón had already been to Europe several times, mostly to Spain and France, including Napoleon's Paris, and was steeped in Enlightenment reason and romance. From France he hiked into Italy, where he pledged himself to Spanish America's liberation, either—depending on the legend—on the peak of Mount Vesuvius or among the ruins of Rome. This was around August 1805, about the time Miranda was lobbying Jefferson for help freeing Spanish America.

The return of Miranda and Bolívar to Venezuela in December drove *caraqueños* faster toward independence. The two men helped found a new organization, the Sociedad Patriótica, or Patriotic Society, to defend the revolutionary movement against both royalists and conciliators, political elites willing to settle for greater representation within the empire (as opposed to fighting to break with the empire). The society's job, wrote one skeptic, was "to educate the people in both republican virtue and republican demagogy, to stimulate the power of the public and to be the lever of the revolution."[4]

In June 1810, the Junta called for the creation of a congress, which was formally meant to amplify its power but wound up replacing the Junta altogether. Elections for deputies, representing Caracas and all of Venezuela's provinces, took place through the last months of the year, and Spanish America's first legislature was inaugurated on March 2, 1811.

The archbishop of Caracas, Narciso Coll y Prat, blessed the congress with a High Mass in the city's cathedral. Coll y Prat was no Lascasian emancipationist. He said in his sermon that he shared the "hopes and desires" of the delegates but begged them to remember holy religion, which has "coursed through the ages like a majestic river from Adam to Moses, crossing through centuries of barbarism and idolatry" to light the world. Only religion "ennobles submission" and "softens the yoke of obedience, of the kind that is indispensable in all civil societies." Only the Holy Roman Church, with its "sweet concert of ideas, sentiments, and rituals," creates and protects the common good, teaches virtue and condemns vice, and instructs children to use a soft and docile voice when speaking with their parents. Only the Church kept chaos at bay. The archbishop said nothing one way or the other on the question of independence. But the meaning of his homily, on the sanctity of hierarchy and obedience, was clear.[5]

When the Mass had ended, the delegates, including Francisco de Miranda, swore an oath on the Holy Scriptures that they would unhesitatingly defend the authority of Ferdinand: an empty gesture to a missing sovereign. Congress then got busy passing laws undermining the authority of Ferdinand, stepping stones to full independence.

Spain was losing its hold on America. A month after Caracas expelled its Spanish administratives, Buenos Aires did the same, in May 1810, with local creoles governing through its Junta. In other areas of Spanish America, Spanish officials managed to stay in power and in control of the troops. Royalist suppression of the budding anticolonial movement was violent. On August 2, 1810, in Quito, the Crown's soldiers murdered at least eighty protesters who had been surrounding the city's prison, demanding the release of arrested independence leaders. News of these deaths reached Caracas in October and galvanized revolutionaries primed to be galvanized. A solemn memorial was held in the Church of Altagracia, a poor parish with congregants considerably darker than those who attended Mass in the city's *mantuano* cathedral. After the service, the mourners filled the street in a boisterous outpouring of independence sentiment. "A tumult of *pardos*, *negros* and *zambos* claiming to have patriotic feelings," wrote the city's archbishop, roamed the city looking to avenge Quito. They "demanded that Spaniards and diffident creoles be arrested."[6]

The greater province of Venezuela was about evenly divided, with half of its rural townships standing with Caracas and the other half remaining loyal to Spain. Congress sent troops into the loyalist half, deepening the polarization. For its part, the Sociedad Patriótica ramped up its revolutionary rhetoric, winning over much of the city with its "egalitarian oratory" and steadily strengthening its position to force the question of independence.

To Hesitate Is to Perish

No declaration, law, or act announced Caracas's emotional break with Spain, but rather music, dance, songs, poems, and processions. On April 19, 1811, city residents celebrated the one-year anniversary of having sacked the Spanish governor, a day the Sociedad Patriótica turned into a revolutionary bacchanal. Unsympathetic observers had, over the course of the prior year, begun noticing that public crowds were getting darker, and this festival seemed especially so. Venezuelan historian Manuel Palacio Fajardo writes that this was the moment when "the people" entered the public sphere as a "new factor in the political life of the country," when a new "Venezuelan national identity" was created.[7]

Black, brown, and white marched through the streets wearing yellow, blue, and red. Those were the colors of Venezuela's new national flag, modeled on the one Miranda had carried with him on the *Leander*, which also contained an image of a proud Native American sitting on a rock holding a pike topped with a Phrygian cap, a symbol of the French Revolution. They sang patriotic songs and set portraits of Ferdinand alight, tossing effigies of royal officials into the river. Shouts of "Down with the Spaniards!" bounced off the adobe walls of the city's narrow cobbled streets. Houses were decorated with paintings depicting republican martyrs who had been executed for their involvement in earlier independence plots. Allegories symbolizing *Liberty* and *Justice* adorned the headquarters of the Sociedad Patriótica.

The society's members erected a "Liberty Tree," just as Boston patriots had in 1776, and painted a Freemason "eye of vigilance" on its trunk, keeping watch against enemies of the revolution. An even more militant club called the Sin Camisas, the Shirtless Ones, had just been organized. The group hosted mixed-raced gatherings where, as one royalist described, the dances were "strange and grotesque." The name of the club echoed Paris's sansculottes and came from the popular French revolutionary song "La Carmagnole": "The shirtless ones are dancing, and if anyone wants to know why I am shirtless, it is because the king has undressed me with his taxes." Sin Camisas were out in numbers that April night singing this and other songs borrowed from France.[8]

As the sun set, Caracas blazed with candles and gaslights, nearly every building a farrago of light and shadow. Insurgent carousing, the mixing together of people of all colors, continued for days. "Universal joy," was how one observer recalled the event. A more conservative opinion feared the city was "running headlong into the French abyss," with most of its *mantuano* families sitting out the festivities. The great doors to their compounds were closed and bolted. Dancing Jacobins, as one Venezuelan scholar has pointed out, are dangerous Jacobins.[9]

Miranda, in addition to being a member of the Sociedad Patriótica, had been put in charge of building a revolutionary army. He still hoped that a larger country named Colombia could be cobbled together before various regions began declaring their independence separately from one another—if not all Spanish America, then at least Caracas joined with Bogotá and perhaps Quito. But Bolívar, who later would campaign to unite Spanish America in confederation, thought Venezuela *had* to act immediately. First and alone.

"To hesitate is to perish," Bolívar, who was serving as lieutenant under Miranda's command, said in his first public speech, given on the eve of the Fourth of July, a date he picked to synchronize with the thirty-fifth anniversary of the revolution that created the United States. It was time to break the "ancient chains."[10]

That night and through the next day, *caraqueños*, led by the Sociedad Patriótica and the Sin Camisas, again came out rowdily into the streets, this time to celebrate the independence of the United States—and to force congress to act. On July 5, 1811, lawmakers passed an act declaring the United Provinces of Venezuela to be "absolutely independent" and charged a group of delegates, the most prominent being the forty-eight-year-old lawyer Juan Germán Roscio and the sixty-one-year-old medical doctor Francisco Isnardi, with drafting a fuller declaration.

Miranda led a procession of members of the Sociedad Patriótica to the archbishop's residence and asked the priest to shout *¡Vivas!* from his balcony, in support of independence. Archbishop Coll y Prat refused, even though he said he felt threatened by Miranda's "mob of zambos y negros." Independence would bring nothing but the terrors of France and Haiti. "Devastation," he said. "So much Spanish blood would be spilled by Blacks it will flood the country," the archbishop later wrote, recounting the day's events.

History, the prelate said, confirms the truth of the adage: "The Liberty Tree bears no fruits of equality unless watered with blood."[11]

Insurgents of Another Species

Outside of Caracas, rural people long subject to various schemes of forced labor had their own idea of what freedom meant. One observer described the rolling slave and peasant uprisings that had broken out in the provinces as led by *insurgentes de otra especie*—insurgents of a different type, or species.[12]

In Venezuela's interior, across its expansive grassland plains, *pardo*, *zambo*, and *negro* workers, some free, some enslaved, drove feral cattle and pigs to the market for meat and hides. Most farms were household ranches growing patches of cacao, indigo, tobacco, coffee, cotton, and sugar. Workers and their families from these smaller operations might join regional uprisings, fighting either for or against the republic. Others, though, simply self-emancipated. They dropped their tools and left with their families for the forest frontier or the grasslands.

In some areas, plantation slaves and indigenous communities understood freedom to mean being free to remain loyal to Ferdinand. They calculated that their lives would be better lived staying loyal to the Church and a far-away monarch than under the unshackled power of capricious *hacendados.* In other places, it meant claiming the estate lands they worked on as their own. Congress ratified many of these spontaneous expropriations. It justified doing so by defining slavers who opposed the republic as insurrectionists, and the penalty under colonial law for insurrection was the confiscation of property. Several counterrevolutionary aristocratic families lost a good deal of property.

Two serious revolts broke out almost immediately, within days of congress issuing its declaration of independence. The first, led by a group of Canary Island merchants, was quickly put down. The second took place in Valencia, a city west of Caracas. This uprising was more serious, launched as a defense of Church and king. "Long Live the King and the Virgen of Rosario—Death to the Traitors" was its rallying cry. Before long, royal troops had moved into Valencia to reinforce the popular uprising. Miranda and his lieutenant Simón Bolívar laid siege to the city.

Miranda wasn't squeamish when it came to spilling blood. He had over the years fought in battles in northern Africa, the southern United States, France, and elsewhere, where he killed many an enemy. Now, he set out to retake Valencia with a surety of purpose, fighting and winning a bloody two-week battle that left thousands dead. This was Bolívar's first military battle and command, and he distinguished himself fighting the king's soldiers on Valencia's narrow cobblestone streets. Over the next few months, Bolívar took over the campaign to push back royalist advances in eastern Venezuela.

Elite opposition to revolutionary reforms began to be felt within Caracas. Congress set up a "tribunal of vigilance" authorized to enter private homes and assess family loyalties and established schools for "patriotic education." The Sociedad Patriótica likewise sent out night patrols, which reportedly executed known royalists.[13]

The new republic, though, avoided a descent into siege-induced terror. Seven of the leaders of the Canary Islander revolt were executed. Yet no guillotine was erected in Caracas's Plaza Mayor. Political repression remained contained. Republican troops established a semblance of order in much of the countryside, especially in the important port town of La Guaira and in the western farmlands, which supplied Caracas with food. Insurgent privateers easily broke Madrid's feeble sea blockade. The revolution was taking hold, or so it seemed.

Colombiano

Spanish America's first republic, the American Confederation of Venezuela, ratified its constitution on December 21, 1811. Two hundred and twenty-eight articles set the rules for a three-branch government: a bicameral legislature, judiciary, and executive. Many of the constitution's long list of rights would have been compatible with United States laws, limiting the power of the state to allow the maximum amount of individual liberty. The drafters defined *liberty* as: "the ability to do what one wants as long as it doesn't infringe on the rights of others."[14]

The new nation was to be led by an enlightened, educated elite chosen by a complicated formula of indirect representation, again much like in the United States. All free, adult men, regardless of whether they owned property or the color of their skin, could vote—that is, vote for a much smaller group of electors who in turn would choose representatives to a lower and upper house, who then would pick the executive. To satisfy Miranda's dream of a continent-wide republic, the constitution contained a simple mechanism for expansion. Once another Spanish American province achieved effective independence from Spain, it could be admitted into an enlarging union until the entire continent was free. The name given to this expected nation was *Colombiano*.*

Congress got to work. It abolished the Inquisition, outlawed torture, and

---

* Not all Spanish America's independence leaders shared a desire to honor Columbus. When in 1817 General Charles Wooster sailed his heavily armed bark, *Columbus*, from New York to Santiago to make it available to Chilean rebels, the rebels didn't like the ship's name. They thought it more proper to fight in a vessel honoring the continent's conquered people than its

did away with the privileges and prerogatives of the nobility and clergy. It ended the slave trade but held off emancipating slaves until republicans could gain better control of the feudal countryside. The revolution wasn't secular. The constitution made it clear that Venezuela was a Catholic country. Still, conservative clerics saw danger. Republicans might claim to be Catholic, but they were still influenced by that utilitarian ridiculer of religion, Bentham, who said that no morality existed beyond the stimuli of pain and pleasure. And congress was passing legislation allowing freedom of the press, with new journals printing cynical and satirical articles skewering the Church, and even the Vatican. The city's archbishop feared that religious tolerance would open the door for Lutheranism.[15]

Freer speech and a loosening of the rituals of caste changed everyday life. Suddenly, "negroes and mulattoes had the privilege of greeting any person," wrote one British observer hostile to republicanism, "with the familiar appellation of *citizen*." In Caracas, people of color were invited to public balls and allowed to ask white women to dance. Brown- and Black-skinned people were even extended such invitations with "particular preference."[16]

The precedent set by the United States helped Spanish Americans justify their claims to republican sovereignty. In response, royalists brazenly cited Vitoria. They said that if the claims of independence leaders were to be taken to their conclusion, then Venezuela should be returned to its true sovereigns, to the "Caribes, Motilones, Guagiros, Quiripiripas, Guaranos, and other indigenous Indian nations" who ruled Venezuela before Spain's arrival. This wasn't an easy-to-dismiss criticism, and the best independence leaders could do was say that over time history created new obligations. There was no going back to the past. If Spanish Americans were required to return America to its original peoples, then Spain, republicans said, should give Iberia back to the Phoenicians or Carthaginians, "wherever they may be found."[17]

---

conqueror, so the bark was renamed *El Araucano* in tribute to the Mapuche (*Araucano* was the name the Spanish used to refer to the Mapuche).

Sweeter, More Peaceful Rights

The United States Constitution is famously a document of restraint. The text is Mosaic in its prohibitions, enshrining the phrase *shall not* to limit the power of the federal government and carve out a realm of freedom for both the individual and individual states. Venezuela's first constitution exhibited a similar proscriptive spirit. Its drafters understood that one function of law was to protect individual rights. Among the grievances that drove Spanish Americans to break with Spain were royal limits on the right to hold property, to publish, and to trade freely. Venezuela's constitution guaranteed all three. It stipulated that "property is a right" at least nine times, defining that right as the ability "to enjoy and dispose of the goods that have been acquired by work and industry."

Spanish American republicans veered away from their English-speaking counterparts, however, when they insisted that the rights of the individual had to be balanced by *el bien común de la Sociedad*, or the common good of society. If you failed to protect both (the individual and the community) you would have neither.[18]

Venezuela's constitution makes mention of the word *social* nine times, and *sociedad*, or *society*, fifteen more. Neither word appears in the United States Constitution. "Society fortifies the individuals who comprise it," Venezuela's constitution stated, and makes possible the "enjoyment of life, liberty, property and other natural rights." The constitution provided a series of checks and balances not just to moderate the government, but individualism as well. "The establishment of society presupposes the renunciation of the dangerous right to unlimited freedom," the text read, in exchange for the acquisition of "other, sweeter and more peaceful rights" that come from living in harmony with others.[19]

Venezuelans even previewed what later would be called *social rights*, mandating that the government not just *stand down* to protect freedoms inherent in individuals but *stand up* to take action that nurtures the commonweal: "Because governments are constituted for the common good and happiness of men, society must provide aid to the destitute and unfortunate and education to all citizens." True freedom, the constitution argued, "means the renunciation of unlimited and licentious freedom," which easily leads to anarchy, where everyone pursues their "private passions in a savage state." The echo is clear of Las Casas's and Mendieta's belief that New World freedom turned Spanish colonists into beasts, ferocious animals despoiling all.

Many an independence intellectual wanted to sweep it all away, all inquisitional prohibitions, the scholastic deductions justifying absolutism, the Latin-only Bibles and superstitious rituals, and realms of immunity that protected public officials: all of colonialism's many evils and inconsolable sorrows, its corruptions and cruelties.

Caste categories had to go, starting with the original unholy trinity, *indios, negros, y españoles*, followed by their endless permutations. The whole system, just before it toppled, had turned into a pyramid scheme, with Spain authorizing officials to sell variances, *cédulas de gracias*, allowing individuals to change their racial status. For seven hundred pesos, a *pardo* (half Indian, half Black) could be reclassified as a *quinterón* (seven-eighths white). Royal officials worried that free people of color might join the republican cause. So they proposed securing their loyalty by allowing qualified *negros* and *pardos* to be "registered as white." Just like that.[20]

"Our laws are ghastly relics of ancient and modern despotisms," Bolívar once said. "May this monstrous edifice shudder, collapse, and break into ruins, over which we will erect a temple to justice."[21]

Miranda had called for the freeing of all slaves during his failed 1806 campaign. In November 1810, Mexico's insurgent priest, José María Morales, proclaimed the end of all caste categories, including slaves. All Mexicans from this point forward, he said, will be called Americans. "Slavery is the negation of all law," Bolívar said. Racial differences were merely "accidents of skin" and not the immutable categories created by the Spanish Empire.[22]

The drafters of Venezuela's first constitution used an awkward but optimistic phrase to describe one group of residents who would live free under the republican government: "those citizens who until today were called *indios*."

Until today: a newer world not yet born but being so.[23]

Historians often peg the kind of communitarianism—the idea that the rights of the individual need to be balanced with the needs of the common good—found in Venezuela's first constitution as leftover Catholic medievalism, a worldview that values social integration and insists on the whole-ism of existence. But there's more to it.

The Spanish Empire in the Americas had yielded, by the early 1800s, to a republicanism that was both more *inclusive* and more *activist* than its counterpart in the United States.[24]

More *inclusive*, in the sense that republicans were heirs to a colonial regime that claimed to be universal, the legacy of the oneness of Catholic creation—even as it built an administrative structure that accommodated an ever-expanding catalog of racial differences. Everything and everyone had its place, as Octavio Paz pointed out. Washington's first consul to Venezuela, John Williamson, noted the sociality of the Spanish "colonial system," which had created a people "absolutely woven into a chain and their subsistence, their pleasures," and their "necessaries are absolutely dependent one upon the other." It took, Williamson said, about a quarter of all the poor women of Caracas to make the city's daily corn bread, or *arepas*. In the United States, one "solitary mill" could grind out flour for the day's bread in an hour.[25]

More *activist*, in that republican insurgents knew they would need a strong, empowered central state to transcend the regime they had inherited, to bring about a hoped-for world of law and political equality. Centuries of colonialism had left the region divided between a subjugated, dark-skinned majority and an entrenched, paler oligarchic elite. It would take more than the unleashing of individual interests or republican declarations of equality to free the present from such a past. It would take an executive fully "clothed in power" (to use Hamilton's phrase) to break the political, economic, and cultural hold the landed and slave-owning class had over daily life. Only then would subservience come to an end.[26]

Compare, for example, Venezuela's independence manifesto, written by Juan Germán Roscio and Francisco Isnardi, to Thomas Jefferson's Declaration of Independence. History barely gets a tug from Jefferson. All is nature, freed from the burdens of society. All the New World's evils are placed at the feet of King George. The original settlers and their heirs who claimed the land and drove off its original inhabitants did no wrong. They only suffered wrongs. For John Adams, North America was "not a conquered, but a discovered country." Nature for the taking, not granted by the king's grace, but explored, cultivated, surveyed by English-speaking settlers.

In contrast, for Roscio, a Venezuelan *pardo* with a doctorate in canon and civil law, and Isnardi, a physician born in Spain, the New World wasn't discovered but "conquered." They knew that America was a stolen continent. The Conquest hovers over their independence manifesto, an event so vile it set the course of centuries of human events. The Spanish arrived like "wild animals," carrying with them Europe's entire "history of bloodshed and perversity." The existence of the New World affirmed the oneness of humanity, bringing about wondrous advances in "human consciousness" and human knowledge. But Spanish bloodlust allowed only for domination and exploitation. A free Venezuela, a free Spanish America, would give the world a second chance: to "accelerate, consolidate, and perfect the happiness of *both* Worlds."[27]

America was a redeemer continent.

Such optimism existed alongside deep pools of fatalism. There's a sense, reading the public and private writings of independence leaders, that the Spanish Empire had driven them mad, that it had entered their dreams like some kind of minotaur. The half-human, or humanist, part pulled along a mountain of law books and philosophical treaties insisting that all existence, all humanity, was one. The other monstrous half rampaged through history, leaving corpses in its wake.

Race and racism persisted. Many elites wanted a break from Spain that would allow them to keep their considerable privileges, including control over a cheap and compliant workforce. Everyday life remained filled with the jumble of caste slang and slurs, a lexicon that continues to this day. Indians continued to be called *indios*, no matter what Venezuela's constitution said. Bolívar did what his counterparts George Washington and Thomas Jefferson wouldn't: he freed the slaves on his family's estate, hundreds of them. Yet proclamations, laws, and constitutions were one thing, entrenched social power something else. Some of Bolívar's family slaves claimed their freedom. A few joined the fight against Spain. But many simply continued to work the Bolívar estates in some form of servile condition now called freedom, bowing their heads when the family's administrator walked by.[28]

16.

War to the Death

Thursday, March 26, 1812, Caracas: What image better captures the cusp between old and new than Simón Bolívar standing defiantly on a mountain of rubble? His audacity signaled not just the beginning of the end of Spanish colonialism but the breaking of the chain that linked slave, peasant, servant, man, woman, priest, master, lord, and king in a hierarchy reaching to the sky, a sky crisp and clear that tragic Thursday. The earthquake had destroyed most of the city and its hinterlands. At one point, Bolívar, who was back in Caracas from his military campaigns when the quake hit, drew his sword on a priest and ordered him to stop praying for souls and start saving lives. Pull bodies out of the rubble, Bolívar ordered the cleric. After scrambling atop a high pile of stones from a ruined convent, Bolívar came face-to-face with José Domingo Díaz, a medical doctor loyal to Spain who for two years had written weekly polemics against the foolish dreams of republican liberation. Bolívar, as Díaz described him, looked desperate.

"What now?" Díaz asked, as if mocking the republican arrogance that it was *history* that mattered, that it was *history* that could be overcome by man's will—that it was *history* and not *nature* that decided who ruled. Bolívar's answer came back quick: *Si se opone la naturaleza lucharemos contra ella y la haremos que nos obedezca*: If nature itself opposes us we will fight nature and make it obey.[1]

Appealing to nature to argue politics had become especially popular during the Age of Revolutions—used to justify every position and its contrary. "The laws of nature and of nature's God" reads the first sentence of Thomas Jefferson's Declaration of Independence, meant to convey the idea that individuals possessed natural, inherent rights, and that a government's legitimacy was measured according to its ability to protect those rights. Jefferson took that line verbatim, minus a comma, from an Anglican priest and Tory ultra who used the phrase to argue the exact opposite. In a 1761 poem, Myles Cooper, the president of King's College (now Columbia University), said that those who presume "to defy The Laws of Nature, and of Nature's God" by opposing royal authority would be struck down with "impious Force."[2]

There's *nature* as reason, as a justifier of beliefs and ideals. And there's *nature* as force, impulsive, terrifying, and marvelous. Bolívar, climbing the convent's rubble and pledging that he would compel nature to submit to republican will, was defying both. He wasn't disputing the royalist argument that the natural disaster was a manifestation of God's displeasure. But if true, then God's will had to be defeated and the old world He presided over had to end. During this moment of earthshaking crisis, Bolívar was Milton's rebel angel hurling defiance toward the vaults of heaven. If nature stood in the way, nature would be destroyed.

After surviving Caracas's 1812 earthquake, Bolívar would spend the next twelve years of his life waging war against Spain, and against the institution that enriched Spain: slavery, in all its many guises.

Apocalypse Angel

Caracas had been suffering from a long drought that spring, and the sky was blue on the day of the quake. But a few raindrops fell just before the church bells started to ring: at 4:07 in the afternoon, not to mark time but because their towers were swaying. The undulations of the earth came from different directions, north to south, and east to west, like two waves cutting across each other.

The city sat at the intersection, and the waves crashing together sounded like thunder rising from "hell," one survivor said, like the "voice of the Angel of the Apocalypse."[3]

Columns gave way. Balconies fell. The timing of the earthquake was uncanny. The twenty-sixth of March in 1812 was Maundy Thursday. On that day two years earlier, Caracas had expelled its royal overseers. On that day one year earlier, the city had commemorated the expulsion in a wild night of revolutionary exuberance, and then shortly thereafter declared independence. Believers were in the city's many churches and convents celebrating Mass when the buildings started to collapse, and many of them, maybe most, were crushed to death. When the sun went down at 6:10, the dust rising from the rubble deepened the darkness. The "lamentations" of those buried beneath the ruins "lacerated the heart," recalled one witness. The destruction was near total, the terror absolute. Washington's envoy to the new republic estimated that twenty thousand people had died immediately, and tens of thousands more would perish in the weeks to come from hunger, disease, and injury. Church buildings in wealthy *mantuano* parishes were made of heavier stone, with larger buttresses, so most of them remained standing. Casually built churches in poorer areas of the city nearly all collapsed, crushing the city's servants, along with their children. This meant that there was a shortage of laborers and domestics to help upper-class families recover: a preview of what a world without slavery might look like.[4]

The quake radiated hundreds of miles beyond Caracas. Town after town fell, with waves felt as far west as Bogotá in Colombia. Storehouses collapsed, burying shovels and other needed tools, medicines, linen, and food. Rescuers used their bare hands to dig survivors out from the rubble. The quake blocked springs and broke pipes running to public fountains, so there was little safe water to drink or to clean wounds. Suddenly, for the well-off, the abstractions of revolutionary slogans proclaiming liberty and equality were materialized in their worst fears: the city's poorer survivors were seen "entering the houses that were still standing" and "carrying off everything they could lay hands on." Some called it looting, though it might more rightly describe survival. To prevent the spread of disease, bodies were burned by the dozens. Corpses were carted to the beach of La Guaira, Caracas's port town. There, they were burned "about forty at a time in one fire," with the flames visible to ships far out in the Caribbean.

"The City has disappeared," wrote the Prussian naturalist Alexander von Humboldt, who had visited Caracas during his American travels, upon reading of the catastrophe. So too, for many, republicanism. Congress held its last session on April 6, 1812.[5]

Nine out of ten prosperous *caraqueño* houses, compounds in the Andalusian style, thick adobe chambers surrounding lush courtyards, were destroyed. Simón Bolívar's, just off the Plaza San Jacinto, survived. Its beams buckled but held. Witnesses recalled the twenty-nine-year-old Bolívar in a tattered, stained shirt with sleeves rolled up, alternating between pulling people from the wreckage and arguing with those who said the calamity was a divine strike against republicanism, against the "sin of independence."

Disaster Royalism

Republicanism in Venezuela, as mentioned, wasn't anti-Catholic. In Caracas, as well as in key provincial cities, especially in the Andean city of Mérida, there existed emancipationist priests, of the kind that might read a passage from Las Casas rather than a chapter of the Gospel while saying Mass. But a larger, opposing group was mobilized by Archbishop Coll y Prat. A few conservative clerics had been preaching for years against republican perversity, warning of the wrath that might befall a people arrogant enough to believe they could rule themselves. Others held their tongue. Until Caracas collapsed.[6]

The archbishop, born in the Cataluña foothills of the Pyrenees, urged his priests to preach disaster royalism. They were to tell people that "hell was opening to swallow them." Clerics cited the fact that the city's buttressed cathedral was spared destruction as evidence that God protected the faithful. Christ's Crucifixion, people were reminded, was followed by a similar upheaval: "And the earth did quake, and the rocks rent." The destruction was "terrifying," Coll y Prat remembered. But "well deserved." The earthquake "confirmed for our times the timeless prophecies revealed by God to men about the ancient cities impious and proud: Babylon, Jerusalem, and the Tower of Babel."[7]

Royalists who had previously fled republican Caracas, many to Caribbean islands where no integrated balls were held, came home. They brought with them a new stock of servants and a strong dose of Catholic revivalism, including exaggerated displays of public penance. Survivors and returnees roamed the streets in impromptu processions, dressed in sackcloth, dragging makeshift crosses, and confessing their sins. The churches left standing were packed day and night, and anyone who didn't, according to one account, "surrender himself to the ridiculous mania of living in penance was regarded as a dissolute libertine who provoked the anger of heaven." Not just republicanism but all transgressions were regretted. Couples living together out of wedlock sought out priests to marry them. Fathers recognized their bastards. Republicans lost their audience.[8]

The drought let up after the quake. Hard rains that would have been welcome in any other year now tormented a city not given time to repair its roofs or drainage systems. Those still committed to the patriot cause found it impossible to speak "of liberty and national duties" to survivors seeking to stay dry under rubble, "clasping the sepulchers" with an "intense sorrow."

Earthquakes "strike the imagination," Humboldt had said upon learning of the political and religious repercussions of the quake. "Tradition seizes in preference whatever is vague and marvelous." Caracas's conservative clerics were quick to seize on the marvelous to strike at the republic. Aftershocks continued for weeks; another large quake on April 5 threw the ground into a "state of perpetual undulation." For many, there existed "only one recourse."[9]

Make peace with God. And stop calling one another citizens.

Chastisement of Heaven

In Spain, the Cortes de Cádiz had been too occupied fighting Napoleon to mount a full military campaign against republican Venezuela. It left the pacification initiative to a loyal, poorly armed frigate captain named Domingo de Monteverde. Short on men, Monteverde had begun to try to win over some of those *insurgentes de otra especie* who were stirring in rural Venezuela. Before the earthquake, Miranda and Bolívar, as leaders of the republic's defending army, had kept Monteverde in check. After the quake, though, with disaster Catholicism spreading fast through the land, the counterrevolution grew.

The United States hadn't officially recognized the Venezuelan republic, but it did send a consul, Robert Lowry, to Caracas's port city of La Guaira to monitor events. In June, he reported to Secretary of State James Monroe that royalist forces had "penetrated" deep into the interior. Monteverde's army was growing with "superstitious" recruits who had been "excited by the Priesthood." The earthquake, they were told, "is a chastisement of Heaven for abandoning the cause of Ferdinand the Seventh."[10]

Baltimore merchants had received news of the quake through ships docked in their city's harbor, and they lobbied Washington to help save the republic. In response, the United States Congress approved its first foreign aid package, appropriating money to buy grains to send to La Guaira. The wheat was commandeered by Monteverde, who sold the grain to merchants rather than distribute it to the hungry.

The counterrevolution had begun to consume the revolutionaries. The Sociedad Patriótica successfully demanded that the government name Miranda "dictator," giving him extraordinary powers to put down royalists.* Miranda ordered the arrest of all Spaniards and Canary Islanders (mostly merchants who had prospered under Spanish mercantilism and were thus hostile to the independence movement). The republican army had been enfeebled by the quake and the chaos of its aftermath. So Miranda took steps to bolster its ranks by finally fulfilling a promise that he had made to Wilberforce to end slavery. The revolution had already ended the slave trade. Now, Miranda issued a decree promising "liberty for all slaves that take up arms for Venezuela." The city's white elite and conservative clergy were

---

* The term *dictator* did have some negative connotation at the time, but it wasn't synonymous with *tyrant*. Rather, based on Roman law, it designated someone given executive authority to respond to an emergency until the situation is stabilized. A dictator is granted power; a tyrant seizes power.

outraged. They understood Miranda's edict as "an attack on their property and dissolvent of the social order," a perilous unleashing of forces best kept chained.[11]

A tipping point had been reached. In response to Miranda's decree, anti-republicans did the same. They began to mobilize people of color. Archbishop Coll y Prat sent secret instructions to priests in the provinces to encourage enslaved and free Blacks to fight in defense of our "legitimate sovereign." A rumor spread throughout the provinces that the archbishop had been taken prisoner, and soon a column of armed people of color was marching on the city to rescue the cleric and "end the republican government." By the end of June, reports came in that large stretches of the coast east of La Guaira were under the control of royalist *negros* and *pardos*. Miranda had pulled troops out of the city to attack Monteverde, leaving Caracas undefended against the archbishop's would-be rescuers, whose battalion was twelve leagues from the city's gates and moving fast.[12]

Miranda didn't have the will or heart to fight back. He was, at this point, carrying on back-channel communications with London officials, who were urging moderation. Don't, they said, replicate the measures he used to pacify Valencia. Maybe it was because of his age; maybe because he was disheartened by how many poor people of color had, after the earthquake, fallen back into the reactionary Church or joined with Monteverde; maybe because of memories of Jacobin France. Whatever the reason, he succumbed, according to one of his biographers, to a "spiritual" lassitude of "doubt and vacillation." At key moments when battlefield leadership was needed, Miranda was nowhere to be found. He spent one day in his tent regaling young cadets with stories of his travels in the United States, including his impressions of Thomas Jefferson and John Adams. Miranda opened talks with Monteverde, and, in exchange for being allowed to return to London, surrendered on July 25, 1812. Spanish America's First Republic was no more.[13]

Bolívar was enraged. Miranda might have believed he had no choice, but his former comrades charged him with treason. Still, Miranda, caught in his lassitude, delayed his departure for London. He may have felt he had no place left to go, that to return to Grafton Street to recount his failure to Bentham, Mill, and others would be unbearable. His delay allowed a group of revolutionaries, including Bolívar, to capture the old general and turn him over to the royalists. What exactly happened next is unclear, but Monteverde's promise of safe passage was revoked. Royalists sent Miranda to Spain, where he died in a prison cell on July 14, 1816, on the twenty-seventh anniversary of the fall of the Bastille. Bolívar, after giving up Miranda, gave up the fight as well, for the moment. Monteverde's troops allowed him and a handful of revolutionary officers to escape to the English island of Curaçao, on a small sailboat named *Jesús, María y José*, where the exiles were given shelter by Mordechai Ricardo, an Amsterdam-born Jewish lawyer (and cousin of the economist David Ricardo).[14]

Monteverde entered Caracas at the end of July and began arresting the city's remaining republicans, including the drafters of the Declaration of Independence and the constitution. Calling them "monsters of America," Monteverde imposed, according to the United States envoy charged with delivering food relief, a "system of proscription, sequestration, imprisonment, and cruelty almost unexampled." They were put in irons and thrown into dungeons, "noxious in all countries, but doubly fatal in a climate like this."[15]

Around this time, Spanish military officers began to draw favorable analogies between their pacification campaign and the war waged by Spain's first conquistadores. "Caracas must be treated," Monteverde said, "according to the Law of Conquest."[16]

The Country Is America

Taking control of Caracas was relatively easy. More difficult for Monteverde was putting down the rural *insurgentes de otra espiece*, including those he had mobilized himself. The column determined to rescue Archbishop Coll y Prat was now camped on the outskirts of the city. The archbishop sent a message ordering slaves and peasants to return to their masters. The church was safe, I am safe, he said. The leaders of the march refused to disperse. Instead, they invoked Miranda's decree, saying that by fighting for king and Church they should receive their freedom. "Nonsense," said the archbishop. We "promised you nothing."

The leaders of the assembled masses let Spanish officials know that their allegiance was conditional. They had already killed several of their "masters, overseers, and many whites" and could easily expand their ranks, raising an army of thousands of enslaved and free Blacks. "All armed," as the archbishop's envoy noted. Suddenly, victorious royalists were faced with the prospect of having to fight the forces that helped carry them to victory. As the archbishop's envoy noted, the ragtag army bivouacked outside of Caracas could easily live off the land. "They all have been hardened by labor and the torrid heat." Rumors began to circulate that their leaders were in contact with republicans, who didn't hesitate to confirm that if they switched sides, they would indeed be emancipated.

Negotiations averted a siege of the city, and the "black corsairs," as the archbishop called them, retreated. But Venezuela fell into chaos. Monteverde was injured in battle in October 1813 and eventually relieved of duty.

To the fore of the royalist pacification campaign came a ruthless horseman from the eastern *llanos*, or grasslands, named José Tomás Boves. Royal officers had released Boves from prison, where he was being held on charges of smuggling, and, after witnessing his merciless efficiency in the field, set him loose.

Essentially operating as a paramilitary field marshal, Boves practiced a unique form of royalism, which consisted in the waging of relentless class and race war. He held an implacable hatred of both republicans and Venezuela's antirepublican landed aristocrats. His army, at its height, counted seven thousand men, mostly former slaves, cowherds, and peasants, who raised a piratical black flag—what he called his "banner of death," adorned with a skull and crossbones and the words "Liberty or Death"—in every town they occupied. They slaughtered republicans by the thousands and terrorized white aristocrats, threatening to divide their great estates among the impoverished masses. All in the name of King Ferdinand.

Meanwhile, Bolívar, who had eventually made it to Cartegena, in Colombia, regrouped. He raised troops and rode back to Caracas, defeating all opposition and taking the city again in 1813. But in the countryside, Boves's army was growing, cutting a line of mayhem through the provinces. Caracas, at least, was again in the hands of republicans, the capital of a "Second

Republic." But Bolívar was no longer interested in creating a besieged backwater nation on the littoral of a vast continent. He became the agent of his mentor Miranda's grander vision, pledging himself to fight for a greater America. *"Para nosotros la patria es la América"*—For us, the country is America, he declared in one field speech.[17]

Bolívar, on June 15, 1813, in the city of Trujillo, decreed a "war to the death." It wasn't just a figure of speech. Earlier, he had been infuriated when Venezuela's congress granted amnesty to Valencia's royalist rebel leaders, believing such mercy only disincentivized allegiance to the cause of independence. The struggle to recapture Valencia had given Bolívar a sense of how deep-rooted royalism was in the countryside and an awareness that it would take significant coercion to defeat monarchical allegiances. He wanted his troops to terrorize Spanish loyalists, to avenge the "horrific desolation" left behind by Monteverde and the atrocities committed by Boves. Tactically, he wanted the remaining "accursed race of European Spaniards" to know they had three choices: accommodate to independence, return to Spain, or die. Spaniards who conspired with the enemy would be considered traitors and executed. Those who joined the rebels would be given an "absolute pardon."

Bolívar was drawing a line and making it clear that the war was not simply a colonial rebellion but a conflict between two nations, Spain and America. Once set loose, such furies were hard to contain. The more Spanish heads his soldiers took, the faster they rose in the ranks. Some of the first such trophies to arrive at Bolívar's camp were cut from the corpses of an elderly aristocratic husband and wife, along with a note written in the victims' blood.

Churches Filled with Blood

Boves continued his own war of extermination. In early February 1814, in the town of Ocumare, his army pillaged, raped, and murdered, cutting off "the noses and ears of inhabitants, the penises of the men and the breasts of women." "Blood was everywhere." Survivors took refuge in the Catholic Church. Boves's marauders used axes to hack the door to splinters, and then murdered everyone they found inside. In retaliation, Bolívar ordered the execution of hundreds of Spanish prisoners. Archbishop Coll y Prat pleaded for their lives, but the killings went ahead. Historians guess that, between February 14 and February 16, 1814, as many as a thousand Spanish prisoners were shot or macheted to death. An upward spiral of violence gathered force.[18]

Earlier, during the First Republic, political terror had been relatively contained. That restraint now fell away. Bolívar thought mass executions would force Spanish officials to curb Boves. If the Spanish knew that they'd pay "dearly" for Boves's "atrocities," they would rein him in. Bolívar was wrong. Royal officers had no control over Boves.[19]

By June, Boves had begun his march on Caracas. Along the way, his men killed sixteen hundred republicans in the town of La Cabrera, "right down to the last child drummer." Boves took the city of Valencia and ordered the slaughter of every white man, no matter their political allegiance, no matter where they stood during the earlier royalist revolt. With whip in hand, the cowherd turned royalist avenger forced surviving "wives and daughters to dance his favorite Venezuelan folk dances." Massacre followed massacre, with Boves's men building pyramids with the heads of decapitated victims.[20]

Bolívar couldn't defend Caracas. His generals and their troops, having suffered staggering losses, were dispersed, and Bolívar didn't want to test the loyalty of the people of the provinces, who he feared would join with Boves upon his advance. On July 6, 1814, he ordered Caracas evacuated. Thus ended the short-lived Second Republic. Twenty thousand residents hastily gathered what they could and left their homes, with republican officers stripping the churches of silver to finance the fight. With Boves descending on the city from the west, thousands fled eastward, while Bolívar escaped by sea. Boves entered Caracas and once again ordered the execution of all remaining white residents. There weren't many left. He also ordered troops to pursue the refugees.

The exodus was chaotic. From the western plains to the eastern marshes, Venezuela was filled with roving armed men with shifting allegiances. Some refugees made it into republican-controlled territory. Others straggled. Thousands died, of snake bites, dysentery, and hunger, among other causes.

Boves's troops moved fast. In October, his army arrived at the town of Cumaná, where a group of Caracas's exiles had taken refuge. Another day of carnage. Another dance. This time, though, he had in his custody Caracas's republican orchestra, headed by Juan José Landaeta (the composer of Venezuela's national anthem, "Gloria al Bravo Pueblo"). He ordered the thirty-member group to begin playing their instruments as his soldiers waltzed with the city's widows. Blood from the day's killing still moist on their boots turned the dance floor red. As the orchestra played, Boves took one musician out at a time to be executed. He ordered them to continue to play as he shot them in the head. When the last musician had been executed, Boves announced that the "party was over." Then the rapes began.

"The roads and fields are filled with unburied corpses, the towns are leveled," said a royalist tax collector, "the churches defiled and full of blood."[21]

Everything Will Become Nothing

Boves was a phenomenon difficult to explain. He turned everything on its head, a black flag–waving royalist waging a counterrevolution to spark a more profound revolution. He terrorized those who presumed themselves, due to their Spanish blood and white skin, immune to terror.

Boves shook Bolívar. Bolívar would continue to fight for more than a decade longer—as if he were sure the fight was worth it, as if he were certain that what came after Spanish rule would be better than Spanish rule. But he wasn't sure. Boves represented a greater chastisement than any earthquake, a warning that the war against Spain would unleash powers resistant to reason, forces pulling Spanish America apart more powerful than those fighting to hold it together.

"All will return to its most basic element: matter," Bolívar lamented during one of his dark moments. "Everything will become nothing." His experience defending Venezuela's republic deepened his conviction that a strong executive was needed to hold the forces of disunion at bay. Bolívar could express world-weariness in racist terms. "Guinea and more Guinea we will have," he wrote, as it became clear that his enemy would not just be royalist troops and accursed Spanish but, in some places, masses of poor people of color. Yet for all his pessimism, Bolívar never posited *race* as an ontological category, an essence found in drops of blood.

Race was for Bolívar an artifact of history. Like Las Casas, whom he read and hailed as an "apostle" of freedom, Bolívar believed the Conquest was a crime, not just because of its violence but because it imprinted racial difference in its legal codes. "Everything that has come before us is wrapped in the black cloak of crime," he sighed. The fight for independence wasn't sparked by a divine touch from on high but came up through muck and mire, centuries of colonial exploitation: Spanish Americans, those who fought for and against independence, were "the abominable offspring of those raging beasts who came to America to spill her blood and to breed with their victims before sacrificing and discarding them."[22] Some of those beasts, like Boves, still prowled the land.

And Bolívar remained committed to emancipation, both as part of the republican ideal and as a military tactic, even though he feared that emancipation would evaporate elite support for republicanism. In Haiti to regroup and request assistance, which the free Haitian government provided (a thousand rifles, gunpowder, clothing, and military advisers), Bolívar pledged to continue to work to free South America's slaves. "That portion of our brothers who have labored under the miseries of slavery is now free," he said upon returning to the mainland; "From here forward, in Venezuela there is only one class of men: all will be citizens."

Bolívar would continue to issue horseback emancipations, galloping from one hacienda to another and freeing its slaves if they promised to join his fight.* Other revolutionary leaders in Argentina, Chile, and Peru—such as José de San Martín—did the same. Battalions of emancipated slaves helped win some of the most important battles of the independence movement, at Junín and Ayacucho, for instance. Montevideo, dubbed the New Troy after

---

* Bolívar's ongoing success in mobilizing enslaved peoples was noticed in the United States, setting a precedent that would be invoked in debates leading to Abraham Lincoln's Emancipation Proclamation. "The early experience of South America," the president of Argentina Domingo Faustino Sarmiento later wrote, proves that the U.S. Union Army had nothing to fear by raising battalions of emancipated peoples.

it lived under Spanish siege for more than a decade, never fell, thanks to its African defenders.[23]

Nor did Bolívar, with Las Casas imprinted onto his consciousness, blanch from admitting that republicans were founding their new "free" nations on stolen land, that nationalism entailed its own form of colonialism. "We find ourselves engaged in a dual conflict: we are disputing with the natives for titles of ownership, and at the same time we are struggling to create a new country."

Whether such a new country could come into being or not—much less be a vehicle for justice—was a question left for the future. The fight itself was what Bolívar called an "obligation of atonement" to those who came before, especially to the "annihilated Indians" and their descendants. To break Spain's hold on the New World was a debt "of the greatest transcendence." Be there earthquakes or be there beasts like Boves, he'd fight on, even if "heaven has determined that our conquerors shall be our brothers."[24]

Boves was killed in battle by one of Bolívar's men in 1814. Spain followed by dispatching an expeditionary army of ten thousand soldiers, along with a new suite of royal officials to impose order. The troops were led by Field Marshal Pablo Morillo. There wasn't much left of Boves's counterrevolutionary army, and those soldiers who had survived were in rags.

"If these are the victors," Morillo asked, of the men who had defeated Venezuela's Second Republic, "who are the vanquished?"

In the years to come, Bolívar would march through indigenous communities, cattle lands, and haciendas worked by peons and slaves, continuing to offer freedom for all who joined the fight. Bolívar the utilitarian thought, abstractly, that racial divisions could be transcended with education. Bolívar the military leader hoped that war would create unity. Bolívar the existentialist doubted that any of it would matter.[25]

By 1819, Bolívar was leading an increasingly unified revolt against the Spanish Empire. That year, he helped found the republic of Gran Colombia, a sprawling nation with its capital in Bogotá, uniting what is now Venezuela, Colombia, Ecuador, Panama, parts of northern Peru, and western Guyana.

Mexico won its independence three years later, in 1821, and it was expected that combined, these two large nations would be formidable, capable of representing the interests of a free Spanish America to Washington.

Spain, though, still controlled much of Peru, forcing Bolívar to command an exhausting trek up the eastern slope of the Andes, across floodplains and frozen plateaus to ambush Spanish troops. Bolívar won that battle, which he hoped would be the last. But royalism regrouped and dug in, in the uplands west and south of Lima. There, the Crown enjoyed support from hacienda slave owners, a dark crimson-and-gold redoubt in a tricolor hemisphere.

And so in 1824, Bolívar camped outside the port city of Trujillo mustering for his second Andean ascent, this time from the west, his army growing daily by the hundreds, weekly by the thousands. Enslaved peoples abandoned their masters and signed up to fight the Crown in exchange for their emancipation. Indigenous peoples came down from their highland villages, hoping that, after centuries of colonialism, their lot would improve under republican rule. One of the last battles of the long war for independence would take place in August, in the marshy highland plains of Junín, with Bolívar's eight-thousand-strong army routing Spanish troops.

Save for a few last skirmishes, Bolívar had decisively defeated Spain.

Still, in victory, he remained haunted. He'd return again and again in future writings to history's capriciousness, to a gloom that could rival the prophet Amos:

"My time is a time of catastrophes: everything created is destroyed in a flash, like lightning," he wrote to his former vice president. "How foolish I was to believe I could stand firm in the midst of such convulsions, in the midst of so many ruins, in the midst of the universe's moral upheaval. . . . It would be madness to see the storm that is coming and not take shelter."[26]

PART IV

UNION/DESUNIÓN

Andrew Jackson   *Simón Bolívar*

17.

A Kind of International
Law for America

On June 3, 1792, Thomas Jefferson, then Washington's secretary of state, hosted a private dinner for George Hammond, London's envoy to the United States. Jefferson suggested the two men dine *solus cum solo*—alone with the infinite, or alone with God, in Latin. He wanted to speak frankly about "what is to be done" about the Indians.[1]

The food was served, the servers retired, and Minister Hammond casually mentioned to Jefferson that he, speaking for London, assumed that the United States would "exterminate the Indians & take their lands."

On the contrary, said Hammond's host. Jefferson imagined a good use for them as a "maré chaussée or police, for scouring the woods on our borders." *Maréchaussée* is French for *constabulary*, or local guard, the origin of the word *marshal*. Jefferson thought Indians might serve as an early border patrol to prevent "rovers and robbers," along with British fur traders, from establishing a presence.

Hammond followed up: What was Jefferson's understanding of his nation's rights regarding "Indian soil"?

The United States claimed two rights over Indian soil, Jefferson said.

First: "A right of preemption of their lands, that is to say, the sole and exclusive right of purchasing from them whenever they should be willing to sell."

Second: "A right of regulating the commerce between them and the whites."[2]

Hammond then asked Jefferson if such a "right of preemption prohibited any individual of another nation from purchasing land which the Indians should be willing to sell?"

Yes, Jefferson answered. He considered such entitlement a "kind of *jus gentium* for America"—a kind of international law for America. A "white nation settling down," Jefferson said, has the right to defend its interests.

"A kind of international law for America" is an interesting twist on the arguments presented by those early critics of the Spanish Conquest, who laid the foundation for a different "kind of international law," a law that recognized that Native Americans enjoyed the right of possession over their land. Jefferson, whose Monticello library was stocked with early chroniclers of the Conquest (including numerous editions in many languages of Las Casas), flipped that law on its head to argue that "white nations settling down" among Natives enjoyed mandatory powers. Washington claimed the authority to decide to whom they could sell their land, with whom they could trade, as well as the right to use them as national security proxies, as a patrol to prohibit European meddling.[3]

The British no longer controlled any territory in the Mississippi Valley, but its fur traders and political agents were still active, working with indigenous nations that had been its allies during both the Seven Years' War and its fight against the American Revolution. Minister Hammond, here, was trying to clarify what the United States' position was toward this activity.

Did Jefferson's new kind of international law "prohibit the British traders from coming into the Indian territory?"

"That has been the idea," Jefferson answered.

"This would be hard on the Indians," Hammond replied.

It was.

Wars of 1812

Desire for an unimpeded sphere of influence in the West was one of the reasons the United States waged a second war against Great Britain and their Indian allies. Washington charged London with continuing, from its base in Canada, its "intrigues" among tribal nations in the upper Mississippi Valley and Northwest Territory, around the Great Lakes, working with the Shawnee leader Tecumseh to create a trans-indigenous alliance to halt U.S. expansion. President James Madison signed a congressional resolution declaring war on June 18, 1812, just a few months after the Caracas earthquake, around the time that Bolívar began waging his "war to the death" against the Spanish.

The two conflicts are never discussed in tandem, yet they should be for they set republicanism on divergent paths in North and South America: in one direction led the United States, its sense of national identity consolidated after beating the British a second time, toward, notwithstanding the looming crisis over slavery, greater economic consolidation, toward a greater *union*; in the other direction, it led Spanish America, despite soaring visions of continental unity, toward constant crisis and disaggregation, toward *desunión*.[4]

The two wars were waged in a shared theater of operations, the greater Caribbean basin. New Orleans and Cartagena faced each other across the sea, both bustling slave ports. Merchants from the interior of the United States would float down the Mississippi, sail across the Caribbean, and then up the Magdalena River Valley—"Colombia's Mississippi"—to Barranquilla and other river towns, selling cloth, shoes, and rifles, cash on the barrel.

Battles took place simultaneously. In late 1812, Simón Bolívar, having arrived in Cartagena from Curaçao, brazenly, against the wishes of Colombian independence leaders and with only a small detachment of troops, attacked royalist-controlled towns along the Magdalena, winning control of the waterway for the rebels. At the same moment, across the Caribbean, Andrew Jackson was receiving his first military commission, as a major general with instructions to "call out, arm and equip fifteen hundred of the militia of Tennessee," to march down the Mississippi on New Orleans. Both campaigns introduced their respective leaders as world-historical figures. Bolívar's victories along the Magdalena River built momentum that drove him forward, first to retake Venezuela and then toward his final victory over the Spanish. Jackson's stubborn, reckless, and ruthless actions during the war propelled his growing fame, putting him on the path to the presidency. In the years to come, Bolívar and Jackson would serve as contrasts on how Anglo-Saxon and Spanish American republicans dealt with, or didn't, people of color.

Both wars radicalized race relations and hardened racial identity. Great Britain, as Spain did in Venezuela, fought its war by rallying people of color against republicanism. Creeks and other indigenous groups joined with the British. Tecumseh's transtribal confederacy defended Canada. The British Navy called on enslaved peoples to join the fight. Hundreds quit their Chesapeake plantations to march alongside redcoats on Washington and set the White House ablaze. The British Navy evacuated four thousand escaped slaves to Canada and Bermuda.

People of color also fought on the side of republicans in the United States. Jackson had a talent at playing up internal conflicts among the Creeks, between the so-called Red Sticks who refused to accommodate to settler society and those Creeks who sided with the United States. Jackson, with some Cherokee and Choctaw allies, used the war to destroy the Red Stick Creeks in Alabama and force on them a humiliating treaty that included ceding a massive amount of land. Nearly "the whole of Alabama," as Jackson described the Creek handover to the federal government, some twenty-two million acres.

Jackson moved on to New Orleans. United States troops had mostly refrained from enlisting slaves in southern states. Jackson, though, in preparation to defend the city in December 1814, visited local Louisiana plantations and promised enslaved workers freedom. "If the battle is fought and the victory gained," Jackson said, "you shall be free."

Jackson ordered plantation owners to put their slaves, as slaves, to work on building ramparts, barricades, trenches, and canals across New Orleans, a dense network of breastworks key to Jackson's coming victory. Out of the bayou came Joseph Savary, leading a regiment of formerly enslaved Haitian and Cuban refugees, entering the war on the side of the United States. Savary's men, Jackson himself said, were decisive in defeating the British.

The war ended and Jackson broke his promise. There would be no emancipation for enslaved peoples who fought the British. Jackson said he couldn't "take another man's property and set it free." "Go home and mind their masters," he said, when asked what the future held for his enslaved recruits. He ordered "men of color" to leave the city and refused to allow Black regiments who fought on his side to participate in the victory parade. Jackson's glory was undivided.[5]

Joseph Savary marched his men anyway. Former Cuban and Haitian slaves turned republican internationalists filed through the streets of New Orleans, taking pride in having driven the British out. When the parade was over, Savary sailed south to put his army at the service of Bolívar and Mexican insurgents, helping to briefly establish a piratical republican free zone in the Bahia de Gálvez, later known as Galveston Bay, after the Spanish officer who helped North American rebels win their revolution.

Barrier of Savages

Negotiations to end the war began in 1814 in Ghent. Early in the talks, the British kept bringing up the fate of their indigenous allies, referring to them as if they were sovereign nations. London, despite Jefferson's earlier categorical rejection of the idea, hadn't given up on trying to shore up Native American autonomy in the Mississippi Valley. The British insisted that the peace treaty recognize Indian boundaries and that the United States commit to honor treaties London had signed with indigenous groups.

The United States delegation, led by Henry Clay and John Quincy Adams, had had enough of such proposals, enough of Europeans trying to use Native Americans to block the territorial growth of the United States. Clay, who hailed from Kentucky, was eager to end British meddling in the Mississippi Valley. The young Adams was at this point in his life an avid expansionist. He put forth a series of justifications for the dispossession of Indian soil that could have come straight out of John Locke, or Juan Gines de

Sepúlveda. Most Indians refuse to establish towns but rather roam and hunt, he said. "It was impossible for such People ever to be said to Have Possessions," Adams insisted.

It was out of the question, he wrote in his diary, to "condemn vast regions of territory to perpetual barrenness and solitude that a few hundred savages might find wild beasts to hunt upon." Adams rejected what he called London's "barrier of savages." British proposals regarding Indian autonomy were an "outrage upon Providence; which gave the earth to man for cultivation and made the tillage of the ground the condition of his Nature and the Law of his existence."[6]

Adams issued an apocalyptic warning. The population of the United States had just passed eight million people. It would continue to grow, and grow fast—so fast that nothing, certainly not a treaty, could stop it. If London really wanted to contain the United States, it should break off talks and prepare to wage a war of "utter extermination." Unless the United States was wiped off the face of the earth and its people eliminated, war would be eternal. New generations of settlers would swell and sweep westward—requiring yet another war, and another, and another, to slow their progress. No "bond of paper" that came out of Ghent could stop the westward expansion of the United States.[7]

Adams, who later would be known for his humanism, triumphed, in a bellicose attack on the rights of "Indian soil." He revived the doctrine of conquest as part of Jefferson's "kind of international law for America," a law that would sweep away all obstacles to the Pacific and remove European powers from the field.

Like Bolívar, most of the founders of the United States blamed their new nation's Indian problem on European colonialism. But unlike Bolívar, they had no doubts, no despairs, no compulsion to atone. Thomas Jefferson, for instance, was a man of the mind who ordered his generals to act. He accepted with hardly a qualm that extermination might be the consequence of acting: "We shall be obliged to drive them with the beasts of the forest into the Stony mountains." The United States would be forced "to pursue them to elimination," he wrote early in the War of 1812, if the British didn't stop their meddling. "If we are constrained to lift the hatchet against any tribe, we will never lay it down until that tribe is exterminated, or driven beyond the Mississippi," he wrote elsewhere, as president to his secretary of war. Surely this must be among the most liberal uses ever of the word *constrained*.[8]

London's delegation ultimately gave up on demanding that the United States recognize the sovereignty of indigenous nations. Clay and Adams did agree to an unenforceable provision incorporated into Article Nine of the final treaty, which required the United States to return all land taken from Indians during the war and recognition of tribal boundaries as they existed in 1811.

To Last Forever

The defeat of the British was catastrophic for Mississippi Valley Indians, eliminating an important ally of theirs from the field. Even as indigenous refugees fled west, across the plains to the Rocky Mountains or down into East Texas, momentum grew among Anglos for a comprehensive plan of removal of Indian nations who cluttered the eastern side of the valley, who clung to their land, who entered alliances with European powers, got in the way of constituting new states and growing the union. Five nations in particular had to go: the Cherokee, the Choctaw, the Chickasaw, the Creeks, and the Seminole.

The war had deepened pessimism among those who set the political and intellectual tone of the nation, about the possibility of incorporating Native Americans into the new republic. Lewis Cass, for instance, published a series of essays in the influential *North American Review*, meant to quiet religious opposition to removal. "The Indians are impelled to war by passions," Cass, who fought in the War of 1812 before serving as territorial governor of Michigan, wrote. "They have not only no principles of religion or morality to repress their passions, but they are urged forward in their career of blood by all around them." Slavers wanted Indian land to stake out plantations, but they also wanted to do away with the "little sovereignties" of indigenous peoples, lest they provide sanctuary for escaped slaves.[9]

Along with increased hostility toward Native Americans came legislation formalizing the subordinated status of free peoples of African descent. Free-men who had been able to vote in several states were now no longer allowed to do so, and other laws went into effect that segregated housing and educa-tion. State legislatures codified the one-drop rule, which previously had mostly been adhered to as social custom. A "belligerent white supremacism" rose in the North, in cities like Philadelphia, where Black neighborhoods and Black churches were attacked by white mobs. Textile mills in Lowell, Massachusetts, and Manchester, England, among other places, demanded ever more cotton, which the southern United States—with its cotton gin, slaves, and land taken from Indians, including those many Creek acres— was well placed to satisfy.[10]

As Indians were pushed west, free people of color were urged—by the American Colonialization Society, founded two years after the end of the War of 1812—to remove themselves east, to Africa. At the same time, argu-ments making the case that slavery was a positive good were becoming com-mon, advanced not just in the plantation South but in the manufacturing North, where much of the profits from sugar and cotton were distributed. Sixty percent of all proslavery clergymen who received degrees did so from universities or colleges north of the Mason-Dixon Line.

Most of these degrees were issued by Yale University. Yale theologians and sociologists pushed back against the rising abolitionist movement, against the idea that slavery would eventually be legislated out of existence. God not only sanctioned slavery but himself dealt in slaves, said Parson Theodore Clapp, Massachusetts born, Yale educated. The Lord distributed bondmen and bondwomen to his favorite patriarchs, including Abraham. Read verses 44, 45, and 46 of Leviticus 25, Clapp, who had become a pastor at the First Presbyterian Church of New Orleans, said. There, you will find "an exact description of slavery as it exists in Louisiana, and the Southern States generally." "Strangers," which for Clapp meant Africans, "are freely bought and sold among us." These "possessions," he said, are passed down to children and their descendants like all other possessions, "by inheri-tance."[11]

"And this state of things is to last forever."

Napoleon of the Woods

James Monroe, another Virginia slaver, took over from James Madison as president, and in late 1818 told his secretary of state, John Quincy Adams, that he planned to issue a declaration recognizing "South American" independence.

"What part of South America?" Adams asked.

"All South America, and Mexico, and the islands included," Monroe answered.

Wait a bit, Adams told Monroe.

There were loose ends the secretary wanted to tie up with Spain while it still had nominal authority over its colonies. At stake were the two Floridas, as well as the need to establish a firm western boundary line. Anglos around Natchitoches remained restless, demanding that the United States border be extended as deep into East Texas as possible.

Adams still hoped for Cuba, and perhaps Puerto Rico. "There are laws of political as well as of physical gravitation," he told Spain's foreign minister: just as "an apple severed by the tempest from its native tree" couldn't not but "fall to the ground," Cuba would soon fall into the "North American Union." Better for that to happen before an independent Mexico grabbed the island for its own.[12]

In addition, there was ongoing disagreement between Washington and London over Article Nine of the Treaty of Ghent, related to the restoration of indigenous land lost during the war. The British understood that land to include those Alabama acres Andrew Jackson took from the Creeks. The United States read the clause differently, citing the treaty Jackson imposed on the Creeks as placing it outside the scope of matters covered in Ghent.

Besides, Jackson wasn't finished.

In May 1818, General Jackson, then in residence at the Hermitage, his Tennessee plantation, received an order from President Monroe and Secretary of War John Calhoun to defend the United States against Indian raids originating in Spanish Florida. Jackson took the directive not as a command to secure the border but a warrant to rage through Florida, burning towns, destroying villages, and murdering Indians and their British allies.

Jackson's campaign is known as the First Seminole War. In many ways, however, it was the last battle of the War of 1812. One part of the twenty-two million acres of Creek land that Jackson had confiscated in that war entailed about half of what is today the state of Alabama. Another part ran across the top of the Florida Panhandle. Many of the Indians who had lived on this land had fled, during the war, into Spanish Florida. This was the immediate source of the border conflicts—the so-called Indian raids were dispossessed Creeks trying to return home, or trying to stop white settlement on what had been their land.

In addition to the Creeks, Spanish Florida's Panhandle had become a longleaf pine and wiregrass sanctuary for escaped slaves and refugee Indians.* "All the runaway negros, all the savage Indians, all the pirates, and all the traitors to their country" had assembled there under London's tutelage, Adams complained, to "wage an exterminating war" against the United States.

By this point, London had formally given up trying to use official channels to force Washington to abide by Article Nine. Yet on the ground in Florida, London's agents were telling the Creeks and Seminoles that Washington was indeed obligated to return conquered land. British officials and merchants were also encouraging refugee peoples of color to align themselves with Bolívar's war for independence. London assumed, wrongly as it turned out, that Florida would become part of whatever new nation was established after Spain's defeat, either as part of Mexico or Colombia.[13]

Jackson marched his men through the Panhandle, razing Seminole towns, massacring Black farmers on the Suwannee River, and murdering Red Stick refugees. His men also captured two British subjects who had been advocating for a restoration of Creek land. Jackson had both executed, one shot, the other hanged.[14]

Even as Jackson was advancing through Florida, the federal government was putting the previously appropriated Creek land in Alabama and along the Panhandle up for bid, leading to a real estate boom that would make

---

* The Seminoles were related to the Creeks, but by the early 1800s had become a distinct people, incorporating escapees from slavery along with Red Sticks into their community.

Jackson rich. Jackson and his associates claimed about forty-five thousand acres, and, with cotton prices at an all-time high, established a chain of plantations. Jackson, writes the journalist Steve Inskeep, "both created and scored in the greatest real estate bubble in the history of the United States up to that time." Jackson's assault on the Creeks was but one instance of a larger "mania" of confiscation and privatization of tribal land going on since at least 1781.[15]

Jackson's business partners and family members had invested in Panhandle land too, around Pensacola, which would lead to another real estate windfall once Florida was transferred to the United States.[16]

Great Britain threatened retaliation. Spain protested. France called Jackson *"ce Napoléon des bois"*—this Napoleon of the woods. Secretary of State John Quincy Adams was roused from bed and made to read urgent notes complaining about Jackson. Monroe and his cabinet were shocked at Jackson's assault.

Everyone except Adams, who argued that Jackson's campaign fell within the bounds of established international law. It was, he said, national self-defense.[17]

Monroe authorized Adams to compose Washington's official response to Spain. Adams did, in a blast of unapologetic just war theory: Spain had a responsibility to control its territory. "The obligation of Spain, to restrain *by force*, the Indians of Florida, from hostilities against the United States and their citizens, is explicit, is positive, is unqualified," wrote Adams. Spain countered that it hadn't instigated the raids and was powerless to stop them. Adams said that Spain's confessed incapacity provided Jackson all the justification needed. The question of whether the raids were a result of Spain's "weakness" or its "will" was moot. It mattered little whether Madrid intended that Florida become a base of operation for enemies of the United States. The fact that it did become a base of operation for enemies granted Washington the right to do what it must to protect itself.[18]

If Spain couldn't exercise effective control over the hostile Indians and runaway Blacks within its territory, then it had no right to call itself the sovereign of said territory. The land was "derelict," and Spain should cede it to a nation that could exercise dominion.[19]

Later, Adams recalled to a journalist that he "alone defended" Jackson's actions in Florida "and put him on the high ground of international law, as expounded by Grotius, Pufendorf, and Vattel." When told by a reporter about Adams's remarks, Jackson answered: "Damn Grotius! Damn Pufendorf! Damn Vattel!"

"Jackson made law," the reporter noted, while "Adams quoted it."[20]

The Spacious Transcontinental Treaty

Adams's note calmed London, angry over the execution of two of its subjects, and left Madrid with little leverage. Even before Jackson's assault, Spain had come to accept the need to give up the Floridas.

They were indefensible, and anyway, Madrid was more concerned about protecting Texas. At issue was defining the western boundary of the Louisiana Purchase, a territory that, in the public imagination at least, grew bigger every year. Spain was eager to negotiate with Adams to establish firm, fixed borders.[21]

Talks between Adams's State Department and Madrid's chancery were ongoing when Jackson raided Florida. Adams used the momentum generated by the assault to demand a border that ran "straight to the Pacific Ocean." Spain's foreign minister, Luis de Onís, was shocked at this proposal. "You are trying to dispossess us also of the whole Pacific Coast," he said indignantly, pointing out that since the 1500s Spain, by the right of discovery, had claimed the coast up to just south of Russia's Alaska.

Onís was of that aristocratic cohort who had thought it a mistake to help the United States break from London. He wasn't impressed with United States diplomats. The new country, he felt, lacked a national character, other than what he called *anglomanismo*—Anglomania—a cheap knock-off of British culture. Demagogues held the public in thrall, while moralists seemed only to be concerned with the free "pursuit of interests." They believe themselves "beautiful in their wisdom," called "to extend, immediately, their dominion to the isthmus of Panama and in the future to all the New World."[22]

Adams cared little for Onís's opinion. He held a trump card: Jackson, and the threat of letting him loose to permanently take the Floridas and maybe Cuba. So Onís, after a few go-rounds, gave Adams almost everything he wanted, everything except Texas.

The "spacious transcontinental treaty" signed in Washington in February 1819 transferred West and East Florida to the United States and fixed a northern boundary line that ran straight to the Pacific. This land was home to, on the eastern side of the Rockies alone, hundreds of thousands of Native Americans comprising more than a hundred indigenous tribes. Adams took the whole Columbia River basin and all its many tributaries. But he set Louisiana's border at the Sabine River, leaving Nacogdoches in Spain. It was an enormous territory and Adams was satisfied—he had made it to the Pacific. Writing in his diary, Adams thought the finished treaty "the most important event of my life. It was an event of magnitude in the history of this Union."

Adams had negotiated his border treaty at a time when the crisis over slavery in the United States was coming to a head. Tensions were lessened, for the moment, by the admittance of Missouri as a slave state and Maine as a free state, with the idea that future Southern states would allow slavery and Northern ones would be free. The so-called Missouri Compromise took slavery, a problem related to politics, economics, and morality, and turned it into a conflict over geography. Adams's treaty gave those opposed to the expansion of slavery a good deal of northern territory to potentially turn into free states, which would tip the balance of power in Congress in their favor. Slavers needed a counterbalance: hence their desperation to break Texas from Mexico and annex it to the United States.

Slavers began to conjure their own *reconquista* legend, insisting that Texas had been included as part of the original Louisiana Purchase. Texas wasn't land that they wanted, but land that they once had, already ancestral. Adams's treaty had its supporters, including those who had invested in Florida real estate. But over time a backlash built around the idea that Adams had forsaken Texas, anger that led to an early attempt to annex Texas, launched from Natchitoches. That effort failed. *Reconquista* ressentiment simmered.

"Texas was once a part of our country," President James Polk said decades later in his first inaugural address, and it was Polk who would preside over the successful taking of Texas and the launching of a war of conquest against Mexico, annexing about a third of its territory.

For now, though, with the western border fixed on paper if not in opinion, and the United States now in possession of Florida, Secretary of State Adams could turn his attention to the question of Spanish American independence.

The Balancing Power: Monroe's Doctrine

The men who mattered when it came to questions of state weren't sure what to do about Spanish America's independence movements.

Thomas Jefferson's enthusiasms waxed and waned. He was a realist. He worried that were Spanish America to form a single nation, it would be too "formidable" a "neighbor." Better that it break up into three or more "confederacies," then the United States might be able to serve as "the balancing power" and leverage one part against the other. He was also a dreamer, fantasizing that if the hemisphere broke with Spain, then the New World might fill up with Saxon stock.

Henry Clay, then a Kentucky congressman, thought a free Spanish America would be a boon to the United States. Clay considered Spanish American republicans his "brothers" in the freedom struggle and proposed turning the New World into an alliance of "liberty," a "counterpoise" to the Old World. He first used the phrase "American System" in 1820 to describe his vision for the organization of the Western Hemisphere, with a developing manufacturing economy in the United States at its center, protected by tariffs. Spanish America, in Clay's system, would be a provincial supplier of resources, which in turn would allow all the United States, including the slave South, to be turned into a prosperous, progressive, humming New England factory: "In relation to South America, the people of the United

States will occupy the same position as the people of New England do to the rest of the United States. Our enterprise, industry, and habits of economy, will give us the advantage in any competition which South America may sustain with us."[1]

Specifically, such a system would let the United States catch up with manufacturing in Great Britain. The British were already heavily invested in Colombian and Mexican mining. And even as London was establishing greater control over India, it was laying the footings for a financial empire in a free Spanish America, one that aggressively used trade treaties and loans to establish dominance.[2]

John Quincy Adams wasn't impressed with Clay's idea. We already have an "American system," he wrote in his diary, and it had a name: the United States. "We constitute the whole of it," he wrote, "there is no community of interests or principles between North and South America."

"There was danger in standing still," President Monroe complained to Jefferson in March 1822, worried that London's commercial agents had gotten a head start on the U.S. signing trade treaties. And peril in "moving forward": Madrid and Paris might retaliate were he to recognize Spanish American independence.

This Sets Our Compass

Monroe hoped to maintain, as long as possible, the appearance of neutrality, quietly accepting the credentials of envoys from insurgent armies in control of territory. He also allowed merchants to sell arms and other matériel to the rebels, sending barks laden with rifles, cannons, balls, and powder to Buenos Aires, Valparaíso, Callao, and Caracas.[3]

By January 1823, it was impossible to deny that insurgents in Chile had defeated royal troops and established a viable, independent republic, and so Monroe recognized the new government. A few months later, Great Britain's foreign minister George Canning sent a note to Monroe and Adams proposing that a joint statement be issued regarding Spanish American independence. It was Canning's opinion that Spanish America's break with Spain was irrevocable, and that London and Washington should warn Madrid, Paris, Moscow, and other European powers against trying to reconquer the continent.

The proposal led to weeks of debate in Monroe's cabinet, which was torn between wanting to use Great Britain's power to scare off the rest of Europe and fearing London's economic might. Monroe was eager to join with Canning. He was certain that Europe's conservative monarchies would launch a military campaign to return America to Spain. France, now under a restored Bourbon king, remained an evergreen threat, offering to help Madrid retake its colonies in exchange for Cuba.

Always Cuba. The London *Courier* around this time called the island the "Turkey of transatlantic politics, tottering to its fall, and kept from falling only by the struggles of those who contend for the right of catching her in her descent."[4]

Secretary of State John Quincy Adams was suspicious of Canning's motivations. He had had his fill of British tears for Indians at Ghent and thought that the United Kingdom would use whatever statement was produced to better its own position in Spanish America.

No, Adams did not want to join with London. "We should at least," he advised, "keep ourselves free to act as emergencies may arise." Adams concluded the United States had to act and act unilaterally, and he convinced President Monroe of the same.

What eventually became known as the Monroe Doctrine was announced in President Monroe's State of the Union message on December 2, 1823. Monroe's hesitancy is reflected in the form of the announcement itself, which took up just a few, nonconsecutive paragraphs in a document of more than six thousand words. A long discussion of the increase in postal roads separates its two most important points: a warning to Europe against intervening in American affairs; and a declaration that even though Washington would not intervene in Spanish America's wars for independence, it was "obvious" that Spain had lost its colonies.

Summed up, the "doctrine" made these five points:

1. The New World was henceforth off-limits "for future colo-
    nization by any European power." Any effort to "extend"
    Europe's "system to any portion of this hemisphere" would
    be viewed by the United States as a threat.

2. Washington will view events that take place anywhere in the
    Americas as bearing on its "peace and happiness"—and re-
    serves the right to intervene throughout the hemisphere to
    protect its interests.

3. Europe is "essentially" different from the United States,
    though Monroe didn't specify the nature of this difference.
    He did, though, imply that he meant the distinction between
    republicanism and monarchism.

4. The United States would continue to recognize existing Eu-
    ropean possessions in the New World (Cuba, Puerto Rico,
    Jamaica, British Guiana, Canada, among others).

5. Washington considered Mexico, Chile, Gran Colombia, and
    Argentina to be free.

"This sets our compass," said Jefferson of Monroe's remarks, "and points
the course which we are to steer through the ocean of time opening on us."

If so, it was a compass that would point north any direction the holder
desired. The doctrine's magic, and the source of its enduring influence, is
found in its ambiguity, in its ability to reconcile contradictory policy impulses.* The statement's vision of shared New World interests appealed to

---

* Observers have long had a hard time determining what, exactly, the Monroe Doctrine
meant. "It might be a good thing," said one-time presidential candidate Samuel Tilden, "if
one could only find out what it was." Woodrow Wilson complained that when he tried to define the Monroe Doctrine, "it escaped analysis." Also, Monroe's 1823 pronouncement
wouldn't get upgraded to "doctrinal" status in public opinion until around the 1840s, when
the United States press began to use the phrase "Monroe doctrine" or "the doctrine of Monroe" to protest Great Britain's effort to build a canal through Nicaragua. At around the same
time, British writers began to describe Washington's hemispheric policy as a "doctrine" to
ridicule its self-importance: the North American man "has made maps of his empire, including all the continent, and has preached the Monroe doctrine as though it had been decreed by
the gods," wrote London's *New Monthly Magazine* in 1862. For simplicity, I'll mostly use
Monroe Doctrine throughout.

Clay's internationalism, while its warning to Europe to keep out satisfied Adams's unilateral go-it-aloneness. It also satisfied statesmen who viewed diplomacy as a balance of power between the Old and New Worlds and those who believed that the fulcrum of geopolitics had shifted to the New World. And it sanctioned the idea that the United States has a right to project its powers beyond its official borders, to resolve matters anywhere in the Americas that threatened its domestic peace and happiness.[5]

Earlier, Jefferson had written to Monroe saying that he believed Spanish America's independence to be inevitable, and that it both served the United States' *interests* and reflected its *ideals* to promote such a cause. "Interest, then, on the whole, would wish their independence," Jefferson said, "and justice makes the wish a duty." The founders of the United States rarely distinguished between their material ambitions and their moral faith: the Monroe Doctrine was the first formal pronunciation of this imagined harmony, cited down the centuries as the United States pursued its national interests in the name of universal ideals.

Beyond the practicalities of diplomacy, Monroe's statement marked a broader cultural shift. Writers in literary journals who had earlier basked in the uniqueness of the United States, in the *solitude* of its continental wilderness, now wrestled with the fact that they were not alone, that they now shared the hemisphere with other republics. William Thornton, the lead architect of Washington's Capitol building, published an outline of a constitution for a unified Western Hemispheric nation, a United North and South Columbia to be governed by an Inka and twenty-six sachems. Thornton named the political offices in honor of Native Americans to distinguish them from the "titles of the dignitaries of other empires."[6]

A minority of reformers believed Spanish Americans were putting forward a higher-minded form of republicanism that grappled with the implications of extending the ideals of freedom and equality to all. Abolitionists, for example, who helped refugee slaves flee into Mexico saw in Spanish America, however chaotic and crisis ridden, a more coherent humanism, less conflicted about the rights of man and the rights of property. Freedom meant freedom. It could mean freedom of property. But it didn't mean that human beings could be property. "No slave clanked his chains" in Mexico, said Ohio's radical Republican Joshua Reed Giddings.

The United States was going to have to share the hemisphere with other republics, that much was clear. That didn't mean the New World's first republic had to abandon its title to uniqueness, to exceptionality, even if it was no longer alone in the wilderness. New editions of Las Casas revived the Black Legend, leading to predictions that a free Spanish America would devolve into a burlesque form of self-government. For Edward Everett, a professor of Greek literature at Harvard and editor of the *North American Review*, Spanish America's "corrupt and mixed race of various shades and sorts" highlighted the singular virtue of the United States. Spanish America, with its "wealthy aristocracy and a needy peasantry," had more in common with Europe than with the United States. The seemingly interminable, property- and people-destroying revolutions that tormented Spain's former colonies offered a close-to-home warning of the risks of a republicanism taken too far, a dangerous migration of the ideas of the French Revolution to New World soil.

"Before any good omen is drawn from the analogy of our revolution," it must be remembered, Everett wrote, that absent a free civil society based on private property, it mattered little whether any given nation was a monarchy, colony, or republic.[7]

Lonely Places Made Glad

The Monroe Doctrine's ignoble history is well known today. Over the course of two centuries, the United States would cite the doctrine as a self-issued warrant to intervene against its southern neighbors, from the taking of Texas to more recent efforts at regime change in Venezuela and Nicaragua. Spanish- and Portuguese-speaking Americans, even before they had started to regularly use the word *imperialismo*, would in the early twentieth century coin the phrase *Monroísmo* to describe the arrogance of a great power that claimed a writ to police the hemisphere. Washington attached addendums on Monroe's original policy statement as needs dictated and ability allowed.

Initially, though, Spanish America's independence leaders read Monroe's pledge with great sympathy, as an amicus brief supporting their own radical republican revision of international law. Spanish Americans celebrated Monroe's remarks because they seemed to confirm their own anticolonial premises, that the old justifications of dominion no longer held. They thought they heard Monroe saying that there is no part of the New World that can be conquered, no part that is *terra nullius*.

Spanish American insurgents should have read Monroe's entire State of the Union Address more closely, for elsewhere in the text, the president gave a rousing defense of conquest.

The union was sound, Monroe told Congress. Its population was growing fast, not because of immigration but nearly entirely from new births, signaling vigor and vitality—and opportunity, so long as "Indian soil" was available for the taking. "New territory has been acquired of vast extent"— Louisiana, Florida, and northwestern additions—and "our population has expanded in every direction." Territorial expansion and population increase has had, the president reported, "the happiest effect" on the nation. Such enlargement, Monroe continued, prevents "disunion." Cotton plantation slavery was fast expanding, as was the fight against slavery. Yet that conflict need not tear the nation apart so long as the nation kept growing. Earlier, Monroe suggested that there was no limit to his hemispheric vision, that soon "our rapid multiplication" will "cover the whole northern, if not the southern continent, with a people speaking the same language, governed in similar forms and by similar laws."[8]

The Supreme Court that year, in 1823, likewise affirmed the doctrine of conquest as the foundation of United States sovereignty: "Conquest gives a title which the Courts of the conqueror cannot deny."[9]

Monroe's hymn to conquest and population increase—which should be taken as part of his doctrine—was one voice in a choir. There was John Quincy Adams at Ghent, warning British negotiators that his country's move across the continent was unstoppable, that a fast-growing population meant an unending supply of settler-soldiers to fight any effort to pen the United States in. There was Jefferson, who wrote that the people and soil of the United States was so fertile that soon the country would boast over a billion inhabitants, "a number greater than the present population of the whole globe."[10]

Some saw the multiplication of new Spanish American republics as part of this shared history of progress, equal to the multiplication of new Western U.S. states, adding to the "glory of the New World." Speaking to Indiana's legislature, Governor James Brown Ray happily equated Spanish American independence with the "tides" of settlers moving west. "Our forests are daily yielding to the axeman and disappearing before his strength" as "the children of nature"—Native Americans—"fly still further towards the setting sun."

America's "solitary places," Ray said, are being made "glad."[11]

Adams had Monroe's message translated into Spanish and distributed in South America, though news of the declaration first reached Simón Bolívar on March 15, 1824, via a Jamaican newspaper that had reprinted an item from the London press. Bolívar was then camped outside Peru's port city of Trujillo, making plans for his last climb up the Andes to confront Spanish forces.

Desperate rebel leaders had put forth desperate proposals while waiting for Washington to take a stand. In Buenos Aires, a prominent insurgent faction proposed placing the heir to the last Inka king on a restored Inka throne, based in Cuzco, aligned through marriage with a Brazilian aristocratic family to create a new royal house—an Inka American dynasty to rival the Bourbons and Hapsburgs, a bid to find a unifying symbol to replace Spanish power. At one point, Argentines thought that Ferdinand's brother, Prince Francisco de Paula, might be appointed regent of an autonomous American kingdom.[12]

More realistic was Bolívar's fear that he would have to ally with London to stop a major sea invasion launched by Europe's Catholic powers. Or that he would continue to struggle alone. "America stands together because it is abandoned by all other nations," Bolívar wrote in 1815. "It is isolated at the center of the world."

Word of Monroe's pronouncement, then, was electric. "Unaffected joy," was how the United States envoy to Bogotá described local reaction to Monroe's doctrine. Gran Colombia's vice president sent a formal letter of appreciation to James Monroe, calling his words "majestic." Spanish Americans ignored the ambiguity, reading the statement as a rousing New World manifesto: anticolonial and republican.[13]

"The United States of the North," as Bolívar—who at this point was serving as Gran Colombia's president as well as the head of the revolutionary army—summed up his understanding of Monroe's remarks, "have solemnly declared that they would view any measures taken by continental European powers against America and in favor of Spain as a hostile act against themselves." As was custom for the time, especially among Spanish-speaking republicans, Bolívar here used the plural *have* and *they* to refer to the United States, referring to the multiplicity of states that made up the New World's first republic, then numbering twenty-three.[14]

As also was the Spanish American custom, Bolívar used the phrase *of the North* instead of *America* since *América* was home to all.

By 1823, most of the New World's former Spanish colonies had asserted their independence. By 1826, victory was complete. Spain had withdrawn its troops, save for those left on Cuba and Puerto Rico, back across the Atlantic.

19.

As You Possess

S panish Americans thought they glimpsed something idealistic in
Monroe's statement, the seed of a different kind of diplomacy, distinct
from European balances of power, which balanced nothing but only
encouraged rivalries that inevitably led to war.[1]

America stood timorously in the morning light. "The great day of
América has not yet dawned," Bolívar wrote on the eve of full independence. "We have expelled our oppressors, broken the tablets of their tyrannical laws and founded legitimate institutions." Such a new "social compact"
will "form of this world a nation of republics." "Who," he asked, "will resist
América reunited in heart, subject to one law, and guided by the torch of
liberty?"[2]

Bolívar was as vague as Monroe. He didn't say what the terms of this
compact would be nor define what he meant by America. America, as an
idea, was up for grabs in the early 1800s. Over time, though, Bolívar's question would have its answer. Who will resist América? The country that
would go on to call itself *America*: the United States, whose leaders and
courts regularly insisted that the doctrines of conquest and discovery were
still valid.

Red Lines

In breaking from Europe, Spanish America, together with still royalist yet independent Brazil, came into existence as a community of nine free countries, an already constituted league of nations. Their formal names were República de Gran Colombia; Los Estados Unidos de México; Las Provincias Unidas de América Central; República de Chile; República de Bolivia; Las Provincias Unidas del Río de la Plata; República del Paraguay; República del Perú; and Império do Brasil. The République d'Haïti made it ten.

Yet casting off divine rule created a vacuum. By what higher law did the fledgling nations not devour one another? Independence leaders faced a paradox, for the new countries they created simultaneously legitimated and threatened one another. *Legitimated* in that they collectively broke from Spain (and in the case of Brazil, Portugal), validating their right to independence. *Threatened* in that under the existing protocols of great-power diplomacy, what law would stop a new nation from accumulating power to dominate the others, what would stop a country from conquering and annexing another?

The United States didn't have to worry about such questions, founded as it was as the only republic on a vast continent. Its main theoretical challenge was to figure out a way to reconcile the ideal of republicanism, which many philosophers believed could only work in a small polity, with expansion. Its founders answered the challenge with what they called the "federative principle," the constitutional procedure that allowed new territories to join the union as states. That principle not only allowed the United States to grow, but to use that growth to dilute domestic tensions. "Extend the sphere," wrote James Madison in the debates that preceded ratification of the U.S. Constitution, and "you make it less probable that a majority of the whole will have a common motive to invade the rights of other citizens."

The admission of new states under the federative principle would "bear indefinite extension," one Mississippi senator put it. It could go on forever, said another senator, from Illinois: "No more disputes about boundaries or red lines on maps." With "conquest" affirmed by the courts as the foundation of United States territorial sovereignty, the United States could continue to roll west until the land gave out.[3]

Spanish America had no such option. Imagine Argentina trying to claim sovereignty in the same terms that did the United States, sending its merchants, settlers, slavers, and speculators over the Andes to take Chile and its Pacific ports as its own. That option was unthinkable.

Argentina might not have marched to the Pacific, but a gaggle of new states sharing a crowded continent with vague borders provided no end of opportunities for potential conflicts. At the time of independence, large stretches of South America were outside administrative control, with much of the hemisphere still effectively governed by indigenous peoples—in the Mexican north, the Patagonia south. Tens of thousands of people lived in the Amazon—one of the world's largest river basins, almost the size of the continental United States—beyond the reach of the new nation-states.

If the Amazon had bordered the edge of human settlement, as the Mississippi had for a time, it might have been thought of as a frontier. Instead, Amazonia sat at the heart of the continent, surrounded by every new mainland nation except Chile, Paraguay, and Argentina. Statesmen could peer down at its swelter from the peaks of the Andes, wondering where the borders lay. They could imagine themselves eyeing their counterparts across the verdant expanse, maneuvering to grab a bit more territory before national boundaries became fixed. The great forest was the ultimate *terra nullius*, a more intimate sort of nothingness than other blank spots on the map. It was like having a black hole floating in the living room. The United States had the Mississippi River, a line to cross over. Spanish Americans had the Amazon, a void to circle around.

In addition to the Amazon, hundreds of coastal islands, vast grasslands, formidable mountains, and deserts mocked the idea of sovereignty. Valuable resources (minerals, good soil, grassland, guano, nitrates, rubber, for example) were found on one side of a border or the other, leading to more than a century of episodic fighting and occasional full-scale wars. If they were to survive as independent nations, Spanish American republics needed their own theory of sovereignty, one based on cooperation, not conquest.

As You Possess, So Shall You Possess

Before conflict broke out, the leaders of Spanish America's independence movements knew they had to come to agreement on borders. After his experience fighting Boves and other local caudillos, Bolívar accepted the fact that independence would bring into being many nations. There were too many passions, too many crosscutting interests at play in Spanish America to create a single country. The factionalism that Madison said could, in the United States, be dispersed through expansion must, in Spanish America, be contained by reasonably sized states with strong executives: lest "demagogic anarchy" reign.

To that end, Simón Bolívar in 1824, acting now not as a rebel general but as a statesman, president of Gran Colombia, dispatched representatives to the region's governments-in-formation to sign treaties of friendship and to establish boundaries. Several theories were circulating around this time as to how best to bound a nation. Bolívar and his advisers rejected so-called natural boundaries—a theory that rivers, mountain ranges, or other accidents of topography form organic political boundaries.[4]

They likewise rejected using their revolutionary break with the past to draw new borders by fiat, *de novo*. Just draw a new red line on a map. Thomas Jefferson imagined imposing a perfect mathematical grid over the Western territories of the United States, and Aristotelian symmetry had appealed to the Spanish, who laid out their colonial cities along straight, intersecting streets spreading out from a central plaza. Bolívar, though, had too much respect for history, for the dull affection of routine, to impose new national borders based on abstract geometry.

Bolívar thought Spain's old colonial borders—used to mark out viceroyalties, captaincies general, and other administrative divisions—were as good as any. In his 1824 diplomatic dispatch, he recommended that nations sign treaties that guaranteed "keeping boundaries" as they existed during Spanish rule. There was urgency to settle the question. Bolívar and his allies feared that now that the fight against Spain no longer focused passions, revolutionary armies or dissident renegades would start fighting one another over territory. He was especially concerned about tensions between Gran

Colombia and Peru. Both republics claimed they had rights to Quito and Guayaquil. The precariousness of the situation demanded clarity—not just on where a border might run but also on their legal justification.

To settle the matter, Colombia's foreign minister Pedro Gual had the idea of modernizing an old Roman law doctrine, *Uti possidetis, ita possideatis*: As you possess, so shall you possess.[5]

Uti possidetis had been one of those legal principles associated with conquest: the war had been won and the winner got to keep the territorial spoils. As you possess. Gual first referred to the doctrine in negotiations with Peru, posting a letter to Bolívar in July 1822 reflecting confidence that when it came to the possession of Guayaquil, "our rights are without doubt" based on the principle of "uti possidetis at the time of the foundation of the republic."[6]

Gual here was just making a routine self-interested assertion, citing the commonly used doctrine in a matter-of-fact way. It was true that Guayaquil was, during the colonial period, within the Viceroyalty of New Granada, and Gran Colombia roughly corresponded to the viceroyalty's borders.

But Gual soon would go further, relating the doctrine not, as it had been for centuries, to war and conquest, but to peace. Spanish America, Gual said in his first public use of the phrase, must take *uti possidetis* "as a rule" to "guarantee the territorial integrity" of each nation, a recognition that each state was "sovereign."[7]

Even in its standard usage, *uti possidetis* had a kernel of idealism embedded in hard-heartedness, since the doctrine was used to end wars, settle conflicts, and set the terms of peace. It wasn't a stretch then for Gual to claim the doctrine for peace itself, to use it not to settle conflicts but to prevent them. The doctrine quickly became used in the arguments of Spanish American jurists to negate the right of conquest and the doctrine of discovery.

Uti possidetis resolved the paradox mentioned earlier, allowing republics to exist in tight quarters without, in theory, one threatening another. The leaders of Spanish American independence, in other words, founded not just their own nation, but a league of nations.

An American Translation

The embrace of *uti possidetis* didn't create peace. It did give Spanish American republicans, along with their royalist Brazilian counterparts, a framework with which to imagine peace. In principle, Spanish Americans held to what they called *uti possidetis de 1810*, that is, an acceptance of colonial administrative lines as they existed on maps and surveys at the time Bolívar and Miranda established Spanish America's first republic in Venezuela.

But these weren't always clear. Diplomats argued over which royal edict or survey establishing which border was valid. Some nationalists in Buenos Aires fantasized of recomposing the sprawling colonial Viceroyalty of the Río de la Plata, which in 1810 included Bolivia, Uruguay, and Paraguay. But those provinces would become their own independent republics. There would be no reestablishment of the greater Viceroyalty of the Río de la Plata, *uti possidetis de 1810* notwithstanding.[8]

Most importantly, statesmen agreed on foundational principles: that there existed no *terra nullius* in the New World, that the hemisphere's new governments now possessed the sovereignty once held by Spain and Portugal, and that borders previously defined by Madrid and Lisbon would be the borders of newly independent states.[9]

Border clashes and all-out, catastrophic wars continued to break out throughout the 1800s. Yet no nation challenged the legitimacy of *uti possidetis*, while diplomats unerringly appealed to the doctrine to settle disputes, and to end wars. *Uti possidetis* was an "American translation" of Roman doctrine, wrote the Bolivian Ricardo Mujía, as he negotiated a border dispute with Paraguay. In its original, Mujía said, the doctrine was used to end conflicts between "enemies." Now, in the New World, it was used to prevent conflicts among friends.[10]

More critically, the doctrine of *uti possidetis* allowed the new rulers of America to sidestep the dilemma that both Las Casas and Bolívar, among others, confronted directly: the fact that the region's new nations, ruled by descendants of Europeans, were founded on indigenous land. The United States dealt with this dilemma by waging an all-out assault on, as Jefferson put it, "Indian soil," a more than century-long war that pushed Native Americans to the brink of disappearance, or into concentrated reservations.

In Spanish America, in contrast, *uti possidetis* removed the imperative for genocide: the lines were fixed, and indigenous peoples—be they Mexico's Maya, Chile's Mapuche, or Gran Colombia's Wayuu—could stay put. First peoples would continue to lose their lands, especially as export agriculture spread. And no matter what the new constitutions said, they would continue to be abused and misused, treated as second-class citizens. But, unlike in the United States, their dispossession, and their disappearance, wasn't integral to territorial aggrandizement nor a requirement for the realization of national sovereignty.

Spain and Portugal had in the late 1700s surveyed much of the continent. Yet South America's leaders had no easy access to the information gathered by colonial geographers, so they sent out new surveyors to map their boundaries. The work of these surveying commissions went on for years. Maps were drawn up. Then a republic would split apart, as Gran Colombia did, and new commissions had to be sent out to draw up yet newer maps.[11]

When possible, after relations with Spain improved, foreign ministers sent their underlings to archives, mostly in Seville, to search for maps, surveys, and royal decrees to reinforce their claims. These bureaucrats were mystified by eighteenth-century cursive that looked more like Arabic than like Spanish or Portuguese. "I am trying to master the shapes of the letters and the most curious abbreviations," said the secretary of Chile's legation in France, who had been sent to Spain to find documents to support a dispute with Argentina over Patagonia. Foreign service officers, not trained in doing archival work, complained of the "disorder of the documents," lack of classification, and "wormy, moth-eaten pieces of paper."

Within a century, each border hot spot—between Colombia and Peru for example, or Bolivia and Paraguay, or Argentina and Chile—had produced a small library documenting the history of surveys, negotiations, and archival evidence.[12]

Key to the adoption of *uti possidetis* was the establishment of an arbitration commission to settle boundary disputes. The use of third-party mediation to settle border disputes was an old practice, dating back to the ancient Greeks. But in the decades after their break with Spain, Spanish American jurists turned the ad hoc exercise into a permanent protocol. There wasn't one border in Spanish and Portuguese America that wasn't surveyed, resurveyed, arbitrated, and mediated. Diplomacy over any given disputed line could go on for decades, even centuries. Negotiations between Peru and Colombia lasted until 1998.[13]

Over the years, the United States and Great Britain would serve as mediators. Peru and Ecuador even asked the Spanish Bourbon king to adjudicate, to come back to America and measure what would once have been his birthright. The decades after independence witnessed two major wars, with staggering numbers of casualties: Argentina, Uruguay, and Brazil against Paraguay (1864–1870) and Chile and Peru against Bolivia (1879–1884). These, along with frequent skirmishes, were all fought over borders. Yet ceaseless arguing over the baseline of where to start *uti possidetis* claims, if not the doctrine itself, generally kept the peace. "I am going to insist one more time," an Ecuadorian envoy told his Peruvian counterpart at an 1889 Quito conference convened to determine a common border, "that the only line that can possibly serve as a basis for agreement is that of *uti possidetis* of 1810."

Bolívar and Gual took something old to make something new. In trying to overcome the past, they turned to the past, and seized on a doctrine that encouraged war (by promising spoils to the victor) and turned it into a premise that promoted peace, that would set the boundaries of the modern world.*

---

* *Uti possidetis* would escape its New World origins and become the basis of a new multilateral order, serving as the foundation for the nonaggression principle found in the charters of the League of Nations and the United Nations and providing the framework for decolonization in Africa. The Organization of African Unity, at its founding meeting in Addis Ababa, affirmed *uti possidetis* as its governing doctrine. "We must," said President Modibo Keita of Mali, "take Africa as it is, and we must renounce territorial claims." "It is no longer possible, nor desirable," President Philibert Tsiranana of Madagascar seconded, "to modify the boundaries of nations on the pretext of racial, religious, or linguistic criteria." And in 1986, the

Bolívar, Gual, and other independence leaders insisted that their revision of *uti possidetis* was a different way of saying what Monroe was saying. And they immediately began to ask Washington to "internationalize" Monroe's message, to issue a hemisphere declaration rejecting the doctrines of discovery and conquest. In early 1824, the republican government in Buenos Aires dispatched Carlos María de Alvear to Washington to ask if Monroe might consider adding an amendment to his 1823 statement recognizing the doctrine of *uti possidetis*. Monroe met with Alvear for two hours, speaking "vociferously" against Europe's opposition to republicanism.[14]

As to accepting the legitimacy of *uti possidetis*, Monroe refused.

International Court of Justice described *uti possidetis* as the foundation of the modern state system. *Uti possidetis*, though, was no panacea. For reasons having to do with Africa's colonial history, it has proved much less successful in containing interstate wars than in Latin America. And the doctrine itself, by guaranteeing the integrity of the nation-state, undermines claims for self-determination by indigenous communities that span borders. That the borders of the nation-states of Rwanda, Burundi, Uganda, and the Democratic Republic of the Congo were superimposed over the Tutsi, and that those of the nation-states of Somalia, Ethiopia, Kenya, and Djibouti were likewise laid over the Somali people, have been ongoing sources of conflict in their respective regions. Likewise, it was one thing to accept borders imposed by a foreign power when those doing the acceptance were leading a hemisphere-wide anti-imperialist movement, as in Spanish America. It was another thing for an empire to demand that peoples accept imposed, arbitrary borders, such as what London did in South Asia and Palestine, where the results have been catastrophic.

20.

This American Party

J oel Poinsett, a Carolina slaver, arrived in independent Mexico and presented his credentials to President Guadalupe Victoria in July 1825, beginning an eventful four years as ambassador. Poinsett's time in Mexico is a useful illustration of how the Monroe Doctrine played out locally.

Poinsett came with a full agenda: limit British influence; buy Texas, or, short of that, renegotiate the Adams–Onís border treaty, to gain more territory for the United States; compel Mexico to agree to return fugitive slaves; defend the right of Anglos settled in Mexico to own slaves; sign a trade treaty; and prevent Cherokees and other indigenous groups from establishing communities in northern Mexico, which might be used as stalking horses by the British to hinder United States interests.

Poinsett was an appointee of Henry Clay and shared his vision of a great Western Hemispheric alliance organized around commerce, directed by a strong federal government based in Washington. He was also a hard-line polygenesist.[1]

Natural Progress

Ambassador Poinsett didn't believe that "all humanity is one." He didn't even believe that societies evolve over time toward greater complexity. He once delivered a lecture to Charleston's Literary and Philosophical Society on the "Natural Progress of the Human Race from Barbarism to Civilization." In it, Poinsett put forth a more absolutist position than those Anglo supremacists who drew from Father Acosta to say that different races progress over time from a state of savagery to a higher culture. For Poinsett, hunters stayed hunters. Gatherers stayed gatherers. And pastoralists stayed pastoralists. Caucasians were the only race to advance to the level of agriculturists, a "zoologically" higher state of civilization.[2]

Poinsett told a story he had heard during his travels in Brazil, where Jesuits, no matter how much success they had in convincing native Tupis to adopt Western clothing, couldn't get them to give up the taste of human flesh. A mission priest tending to an elderly Tupi woman, whose stomach couldn't hold anything down, asked if he couldn't get her "a little sugar" or a European sweet. "Do you think you could eat it?" the Jesuit asked. "Ah," said the dying convert, "my stomach goes against everything—there is but one thing which I think I could touch. If I had the little hand of a little tender Tapuya boy, I think I could pick the little bones—but woe is me, there is nobody to go out and shoot one for me." Poinsett concluded from this tale that it was possible for hunters and cannibals to dress like civilized people but impossible for them to be civilized. Only Caucasians, Poinsett said, could "progress to the most perfect state of civil society."

Educated in the best schools in the United States and Europe, supported by his planter-slaver-doctor father, Poinsett was an amateur naturalist, ethnographer, and slave owner himself. He took at least one slave with him on his postings to Spanish America.* His "faithful negro Sam," as Poinsett described his slave while applying for his passport, lugged his sample cases from

---

* It was common in the early years of the United States for its envoys to bring their enslaved servants with them overseas. Earlier, John Jay took an enslaved woman, Abigail, to Bourbon Paris to negotiate the Treaty of Paris. Abigail died there, after being imprisoned for trying to escape. Thomas Jefferson also, when he served as ambassador to France, took his slaves to

spot to spot. Along with the correspondence he dispatched to Washington, Poinsett sent rocks and plants back to Virginia for his collecting cabinets, including *flor de Pascua*, a red-leafed ornamental that in the United States became known as a Poinsettia. And like many early Virginia gentry diplomats, Poinsett was eager to compare the sorry condition of "free" peasants to enslaved people in the U.S. South. "I certainly never saw a negro-house in Carolina so comfortless," he said, than the huts of peasants in rural Mexico.[3]

Poinsett landed in Mexico and became immediately alarmed at the influence London held over President Victoria's government, especially over the conservatives, the *centralistas*—politicians who wanted a strong executive government and who looked to Anglican Great Britain as an ally, the new nation's main source of capital, loans, investment, and imports.

"When I arrived here," he wrote, "the English men were completely master of the field, and I really feared that Mexico would never become a member of the American family."[4]

Everything to Fear, Nothing to Hope

One such archconservative and centralizer was Mexico's foreign minister, Lucas Alamán, whom Poinsett had to deal with to renegotiate the Adams–Onís treaty. Alamán was thirty-two years old and from a rich Guanajuato mining family that had abandoned their provincial gentry life for the safety of Mexico City during the wars of independence. Neither in sentiment nor philosophy was he a radical like Bolívar. Yet like Bolívar he was committed to independence, not just for Mexico but for all Spanish America. By that, he meant not just breaking formal ties with Spain, but avoiding falling under the sway of the United States. Like many conservative centralizers, he supported the abolition of slavery largely because slavery in most of Mexico was already on the decline, and because abolition would weaken Anglo settlers, who were beginning to act as if Texas was an independent country.[5]

Paris, including Sally Hemings, from 1787 to 1789. Laws prohibiting the slave trade made the practice more difficult.

Alamán knew Washington wanted more Mexican territory, and so in his first meeting with Poinsett, the Mexican minister went on the offensive. He handed his counterpart a map and asked if he knew where Spain's border with the United States existed in 1795, before the Louisiana Purchase. Poinsett did. The Mississippi River, he answered. What, the U.S. diplomat asked Alamán, was the point of the exercise? Alamán told Poinsett that was where Mexico wanted its border reestablished. The Mexican implied that Spain's transfer of Louisiana to France was illegal, and therefore France's sale of Louisiana to the United States should be voided. Cheekily, Alamán cited nothing less than Monroe's doctrine, which had declared that the "transfer" of New World territory from one power to another was prohibited.[6]

Alamán knew that Poinsett could never consider such a radical retrocession of United States territory. He was just making a point.

Alamán was afraid his new country was being picked apart north and south. Mexico had just lost the five states that made up Central America. Guatemala, El Salvador, Nicaragua, Honduras, and Costa Rica had been part of Mexico at the time of independence in 1821 but had since broken away to form their own federation. So Alamán stalled Poinsett on the question of the northern border, hoping to have better leverage in the future. He insisted that no line could be formally fixed until a surveying commission did its work, which would take years.

Reporting back to Mexico's congress on the negotiations, Alamán, in a secret session, said that Mexico "had everything to fear" from the ambitions of the United States and "nothing to hope" from its friendship.

The American Party

In response to "the machinations" of Alamán and other London-aligned conservatives, Poinsett staged the United States' first coup—a "soft" one—in Spanish America.[7]

Poinsett was a Freemason, and he noticed that the conservative *centralistas*, including President Victoria, were all members of so-called Scotch Rite lodges, where they socialized with British businessmen and politicians. Class interests, status, ideas, and politics were so tightly linked within this network of lodges that, Poinsett said, it essentially functioned like a political party.* So Poinsett set out to organize an "American Party," made up of several "York Rite" lodges, as a counterforce, for federalists, who opposed the conservatives and preferred a weak presidency along with a significant amount of local state autonomy, including autonomy for Anglo colonists.

These new lodges became what Poinsett called the "political machine of the opposition," places where federalists sympathetic to the United States could meet and strategize.[8]

In October 1825, Poinsett called prominent *Yorkinos* to a meeting in his residence, to plot, again in Poinsett's words, a "palace revolution." Acting with a unity of purpose, Poinsett's masons forced Victoria to reorganize his government, replacing members of the Scottish Lodge with politicians from the Partido Yorkino. Gone were Alamán and his allies. Victoria remained president, but his ministers were now all close to Poinsett. *Yorkinos* became a majority in congress and took control of the army and the "majority of civil and political offices."[9]

Poinsett later said he had done "more to develop an American party than any other citizen of the United States could do in Mexico." As part of their putsch, the *Yorkinos* established republican Mexico's first paramilitary organization. London's ambassador Henry George Ward described the group as a "corps of 3,000 men" composed entirely of officers and men affiliated with the York masons, ready to follow any order that would "afford a prospect of plunder." Its officers thought themselves the "new guardians of the public peace," working as the "main-spring" of the purge of *centralistas* from government. Ward's upper-class sensibilities recoiled at such mass mobilization. He called them Mexico's "dregs," criminals responsible for a "dreadful increase in robberies, and assassinations."[10]

Thus went the United States' first regime change in Spanish America. The most immediate effect of the *Yorkino* coup was to convince a now pliant

---

* Simón Bolívar was a Scottish Rite Freemason. In London as a young man, he frequented a lodge established by Francisco de Miranda, La Gran Reunión Americana, and in Paris he became a Master Mason at the Mother of St. Alexander of Scotland Lodge.

Mexican government to give up its plans, hatched when Alamán was the head of the foreign ministry and working in alliance with Colombia, to send a naval expedition to liberate Cuba and Puerto Rico from Spain. John Quincy Adams, still hoping the Cuban apple would drop into the U.S. basket, thought it would be easier for Washington to acquire the island if it remained a colony of Spain. President Victoria bristled at Poinsett's insistence that the military campaign to free Cuba be called off. Yet, barely in control of his government and military, he had little choice but to agree.

What Will Become of Texas?

Meanwhile, the borderlands, especially around Nacogdoches, grew ever more anarchic. More people poured in overland from the east: revolutionaries, refugee Indians, slavers, slaves, smugglers, missionaries, horse traders, and gun merchants. Andrew Jackson had recently been appointed governor of Florida, launching another brutal assault on Native Americans, which produced another refugee exodus into Mexico. More settlers came through looking for their "fertile paradisiacal piece of Texian lands, a mile square." It became common sense among would-be colonizers and their advocates that the Rio Grande was Texas's "natural border," with adventurers maneuvering to break everything north of it from Mexico and attach it to the United States.[11]

The British in Mexico City warned Victoria about Poinsett's ambitions, to "embroil Mexico in a Civil War" so to acquire Texas. Victoria sent General Manuel de Mier y Terán, a revolutionary war hero, to investigate matters. Mier y Terán traveled extensively through northern Mexico. He wasn't impressed with the white settlers in and around Nacogdoches. He thought them the lowest sort of criminals. Nacogdoches was a tinderbox, filled with the rough and the rowdy, drunks, disaffected Cherokees, abolitionists, revolutionary republicans, smugglers, con men, gunrunners, and swindler-speculators who called themselves settlers.[12]

The city's tumult allowed greater degrees of racial tolerance, as Anglo and Mexican politicians entered alliances, or tried to, with the Cherokees and Kickapoos settled on the town's outskirts. A multiracial revolt declared Nacogdoches the capital of the short-lived Fredonia Republic, which proposed dividing Texas in two parts, one for poor white settlers, the other for Cherokees.

Stephen Austin thought such a plan a horror. Austin's father, Moses, had received permission in the last days of the Spanish Empire to establish a colony of Anglo settlers in Texas, a grant that Stephen renegotiated with Mexico's independence government. Settlers, mostly from Louisiana, started arriving at the lower end of the Colorado River in December 1821, establishing the nucleus of what would become Anglo Texas. By 1825, the colony counted 1,790 settlers and 440 enslaved African Americans. By this point, the settlement was doing well and the idea of a biracial confederation, such as the one Fredonia presumed to establish, was an abomination. "Great God, can it be possible that Americans, high minded free born and honorable Americans," Austin said, would "league with barbarians and join a band of savages in a war of murder, massacre, and desolation?" Austin organized a settler militia to join with the Mexican government to put down Fredonia—the "Nacogdoches madmen," as he called the leaders of the doomed republic.[13]

Mier y Terán predicted, rightly, that Anglo settler-slavers themselves would soon launch their own separatist movement. They treated their chattel with exceptional brutality and constantly complained of Mexico's efforts to limit slavery. Mexico's congress wouldn't completely abolish slavery until 1837, yet by the mid-1820s, a series of emancipation decrees by rebel leaders and presidents had effectively outlawed slavery. In response, white settlers called their slaves "servants" and obtained pledges from local legislatures not to interfere in their labor relations.

Over time, Mier y Terán grew increasingly despondent, having concluded that "no physical force is capable of stopping the North Americans." The general committed suicide, falling on his sword in full dress uniform in a dark corner of a dusty church. *En qué parará Texas?* he asked three times in a letter to Lucas Alamán he posted just before he took his life: What will become of Texas? He provided his own answer: *En lo que Dios quiera.* What God wills.[14]

On Mexican Soil

Meanwhile, thousands of refugee Cherokees from the United States had petitioned Mexico City for a grant of land near the border. Encouraged by the British, President Victoria considered the proposal, but the *Yorkino* soft coup had tied his hands. Poinsett made clear his opposition. He feared that the British-backed Cherokee proposal would turn Texas into what West Florida was before Andrew Jackson's rampage: a refuge for hostile Native Americans. Poinsett also said that London's encouragement of the settlement was a violation of the Monroe Doctrine's prohibition against European interference in the New World.[15]

"I do not think it would be politic on the part of the United States," Poinsett wrote Henry Clay in April 1826, "to suffer the emigration and establishment on the Mexican frontier of so large and powerful a body of Indian warriors."[16]

During trade talks, Poinsett took up an old complaint: escaped slaves. Mexico's emancipation decrees were read by enslaved peoples in the United States "as an invitation for them to escape," said Poinsett, and Washington would refuse to sign any trade treaty that didn't include a clause promising that Mexico would return fugitive slaves to their masters.

Victoria was eager to facilitate better commercial relations with the United States. Wealthy Spaniards hostile to independence had left for Spain, carrying with them nearly all of Mexico's portable mineral wealth. The Mexican government was desperate to jump-start trade and reopen shuttered mines. Still, both houses of Mexico's congress, comprised of many *federalistas* aligned with Poinsett, rejected the proviso. "Slaves," the government's negotiators told Poinsett, "could not exist on Mexican soil."[17]

Poinsett pushed, but Victoria wouldn't budge on the issue, continuing to insist that by simply crossing the border into Mexico, enslaved peoples were emancipated, protected by the "inalienable rights" to liberty granted by the "author of nature."[18]

Poinsett concluded that Mexico's stubborn refusal to agree to return escaped slaves was proof that its leaders "dislike our republican institutions."

President Victoria had had enough of Poinsett, who, apart from badgering Mexico to sign a fugitive slave treaty, refused to take a stand against ongoing Spanish efforts to reconquer Mexico. In a public speech, Victoria lamented Washington's betrayal of the anticolonial principles laid out in the Monroe Doctrine, in doing nothing to defend Mexico against European intrigues.

The speech earned Victoria a rebuke from John Quincy Adams's ambassador to Spain, Alexander Hill Everett—not for its content, but for the way the Mexican president addressed the United States.

Until now, it was common enough for Spanish American statesmen to use the phrase *United States of the North*, in the friendliest of exchanges, a kind of New World comradery: We are all Americans. But Everett, Boston born, Harvard educated, and a member of Adams's law office, found it offensive.

The proper name of his country, Everett said, was the United States of America. "The chief magistrate of a great republic ought to know that it is usual," Everett wrote, "to designate friendly powers under the names they assume, unless it is intended to contest them, which I hope is not the case here."

Moreover, Everett was also bothered by Mexico's official name, Estados Unidos Mexicanos. He felt that *Estados Unidos*, or, in English, the United States, was proprietary to his country, the United States of America. Mexicans were both plagiarists and thieves, "borrowing one half our name" only "to rob us of the other." This, as far as I know, was the first time that the name *America* was politicized in such a pointed way.

As for Poinsett, his presence in Mexico grew untenable. He returned to the United States in 1830, in time to see the passage of Andrew Jackson's Indian Removal Act. In a few years, Poinsett, as Martin Van Buren's secretary of war, would be in charge of executing the act, driving tens of thousands of Native Americans west, across the Mississippi and, many of them no doubt, into Mexico.[19]

21.

Sister Nations

Simón Bolívar sent out the first round of invitations for a Continental Congress on December 7, 1824, two days before the Battle of Ayacucho, the last great insurgent victory. A few more minor battles, including the final liberation of Alto Perú, or Bolivia, and America would be free. Bolívar called his planned gathering the *Congreso Anfictiónico de América*, in tribute to the fabled ancient Greek Amphictyonic League, or League of Neighbors.

Greece was then fighting for independence from the Ottoman Empire, and many cheered the struggle in the Peloponnese as part of a general uprising against tyranny, of the kind the United States and Haiti had won, and Spanish America was about to win.

There was worry, though, in Bolívar's learned reference. The fate of ancient Greece was exactly what a free Spanish America wanted to avoid becoming: an unstable confederation of weak republics easily upended by ambitious powers, where submission to a conqueror, like Alexander, or an empire, like Rome, was the only way to establish order. Bolívar and other independence leaders feared such a fate, since the social base for liberalism in Spanish America was weak. Servility was deeply seeded. Jacobinism militant. And oligarchic reaction ready with the lash. Bolívar didn't want to be Alexander. He didn't want a continent of microrepublics, *patrias chicas*, or city-states. And he didn't want to place free Spanish America under the protection of Great Britain, which he thought of as a liberal Rome. He wrote his Colombian vice president complaining that the leaders of both London and Washington were "*muy egoístas*," but at least London's Royal Navy was enforcing the abolition of the slave trade.[1]

There was no existing model for the kind of confederacy Bolívar thought necessary to escape the repetitions of history. Not balance-of-power Europe. Not the United States' expansionist union, which insisted on the legitimacy of the doctrine of conquest. He and his allies wanted a confederacy of substantial republics where the working assumption was that each nation shared interests with the others.[2]

Bolívar's Congress would take place in Panama, then a province of Gran Colombia, in the summer of 1826. The venue was chosen for obvious symbolic reasons related to its geography. In his invitation, Bolívar said that Panama sat not just at the center of America but of "the globe, having on one side Asia, and the other Africa and Europe." What better place to bring forth new laws, new ways of organizing international politics? "When after a hundred centuries, posterity shall search for the origin of our public law," it will find Panama. "What, then, shall be the Isthmus of Corinth compared with that of Panama?"[3]

Spanish American nations were something entirely new in the world. Not because they were republican. But because they were republican *together*. Historians sometimes cite the Peace of Westphalia or the Congress of Vienna as establishing the first association of nation-states. But those arrangements grouped together dynastic monarchies that, anyway, were empires, not bounded nations. France, Holland, and Great Britain flitted about the earth's oceans in their gunner ships, starting wars, constructing slave-trading forts on the coast of Africa and the Indian Ocean, capturing humans and selling them halfway around the world, tendering joint-stock companies to establish territorial and commercial dominance in Asia, setting up plantations built on forced labor, putting down rebellions in Java and India, and funneling the world's precious metals and raw materials back to Europe.

Spanish American revolutionaries sought to build a community of nations without colonies or empires, dedicated to an idealistic conception of how the world *should* be ordered.

Youthful and Stirring

Bolívar had been planning the Panama Congress for years. The founders of independent Spanish America were anti-expansionists when it came to territory, thinking that the only way to ensure peace was for each nation to adhere to its defined borders. But they were expansionists when it came to their faith in the universal appeal of republican values. Like some of his counterparts in the United States, Bolívar believed that one day there would exist "a single nation spanning the universe—a federation." This expansion would not take place through settlement, conquest, and dispossession but through emulation and voluntary confederation. The whole world would follow the path opened by *América*.[4]

Bolívar pushed for a confederation that could mediate conflicts among member states and, as he wrote in 1824, "function as a council in great conflicts" and serve as a "trusted arbiter" of treaties and disputes.[5]

Bolívar put Pedro Gual, the theorist who moralized *uti possidetis*, in charge of organizing the conference. Born in Caracas, Colombia's foreign minister had graduated from La Real y Pontificia Universidad de Caracas with a doctorate in theology, having studied under the lawyer who had drafted Venezuela's first declaration of independence, Juan Germán Roscio. The Venezuelan university had continued, up to the time Gual was enrolled, to follow much of the curriculum used by the University of Salamanca in Spain, but supplemented with the new Enlightenment canon of Voltaire, Rousseau, Locke, and other philosophers.[6]

It was a powerful mix. Scholasticism taught that to accept the first principle of an argument was to accept the whole argument. The Enlightenment's first principle was that humans were free, rational, and moral beings. In briefing Gran Colombia's congress, Gual said the point of the Panama meeting was to lay the foundation for an eventual confederation, not of rulers against their own people, as in Europe, but of the people themselves.

"Ours must be a society of sister-nations, separated *for now* in the exercise of their sovereignty by the course of human events, but united, strong, and powerful enough to defend against the aggressions of foreign powers."[7]

The precondition to confederation, Gual said, was recognizing the absolute sovereignty of individual nations. With borders defined and respected, sovereign nations could join together in a way that achieved something more transcendent than a mundane balance of power. Gual also made clear that he hoped that the meeting in Panama would begin the codification and standardization of continental law. All residents of America, Gual told Colombia's congress, would enjoy equal rights and live under the same laws, no matter what country they were born in, traveled to, or settled in.

The agenda of the proposed conference kept changing, but one thing became clear as Bolívar, Gual, and their allies debated the matter: the Panama Congress, if it was to come off, would be unprecedented in the history of diplomacy, unrivaled in its ambition. It included, among other objectives:

- Mutual defense against European efforts at reconquest.

- The publication of a manifesto condemning Spain and the suffering it had caused in the New World.

- The promotion of the independence of Cuba and Puerto Rico, along with the Canary Islands and the Philippines.

- The formalization of the Monroe Doctrine as international law (meaning the formal repudiation of doctrines of discovery and conquest).

- The total abolition of New World slavery.*

---

* Slave emancipation was a long, chaotic process in Spanish America that started with the Haitian Revolution in 1791 and continued with Venezuela's first Republic—with Miranda's and Bolívar's pledge to free any enslaved person who joined their rebel armies. Throughout the fifteen-year war for independence, insurgent leaders issued many abolition decrees. Yet once independent republics were established, new governments might or might not officialize such decrees. Still, there existed a generalized belief among independence intellectuals that freedom from Spain included freedom from servitude, in all its many varieties. The abolition of chattel slavery was but one element of a larger emancipationist ethos. And it was clear to most that abolition was inevitable, and, once the break with Spain had been achieved, a

- The recognition of Haiti.

- The legalization of borders based on *uti possidetis de 1810*.

All the basic principles that would later go into the founding of the League of Nations and the United Nations are present in the early years of Spanish American independence: the rejection of aggressive war and the doctrines of conquest and discovery, the ideal of anticolonial nationalism, an embrace of territorial sovereignty tempered by multilateral self-defense and cooperation to solve problems bigger than the nation-state, a belief in the equality of nations, and a commitment to the dignity of humans, which included, as soon as possible, an end to slavery.

Horrors, Calamities, and Crimes

Ideas were one thing. The social context in which ideas root or wilt another.

Spanish America was in bad shape when Bolívar sent out his invitations, greatly indebted due to loans taken out to pay for arms and provisions to fight Spain. When Bolívar sent two envoys to London to acquire matériel on credit, both were thrown in debtor's prison for not being able to pay what insurgents already owed to merchants. "A cruel humiliation to beg for help from men," Bolívar said of London creditors, "who are as uncaring as gold itself."[8]

Under Spanish rule, the paying of taxes and tribute was a burden, but it was a comprehensible burden. Now, their nations free, republicans had to deal with more mysterious forms of tithing to the City of London: interest and fees on loans and trading bonds. British merchants and banking houses

---

second war, a civil war (of the kind that would nearly break the United States), would not be needed to end slavery (which turned out to be the case, except for one short conflict in Colombia in the 1850s). Around the time of the Panama Congress, slavery had been ended in Chile, Bolivia, and in parts of Mexico. Central America abolished slavery in 1824. Bolívar as president of Gran Colombia said slavery was no more, but the component regions of the sprawling nation decided the matter for themselves. Venezuela had begun to abolish slavery in 1821, with complete emancipation not coming until 1854. Bolívar tried to abolish slavery in Peru, but slavers in the countryside paid him no mind. And so despite the consensus that slavery should have no place in an emancipated New World, slavery continued in Peru, as well as in the United States and Brazil. Thus abolition's inclusion in the Congress's agenda.

took a godlike role in the creation of a New World of nation-states, extending credit and collecting debt; financing weapon purchases; advancing loans to feed armies; and organizing the shipments of Yorkshire clothing, Sheffield swords and muskets, and Irish horses straight to battlefields.

Then the bill came.

London suppliers began presenting staggeringly high invoices for matériel they said they had shipped on credit during the early years of the war against Spain. Debt piled up, requiring the securing of more loans to service interest. When Spain ruled, imperial treasure fleets would depart twice a year filled with the continent's wealth, its silver, gold, pearls, lumber, tobacco, silk, and other goods. Now it went to London, as British warships carted off millions of pounds of Potosí silver as interest payment. Spanish America's republics were hamstrung from the get-go.

The wrecked economies that emerged from the freedom wars hindered the formation of a stable governing class and hastened the fragmentation that terrified Bolívar and his allies. There was, the sociologist Miguel Centeno writes in *Blood and Debt*, no "anchor on which to base institutional development." New states issued paper money backed up by what Bolívar called "imaginary rents"—imaginary because no civil service existed that could collect taxes, and what money that was collected went to service debt. Inflation became chronic, viewed by citizens "with more horror than they did servitude."[9]

New World independence offered London banks endless opportunities to come up with new speculative instruments, and new ways to skim more off the principal and the payments. Bank officials in London worked Spanish Americans hard, and forced loans on envoys that their governments didn't ask for. General William Miller, a British officer who fought on the side of Chile's republicans, noted the corrupting power of easy lucre. The arrival of London gold in Santiago, Miller said, gave rise to levels of theft from public coffers that made a burlesque out of the idea of republican virtue. "The masters of the mines and the owners of Andean silver and gold," Bolívar complained, leveraged their properties to borrow money. Yet they didn't use their loans as capital, as investments to increase production. Rather, they lent the already borrowed money out at high interest rates.

London banks lent money to Spain to reconquer Mexico and lent money to Mexico to fend off the reconquest. Loans had to be paid back in pounds sterling, according to the official exchange rate, and the mere rumor of political unrest could send the value of local currency, in relation to the pound, plunging, increasing the burden of the original note tenfold.

Catholicism had bequeathed to Spanish American republicans a strong prejudice against usury, profits made from unjust interest rates. Saint Thomas Aquinas, followed up by scholars of the Salamanca School, wrote not just on law and politics but economics, insisting that trade and finance should be regulated by ethics, that goods should be sold at a "just price." Aquinas condemned moneylending at interest. An investor might put up money and earn a profit or accept a loss depending on the success of the venture. But lending money solely for purpose of collecting interest was, for Aquinas, a mechanism of domination, and hence a sin.* In general, economics should be regulated by moral customs that help reinforce the greater good.

Independence brought the opposite reality. Compulsory payment of debt was internationalized, interwoven into great-power diplomacy. Paris, in one infamous example, threatened to destroy Haiti if it didn't agree to pay 150 million francs in indemnification to exiled slave owners for lost property— that is, for their former slaves—a debt whose interest compounded to the heavens. Not only was debt not governed by morality: debt became the measure of morality. To be sovereign, a country needed to be solvent. Yet not one Spanish American republic in the decades after independence could keep up with interest payments. Nations that couldn't pay back what they owed weren't so much denied credit as forced to accept ever more onerous terms.

---

* John Maynard Keynes, in his *General Theory*, recalls how Anglo economists ridiculed the Salamanca School's economic arguments. Keynes, though, came to concede that their ideas were formidable: "I was brought up to believe that the attitude of the Medieval Church to the rate of interest was inherently absurd, and that the subtle discussions aimed at distinguishing the return on money-loans from the return to active investment were merely Jesuitical attempts to find a practical escape from a foolish theory. But I now read these discussions as an honest intellectual effort to keep separate what the classical theory [of economics] has inextricably confused together, namely, the rate of interest and the marginal efficiency of capital. For it now seems clear that the disquisitions of the schoolmen were directed towards the elucidation of a formula which should allow the schedule of the marginal efficiency of capital to be high, whilst using rule and custom and the moral law to keep down the rate of interest."

Aquinas would have been horrified. Bolívar was. "Public debt is a chaos of horrors, calamities, and crimes," Bolívar said. "Colombia's entrails are being picked to pieces by vultures."

Republics of Air

The crises were many. The new republics were fragile and seemed likely to fall. They were, Bolívar complained, *de aire*—of air—delicate and utopian. Confederating would at least allow for better bargaining power when dealing with London banks.

The United States had also won its revolution on borrowed money, and with freedom came inflation. The new nation, writes the historian Michael Blaakman, "was born in debt and swaddled in fiat currency." But the fledgling U.S. had something Spanish Americans didn't: Western lands, including Indians lands—which served as, among other things, collateral. As a result, debt and speculation in the fast-growing United States weren't engines of chaos and crisis, as they were in Spanish America. Rather, thanks to the frontier, they were sources of power.[10]

In Spanish America, the problem wasn't just debt. There were too many poor, too much wealth was held by too few families, and the Church controlled too much land and had too much influence. Wage labor was not developed enough to create virtuous "free" citizens, much less break the bonds of peonage and servility. Years of insurgency had upended the social order, unleashing common crime and political repression.[11]

All it took, it seemed, for a civil war to break out, for a local caudillo to raise an army and make a bid for power, was for Bolívar to leave town. Peru was a warren of royalist intrigue and landlord obstructionism, leading republicans to appoint Bolívar, still president of Gran Colombia, "dictator" in the hope he could put down episodic revolts and form a working government.

Independence also cost blood. Some estimate that three million Americans had perished in the fight against Spain, while the number of soldiers who lost their lives defending royal rule is unknown. Added to the human suffering was the destruction of mines, plantations, cities, and villages. Rebuilding what was, much less building something new, seemed impossible. Political differences added to the chaos. Ideologies crisscrossed and clashed: liberals, conservatives, *federalistas*, *centralistas*, republicans, monarchists, slavers, Jacobins, abolitionists, and *hispanoamericanistas* (conservatives who wanted to maintain cultural fidelity to Spain), all had competing variants and radical wings.

Hence the fantastical embrace by Bolívar and others of *América* as a transcendent ideal to create unity. And though there was much love for the whole of *América*, there was some hate, especially among political elites, among its component parts. "The south hates the north, the coast hates the highlands," Bolívar complained, speaking of the forces pulling Gran Colombia apart. And not a few independence leaders didn't care much for Bolívar, wary of his obsessions.[12]

Nationalism began to pull on peoples' affections: *lo mexicano, lo chileno, lo venezolano*. Some identified with smaller *patrias chicas*, or little homelands, those microrepublics Bolívar hoped to avoid, which in the countryside orbited around great families and their caudillo patriarchs. "Hooligans," Bolívar called them. And others understood themselves primarily as residents of one or another of Spanish America's ornamental and well laid-out cities—where everything beyond the boundary of the civilized *urbe* was barbarism. *Fuera de México todo es Cuautitlán*, which loosely translates as: the only thing outside of Mexico City are Indians, corn, dust, and farm animals. Venezuelans said something similar: *Caracas es Caracas*; *todo lo demás es jungla y serpientes*—Caracas is Caracas, and everything else is jungle and snakes.[13]

Bolívar and his allies hoped *América* could cradle all these many identities and that confederation could work to slow the centrifugal forces threatening to tear the new republics apart.

Bolívar tried to hold it together by rhetorical will. In practical terms, he didn't think that all Spanish America was near ready to unite as a single political unit. The proposed Congress of Panama was meant to be something of a speech act, or, as he put it, a "theatrical representation." Unity and solidarity would be forged from talking about unity and solidarity.

Bolívar sought to use the whole to keep the parts from flying away. He hoped the Congress would create a world bound by a common set of laws, where "differences of origin and color would lose their influence and power" and where no nation "would be weaker than the other, nor stronger." Not just a balance of power but a "perfect balance established in this true new order of things."[14]

Aspirations, the fancies of republics as tangible as, Bolívar feared, ether.

Torments

John Quincy Adams followed Monroe as president, taking office after the contested 1824 election, when the House of Representatives gave him the White House even though Andrew Jackson had won a majority of both popular and electoral votes. The fallout from that dispute marked the beginning of a momentous domestic realignment, ending the old two-party system. Soon gone would be both the Federalists and the Democratic-Republicans. The conflict over slavery was hardening, and nearly every debate, especially if it had to do with territorial expansion and foreign policy, had the future of slave labor as subtext.

President Adams announced his decision to send delegates to Simón Bolívar's Panama Congress in his first State of the Union message, in December 1825, an address famous for laying out a robust program of national integration. Adams's agenda was ambitious, including the building of roads, canals, and harbors; the extension of postal routes; the carrying out of surveys and western exploration; the bringing of new territories into the union and the forging of new states from those territories; the adoption of common weights and measures; and the expansion of the navy to protect whalers wherever they hunted, in the islands of the Pacific, or off the coast of Chile, Peru, and even in the China Sea. Revenue from the sale of public land in the Western territories would overflow the national coffers and pay for all this "improvement." President Adams also wanted to build the first astronomical observatory in the Americas. He noted that while Europe had over a hundred such heavenly "lighthouses," our "half of the globe and the earth revolves in perpetual darkness to our unsearching eyes."

Adams was putting forth a sweeping interpretation of executive power. The Constitution, he said, granted the president the power to do all these things, to collect taxes, impose duties and tariffs, regulate commerce, maintain an army and navy, and administer territories.

Such a broad vision of an empowered presidency worried members of what would be called the Jacksonian coalition, which had already begun to associate the vitality of slavery and settler expansion with limited government.

Not limited in its coercive capacity, in its ability to catch and return fugitive slaves or remove Indians from their lands. But limited in its ability to plan the economy and integrate the nation. Adams mentioned using the navy to suppress the slave trade, and his description of slavery as "abominable" riled Southern representatives. At the same time, though, he pledged to push London to pay reparations for "slaves carried away" in the War of 1812. (True to his word, his government, the following year, received $1,204,960 in compensation from the British government, the estimated value of 3,601 enslaved people emancipated by royal troops from New Orleans and Chesapeake plantations.)

Adams made only one quick reference to Bolívar's Congress, downplaying its importance. Elsewhere, he and his secretary of state, Henry Clay, presented the proposed gathering as trivial, little more than a discussion on trade, navigation, and questions of neutrality. They insisted that United States participation would not expand executive power into the realm of foreign policy.

Still, rumors were already circulating around Washington that Bolívar and his allies planned to use the conference to touch on the tenderest parts of United States politics: slavery, continental expansion, borders, Haiti, and Cuba. The backlash against Adams for having accepted the invitation was harsh, revealing a fear that would haunt reactionaries in the United States down the centuries: that foreign policy would be used to restructure domestic politics, that submitting Washington to even the mildest forms of international jurisdiction would impose insufferable constraints. That fear jolted the Age of Jackson into existence.

Utterly Ultra

Opposition to Bolívar's Panama Congress came from all parts of the United States. In Missouri, Senator Thomas Hart Benton warned of a trap. If Washington's delegates opposed resolutions, they would be seen as enemies of Spanish America. Yet if they voted with the majority, the United States would become "trammeled and controlled" by Spanish America. "To become a single satellite to a larger planet, and with no more power in the great Continental Confederacy than Peru or Guatemala," said New Hampshire senator Levi Woodbury, would undo the work of the founders and throw the protections provided by the Constitution to the wind.

Pennsylvania senator James Buchanan said that the United States had "grown great" by "standing alone." Buchanan was worried that joining Bolívar's alliance would tie Washington's hands. The United States wouldn't be able to wage war against any of the alliance's members. Yet if Washington didn't join and the United States were to attack a member country of the alliance, the "whole continent of America, South of our own territory, will be marshalled in hostile array against us." The future president warned "War with one must be war with all."[1]

Aside from the fact that Bolívar and his allies call themselves republicans, said New York senator Martin Van Buren, "we are unalike in all other things."[2]

From Tennessee, Representative James Polk accused Adams and Clay of favoring New England merchants to the disadvantage of Southern planters and interior settler states, since any alliance with Spanish America would foreclose on the possibility of taking Mexico, or at least Texas, and the hoped-for expansion of slavery into those regions. Later, as president, Polk would annex Texas, invade Mexico, and urge the Senate to incorporate the Yucatán into the union. Now, though, he spoke out against an interventionist policy in Spanish America, citing George Washington's warning that the United States must avoid "entangling alliances."

Detractors focused on executive overreach, emphasizing the impropriety of the executive branch's involvement in a conference convened to establish an international alliance. At stake though, clearly, was the content of the planned conclave, its agenda, especially the fear that Spanish Americans would issue a resolution calling for the hemispheric abolition of slavery. Southerners were "especially apprehensive of any and every scheme proposed by Simón Bolívar." They feared that his proposed summit would call for hemispheric "emancipation of the enslaved Negroes" and that Bolívar "would not cease operations . . . until they were wholly emancipated."[3]

Adams and Clay had their supporters, and they eventually won a congressional vote to fund the travel expenses of two agents to observe the proceedings. But the fight in Congress went on for more than four months, with those opposed to the appropriation of funds getting, rhetorically at least, the upper hand. "No question, in its day," wrote Senator Benton later, "excited more heat and intemperate discussion, or more feeling between a President and Senate, than this proposed mission."[4]

The press, including abolitionist journals, reported on both the Congress of Panama and the continental emancipation of slaves as of a piece. The Senate debate took place as Colombia and Mexico were making plans to liberate Cuba, and many Southerners warned that Bolívar's schemes would provoke a "slave rebellion in Cuba." Virginia's Senator John Randolph raised the specter of Cuba's unchained "immense negro population" escaping to Florida "in row boats."[5]

The debate over Panama moved Vice President John Calhoun toward becoming what he called a "systematick" opponent of Adams's administration and an "utterly ultra" defender of states' rights. Calhoun, who presided over the debate, used procedural rulings to give Adams's opponents free range while stifling allies. The force of hostility to the mere idea of attending an international conference helped the fledgling Jacksonian coalition bring "together their constituencies in the North and South." Just the presumption that the nations of the Americas shared common ideals and interests reconciled longtime foes.[6]

First among Calhoun's foes was Virginia's flamboyant Senator Randolph. Calhoun didn't like Randolph but gave him the floor and let him talk. And talk. And talk. Described by one of his first biographers as the "great rallying officer of the South," Randolph worried that the white emissaries Adams had named to attend the Congress would be forced to "take their seat" at the conference table next to "the native African, their American descendants, the mixed breeds, the Indians, and the half breeds." Until recently, diplomats took their slaves along to serve them on their travels. Now, they were expected to negotiate, as equals, with people who should be slaves.

Furthermore, said Randolph, protocol would prohibit them from taking offense, or their position might be canceled. Randolph wrongly believed that Panama was a province of Guatemala, and that Guatemala was "as much a black Republic at this time as Hayti itself." Even ambassadors from the so-called white republics of Spanish America were suspect, since a "great deal of African blood" flowed through their veins. "What would be our social relations with a Black minister" were Spanish America to send one to Washington, Vice President Calhoun wondered. "Must he be received or excluded from dinners, our dances and our parties, must his daughters and sons participate in the society of our daughters and sons?" Randolph painted Bolívar's wars for independence as one grand integrated dinner party: the "ball of Spanish American Revolution."[7]

Lighthouses in the Sky

The congressional debate over Bolívar's Panama Congress drew out and honed three arguments key to the United States' incomparable sense of itself.

The first upheld the idea of its uniqueness, that alone among the revolutions that rolled across the Atlantic world, only the United States struck the sweet spot between liberty and licentiousness. To take the ideal of liberty too far leads to the "frantic orgies of the French Bacchanals of the Revolution," as Randolph described the Jacobin terror, a "politico-religious fanaticism" that was the opposite of the "manly and rational piety" adopted by the United States.

"Fanaticism, political or religious, has no stopping place short of Heaven—or Hell." That idea was explicitly racialized in the Panama debate. Randolph called Spanish America's abolitionist movement a "black crusade," a cause alien to the United States. The Virginia senator singled out Bolívar's battlefield emancipations for special concern. A promise of emancipation was bad enough. Much worse was that Bolívar mustered slaves to cut "their masters' throat."[8]

The second argument expressed a widely held fear that foreign policy would be used to rearrange the domestic order, used to equalize not just civic relations but social ones as well, even in the most intimate realms of home and hearth. The "safety of our families" was at stake, South Carolina's Senator Robert Hayne said, "our firesides." Opponents of Bolívar's Congress were especially concerned with the danger of submitting the issue of slavery to international opinion. "The question of slavery," said Hayne, "must be considered and treated entirely as a DOMESTIC QUESTION," the transcript of his remarks using capital letters for emphasis. Therefore, Hayne went on, it cannot "be touched" or "brought into question," neither by "sister States" nor the "Federal Government," much less by foreign nations. "To touch it at all, is to violate our most sacred rights," and to "attempt to instruct us on the subject, is to insult us. . . . There is not a nation on the globe with whom I would consult on that subject, least of all, the new Republics."[9]

Third was the rehearsal of the argument for minimal government—against an empowered executive branch and in favor of muscular states' rights, with Panama providing an opportunity to reconfirm that the founders' Constitution was meant to restrain not empower the presidency. This position intensified in the years leading to the Civil War, as its proponents hoped to counter federal action against slavery.

Here, thirty-four years before the election of Abraham Lincoln, Southerners like Randolph and Hayne knew that Adams's ambitious agenda was a threat to chattel slavery, for it was based on the idea that the Constitution invested formidable power in the presidency. The ongoing vigor of slavery needed the executive branch constrained. Any policy, even if it had nothing directly to do with slavery, that strengthened the federal government—be it the building of an astronomy observatory or the sending of observers to attend a conference—was taken as a threat and characterized as a perversion of the founders' intent. Adams no doubt thought his reference to observatories as "lighthouses *of* the skies" felicitous phrasing. Randolph, in one of his stem-winders against the Panama Congress, dismissed them as "lighthouses *in* the sky," a mockery that followed Adams to his grave.

Andrew Jackson read about the Panama debates on his Tennessee plantation. The Panama mission, he said, was "one of the most dangerous, and alarming Schemes that ever entered into the brain of visionary politicians."[10]

Henry Adams, John Quincy's grandson, described the debate over the Panama Congress as taking "every loose element of opposition in the Senate" and tying them "together in a new party," one that would "consolidate the slaveholding interest." For the budding Jacksonians, rhetoric equating Adams with Bolívar allowed slavers in Congress to unite behind "the banner of states' rights" to defend slavery even as they depicted expansion of the executive government as an "instrument of slavery"—the slavery of free white citizens. For the ascendent Jacksonians, the high dudgeon of their oratory was the point, much as Bolívar himself imagined the Congress: a "theatrical representation."[11]

Leaders of the fledgling new coalition came from all regions, represented in the North by future presidents Martin Van Buren and James Buchanan; in the West by another future president, James Polk, a vocal advocate for taking Texas; and in the South, where Calhoun and Randolph, among others, led the opposition against Adams. The reaction to Adams's State of the Union agenda and the condemnation of Bolívar's Congress also pulled in nascent labor radicals. Labor leaders opposed raising revenue from Western land. They wanted to distribute that land to poor homesteaders.

The monthslong congressional fight let Andrew Jackson—already celebrated for his destruction of the Creeks, defeat of the British at New Orleans, and pacification of Florida—emerge as a tribune of minimal government, a defender of settler rights, and a protector of the founders' original intent. Signing commercial treaties made sense, Jackson said. But he rallied his followers against "entangling alliances"—this from the man who once swore allegiance to the Catholic king of Spain.

From this quarrel over the meaning of the Panama Congress emerged the country's second two-party system: the Federalists and the Democratic-Republicans gave way to the Whigs and the Democrats.[12]

For the next three decades, the Democrats, made up of "Jacksonians, Radicals and Calhoun men," dominated domestic and foreign policy. United as "one man," said Senator Hayne, referring to the concord forged out of complaining about Bolívar.[13]

That man was Andrew Jackson, who, winning the White House in 1828, would make Adams a one-term president.

Torments in the Name of Liberty

The timing of the Panama Congress, in June 1826, seemed auspicious, coming as it did after the complete defeat of Madrid. The Spanish Empire, from the Sabine River to Cape Horn, was, save for Cuba, Puerto Rico, and the Philippines, gone.

The Congress was a bust. Bolívar, earlier, had acknowledged the meeting's goals would be practically impossible to achieve. Still, the illusion was worth chasing, he thought, since it would set the terms of what America *should* be, even if it yet couldn't. The venue itself captures the mirage. Panama City was a shambles at the time, its neighborhoods abandoned and overgrown. Bolívar, worried about summer pestilence, had considered moving the proceedings to highland Quito, but invitations had already been sent out. Sessions were held in the Chapter Hall of the Convent of San Francisco, among the oldest buildings standing in the Americas, its rectangular stone walls sheltering a lush garden. An antique building to launch New World political modernism.[14]

Once the conference got under way, delegates—from Gran Colombia, Central America, and Mexico—talked much, showcasing the topics that so vexed the United States: slavery, Haiti, Cuba, alliances, sovereignty, and borders. They accomplished little, other than agreeing on the wording of Gual's Treaty of Union, League and Perpetual Confederation, which obligated member nations to mutually defend the borders of the territories they held on becoming free. Mexico's envoys, allies of Poinsett, were hostile.

Adams's representatives were absent. One died of dysentery along the way; the other arrived after proceedings had ended.[15]

Bolívar didn't participate in the Congress. He was in Lima, trying to use his extraordinary "dictatorial" powers to tame the landed class and build a nation. He was too pressed from all sides. He was still president of Gran Colombia, and that nation was coming apart as secessionists in Venezuela and Ecuador threatened civil war. Hoping to hold the union together, Bolívar quit Lima on April 10, 1826, moving on to western Venezuela, where he began to muster troops, though his mere appearance, along with a general amnesty, was enough to quell the separatists. By early 1827, he was in Bogotá. While he was away, his adversaries, many from the provinces who opposed a strong executive, had grown in strength.

The establishment of Washington's diplomatic corps in Spanish America added to Bolívar's troubles. United States consuls, following the example of Poinsett, were hostile to his vision of a united Spanish America, cultivating local politicians friendly to Washington who wanted a weak central government. William Tudor, Washington's man in Lima, dismissed Bolívar as a vainglorious tyrant; "Bolívar's model is now Napoleon and his ambition is equally unbounded," Tudor said, as he worked with Bolívar's opponents to destabilize Gran Colombia. London's ambassador to Peru reported on the "malign" hostility Washington's representatives had for Bolívar. One, probably Tudor, went to the "extreme" of openly hoping that the Spanish American Caesar—that is, Bolívar—would soon meet a Spanish American Brutus. Soon enough, Bolívar barely escaped the knives of an assassin. Washington's new envoy, William Henry Harrison, later president of the United States, arrived in Bogotá shortly after the assassination attempt to lecture Bolívar on the dangers of despotism.[16]

The Panama Congress then marked the beginning of an era not of confederation but of political schism, as many of the original independent Spanish American republics splintered. The United Provinces of Central America broke up into Guatemala, El Salvador, Honduras, Nicaragua, and Costa Rica. War between Brazil and Argentina led to the creation of the Republic of Uruguay.

In Lima, Consul Tudor flamed long-standing tensions between Peru and

Gran Colombia over the port city of Guayaquil, leading to a breakout of hostilities. The war didn't last long and ended with a peace treaty that, citing *uti possidetis*, recognized that Guayaquil belonged to Gran Colombia. Still, though short-lived, the crisis ricocheted within Gran Colombia, worsening tensions between political factions and hastening that nation's split into Venezuela, Colombia, and Ecuador.

The United States, Bolívar said, "seem destined by Providence to plague America with torments in the name of liberty."

Bolívar resigned Gran Colombia's presidency on January 20, 1830, shortly before the country's final breakup. He set out on a riverboat down the Magdalena toward the Caribbean, making plans to seek exile somewhere in Europe, possibly in Paris.

Along the way, Bolívar posted a last letter to a friend, saying that after nearly two decades of endless warfare he was certain of only a few things, among them:

1. America is ungovernable;

2. To serve the revolution is as futile as plowing the sea;

3. History is running in reverse; America is heading toward "primitive chaos."

Bolívar died on December 17, delirious from tuberculosis, on a rum hacienda near the coastal town of Santa Marta. He was forty-seven years old.

A few days earlier, he had asked: "How will I escape this labyrinth?"[17]

PART V

YOUNG AMERICANS

The twenty-day siege of Veracruz, beginning March 9, 1847,
was a major escalation of Washington's war on Mexico.

23.

The March of God

What is history? The first generation of American revolutionaries thought they knew. Jefferson believed it was progress, an evolution away from a primitive past toward civilization, away from servility toward freedom. Revolutions were engines of history, expanding the radius of liberty, allowing men to overcome the constraints of necessity. Even Spanish America, he said, might be able to break its chains of "ignorance and bigotry," because, as he wrote to the French political theorist Madame de Staël, the revolutionary experience itself nurtures freedom. The wars for independence have awoken in Spain's former vassals the "common sense which nature has implanted into everyone," and the struggle for freedom "will go on advancing towards the lights of cultivated reason."[1]

Staël was doubtful. She had been forced into exile twice, first by the Jacobins and then by Napoleon's dictatorship. "Liberty was ancient," she said; revolution made "despotism modern." If true, then history wasn't a movement toward greater freedom but toward more formidable means of social control.

A similar pessimism, already voiced by Bolívar, had spread throughout Spanish America, as the equalitarian energies of the early years of freedom faded. Throughout the region, wealthy families acted as if all independence meant was an increase in their private power, as if the new republics were but their own private haciendas. Reports from Haiti of ongoing racial violence and instability contributed to the pessimism, as did the restoration of Bourbon rule in France.

Maybe Bolívar was right. Maybe history was not the progress but rather the regress of humanity, toward savagery.

In the United States, Jackson's Indian Removal Act sparked sentimental interest among artists and scholars to capture Indian life before it was broken up and its remnants driven across the Mississippi. Some preachers and writers protested Indian removal, and the abolitionist movement grew. Yet only a few intellectuals—among them Ralph Waldo Emerson, Henry David Thoreau, Margaret Fuller, and eventually Herman Melville—grappled with what it meant to have a democratic culture underwritten by stolen Indian land and slave labor. Fuller savagely dissected the justifications of Indian removal, blaming the degradation of indigenous life completely on the "white thinker" and the "white man," whom she called a "half-tamed pirate." "A veil of subtle evasions and chicane," Fuller wrote, covers up the horrors of what "civilization" has done to Native Americans. Still, though she fully opposed removal and was alive to the hypocrisy in which public men debated the issue, Fuller feared that elimination was inevitable: Indians were, she thought, "fated to perish."[2]

But then a blast of cultural revival broke through the melancholy, not just in the United States but throughout the hemisphere. Much has been written on the "American Renaissance," by which is meant a United States Renaissance—a broad affiliation of philosophers, propagandists, writers, utopians, reformers, journalists that flowered from the 1830s and lasted until the eve of the Civil War. Emerson gave the revival its name. Who, he asked in an 1844 lecture, should lead the nation and the world in "generous sentiment"? Who should "stand for the interest of justice and humanity?" Who but the "Young Americans"? Scholars of United States history tend to discuss this Renaissance in isolation. But its span was broader, part of a larger intellectual awakening elsewhere, especially in Spanish America and Brazil, where a new generation of writers and activists, reared in liberty, were trying to figure out why history seemed to have stalled, why the potential of their freedom movements appeared wasted.[3]

There was Young America, and there was Young América.

Young America

They took Emerson's phrase as their own, but democratic bohemians tended to disdain priggish and high-minded transcendentalists, whose ethereal essays added up to one "all-embracing baccalaureate sermon." Young Americans, who preferred the bustle of New York City to meditative Concord, were earthier than the sainted New Englanders, their drive to create an organic, republican culture bound up with a rejection of aristocratic Anglophilia. Nearly all took America, by which most meant the United States, as spirit, as potential, as a nation whose destiny was yet to be manifest but would soon be.[4]

Young Americans wanted to speed up their nation's democratization of politics and culture, a forward motion propelled by extending the vote to illiterate and unpropertied white men. Conservatives worried that doing so would sharpen class conscience and add momentum to already existing labor parties, some of the world's first, which had sprung up in Eastern cities at the start of Andrew Jackson's presidency.[5]

The United States avoided this consequence largely thanks to the western frontier. The government's distribution of low-cost Western land—land that until recently had belonged to Native Americans—to settlers dispersed social tensions in the east. The frontier offered working-class migrants an alternative to taking low-wage jobs in sooty factories and paying high rent to live in crowded tenements. Many of the leaders of what became known as the Free-Soil Movement, which included the National Reform Association—founded in 1844 by George Henry Evans and other radicals—had capacious visions of reform. They were abolitionists, feminists, and socialists. Many were defenders of Indian sovereignty. "Loud applause" greeted a resolution put forward at a New York meeting by the National Reform Association declaring that Indians have rights and that their "oppression should cease." Evans condemned Indian removal. In the mid-1800s, his National Reform Association was the closest the United States had to the kind of working-class and socialist parties being organized in Europe, a "great working men's party," expressing international solidarity with all the earth's wretched, with the "chattel slaves" of Brazil and the South, Russia's serfs and Mexico's peons, the wage slaves of the United Kingdom and the United States, and the poor of India.[6]

"Free soil for all people," said reformer Van Amringe, "whether God has painted them white, red, or black."

Yet Free-Soilers saw the frontier as a great social leveler, and worked closely with Andrew Jackson's party of slavery, war, and removal: the Democratic Party, which followed its ratification of the Indian Removal Act with a series of laws allowing settlers to squat on "public" land—that is, on what had been Indian land.[7]

The promise that social conflicts could be mitigated through expansion, through free land, was too powerful a temptation to resist, leading even the most radical advocates of equality into supporting, even if only tacitly, the taking of Western lands from Native Americans and Mexicans. There was no way around the fact that when the NRA held up "free soil" as an answer to humanity's affliction, it meant Indian soil, or it meant Mexican soil.[8]

In 1836, Texas settlers broke from Mexico. In 1845, the territory was annexed by the United States to become the twenty-eighth state, a slave state. Then, the following year, President James Polk manufactured a crisis at the Mexican border as pretext to launch a war on Mexico. Fighting lasted two long years, with Mexicans putting up more effective resistance than anticipated. The United States eventually won, taking 55 percent of Mexico's territory—from Arizona's desert sands to California's Pacific beaches to Utah's winter snows—and turning some hundred thousand Mexican citizens, of all races, into United States subjects.

As with Indian removal, some intellectuals, reformers, and abolitionists did oppose Polk's war on Mexico. William Lloyd Garrison called it "atrocious," a bald-faced bid to extend and preserve slavery. Frederick Douglass and Margaret Fuller thought the same. Elizabeth Cady Stanton saw the war on Mexico as a continuation of the campaign against the Seminoles, and wrote that if women had political power such "aggressive warfare" would be a thing of the past.

Yet the romance of the frontier, of making something new in history, lent itself to eliminationism—a nearly century-long race war that the journalist John O'Sullivan, in 1845 in *The Democratic Review*, dubbed *manifest des-*

tiny. (Some scholars, though, think Jane Cazneau, a Young American even more zealous in her support for expansion than O'Sullivan, was the actual author of the unsigned article.)

George Henry Evans, thunderous from the podium when it came to defending workers' rights, was mute on Polk's trumped-up invasion. The antiracist Young American socialist Lewis Masquerier got turned around by the war, coming to support an odd formula of dispossessing the dispossessed to help the dispossessed: use the land taken from Mexico, he said, to "invite every landless American, Mexican, Indian, White, or Black Slave throughout the earth to claim his right to an equal, individual and inalienable homestead."

That didn't happen. Tens of thousands of Native Americans, maybe more, were murdered after California passed to the United States, and tens of thousands more were taken for forced labor—even though California, formally, would quickly be admitted into the union as a free state. Congress gave war veterans a 160-acre plot of bounty land for helping to defeat Mexico, a grant that, as the historian Paul Foos writes, gave a "free-soil tint to the war." The war, and the expansion it allowed, reaffirmed the promise of American newness, the promise of history as forward movement realized in the movement of settlers across the West.[9]

The United States formally ended its war on Mexico on February 2, 1848, when representatives from Washington and Mexico City signed the Treaty of Guadalupe Hidalgo. Three weeks later, workers in Paris took to the streets to stage an uprising, the first of many that would roll across the continent that spring and summer.

Everywhere in Europe—in Prague, Vienna, Munich, Berlin, Milan, Geneva, Pisa, Rome, and elsewhere—the old order seemed on the verge of collapse, and many a Young American enthusiastically supported Europe's season of revolution. Yet applied to the Western Hemisphere, this enthusiasm couldn't be disassociated from slavery and conquest. John O'Sullivan and Illinois senator Stephen Douglas visited the White House shortly after the Paris uprising and urged President Polk to redeploy U.S. troops stationed in Mexico to the Caribbean, to keep faith with 1848 by liberating Cuba from Spain. Never, Douglas said, was there a people "more unanimous in their longing for emancipation from their tyranny" than Cubans.

To keep true to the nation's revolutionary heritage was to back "full expansion north, south, west."[10]

The March of God

Westward movement kept the nation's intellectual revival at a boil, capturing the imagination of the nation's first historians. George Bancroft had returned to New England from Germany in 1822, where he took a doctoral degree from the University of Göttingen. The Germanic imprint on U.S. intellectuals and politicians like Bancroft is sometimes hard to spot, for they had a knack for transforming heavy Teutonic prose with American vim. Bancroft had attended lectures in Berlin given by Georg Wilhelm Friedrich Hegel, a philosopher associated with systematizing the idea that history was progress, that it moved forward through various definable stages each defined by dominant ideas that reflect an epoch's spirit, or the *geist*, and reveal its contradictions. Bancroft said he hadn't understood Hegel, that he found the philosopher's thick Swabian accent "sluggish." But he, along with other Young American intellectuals, intuited what Hegel was saying.[11]

Bancroft had a modern sensibility when it came to the study of history. The historian's task, Bancroft wrote in 1835, is to "write the changes in humanity" by placing "events in connection with each other" and "observing the general principles by which that succession is controlled."* To study

---

* Frederick Jackson Turner was the most influential ventriloquist of European critical theory, including the works of Hegel and Marx as well as the Italian sociologist Achille Loria and the German geographer Friedrich Ratzel. Historians and legal scholars have identified a roundabout of influence, in which German romanticism shaped the providential exceptionalism that justified U.S. westward movement and removal; and exceptionalism, in turn, informed will-to-power Nazism. Among others, James Q. Whitman in *Hitler's American Model*, Edward Westermann in *Hitler's Ostkrieg and the Indian Wars*, and Carroll Kakel in *The American West and the Nazi East*, have documented that German Nazis looked to U.S. expansion and Indian removal as precedent for their *Lebensraum* genocide. Karl Haushofer, a geography professor at Munich Polytechnic University, was a leading theorist of *Lebensraum*—technically defined as "living space," more rightly a German analogue of Turner's Frontier Theory—and the leading Nazi jurist Carl Schmitt often cited the Monroe Doctrine to legitimate Third-Reich expansionism.

facts and ideas in isolation, to segregate them from their political and social context, Bancroft wrote, borrowing from Hegel, leads the historian into "mazes of speculations" where they chase "formless shadows" and become entranced by "mystic visions." A philosophy of history was needed to escape the mazes and fill out the shadows. Everything is connected.

Hegel wasn't just popular with historians but poets as well. "Only Hegel is fit for America," Walt Whitman said, only his vision of history's sweep "is large enough and free enough." The name Young America nods to the Young Hegelians, a group of idealistic philosophers in Germany who carried on the master's work after his death, and which included, for a time, Karl Marx. Whitman welcomed Polk's invasion of Mexico in stark Hegelian terms. The United States was thesis; Mexico antithesis. The synthesis would be an expanded republic, a higher unity resulting from victory. Dilemmas and doubts—what German philosophers would call contradictions—would "resolve themselves away," Whitman wrote in 1846. "Mexico will be a severed and cut up nation," a fate its people "deserves" because the country "has been more a libel on liberty than liberty itself." "We pant to see our country and its rule far-reaching," he wrote, not merely for territorial aggrandizement but to reach the "truer good."[12]

Bancroft's 1834 *History of the United States* is saturated in Hegelian notions of progress. To fully understand a given historical period, Hegel had written, is to understand its manifest potentiality, its capacity to change, to break free of the past. That's how Bancroft describes the whole of North America prior to the arrival of Europeans—as "unproductive waste," the potential fertility of the soil untapped until the arrival of Anglo settlers. "Our land extends far into the wilderness, and beyond the wilderness," Bancroft wrote. Hegel's vision of progress, of "overcoming" the past—which many in the United States understood as "overcoming" Native Americans and Mexicans—easily mapped onto the republic's history of territorial enlargement: expansion as manifestation of a nation's will and realization of its spirit. What Hegel called the unfolding history of the "march of God in the world" was, for historians like Bancroft and propagandists like John O'Sullivan, the unfolding history of the United States.

That march was a conqueror's march, not just across the homelands of

Western Indians but of all the world's darker peoples. John O'Sullivan became a vocal supporter of the early phase of European colonialism in Africa and Asia. He was "glad" to see "our common race and blood overspread all Africa under the French flag, and all India under the British," just as the United States was to "overspread all the Western hemisphere."

Manifest Destiny, O'Sullivan said in 1855, describes not just the United States' move west but European imperialism's drive south and east.[13]

Americanos Jóvenes

Bolívar, in his last despair, didn't make it to France. But the generation that came after him did. The stultifying power of the Catholic Church still held sway in much of republican Spanish America, and intellectuals looking to breathe freer, to think with more liberty, made their way to Paris. Some of these exiles included young men who would become the continent's leading lights in literature, law, and politics. They included the Argentine Domingo Sarmiento, Juan Bautista Alberdi, and the Chilean Francisco Bilbao. They were, even before they set sail for Europe, already frenchified. Literary societies and intellectual salons, or *tertulias*, had sprung up in many cities after independence, after the Inquisition was dismantled. Members argued over books by Victor Hugo, Alexandre Dumas, Honoré de Balzac, and Jules Michelet, along with now more obscure Christian and utopian socialists.

Popular were historians who rehabilitated the French Revolution, who argued that neither terror nor, as Staël had it, modern despotism was inherent to its principles. In Argentina, the historian Esteban Echeverría founded a political society called Joven Argentina, or Young Argentina. In 1837, he published a "Socialist Dogma" that defined "Symbolic Words," a set of keywords to create a common radical vocabulary. *Progress*: "the desire to improve, to hope, and to take creative action." *Democracy*: "liberty of the individual, welfare of the people, and a government formed of popular reason." *Dogma* had no negative connotation, defined by Echeverría as: "the world marches forward; march with it to achieve the dignity of free people."[14]

We were raised waiting for the revolution, wrote the Chilean Benjamín Vicuña Mackenna. "We saw it coming," he said, referring to Europe's social revolts of 1848. When news did come that the French monarchy was no more, crowds filled the streets of Santiago singing "La Marseillaise."[15]

Francisco Bilbao was twenty-five in 1848. He had learned carpentry at a young age and committed to memory the Gospel of Saint John. Francisco could "chant" Rousseau's *Social Contract* "as if it were the Koran." Born the year Monroe issued his doctrine on hemispheric affairs, Bilbao grew up into an archetypal Spanish American romantic polymath, living close to destitution as he wrote, edited, reported, and agitated. Like Emerson, who told scandalized religious elders at Harvard Divinity School that he preferred "the Soul" to "the Church," Bilbao provoked Santiago's Catholic hierarchs by declaring his support for a radical Catholicism, one that rejected in full the authority of the family. Influenced by French Christian radicals, Bilbao early on caught how the patriarch—the *pater familias*—was the keystone of Catholic colonialism. His equation of Catholic patriarchy to chattel slavery and wives and children to slaves got him in trouble with authorities. He sought refuge in Europe.[16]

Bilbao was Bolívar purified, with all the Liberator's dictatorial, race-obsessed dross skimmed off. Like many of the radicals of his time, Bilbao was self-consciously antiracist, insisting that independence wouldn't be complete until all Spanish America's inhabitants had absolute equal rights, no matter blood lineage, skin color, or sex. Rather than fret about the dangers of *pardocracy*, as did Bolívar, Bilbao embraced the region's diversity: "*América* is destined to be the altar of human fraternity in all the varieties found in moral and natural creation, the meeting place," he wrote, "of all humankind, north, south, east and west, blacks, Indians, and whites."[17]

Bilbao was everywhere in Europe that summer of 1848, an eyewitness to revolts and counterrevolts. In the end, the revolutions failed. All were suppressed, though they did put the "social question" on the table, spurring modern labor movements, labor parties, and nationalist movements in Poland, Germany, and Italy. Bilbao eventually returned to South America where he, along with other radicals, remained committed to keeping the revolutionary flame alight.

Back in Chile, he helped found the Society of Equality, which in 1851 staged a nationwide insurrection. Leaders of the Society spent the night before the revolt reading books on the French Revolution to choose their nom de guerre. Bilbao picked Saint-Just. His colleague, Santiago Arcos, went by Marat.

That revolt was defeated, and Chilean elites remained in power. Bilbao, undeterred, fled to Lima, where he established yet another revolutionary society. Chile had abolished slavery with independence, but it still existed in Peru, and one of the goals of La Sociedad Republicana was abolition, not just of chattel slavery but debt peonage, and all the many forms of servility and unfreedom that existed in a nominally "free" Peru. Peru's young bohemians and radical artisans—some of whom had also witnessed Europe's social revolutions firsthand—were drawn to Bilbao. If France was able to "reconquer its primitive rights and overthrow crown and throne," proclaimed the cobbler Miguel Guzmán, then Peru can do the same to "the handful of men" who think that "this nation is their private property, and we their slaves." La Sociedad Republicana was broken up, yet its abolitionist energies continued, with both slavery and the hated tithe (which was still being collected from Indian communities) ending in 1854.[18]

Radicals elsewhere also pushed politics toward the insurgent. Liberals became more reformist, reformers converted into socialists, socialists turned militant. In Colombia after 1848, "communism" became a familiar term, as newspapers engaged in serious discussions of various kinds of socialism. There, a reform movement successfully pressed the government to expand the rights of citizens, end the death penalty for political crimes, and, eventually, abolish slavery. France's revolutionary hopes were likewise shared in Argentina, leading to the downfall of Argentina's dictator Juan Manuel de Rosas. Even royalist Brazil was rocked by a long uprising in the state of Pernambuco. Over three hundred soldiers were killed, along with more than five hundred insurgents. One observer blamed Brazil's "socialist ferment" on France: the fall of the French monarchy in February 1848 "shook our political world to its depths." In the years to come, governments throughout the region passed legislation that delivered basic services to poor working-class families: building schools, hospitals, and hospices; organizing fire brigades; laying sewer lines; implementing tariffs to protect artisans; raising wages; and establishing pensions and burial funds. The outlines of what would eventually be called social rights were coming into view.[19]

Progress was being made, yet for impatient intellectuals, Spanish America's promised social republic remained forever delayed, "a thing," one traveler observed, "that seems to all of them like a millennium, always at hand, but alas! never yet seen."

A Philosophy of History

As in the United States, political activism in Spanish America was accompanied by intellectual innovation, including arguments over how to draw meaning from history. There hadn't, though, been much history writing in colonial Spanish America, and rates of literacy remained low. Yet historical thinking was a part of Spanish humanism, and republican intellectuals debated the best way to approach the past.

The question of history was especially intense in Chile, with its government-subsidized penny press. Two intellectual camps raised battle flags. Young writers offered sweeping syntheses laden with moral meaning. Traditionalists wrote chronicles backed by facts. The disagreements between the two camps are uncannily familiar from the vantage of today. Restless thinkers wanted an analytical method that was useful, interpretive. They dismissed antiquarians who wasted time grubbing facts as antiques themselves. "In America we do not need mere collections of facts," wrote Domingo Sarmiento, an Argentine then living in Chile, "but the philosophical explanation of causes and effects."[20]

José Victorino Lastarria, an ally of Bilbao, composed a historiographical manifesto calling on Chileans to construct a "philosophy of history." In 1844, he told an audience of older academics at Chile's Instituto Nacional that the point of studying the past was to critique the present, to reveal the contradictions embedded in dominant ideas. Spain, Lastarria said, had reduced Chileans to "servile dependence under a tyrannical system of laws." The goal of history writing, he said, should be to show how the past continued to weigh on the present, how a feudal mentalité deformed republican rule. "The philosophy of history consists in connecting what was to what will be," said one young Argentine historian. History writing should serve as a rhetorical weapon to advance liberation.[21]

Traditional scholars scolded Lastarria and other young historians, telling them to stop trying to deduce an era's "soul" or "spirit" and stick to the facts. "Leave the reader free to draw his own conclusions," the historian Claudio Gay admonished.

Radicals didn't just focus on history writing but on the Spanish language, believing that *América* needed to break from the dictates of Spain's Royal Spanish Academy, a linguistic Vatican charged with ensuring the "propriety, elegance, and purity" of proper Spanish. These young cultural insurgents complained that universities and writers were too submissive to Academy orthodoxy, that each new republic should celebrate its vernacular and encourage a popular writing style. "There is no spontaneity," no "imagination," wrote Sarmiento.

The classically trained scholar Andrés Bello, who was born in Caracas and moved to Santiago in 1829, held the line against overly politicized, overly interpretive, and overly anti-Hispanic students. He cared little for Lastarria's "German method," describing it as convoluted "multiform historical reality." Bello, who for a short time tutored a young Simón Bolívar, defended a standardized language as necessary to create the continental identity radicals claimed they wanted. In this, Bello echoed John Adams, who believed that "Americans" should speak English: "We have not made war against the English language." Bello wondered what kind of unity would be achieved were Spanish to fragment into local vernaculars salted with Guaraní or Mapuche slang words? Guatemala alone counted over twenty Mayan languages and one hundred dialects. The continent, he said, would be turned into a Tower of Babel if radicals had their way.[22]

Traditionalists complained that Spanish America shouldn't be borrowing from foreign theories and were especially hostile to what one conservative called "that method coming from Germany, which sees in every fact the sign of an idea and in human events a continual mad development."[23] Hegel is the philosopher most famously associated with the "German method," and he had his followers in Latin America.

But a different, now obscure German scholar had a far greater influence: Karl Christian Krause. A contemporary of Hegel's, Krause was more interested in the practical implications of metaphysics, how to apply theory to law and politics. Krause's philosophy echoed, in a way, Simón Bolívar's worldview, in that both men struggled to find balance: between the greater good and individual freedom; between nationalism and internationalism; and between pragmatism and romanticism. Krause and Bolívar both hoped that history was moving toward the creation of a "single peaceful and prosperous state," in which individual rights would harmonize with the interests of society.[24]

Krause's ideas entered Spanish America via the region's exiles in Paris. Bilbao read Krause's French followers. *Krausismo* was as much a persuasion as a defined school of philosophy. In Spain, liberal followers of Krause fashioned their own style, almost a parody of constrictive conservative orthodoxy. They dressed in black, writes the historian Juan López-Morillas, and "their faces were fixed in an impassive and severe expression, they walked with a preoccupied air, cultivated taciturnity, and when they spoke did so in a quiet and slow voice, sprinkling their sentences with axioms that were often intentionally obscure." Spanish America intellectuals didn't imitate the fashion, but *Krausismo* idealism lasted into the twentieth century and shaped the disciplines of sociology, philosophy, education, and, importantly, law. Cuba's José Martí and Guatemala's Juan José Arévalo were *Krausistas*. The historian Richard Gott traces the ideological roots of the 1959 Cuban Revolution to Krause, especially to his fusion of pragmatism and romanticism. Revolutionaries valued useful knowledge. They became engineers, agronomists, economists, and physicians. And they were romantics who kept their Cervantes and Goethe close (like Ernesto Guevara, the Argentine medical doctor who joined Fidel Castro's revolution, who was famously photographed reading *Faust* in his guerrilla camp bed).[25]

Young Spanish American revolutionaries preferred Krause because they read him as being more open to the idea of free will and contingency than

Hegel, whose argumentative structures could feel suffocating—and his view of history mechanistic and ultimately reactionary. Conservative intellectuals might not have had much use for the "German method," yet they understood the value of an epochal or stagist interpretation of the past: not in the service of liberation but exculpation. Viewing historical progress as a series of inexorable stages let them relativize the atrocities of the Conquest and colonial rule as both *acceptable* (for their time) and *required* (to move history forward). "Deeds common to their era," was how one apologist of Spanish colonialism justified the violence of the Conquest.[26]

Bilbao denounced such self-forgiving "fatalism." He showed little patience for "charlatan professors of progress" who shrugged off the elimination of Native Americans and enslavement of Africans as "providential necessities." Apologists for colonial rule write as if "all the horrors of the past and present were *golpes de estado de la divinidad*," or "divine coups d'état prophesied since the beginning of eternity in God's infinite wisdom." Such was Bilbao's forceful rejection of Hegelian determinism, Calvinist-like in its belief that history was fate, unbending to will, behavior, or reason. Having witnessed the force of political reaction in both the Old and New World, Bilbao knew that neither war nor revolution inevitably advances the human cause. "Justice can be defeated," he wrote.[27]

In place of historical inevitability, Bilbao emphasized political struggle. He described postindependence Spanish American society as rent by a "dualism" between two forces in conflict: republican liberty and rationality stood against a monarchical, theocratic, patriarchal worldview.

The "old synthesis" of feudal patriarchy, the fading spirit of the colonial age, still had power and force but no longer had legitimacy. The outlines of a "new synthesis" of reason and freedom could be seen, could inspire men to act. But it was not yet realized, not yet capable of vanquishing the forces of reaction. The Catholic Church was fighting back, becoming more militant, with Santiago's Catholic priests urging the faithful to be the "vanguard" in the "fight against socialists and communists." The fight was really against broader changes in society, against secularization and liberalization. But by directing their ire at radicals, Catholic conservatives could focus their critique. Bilbao was among the first to be branded a Communist as a political insult, his enemies conjuring something that had so far been absent from Catholic theology: a pariah.[28]

Chileans too had a frontier, but not the kind whose conquest could animate the spirit of a nation on the march. Chilean elites did talk about opening the south for development and invoked the United States as a model. Wheat production, a useful marker of where Chile's frontier lay, had begun to creep below the Bíobío River. But a full-on assault couldn't be launched. The Mapuche, who held the Spanish off for centuries to retain a significant degree of autonomy, weren't fully unified but they were more united than Native Americans in the Mississippi Valley. There was nothing like the Choctaw, whom Jackson allied with to break the Creek. The Chilean state didn't have the military capacity the United States brought to bear against the Seminole in Florida. Similar to the situation in Mexico, no slaver-settler-speculator combine pushed into uncharted territory, turning indigenous land into plantations.[29]

And so, instead of putting forth a "free soil" demand—the idea that giving workers free or cheap frontier land would create "free men"—Chilean radicals instead argued for a breakup of landed estates, the haciendas, or *latifundios* that dominated the country's central plain and kept tens of thousands of peons in a state of indebted servility. "It is necessary to take land from the rich and distribute it to the poor," said one of the founders of the Society of Equality. Radical liberals and socialists wanted a restructuring of land tenure, a destruction of *latifundios,* and the creation of a republic of yeoman farmer-citizens who owned their tillage and pastures.[30]

In the United States, a faith that the frontier was limitless allowed agrarian radicalism to coexist with landed barons. Such coexistence meant that Indians had to go. In Chile, radicals believed that the prerequisite to democratization was that the landed barons had to go. The nation would be realized not by race war but by class war: the enemy blocking progress was the "*casta de los ricos.*"[31]

The historian Frederick Jackson Turner would famously identify the United States' frontier as an incubator of political equality, as the place where the promise of the nation was made manifest. Few Spanish American intellectuals, of any period in any country, would make a similar argument. They viewed their frontiers as historic theaters of terror and domination.*

Lastarria, in his 1844 manifesto, said that the source of all of Chile's national pathologies—fanaticism, intolerance, dissimulation, and fear—could be traced to the war of conquest the Spanish waged against the Mapuche. Rather than forcing Indians to recede so that the nation could proceed, Lastarria said that the historic struggle of the Mapuche for dignity and autonomy against the Spanish was the essence, the spirit, of the true Chilean nation, the yet-to-be-realized social republic. Later in the century, the Brazilian geographer Euclides da Cunha, a contemporary and admirer of Turner's, described those who settled the interior of Brazil, especially the Amazon, as the nation's wretched, driven out of their parched, drought-stricken homelands to look for a new place to live. They were "terrifying starvelings, burning with fevers and pox," and their flight into the interior was no march of God. Da Cunha described it as "disordered flight . . . All the weak, the used up, the worn-out, the sick and suffering were sent off willy-nilly to that wilderness."

Their "painful mission" wasn't to make manifest the destiny of the nation. Rather, it was to go away, "to disappear."[32]

---

* Later in the 1800s, a new generation of authoritarians across the hemisphere would dispossess Native Americans of their land and force them into the labor market, thinking that the suppression of indigenous culture was required to create a modern state. Even then, racial frontier violence was never as central a component of national identity for Spanish America and Brazil as it was for the United States.

24.

Two Americas

As the sectional crisis over slavery in the United States worsened, as slavers dug in and abolitionists gained ground, the United States flung itself further across the hemisphere: west now that California was secured, but also south over Central America and around the Cape of Good Hope, to get to California. Southerners, who dominated the Democratic Party and stood "at the helm" of the federal foreign policy apparatus, continued to push outward. They looked for new lands in which to expand slavery and they defended slavery in the few countries where the institution still existed, like Brazil.[1]

Southerners and Democrats said they were advocates of limited government, at least when it came to ensuring that the executive branch was disempowered from acting on abolition. Yet in the decades prior to the Civil War, they turned the executive branch into a powerful engine of outward movement; capable of expelling Native Americans from their homes, fighting pacifying campaigns when Indians resisted, waging war on Mexico, and defending settlers.

They built Manifest Destiny's infrastructure: its presidios, roads, bridges, railroads, telegraph posts and lines, and canals. By 1838, Congress had doubled the size of the Army Corps of Engineers, which dredged and widened rivers, built dams (which often flooded indigenous land), removed sandbars, tamed the Mississippi, and laid a road from Maryland across Appalachia to Illinois, among other public works. They finished building the United States Naval Observatory, among the world's most technologically advanced "lighthouses in the sky," whose construction began during the administration of John Quincy Adams.

There existed a minority of politicians and intellectuals grouped around the remnants of Northern Whigs, Free-Soilers, and abolitionists who would go on to create the Republican Party in 1854. They advocated for limits. Illinois congressman Abraham Lincoln, who opposed the war on Mexico, called for a modest foreign policy. Restraint, he said, was the intent of the founders. The dominant Democratic Party, though, was full-on and full-ahead for empire, ridiculing anti-expansionists as "do-nothings" and "stay-at-homes."[2]

Most wanted to do something, expecting the United States, having filled out its Western territories, to turn its attentions to the Caribbean, Central America, and Asia. Into the wilderness, and beyond the wilderness, as Bancroft put it.

No land taken from Mexico became a state before the outbreak of the Civil War, except for Texas, which joined the union as a slave state in 1848, and California, which entered as a free state two years later. Oregon, not part of the Mexican land grab, became the thirty-third state in 1859, a free state, but with some of the most venomous race laws on the books. A congressional "compromise" in 1850 strengthened fugitive slave laws, mandating Northern states to return refugees. Yet slavers, able only to develop slavery in Texas, felt besieged. They pushed their "proslavery imperialism" that much more. The "slaveholders' Monroe Doctrine" was how one nineteenth-century historian described Southern-driven expansion.[3]

Southern politicians coveted Nicaragua and Panama as stagecoach and possibly railroad and canal routes. The islands off Peru and Ecuador, including the Galapagos, were a source of guano to fertilize sugar and cotton lands, both for the exhausted soil in the Old South and the new plantations being opened in Alabama, Louisiana, and Texas. Visionaries looked beyond Central America to the Amazon Valley as a place where chattel slavery might be established. Matthew Fontaine Maury, an oceanographer, mapmaker, and a U.S. (and later Confederate) naval officer, used his observations of wind and current to make the case that the U.S. could claim the Amazon as "a continuation of the Mississippi valley."

Expansionists had Puerto Rico, Haiti, and the Dominican Republic in their sights. Some thought the Yucatán might be added to the Union as well. As always, they wanted Cuba. For many reasons. Seizing Cuba would hold true to Monroe, since they would be limiting the influence of always-meddling London in the New World. Northern merchants were heavily invested in trade with the island. By the middle of the nineteenth century, around thirteen million dollars' worth of Cuban imports, mostly sugar, entered the United States every year. Some Southerners wanted the islands to expand slavery. Others hoped to defuse the escalating crisis over slavery by turning Cuba into a place they could ship their free people of color, which, some said, would lessen racial tension.[4]

Even better, thought *The New York Times*, a war with Spain over the island would distract from the crisis at home. "Why not," the paper asked, referring to the possible acquisition of Cuba, "give the public something else to talk and think about" besides "the everlasting Slavery question?"[5]

Texas All Over Again

In 1854, the USS *Cyane* burned Greytown, a dusty community on Nicaragua's Atlantic coast, to the ground. The pretext for the assault was to assist a white U.S. citizen threatened with arrest by local authorities for the murder of a Black man. The backstory was that Cornelius Vanderbilt wanted to gain monopoly control for his steamboat and stagecoach business, which was conveying travelers rushing across Nicaragua for California gold. The *New York Tribune* reported that Vanderbilt had "long desired to get rid" of Greytown, which served as a base of operations for British rivals. Got rid of the town was. President Franklin Pierce defended the ruin: Greytown was "a pretended community," Pierce said, a recently created boomtown made up of "a heterogeneous assemblage gathered from various countries," comprised mostly of "blacks and persons of mixed blood." Greytown, the president said, could expect nothing other than to be treated as a "piratical resort of outlaws or a camp of savages." Washington was also competing with Great Britain for a canal through Nicaragua, and the obliteration of Greytown was a dramatic pushback against London's Central American ambitions.[6]

A year later, in 1855, William Walker sailed out of San Francisco with a detachment of fifty-five soldiers, whom he called La Falange Americana, toward Nicaragua. A Tennessee mercenary who earlier had tried and failed to seize territory from Mexico, Walker was backed by both Southern slavers and Northern investors, including Vanderbilt, who hoped to build on the destruction of Greytown by installing a proxy to rule on his behalf in Nicaragua. Spanish Americans across the hemisphere were horrified when Walker, after a five-month war, grabbed power and proclaimed himself Nicaragua's president. Even more so when he reestablished slavery, in a country that had abolished the institution three decades earlier.

Walker was popular in all the United States, one of those Sons of 1848 mercenaries said to be carrying the light of liberty to "darkling" lands. *Nicaragua*, a play celebrating Walker's conquests, opened at Manhattan's Purdy's National Theatre, near the Bowery. The San Francisco Minstrel Company also put on a show about Walker. Migrants from the United States flocked to Nicaragua to settle, as if it were now the frontier. Walker offered them hundreds of acres of land and Vanderbilt sold them discount tickets on his steamers. President Franklin Pierce quickly recognized Walker's government.

A nation of "ingenious rogues," Lord Palmerston, referencing Walker, called the United States. Nicaragua was "Texas all over again," Palmerston said, referring to the settler takeover of a large part of Mexico. Central Americans, he said, should dispatch Walker and his followers "with Bullets through their Heads."[7]

Meanwhile, United States gunboats were sailing further in Latin American waters than ever: down the Atlantic; up the Amazon and Paraná rivers;

along the coast of Argentina into the Pacific to Chile and Peru. In February 1855, Paraguayan soldiers fired on the USS *Water Witch*, killing its helmsman. The U.S. Senate was already annoyed with Paraguay for drawing up a commercial treaty that had contained the phrase the *United States of North America*. And so, in response to the attack and to satisfy congressional demands that Latin American nations refer to the U.S. by its proper name, President James Buchanan dispatched a fleet of nineteen ships carrying twenty-five hundred men and two hundred guns to deliver a revised treaty, with the word *North* struck out. Such a show of force left Paraguay little option but to sign the treaty, which opened the nation's waters and markets to the United States.[8]

Securing economic interests was important to Buchanan, but his aggressive foreign policy also helped with domestic polarization. Any war, wrote *Harper's Weekly*, would "under almost any circumstances, be popular with the masses of this country." Punishing Paraguay would have the "singular advantage of diverting attention from the slavery controversy." "War," wrote *The (London) Daily News* of the incident, "is so obvious a means of distracting a nation from its own internal affairs."

Archimedes's Fulcrum

The light of 1848 had dimmed, and radicals in Spanish America gave way to top-down strongmen, national consolidators who may have called themselves liberal but weren't much concerned with liberty. Instead, they established order and built secure states to preside over an export-driven economy, with California, New Orleans, Philadelphia, New York, Liverpool, Manchester, and Hamburg importing the region's coffee, beef, hides, rubber, copper, hemp, sugar, cotton, and other commodities.

Radicals still pushed for domestic reform, yet their priority shifted to counter the growing threat of the United States. The foreign ministers of Mexico and Colombia had already, before Walker's invasion of Nicaragua, organized several international conferences in the hopes of checking

Washington. David Starkweather, consul to Chile, reported a rising fear among Chile's leaders of "imminent annexation" by the United States. Walker's seizure of Nicaragua prompted Peru, Chile, and Ecuador to sign, in 1856, a "continental Treaty," pledging mutual defense against Washington's aggression.[9]

The Democratic Party controlled foreign policy, and their diplomats to Latin America mocked these meetings in terms not unlike those that three decades earlier mocked Bolívar's Panama Congress. The idea, put forward by the region's statesmen, of convening an assembly of "all the American States of Spanish origins from Mexico to Chile," wrote U.S. ambassador to Colombia James Bowlin, is a "ridiculous farce." Bowlin dismissed the "mad pranks, and silly nonsense of pretended Statesmen." "Perched up here amidst the peaks of the Andes, with a limited communication with the world," the ideas of Colombian statesmen were as "rarified as their atmosphere."[10]

The Chilean Bilbao, still active in continental politics and Spanish America's most elegant spokesperson, devoted the last decade of his life to the fight against United States imperialism. "They would concentrate the universe in themselves," he complained in the wake of Walker's invasion of Nicaragua, referring to U.S. politicians and intellectuals who cheered the invader's exploits. Bilbao lamented a lost promise: the birth of the United States had "caused rejoicing on the part of sorrowing humanity . . . and provided a field of utopia." But now, the "Yankee has replaced the American; Roman patriotism has displaced philosophy"; and "self-interest has supplanted justice."

Paris, for radicals, was still a refuge. There on June 22, 1856, at a gathering of Spanish American exiles, Bilbao gave a speech proposing to hold a congress to finish what Bolívar had started, to create a Latin American confederacy. "We need to unify the soul of América," Bilbao said. If not, no resistance to Washington would be effective. "Look," he said, "you can see the smoke from the campfires getting closer. Listen, the soldiers' footsteps are ever nearer."

Panama, then a province of Colombia, was strategically important as the potential site of a interoceanic canal or railroad. Bilbao called it "the fulcrum that the Yankee Archimedes is using to lift South America and suspend it over the abyss," so to "devour the continent in pieces." Bilbao assumed that Walker was the advance guard toward taking all Central America. And once that happened, nothing would be able to "contain the rush of Saxons."

"Walker is the invasion. Walker is the Conquest. Walker is the United States," he said.[11]

Central Americans did finally unite to drive out Walker in 1860, with soldiers doing what Lord Palmerston suggested. They put a bullet through his head on a Honduran beach. A year later, Spain, taking advantage of the distraction caused by the outbreak of the United States' Civil War, sent thousands of troops into the Dominican Republic. France also made a move in 1861, sending troops to invade and occupy Mexico. Paris was acting in response to Mexico City's announcement that it considered a portion of its foreign debt illegitimate. "Europe can't even civilize itself and yet it would civilize us," wrote Bilbao of these interventions.

Mexican liberals launched a guerrilla war that ended France's occupation, and Dominican insurgents defeated Madrid's occupying army. Still, Walker in Nicaragua, Spain in the Dominican Republic, France in Mexico, and an endless parade of plots and plans to take this or that piece of territory: Spanish Americans at midcentury, especially the first generation to grow up republican, were vulnerable.

And then they still had the United States to deal with.

Becoming Latin America

Variations of the term *Latin America* had probably been floating around in conversation in Spanish America and Paris before Walker's invasion. Yet the phrase wasn't captured in print, as far as historians know, until February 1856, when a Costa Rican newspaper warned that Walker threatened the whole of the "Latin-American race." Bilbao then used the phrase *América Latina* in his Paris remarks condemning Walker. It was common at the time to classify the world's peoples by grand, ineffable, and romantic associations: Asians, Slavs, and Saxons. Bilbao was influenced by his French Catholic socialist mentor, Félicité Robert de La Mennais, who, along with others, looked to *latinize* the fragments of Catholic empires that shared a Romance language. The point was to protest the conceit of English-speaking intellectuals that Protestant Great Britain stood at the apex of civilization.[12]

Yet it wasn't until Walker's conquest of Nicaragua, and U.S. recognition of the conquest as legal, that the term *América Latina* took hold. Throughout Spanish America and Brazil, there was a growing sense—after Texas, after Mexico, and especially after Walker—that the United States was driven by, as the Brazilian diplomat Felipe José Pereira Leal put it, the "dizzying spirit of conquest."[13]

The descriptor *Latina* had the advantage of appealing to various constituencies. To use a Bilbaoian idea, *América Latina* was a "new synthesis," one that spoke not just to liberals and radicals opposed to Anglo supremacy but conservatives as well. Elites in Spanish America and even Brazil, with their Parisian tastes, were fine calling themselves *Latin*. Those obsessed with racial and cultural degeneration, now that they no longer had Spain or Portugal to issue chits proving the purity of their bloodline, might hide behind the idea that they were Latin to distinguish themselves from, as an adopter of the term put it, "apaches, comanches or lipanes." The Argentine jurist Juan Bautista Alberdi understood *Latin* and *Saxon* not in opposition but in unity: "Everyone who is not *Latin* or *Saxon*, that is, *European*, is a barbarian." Many, though, used *América Latina* to set themselves off from Saxon America, to promote an inclusive, egalitarian republicanism that could encompass the broadest humanity possible.[14]

Poetry and diplomacy joined hands. Bards and statesmen, in an unending production of literary magazines and international conferences, seized on *la latinidad* in its many forms: *latinoamericanos* to refer to the region's inhabitants; *países latinoamericanos* or *pueblos hermanos latinoamericanos* to describe the collection of republics that made up a shared region; and *la raza de la América Latina* to invoke not a specific race but rather the spirit of a common community. "The New World will be the synthesis of all the old worlds that came before," Bilbao wrote, "the meeting place of all the elements of humanity, north and south, east and west, the Black, the Indian, the White."[15]

In 1857, Colombian poet José María Torres Caicedo published a long poem, set not only in the shadow of Walker in Nicaragua but of Bleeding Kansas—the violence in Western territories between slavers and abolitionists that previewed the coming Civil War, that conveyed a sense that the fight over slavery was going to destroy republicanism in the United States. The "Union," Torres wrote, is "mined" and ready to explode. As to Spanish Americans, they were a "people born to ally:"

> *La raza de la América latina*
> *Al frente tiene la sajona raza*
> *Enemiga mortal que ya amenaza*
> *Su libertad destruir y su pendón.*

> (The Latin American race
> Confronts the Saxon race
> Deadly enemy that now threatens
> To destroy Liberty and its banner.)

Torres continued:

> America of the South is called
> To defend the true liberty,
> The new idea, the divine morality,
> The holy law of love and charity.
> The world lies prostrate in deep darkness
> In Europe, despotism dominates
> In America of the North, selfishness,
> Thirst for gold, and hypocritical piety.

Torres was among the first to write of "two Americas"—Latin and Saxon—defined in opposition.[16]

As Anglo-Saxons calibrated their own superiority against Spanish-American *mongrels* and *zambos*, and as Washington rehabilitated the doctrine of conquest to justify its dispossession of both Native Americans and

Mexicans in North America—not to mention Nicaraguans in Central America—*Latin America* had to stand for, if it were to stand for anything, the opposite of what the United States stood for. *Peace* rather than *war*. *Co-operation* and not *conquest*. The *American* versus the *Yankee*.[17]

Latin Americans love "everything that unites," Bilbao wrote, "we prefer the social over the individual, beauty over wealth, justice over power, art over calculations, duty over interest." Over the years, what has often been taken for "anti-Americanism" in Latin America is better thought of as a competing version of Americanism.[18]

By the time Bilbao died of tuberculosis in Buenos Aires in 1865, the term *Latin America* was in wide circulation.

Spanish Americans are often assigned responsibility for this New World split, for their embrace of *Latin* in opposition to *Saxon* America. Yet decades before the adoption of *Latin America* in the 1850s, it was the Jacksonian backlash against Bolívar's Panama Congress that charged the term *South America* with racial current, that contemptuously stressed the *South* in *South America*.

Webster's 1828 *American Dictionary* defined *America* as divided by *North* and *South* at Darién, or Panama, but still as comprising a single continent. An *American* was "a native of America; originally applied to the aboriginals, or copper-colored races, found here by the Europeans; but now applied to the descendants of Europeans born in America." Two years later, *Webster's* dropped the reference to Panama from its definition and simply described America as "one of the great continents," still implying a unified geographical area. Yet from this point forward, the growing list of entries defining variations of *America* (*Americanism*, *Americanize*, for example) suggests an evolution, from *America* referring to the entire New World to *America* referring to one nation in particular.

A-MER/I-CAN-ISM, *n*. An American idiom;
the love which American citizens have for their own
country.

A-MER/I-CAN-IZE, *v.t.* To render American; to naturalize in America.

Webster, cited here in 1842, isn't referring to naturalizing in just any of the many American nations but the United States specifically. Then, in 1847, the dictionary added to its definition of *American* the clause: "especially to inhabitants of the United States."[19]

25.

Lincoln Belongs to Us

Even before Abraham Lincoln's election in 1860, some of his supporters in the Republican Party had begun to cast about for a place they might deport free people of color and emancipated slaves in the hope of avoiding a civil war. Maybe Venezuela. Or off the coast of Haiti, on Île-à-Vache, Cow Island. Panama was a possibility, where those transferred could provide the labor to build a railroad across the isthmus.

The Blair family of Missouri—father Francis and sons, Frank and Montgomery—were influential promoters of what was called colonization, the idea that the United States, by purging itself of its African American population, would not only remain united but as a purified white nation would grow even more prosperous, even stronger. The Blairs owned slaves. Yet unlike the planters who had dug themselves in throughout the Missouri River Valley, they were opposed to spreading slavery west. Montgomery fought in the Seminole War in Florida. Frank served in the war on Mexico and fought against Indians with what he called the "Rangers of the Rocky Mountains." The Blair family saw its state as a gateway to the West, and wanted a Free-Soil, freemen, and free-labor frontier, a place where servility would end and political equality, for white mechanics, craftsmen, and farmers, would deepen.[1]

Frank Blair gave a speech in early 1859 to Boston's Mercantile Library

Association, titled "The Destiny of the Races of This Continent." At once sweeping and desperate, Frank put forward a bold vision of an impossible future, offered as a way to avoid the coming war over slavery. The Missourian called for the establishment of continental apartheid, insisting that white man's equality *required* racial segregation.

Blair was a "scientific" racist who believed that the Atlantic slave trade had disrupted a natural evolutionary sorting, in which Blacks gathered in sweltering Africa and Anglos thrived in pleasant climes. Native Americans didn't figure much in his vision, having been, as Blair said, neutralized, killed, or pushed beyond the frontier. The two real, vital races left in the United States were Anglo-Saxons and Africans, and if they continued to occupy the same territory, all future generations would be admixtures of the two. Except, Blair warned, the result wouldn't be *mestizaje*, a blending of both races. Rather, one racial type would inevitably come to dominate the other. North America would either become essentially African or Anglo-Saxon. Different races "repel each other," similar to, Blair said, using a metaphor drawn from the study of electricity and magnetism, "two positive poles." Look at Spanish America, he said, where the once "proud" Spanish succumb to the "Negro," which is "now fast racing to become the ruling race in those regions."

There was a solution, he said. Send the Blacks to the tropics and give the "temperate regions of this hemisphere" to the whites. Blair cooed the word *temperate* so often, and repeated the word *tropic* with such irritation, he seemed a man plagued by a nettle rash no balm could soothe. "A separation of the races is the only perfect preventive," Blair said. "Nothing can save us from pollution but a complete separation." Such a vast demographic rearrangement would begin to dissolve the institution of slavery in the United States. Only when North America was purged of African-descended peoples could Anglos complete "the conquering march" of Western expansion.

The "Anglo-Saxon race" was ready to "leap through space" with the "all-pervading power of electricity and steam" and create new states in the Mountain West's mild climate, where grass turned to hay naturally, unlike in the tropics, where it rotted into disease- and death-dealing miasmas. "I have trod much of this vast scene," Blair said, striking a Whitmanesque note. Meandering rivers, forest shade, luxuriant pastures, and rich minerals jutting out of mountain crests filled Blair's arcadia. It would soon teem with "busy people," with white people. The war with Mexico redeemed California from the Spanish, he said, who were too indolent to notice the gold glistening in its sand.

The transfer of millions of emancipated slaves to South America would be an enormous endeavor, Blair admitted. Yet wasn't the great movement of people that inaugurated the modern world—the arrival of Europeans to America, followed by the enslavement of Africans and removal of Native Americans—an equally mammoth undertaking? The benefits of such a removal would be incalculable. Slavery would collapse. War would be averted. White wage workers would fill the South, and the West would become the motor of national energy, with a continental railroad offering Europeans a faster way to get to the Asian market than London's proposed canal through the Suez. Rendered white and free, the United States would become the New World's "overshadowing power," with the "Indian" and "African" republics of Spanish America turned into informal "dependencies."

Blair was proposing an alternative to what the British were putting into place in South Asia, where after the 1857 "Mutiny"—a massive uprising against incipient British colonialism in India—London consolidated its imperial rule, with Queen Victoria eventually taking the title Empress of India. Blair hoped the United States could maintain a more informal sphere of hemispheric influence. Spanish America, he said, would "become our India." Yet Washington would be unburdened by the demands of direct colonialization. Latin Americans will be "with us, though not of us."[2]

Freemen I Suppose

On August 14, 1862, one year into the Civil War, Abraham Lincoln received a deputation of free Black leaders at the White House, where he suggested Central America as a place they might go. Lincoln was committed to finding some spot, preferably not too far away, where the nation's emancipated could live in peace. Upon taking office, Lincoln asked Secretary of

State William Seward and Montgomery Blair to sound out the governments of Mexico and Central America to see if any might be amenable to taking in the United States' population of African Americans. Lincoln also named Reverend James Mitchell, who headed Indiana's American Colonization Society, to run the federal Office of Emigration, which oversaw various schemes to encourage the self-deportation of free people of color.[3]

"You here are freemen I suppose," Lincoln greeted the delegation. "Yes sir," a voice from the crowd answered. Lincoln then recited the many reasons the "two races on this continent" could not live together. "It is better for us both," he said, "to be separated."

The president admitted that Liberia, established in western Africa decades earlier to promote the migration of free people of color, was too far away. Free people "would rather remain within reach of the country" of their "nativity," he said. For that reason, Lincoln suggested Panama, and specifically Chiriquí province (then being considered as a canal route to connect the Atlantic to the Pacific). Lincoln made it clear to the deputation that the people they represented were not welcome. The Union was fighting a bloody war for their freedom, the president said, even though "many men on both sides do not care for you one way or the other."[4]

Bolívar and Bilbao hoped Panama might become the center of world republicanism. Lincoln, Blair, and others thought to turn it into a repository of the world's castoffs. "Nearer to us than Liberia," Lincoln told the delegates.

A month later, on September 22, 1862, Lincoln made public his Emancipation Proclamation, which he wouldn't formally decree until New Year's Day. On September 24, he called a special meeting of his cabinet to discuss that status of treaties with foreign governments to promote the "colonization of blacks." Salmon Chase, in charge of Treasury, didn't think much of the idea. Black labor, he wrote in his diary, was needed within the country. In this, Chase was representing a common opinion among Republicans regarding the value of the labor of emancipated peoples: it was needed during the war and would be needed after war's end. Chase also made a more subtle point, about how such removal schemes allowed for moral evasion. Rather than look for empty space to deposit people of color, "how much better would be a manly protest against prejudice," how preferable it would be to give "Freemen homes in America!"

He did think Lincoln's Panama plan might help the United States gain a "foothold" in Central America. The White House went ahead with the idea, authorizing Kansas senator Samuel Pomeroy to travel to Chiriquí with "500 able-bodied negroes" as "pioneers to smooth the way of others"—and to establish a settlement called Lincolnia.[5]

The nascent colony was scuttled when abolitionist leaders, Black and white, objected. Lincoln's enthusiasm for colonization displayed all his "inconsistencies," said Frederick Douglass, "his pride of race and blood, his contempt for Negroes and his canting hypocrisy." "Puerile, absurd, illogical, impertinent, and untimely," declared the abolitionist William Lloyd Garrison. Having just defeated William Walker, Honduras, Nicaragua, and Costa Rica also opposed the plan. The United States would have to solve its slavery problem without the help of Central America.

Lincoln, though, persisted in hoping colonization might become a key element of postwar reconstruction and reconciliation, freeing up funds to send nearly five thousand escaped slaves seeking refuge in Virginia's Fort Monroe to Île-à-Vache, a rainforest island twelve miles off Haiti's southern peninsula that served as a haven for privateers. The idea was to create a large cotton plantation. On June 1, 1863, nearly five hundred Fort Monroe refugees were dumped on the island, without housing, what money they had confiscated by Bernard Kock, the merchant overseeing the venture. The castaways had nothing to eat but moldy corn and salted pork, and within a short time about half the colonists had died and seventy fled. The survivors wasted away on the island for over a year, even as the merchants in charge of the venture grew rich off public funds and stripped Haiti of mahogany. The White House didn't know what to do. "For God's sake, don't bring those people back to the United States," said Secretary of State Seward. Finally, on Lincoln's orders, the merchant ship *Marcia C. Day* transported the survivors to northern Virginia in March 1864, where they were resettled in the newly created Freedman's Village, founded on Robert E. Lee's Arlington estate.[6]

Lincoln gave up promoting large-scale removal after the fiasco at Île-à-

Vache. Following his assassination, however, the Blairs once again began pushing his successor, Andrew Johnson, to deport emancipated peoples. Establishing a colony somewhere in Spanish America for freemen, the Blairs said, would be better than letting them vote. Johnson faced "strong pressure" from Southerners, said Charles Sumner a few months after Lincoln's death, "to enforce the Monroe Doctrine as a safety-valve now, and to divert attention from domestic questions."[7]

Forward, Lincoln, Forward!

Frank Blair's proposal was crude and clear-cut. Blacks go there, whites stay here. His call to create an Anglo-Saxon-superintended world foreshadowed later international relations theory and grand-strategy thinking. Blair's intellectual successors, such as Alfred Thayer Mahan and Brooks Adams, made big balance-of-power arguments that explicitly divided the world by race. How best to keep Japan down? Who should get what of China? And they also had more intimate concerns, of the kind that obsessed the early Jacksonians when Bolívar invited the United States to his Panama Congress: miscegenation, biological degeneration, and making sure enough white women went to the tropics to serve as wives and mothers for white administrators.

The color-coded grand strategies that charted the rise of the United States as a world power should be read alongside later essays by Cuban independence leader José Martí, especially *Nuestra América* (*Our America*) and "Mi Raza" (My Race), published respectively in 1891 and 1893. Martí would continue Bilbao's purge of racism from Bolivarianism. Gone, in Martí's imagination, is *race* as a historical burden that must be overcome. Martí saw the New World's diversity as a wellspring of spiritual and material strength.

"Man is more than White, more than Mulatto, more than Black," Martí said, updating Las Casas's universal humanism for a republican world, "everything that divides men, everything that specifies, sets them apart, or corners them, is a sin against humanity."[8]

Washington after the Civil War treated not just Panama but the entire continent as its fulcrum, lifting the United States to unprecedented heights of power. By the 1870s, it had pacified the "Lords of the Southern Plains," the powerful Comanche nation, and within but a few more decades would win the West. The nation doubled its production of wheat and corn, and increased the extraction of coal eightfold. The United States indeed had leapt through space with the pervading power of electricity and steam, quintupling the amount of existing railroad track since the end of the Civil War. Steel mills were, within a few decades, rolling out nearly eleven million tons of castings and ingots. Three million barrels of crude oil pumped in 1865 grew to more than fifty-five million in 1898.[9]

Northern intellectuals and Washington officials in the years after the Civil War tended to imagine Latin America as a vast extension of the United States' South, undeveloped, manorial, feudal, and servile. When nationalists from the region criticized the United States, U.S. diplomats tended to dismiss critics as antimodern, Hidalgos who refused to keep stride with the modern world.

It is true that many Latin American radicals and reformers were steeped in romanticism. Yet it was not the romance of Confederate cavaliers. Latin American nationalists had little but contempt for ex-Confederates who, in their efforts to rehabilitate the South, cultivated a "moonlight and magnolia" myth of a cultured and genteel land overrun by industrializers and money-grubbers. Grown fat and rich off inhumane bondage, they now claimed they were defending the old ways, a noble world against a "commercial, industrial, plebeian" North, with its machines, soot, and mass migration.[10]

Most Latin American critics were hell-bent on overcoming the old ways, committed to liquidating their region's seignorial past. Their romance was of what could be, not what was. They wished their countries could roll out so much steel.

Spanish American intellectuals and activists appreciated those in the United States they thought represented an authentic Americanism. Lincoln was cheered, his death mourned, and his martyrdom eulogized across the political spectrum. The experiences of two Cubans who fought in the Union

Army and were present when Lincoln gave his Gettysburg Address were shared across the island. *Avance, Lincoln, Avance* was a refrain heard among sugar workers in the island's cane fields. Later, a 1952 Cuban history textbook reported that images of Lincoln hung both in poor huts and wealthy manses, representing "the deepest Cuban aspirations." "Lincoln belongs to us," Fidel Castro would say.

Abolitionists in the United States were hailed in Latin America. Enriqueta Beecher Stowe's famous novel *La Cabaña del Tío Tomás* was published widely and repeatedly in Spanish- and Portuguese-speaking America.

With Protestantism finally experiencing a moral reckoning over slavery equivalent to the one Catholicism had centuries earlier over the Conquest, historians drew lines connecting the "abolitionist" Bartolomé de las Casas to the "abolitionist" Abraham Lincoln. Lincoln embodied the "spirit of Christ," Martí wrote. John Brown was celebrated. Translations of Victor Hugo's passionate defense of Brown's attempted uprising, which included Hugo's sketch of Brown's Crucifixion-like hanging, circulated widely. "For Christ and like Christ," Hugo had written underneath his drawing in Latin. Brown was to Lincoln, one Venezuelan wrote, what Miranda was to Bolívar: a precursor of emancipation.[11]

Heir to the World

The Democratic Party had been the main agent of expansion prior to the Civil War. The Republican Party became so after Appomattox. Republican ambassadors were, at first, a welcome relief after the Jacksonian era's slaver-envoys, raising the hope that the United States would stand with Latin America. Yet as the United States resumed intervening in the affairs of other nations, and Republican administrations took up the task of completing the conquest of the West, the goodwill faded.

As it did, Latin American intellectuals stepped up their criticism. The Civil War matured Walt Whitman, who had abandoned his youthful imperialism. Modernist intellectuals like Martí ignored his early writings and now invoked the poet to fight back, rhetorically, against conquering Saxonism.* Martí attended one of Whitman's last public appearances in New York in 1887 and lauded the aging poet's ability to join "reason to grace." Martí pronounced him an "heir to the world" who represented an alternative to the South's romance of racism and the North's grasping materialism. Whitman's promiscuous use of Spanish words such as *libertad, americanos,* and *camarada,* Martí felt, suggested an inclusive and diverse Americanism. "His soul seems a mirror of the infinite," wrote the Nicaraguan Rubén Darío, considered the founder of Latin American literary modernism. He is old and tired. His brow is furrowed. But he "sings his song like a new prophet" of "a better day to come."[12]

Whitman's Spanish notwithstanding, most writers in Latin America remained wary of the United States. Critics rarely defined themselves as "anti-American." They tended to use the terms "anti-interventionist," "anti-Yankee," and, increasingly after 1898, "anti-imperialist." Literary nationalists from every Latin American country produced an impassioned, lyrical body of work that censured Washington for not matching its actions to its ideals. Their names now are barely remembered in their own countries, but writers such as Brazil's Eduardo Prado, Mexico's Isidro Fabela, Venezuela's Rufino Blanco-Fombona, Bolivia's Franz Tamayo, Cuba's José María Céspedes, Guatemala's Máximo Soto Hall, and Colombia's José María Vargas Vila contrasted what they imagined to be the utilitarian, alienated, sterile, cunning, instrumental United States, driven by brute political and eco-

---

* In July 1883, from Camden, New Jersey, a sixty-four-year-old Walt Whitman used the 333rd anniversary of the founding of Santa Fe, New Mexico, to write a love letter to Latin America. "We Americans," he said, "have yet to really learn our own antecedents, and sort them, to unify them"—antecedents that, according to Whitman, were not to be found just in Europe but within America, especially within what he called the "Spanish element in our nationality." He dismissed the Black Legend as a child's tale told by New England schoolmasters. ("It is time to realize—for it is certainly true—that there will not be found any more cruelty, tyranny, superstition, &c., in the résumé of past Spanish history than in the corresponding résumé of Anglo-Norman history. Nay, I think there will not be found so much.") The poet who decades earlier urged the United States to take Mexico now suggested that in the face of the "seething materialistic and business" growth of the United States, with capitalist rapacity "controlling and belittling" everything that stands in its way, Spanish America was necessary to help socialize and humanize the United States with values other than conquest.

nomic power, with the more authentic, humanist, aesthetic, and spiritual republics of Latin America.[13]

In 1900, Uruguay's José Enrique Rodó published *Ariel*, a book described as the "spiritual breviary" of Latin America's romantic youth. Rodó cast Latin America as the sublime Ariel and the United States as the grubbing Caliban, fated to destroy Latin America if not contained.[14] At the same time, mass political opposition to U.S. expansion was beginning to take shape with the organization of socialist parties, anarchist movements (especially in Argentina), and militant labor movements. The radical leaders and intellectuals of these movements continued to draw on allegorical representations of Washington's ambitions, while paying increased attention to the economic dimensions of U.S. expansion. "Modern conquests," the Argentine Manuel Ugarte wrote, are "subterranean," carried out through financial manipulation. In the late 1800s, corporations and banks steadily replaced gunboats as the main agent and symbol of United States power, though Marines and private companies continued to fight their "banana wars" throughout the Caribbean and Central America. The United Fruit Company regularly overthrew governments in Guatemala and Honduras, and its chief shareholder, Samuel Zemurray, said that in Central America, he could buy a congressional deputy cheaper than he could a mule. A president or high judge might cost the price of a good gelding.[15]

Latin American novelists began to take on the indignities of everyday life under the growing influence of United States corporations as experienced in mining or agricultural company towns, or in cities where electricity, transportation, and finance were monopolized from abroad. In Chile in 1904, Baldomero Lillo, the son of a mine foreman, published a volume of short stories that captured proletarian miseries, including abuses at the hands of one "Mister Davis," the first of many unsympathetic "misters" who would populate twentieth-century social and magical realist prose. In his 1929 novel *Doña Bárbara*, Rómulo Gallegos introduces readers to "Mister Danger," a blue-eyed, pink-faced, land-grabbing, "scornful foreigner" who spends his days swinging in a hammock and shooting alligators. Later, "Mister Brown," in Gabriel García Márquez's *One Hundred Years of Solitude*, is the head of a foreign fruit corporation who presides over the execution of thousands of striking workers, summoning a biblical storm that wipes away the town of Macondo.

Starting with the agenda of Simón Bolívar's 1826 Panama Congress, Latin American intellectuals had, by the end of the 1800s, produced a remarkably coherent ethical worldview: the New World had a providential role to play in history; nationalism need not vitiate internationalism, nor sovereignty justice; the defense of borders didn't involve restricting migration; the needs of society had to be balanced with the rights of individuals; and doctrines of discovery and conquest had been abrogated.

Political stability, though, remained elusive. Wars, civil wars, insurgencies, interventions, coups, and dictatorships roiled domestic politics. In no country was a ruling class able, for any length of time, to establish an enduring governing coalition unless, as in Mexico, Chile, and Argentina, a significant amount of repression was deployed.

Most nations, though, including small ones like El Salvador and Honduras, did develop capable foreign services. Argentina and Brazil, especially, counted on a diplomatic corps that could rival any in Europe. Even the independence movement in Cuba, still a colony, assembled a shadow cabinet of jurists who argued in favor of independence and national sovereignty. These diplomats carried forward Bolívar's dream: the idea that domestic politics might be stabilized if only the hemispheric order could be stabilized.[16]

For that to happen, a new "kind of international law for America," to use Jefferson's phrase, would be needed.

26.

Twilight

Cuba drove José Martí near to a breakdown. "My lungs constantly complain, and my heart beats faster than it should," he wrote a friend in the summer of 1890 from his Catskills retreat in Haines Falls, New York. The mountain air calmed him. "I'm moving ahead with Emerson," the thirty-seven-year-old writer said, and "studying insects" in order "to understand humans better." "They are not as bad as they seem, and they are as smart as us." "It is a savage pleasure," he said, of his time alone, "to be able to think and speculate without having to speak."[1]

Martí was born in Havana in 1853 to Spanish parents of humble origins. His father, Mariano Martí, was a sergeant in Spain's colonial army. José described him as if he were Spain itself: "a strong character, despotic and rustic in the extreme; he was a living transcript of *pater familia romana* in all matters, moral and material, a jealous defender of his home" who maintained "ominous authority over what was his."

His mother, Leonor Pérez, was loving, though she objected to José's constant questioning of authority. A revolution for independence had broken out in 1868; soon Martí, a seventeen-year-old secondary school student, would be arrested on charges of sedition and sentenced to hard labor in a Havana jail. Later, he'd say that his opposition to Spanish rule came from having witnessed a slave being whipped. Las Casas echoes down the years: "*Yo lo vi*," Martí wrote of the experience. "I saw it. I saw it when I was a child, and I am still ashamed." His stint doing forced, shackled labor also influenced his politics. Released from prison in 1871, Martí would go on to read a library of romantics, socialists, realists, transcendentalists, theosophists, and social engineers: Krause, Whitman, Marx, Emerson, Spencer, Hugo. But as one biographer noted, it was prison that made him. Martí came out of jail "fully formed."[2]

He left Cuba for Spain to take advantage of a recent law providing free access to all levels of education. Martí enrolled in the University of Zaragoza, taking courses in Hebrew, literature, metaphysics, and something called "critical studies." He passed seven oral exams and then went on to focus on Roman and Greek law. Martí was allowed to return to Havana, but he couldn't practice law because he couldn't afford to pay the fees to receive his degree. Learning was free in Spain. Diplomas weren't. Within a year, his speeches and writings again brought him to the attention of Spanish officials. He left for France, Mexico, and Guatemala, working as a teacher, tutor, and reporter.

Martí arrived in New York in 1880, at once fascinated by the city's dynamism and troubled by its poverty amid plenty. For his Spanish readers, Martí described Jim Crow segregation, the treatment of Native Americans, and violence directed at unions, especially the deadly response to Chicago's Haymarket protest. Martí generally was in favor of free trade, in reaction to Spain's tight control of Cuba's economy. Yet he recoiled at the mix of commercial materialism and libertarian individualism that he thought was driving the United States toward madness.

A nation is not a "wild horse race"; people must be "harnessed together" by something other than self-interest, he wrote. He predicted that class war would lead to a second civil war.[3]

His wife, Carmen Zayas-Bazán, and son, José Francisco, stayed in Cuba as Martí, living in Brooklyn and working in lower Manhattan, engaged in a bewildering array of activities. He wrote plays, poems, novels, and political essays, which were published across the hemisphere. He started newspapers and a monthly magazine for children.* And he composed scores of lengthy obituaries. One described a memorial for Karl Marx, held in Cooper Union's Great Hall on March 19, 1883, five days after Marx's death. The Hall was overflowing with artisans and laborers, with "more honest faces than silken scarves." Martí said that he appreciated Marx's efforts "to topple the cracked pillars" of the old order, but worried that he went "too fast in the darkness." That is, Martí thought Marx underestimated the danger of reaction. He translated dozens of English, French, and Irish works, including the poems of Ralph Waldo Emerson, one being "The World-Soul": "He will from wrecks and sediment / The fairer world complete."

Martí kept Latin American readers appraised of what Washington was doing, its designs on Cuba and Central America. He took visiting Cubans to Coney Island, with its "melancholy dwarves and stunted elephants," and P. T. Barnum's circus. He lectured regularly on politics, metaphysics, the relationship of society to nature, and the experience of exile, and threw himself into the movement for Cuban independence. He was one of those Latin American intellectuals who saw no conflict between nationalism and internationalism.

"Homeland is humanity," he wrote.

At the Feet of Cadmus

Martí finished his most famous poem in the Catskills, *Versos Sencillos*, or *Simple Verses*—forty-six stanzas of four lines each, some later worked into the Cuban folk song "Guantanamera": "I am a sincere man," goes its opener. Latin Americans like Martí shared the concerns of philosophers like

* *The Golden Age* moved children's literature out of bewitched forests and feudal castles and into modern "factories and laboratories," where science created stranger and more powerful things than old-fashioned magic. One issue contained a didactic biography of Bartolomé de las Casas, describing the priest as *feo y flaco* (ugly and thin), but whose "sublime soul burned in his eyes like a clean fire." Martí used the essay to teach young readers about historical time and virtue: "Four centuries is a long time, four hundred years. Father Las Casas lived four hundred years ago, and if he seems to be alive today it is because he was good."

Emerson about the artifice of modern life. "Let us speak with sincerity," wrote Uruguay's Rodó at around this time, "let us think with sincerity."[4]

The cabin compound where Martí stayed was run by the Twilight Club, one of many dinner societies that sprang up in bustling United States cities in the decades after the Civil War, less covert and esoteric than Freemason lodges. Twilight shared membership and philosophy with the more famous but shorter-lived Metaphysical Club, which had only operated as a gathering society for a few months. Oliver Wendell Holmes attended both. Emerson hovered over all. The Twilight Club's name referred to its after-the-workday meeting time, but also the idea that wisdom came at dusk, at the end of the day, or at the twilight of a historical epoch, in a nod to Hegel's aphorism: "The owl of Minerva spreads its wings only with the falling of dusk."

Returning to New York at the end of summer and satisfied with the final draft of *Versos*, Martí was asked to give one of the Twilight Club's after-dinner "Owl Talks." The topic Martí chose was "Memories of Summer," which he said would be a meditation on nature.[5]

The club's expected tone was jovial; no party politics allowed, no long speeches. It was more democratic than other similar associations. Women attended. And though Twilight had a few millionaire philanthropist members, including Andrew Carnegie, dues were affordable to writers, poets, and exiles like Martí. The real entrance requirement was to be clubbable, which in this case meant being engaged with the spirit of the times. Members enjoyed eight months of socializing in New York City, then to the Catskills in August, where the conversations continued.

The joviality seemed forced. Slavery had been abolished, the Union saved, and the frontier settled. Still, something felt wrong. Behind the jokes was a fear that modern society had no moral compass, that the Gilded Age's mix of enormous, concentrated wealth and mass politics was unsustainable, and that the dominion of a handful of European empires over the world's darker peoples was moving toward conflict. Each financial crash felt a little longer, cut a little deeper, than the last. The end of Reconstruction led to a restoration of white power in the South, backed by racial violence. The drive west directed passions outward, but society remained violently polarized. Serial crises—a contested presidential election in 1876, a railroad strike a year later, and the 1881 assassination of President James Garfield—led some to comment that the United States was become too much like unstable Latin America, that the "Mexicanization of the country" would lead to "the ruin of the republic."[6]

One era had opened to another, as slavery gave way to the industrial revolution. Yet the owl's great wings brought not wisdom. They cast shadows and doubt. The Scottish labor radical and journalist John Swinton was a Club officer, and he injected a sense of social urgency into its dinners, or, as the Twilighters called the gatherings, Feasts of Reason and Flows of Soul. Swinton was infamous for a talk he had given at a formal press dinner, where he told the journalists, editors, and publishers in his audience that they were "all slaves," including himself, "tools and vassals of rich men behind the scenes. We are jumping-jacks. They pull the string and we dance. Our time, our talents, our lives, our possibilities, are all the property of other men." Free speech, like free labor, was subordinated to the men of real power.

After returning from a trip to Europe, Swinton addressed the Twilight Club on the topic of socialism, and the agonies and dangers of capitalism. Everywhere in Europe he went, he "saw the many-headed and many-minded mob suffering untold misery in silence." The silence would not last long, he warned: "Caliban is sitting at the feet of Cadmus and learning his letters." Others gave lectures with titles such as "Have You Lost Faith in Democracy?," "Have Workingmen Real Grievances?," "Shall We Annex Hawaii?," "The Silver Question," "How Should Girls Be Trained?," and "What Should We Do with Our Slums?"[7]

To Shake Hands with the Cuban

Martí began his remarks with Emerson. In Ralph Waldo Emerson, especially Emerson's essay "Nature," Martí heard echoes of a kindred soul. "The forest returns man to reason and faith," Martí had written earlier, in his obituary for Emerson. Nature, Emerson taught, "inspires, heals, consoles, fortifies, and teaches virtue." Humans cannot be complete beings, nor can they sense the infinite, "without an intimate relation with nature."[8]

Important differences need acknowledgment and metaphysical hairs split: Martí was exceedingly more outer-directed, more political than Emerson, more expressly concerned with poverty and the oppression of the working class. We don't know what Martí made of the New Englander's extreme emphasis on self-reliance, which clashes with Latin American *sociabilidad*. Maybe the Cuban thought Emerson's emphasis on autonomy was but a gateway to the whole, a way to appreciate how each person's life, as Emerson wrote, is "a bundle of relations, a knot of roots."

In any case, Martí finished with Emerson and then turned to what he really wanted to talk about: Cuba.

Every administration since Grant's had devoted attention to Cuba, as Spain responded with increasing repression to the island's independence movement, which, in the decades after the Civil War, flared, faded, and flared again. In 1872, Colombia's president proposed forming a hemispheric coalition to support the insurgents, to save the island from becoming "a field of ruin and desolation." Washington brushed off the idea, preferring to keep its options open unburdened by alliances.

Earlier, the back draft of Europe's revolutionary 1848 let expansionists imagine themselves carrying liberty to benighted lands. Cuba represented a great leap in this use of idealism to justify intervention. As Cuban rebels gained ground, Spain's royal troops let loose a bloodbath, a pacification campaign that gave no quarter. Washington for the first time cited the protection of "human rights" as an objective of foreign policy.[9]

Martí wasn't convinced by this newly professed humanitarianism. He found little to redeem in anything he heard in the United States about Cuba. Those opposed to annexing the island were racist. The *Chicago Tribune* said that its mixed-blood population would be more "tedious and difficult" to "Americanize" than it had been to Americanize New Mexico and Arizona. Those who wanted to annex the island saw it as a stepping stone to greater power, a chance to launch a larger war against Spain to take the Philippines and secure Asian markets for U.S. producers.[10]

The drumbeat for annexation was loud, and Martí at the Twilight Club chose his words carefully. Some club members had a defined politics, like the socialist Swinton and the anti-imperialist Carnegie. Most occupied a squishier place, influenced by the theosophists, mystics, and swamis who came to lecture, who said that universalism meant respecting not just other nations but other planes of existence. Their support for the "brotherhood of man" might justify taking Hawai'i, or not, depending on the opinion of the last person they spoke with. Many thought, when they thought about Cuba at all, that Washington should do something to stop the carnage.

Martí reminded his audience of all the past efforts by the United States to take Cuba "in the name of freedom." He wanted an independent Cuba and wasn't opposed to accepting aid from the United States, providing that Cuba's sovereignty was respected. He told his audience that he feared that wouldn't be the case. A "violent union"—forced annexation—was being plotted, Martí warned, and a war with Spain would not be to free Cuba but to take Cuba.

Martí was insecure about his English skills and outraged at the arrogance of monolingual English speakers. "One feels constantly beaten up" was how he described trying to communicate with strangers. He must have carefully prepared his remarks, pitching his closing words to his audience's ecumenical humanism. A free Cuba, he said, "is possible," as is an alliance with the United States, based not on conquest but friendship, on "righteous" respect and truth—the very ideals that motivated the founders of the Twilight Club, "before whom this humble foreigner offers his grateful heart."[11]

As Martí finished his remarks, he looked out at a sea of silent "white heads" that he at first thought "censorious." Then, suddenly, the crowd rose as one "from its seats and gave him thunderous rounds of applause." When the clapping ended, audience members rushed to the podium to "shake hands with the Cuban."[12]

Who Defends America?

The immediate cause of the exhaustion that took Martí to the Catskills—aside from his nonstop writing, publishing, and activism—was his experience attending the First International Conference of American States, which had been hosted in Washington by Secretary of State James Blaine from late

1889 to early 1890. Martí had joined the conference as a journalist and as a member of the Uruguayan and Argentine delegations (since he worked as the New York consul for both those countries).[13]

For decades, State Department officials had watched as Spanish Americans held their conferences. Jacksonian diplomats ridiculed these gatherings, likening them to conclaves of Talmudic rabbis. But now the United States was led by Republicans who thought the moment was right for a summit of the Americas. It was time to organize the hemisphere.

Latin Americans began arriving in East Coast ports in late 1889, assembling as a group in an unseasonably warm December in New York to attend a series of preliminary events. They disembarked in Brooklyn and fell into a Walt Whitman poem. The visitors looked with awe at the vast expanse of the Narrows. They watched as ferrymen shuttled throngs of people across the East and Hudson rivers. Docks filled every inch of shoreline around Brooklyn and both sides of Manhattan, with ships in every slip, masts fluttering, ropes taut, as stevedores with pulleys and grappling hooks loaded and unloaded cargo. Vessels of all sizes crisscrossed the harbor, passing Beldow Island, home to the recently completed Statue of Liberty, its copper cloak and skin still mostly reddish-brown. Horse carriages carried the delegates across the Brooklyn Bridge, under its web of steel cables and soaring arched anchorages, escorted by mounted police.

The day's events included a tour of the Stock Exchange and the Chamber of Commerce, where the aged Civil War hero General William Sherman arrived to recount his March to the Sea. Sherman looked to reassure the delegates. He told them that the United States was finished growing. "We have forty-two States and some territories. That's about as many as should be united under one system of government." You have nothing to fear, the general was saying, from the United States.

That night, the diplomats retired to the Scottish Rite Hall, on Madison Avenue and Twenty-Ninth Street, for a reception in their honor. Dinner was at Delmonico's, transformed by palms and "all manner of southern plants" into a "tropical wilderness." Flags of all nations were draped over the restaurant's mirrors, with two large portraits of Washington and Bolívar placed behind the head table. The mayor's office had appropriated five thousand dollars for entertainment. No expense was spared. Hanging from the center ceiling of the great hall was a floral, deep green globe, its surface traced only with the outline of the Western Hemisphere. Red, white, and blue garlands ran to the various corners of the room, "like resplendent latitudinal parallels."[14]

The delegates had arrived shaky. The trip was long. Most didn't speak English. Many were only meeting one another for the first time, and the itinerary was confusing. Press coverage was favorable, though some newspapers countermanded General Sherman's reassurances. *The New York Herald* "pleaded for an occupation of all America." The United States, wrote *The Sun*, had recently purchased Alaska as part of a plan "to form a union of the whole northern part of the continent, with the flags of the Union floating from the polar ice to the Isthmus, and from sea to sea." Such statements were swagger, the newspapers using the festivities to entertain imperial fantasies.

Latin America's representatives didn't know what to expect from the United States. And there were enough quarrels and even wars among their nations to prevent a united front. War, debt, and domestic revolts created a sense of urgency among Latin American delegates to reform the international order. Delegations from Chile, Uruguay, Bolivia, and Argentina were expected to be confrontational. Mexico, which since the end of the Civil War had become tightly integrated into the United States market and dependent on United States capital, was likely to be deferential. Small Central American nations had little power and many grievances. Their diplomats would be among the most vocal advocates of using the conference to reorient international law even as they competed against one another for a canal.[15]

Martí received Uruguay's and Argentina's envoys in the small office Montevideo had provided him for his consular work. The room was spare, adorned only with an iron link from his old prison chain, which his mother had sent him. Martí was even sparer. His visitors thought he looked cold and hungry. Writing paid little, publishing cost money, and the Cuban lived on what salary he made issuing visas and processing passports. The Argentines gave him a blanket to keep his legs warm when he typed and treated him to some good meals in Manhattan's finer restaurants, where they discussed what other nations wanted from the conference.

Martí didn't trust Blaine. He thought him an opportunist who used dishonest rhetoric in his speeches to manipulate the public. It was clear to Martí that the secretary of state was hoping a successful Pan-American conference would set him up for a run for the White House. "If he had this country in his hands," Martí wrote, he "would use its army for a horse and navy for spurs," kicking it out to "conquer the world."

The conference, Martí wrote in his first essay on the gathering, will "soon reveal who defends America, and who does not."

American International Law

The Latin American delegates would be negotiating mostly with wealthy businessmen picked by Blaine, including Andrew Carnegie. Others representing the United States were the wagon- and carriage-maker Clement Studebaker; Boston merchant Cornelius Bliss; Charles Flint, later to found IBM; W. R. Grace; T. Jefferson Coolidge, a great-grandson of Thomas Jefferson, who made his money in textiles, railroads, electricity, and bananas (he'd soon help found the United Fruit Company); Georgia's John Hanson, a textile and steamship tycoon; and the railroad millionaire Henry G. Davis.

These men thought the meeting was convened to talk about trade and the possible building of the Pan-American Railroad.

Latin Americans wanted to talk about something else.

The foreign delegates had arrived carrying arguments gleaned from decades of thinking about international law and what an American system should look like. The jurist Juan Bautista Alberdi, who was born in Argentina but lived and worked mostly in Uruguay and Chile, had given a name to the complex of interlocking principles that the region's statesmen believed should form the basis of a new global order: a rejection of doctrines of discovery and conquest; insistence on formal equality of nations despite their size; nonintervention; *uti possidetis*; and impartial arbitration. Alberdi, in 1844, called this set of ideals American International Law.[16]

Alberdi believed that a shared opposition to "colonial slavery" had produced a unique hemispheric jurisprudence. Such a body of law was distinct from what was generically called "international law," which pretended to be universal but merely reflected the interests of the European conquerors.[17]

Conventional international law, for instance, recognized the rights of nations to protect their citizens abroad. Great powers made full use of this right, in its broadest sense. The United States left Nicaragua's Greytown in ashes as punishment for a reported crime committed against a U.S. citizen (and to help out Vanderbilt). Swiss, French, German, Dutch, British, and even Italian creditors swarmed the indebted American republics like flies, demanding that their governments use gunboats to collect debt, which they often did. France had leveraged a dispute over a bond issuance to justify its 1861 takeover of Mexico.[18]

In response, the Argentine lawyer Carlos Calvo, in 1868, insisted that America was comprised of free, independent nations: all sovereign and equal no matter their size or strength. Such sovereign equality prohibits "intervention of any sort" by foreigners (*ingérence d'aucune sort*, in the original, as Calvo's six-volume textbook was first published in Paris). The Calvo Doctrine, as his most famous argument became known, held that foreigners, be they businessmen, investors, residents, or travelers, were to be protected absolutely and equally by national law. They were owed all the rights of national citizens. But they were not owed additional rights, rights that national citizens didn't have, such as the right to call in gunboats to defend their interests. There could be, Calvo in essence said, no political sovereignty without economic sovereignty. Soon, Latin American lawyers were inserting "Calvo Clauses" into contracts with foreign companies, denying them the right to call on their home governments to adjudicate the contracts.[19]

No Latin American jurist, as far as I know, believed that the adjective *American* in the phrase American International Law meant the ideals they advocated for pertained only to the Americas. Their origins were hemispheric, but their values were believed to be universal.

"The law," Alberdi wrote, "is one for all the human race by virtue of the unity itself of the human race." "One god, one species, one law—the law of the human species."[20]

Washington, as might be expected, generally opposed the idea of American International Law on all its points, since, as its ambassador to Peru noted, it would clearly limit "the power of the United States." A few Latin American jurists held on to the idea that the principles of American International Law were merely an expansion of the ideals found in the Monroe Doctrine. The Monroe Doctrine, a Colombian historian writing about border disputes with Peru said in 1893, "is simply the application of the principle of national sovereignty to the republics of this continent." By this point, though, most of his contemporaries had begun to accept that the doctrine was what Washington said it was: something akin to the original New World Papal Donation, a warrant that granted the United States mandatory power to use as needed, to project its authority and protect its interests.[21]

The delegates might have had a sense of purpose. Yet the quickness with which some of their countries had recently fallen into catastrophic wars had rocked the region's chanceries. The motives behind the conflicts—control over resources, a drive for territorial aggrandizement, geostrategic maneuvering—violated every principle Latin America was said to represent. Yet, most jurists continued to insist, the doctrines and ideals weren't the problem. The problem was the failure to apply the doctrine and live up to the ideal. In 1870, toward the end of the War of the Triple Alliance, when Brazil, Argentina, and Uruguay nearly destroyed Paraguay, Alberdi—the jurist who coined the phrase *American International Law*—wrote a cry-of-the-heart treatise. *The Crime of War* anticipated many of the arguments that justified future war-crime tribunals, starting with those held in Tokyo and Nuremberg after the Second World War. The legal phrase, "law of war," Alberdi wrote, was a monstrous sophistry, a sacrilegious perversion of common sense, as if there could be a law of murder, or a law of thievery. War is nothing but collective crime, and it can no more have a law to legitimate it than can homicide.[22]

Alberdi's plea didn't stop Chile from attacking Peru and Bolivia, a conflict goaded on and financed by British mining and financial houses that were invested heavily in nitrate in the country's northern deserts. Chile won the war, seizing in 1883—just six years before the convocation of the Pan-American Conference—coastal territory and turning Bolivia into a landlocked country. Chile had also sacked Lima, carrying away animals from the city's zoo and a trove of colonial papers from its archive, which hindered Peru's ability to use the documents to make *uti possidetis* claims on conquered territory. Blaine called it "an English war on Peru, with Chile as the instrument." He was right. But Washington, along with U.S. banks and companies such as the guano exporter W. R. Grace, had backed Lima.[23]

The fact that regional conflicts were aggravated and manipulated by foreign interests likewise confirmed a belief that international public law had to be strengthened and an interstate system had to be founded, one that would reenforce national sovereignty and establish effective arbitration. Such arbitration would prevent the kind of "conquests" that had turned Bolivia into an "island surrounded by land" and had dismembered Mexico, which Latin American jurists began likening to partitioned Poland.[24]

Martí was steeped in the ethics and history that gave life to American International Law. While a law student, he had read Thucydides, whose description of Athens's victory in the Peloponnesian War is often taken as the first expression of political realism. Athens lays siege to Melos, a small island (like Cuba), after Melos is unable to meet its tribute obligations. Thucydides has Melos making all sorts of appeals to law to prevent its destruction. The Athenians respond by insisting that justice is a matter only "between equals in power." In all other cases, "the strong do what they will, the weak suffer what they must." Athens attacks Melos, massacres its inhabitants, and then colonizes the island.

It takes little imagination to see the relevance of the story to the Americas, in the obliteration of Greytown, in the taking of Texas and the destruction of Mexico's sovereignty in other northern regions, in William Walker, and in Washington's endless menacing of Cuba—in the countless incidents where Washington did what it would and Latin Americans suffered as they must.

Now, Latin America had the chance to avenge Melos by insisting on sovereign equality for all, not only for those equal in power.

Delegates from Brazil came as monarchists. But in the middle of the conference, a military coup overthrew Emperor Dom Pedro II. Its envoys in

Washington didn't miss a beat. Having arrived as royalists, they now parlayed as republicans. Haiti's envoys came late, only after receiving a promise from Blaine (brokered by Frederick Douglass, who had been named ambassador to Port-au-Prince) that the United States would discontinue the occupation of a stretch of land it used as a coaling station.

Washington's Arlington Hotel housed the Latin Americans, and the Wallach Mansion, on the corner of Eighteenth and I streets, hosted the proceedings. Introductions were made, toasts were raised. Rules of order were established, the conference officers selected. Blaine was named president.

His first order of business was to put the proceedings on hold for a few days and invite the delegates to board a special train organized by the State Department for a five-thousand-mile ride. The point of course was to awe the Latin Americans as they passed plains, mountains, and pulled into busy depots. The trip was also designed to sell the delegates on the idea of building a Pan-American Railroad to crisscross the hemisphere the way the transcontinental crisscrossed North America. The train—five sleepers outfitted with feather beds, a bathroom car, press car, library, barbershop, bar car, and a French restaurant—traveled north to Niagara and west to Omaha, stopping at West Point and passing copper mills in Detroit, oil wells in Ohio, ports, factories, breweries, ranches, wheatfields, slaughterhouses, and universities.

Envoys from Argentina, Bolivia, and Chile, along with Martí, stayed back. They wanted to work on their conference strategy.

27.

America for Humanity

T he Pullman train returned to Washington and the conference got under way. Latin American delegates heard one thing from United States officials during the day. Then, over drinks, they were told something entirely different by the businessmen delegates, who were too busy to be prepped by the State Department. Blaine was pulled away from the conference after the sudden deaths of two of his children from influenza and could only attend sessions that dealt with pressing issues. All parties were frustrated by slow translations, and so delegates began to talk over the military interpreters, in some blend of Spanish and English. Many got mixed up, thinking they understood something when they hadn't. Martí was impressed with one U.S. official, a lawyer, Arthur Fergusson, who could "catch Spanish on the wing and translate it without adding either sugar or gall."

Marti's skill as a narrator and analyst is on display in his dispatches back to Argentina, published in the widely circulated *La Nación.* He was a good guide to what he called the "entrails" of the conference, paying close attention to the slow overcoming of differences among the Latin American delegates and their rallying behind Buenos Aires' representatives: Roque Sáenz Peña and Manuel Quintana. In a strange land, the delegates gravitated toward one another, establishing camaraderie in the meeting hall and outside, often at the expense of their United States counterparts, whom they ridiculed and complained about.[1]

They soon got their footing. The more time they spent with United States representatives, the less intimidated the Latin American statesmen were by them. Washington's businessmen-delegates knew little of Latin America and even less about international law. They grew uncomfortable as the discussion turned confrontational. Some gazed at the ceiling. They "smoked, pulled at their vests," and "smoothed their hair."

The first fight was over Blaine's customs union, an idea the secretary of state based on Prussia's *Zollverein*, a common market founded in 1834. In Central Europe, the *Zollverein* had not only stimulated manufacturing but facilitated the 1871 unification of German provinces.* Blaine imagined that a New World common market might result in similar benefits, creating a hemispheric economy that would ensure United States supremacy. State Department envoys wouldn't describe the proposal for the union in such blunt terms. Nonetheless, they presented the idea with a phrase sure to raise hackles: they said the United States had given up "annexing the territory" of Latin America and now was only keen on "annexing its trade." Oddly, they thought this wordplay would placate the region's delegates.[2]

Latin America's envoys didn't like any proposal with the word *annexation* in it. The Argentines especially were convinced that the customs union was meant to build a protectionist wall around the Americas that would benefit United States industry. When pressed, U.S. delegates couldn't say how the union would supersede the United States' already extremely high tariff rates imposed on Latin America. They admitted that one set of common tariffs might be levied against European imports into the hemisphere, and another set against Latin American products entering the United States.

Argentina's Roque Sáenz Peña gave a stem-winder of a speech that put the issue to rest. Compared with the protectionist United States, Sáenz Peña

---

* Blaine's proposal was not just modeled on Germany's economic policy but was also meant to counter Germany. Washington, since German unification, had grown steadily concerned that Berlin both planned to expand its *Zollverein* to cover all Western Europe and had designs on Latin America, that it meant to challenge the Monroe Doctrine. For his part, Bismarck called the Monroe Doctrine a "special manifestation of American arrogance."

said, Latin America's ports were open to the world, its rivers welcoming ships flying all flags, its factories taking in all migrants. Latin American nations already had commercial relations consecrated in treaties with France, Germany, and the United Kingdom that promoted the liberty of trade under moderate tariffs. Were these to be abrogated? the Argentine asked. Sáenz Peña went into detail on how Blaine's *Zollverein* would make trade with Europe prohibitively expensive. Manufacturing in the United States was a wonder—of that there was no doubt, Sáenz Peña said. The entire nation was a "vertigo of production." But the United States couldn't possibly consume all that it produced. This meant that it needed Latin American markets to purchase its surplus production. The customs union, Sáenz Peña said, was nothing but the United States trying to "defend itself from its own success."[3]

Sáenz Peña ended with a call for universalism. Washington, with its proposed customs union, says *America for America*. No, said Sáenz Peña, bringing his speech to a close: *¡Sea la América para la humanidad!*

Let America be for humanity!

A Chinese Box

The most dramatic day of the conference was devoted to the question of arbitration. The topic seems dull, the dusty stuff of law and economics. But, at some point, Martí realized that arbitration was the key to realizing Latin America's entire legal reform agenda: "The conference had been like one of those Chinese Boxes that have many chambers, one inside the other. Every time you open up one, there's another, until you reach the last box and the mystery is revealed: *arbitration*."

For the Latin American delegates, the need to set up a truly fair and binding arbitration system, one that wasn't dominated by "great powers," was the hub around which all other issues revolved, the prerequisite for the remaking of international law. In focusing on arbitration, Latin Americans were asserting the first principles of political liberalism: due process and equal protection, that all nations—no matter how poor or rich, how big or small, how powerful or weak—be judged the same before the law.

Latin America's experience with arbitration, which had been an ad hoc element of international relations for centuries, hardly instilled confidence. In 1868, for instance, Washington and Mexico City established a binational tribunal to hear claims made by the citizens of one nation against the other. The tribunal, dominated by the United States, was scandalous, with U.S. citizens and businesses greatly inflating the value of the supposed losses— losses that were the result of decades of crisis unleashed by Washington's 1846 war on Mexico. At the end of the day, the tribunal awarded United States claimants $4,000,000 and Mexican supplicants only $150,000. Mexico City, fearing that Washington would seize Sonora as a "protectorate," had no choice but to start making monthly payments with interest.

And so Latin America at the Pan-American Conference insisted that arbitration alone wasn't sufficient to ensure peace and justice. For arbitration to be effective, for it to be a true mechanism for the prevention of war, it *had* to be linked to the both the renunciation of the right of conquest and the recognition of sovereign equality. No more threatening wars of conquest to collect debt.

Advocates in the United States and Europe within the nascent international peace movement paid attention to the debate. John Greenleaf Whittier, the Quaker poet and aging abolitionist, wrote to Blaine to say that if delegates came to an agreement on rules of arbitration, the conference "will prove to be one of the most important events in the world's history." Such a breakthrough would "herald a new era of 'Peace on earth and good will to men.'"[4]

Latin Americans had already at a conference held in Caracas in 1883 issued their most forceful denunciation of the doctrine of conquest yet. Now in Washington, delegates took up the question again, led by the Argentine Manuel Quintana. Arbitration won't work, he said, if the presumption of inequality—"of a strong nation" lording "over a weak one"—continues to hold sway. Blaine, who attended these sessions, opposed Quintana's linkage of arbitration to a renunciation of the doctrine of conquest.[5]

After some debate, a compromise was reached, with the delegates agreeing to vote first on arbitration, which would remain in effect for a twenty-year period. That resolution passed unanimously. Then the delegates moved on to the discussion of conquest. Quintana offered this resolution:

> Whereas there is, in America, no territory which can be deemed *res*
> *nullius* . . . therefore . . . the principles of conquest shall never hereafter
> be recognized as admissible under American public law.[6]

The wording of Quintana's full proposal suggested that old conflicts
might be subject to readjudication, that Mexico might be able to retroactively contest its 1848 cession of territory to the United States, or Argentina
might be able to expel Great Britain from the Malvinas, also known as the
Falkland Islands.

Latin American nations represented at the conference were hardly virtuous when it came to conquest, to the destruction of their native people or
the seizure of land. In Argentina, an extermination campaign against
Pampas and Patagonia Indians had just ended. Chile's delegation was torn
between the ideal and the real. Ideally, Chile's envoys supported the nullification of conquest. Really, their nation was holding land that had recently
belonged to Peru and Bolivia.[7]

Latin Americans had learned how to live with such contradictions, since
they not only had to deal with one another but had to hold off an aggrandiz-
ing United States. And so a set of fledgling ideals put forth by independence
leaders like Gual and Bolívar in the 1820s had by the 1890s sharpened into
a coherent and stubborn challenge to standing international law. There is no
territory anywhere in the New World that can be deemed *res nullius*; all
space was already social, already claimed, they said. The doctrine of conquest was a relic that had to go.

A Compromise

Blaine opposed Quintana's resolution, especially the part that suggested that
past conquests might be readjudicated. By this point in United States history, the "right of conquest" had weaved itself into republican jurisprudence,
justifying, well, everything, from the landing of the Puritans and the founding of the nation, from westward expansion to the establishment of the
modern right to private property. The right of conquest had been taught to

generations of law students. "The title of European nations, and which passed to the United States, to this vast territorial empire, was founded on discovery and conquest," lectured James Kent at Columbia Law School in the 1790s. From an 1857 textbook: "It has become a cardinal maxim of their public jurisprudence that the system under which the United States was settled has been that of converting the *discovery* of the country into *conquest*, and the property of the great mass of the community originates in this principle."

For decades United States judges, both on the Supreme Court and in lower tribunals, had cited the doctrine of conquest to justify both the pacification of Native Americans and the dismemberment of Mexico. And Indian wars in the West were still ongoing. The assault on Wounded Knee, where the U.S. Army massacred over three hundred Lakota, was still months in the future (it would take place on December 29, 1890), after which would come years more of occasional battles against Indians who refused to submit to federal authority.

And now, as the United States was about to move from landed expansion to overseas empire, lawyers in the State Department were especially loath to give up such a right. The world was wide open and much of it was for the taking.[8]

By this point, the entire room was focused on the standoff between Quintana and Blaine. Blaine proposed an amendment to the resolution, that the prohibition against conquest last for twenty years, for the time span of the agreed-upon arbitration system. Quintana scoffed. "If conquest is a crime," he asked Blaine, "how can we declare it so for only twenty years?" A crime is a crime. "Will this be our amendment?—that Conquest is declared inhumane for twenty years?"

Blaine didn't answer. He crumpled the papers he had gathered in front of him on the table and waited, hoping that silence might reveal disagreement among the Latin American delegates. It didn't. Nobody came to his defense, not his friend, the Mexican minister Matías Romero, and not Chile's envoys. Blaine begged Quintana to reconsider. The Argentine refused.

A vote was called: Quintana and Martí feared that Chile, because of its conflict with Peru and Bolivia, would vote no. But Chile's minister abstained. Certainly, the five small Central American republics, vying with one another for a possible canal route, wouldn't buck Blaine. They did. The United States delegation "listened in astonishment" as each Latin American nation voted in favor of the resolution outlawing conquest: fourteen Latin American *yeses* and one United States *no*, and Chile's abstention. Thus began a long tradition of Washington standing against the majority in multi-lateral meetings. The Latin Americans were elated, both at the content of the resolution and at their unexpected near unanimity against the full rhetorical power of James Blaine.

The United States didn't hold a formal veto over the proceedings, as it would in future international organizations. But when Blaine, followed by his gaggle of businessmen, left the room after the vote, it had the same effect. What good would a system of arbitration be if it didn't include the United States? Latin American delegates, including Quintana, knew, despite their victory, that they would have to compromise.

Andrew Carnegie took charge. Martí described him as "the little one," an "astute Scot with round eyes," a "conciliator." He approached Quintana with a smile, saying it is a "sin to fight." This is only a conflict over words, Carnegie said, and with "words it will be resolved." Tell me what you accept, and I'll bring it to Blaine. Quintana said that if seizures of territory were subject to international arbitration, then he could live with the "mutilation" of his resolution. He'd accept limiting the ban on "conquest" for twenty years, with a commitment to revisit the question after that time. Carnegie took the offer to Blaine, which Blaine accepted. Another vote was taken, and the revised resolution passed.[9]

Still, Quintana wanted to know: What kind of punishment might apply to a crime that would only be a crime for twenty years?

Common Law of the Civilized World

More resolutions passed. Fifteen *yeses* to Washington's single *no* affirmed the Calvo Doctrine, the principle that held that foreigners were entitled to absolute equality under the law of the nation they invested in, but couldn't appeal to their own nation for backup force. Also passed by the same margin was a vote on the "principles of American International Law," that complex of jurisprudence discussed earlier, which outlawed military intervention; affirmed *uti possidetis* and the sovereign equality of all nations; and insisted that cooperation, not competition, should be the foundation of global politics. Since the conference was nearing its end, it was left to William Henry Trescot, one of only two diplomat-lawyers on the ten-man U.S. delegation, to file a dissent.[10]

Trescot is an interesting figure, a supporter of secession who had owned his own slave island, "Barnwell Island and its slaves," off the coast of South Carolina, as if he were an *encomendero*: with a great house surrounded by scores of slave huts. Mrs. Trescot complained of the hardships of running an entire island and its bonded peoples. "When people talk of my having so many slaves," she said, "I always tell them it is the slaves who own me. Morning, noon, and night, I'm obliged to look after them." When war broke out, Mr. Trescot entered the diplomatic corps of the Confederacy. After Appomattox, he represented the interests of South Carolinian planters to the federal government, arguing for states' rights the way Latin Americans argued for national sovereignty. Trescot used his time in Washington to reenter the federal foreign service. In this, he was typical, as the State Department proved willing to recommission antebellum Southern diplomats and military officers, often sending them to Latin America. Trescot was named a consul to Chile in 1881.[11]

Trescot was a reasonable-sounding racist who before the Civil War hoped the United States and Great Britain would establish an Anglo-Supremacist alliance to dominate global politics. What he thought of Blaine's catering to a group of self-serious Latin American jurists who were certain they had found the key to world peace is unknown.

We do know his opinion of American International Law. "I object to the term 'American International Law,'" he wrote in his dissent. "There can no more be an American international law than there can be an English, a German, or a Prussian international law. International law has an old and settled meaning. It is the common law of the civilized world, and was in active, recognized, and continuous force long before any of the now established

American nations had an independent existence." There's only one law, Prescott told the delegates. It's not your law.[12]

Ecuador's José Plácido Caamaño took exception to Trescot's objection. What nation, in what conference, Caamaño asked, has the right to say what is and isn't international law? Should we only follow the resolutions of conferences "held at Vienna, Geneva, Paris, or Berlin?" Existing international law, Caamaño said, has taught us how to "make war upon each other." Have "we Americans not the right" to teach ourselves how to make peace?

The United States didn't ratify the conference's treaties or decrees, so most Latin American nations didn't bother presenting the meeting's proceedings to their legislatures. The main accomplishment was to create a "bureau," eventually called the Pan-American Union, based in Washington, D.C., that functioned as an adjunct of the Department of State.

The Pan-American Union began to tie the hemisphere together, mostly through a series of affiliated institutes focusing on social issues, on health, labor, education, agriculture, the teaching of geography and history, and the role of women in society. The Union held about two plenipotentiary summits per decade, and the dynamics of the discussion were usually similar. Goodwill reigned over technical and most policy issues. Everyone cooperated when it came to standardizing postal practices. Nations in dispute aired their grievances and agreed to third-party mediation. But when Latin American delegates denounced the latest barbarity committed by Washington, their U.S. counterparts simply ignored them.[13]

A good gauge of the historical significance of the first Pan-American Conference would be a comparison with the more well-known Berlin Congress, held in 1884. The two gatherings stood at opposite ends of a moral spectrum.

The opening premise of the Pan-American delegates, or at least most of them, was that peace based on the recognition of sovereignty among all nations, small and big, weak and strong, should be the foundation of a new global order and that "conquest" was a vestige of medievalism that needed to be purged from modern life.

The forceful stand Latin American delegates took against conquest was technically an opposition to wars of aggression and territorial annexation. But really it was about a more general principle: that no powerful nation had the right to intervene in any way—*ingérence d'aucune sort*, as Carlos Calvo put it in 1868—in the politics of other nations. *Conquest* here was being redefined to include not just land grabs but economic domination and diplomatic manipulation. In turn, this prohibition against conquest—against intervention—opened the way for Latin America to put forth an even more ambitious ideal: *absolute sovereign equality*, that all nations, no matter how small their navy, how poor their treasury, how feeble their factories, had the right to organize their own affairs, to decide their own destinies. The world, ideally, should be organized as a community of nations enjoying equal rights and protections.

At the Berlin Congress, Europe was going in the other direction, setting loose its nations to "scramble for Africa." Its statesmen thought they'd have another go-round, making their case for why a new conquest of yet another continent was morally justified. The contrast could not be sharper.* European jurists updated the doctrines of discovery and conquest for new times, launching Europe on yet another round of imperialism. Across the Atlantic, Latin American jurists were pushing as hard as they could to nullify that doctrine, laying the legal basis for the world to come after imperialism.[14]

The Final Verse

The Pan-American conference was a turning point for Martí. Latin Americans had achieved an important rhetorical victory. He knew, though, that

---

* Both the State Department and the Senate's Foreign Relations Committee felt the Berlin Congress could further United States interests in Africa, especially if Congo, ruled by Belgium, were declared a "free trade" zone. Washington, now that Reconstruction had ended and the power of Southern planters was restored, was *still* on the hunt for some *res nullius*, for some *vacuum domicilium* where it might ship its emancipated Black population. Alabama's Senator John Morgan, a member of the Foreign Relations Committee, was an especially vocal publicist for moving people of color to the Congo. So was John Kasson, an Iowa Republican who represented the U.S. at Berlin and supported Belgium's claim on the Congo. In exchange for this support, King Leopold II deemed the Congo a "free trade" zone. Kasson, a Republican who exalted "free labor," said that such a zone would encourage the spread of modern labor relations: free trade, free men. Some historians liken what happened next to a horror equal to that of the Spanish Conquest.

the United States was still the United States—powerful, unignorable, its economy exerting an ever-greater gravitational pull, inevitably more appealing than Europe's. Martí had to fight that attraction every day, even in the ranks of Cuban revolutionaries, some of whom wanted to break with Spain only to follow the example of Texas and annex themselves to the United States.

A sharp economic crisis, beginning in 1893, increased pressure for the United States to move further outward. Agendas differed. Militarists dreamt of national regeneration; farmers and industrialists looked for international markets; labor leaders hoped for social peace and a piece of the pie; and intellectuals searched for an outlet for individualism in a world of corporate concentration. Yet all came to share a vision in which the solution for domestic crisis was foreign expansion.

Cuba came into the crosshairs. "You furnish the pictures and I'll furnish the war," the publisher William Randolph Hearst telegraphed the photographer Frederic Remington.[15]

Martí walked a narrow path. The decades-long independence movement had, by now, turned into a full-scale, island-wide insurgency against Spanish rule. Martí wanted Washington to recognize the insurgents as a legitimate belligerent force. But he was afraid that imperialists would take advantage of such recognition to push for military intervention. And intervention could easily lead to annexation. Press coverage of Spain's brutal pacification campaign allowed reporters to imagine themselves humanitarians. After listing several self-interested reasons, including "honor," for why the United States should declare war on Spain, Hearst's Cuban correspondent Richard Harding Davis editorialized: "Why not go still further and step higher, and interfere in the name of humanity?"

Soon, Martí gave up his writing and translating and devoted himself to revolutionary politics. In 1895, he decided to join his fellow rebels in the field. "The poem of 1810"—the poem of independence started by Bolívar—"is missing a final stanza," Martí said. He "wanted to write it."

Martí wouldn't get the chance. He was killed in battle shortly after landing on a Cuban beach in May 1895, leading a botched two-person charge on Spanish troops.

The rebel army Martí hoped to join was a living embodiment of his ideal that strength and social solidarity could be found in diversity. White and Black Cubans fought side by side, with free people of color and former slaves obtaining the highest military ranks. Black officers commanded ordinary soldiers of lighter skin, marching through the Cuban countryside, taking over plantations, setting cane fields ablaze, and occupying villages and cities. In the years after Martí's death, Spain's army had fallen back, disordered and demoralized. There was little doubt that the insurgents would win.

Then on February 15, 1898, the gunpowder magazines on board the USS *Maine* exploded, killing most of its crew and sinking the ship, which had been anchored in Havana's harbor. President William McKinley used the explosion, which he blamed on Spain, as a pretext to enter the war, dispatching the U.S. Navy to Puerto Rico, Guam, the Philippines, and Cuba. United States troops easily took Spain's island colonies, and, in Cuba, shunted aside the rebel army. A new government, supervised by a military staff that included ex-Confederates like Fitzhugh Lee, Robert E. Lee's nephew, imposed a system of racial segregation roughly based on the model of the post-Reconstruction South. Washington kept Puerto Rico, Guam, and the Philippines, but granted nominal independence to Cuba. The United States did insist that the new republic include in its constitution a clause, called the Platt Amendment after Connecticut senator Orville Platt, that granted the United States the right to intervene in the nation's affairs at will.

A few days before his death, Martí wrote the fourteen-year-old María Mantilla and gave her a translation task. María was Martí's goddaughter and maybe his actual daughter as well. Historians aren't sure. Her mother was Carmen Miyares de Mantilla, a Venezuelan émigré who ran a Manhattan boardinghouse on East Twenty-Ninth Street popular with Cuban revolutionaries and Pinkerton agents paid by Spain to keep an eye on the revolutionaries. Over the years, Martí had gently attended to María's education, adding research and translating tasks to what he called the "Yankee details" she learned in public school. She should think herself "equal" to all and not be "slave" to any man, Martí told her. Get *Bulfinch's Mythology* and look up *Athos* and *Atlas* was one typical assignment.

"Do you think about the truth of the world?" he asked in his last letter. He wanted María to have knowledge and to experience desire, freedom, and love. "Do you know? Do you want? Do you know you can want, want of your own free will?"

In this last communication, he urged María to read Arabella Buckley, *The Fairy-Land of Science*, and John Lubbock's *Flowers, Fruits, and Leaves* and *Ants, Bees, and Wasps*. He admitted he had given up reading poetry, since he found most poems artificial, stale with forced sentimentality. He gave María one final hectoring, loving lecture against frivolity and the runaway consumerism of Manhattan emporiums.

"Those who are full inside," he wrote, "need little outside."

Tar Wars

T he United States swung wildly in the years after the War of 1898. In one direction, it brutally asserted the Monroe Doctrine to back up boots-on-the-ground invasions. In the other, it gingerly began to participate in the early construction of a system of international law. This wasn't hypocrisy. It was carburetion, figuring the most efficient mix of fuel and air, of empire and law, domination and arbitration—of going alone and working together.[1]

Lawyers like Theodore Roosevelt's secretary of state Elihu Root and the Carnegie Endowment's John Brown Scott understood the Cuban intervention and the Platt Amendment not as a violation of international law but as law's genesis, the birth of a new world on the eve of a new century. Europe did nothing as the Ottomans slaughtered Armenians, a repression that caught the attention of the United States press. The United States, in contrast, stood up for "human rights" and quickly ended Spain's violent counterinsurgency in Cuba. Washington's newly expanded navy had fast knocked Spain out of Manila, Havana, and San Juan, in contrast to previous drawn-out conflicts, including the devastation of the Civil War and the traumatic, century-long pacification of Native Americans. Confidence ran high.[2]

The United States, said Senator Henry Cabot Lodge, enjoys a "rightful supremacy in the Western Hemisphere." It was as if victory in Cuba was the real liberation of Spanish America, rendering Bolívar's more than decade-long fight but an overture. God, said Senator Albert Beveridge, "has marked the American people as His chosen Nation to finally lead to the regeneration of the world." The defeat of Spain invested the United States with the moral authority to try to reform the rules of the world, to support a world court and maybe a world assembly, a chance to create a parliament of man.[3]

Empire, for some, was not a disrupter of peace or violator of law but peace and law's precondition. There must be, said Reverend Lyman Abbott—an antiwar advocate of labor rights who took over as pastor of Brooklyn's Plymouth Church after Henry Ward Beecher's death—"a new imperialism, the imperialism of liberty."

The New Empire had energy. It was during these years that Roosevelt's gunships and J. P. Morgan's money helped break Panama off Colombia to start digging a canal. Marines landed in Guatemala, Mexico, Cuba, and Honduras for short periods, and occupied Nicaragua, Haiti, and the Dominican Republic for decades, fighting bloody wars against Nicaraguans, Haitians, and Dominicans who didn't want them there. Many politicians and intellectuals still hoped that Cuba would become a state in the union. Others thought there was a chance of scratching a bit more out of Mexico. With their U.S.-owned mines, ranches, and railroads, along with villages that sent harvesttime migrant laborers into the United States to work in the fields, states like Sonora and Coahuila were practically extensions of Texas as it was.[4]

The slaver's Monroe Doctrine was dead. So associated was it with the stench of branded flesh that Republicans after the Civil War were loath to make mention of it. Now, though, enough time had passed. Monroe's proclamation was ecumenicalized. In Brooklyn, Reverend Abbott said that the new imperialism wasn't "inconsistent with the Monroe Doctrine" but rather its extension to "a new and larger sphere." On the other side of the country, in Natchitoches, scene of many a borderland drama, the Catholic bishop Anthony Durier gave a sermon that held that "by his Monroe Doctrine and his army of free men, Uncle Sam rules from ocean to ocean, from pole to pole." United States politicians increasingly invoked the Monroe Doctrine to ward off Europeans, especially Germans, believed by the new empire builders to be a special menace. Berlin "will make us either put up or shut up on the Monroe Doctrine," Roosevelt said, when he was still governor of New York. Time "for the eagle to scream," wrote *The Philadelphia Times*, on the need to check a rising Germany.[5]

"Ye could waltz to it," said the Chicago humorist Finley Peter Dunne, of such imperial fantasias.

The Hog Combine

More than a decade before the New York–based Caribbean Petroleum Company sank the first oil well in Venezuela, Caracas tested this new empire. There, a conflict over asphalt tar pitch provides a good snapshot of how the United States was compelled to accept some of the ideas of American International Law—put forward forcefully by the hemisphere's delegates at the first Pan-American Conference—even as its lawyers kept saying there could be no such thing as American International Law.

Asphalt was a vicious business *in* the United States, where corrupt machine politicians were handing out millions of municipal dollars to tar their city's streets. Around this time, a well-capitalized gang led by John M. Mack, president of the Mack Paving Company, was making a bid to take control of the entire industry. The result was the creation of the National Asphalt Trust.[6]

Mack was part of a group of Philadelphia businessmen collectively known as the Hog Combine, because they "hogged everything in sight." A former bricklayer, Mack became a real estate speculator and railroad financier. He controlled most of Philadelphia's garbage trucks, headed up the city's electric and telephone companies, and ran the trolley lines. Over the years, City Hall's political bosses had given the Mack Paving Company some four thousand contracts worth over thirty million dollars. "My friends and I," Mack later testified in a graft trial, "spent much money" to secure those contracts. With the National Asphalt Trust, Mack and his partners would attempt to secure control over all sources of asphalt coming into the United States, mostly from Mexico, Venezuela, Trinidad, and Cuba.[7]

Mack's intrigues caused havoc in Venezuela. The details of the sordid story are too many to relate here, but a sketch of the conflict is enough to convey its stakes. The fight was over control of Bermúdez Lake, an enormous pit in remote eastern Venezuela filled with thick, bubbling black pitch. The tar was heavy enough for the Spanish to use it to caulk their ships. A subsidy of Mack's Asphalt Trust, New York & Bermudez Company, claimed the lake. So did rival companies. The trail of titles, deeds, and concessions, granted by previous Venezuelan presidents, reached back decades, and like Mack's many contracts in Philadelphia, were often handed out in exchange for under-the-table money. Before long, hired thugs were fighting it out gangland style, battling for control of the tar lake like mobsters battling for control of a city's gambling rackets.[8]

A powerful Philadelphia party-machine Republican, Mack was better connected than his competitors. The tentacles of the Asphalt Trust reached to the highest levels of the United States government. Both Pennsylvania senators were investors, as was Assistant Secretary of State Francis Loomis. U.S. diplomats stationed in Venezuela not only held stocks in the Asphalt Trust but received direct payoffs from Mack's men. General Vinton Greene, the Asphalt Trust's president, was close to President McKinley, having overseen the finances of the U.S. military government in the Philippines. Greene also was a former colleague of Vice President Theodore Roosevelt, from their days working on New York City's police force.

So when Venezuela's president Cipriano Castro refused to settle the dispute on the Asphalt Trust's behalf, it was nothing for Mack to get the White House to send three battleships to cruise Venezuela's coast in a show of support.[9]

That was just a start. Mack and his allies then financed a Venezuelan banker and Castro rival, Manuel Antonio Matos, to launch a revolution against Castro. They paid to outfit a steamer, the *Ban Righ*, renamed *Libertador*, as a gunboat, and gave Matos another $140,000 in supplies and weapons, drawn from a Trust account earmarked for "government relations." Castro survived the revolt, though the uprising led to the deaths of thousands of Venezuelans and the destruction of much public infrastructure, including roads and ports. Meanwhile, the State Department, working closely with Vinton Greene, pressed Castro to confirm the Asphalt Trust's claim. Both Mack and his allies in the U.S. government controlled the only English-language reporter in Venezuela, Albert Jaurett, himself an investor in the Asphalt Trust. All news that came out of the country, picked up by the world's wire services, came from Jaurett. He hyped Matos's revolution and smeared Castro's government, generating panic among Venezuela's creditors. The value of the nation's currency collapsed. Venezuela's debt soared.[10]

The Trust's war on Venezuela was taking place even as next door in Colombia Theodore Roosevelt, who became president after McKinley's assassination, was pressing Bogotá to give up Panama. Roosevelt would soon dispatch the USS *Nashville*, USS *Dixie*, and USS *Atlanta* (the ships' names give a sense of how the War of 1898 helped rehabilitate the Confederacy) to land Marines at Colón, Panama, to make sure Bogotá couldn't put down the provincial rebels. The insurgents were little more than a Panama City fire brigade in the pay of the U.S.-owned New Panama Canal Company, yet with the *Nashville*, *Dixie*, and *Atlanta* backing them up they won their revolution. Most Panamanians didn't know they were in the middle of a revolution for independence from Colombia until an "American officer raised" Panama's "new flag." The United States recognized an independent Panama in November 1903. Work began on the canal on May 4, 1905.[11]

Back in Venezuela, Castro was tenacious in fighting what he called the "business invasion of foreigners," the "invasions of the barbarians of Europe and the other America." Castro's government commandeered the Bermúdez pitch field and began shipping asphalt directly to Mack's competitors.[12]

There still wasn't enough revenue coming into the treasury to pay Venezuela's debts, so Castro convened a national commission to review the legality of past loans, some of which dated back to when Venezuela was part of Gran Colombia. He threatened to default on loans owed to both U.S. and European creditors.[13]

Spank It

In response, Germany, Britain, and Italy, in late 1902, sent their own gunboats to Venezuela, sinking and seizing Venezuelan ships and bombing the coastline. Villages made up of mud huts and adobe houses were besieged by ironclad warships armed with state-of-the-art artillery, including cannons and mortars. The firepower was awesome, its effect terrifying. One of the causes of the soon-to-be world war was competition among European powers for overseas colonies. And so the Venezuela skirmish, made up of many future belligerents, can be seen as an augury of much worse to come.

Washington supported Europe's demand that Caracas pay its debt. "You owe money," a United States envoy told Castro, "and sooner or later you will have to pay."

But Washington didn't want German or British naval vessels darting around the Caribbean.

Neither did Argentina want Europeans threatening Latin American nations over debt. Its foreign minister, Luis Drago, protested, urging the countries of the world to recognize the principle "that public debts cannot occasion armed intervention." With its fast-growing economy, Argentina was challenging Washington for regional leadership.

Roosevelt and Root sympathized with Drago, to a point, to the degree that his protest helped Washington limit Europe's actions in the New World. But Roosevelt and Root rejected what became known as the Drago Doctrine, an absolute opposition to the use of military force to collect debts. Roosevelt was especially annoyed that Latin Americans were citing the Monroe Doctrine to argue that that Europe couldn't send its ships into hemispheric waters to force debt collection. "The Monroe Doctrine," he told France's ambassador, "could certainly not be used by southern Republics to shield them from the consequences of their own torts."[14]

"If any South American country misbehaves toward any European country," Roosevelt had declared earlier, when he was vice president, "let the European country spank it."

Roosevelt wavered between deference to Europe on principle—"spank it"—and a sense that he had to act to check Berlin. Talk of war was constant in Washington. Anonymous sources told *The New York Times* that "persons of considerable importance in the War, State, and Navy Departments" believe that a confrontation with Germany was inevitable: "the war might as well come over Venezuela as over anything else" was the feeling of many in the Roosevelt White House; like measles, "it would be better to have the thing right away and be done with it." War with Germany would come, but not yet, and would be sparked by a different set of immediate causes. Meanwhile, Venezuela simmered.[15]

Roosevelt successfully pressured Rome and London to pull back. Berlin, though, ordered its gunboats to bomb Venezuelan forts, a defiance that had the side effect of drawing the United States and Great Britain closer to each other, setting the stage for its future world war alliance.

Roosevelt considered going into Venezuela himself. He ridiculed Castro, calling him an "unspeakable villainous little monkey." The press painted the Venezuelan leader in extreme racist terms, creating a new standard of dehumanization of foreign leaders, especially leaders who threatened the property rights of foreign investors. The diplomat Francis Huntington Wilson, Yale educated, described another economic nationalist, Nicaragua's president José Santos Zelaya, as "unspeakable carrion." Roosevelt thought Colombians "contemptible little creatures" for opposing his Panama grab.

From savages and barbarians to carrion and villainous monkeys, it seemed that modern capitalist property law had to arm itself with the worst images from the days when Europeans were debating whether Indians were humans or beasts, or some species in between.

Root was a restraining hand. Instead of having the United States join the assault on Venezuela, he brokered a deal to have all parties accept arbitration at the Hague.[16]

Claims and counterclaims were many. Appeals went on for years. Arbiters mostly ruled against Venezuela. But Caracas won on several key points. One Hague judge affirmed the doctrine of sovereign equality, saying that all nations, despite their size or power, had the right to due and equal process. The judge went even further and said that behavior had no bearing on jurisdiction. That is, a large power couldn't justify ignoring the rules of international law simply by pointing out the irresponsibility of its adversary.

Can it be inferred, the judge asked rhetorically, that only "civilized, orderly" nations are protected by international law? Should countries that are "revolutionary, nerveless, and of ill report" be relegated to "a lower international plane?"

Roosevelt and Root, if asked these questions, would have said yes, most definitely. London would have agreed. Civilization and barbarism. Virtue and vice. Solvency conferred sovereignty. The Hague judge thought differently, saying that it was his "deliberate opinion" that all nations, regardless of comportment, enjoy "equality of position and equality of right." The finding directly contradicted Roosevelt's insistence that Venezuela was a pariah nation. The United States, Roosevelt said in December 1904—in what became known as his "corollary to the Monroe Doctrine"—would "exercise international police power" against "wrongdoing."[17]

And it wouldn't wait for a warrant issued by The Hague to do so.

Still, the United States couldn't completely disregard Hague opinion. International claims commissions run by The Hague or other respected entities were by this time citing Latin American jurists, including Carlos Calvo and Luis Drago, as legitimate sources of authority. Principles such as the Calvo Doctrine and *uti possidetis* were now found in textbooks, footnotes, and arbitration decisions. Soon the Drago Doctrine would be too. An elderly Carlos Calvo himself noted this spreading influence. "Not one book on international law has been published" in English, German, and French, he said, "in which Latin America does not occupy the rank that belongs to her among civilized nations."[18]

In 1907, Venezuela's high court fined Mack's subsidiary, the New York & Bermudez Company, five million dollars for damages incurred in the revolution that its parent company, the Asphalt Trust, had funded. Naturally, both the company and the State Department dismissed the court as corrupt and its ruling void. The Asphalt Trust toned down its confrontational rhetoric even as it began to support, more quietly, another armed movement against Castro. This time, Castro, sick from kidney disease and having no money in his treasury, couldn't hold his political coalition together. He left Venezuela in December.

A new, more compliant government reached a deal with Washington. The Asphalt Trust had its claim certified in exchange for paying a small fine to settle the accusation that it supported Matos's revolt.[19]

An estimated fifteen thousand Venezuelans had lost their lives in that pointless uprising, financed by a Philadelphia contract man looking to control a sputtering tar pit, compared by more than a few to a gate of hell, near which no trees could grow nor birds fly.

Soon the hunt would be for petroleum proper. In other countries it would be other resources. Later, W. E. B. Du Bois, considering the causes of the coming world war, identified the rich world's dependency on the poor world's resources: "Rubber, ivory, and palm-oil; tea, coffee, and cocoa; bananas, oranges, and other fruit; cotton, gold, and copper—they, and a hundred other things which dark and sweating bodies hand up to the white world from pits of slime, pay and pay well."

Laying Down the Law

Root held Roosevelt back from "spanking" Venezuela in part because he worried that military aggression would poison the prep work he was trying to do for the upcoming 1907 Hague Peace Conference.

The conference was to formalize a set of issues agreed to at an earlier Hague Conference. That 1899 meeting had been a "great power" affair, a throwback to the days when a handful of European statesmen met in some villa to settle a war or redraw a map. The second Hague meeting, convened on June 15, 1907, pointed toward the future. Forty-four nations, eighteen of them Latin American—the largest regional group by far—would attend.

Root and Roosevelt could see how a system of global rules capable of preventing the kind of chaos that took place in and around Venezuela would benefit the United States. It would keep Europe at bay. The more mechanisms of arbitration that existed the fewer opportunities for Europe to send its gunships to collect debt. It would take the pressure off Washington to come to the aid of every aggrieved U.S. investor and bondholder. And it would, maybe, tame financiers and speculators who, as Roosevelt and Root came to see, were men of mayhem.

For years these men had lent money in sketchy deals knowing they had the State Department to cover their backs if things went sideways. They advanced guns to this or that armed group to press domestic conflict to their advantage and used the chaos they caused to justify advancing loans at high interest rates. "The system of forcible collection of debts generated speculators who live on the people of the country," Root admitted, "who promote revolutions by advancing money for arms and ammunition," taking advantage of governments that are "seeking to avert complete destruction."

The United States wasn't considering giving up part of its sovereignty, nor the Monroe Doctrine, considered by many an extension of that sovereignty. But in the decades to come, the tension between nationalism and internationalism would become a permanent fixture in U.S. diplomacy. And slowly, out of the chaos of Venezuela's debt crisis—with Roosevelt wavering between wanting to send in his gunboats and moving to file the paperwork for The Hague to begin arbitration—came the first tentative steps toward building the "globalist" institutions that over the next century would expand their jurisdiction in regulating disputes.[20]

Latin America was key to Root's strategy for dealing with Europe. A hemispheric alliance system managed by the United States would have great sway over the international order, and the international order was ultimately what the United States expected to manage.

For their part, Latin Americans saw the Hague Conference as another scrimmage to push forward their interpretation of international law. Already, their ideas concerning multilateralism and sovereignty were spreading beyond the Americas. At The Hague, they "took hold."[21]

The most contentious item on the agenda was how to appoint judges to a permanent court of arbitration. Latin Americans demanded that all nations have equal say in the selection. Brazil's foreign minister, Ruy Barbosa, pressed the issue, attacking the existing arrangement where nations with "preponderant power" decide on who gets to judge. "Sovereignty means equality," Barbosa said, or it means nothing. Guatemala's delegate, José

Tible Machado, seconded Barbosa's point, saying that only the appointment of impartial judges in a fair process would ensure "the fixed principle of sovereign equality."

No major power inside the conference dared dispute the principle of "sovereign equality." Outside, though, newspapers said what delegates couldn't. Great powers, wrote the London *Times*, "will not, and can not, in any circumstances" allow small states "to have an equal right with themselves in laying down the law." To elevate small states to equal status of great ones "would involve the subjugation of the higher civilization by the lower," and "condemn the more advanced peoples to moral and intellectual regression."[22]

Roosevelt and Root agreed with the *Times*. But they also wanted to leverage Latin America against Europe. Root pressed Barbosa, imploring the Brazilian to give way on the judgeship question. Root proposed that they defer the matter to Europeans. Let them organize the Hague court as they want, Root said, and we, "the Americans," can "arrange our own conferences exactly as we wish." It was a desperate bid to salvage the talks. Barbosa wouldn't back off, and the conference ended without a clear mandate on how judges would be selected.[23]

Root didn't see a way to reconcile the ideal of sovereign equality with the reality of inequality, with the fact that the world was, undeniably, divided between nations alternatively called "great powers," "great nations"—or, matter-of-factly, "the principals"—and poorer, weaker countries and colonies. "All of the small nations clung with great tenacity to their rights of equal sovereignty and would not permit any great nation to have a greater voice in the constitution of the court than they had," said Root, while the great nations "were unwilling to be overwhelmed by the numerical superiority of the smaller nations."

Root blamed Barbosa's stubbornness on the legacy of Catholic scholastic absolutism. "A peculiarity of the Latin races," he wrote to a friend, "is that they pursue every line of thought to a strict, logical conclusion." To insist that A leads inexorably to X allows no room for compromise to "achieve practical benefit as the Anglo Saxons do."[24]

Practical or not, Barbosa did see the coming storm. He warned the great powers not to be too cocky, to consider the aspirations of the world outside their dominion, and the danger of colonialism and the global arms race. Japan's military defeat of Russia in 1905 had awakened the subjugated world. Things change. Those on top now might not always be so.

We live in "fast times," Barbosa said, seven years before the world war would break out. "The future invades the present. And the future is always full of reversals and surprises."[25]

PART VI

TOWARD A WORLD DOCTRINE

A Tampico gusher

Mexico's Revolution

Woodrow Wilson already had, when he was first running for president, a small encounter with the perils of revolutionary Mexico. His twenty-year-old daughter, Nellie, had gone to visit family friends in Sonora in April 1912. On her way home, she found herself stuck on a train out of Chihuahua to El Paso. Revolutionaries had burned a bridge on the line ahead and the train couldn't proceed. Newspapers in the United States reported the story in lurid tones. Reporters tended to paint Mexicans as lawless and lascivious, amplifying every insult suffered by a U.S. citizen, especially by a young woman like Nellie. But El Paso's train dispatcher sent a reassuring telegram to Wilson, who was then running for president. "Don't think your daughter in slightest danger." Insurgents held the train for a few days before eventually driving Nellie to El Paso. There was nothing interesting to report, she told a gaggle of waiting reporters. Wrapped in an Indian shawl, Nellie said she was sorry "to leave the rebels, who were most polite."[1]

The Mexican Revolution by this point was two years on. On November 20, 1910, Francisco Madero, the thirty-seven-year-old heir to Mexico's fifth-richest family, had called for an uprising to topple Porfirio Díaz, Mexico's ruler for more than three decades. Mexicans answered the call and as revolutionary armies rallied and insurgents occupied cities, Díaz, facing widespread desertion among his officer corps, resigned.

On May 31, 1911, the aging ex-president boarded a German steamer at Veracruz, bound for France. On November 6, 1911, over 90 percent of Mexicans cast their ballots and elected Madero president in the country's first truly free vote.

Madero inherited decades of built-up problems. Díaz had presided over an intense concentration of wealth. Low wages and rising food prices (which rose higher during the many droughts that preceded the revolution) made life miserable for most. There were too many demands to satisfy, too many classes, castes, power blocs, and factions with too many antagonistic interests for Madero's credit-starved government to forge a stable government.

Emiliano Zapata's peasant army, tired of waiting for promised land reform, patrolled perilously close to Mexico City. Peasants had historic land claims going back centuries to the invasion of Cortés: when U.S. soldiers had occupied Mexico in 1847, they were surprised that memories of the Spanish Conquest were so vivid that peasants could recount the details of how the Spanish, in the early 1500s, dispossessed them of their land. More recently, rural communities had lost more land, as expanding plantations, mines, railroads, and ranches encroached on peasant farmland.

For their part, Mexican capitalists in the north of the country had embraced economic nationalism. They were represented by Venustiano Carranza, from a wealthy Coahuila mine-owning family, who headed his own insurgent army. These northerners wanted to industrialize, to develop manufacturing industries, freed from United States control. Then there were the ranch hands, miners, and cowboys who worked for men like Carranza. They filled the ranks of Pancho Villa's powerful Division of the North. Villa's followers wanted the large estates they worked for broken up and distributed among the workers. Unions, including those organized by anarchists connected with the Industrial Workers of the World, staged strikes, seized factories, and demanded not just better pay but the nationalization of industries.

The Mexican Revolution, which began in 1910 and would roll on for decades, was a shock. It was a revolt by a poor country not just against Anglo-Saxon capitalism but also against its justificatory myths and enabling laws. The United States had, by the eve of the revolution, billions of dollars invested in Mexico, in copper, silver, and coal mines, agriculture, petroleum, electric plants, telephone and telegraph companies, jute plantations, railroads and city trolley lines, ports, roads, and factories. Combined, U.S. foreign investors, along with some seventy thousand U.S. citizens living in Mexico, owned nearly half of all Mexican property value. Much of that value would be lost during the revolution, as insurgents destroyed or seized foreign holdings. More was at stake, though, than individual fortunes. The Mexican Revolution would redefine liberal property rights, kicking off a great century-long wave of government nationalization of foreign industry—not just in Mexico but throughout what eventually would be called the third world.[2]

Until now, Latin American dissent had been voiced mostly in somber chambers and through the muted formalities of diplomatic notes. Heated arguments took place around seminar tables. Mexico changed that. The twentieth-century's first great social revolution added new intensity to the debate—pushing forward the transformation of international order and advancing the broad ethical vision of American International Law.

The revolution would soon spiral out of control, but around the time of Woodrow Wilson's campaign for the White House, the situation was relatively calm. Madero, broadly popular, had the loyalty of most federal troops. The Taft administration had menaced the courtly Madero for months, demanding that he do better in protecting the property of United States citizens from rebel violence. Taft's State Department pressed hard for compensation, while U.S. banks made it difficult to lend Madero money.[3]

But Woodrow Wilson's November 1912 victory boosted Madero. The Mexican president thought he might have a partner to work with. Madero's advisers liked that Wilson was the "author of works on the theory of Government and political economy." With two progressives in charge on either side of the border, relations between Mexico and the United States might improve. And so the Mexican president waited anxiously for Wilson's March 1913 inauguration.[4]

Madero didn't live to see it. He'd be executed two weeks before Wilson took the oath of office.

The Ambassador

Complicit in Madero's murder was Taft's ambassador to Mexico, Henry Lane Wilson.

Wilson, no relation to Woodrow, was a short, toupee'd, ashen-faced Son of the American Revolution who had entered the foreign service after he failed as a real estate broker. The ambassador was quick, capable of moving at a "truculent, trotting pace" to waylay Mexican officials and start lecturing them on mind-numbingly trivial matters for long lengths of time. Taft appointed Wilson to his position in 1909, and as he witnessed the collapse of Díaz's government, Wilson committed himself to defending the interests of U.S. investors.[5]

Preoccupied with his own presidential campaign, President Taft left Wilson to set policy on Mexico. He acted more as a viceroy than a diplomat, expecting Francisco Madero to be a pliant apprentice—a good "lad," as one journalist put it, noting that the ambassador always looked like he was patting Madero on the head. Madero, in turn, was polite, not outlandishly so, dignified in a modern manner, with a narrow face and well-kept beard. He went out of his way to praise the "great and honest sympathy of the American people" for the Mexican cause.

Shortly after Madero's election, the ambassador gave a speech at a dinner party held in the new president's honor. The event was hosted by the American Colony, in the suburb of Churubusco, home to the wealthiest of Mexico City's fifteen thousand U.S. residents, many of them associated with railroads, oil, mining, ranching, or diplomacy. They lived in spacious hacienda-style houses laid out around a country club and golf course. The point of the dinner wasn't to toast Madero but to geld him, to let him know that they expected that the close and lucrative relationship that had existed with Díaz would continue with his government.

In his after-dinner remarks, Ambassador Wilson lectured Madero, impressing on him how "we"—that is, the United States citizens at the dinner—wanted him to govern. Members of the audience applauded loudly throughout the speech. They thought that they were finally "coming into their own" and that the ambassador "had gentled Madero." Wilson in fact had infuriated the incoming president. Madero was quiet during the speech, but one reporter noticed him tugging on his beard and wincing his eyes. When the ambassador had finished his remarks, Madero stood up and quietly left.[6]

The relationship between the president and the diplomat deteriorated after this point. Wilson began sending alarmist cables back to Washington, exaggerating the danger to United States' residents, overstating Madero's difficulties, and building up would-be substitutes. He told Secretary of State Philander Knox that he believed Mexico's leader suffered from dementia or some other psychological disorder.* Madero's "French education" was also a problem, having instilled in him a romantic nationalism. Peasants in the central valley and peons in the north were seizing U.S.-owned estates. Wilson pushed aggressively for the settlement of property claims. Most expatriates from the United States lived well, safe behind high bougainvillea-covered walls. Yet reporters, thanks to Ambassador Wilson, heard about every incident of a field worker waving a machete at a U.S. ranch administrator.[7]

Historians tend to treat Henry Lane Wilson as an independent actor, motivated by his own grandiosity. Yet the ambassador's efforts to defend U.S. property rights corresponded closely with the policies of Taft and Secretary of State Knox, who had been proactive on behalf of investors. Earlier, in 1909, the Taft administration had engineered the overthrow of Nicaragua's president José Santos Zelaya, a reformer in the Martí style.

The White House issued more than one warning to Madero to get matters in hand, to take control of the countryside, and to defend United States property, not just against peasant revolutionaries but capitalist competitors. The sprawling Madero family was economically diversified in the north. Francisco, along with his uncles, brothers, and cousins, owned mines and smelters; rubber, cotton, and tobacco plantations; vineyards; and agricultural lands, and had allies among similar families, nationalists who vied with the Guggenheims, Rockefellers, and Aldriches. Mexicans chafed under the exorbitant tariffs they had to pay to U.S.-owned railroads to ship their goods

---

* Ambassador Wilson cited the fact that Madero "believed that the Mexican people should be governed by kindness and love" as evidence of his instability. Another of Madero's faults, according to the ambassador, was that he was too much of an idealist: "The dreamer of Coahuila, who essayed the role of Moses."

to the border or the coast. The Guggenheims wanted the rich Real del Monte mine north of Mexico City and thought a different president would help them get it.

Petroleum was at first a small sector, less than 2 percent of all investment, and its rapid growth took place in tandem with the progress of the Mexican Revolution. It was led largely by the Californian oil executive Edward Doheny, Rockefeller's Standard Oil, and a phalanx of Texas drillers, engineers, surveyors, investors, and lawyers. "Texas was not large enough for all of its would-be oil men," recalled a relative of one of the frontline wildcatters who poured into the coastal state of Tamaulipas, felling thick groves of evergreen breadnut, sapodilla, and zapote trees and replacing them with a forest of oil rigs. Soon, Tampico and Veracruz were the busiest petroleum ports in the Americas, and the second busiest in the world. Oilmen, especially Texas oilmen, despised Mexican economic nationalism, and they drafted Texas Rangers and other vigilantes from the U.S. Southwest to deal with security issues, including demands from workers for better pay.[8]

Madero was willing to make deals, honor claims, pay interest, extend concessions and courtesies. But he had the stench of reform about him. Oil and mine barons wanted to smell compliance. Taft backed away from Ambassador Wilson's actions as events steamrollered forward. It was an election year in the United States, with Woodrow Wilson, Taft's main opponent, promising to tame the country's domestic capitalists. Taft didn't want to appear overly solicitous of the fat cats.

In the event that he did win a second term, Taft had the Department of State and the Department of War draw up plans, making ready if need be to invade Mexico in June 1913. Theodore Roosevelt, who was running for president as a third-party candidate, said he planned to get the Rough Riders back together—a group of men he used to great publicity advantage to take the largely unoccupied San Juan Hill in Cuba during the War of 1898—to lead a cavalry invasion. Even the mystics wanted to punish Mexico. Madame Catherine, a psychic who lived in a lushly tapestried Fifth Street townhouse equidistant from the White House and the Capitol Building and whose forecasts were sought out by D.C.'s high society, predicted that Roosevelt would win the election by a landslide and that the "United

States will go to war with Mexico" and "annex every country between the Panama Canal and the borders of our country."[9]

Madame Catherine was wrong. Wilson won, and Taft's and Roosevelt's war plans were shelved.

Exit Madero

Now began the plotting to remove Madero before Wilson's inauguration, worried that the new U.S. president would seek to normalize relations with Mexico. The proximate events leading to the Mexican president's demise began in an abandoned Mexico City house. There, on February 11, 1913, with Taft still president and Wilson president-elect, a railroad executive named Ernest Pettegrew arranged a meeting between General Huerta, who publicly supported Madero, and Porfirio Díaz's nephew, Félix Díaz. Félix was, according to one source, "financed by a few Spanish reactionaries" and in league with exiled Mexicans. The two men came up with a plan.[10]

After this meeting, Díaz and his men seized the Ciudadela, the city's weapons arsenal, which sat a few blocks from the national palace. Over the next few days, pitched battles took place between Huerta's federal soldiers and Díaz's rebels. Huerta's defense, though, was duck soup, a play-act, presumably agreed upon in that secret meeting with Díaz.

Over the course of a week, hundreds of soldiers and rebels would be killed and maimed, all in the service of manufacturing a crisis that Huerta, acting as if he were still loyal to Madero, would be called on to mediate. Huerta could easily have defeated Díaz. The counterrevolutionary nephew had no support in the cities. No protests broke out in his defense. No recruits flocked to the fight. What Díaz did have was a well-stocked armory, which allowed him to lob mortars into the city, and an arrangement with Huerta to make the siege look like a standoff.

Meanwhile, Henry Lane Wilson aggravated tensions with breathless communiqués to Washington. The ambassador opened the United States embassy, a Moorish citadel-like structure, to the plotters to plan their next move. Wilson also summoned other international envoys to the embassy

and pushed them to start pressuring Madero to resign and for their governments to withdraw recognition.

Latin America's envoys refused the demand unanimously. The ambassador simply cut them out, reconvening Germany, Spain, and Great Britain as
a rump "diplomatic corps" that supported, or at least didn't object to, his
plans. Fighting continued for days. Díaz's men mounted machine guns on
the armory's roof to fire into federalist ranks. At the end of the day's shooting, a truce was called to give each side a chance to pull their dead off the
city streets.

On the morning of February 18, Huerta made his move. At 11:00 a.m.,
he had Madero's brother, Gustavo, captured and handed over to Díaz's men,
who beat him to death. At 1:30 p.m., Huerta had Madero and his vice president arrested. The rebels gave up the armory, and the city's church bells
rang to celebrate the restoration of peace. Wilson had already, two hours
earlier, around the time of Gustavo's murder, telegrammed Washington to
report that Madero's government had come to an end.[11]

Huerta asked Wilson if Madero should be deported or put in an "insane
asylum." "General," Ambassador Wilson answered, "do what you think is
best for the welfare of Mexico." On Saturday, February 22, 1913, the ambassador threw a reception for Huerta at his embassy, attended by prominent
Mexicans, U.S. expatriates, and foreign diplomats. At one point, Wilson
and Huerta retired to the smoking room, where the two men had an hour-
and-a-half-long private conversation. Then, around midnight, Madero and
his vice president were taken from their place of confinement and executed,
a bullet each to the back of their heads. Woodrow Wilson learned of their
murders while in Princeton preparing his inaugural address. He was, he
said, "shocked."[12]

The killing of Madero had the same effect on Mexico that the killing of
Archduke Franz Ferdinand of Austria, a year later, would have on Europe. It
radicalized forces in motion. In Mexico's case: the revolutionary masses,
peasant leagues, and labor activists who wanted to build a new order, and
the old guard who worked to restore the old one. The nation moved toward
total war. Insurgent armies led by Carranza, Villa, and Zapata put aside

their differences and united to oppose Huerta. "Passions and impulses and organizations more radical," the historian John Womack writes, "than any since independence were unleashed." Three to four million people would perish in the coming decades, out of a population of about fifteen million.[13]

What to Do with Mexico?

Madero's killing also radicalized Woodrow Wilson—for a time, anyway.

Wilson faced many foreign policy crises upon taking office. Europe's meddling in China needed monitoring. Japan was protesting a proposed California law limiting the property rights of Japanese subjects. Demands were growing for Philippine independence. Germany was still considered a threat.

But he started with Latin America, devoting his first two cabinet meetings to the region—not to any one conflict or crisis, though Mexico soon would consume his attentions, but to the broad history of the United States' relations in Latin America. He knew that the United States had to move beyond the Monroe Doctrine, or update it into a more universal principle, as Latin Americans themselves had long been demanding. Along these lines, Wilson drafted a hesitant statement of principles that he read out loud to his cabinet, hinting that he thought inter-American relations might serve as a model for a world doctrine of law and peace.

It made sense that Wilson, inevitably described as an idealist, would see Latin America as a testing ground for a new moral diplomacy, based not on the crude pursuit of profits or national interests but on the principles of higher law, of equity and fair dealing. In no other region were the contradictions, paradoxes, and tautologies of United States foreign policy so obvious, the hypocrisies so ham-handed. Wilson, when discussing Mexico and Latin America, had begun to sound like Bolívar and other Spanish American philosopher-statesmen when he criticized the old diplomacy, the old balances-of-power, as absent of virtue, absent of morality.

Huerta, his government yet to be recognized by Washington, soon came to dominate Wilson's attentions. "What to do with Mexico is the great problem and was discussed at length," wrote Wilson's secretary of the navy Josephus Daniels in his diary of these first cabinet meetings.[14]

Wilson had an administration full of officials who owned property in Mexico, many of them from Texas, and most were happy that Huerta was in charge. Even Wilson's populist secretary of state William Jennings Bryan, the "great commoner," owned land in the Rio Grande Valley. The Democratic Party was in a process of realignment, gradually becoming, in the North, a vehicle of reform. But many of its power brokers were concentrated in the Southwest and West, concerned with things other than reform. Democrats in Texas and California, heavily invested in Mexico's extractive industries, played an influential role in the national party, with many of the party's leaders owning large tracts of cotton and ranch land on the Mexican side of the Colorado River Delta.[15]

These men wanted stability. London showed no qualms in quickly recognizing Huerta. Get it over with, was the consensus of Wilson's cabinet. He's a "brute" said Secretary of War Lindley Garrison, but at least the United States would have someone to deal with.

By the time Wilson became president, a tremendous amount of U.S.-owned property had been destroyed. Insurgents seized land, flooded mines, burned factories. Pancho Villa's men raided the Hearst family's 1,625,000-acre ranch (established by George Hearst at the end of the 1800s with land and water taken from Native Americans) and made off with sixty thousand head of white-faced shorthorn cattle. The Mexican Revolution was, says the historian John Mason Hart, the "first great third world uprising against American economic, cultural, and political expansion."[16]

The sooner order was established, the sooner property claims could be processed. Investors wanted a Mexican president capable of both protecting what was left and paying for what was gone. They thought Huerta their man. U.S. citizens living in Mexico, led by William F. Buckley Sr., whose son, William Jr., would become known for editing the *National Review*, thought so too.

"I have to pause and remind myself," Wilson said shortly after taking office, about pressure to recognize Huerta, "that I am President of the United States and not of a small group of Americans with vested interests in Mexico."[17]

As a presidential candidate, Wilson had promised to forgo interventionism in Latin America. Yet he inherited an impossible situation. He could recognize the government that came to power from the U.S.-brokered coup, putting the White House's imprimatur on Madero's murder and overlooking Ambassador Wilson's complicity. Or he could refuse recognition, which, as his experts at State told him, was a tacit endorsement of Huerta's revolutionary opponents.[18]

"I will not recognize a government of butchers," Wilson said, and began to take measures to provide aid to the revolutionaries, including Pancho Villa, Emiliano Zapata, and Venustiano Carranza.[19]

To atone for an intervention, Wilson intervened.

Huerta Digs In

Wilson the Presbyterian saw Huerta as bad both in "origin" (having come to power in an illegitimate coup) and in "purpose" (representing the worst of Latin America's brute militarism and Catholic zealotry). The more Wilson learned about the circumstances of Madero's murder (from the State Department but also from secret reports prepared by agents he sent outside of official channels to investigate the killing), the more he committed to nonrecognition. Wilson was shocked upon learning of Henry Lane Wilson's intrigues. "Indeed extraordinary," he said to Bryan upon reading one report. Marvin Ferree, the night editor of an English-language newspaper in Mexico City, passed a cache of documents to President Wilson filled with photographs and sworn statements apparently proving that Ambassador Wilson had arranged to pay Huerta five hundred thousand dollars in gold to move forward with his coup.[20]

Pressing on Wilson was a group of men, in and out of his administration, who wanted to turn Mexico into a vassal state, on the order of the British model. Colonel Edward House, Wilson's closest adviser, wanted to send someone "into Mexico like Lord Cromer was sent into Egypt." House was referring to Evelyn Baring, the First Earl of Cromer, whom London sent to Cairo in 1877 to oversee the British occupation of Egypt. If not Egypt, then Cuba. "We should treat Mexico very much as we have Cuba," by which House meant intervening in the civil war on the side of rebels and then superintending a cooperative government.[21]

House, part of a Texas family invested in Mexican cotton, was Wilson's main channel to a bipartisan group of powerful Southwestern businessmen. That New Mexico and Arizona had just successfully entered the union as states in 1912 added to a sense, among some, that Polk in 1848 should have gone further and taken all of Mexico. Perhaps the U.S. still could. "We all believe here that there is but one solution" for the Mexico problem, William Buckley wrote House in late 1913, "and that is American intervention." Among this "all-in" group were New Mexico senator Albert Fall, the *Los Angeles Times*' Harry Chandler, *Chicago Tribune* publisher Robert McCormick, Theodore Roosevelt, and William Randolph Hearst.[22]

"Many Americans want intervention," said Secretary of War Lindley Garrison. True, as far as Garrison and a small circle of wealthy families were concerned. The general population of the United States, however, elected Wilson on a peace platform to focus on domestic issues in an election where Socialist Party candidate Eugene Debs pulled just under a million votes, 6 percent of the total. London's ambassador to the United States suspected there was significant approval among the U.S. working class of the beating United States corporations were taking in Mexico. "It is singular how the majority of the Americans are rather pleased than otherwise at the losses of rich Americans in Mexico," he wrote his wife, noting that those "rich Americans" were turning to the British government to protect them.[23]

Huerta dug in. And, after back-channel efforts to negotiate his exit failed, so did Wilson.

"There can be no certain prospect of peace in America until General Huerta has surrendered his usurped authority," the president said at the end of 1913. By this point, Wilson's executive agents in Mexico were establishing contacts with the opposition to get a sense of what a post-Huerta settlement might look like. The rebels all made clear that there could be no settlement that would involve the participation of Huerta. "Revolutions must be implacable if they are to triumph," Carranza had said at an earlier moment. "The revolution which compromises commits suicide."[24]

President Wilson recoiled from such absolutism. He was "deeply disturbed" that the revolutionaries "would trust no one but themselves." Carranza rebuffed all efforts by Wilson's envoys to place conditions on support, to accept that in exchange for providing aid Washington might have some influence in a post-Huerta government. Mexico's revolutionaries, Carranza insisted, could win without the help of the United States. Mexico would not be Cuba.

Wilson wouldn't recognize Huerta. He opposed annexing Mexico. But given the importance of Mexico to the United States, he couldn't do nothing. That left supporting the rebels. Business backers of Wilson, short of recognizing Huerta, thought the upper-class Carranza the safest option. Among all of Mexico's insurgent leaders, he seemed the closest to their habitus, someone they might have to compete with but at least would be able to do business with.[25]

Carranza, though, continued to refuse to make any promises regarding property rights or compensation in exchange for assistance. So, caught between Huerta's tenacity and Carranza's commitment to sovereignty, Wilson drifted left. He aligned, without receiving any concessions in return, with the revolutionary coalition led by Carranza, Zapata, and Villa, representing nationalists, socialists, communists, peasants, workers, and anarchists.

There existed a ban on selling weapons to Mexican belligerents, so the White House arranged for a shipment of ten thousand Krag-Jørgensen rifles to pass through San Francisco customs "cleared for China" before being diverted to rebel forces. Wilson instructed his Treasury secretary to quietly allow train cars full of ammunition to reach the revolutionaries.

In early 1914, the secretary of war and secretary of the navy began making plans to invade Veracruz. Some in Wilson's cabinet and larger circle of advisers saw this move as a chance to secure Mexico's oil, though Wilson, in both public and private comments, continued to frame the invasion exclusively as an assist to the revolutionaries. In early February, he told London's ambassador that "a radical revolution was the only cure" for Mexico's troubles. Mexicans, he said to the journalist Walter Lippmann, possess the "sacred right of Revolution." He "believed" in the "revolution."[26]

In March, Wilson lifted the ban on selling arms to the rebels, saving them from having to waste time on complicated smuggling operations so they could focus on defeating Huerta's troops. It was "incumbent on the United States," John Lind, one of the president's special envoys to Mexico, said, "to put an end to Huerta's saturnalia of crime and oppression." By April, Wilson was so anxious that Huerta was consolidating power and winning the civil war that he gave the order to launch the invasion.[27]

William Buckley thought Wilson a fool. The Mexican Revolution was a race war, he said, a "revolt of the Indian against the white," and the president of the United States was on the wrong side. For United States capitalists, race and property relations were inseparable, as was the belief that democratic majority rule was a form of political subversion. The Soviet Revolution was still years away; Lenin's Bolshevik Party but a few months old. And yet Delbert Haff, a Kansas City lawyer representing U.S. mining and rail interests in Mexican courts, raised the menace of communism. "The Indian is originally, and by tradition, a communist, as is well known," he said. "He practiced it in its most perfect form." Many had thought that the iron-fisted Díaz had "extinguished" the threat of peasant communism once and for all. Yet granting the vote to peasants revived the notion that "democracy is a sort of socialism and communism."[28]

"The white race will be expelled from Mexico and a new empire of the Montezumas set up in the palace of Chapultepec," testified Henry Lane Wilson to Congress after having been recalled from Mexico. "Under the rule of democratic institutions," he said, the slogan "Mexican for the Mexicans" really means "Mexican for the Indians, because if the majority rules the Indian will rule in Mexico." The Conquest, for these men and others like them, wasn't over, nor was, centuries after Vitoria and Las Casas, the argument over the relationship of property and sovereignty.[29]

30.

Wilson's Dilemma

W oodrow Wilson is remembered today as an internationalist, a dreamer, a moralist, and a racist, a president who resegregated the federal bureaucracy and courted Confederate voters for reelection. He is also known as a president who tried and failed, in the post–World War I peace talks, to force New World idealism on Old World realism. He was all these things, but how all these things are connected can't be understood without grappling with his response to the challenge Mexico, and more broadly Latin America, posed to United States authority.

Wilson had long been conflicted over the idea of rebellion and the validity of establishing a new social order based on force. Born in Staunton, Virginia, on the eve of the Civil War, he learned opposing lessons from his minister father, Joseph Ruggles Wilson. As a leader of the Presbyterian Church of the Confederate States, the elder Wilson used a key principle of covenant theology to justify slavery: social hierarchy is natural, and slavery is as elemental as "the family order which lies at the very foundation of the Church." Yet as a Confederate rebel, his father defended the South's break from the North with a different principle of covenant theology: the right to rebel against tyrants. Woodrow Wilson, trained as a historian, would notice that most revolts provoked reaction and ended in despotism. Only the

United States mastered "self-command, self-possession," while other nations, in their periodical revolts, lost self-control.[1]

The reason for this distinction, Wilson once said, was that the Revolution that created the United States wasn't a revolution at all but really a process of self-organization. The new republic did nothing but "methodize its way of living," organizing virtues that existed prior to the Revolution.

The Country Is Theirs

Wilson, to his credit, realized the enormity of what he faced in Mexico. He knew that the country's revolution demanded not just a change in policy but a change in worldview—a change in, well, doctrine.

Wilson would come to appreciate the upheaval as a "revolution as profound as that which occurred in France." He knew how financial imperialism worked in Latin America. He knew how bankers and businesses caused the chaos that justified high interest and, by creating turmoil, required military intervention to restore order. And he knew that international debt was a form of modern slavery, using abolitionist imagery to call for its downfall: "I rejoice in nothing so much as in the prospect that" Latin Americans "will now be emancipated from these conditions; and we ought to be the first to take part in assisting in that emancipation."[2]

Wilson knew all these things, and still he sent eight hundred Marines and sailors into the port of Veracruz on the morning of April 21, 1914, soon to be reinforced by thousands more. The pretext for the invasion was that Huerta's soldiers refused to follow protocol and properly salute a U.S. flag on a ship docked in port. The real reason was to end Huerta's regime and bring one of the revolutionary factions to power. In Veracruz, there were still witnesses alive who remembered the bombs of 1847, which landed on churches, hospitals, and homes, followed "by scenes of rape, pillage, robbery and killings by the invaders." "My heart bled for the inhabitants," Captain Robert E. Lee wrote to his wife, describing the carnage.[3]

The destruction wasn't as bad this time around. Wilson's warships bombed a holdout military academy, killing most of its cadets. U.S. troops took control of the customs house, railroad depot, and telegraph office, as city residents and Huerta's soldiers withdrew into the interior. United States citizens who resided in Mexico filled the port's dockside, escaping what they feared would be Mexican retaliation for the invasion. The navy put them on lighters bound for New Orleans. Some made their way to Washington to demand that the U.S. declare war against Mexico. Bryan turned them away without a meeting. Secretary of the Navy Josephus Daniels opened his door only to lecture them. "You men went to Mexico because you weren't satisfied with business conditions at home," Daniels said. "You went there to get rich quick; and now you want the whole country to raise an army of five hundred thousand men and send it to Mexico at this country's expense to protect you."[4]

Secretary of War Lindley Garrison was more sympathetic. Just weeks after Austria had declared war on Serbia, he urged the president to do what the oilmen wanted: march on Mexico City and occupy the entire country. By this point, Mexico, despite the chaos, was pumping more petroleum than any other country in the world. Wilson, however, rejected this advice. To escalate would unite the revolutionary armies, this time in opposition to Washington. Wilson's objective was to oust Huerta.[5]

He told Garrison that he refused to play the part of historical reaction, the way Europe's ancien régime did to prevent the French Revolution from unfolding according to its internal dynamics. "Mexicans are to sort out their own affairs," Wilson said in August 1914, as the guns of Europe began to fire and his gunboats bobbed off the coast of Veracruz.

"The country is theirs," Wilson said.[6]

Wilson Gives an Interview

On April 27, six days after the navy landed troops in Veracruz, President Wilson enjoyed a dinner with a small group of family and friends. His daughters, Margaret and Nellie, sang a round of songs. Later, Wilson retired to another room to sit for an interview with *The Saturday Evening Post*'s Samuel George Blythe about what he hoped to achieve in Mexico. A "righteous government," he said, justice for "the submerged eighty-five percent of the people of that country."

Wilson that night was in high social-history gear, putting forward a vision of historical progress as emerging from struggle, as made possible only through the fightback of the oppressed. He challenged Blythe to cite one "instance in all the history of the world where liberty was handed down from above." "Liberty is always attained by the forces working below, underneath, by the great movement of the people."

"They want order," Wilson went on, referring to the "aristocrats" and "vested interests" of the "old-time régime," the "great owners of property, the overlords." "I say to you that old order is dead." It was his mission, he said, to help create a "new order, which will have its foundation on human liberty and human rights."

Wilson's most striking remarks in his interview with Blythe had to do with his support for the distribution of land. The interview demonstrated an appreciation of how much had been stolen from indigenous and peasant communities during the Díaz government. His wife, Ellen Axson Wilson, had been reading books on Mexican history and summarizing them to the president, giving him a command of the details, including a sense of how lawyers used juridical methods to steal land from peasants. "Farm after farm passed into the control of the big landowners, and there was no recourse for the former owners or for their families but to work at dictated terms and practically as slaves on the land that had formerly been theirs," Wilson said. The United States, he vowed, would not "insist on an exact procedure of the partition of the land" but would, once Huerta was gone, help with the division.[7]

Wilson vacillated between wistful and resolute, straying from topic to topic, all, in their own way, related to the raising up of Mexico's bottom 85 percent. At the end of the discussion, he returned to the problem of imperialism, the cause of all the trouble. His smile vanished, according to Blythe, and his face became set: "I shall fight everyone of these men who are now seeking and who will then be seeking to exploit Mexico for their own selfish ends."[8]

Because of Mexico, Wilson had revised his opinion about revolutions, coming to see them as legitimate, as the authentic response of the bottom 85 percent against their lot in life. But also because of Mexico, he came to believe that all modern revolutions, no matter how just, were quickly distorted by outside forces, by powerful nations such as Great Britain, Germany, and the United States, and by private interests, who took sides, sowed division, played faction against faction—like the National Asphalt Trust did in Venezuela. Wilson tried to thread the needle. He committed his administration to stand against this manipulation, be it from London, Berlin, Washington, or 26 Broadway, Manhattan, where John D. Rockefeller held court. In so doing, he intervened, believing he wasn't intervening. The United States has "no right at any time to intervene in Mexico," he said to his secretary of war, even as his troops occupied Veracruz.

To prove the sincerity of their pledge to treat Latin America equitably, Wilson had Bryan that April agree to pay Colombia twenty-five million dollars in compensation for its loss of Panama, and offered "sincere regret" for Washington's role in the loss. Theodore Roosevelt went on a speaking tour to denounce the deal as "blackmail" and Wilson a "traitor." There was nothing to be sorry for, Roosevelt said. If there was, then "Panama should at once be returned to Colombia, and we should stop work on the canal and abandon the place bag and baggage." Wilson might have been the first U.S. president to apologize for an act of foreign policy aggression, and Roosevelt the first to condemn such an apology.[9]

In the name of idealism, Wilson thought himself fighting not just the U.S. foreign policy establishment but Great Britain's as well. London's diplomats complained of Wilson's "moral diplomacy." There were valuable material interests at stake, and the world needed a stable Mexican government, the British said. Wilson's stubborn obsession with Huerta proved he was "either ignorant or indifferent" to how diplomacy worked and was "quite inaccessible to argument."

Bryan did manage to secure a pledge that London wouldn't stand in the way of Washington's efforts to oust Huerta. Wilson was pleased, happy to be "pounding elementary doctrine" into Europe's realpolitik diplomats.[10]

Forward Movement

Wilson had less luck pounding doctrine into capitalists at home. His flights of fancy during his interview with Blythe, his soaring rhetoric about supervising revolutionary change in Mexico, contrasted with a recent humbling he had experienced on the limits of his power.

A week earlier in Ludlow, Colorado, on the day Wilson ordered troops into Veracruz, union busters hired by Rockefeller mining interests and backed by the National Guard had fired on a tent encampment of striking families, killing at least twenty, including eleven children and two women. The Ludlow Massacre was the climax of Colorado's Great Coalfield War, which had started months earlier, pitting miners against the owners of mines. After Ludlow, the war escalated, turning nearly the entire northern mining range of Colorado into a battle zone, with fighting threatening to spill into neighboring states.

Armed union members ranged across a long front, from Denver to the New Mexico border, attacking mines and killing strikebreakers, and making the hills of Colorado look a lot like the hills of Coahuila. There were reports that these miners turned guerrilla fighters had made connections with Villa's forces in Mexico. Since the end of the Civil War, the federal financing of railroads had pushed rail lines deep into northern Mexico, creating, despite an international border, a single copper, coal, and cattle economy. Now, with revolution on one side of the border and a workers' uprising on the other, it looked to many like a single battlefield as well.

Wilson himself understood the fight in Mexico and the one in Colorado as related, as a struggle against what his Mexican agents called "Medievalism" and his Colorado envoys described as a "tenth-century mental attitude." Barons like Rockefeller, no matter what side of the border, treated workers as serfs rather than citizens with basic rights.[11]

Wilson tried to deal with Rockefeller the way he fancied himself dealing with Mexico's "great owners of property, the overlords." A day before his interview with Blythe, he had sent an envoy to New York to threaten the Rockefellers, father and son, that he would nationalize their mines if they didn't recognize the mine worker's union and enter arbitration to end the conflict. The Rockfellers brushed Wilson's envoy off and sent a telegram, written by son John, in reply, which arrived at the White House on the morning of Wilson's interview with Blythe.

Rockefeller's answer to Wilson's threat of nationalization: go ahead. The result would be mass unemployment, Rockefeller said, and Wilson would pay the political price. The right to a union-free "open shop," Rockefeller continued, was sacrosanct, and "could not be arbitrated." The Supreme Court had recently upheld the federal government's breakup of Standard Oil's monopoly, so the Rockefellers had had enough of outsiders interfering in their business. If Wilson wanted to settle the conflict, Rockefeller went on, he should do what he did in Mexico: send in troops and make it clear that the purpose of government is to enforce "obedience to the law" and ensure "to every citizen the right guaranteed to him by the Constitution to be protected in his life and liberty, whether he chooses to work as a member of a union or not."[12]

When Wilson had finished reading the cable, he passed it to his adviser, Colonel House, muttering something about the "contempt" he had for men like the Rockefellers. He thought them ruthless. As president of Princeton, Wilson had his request for a donation to the university turned down by Rockefeller Senior. Then, as governor of New Jersey, where Standard's corporate headquarters were located, Wilson found it impossible to reform the state's extremely pro-business laws. Rockefeller Senior treated him the way Ambassador Wilson had treated Madero, like a lad. Wilson turned his conversation with House back to Mexico.[13]

Pancho Villa, Wilson told his counselor, was the "forward movement," a man of action.

Later that day, with Blythe, Wilson would speak with passion in favor of land reform and with confidence he could stop capitalists from plundering Mexico. Yet he couldn't get the capitalists to stop killing workers and their families in his own country. Realizing the limits to reform in the United States, Wilson fantasized that there were no such limits in Mexico. "There shall be no individual exploitation of Mexico," Wilson told Blythe, as he wrapped up his interview.[14]

Knowing that he lacked the power to take on Rockefeller—to nationalize his mines and force arbitration—the next day, Wilson ordered a thousand federal cavalry troops into Colorado. Then he sent a letter to Rockefeller, capitulating. The troops he was sending would not stay neutral but would pacify the rebellion. Soon the Coalfield War would be over, its leaders in jail, the mines running again.

Germ of the League of Nations

Wilson's seven-month occupation of Veracruz was a public relations and diplomatic flop. He had alienated his allies in Mexico for going too far, and angered the backroom boys of the Democratic Party for not going far enough. The press ridiculed the mission as pointless.

What Wilson did next, though, was an innovation. He did what Rockefeller wouldn't in Colorado: he agreed to arbitration. Wilson and Bryan accepted a proposal by the Chilean diplomat Eduard Suárez Mujica to establish a commission comprised of Argentina, Brazil, and Chile to resolve the Mexican crisis. A precedent was being set. The United States had, in the past, participated in international arbitration to settle border and economic disputes, but never to settle the kind of military intervention that Wilson had ordered in Veracruz. And never would it have submitted to a panel comprised *solely* of Latin American jurists.[15]

That the offer was made so quickly (and that Wilson and Bryan accepted within days of landing troops at Veracruz) hints that a plan might have been in the works before the invasion, with Bryan using his embassies in Argentina, Brazil, and Chile to organize the mediation offer. Huerta, besieged, had little choice but to accept the offer. He named William F. Buckley Sr. to the legal team representing his government. Buckley's politics jibed with Huerta's. Both men were conservative Catholics, defenders of order and the social hierarchy. Buckley had been at Huerta's side since the beginning of his rule: he was in the United States embassy with Henry Lane Wilson when Huerta had Madero arrested. He thought the whole arbitration idea was a setup, and he wasn't wrong. Talks got under way in May 1914 on the Canadian side of Niagara Falls, presided over by jurists the State Department had taken to calling the ABC men, from Argentina, Brazil, and Chile. Wilson had by now become as intransigent as Carranza when it came to Huerta. No settlement, he said, would be "acceptable to public opinion in the United States" unless it included the "entire elimination of General Huerta."[16]

Buckley defended Huerta. There was little left to defend. Wilson's military intervention, though condemned by Mexican insurgents, did succeed in cutting off Huerta's oil revenues. Squeezed by Villa and Carranza from the north and Zapata from the south, Huerta resigned on July 15 and fled to Spain, where he cultivated contacts with Germany with the hope that Berlin would aid in his reinstallation.[17]

Carranza became the provisional leader of the nation, though the anti-Huerta coalition soon unraveled. Villa and Zapata would break with Carranza and remobilize their armies, driving the revolution forward into its violent decades.

Still, the two-month-long Niagara Falls summit gave Latin American jurists a chance to showcase what equitable arbitration might look like and allowed Wilson to promote a new kind of diplomacy—with a better claim to legitimacy in a world where demands for democracy and national sovereignty were getting louder.

Wilson followed up this precedent-setting arbitration with another precedent, an affront to those who thought that the United States should decide its foreign affairs unilaterally. After a series of meetings with Latin American delegates, Washington joined with Argentina, Brazil, Chile, Bolivia, Guatemala, Uruguay, Colombia, and Costa Rica in a collective recognition of Carranza as provisional president. Carranza—who was managing to hold Zapata's and Villa's armies at bay—would govern Mexico until a constitution could be drafted and elections held. Wilson hailed the innovation, saying that the collective recognition of Carranza showed that the cooperative relations of the Western Hemisphere could serve as a guide in the future.

The "states of America," Wilson said, will change "the political history of the world."

As early as August 1914, the war in Europe under way, Colonel House wrote in his diary that the ABC mediation effort contained the "germ of the League of Nations." The mediation's triumph impressed foreign policy modernizers.[18]

"Here was an action which future statesmen can and should turn to great advantage," wrote Franklin Delano Roosevelt, then serving as assistant secretary of the navy. "Why shall we not make the work begun at Niagara a permanent Pan-American policy?" asked Representative James Slayden. It "would be a long step towards universal peace." Secretary of State Bryan kept saying that the United States had a moral duty to offer the same kind of mediation that settled the Mexican crisis to end Europe's war. And Andrew Carnegie (who a quarter of a century earlier had listened, hour after hour, speech after speech, to Latin American statesmen as they pressed their version of international law on Blaine and his delegates) wrote to Wilson in September to urge him to build on the mediation's success. Carnegie's letter contained a proposal for a "Union of Peace of the American Republics." "Twenty-one Republics welded into a peace brotherhood would be such an example to the rest of the world as could not fail to impress it." The New World already leads the way, he said, with thousands of miles of borders, untold islands, with nary a fort, soldier, or cannon. A "league of all the American states" Carnegie said, would "banish war from the New World.[19]

Wilson wrote back: "I am warmly obliged to you for lodging in my mind a suggestion which may later bear fruit." He then ordered the withdrawal of Marines from Veracruz in November.

The Call-Up

The diplomatic triumph of the ABC mediation notwithstanding, Wilson's idealism dimmed as the world grew darker, as the Mexican Revolution radicalized and the European war escalated. His worst qualities came to the fore not long after his frustrating capitulation to Rockefeller.[20]

He never gave up what he imagined was the moral high ground; he continued to sign reform bills that came across his desk. But, under pressure from Southern conservatives in his cabinet, Wilson sped up the racist segregation of the federal government, which in turn helped him consolidate his support in Southern states—useful not just for his coming reelection but for his future effort to lead the United States into Europe's war.

Mexico's size and economic importance forced restraint and reflection on Wilson. Not so the smaller nations in the Caribbean, many of which were in a constant state of upheaval owing to European and United States debt bondage. Haiti was unstable and vulnerable, *still* paying off loans it was forced to take out to compensate French slavers. At the end of 1914, in response to a series of payment defaults, Marines landed in Haiti, acting on behalf of New York bankers. They marched to the Banque Nationale and commandeered seventeen wooden boxes filled with gold bars worth half a million dollars. The soldiers transported them to National City's headquarters, located at 55 Wall Street, and deposited them in the bank's formidable vault.* Wilson then, in July 1915, ordered the navy to occupy all of Haiti. Soon, he'd send the Marines into the Dominican Republic, which, like Haiti, had fallen into crisis due to the shenanigans of foreign financiers.[21]

In the United States, a militant strike wave begun in 1915 would go on for years, accompanied by an equally militant counterwave of company thuggery. As with the case of Ludlow, Wilson did little to protect workers and their families from vigilantes. Freedom of speech came under attack as the government cracked down on anarchist groups and other quarters of political dissent. In response to domestic radicalism, Wilson began to emphasize *Americanism*, not in the continental sense but in the jingoist one. "Disloyalty," he said, "must be crushed." "Certain groups" born under "foreign flags" must be policed. Wilson brushed off an old nineteenth-century political slogan for his reelection campaign: "America First," he said in an address to the Daughters of the American Revolution—"America first, last, and all the time."

Conservatives thought that uniting the country behind a xenophobic patriotism helped stem the forces of disaggregation, what some described as the "Mexicanization" of the United States. All of this was a prelude to a more fearsome crackdown to come—the first Red Scare, when Wilson's Justice Department, empowered by the new Espionage Act, prosecuted,

---

* The vault, among the largest in the world in its day, made with more than a million pounds of steel, is now a private party room at Cipriani Restaurant.

jailed, and deported thousands of socialists and pacifists. By the middle of 1915, Wilson had already taken steps that put the country on the road to war in Europe, including drawing up plans that July to greatly increase the size of the army and navy. He still formally held to neutrality—to staying out of the European conflict—and would run on that policy for reelection. But Wilson now took it upon himself to convince the country that it had to "prepare" for war, which was a stepping stone toward, two years later, war itself. [22]

Yet before Wilson declared war on Germany, he'd send troops once more into Mexico, this time under the command of Major General John Pershing and with the mission to capture Pancho Villa. Villa had, on March 9, 1916, attacked the 13th Cavalry Regiment, which was based near Columbus, New Mexico. The raid was tactical. Villa hoped Wilson would overreact and order another intervention, which would embarrass Carranza.

Pershing's wasn't a small operation. He pulled together an enormous force. And though his objective was to capture one man, he ran the campaign as if it were a full-on invasion. Military strategists created maps that divided the entire state of Chihuahua into a strategic grid. As many as 12,000 U.S. regular soldiers operated hundreds of miles south of the border—five cavalry regiments, four infantry regiments, and three artillery regiments. On the border itself, President Wilson, on June 18, 1916, called up the country's *entire* National Guard, about 150,000 men.

The mission failed. "Villa has not been got," wrote *The Cleveland Leader*, months into the chase. Pershing explained his inability to capture the revolutionary with many an old soldier's complaint. In this case it was true: Wilson had tied his hands. Pershing wasn't Andrew Jackson in Florida, set loose by superiors in Washington to hang, murder, burn, terrorize, and torture at will. Rather, Wilson insisted that Pershing proceed with delicacy.

By this point Wilson had lost all sympathy for Carranza, who was unbending in his economic nationalism and uncooperative when it came to protecting U.S. property. Yet, aware by now that the United States would soon enter the European conflict, Wilson couldn't waste resources on a major war in Mexico. He told Pershing to be careful. Catch Villa but maintain "scrupulous regard for sovereignty of Mexico."

The major general had begun his military career fighting the Apache and Sioux, then the Spanish in Cuba, after which he'd put down a Muslim rebellion in Moro Province in the Philippines, all with little regard for human life. Now, though, Wilson had placed tight restrictions on who he could kill, on when, how, and where he could fight. His soldiers were prohibited from occupying towns and taking offensive action against Mexican troops, even if they opened fire on U.S. troops. There would be no torturing of prisoners, as was rampant in the Philippines. Soldiers did have some fun though. Mexico provided a chance for Lieutenant George S. Patton to be the first to use combustion engine vehicles in battle—a couple of Dodge 30-35 touring cars in a skirmish against three of Villa's men. Patton returned to Pershing's base camp in Namiquipa with the three dead Mexicans strapped to the fenders of the car like trophies from a hunt. The incident led to Patton's promotion and to Pershing's affections. "My bandit," Pershing called him.

Wilson pleaded with Carranza for cooperation. The Mexican president would no doubt have liked Villa eliminated, his army broken up. But he refused Wilson's request, demanding that the United States withdraw immediately. Pershing complained that the changing rules of war limited his ability to complete the mission: We snuck "home under cover," he said, "like a whipped cur with its tail between its legs."[23]

"Pershing came in like an eagle," said Villa, "but left like a wet hen." Villa earned his gloat, but, as it turned out, Villa himself was the least important element of the Villa campaign.

Pershing's Mexican run is often presented nostalgically as the last great romantic cavalry pursuit of yesterday's frontier wars. It's better to think of it as a warm-up for future wars. Between June 1916 and April 1917, Pershing and his officers ran a nearly yearlong drill, testing the ability of army and National Guard officers to maneuver large formations of soldiers from one location to another.

U.S. regular army soldiers made and broke down camps, including field hospitals and kitchens. Operating a mobile command center out of a Dodge sedan, Pershing coordinated ground movements with aerial reconnaissance. Motorized truck caravans were used by the army for the first time, moving not only men but heavy artillery, as soldiers laid telegraph wire and set up machine gun nests. Skills learned in these maneuvers would soon be put to the test in the Argonne.

The call-up of the country's entire National Guard turned what had been fragmented, state-based militias into a coordinated fighting machine, an indispensable reserve for the national army. Officers from the 1st Illinois Cavalry Regiment, understanding that what they were doing was in preparation for France, had their men dig long trenches on either side of a large field and, firing blanks, stage a mock battle over a mock no-man's-land. The pursuit of Villa and battles with both rebel and federal troops turned inexperienced soldiers into effective fighters accustomed to operating on open terrain that was close to what they would soon find in Flanders. The Rio Grande anticipated the Marne. And Patton would go on to command U.S. forces in the Mediterranean and Europe during the next world war.[24]

Wilson won reelection on November 7, 1916. By January 1917, all of Pershing's men had been withdrawn from Mexico. On April 2, the United States declared war on Germany. A good many of the soldiers and National Guard troops—perhaps even a majority—who had followed Pershing into Mexico would follow him to France. Enlisted men who spent months slogging through mud chasing Villa were promoted and served as officers in Europe; many reported that their Mexican rehearsal had been invaluable. "I served in France in 1917 and 1918 and I want to tell you that the training and conditions we experienced in Texas along the border were tougher than those we underwent in combat in France," reported one veteran.[25]

Most Latin American leaders had believed that Wilson was an ally in neutrality, and so were caught off guard by his turn to war. Most of the region's governments hoped for an Allied victory, breaking off relations with Germany and the Central Powers. Several small countries, including most of Central America and Haiti, declared war but didn't engage in combat.* Bra-

---

* Honduras also made a unique contribution to the allied war effort. It was then the most important source of the cohune, or corozo nut, from the manaca palm tree, the shell of which when carbonized is an effective filter against poison gas. During the war, the U.S. imported

zil was the only large Latin American nation to send troops to Europe, largely due to the influence of the popular statesman Ruy Barbosa, who at The Hague seven years earlier had predicted just such a world war. Barbosa had qualms about the conflict, but he thought German militarism a dangerous manifestation of amoral realism. It had to be defeated.[26]

Barbosa felt the pulse of history, saw the catastrophes piling up. A profound change was needed to head off even worse cataclysms in the future. For Barbosa, the reform agenda that Latin America had been pushing for half a century—what the region's jurists called American International Law—was the only moral program that could fill the void left by a receding Christianity. Without a reform of the international system, reorganized around American principles, the only "law" that would exist would be the law of force, of "blood and war," of "steel and gunpowder." The "strongest powers" would throw themselves into an unending competition for colonies. "Small states" would be "swept away like the wind sweeps away straw," dismembered by the "gusts which lash at their borders."[27]

Barbosa put his considerable authority behind Woodrow Wilson, believing that Wilson would, at war's end, create a lasting peace.

Mexico, in contrast, came out strongly against war. In mid-February, less than two months before Wilson's declaration of war, Carranza sent a note to the chanceries of Latin America and the United States proposing that the hemisphere's neutral countries collectively threaten a full trade embargo unless the belligerents ceased fire and agreed to mediation.

Carranza shared Barbosa's sense of doom, but he didn't think joining the war in progress would lead to peace. The Mexican president captured the horror taking place in Europe in full: "Death, desolation, and misery." The war seems "as a great plague that ought to have been isolated and limited long ago." On its own, Carranza's proposal is extraordinary, made by the leader of a revolution-wracked, barely solvent nation, itself a bloodbath of insurgent violence. Carranza admitted that his suggestion overstepped the bounds of established international law, which prohibits neutral nations

---

ten thousand tons of these nuts a month from Honduras's Aguán Valley, for use in gas masks on the front.

from intervening in a conflict among other belligerents. Yet set in the context of Latin America's history, it is but another example of the region's persistent efforts to create international mechanisms to nurture peace and cooperation. This war, Carranza said, had no "precedent in the history of humanity." Already, even before the United States had entered, over ten million had been killed and nearly twice that many wounded, some horribly so. It had to be stopped.[28]

Carranza's note was curtly dismissed by the State Department, which insinuated that Mexico's proposal of neutrality was intended to aid Germany. Carranza wasn't put off. He offered to convene a Latin American commission to mediate relations between Washington and Berlin—not unlike the Niagara Falls arbitration that helped resolve Mexico's crisis, the one that was hailed by many, including Wilson himself, as breakthrough statesmanship. The United States declined the offer.[29]

Wilson still wanted Latin American support and would continue to talk about hemispheric relations as a model for postwar peace (so long as those relations didn't stand in the way of the U.S. going to war). But Mexico, which did so much to force him to think deeply about the question of international justice, had, for him, become a problem. Carranza had proven more of an unbending nationalist than Wilson had wanted. Having not long ago gathered Latin Americans together to legitimate Mexico under Carranza, Wilson now did all he could to isolate the country, to turn it into a pariah state.

"Mexico was the plague spot of the Americas; it needed cleaning up."[30]

Monroe Doctrine of the Future

H istorians for the most part have ignored the Latin American influence on Wilsonian idealism, even though Wilson's advisers, and
Wilson himself, understood that what today is called liberal internationalism was a synthesis of United States power and Latin American
ideas. In Wilson's words, the inter-American system entailed a "mutual covenant" that guaranteed the protection of all the hemisphere's states. "This is
Pan-Americanism," Wilson said at the end of 1915, and it has "has none of
the spirit of empire in it."

As Wilson began his push for military preparedness, he cited Latin
America in arguing for *both* war and peace. Wilson invoked the experience
of the United States in Latin America to say that if his country did enter the
war, it would do so in service of high-minded ideals and not base interests.
It is true, Wilson said, that Washington in the past had often acted ignobly
in Latin America, for profit and aggrandizement. But Latin America's protests had humbled and "chastened" the United States—and in so doing had
prepared Washington to assume its role as an agent of impartial global leadership. And he held up the Western Hemisphere as a template for what
world peace might look like once Europe's guns fell silent: a cooperative
community of nations.

It's doubtful Wilson had read the Latin American jurists who for decades had been demanding a reformation of the international order. He was aware, though, of the work of institutions such as the Carnegie Endowment for International Peace, which had chapters in Latin America. In 1912, the U.S. lawyer James Brown Scott and the Chilean Alejandro Alvarez founded the American Institute of International Law to disseminate, in English, the writings of Latin American jurists. The premises of American International Law seeped into the scholarship of jurists, intellectuals, and peace activists in the United States and began to bubble up in editorials and policy proposals. As Wilson told Walter Lippmann in 1916, "Pan-Americanism" was the model for what he had hoped to achieve after the war.[1]

For the United States to hold up the New World as a model for the old, the Monroe Doctrine had to be redefined. It could no longer be read as a unilateral doctrine of national interest. It now must mean what Latin Americans had long said it should mean: a pact of peace, solidarity, and recognition of national sovereignty. Yale's Hiram Bingham and *The New Republic*'s Herbert Croly called for the "modernizing," "idealizing," or "mutualizing" of the Monroe Doctrine. In 1914, John Barrett, the director general of the Pan-American Union, wanted to remove "the hard, unyielding, dictatorial and didactic suggestions of the words 'Monroe Doctrine,' about which every Latin American is a little sensitive." He suggested changing the word *Monroe* to *Pan-American* and the word *Doctrine* to *policy.* "Pan-American Policy"—not exactly the most animating of catchphrases.[2]

Latin Americans had a simpler suggestion. The Chilean Alejandro Alvarez said let's call a reformed system of international law by its proper name: The Bolívar Doctrine.[3]

Monroe Doctrine of the Future

Latin Americans statesmen had watched Europe race toward world war and offered solutions to avert the disaster based on their New World experience. As early as 1912, a number of Latin American nations proposed that the countries of America enter into a nonaggression and nonintervention pact. That same year, the Colombian Santiago Pérez Triana, retired from his posting as ambassador to the United Kingdom but still influential in Latin America, wrote a series of manifestos calling on Europe to give up colonialism and look to New World unity as a model to emulate. Then, even as Europe was carving up Africa and parts of Asia, Pérez Triana posted the manifestos to all the foreign ministers of the Western Hemisphere and asked them to declare that the "era of conquest" is outlawed forever in all places.[4]

Washington, having recently annexed Puerto Rico, the Philippines, Hawai'i, and Guam, along with a swath of Panama, brushed Pérez Triana off. "Belittle the idea," State told its ambassadors.[5]

Once the world war broke out, Pérez Triana urged Latin American leaders to work with President Wilson (then still promising to stay out of the conflict) to build an international order founded on peace. The Colombian blamed the war on Europe's colonial "reign of barbarism," and argued that the only way to prevent even greater wars in the future was to outlaw colonial conquest everywhere, lest the horrors visited upon Europe engulf the New World. *The New York Times* published Pérez Triana's lengthy letter, written in December 1914, three months after the world war had broken out, under the title "A Monroe Doctrine of the Future."[6]

Pérez Triana proposals were too strongly worded, too dependent on ending European colonialism, to be effective. Yet Europe's collapse into war had sparked Wilson's search for some kind of "organized system of international cooperation" that might prevent what was happening in Europe from happening in the Americas. The Wilson administration saw Latin America as a "model for the European nations when peace is at last brought about," as Colonel House put it. "A way to secure peace when the war is over," said Wilson.[7]

By this point, Wilson, buoyed by the success of the ABC mediation, had begun to salt his foreign policy speeches with the idea of upgrading the Pan-American Union (created after Blaine's first Pan-American Conference) into a more formal multilateral antiwar alliance. "If Europe had a Pan-European Union like the Pan-American Union in Washington," said Barrett, the director of the Union, in March 1915, "this great war would have been averted."[8]

Hunting for a practical framework for such an upgrade, Wilson turned to legislation proposed by Texas congressman James Slayden. Slayden, in response to the outbreak of the war, had called on the United States to join

Latin American nations and sign a treaty committing signatories to respect existing national borders. Slayden's bill was buried in committee. But William Jennings Bryan passed a copy of the proposal to Wilson, with a strong endorsement that a treaty respecting territorial rights would go a long way to ensure peace.[9]

"Striking," Wilson said of Slayden's proposal.

House, whose influence on Wilson cannot be overstated, urged the president to use Slayden's bill as a starting point to move forward on "welding together" the "two western continents." Wilson drafted a statement on December 16, 1914, which House then passed on to Latin American leaders to review. The draft statement guaranteed *uti possidetis*, or as Wilson put it "territorial integrity," and contained provisions for the arbitrated settlement of disputes and the obligation of member nations to defend their allies and to "police" infractions.

House described the initiative as the president's effort to "broaden the Monroe Doctrine." Latin Americans supported the idea, some enthusiastically so. Yet nearly all wanted to be sure that what was being "broadened" was the solidaristic, anticonquest, and anticolonial sentiment implicit in the doctrine. Opposed to the expansion of European colonialism, they wanted "conquest" banned once and for all. Peru, looking to keep the New World out of Europe's war, proposed turning the Americas into the world's neutral zone, guaranteeing that trade and commerce be left unmolested in an area from the middle of the Atlantic to the middle of the Pacific.[10]

Negotiations over the treaty started out in a lively manner, but Wilson's entrance into the war angered most Latin American nations. Talks on creating a hemispheric peace alliance, or, as it became known, a "Pan-American Pact," were put on hold.

Wilson, undaunted, still pressed for what in early 1917 he called an "American league." "This is the very time when such a league would make the deepest impression and have the greatest moral effect on both sides of the water," the U.S. president said. Diplomats from the largest Latin American countries, though, wanted to wait and see what the world looked like at the end of the war.

Give Bond

The idea of a multinational hemispheric alliance didn't die at this point but evolved, subterraneously and fitfully, into what we now know as the League of Nations. Wilson had already agreed to London's request that the United States propose such a league, yet the British vision was essentially a police force empowered to administer the rules of war and sanction nations that violated treaties. London hardly wanted to submit to a collective defense structure, nor cede sovereignty to an organization that might question its empire. Wilson, though, thanks to Latin America, had in mind a more robust vision of what a world community should look like.

In June 1918, as some twenty-seven thousand soldiers from Pershing's American Expeditionary Forces were holding a German advance across the Marne at bay, defending the road to Paris, Wilson hosted a delegation of Mexican editors and reporters in Washington.

The newsmen wanted to know the president's plans for postwar reconstruction. Wilson answered by bringing up the shelved Pan-American Pact. He repeated his willingness to issue a "common guarantee" that if any nation, including the United States, violates the territorial integrity or independence of members of the league, "all others will jump on her." The Monroe Doctrine, Wilson said, worked as far as "protecting you from aggression." But there was "nothing in it that protected you from aggression from us." Now, though, Wilson was promising to "give bond" that intervention was a thing of the past. He also linked that guarantee to the proposal for a "universal association of nations," something much greater than a hemispheric alliance, telling the Mexican reporters that he had always thought of his postwar plans as an extension of the Pan-American Pact. "The future life of the nations of the world" depends on a recognition of the sovereignty of all.

"That is the basis, the only conceivable basis, for the future peace of the world," Wilson said, "and I must admit that I was ambitious to have the States of the two continents of America show the way to the rest of the world as to how to make a basis of peace."

Wilson's ambitions sounded like Bolívar's. Wilson's famous Fourteen Points for world peace, enumerated in an address to Congress just before this interview, called for the "political independence and territorial integrity" of "great and small states alike." This ideal would soon animate the League of Nation's final covenant, which pledged nations to "respect and preserve as against external aggression the territorial integrity and existing political independence of all Members of the League." Later, in August 1919, under a long, grueling interrogation by the Senate Foreign Relations Committee, an exhausted Wilson would explicitly say that the League's principles emerged from his peace-treaty negotiations with "the American States, the States of Central and South America," as well as the ABC arbitration of the Mexican conflict.[11]

For their part, Latin American statesmen hoped such ambitious postwar plans would give them a seat at the table, a chance to make their case for the principles of American International Law.

Wilson wasn't always forthcoming about Latin America's contribution. He took the principles associated with the American International Law movement—nonaggression, arbitration, territorial integrity, sovereign equality, mutual defense, and the belief that common interests and not "competitions of power" should form the basis of international agreement— and attributed them not to Bolívar, Calvo, Drago, Quintana, Barbosa, Pérez Triana, or any other Latin American. Rather, he credited them to the "timeless wisdom" of the United States' "Founding Fathers."[12]

This wisdom, Wilson said, was crystallized in the Monroe Doctrine— and "nations should with one accord adopt the doctrine of President Monroe as the doctrine of the world."[13]

Wilson here was being rhetorically strategic, trying to use the popularity of the doctrine—and the sense that the doctrine represented something transcendent, original to the United States—to defend himself against criticism that what he was doing was somehow anti-American. "I am very much opposed to the President's proposition that we shall surrender our independence," said Washington senator Miles Poindexter, to an international organization.

Wilson also constantly had to fend off charges that he was, well, a little like Madero, a dreamer who governed as he thought reality should be, not as it was. Senator Lawrence Sherman from Illinois called Wilson a modern Don Quixote and said that his vision of a world government was as lofty as a "Hague convention up in a balloon." Roosevelt called Wilson's postwar plans a "Judas Kiss." "Let us dictate peace by the hammering guns," he said, "and not chat about peace to the accompaniment of the clicking of type-writers."[14]

So Wilson took cover behind the Monroe Doctrine. He used its quicksilver nature, the fact that it meant many things to many people, to duck and dodge. At times he referenced the doctrine as representing a "higher humanity." At other times, especially as opposition rose to his global aspirations, he cited the doctrine as if it were Old Testament writ. Wilson confessed that he had often tried to pin down the meaning of the Monroe Doctrine, but to no avail. "I will confide to you in confidence," he said, "that when I tried to define it I found that it escaped analysis."[15]

Wilson's effort to use Monroe's statement to sell his postwar program would backfire, for no matter how much he tried to pitch the Monroe Doctrine as a principle of universal international law, the nationalism at its core couldn't be ignored. People might not have been able to define the doctrine exactly, but they knew it presaged power, dominance, and wealth. To play with that meaning, in a country as powerful, dominant, and wealthy as the United States, was to play with fire.

Wilson wrestled with the doctrine. And soon the doctrine would defeat the man.

Subsoil Socialism

Back in Mexico, President Venustiano Carranza moved forward with turning the spirit of the New World doctrine—especially the principle of national sovereignty, especially how it applied to natural resources and other forms of property—into a reality. In early January 1915, he issued a degree requiring companies to sign pledges that they would abide by new laws regulating oil. This was the first significant effort to establish government supremacy over the industry, including over Edward Doheny's powerful Huasteca Petroleum Company, Mexico's largest producer.

Notwithstanding periodic disruptions caused by the ongoing revolution—Villa and Zapata were still in opposition, still marshaling armies—Mexico was annually producing about thirty-three million barrels, a considerable percentage of the world's total yields. In Detroit, Henry Ford was turning out more than five hundred Model Ts a day, each getting about twenty miles to the gallon. Wilson's shift to a policy of war preparedness added to the demand for petroleum. Oil now was Mexico's most critical export. Earlier, some investors in Mexico oil thought that if they couldn't have Huerta, Carranza would do. He was wealthy, and an extractive capitalist himself. They thought he would be sympathetic to their interests. They were wrong. Carranza continued to apply a growing list of regulations, sanctions, and fees on foreign investors.

Wilson regretted championing Carranza. He was angry that Mexican troops repeatedly ambushed Pershing's men and was sure that Carranza was conspiring with the Germans. The world war revealed the limits of New World unity. Diplomats had patted themselves on the back when they jointly announced their recognition of Carranza's government. But the United States bristled that most Latin American nations were committed to a policy of neutrality. Once thought wise and moderate, Carranza was now thought by the State Department to be "obstinate and vain."

Article 27

Carranza was acting as provisional president, in power just until elections could be organized. Before that could happen, Mexico needed a new constitution. Delegates gathered in in November 1916, in Santiago de Querétaro. The setting was notable. Querétaro was the epicenter of Mexico's great central valley, where peasant and indigenous communities had suffered the worst of the whirlwind of dispossession that, under Porfirio Díaz, had transformed peasant farmland into mines, cattle ranches, and wheat plantations.[1]

Carranza's allies dominated the constitutional convention, but they were mixed in with Zapata sympathizers, anarchists, socialists, Marxists, and even many bourgeois liberals, who after a century of national dismemberment— the loss of Texas, northern Mexico, and Central America—believed that what was left of Mexico should belong to Mexicans. They might not be able to get back what was taken. But they would keep what they had.

The document they eventually worked out was the world's first fully elaborated social-democratic constitution. It promised to protect individual rights by restraining state power. At the same time, it promised social rights by strengthening state power, enshrining, years before similar constitutions would do so elsewhere: the right to work, to a minimum wage, to equal pay for men and women, to welfare, education, and health care.

Debates were fierce over some provisions, but not over its most provocative section: Article 27. Running over two thousand words, Article 27 stated

384 | AMERICA, AMÉRICA

that owning property in the form of land and water was *not* an inherent right vested in individuals. Rather, property belonged to the nation, and the right to property was a right granted by the state. Here was the key, the legal incantation that would unlock the future, that would provide the resources, the revenue, to pay for the robust vision of social citizenry laid out in the rest of the constitution. A draft of the article was presented to the plenum near the last day of the convention and read aloud only once. Some particulars were discussed, after which the article passed nearly unanimously.[2]

The committee that drafted Article 27 was headed by Andrés Molina Enríquez, an attorney dealing in property transactions, born in 1868 in Jilotepec, northwest of Mexico City, not far from the Zapatista heartland. "Lawyers were the shock troops of capitalism," the historian Charles Sellers wrote in his 1991 classic *The Market Revolution*, and Molina was a frontline witness to the destruction of family farms, the growth of peonage and vagrancy, the great theft of Indian common lands.[3]

All the committee members agreed that foreign ownership of natural resources and lack of access to planting land were the main causes of Mexico's misery. Some wanted private property abolished altogether, but a majority thought that idea "utopian." So they reached a compromise: everything found in the subsoil would be socialized, and surface territory would constitute "private property." But the right to topsoil property was not absolute: Article 27 granted the state power of confiscation, so as to enact a land reform, which would include the restoration of peasant communes, or what Mexicans called *ejidos*.

Antecedents existed for Article 27. Haiti's constitutions and legal codes had long prohibited foreigners from owning land (though that prohibition would be removed by the United States during its military occupation of 1915–1934). Colombia in 1913 passed a law stating that the "nation should reserve the proprietorship over all petroleum beneath the public lands of Colombia." In 1916, Bolivia issued a decree that established the nation as the owner of all surface and subsurface petroleum. In Europe, in Red Vienna and ever insurgent Paris, intellectuals had promoted the idea of the right to private property being limited according to its "social function."

But Mexico stood at the center of New World extractive capitalism. As the heartland of oil production and silver mining, the country had, since the end of the Civil War, become an integral part of the United States economy. Its revolution inspired reforms across the hemisphere.

And now here was Article 27, which read as if it were a commandment brought down from the mountain: "The nation shall have at all times the right to impose on private property such limitations as the public interest may demand as well as the right to regulate the development of natural resources, which are eligible for expropriation in order to conserve them and equitably to distribute the public wealth."

Everything below the ground, in the subsoil, belonged to the nation: all minerals or metals found in veins, layers, masses; precious stones; rock salt; phosphates; petroleum; tar pitch; and all hydrocarbons, be they solid, liquid, or gas. The constitution also recognized the collective rights of rural communities to water, roads, and planting land. All church land was to be confiscated. Article 27 also included an affirmation of the doctrine put forth by the Argentine Carlos Calvo, who believed that foreigners should be afforded all the rights and protections of citizens but not additional ones. They wouldn't be able to call on their own governments for help in property conflicts.

In the coming years, similar social rights, along with the idea that the "social function" of property supersedes individual rights, would be affirmed in the constitutions of nearly all Latin American nations. Mexico provided them a formula for how to create a modern nation: use their sovereignty over resources to raise revenue (either through taxation or nationalization) and use the money for two things: to distribute a "social wage"; to pay for public health care, public education, and other kinds of welfare; and to invest in local industry to modernize its economy.[4]

To get to this hoped-for future, Molina had to rummage through the past. Before being driven from office, Porfirio Díaz had made great strides in dismantling the property edifice left behind by Spanish colonialism and aligning Mexican law with the United States' understanding of property: that it was an inherent right of individuals not a gift bestowed by monarchs or governments. Molina's committee reversed Díaz's achievement. Molina himself believed Article 27 owed much to colonial conceptions of property law, to the idea that property was not an absolute right of individuals but one that had to be balanced against a greater good. Independence meant that it was no longer the Crown's or Church's but the republican government's role to promote *el bien común*, the common good, which now included the right to education, to a good salary, to health care, to a dignified life, and to labor unions.[5]

To Tax Is to Confiscate

The same industries that had snapped at Wilson for not recognizing Huerta now demanded that the White House do something about Article 27. Before the constitution was even ratified, Secretary of State Robert Lansing (who had replaced Bryan after Bryan resigned in protest over Wilson's war preparedness policy) told Carranza that Article 27 had to be watered down. The constitution, Lansing said, was "fraught with possible grave consequences." The United States would never "acquiesce in any direct confiscation of foreign owned properties."[6]

Yet Carranza was intransigent and the constitution popular. The Mexican president would only promise that he wouldn't apply its terms retroactively to United States companies.

Carranza did, under the authority granted by the constitution, require foreign companies to register with the national government, to survey and disclose their holdings, pay penalties if they failed to do so, and make good on taxes. Most companies refused at first. Some said they would rather shut down production completely. Lawyers had told the oilmen that even just registering their companies and surveying their lands amounted to a tacit recognition of the legitimacy of the constitution. The "right to tax," said Edward Doheny, "is the right to confiscate."

The evolution of United States property law is complex. By the early twentieth century, it had incorporated the idea that public interest could mitigate inherent and inalienable property rights, under the principle of eminent domain. Yet even those legal theorists who accepted this principle still viewed the Mexican constitution as heretical for explicitly stating that pri-

vate property was a privilege conceded by the government. They feared—
rightly, as it turned out—that the Mexican constitution would lead other
countries to a similar conclusion, thus threatening "certain hard to define
but nevertheless well internationally recognized vested individual rights."[7]

The Oil Producers Association, which represented companies drilling in
Mexico, wanted action. Yet however much Wilson now disliked Carranza,
the White House was little interested in intervening in Mexico on behalf of
producers, worried that to do so would push Carranza into an alliance with
Germany. Wilson tried to shunt their concerns to State.

Under Lansing, the State Department had practically become a private
law and lobbying firm for the oil producers, its officials taking large commissions to write company briefs, which then were submitted to the State
Department to make a claim. State's lawyers to a man opposed Article 27.
The diplomat-jurists who dominated the U.S. Foreign Service—many
themselves holding investments in Mexico, the Caribbean, and Central
America—concluded that the socialization of subsoil resources was in violation of international law.[8]

With Wilson preoccupied by the European war, Lansing was left to run
policy on Mexico. He threatened Carranza, instructing his ambassador in
Mexico "to protest against" efforts "to collect royalties from American petroleum interests." The United States will protect its citizen investors, he
told the Mexican president. In early June 1918, Lansing advised Wilson to
station six thousand Marines in Galveston, Texas, to prepare to land at
Tampico if need be. On June 10, Secretary of the Navy Josephus Daniels
told Wilson that a much larger force would be needed since Mexico, now
operating under a consolidated government, would see such an intervention
as an act of war. The days when Wilson could land a gaggle of Marines in
Veracruz were over.[9]

Mexico would eventually, in the 1930s, nationalize its oil industry, and
in so doing expropriate a good deal of foreign-owned property. These developments were still to come. Now, under the terms of its new constitution,
the revolutionary government was mostly concerned with standardizing
permits, tightening regulations, and extracting slightly higher taxes and
export tariffs. In April, Carranza announced that all corporate back taxes

were due. Until this point, United States oilmen had enjoyed free range in Mexico, so these mild efforts to rein them in felt like heavy shackles.

On August 9, the Oil Producers Association, represented by James Garfield, a former secretary of the interior, and Fred Proctor, a lawyer for Gulf Oil, finally got a meeting with the president. Wilson's relations with Carranza were tense. Still, seizing poor and powerless Haiti's gold for the National City Bank was one thing. Acting as petroleum's policeman against a revolutionary government of a large country was another. Wilson said that he wouldn't overrun Mexico the way Germany overran Belgium. He suggested the companies go back to State and file another complaint.[10]

They did. They also started backing a "bandit army" that offered protection to Tampico oil drillers, led by a local chieftain, Manuel Peláez. William F. Buckley Sr. raised money from conservative Catholics, through organizations such as the Knights of Columbus, sending boxcars full of weapons to the counterrevolutionaries. Carranza easily held Peláez off, but this martial-Catholic putsch was a preview of a more serious paramilitary threat to come, in Mexico and throughout Latin America.[11]

Meanwhile, advocates for U.S. oil and mining interests continued their protest, sure that not just Article 27 but Mexico's entire constitution was a communist wolf dressed as a liberal sheep. They quoted Luis Cabrera, an intellectual close to Carranza who, when asked if Bolshevism was a problem in Mexico, answered no. Mexico, Cabrera said, had nothing to fear from Bolshevism, because its "best part" had already been "incorporated" into Mexico's constitution.[12]

These were the years of Wilson's Red Scare, of rolling labor strikes and government crackdown—and the Mexican border became the Red Scare's southern front. There was the faraway Russian Revolution, victorious in October 1917. But, as William Buckley reported, "Bolshevism in this country came from Mexico." Revolution, war, and labor organizing all led to a heightened Anglo racism. The Texas Rangers, along with vigilantes and local police, launched a murderous campaign in Texas, Arizona, and New Mexico against Mexicans and Mexican Americans, whether they dared organize a union or dared to vote. The historian Claudio Lomnitz writes "several thousand Mexicans" were "shot, hanged, or lynched."[13]

The United States had entered a catastrophic war in Europe, a total war with no clear end game, one destined to destroy, as Wilson put it, "the world we had known." Some thought a worse madness lay closer to home. The Mexican Revolution presaged the future, bringing the class and race fears of men like Lansing, Buckley, Doheny, and many others to the fore, the feeling that unless drastic action was taken, there'd be a reckoning, a forced redistribution of power and property both within and between nations.

Carranza answered the propaganda war by following in the steps of his royal and republican predecessors, holding up Mexico as a sanctuary for refugees of Anglo repression. He happily contrasted asylum-granting Mexico to lynching United States. When the California-born Walter Sanborn, a Mexico City restaurant owner, refused to serve the African American boxer Jack Johnson, Carranza sent a few of his generals to change Sanborn's mind. Mexico, the generals told Sanborn, "was not a white man's country." There "are more Negros now in Mexico City than ever before," complained a Texas Ranger ally of Buckley. Johnson grew close to radicals and socialists, giving speeches in border towns warning that "if the gringos invaded Mexico, American blacks would stand alongside their Mexican brothers."[14]

33.

Bolívar Dreamt

The war ended in November 1918, with an estimated death toll of twenty million. By December Wilson was in Paris, heading a delegation that had taken charge of talks to set the terms of the peace, including the creation of a League of Nations. The president at this point was still citing the Monroe Doctrine in public remarks about what he hoped to achieve at Paris. Soon, though, his effort to whip the Monroe Doctrine in support of his postwar agenda would snap back at him.

In late December, Theodore Roosevelt wrote his last *cri pour la guerre.* He'd die in early January 1919, and his attack on Wilson's peace initiatives appeared posthumously, first in *The Kansas City Star* and then *The Washington Post* and elsewhere. Roosevelt's editorial condemned plans for a League of Nations. Would China, Mexico, and Turkey sit as equals at the table with the United States? What power would the League of Nations have over Washington? Would it exercise authority over immigration? Would it prevent the United States from preparing for the next war? From policing Latin America?[1]

"The American people," Roosevelt said, "do not intend to give up the Monroe Doctrine."

Roosevelt's geopolitics were no less inspired by the Western Hemisphere than Wilson's. For Wilson, the vision was a parliament of man, a federation of the world. For Roosevelt, it was a universal police precinct. "Let civilized Europe and Asia introduce some kind of police system in the weak and disorderly countries at their thresholds," he continued, but "let the United States treat Mexico as our Balkan peninsula and refuse to allow European or Asiatic powers to interfere on this continent."

Wilson, just before entering the war, had released an intercepted telegram sent from Berlin to Carranza's government as proof that Germany was a threat to the Western Hemisphere: "Make war together, make peace together," the cable read, and Berlin will help you "reconquer the lost territory in Texas, New Mexico, and Arizona." Wilson made the communiqué available to the public to gin up more support for war. It did. Yet it also strengthened those who took Roosevelt's argument to heart, that the world needed policing, not utopian peace plans. Likewise, Wilson's opportunistic embrace during his reelection campaign of a nativist "Americanism" now legitimated nationalists who opposed his internationalism. Short-term gain and long-term loss. America First.

Our Peculiar Responsibility

When Wilson briefly returned to the United States in February 1919—with talks still ongoing in Paris—there was much goodwill, but he also found that his opponents were gathering to "defend" the Monroe Doctrine the same way John Quincy Adams's foes united behind opposition to Bolívar's Panama Congress. And for much the same reason: fear of ceding sovereignty and fear of losing the prerogative to act at will abroad, especially in Latin America, and especially in Mexico, Central America, and the Caribbean.

Wilson's critics in Congress, churches, and press conferences had questions.

"Suppose we felt the necessity of going to war with Mexico?" asked Illinois senator Lawrence Sherman. "Are not our affairs with Mexico our own affairs, and ought we turn them over for adjustment to the other nations of the world?" Would the United States need approval from the League to continue to occupy Haiti, Nicaragua, and the Dominican Republic? Would the Japanese be allowed to have their own Monroe Doctrine? If so, would Wilson allow them to "encircle the Philippines"? Did joining the League of Nations mean that the United States now was responsible for policing areas of the world outside the Western Hemisphere? Would doing so dilute the doctrine? "If we have a Monroe Doctrine everywhere," said Senator Lodge in Congress, "we may be perfectly certain that it will not exist anywhere."[2]

For all of Wilson's efforts to universalize the Monroe Doctrine as worldwide common law, the doctrine was, in 1919, inescapably synonymous with the United States' unilateral nationalism.

Wilson's administration rushed to calm fears. Secretary of the Navy Josephus Daniels said that the United States would always uphold "the Monroe Doctrine" as "our peculiar responsibility and duty." Contrary to what Wilson had been saying for years, his envoys in France insisted the League of Nations wasn't going to be an *extension* of Monroe's doctrine. Nor, under the League's auspices, would the doctrine be *broadened* or *universalized*. The League of Nations would be a separate body with no authority over the doctrine's interpretation or administration.[3]

Wilson began to realize that he not only had to dedicate a clause affirming the doctrine's authority but had to do so in a way that placated the nationalists. Much has been written on the Paris settlement, how liberals, progressives, and democratic socialists hoping to create a just postwar order had felt betrayed, how the hidebound defenders of the status quo came to dominate the agenda, imposing punitive war reparations on Germany and leaving imperialism untouched—setting the stage for a more awful war to come. Tracking the debate over the meaning of the Monroe Doctrine illustrates this turnabout.[4]

When Wilson traveled back to Paris in March he sensed the mood had changed, that the goodwill he had experienced earlier had dissipated. Secret deals had been struck as the European powers maneuvered to keep their colonies and annex those of Germany and other vanquished nations. There was talk of signing a peace treaty with Germany that didn't include a League of Nations. Wilson, desperate to keep Europe unified, didn't have much leverage. He feared the spread of Bolshevism and he feared the return of war.

"Europe is on fire," he said. On April 4, he fell violently sick with the flu, the worldwide pandemic that had already claimed millions of lives. Incapacitated and reportedly suffering from bouts of delirium, Wilson gave way. To keep the League an integral part of the final peace settlement he let Britain and France take the Ottoman Empire's territories in the Middle East and expand their hold over Africa. Japan got China's Shandong Peninsula, which had been a German colony.

As all this was going on, Wilson in his sickbed in the Hôtel de Crillon received a telegram from the still influential former president William Taft. Taft, a Republican, supported the idea of the League of Nations, and he worked as a mediator between Wilson and his party's nationalists, those Republicans opposed to the idea of joining a world organization. Taft, in his telegram, told Wilson that he was sure the Senate would not ratify the League if it didn't forthrightly uphold the Monroe Doctrine. By this point Wilson himself had mostly given up citing the Monroe Doctrine as a high principle of anticolonial humanism. Instead, he began to enshrine it as a high-handed expression of colonial prerogative.

The World's Doctrine

Still suffering from a high fever and body aches, Wilson, on April 11, rose from bed to preside over the last session of the committee charged with drafting what had become known as the Covenant, a document that would lay out the League of Nation's organizational and ethical principles. The group had been meeting on the Quai d'Orsay, in the French foreign ministry's ornate Salon de l'Horloge, or Clock Room. The "principal powers"—the United States, Great Britain, France, Italy, and Japan—drove the discussion. But Belgium, Brazil, China, Greece, Portugal, and Romania were also invited to participate, along with representatives from the broken-up Austro-Hungarian Empire.

Wilson told the gathered delegates that the United States wanted to insert a phrase in the League's nearly completed covenant upholding the validity of Monroe as a regional doctrine. Great Britian understood that Wilson was responding to domestic pressure, but didn't object since an affirmation of the Monroe Doctrine legitimated its claims to its colonies and spheres of influence. But delegates from other countries wanted clarification.[5]

It would help, several of them said, if the doctrine could be defined. Jayme Batalha Reis, representing Portugal, pointed out that there was no "text" anywhere that explained exactly what the Monroe Doctrine meant. France's Ferdinand Larnaude wanted a "clear definition" of the doctrine. What was it? Did it "consecrate or change" the rules that allowed the United States to intervene where its interests were threatened? The French government worried that future Washington administrations might decide that the Monroe Doctrine trumps obligations to the League. Larnaude kept asking for a definition. Could we at least have a footnote, he asked, explaining what the doctrine is?[6]

China watched the debate unfold with dread. The Chinese delegate to the peace talks, Koo Vi Kyuin, represented a trampled-upon new republic, wracked by Western intervention and threatened by a rising Japan. He could do little but ask if the clause could be restricted to make clear that it pertained exclusively to the United States, that Japan wouldn't be able to claim an equivalent doctrine. Sir Robert Cecil, representing the British Empire, brushed off China's concern. London did want the reference to Monroe to be exemplary, a model for how to organize other areas of the globe.

The Japanese delegation stayed mostly silent. The discussion was breaking in its favor. Like London, Tokyo thought an affirmation of the Monroe Doctrine would help legitimate its own ambitions to create a broader sphere of regional interest. Back in Washington, many welcomed the idea that Japan would get revolutionary China under control, to do there what the United States couldn't do in Mexico. The United States is willing, wrote an adviser to Wilson's delegation, to confer "upon the Japanese much the same guardianship over East Asia as that we asserted over Latin America."[7]

Portugal's Reis asked if the recognition of the Monroe Doctrine would prevent League action in "American affairs." Wilson, dancing on a pin trying to define the doctrine, answered no. "The covenant," Wilson said, referring to the League's charter, would be "the highest possible tribute to the

Monroe Doctrine," adopting "the principle of the Monroe doctrine as a world doctrine." Study action, not theory, Wilson said enigmatically.

None of what Wilson said made sense, the delegates realized. It's what he didn't say that mattered: the U.S. president needed an affirmation of the Monroe Doctrine as an assertion of the right to maintain a sphere of influence to win over nationalists. Everyone knew that such an affirmation would undermine the League, but all kept quiet.

The day was growing late, the delegates tired. There were other pressing issues on the agenda. Wilson's motion on the Monroe Doctrine passed by consensus. The addendum's final version, included in the charter as Article 21, read: "Nothing in this Covenant shall be deemed to affect the validity of international engagements such as treaties of arbitration or regional understandings like the Monroe Doctrine, securing the maintenance of peace."

Principle of Equality

Japan's representatives, quiet during the discussion on the Monroe Doctrine, now raised a demand they had been making since January. Ministers Makino Nobuaki and Chinda Sutemi proposed that the preamble to the Covenant state that the League would uphold the "principle of equality of nations and just treatment of their nationals."

Mildly worded, this proposed addition was seemingly concerned only with recognition of the equality of nations and the rights of foreigners in member countries. Yet the Japanese had touched a nerve, and their proposal fast became known as the "racial equality" amendment. The overreaction to this most judicious of proposals reveals how much, in the minds of the Anglo-Saxons who ran the world, the problem of the equality of nations was also the problem of the equality of human beings, which was also the problem of race.

Sir Robert Cecil, representing the British Empire, said that London couldn't support the proposal since it would involve meddling in the domestic affairs of member nations. Wilson admitted that the Japanese amendment was "innocuous" and absolutely in keeping with the spirit of the

League of Nations. But he couldn't support it for political reasons, for fear of angering conservatives at home, who were ever alert to the possibility that international agreements might be used to reform domestic politics, to address racism or class exploitation. Wilson's delegation worried that the Japanese resolution might be used by civil rights activists to void a California law that prohibited Japanese subjects from owning property or to fight against segregation.

Japan didn't drop the issue happily. Meiji jurists in the late nineteenth and early twentieth centuries had been active in the movement to reform international law, and Japanese public opinion was very much in favor of the proposal. "If the amendment were rejected, it would be an indication to Japan that the equality of members of the League was not recognized," Sutemi said.

A long debate ensued. Lord Cecil said he thought it best that the Covenant "be silent on these questions" to avoid having the matter taken up by General Assembly. If the issue was taken up by the whole assembly, then nations that were especially racist, like "white Australia," might derail the entire League rather than submit to recognizing equality. "Silence would avoid much discussion," he said, advising the Japanese to steer away from potential backlash. Those Australians were rough.

The committee usually passed resolutions by voice consent. Wilson, though, called Japan's amendment to a vote. Eleven delegates voted in favor, and a handful of "principals" against, at which point Wilson ruled that the amendment had failed since it hadn't "received unanimous approval." A few delegates pointed out that other amendments had passed without unanimous support. But Wilson invoked his power as chair to declare the matter settled.

The Japanese press reacted strongly to this defeat. The "only way for Japan to recoup its failure" to pass the resolution, argued one influential Japanese newspaper, was to assert itself more forcefully in the international arena with its "own Asiatic Monroe Doctrine." Intellectuals pushed Japan to create a "union for the awakening and self-defense of Asian races." Wilson's ambassador in Tokyo said that the refusal to include the amendment "will create a lasting bitterness against occidental nations."

Conferences Among Themselves

Delegates from Brazil, Bolivia, Ecuador, Uruguay, Nicaragua, Panama, Honduras, and Cuba participated directly in the peace talks. They brought with them years of thinking about peace, war, and sovereignty, of honing what they still called American International Law. Still, their United States handlers took them for granted. Jordan Stabler, an official in the State Department's Latin American Division, stated that he had "all my Latins carded and tabulated," and expected their support in upcoming subcommittee votes. Mostly, he was right, but he was dismayed to find that several delegates had joined with smaller European countries to press for greater representation.*

Latin American diplomats resented being marginalized to work on side committees with little input into the creation of the league. "They have been left alone too much," Stabler admitted, "and have been having Latin American conferences among themselves." Indeed they had been, since 1826.[8]

Stabler blamed Mexico. Carranza was still president, and Mexico had therefore not been invited to participate in the conference. Relations between Wilson and Carranza had grown acrimonious, not just over property relations but because during the war Mexico offered sanctuary to pacificists, socialists, and any other objector who for whatever reason didn't want to be sent to Flanders to fight Germans.

Carranza sent representatives to Paris. So did the U.S. oil industry. Each lobbied to convince delegates that their understanding of investment and property should take precedent.

---

* Stabler had taken part in a massive federal social science project called the Inquiry, staffed by a phalanx of social scientists, meant to gather as much information about the world as possible, to both identify the location of natural resources and potential flash points of religious and border conflicts. For Latin America, the Inquiry's team updated Father Acosta's schema for new times, proposing a classification system that grouped the "so-called Latin American 'republics'" according to whether they were "mature," "immature," or "criminal." Inquiry experts believed that only "mature" nations "would be allowed to conduct their own affairs in a world to be governed by reason and justice." "How many Cubas are there?" wondered the author of the classification scheme, meaning: how many nations would the United States have to establish "mandatory" power over until they had matured enough for self-governance.

Mexico pushed to have "the ideas of the new Mexican constitution" recognized as international law. The oilmen wanted Mexico's entire 1917 constitution revoked.[9]

Stabler suspected Mexico of working behind the scenes to influence debate, but the other Latin American delegates didn't need the help. Small Honduras pressed the matter of sovereign equality. The nation's delegate, Policarpo Bonilla, was independent minded. During the final plenary session held to ratify the Covenant, Bonilla objected to the Monroe Doctrine clause. Bonilla asked that the doctrine be defined. He also wanted the League's covenant to explicitly affirm that "the republics of Latin America had the right to an independent existence, that no nation could acquire through conquest any part of their territory or embark on any course of action calculated to diminish their sovereignty or impair their national dignity." Bonilla delivered his remarks in Spanish, a language few at the meeting understood. And so other delegates nodded their heads and moved on to the next topic.[10]

Latin America provided the template for Wilson's internationalism and revealed its limits. Most Latin American nations would go on to join the League, making the Americas the single largest regional group within the organization—nineteen countries in all, comprising nearly a third of the General Assembly's total votes, more than those held by the United Kingdom and its commonwealths. If Wilson could overcome opposition at home and convince the Senate to ratify the treaty, the United States, with Latin America voting with Washington as a caucus, would dominate the League's agenda.

But the kind of independence insisted upon even by Honduras, a country so in thrall to the United States, cast doubt that Washington could easily "card and tabulate" the Latins. Nations were multiplying and outnumbering traditional "great powers," and the challenge for those great powers was how to accept the ideal of "sovereign equality" while putting into place a voting structure that ensured that the ideal never became reality. Edward House had advised Wilson to invest all executive power in the League's higher council and leave the assembly for the majority to talk among themselves. "If the smaller nations are taken in," House said, "the question of equal voting power is an almost insurmountable obstacle." "Mexico and the Central American States" alone could "out-vote Germany, England, France, Italy, Japan and the United States." In the end, the League adopted a cumbersome decision-making system heavily weighted to reflect the preference of the "principals." Latin American delegates, at the final plenary session and among themselves, complained that the vote was rigged, that the affirmation of sovereign equality was window dressing.[11]

Latin American diplomats also worried about the harsh terms imposed on vanquished Germany. The consequences, Bolivia's Ismael Montes said, will be resentment.

"The peace is not yet signed," Montes continued, "and one can already see the seeds of a new war."

The peace soon would be signed. The text of the Covenant, including the clause affirming the Monroe Doctrine, was finalized on April 11 and ratified in a plenary session on April 28. The entire peace treaty—240 pages with 440 articles, including both the creation of the League and the harsh terms imposed on Germany—was signed outside Paris, in the Palace of Versailles, in its great Hall of Mirrors on June 28, 1919.

Monroe's Fence

The treaty's affirmation of the Monroe Doctrine confused matters, to put it mildly. It alienated supporters in Latin America, who thought the phrase "regional understandings like the Monroe Doctrine" made no sense. The Monroe Doctrine either was what Wilson said it was—a world doctrine of anticolonialism and equality—or it was what nationalist opponents of Wilson said it was: the unilateral authority of the United States to exercise corrective intervention across the entire hemisphere.[12]

Europeans, imperialists, and would-be imperialists alike weren't confused. British diplomats thought that the reference to the Monroe Doctrine in the Covenant was clear enough, that it meant that "the United States must inevitably become the mandatory power for Mexico," just as the United Kingdom exercised mandatory power over much of the Middle

East and elsewhere. In Germany, Carl Schmitt, the German jurist soon to build the legal foundation for Adolf Hitler's Nazi regime, likewise thought that the meaning of the doctrine was self-evident. Schmitt would model his own theory of *Großraum*, or Great Space, on the Monroe Doctrine, and Hitler repeatedly cited the doctrine, including in *Mein Kampf*: "What we want is a Monroe doctrine in Europe."[13]

Republican senator Henry Cabot Lodge supported the League on the condition that the "fence" Monroe had put up around the Western Hemisphere remain standing. Men like Lodge wanted new international organizations to help administer the world. But they didn't want those organizations to have jurisdiction over the United States. Other nationalists agreed.[14]

And so the Monroe Doctrine was incorporated into the League of Nations not as a warrant to enforce equality but as a means to consolidate spheres of interest. Instead of a great democratic and anticolonial breakthrough, as Wilson had once promised, the League of Nations legitimated imperial domination of most of the world's peoples: Europe's in Africa, the Middle East, and South Asia; Japan's in the Pacific; and Washington's in Latin America.

And still the U.S. Congress declined to ratify it. On October 2, 1919, President Wilson suffered an incapacitating stroke, a month before the Senate definitively refused to authorize United States membership in the League. He died in 1923.[15]

Monroe's fence stayed standing.

One historian has named the fleeting internationalism that reigned in the months immediately following World War I the "Wilsonian moment." His moment, Bolívar's century. "Bolívar dreamt of a League of Nations," Brazilian ambassador Manoel de Oliveira Lima said shortly after war's end. "We call it a dream because the hour had not yet struck for the realization of such a lofty ideal."[16]

Soon the clock would strike ready.

Death and the Salesmen

Until then, though, growing chaos. The League of Nations lurched into existence. Yet without the United States, the organization was ineffectual. Every Latin American country would join the League: Argentina, Bolivia, Brazil, Chile, Colombia, Cuba, El Salvador, Guatemala, Costa Rica, Haiti, Nicaragua, Panama, Paraguay, Venezuela, Uruguay, and Peru were among its first members, followed by Mexico, Honduras, and Ecuador.

The gap between words and policy was wide. Diplomats, because they were diplomats, talked about the League as if it was Bolívar's dream materialized, or Tennyson's Parliament of Man and Federation of the World realized. They knew the reality was much different. The League proved nearly powerless to prevent wars, did little to address economic inequality between nations, and provided little support for anticolonial movements of national liberation. Costa Rica was the first country to announce, in 1925, that it was withdrawing its membership, in objection to the League's sanctioning of British and French imperialism, and to its continued affirmation of the Monroe Doctrine even though the United States wasn't a member. The high fees charged to countries to be a member also was a factor in Costa Rica's decision to exit the League.

Brazil, its economy second only to Argentina's, could afford the League's membership fees. Yet it pulled out the following year. Rio had eagerly followed Woodrow Wilson in war and peace, believing that the war was needed to expunge Germanic militarism from international politics and that the League represented a new stage in human history, when "great powers" stopped defining themselves in terms of military power.

Brazil, though, insisted on having a permanent seat on the League's executive council. It was, Brazil's foreign ministry said, intolerable that not one New World nation sat on that council and exercised power equal to that of Great Britain or France. Rio's representative to the league, Afrânio de Melo Franco, fought to reorient the organization in a way that would support calls for self-determination, grant independence to Palestine and Syria, and advance the "universality of economic interests and the principle of solidarity and the interdependence of states." He also pushed the League to work with the United States to curtail the international arms trade, which was going strong due to all the surplus World War I matériel on the market. When Brazil lost that fight, it decided that it was better to withdraw its membership than continue to participate in a charade, to give legitimacy to an organization largely controlled by Great Britain and France in defense of their empires.[1]

The New World's jurists did what they could with what they had. Many remained members of the League and participated on its various committees—on war, women, colonialism, education, postal facilities, telegraph and radio communication, labor, health, malaria control, opium, and disarmament. In the years after the world war, Latin America's foreign ministries expanded the work of the Pan-American Union, holding more Pan-American conferences, as well as ad hoc meetings, and founded an Inter-American High Commission to deal with technical matters concerning trade—protocols regulating the classification of merchandise; patents and trademarks; the standardization of currency exchanges; weights and measures; and the establishment of a gold standard of value, among other issues. They also put forth multilateral committees and initiatives meant to address pressing problems, especially those related to arbitration to prevent war; mechanisms both to lessen the burden of public debt and to regulate the lending practices of foreign banks; and protocols to advance disarmament.

The region's statesmen didn't know if they should focus their energies globally, through the League of Nations (despite its shortcomings and that it largely ignored New World concerns) or retrench to the hemisphere. Between and betwixt, Uruguay proposed the formation of a "League of American Nations" that would abrogate the Monroe Doctrine and establish the "absolute equality" of all member nations. Washington blocked that proposal, making it "abundantly clear that the United States had no intention of relinquishing her sole right of interpreting the scope and meaning of the Monroe Doctrine and of enforcing it should occasion arise."[2]

The basic infrastructure of what we now call globalization was being built. Weights and measures were being standardized. Yet Latin Americans operated in a void, advancing urgent proposals meant to help the New World avoid the fate of the Old. However, with the United States returning to a stated policy of self-interest and the League paying little attention to the New World, there existed no means to put such proposals into practice, to stop, for example, the flow of arms into the region or to lessen the burden of foreign debt.

Ink was barely dry on the League's Covenant when European governments began to send military instructors to Latin America to teach its soldiers "the science learned on the Marne." That is, the science of large-scale, pointless destruction.

Latin America after World War I became the perfect foreign market for the consolidating munitions industry of Europe and the United States. Arms dealers plied their wares in Japan, in its buildup against China. But there was no place like Latin America: a continent of independent, sovereign republics, each with their own armies, their own officer corps, their own armories, and their own budgets. The salesmen of munitions companies were happy to encourage rivalries and cultivate border conflicts among the nations.

In Latin America, the rapid growth of debt-financed arms purchases, much greater in scale than anything seen prior to the world war, introduced a fatal poison in the imaginations of many Latin Americans, nearly overwhelming the region's humanist internationalism. Flooding the continent with weapons sparked political extremism, especially on the right, facilitating the rise of paramilitary organizations and inciting violence within and between nations, including what became Latin America's worst state-against-state war of the twentieth century: a fight between Bolivia and Paraguay over oil. This conflict, known as the Chaco War, could be thought of as a forgotten coda to World War I. Or, a preview of the Spanish Civil War. Either way, nothing good.

Get Busy

Great Britain, France, Italy, and Germany owed Latin American nations a significant amount of money for the wheat, beef, and nitrates they had purchased on credit during the four-year conflict. They paid off this debt by offering, at cut-rate prices, all their leftover war matériel, including hand grenades, rounds of ammunition of various calibers, armed Ford cars, and planes. The world war led to the widespread repudiation of poison gas, as photographs and newsreel footage of windswept chlorine-gas clouds drifting across battlefields strewn with corpses horrified the public, leaving behind indelible images of blistered faces and autopsied lungs. That didn't stop Europe, and soon the United States, from selling poison gas to Latin America. Private arms dealers passed themselves off as military theorists, whispering into the ears of presidents and generals about the importance of maintaining a regional "balance of power."

Military officials and their allied civilian strategists began repeating slogans they heard from sales agents and military instructors. *Submarines are the weapon of the weak!* So German manufacturers, forbidden by the terms of the Treaty of Versailles from building submarines, set up shipyards in Holland and Sweden and sold the vessels to weak and strong countries alike in Latin America. *Airplanes will decide future wars!* Soon British, Italian, French, and U.S. aviation companies were showcasing their latest flying machines. Italy sent one of its most famous aviators, at the head of an expansive fleet, across the Atlantic. The British sent a carrier to Latin America, loaded with planes for sale. *The only real peace is an armed peace!*[3]

This diplomatic premise—that the interests of neighboring nations are fundamentally in conflict—was utterly opposed to the region's long diplomatic and philosophical tradition of foregrounding the shared concerns of neighbor nations. "Balance-of-power" thinking, catastrophic in pushing Europe to war, had a "magic effect" on Latin America's would-be Clausewitzs, military officers who styled themselves as tacticians. Suddenly, governments were purchasing weapons not with an eye to defend against outside threats but for war within Latin America.

United States dealers were winning a growing share of sales. Just as some of the most storied names in finance, mining, and oil—the Guggenheims, Rockefellers, W. R. Grace, National City, and Chase—got their first foreign experience in Latin America, blue-chip munitions manufacturers accumulated profits by selling to the region. DuPont got its start selling gunpowder to the United States to fight Native Americans, then expanded its operations with government contracts for millions of pounds of powder for the United States to use in its war on Mexico. Now, along with companies like Remington, it was doing business with the poorest nations of the continent.

Colt, Electric Boat Company, Sperry Gyroscope, and Pratt & Whitney Aircraft all fattened their foreign portfolios in Latin America. The Weaver Aircraft Company made special "fighter" versions of its planes for the Latin American market. Machine guns were installed on the VPF-7 prop planes the company sold to Guatemala. Weaver also hawked its most advanced warplanes, mounted with Pratt & Whitney engines and Browning machine guns and able to reach speeds of 175 miles per hour, to Uruguay, Nicaragua, and Cuba. Brazil purchased at least sixty-nine of these units. Weapons technology was advancing rapidly. Steel was getting stronger. Explosives more powerful. The United States and Europe were constantly improving their weapons, freeing up backstock to be sent to Latin America.[4]

United States diplomats and sales agents goosed the race. They kept governments informed about what other countries were buying, heightening competition. If a consignment of surplus material came on the market, dealers would fly, say, first to La Paz, Bolivia's capital, warning officials that unless they "acted quickly, Paraguay would get it." Vickers, a British shipbuilding company, sold an entire fleet to Chile: a battleship, four destroyers, and six submarines. A Vickers agent then whispered news of the purchase to

Brazil and Argentina. And so Rio and Buenos Aires expanded their fleets. In this way, a 1902 disarmament treaty between Chile and Argentina, very successful in encouraging both nations to maintain small navies, fell apart.

Vickers, which sold to Chile, and the Electric Boat Company, which sold to Peru, were supposedly rivals. But Sir Basil Zaharoff, a top officer at Vickers, was a large shareholder of the Electric Boat Company, and it was Electric Boat (based in Connecticut and now a subsidiary of General Dynamics) that built the ships that Vickers sold to Chile.

Whenever agents got word of a brewing conflict, a revolt, or border skirmish, they moved fast. As one Federal Laboratories salesman put it, "These opera bouffe revolutions are usually short-lived, and we must make the most of the opportunity." "Killing the back-country Indians of South America with airplanes, bombs, and machine guns," a congressional investigation wrote about the arms trade, "boiled down to an order to get busy"—that is, to make a fast sale. "When there are wars, prolong them; when there is peace, disturb it," as a *Fortune* article described the arms merchant's "creed."

Remington sold Latin American nations tens of thousands of pounds of TNT to be used as "airplane drop bombs" tossed out of Junkers props outfitted as warplanes. DuPont marketed "military propellants and explosives" and "fragmentation airplane drop bombs."[5]

One might correctly condemn the hypocrisy of Theodore Roosevelt's and Woodrow Wilson's intervention and arrogance, denounce the first's preposterous realism and the other's failed idealism. But the two presidents at least opened room for those committed to peace, mediation, and disarmament to come to the fore. Now, in the 1920s, successive Republican administrations gleefully encouraged border brush fires, so to provide a chance for arms dealers to "get busy"—and get rich.

Very Large Bomb Orders

United States banks financed many of these sales. At least a third of all loans made in the years following World War I to Latin America was spent on arms, amounting to as much as half a billion dollars.

The arms trade, international loans, and resource extraction were parts of a whole. National City Bank floated a bond on behalf of Peru to pay for weapons. But Lima soon ran out of revenue with which to make its payments, so it worked out a deal with United Aircraft and Electric Boat Company to sell guano in the United States to pay off its debt. Freighters sailing to Peru dropped off TNT and weapons and picked up guano. Bombs floated south. Bird shit went north.[6]

The more war, the more profit. Federal Laboratories salesman Frank Jones wrote that "the unsettled conditions in South America" had been "a great thing" for him, reporting "very large bomb orders" from Brazil, Colombia, Peru, and Ecuador. Hundreds of thousands of Winchesters and Spanish Mausers went to countries as big as Brazil and as small as Honduras. Weapons manufacturers ran a shadow anti-diplomacy. Ambassadors and foreign ministers might work to defuse a conflict, even as officials from the Department of Commerce were passing weapons contractors the names of politicians willing to broker a big sale for a "commission," which could go as high as 35 percent. And the salesmen were pitching escalation.

Asked by Washington senator Homer Bone if New Jersey–based Federal Laboratories sold to both Paraguay and Bolivia, two countries on the verge of war, the company's president said: "We did not discriminate."

Weapons were also used for conflicts within nations, against workers and socialists. As in the United States, the Roaring Twenties and depressed thirties saw pitched class conflict across Latin America, which had its equivalents of the Ludlow, Homestead, Blair Mountain, and Columbine Mine massacres. On November 15, 1922, Ecuador's military used its foreign-supplied weapons to kill anywhere between ninety and nine hundred striking workers in Guayaquil—the number of victims remains disputed to this day. In early December 1928, Colombian soldiers used foreign-bought weapons to slaughter about a thousand striking United Fruit Company workers, near the Caribbean town of Santa Marta.[7]

During these years, the United States had begun rudimentary training of Latin American police forces and national guards. Washington provided these forces with truncheons and guns, including machine guns. Private companies, such as Federal Laboratories, sold tear gas to foreign police.

Company sales reps in Latin America advised customers "that when they use gas to use plenty of it. We have found from experience that if the police try to disperse a mob with too little gas, their efforts will not be successful." Federal Laboratories, which also sold its chemicals to the British for use in Ireland, marketed its gas as effective not just against urban protests but also against "rebels who flee to the hills and to out-of-the-way places where only aerial attacks can be made."

The Ohio-based Lake Erie Chemical Company grew rich during Wilson's Red Scare, providing gas to police departments across the United States. Lake Erie, which also supplied the Japanese in Manchuria and the Italians in Ethiopia, likewise helped Colombia's army manufacture all "necessary war gases." The company would construct and supply all the buildings and machinery needed to produce *chloroacetophenone* (now commonly known as Mace); *diphenylchloroarsine*, a "sickening gas" that affects its victims much more severely than tear gas; and skin- and lung-blistering mustard gas. Lake Erie promised Colombia "all equipment necessary" to wage "complete gas warfare," including building a "shell-filling plant for all gases, smokes, and liquid fire," a "stokes mortar bomb–filling plant," and a "gas candle and grenade–filling plant."

United States law prohibited the sale of weapons directly to private armies, so Lake Erie labeled the contents of its shipments "chemicals" and delivered them to Klein & Co., a Chilean drug company, which then distributed the gas to the militia. Lake Erie's traveling agent for Latin America, D. B. Richardson, demonstrated the use of gas bombs for leaders of the militia, along with police and military officers. At Santiago penitentiary, Richardson fired a 20-gauge shotgun shell of gas into a cell filled with 120 prisoners.

The violence and trauma of the world war had given rise to a new political force: fascism, a virulent, mobilized nationalism, and the same mix of fascists found in Europe—Italian futurists, German Nazis, and French, Portuguese, and Spanish Falangists—began to appear in Latin America. Militants came together and broke apart, founding, disbanding, and re-founding a farrago of parties and associations. Some borrowed from Europe and called themselves fascists, Nazis, Falangists, and integralists. Others coined new monikers. In Chile, national socialists replaced the z in Nazi with a c, and went by *nacistas*, to emphasize their homegrown origins. In Mexico, militant right-wing Catholic fascists called themselves *sinarquistas*. All were antiliberal and antiprocedural, and most emphasized will and action and understood violence to be a feature of modern politics. Some were secular, though most cultivated close alliances with the conservative Catholics.

Chile's Republican Militia, established in July 1932, was at the fore of this new extremism. In May 1933, it led a march of fifteen thousand fascists through the streets of Santiago. A militant faction within its ranks, tired of working with Hispanic traditionalists and wanting a purer, modernist fascism, took a more confrontational approach. They began using the gas and guns supplied by Lake Erie to break up union meetings and socialist protests. In 1937, they gassed the country's president as he rode in a carriage on his way to open a new congress.[8]

Called to War

Despite this postwar arms buildup, most nations in Latin America, apart from a few border skirmishes, miraculously managed to avoid prolonged war—except in the tragic instance of the Chaco War, fought between Paraguay and Bolivia, two landlocked countries, among the poorest in the Americas.

Bolivia in 1908 had no foreign debt and a small army. Two decades later, the country owed forty million dollars, much of it to Rockefeller's Chase National. A significant portion of the loaned money had been used to buy foreign weapons. By 1929, 37 percent of government revenue went to service debt, and 20 percent went to the military. As the military grew, and grew more politically powerful within Bolivia, civil politicians were increasingly subordinated to its edicts.[9]

As Bolivia was falling into debt, successive governments, both civilian and military, had eagerly handed out concessions to nationals and foreigners to encourage petroleum production. There was oil. Petroleum seeps out of the eastern folds of the Bolivian Andes—the Spanish had used it to caulk and tar their ships. Underground deposits were found in the late 1800s. It was difficult, though, for independent, undercapitalized operators to produce much oil. Even when they did strike a gusher, there was no easy export route to either the Pacific or Atlantic. Bolivia was landlocked. So speculators obtained oil leases from the government not to develop fields but to sell the leases to Standard Oil, which by 1921 had taken control of fifty million acres of Bolivian land. Progressive peace activists called the tight linkage between the arms trade, oil extraction, and finance a "subtler kind of imperialism" than what came before. The scholar Bret Gustafson writes that this form of "bond-based oil imperialism" was applied to many countries in Latin America and beyond in the 1920s, a system in which default, conflict, and crisis weren't unwanted outcomes but triggering "mechanisms that further tightened the control of US banks and dependence on future dollar debt."[10]

Standard didn't invest in much production either, but rather mostly held its Bolivian concessions as a hedge against possible shortfalls from profitable fields elsewhere, in the United States or Mexico. The company pumped minuscule amounts of oil that generated little revenue in the way of taxes or tariffs—not even enough for Bolivians to make its debt payments, much less build a nation.

Decades of nationalist frustration—of knowing your country sat on oil but having one of the world's wealthiest companies blocking its extraction—exploded when a geological survey, produced by Standard, reported that large deposits of petroleum existed in a lowland region called the Chaco Boreal.

Many miles separated the Shangri-la–like heights of Bolivia's capital, the twelve-thousand-feet-above-sea-level La Paz, from the port-town bustle of Paraguay's main city, Asunción, on the eastern bank of the Paraguay River. In between sits the Chaco, a mostly dry and hellishly hot grasslands that, before the oil rush, was home to a few settlers and about thirty thousand Native Americans—Guaraní, Wichí, Mbayá, and others. The border between Bolivia and Paraguay runs through the scrub, but for over a century few gave it much thought. The Chaco was a forlorn place, a moonscape filled with squat *quebracho* trees (so named because their hard wood broke axes) and *palo borracho* (a Ceiba tree with a pear-shaped trunk that soldiers would soon hollow out and use as sniper blinds).

Now, though, as Bolivians began encroaching into Paraguay to drill wells looking for oil, the militaries of both countries began to mobilize. Law students in both nations pored through colonial archives looking for evidence that might support a more aggressive border claim—edicts or maps that might allow Bolivia to say that the *uti possidetis* line ran further south than was previously thought, or help Paraguay prove that it ran further north. Newspapers and radio broadcasts in both countries stirred up a toxic patriotic rivalry, a demonic counter-beat to all the songs of Latin unity.[11]

Bolivia drove the conflict, frustrated by its loss of access to the Pacific and conflicts with Standard Oil. But a similar dynamic played out in Paraguay, with officials from British Royal Dutch Shell assuring government officials that the "richest and finest wells in the world" were waiting to be tapped in the Chaco.[12]

The first skirmish between Paraguayan and Bolivian troops took place in 1927, followed by five years of one-off clashes. Argentina, the Pan-American Union, and the League of Nations dispatched mediators to try to broker an end to the conflict, but Bolivia and Paraguay, emboldened by easy credit and cheap weapons, and intoxicated by the idea of a vast underground sea of oil, brushed them off.

The war broke out in full in September 1932, and by the time it was over three years later had claimed the lives of about 150,000 soldiers and wounded tens of thousands more. Most of the dead on both sides were Native Americans, Guaraní in the Paraguayan army, Aymara and Quechua in Bolivia's. Conscripts were issued hand-me-down World War I uniforms yet made to march barefoot.

Paraguay hadn't fought a war since the 1860s. Combat then meant firing single-shot flint rifles and even muskets. Now infantry and cavalry columns marching from Asunción into the Chaco to confront Bolivian invaders looked up and saw, most for the first time, flying machines swooping down like condors from the Andean slopes. The soldiers below didn't, at first, link the flashes of light they saw above to the machine-gun bullets popping at their feet in the sandy dirt. As the shots hit their marks, survivors made the connection and ran into the bush, leaving behind "writhing bodies" and "thrashing horses." The horses, as Paraguayan officials would soon learn, were useless anyway, since the Chaco didn't have enough water to keep them hydrated.[13]

As the war ground on, the backwash of Europe's recent history spilled out over the Chaco. The terrain soon took on the cast of European battle-fields. Trenches and barbed wire divided a no-man's-land shrouded by smoke and gas, with each side dug in on the ground as air battles took place in the sky above.

Several White Russians, former officers in the overthrown czarist empire, joined the Paraguayan army. Ivan Belaieff, who had fought the Soviets in southern Russia in 1920 and 1921, took the rank of general. He was sent to Europe to recruit Cossacks, who would be offered land in the Chaco in exchange for service against Bolivia. Recruitment offices were established in Paris and Belgrade. As for Bolivia, La Paz turned its army over to a German officer, Hans Kundt, who had earlier captained a regiment on the Russian front in World War I. British mercenaries under the command of Kundt allowed a kind of European reconciliation, with soldiers on opposing sides in the world war now brothers-in-arms. United States mercenaries, paid twenty double-eagle gold dollars a day, fought for Paraguay.[14]

Bolivian veterans—many of them conscripted highland tin or silver miners put on trains and trucks bound for the lowland killing fields—reported, after the war had ended, a kind of sleepwalking to disaster: "We had been called to war," Trifonio Delgado Gonzales wrote in his diary, called "by the oil."

The Chaco veteran described the insanity that had come over Bolivian nationalists, an "absurdity" heightened by the battlefield's otherworldly landscape. "We killed, we died, anonymously." But he also hinted at a political awakening to come, like the resource nationalism that fired up Mexican revolutionaries. Those who lost their lives in the Chaco War died needlessly, Gonzales wrote, "defending the oil of the Standard Oil Company of Bolivia."[15]

International law couldn't stop the Chaco War. It couldn't prevent Italy's taking of Ethiopia, Japan's invasion of Manchuria, Europe's divvying up Africa, the Nazis coming to power in Germany, or Franco's fascist uprising in Spain. Washington insisted the Monroe Doctrine *was* international law. So did Tokyo, which, as its imperial army marched through Manchuria in 1933, declared a "Monroe Doctrine for the Orient." Rome used the doctrine to defend taking Eritrea. London considered declaring its own Monroe Doctrine over all of Africa to slow fascist colonialism. Hitler would cite the Monroe Doctrine when Germany annexed Austria.[16]

Uti possidetis, held up by Latin Americans as the keystone of a new world order, had failed to stop Bolivia and Paraguay from ravaging each other. "Words, words, nothing but words," said Colombia's foreign minister Francisco José Urrutia, referring to the gap that existed between law and practice.

In the United States, in the late 1920s, the same coalition of investors in Mexico that had come together under Wilson was again pushing Washington to start a war with Mexico. The State Department accused Mexico of being Moscow's proxy; President Coolidge sent battleships to cruise Mexican waters.

The Roaring Twenties, though, with the Great Bull Market starting in 1927, were a hard time to work up a big war.* The moral intensity associated with Theodore Roosevelt and Woodrow Wilson had dissipated. Hedonism, apathy, cynicism, intolerance, xenophobia, and graft better described the decade's *geist*. Small wars were still a go. In Paris, Secretary of State Frank Kellogg was negotiating with his French counterpart, Aristide Briand, a celebrated treaty to "outlaw war," for which Kellogg was granted the Nobel

---

* A story goes that Plutarco Elías Calles, then Mexico's president, had blackmailed Coolidge to call off his war plans. An Italian janitor employed by the U.S. embassy apparently had passed on to the Mexican government a bundle of U.S. papers, revealing a vicious racism that ran through the ranks of the U.S. foreign service, along with U.S. military plans to seize Mexico's oil fields. Calles couriered copies of the documents to the White House, signaling that he'd make them public if the U.S. attacked Mexico. Apparently, according to rumors, the threat worked. The White House pulled back the ships it had stationed off Mexico's coast. War was averted.

Peace Prize. At that moment in Nicaragua, Marines, who had been occupying the country for years, were waging a brutal counterinsurgency campaign against peasant rebels. They burned villages, raped women, tortured and murdered with impunity, and used De Havilland biplanes to strafe and bomb refugees.[17]

"Virtual chaos" was how Cordell Hull, Franklin Delano Roosevelt's secretary of state, viewed the world order in the early 1930s. "Chaos, chaos, chaos."[18]

Meanwhile, the war over the Chaco dragged on, winding down in 1935 with no clear victor. No oil windfall either. The surveyors' reports were wrong. The fabled lake of petroleum below the scrub didn't exist.[19]

PART VII

LABORATORY
OF THE WORLD

FDR on the deck of the USS Indianapolis, *receiving a salute from the Argentine navy as he arrives in Buenos Aires, November 30, 1936.*

To Montevideo

F ranklin Delano Roosevelt, in the early fall of 1933, asked his secretary of state Cordell Hull to represent him at a Pan-American Union conference, to be held later that year in Montevideo, Uruguay, the seventh since Secretary of State Blaine convened the hemisphere's foreign ministers four decades earlier. FDR had been president for only a few months, elected three years into the global Great Depression, which had thrown much of the world into crisis. Already his administration had participated in two high-profile world conclaves, in London and Geneva. Both had failed spectacularly. Hull knew that Latin Americans planned to raise big issues in Montevideo—not just the perennial demand of nonintervention but proposals related to debt, trade, investment, the Chaco War, arms control, and the United States' involvement in Cuba and Haiti. FDR wanted the laissez-faire Hull to hold off signing any possible free-trade treaty that might interfere with the experimental New Deal, whose programs entailed considerable government intervention in the nation's economy.

"We don't think you need to undertake much down at Montevideo," a presidential aide told Hull. "Just talk to them about the Pan American highway."

Hull asked Roosevelt if someone else could go in his place. Negotiations to normalize relations with the Soviet Union were ongoing in Washington, and he, as the nation's top diplomat, wanted to be there. Recognition of the government in Moscow would go a long way toward stabilizing a shaky world. The Nazis had already, within months of FDR's March 1933 inauguration, seized control of most of Germany's political institutions. Japan, after consolidating its occupation of Manchuria, had withdrawn from the League of Nations.

But Roosevelt insisted that Hull lead the delegation, even as he dampened expectations as to what the conference might accomplish. Maybe, the president said before Hull's departure, "the question of radio communications will be taken up with a view to their improvement." Offer them some beacons so they can land their planes at night.

"There never had been anything more stupid," Hull thought, "than to send a delegation to the Pan-American Conference empowered only to build a road."[1]

Orderly Mutual Efforts

A small group was to accompany Hull, including a handful of ornamental ambassadors, a brace of legal experts from State, and the first woman to serve as an official delegate to a state-level conference, Professor Sophonisba Breckinridge from the University of Chicago. Also accompanying Hull was the unlikely Ernest Gruening, a sharp critic of Washington's ongoing occupation of Haiti (which started under Wilson), a contributor to and former editor of *The Nation*, a left-wing weekly. Gruening was no doubt the first Jew to attend such a meeting.

The delegation sailed on November 11, 1933, leaving from Manhattan's Twenty-Fourth Street Pier on the SS *American Legion*, a creaky World War I transport converted by the Munson Line into a passenger ship for South American runs. A crowd had assembled to send off the envoys. Reporters and well-wishers, along with peace campaigners, labor organizers, and feminists crowded the dock.

Trade unionists wanted the conference to establish an Inter-American Bureau of Labor and pass a Pan-American labor code that would prohibit child labor, shorten the workday, offer health care and insurance to workers, and provide a dignified retirement. Representatives from the Women's International League of Peace and Freedom arrived to bid bon voyage to their fellow league member, Professor Breckinridge. For some time now, "Pan-American" feminists had been meeting regularly at diplomatic conferences, advocating for suffrage and equal rights. The League presented Hull with a resolution urging him to do his utmost to end the war between Paraguay and Bolivia and to "discover the weaknesses existing in the present peace machinery." The more radical National Woman's Party was also there to send off its representative, Doris Stevens. Stevens was going to Montevideo to lobby the Pan-American Union to adopt an Equal Rights Amendment and encourage member nations to pass laws ensuring that citizenship wasn't dependent on a woman's marriage status.[2]

Hull entertained journalists in the *Legion*'s smoking room, where he gently contradicted Roosevelt. The conference would indeed focus on economics, he said. He floated the idea of a Pan-American bank, or some other mechanism to get needed capital to key industries. The shock of the 1929 market crash and subsequent Great Depression had fallen like one of those DuPont "airplane drop bombs" on Latin America, destroying economies, increasing desperation, spawning militancy. Several governments had suspended their debt payments. Neither continents nor nations, Hull said, can any longer afford to "engage in helter-skelter economics."

"We are living in a new order calling for orderly mutual efforts," he said.

Hull understood himself as an internationalist, a free trader at odds with the economic nationalism on the rise both in Latin America and among his own colleagues in the FDR administration. He wasn't doctrinaire. He had helped Wilson draft the nation's first income tax bill and accepted that the complexity of industrial society required regulation and that the intensity of the Depression demanded government intercession. But he thought that someday, when the world was spinning more smoothly, nations would move back toward free trade, and free trade would bring peace and prosperity.

Roosevelt, like Wilson before him, acted as if he were not just president but secretary of state, issuing foreign policy statements and forcing Hull to play catchup. So, Hull, though annoyed he'd be missing negotiations with the Soviets, looked forward to putting some distance between himself and the White House. Maybe he could do some diplomacy in far-off Montevideo. He didn't have much hope but thought he would try to resurrect the idea of trade reciprocity—that is, bilateral agreements wherein two nations agree to lower their tariffs. He worried, though, that he would be vetoed by "the New Deal group," as Hull, without much love, called FDR's advisory group of progressive intellectuals, the fabled Brain Trust. Maybe the conference would be a waste of time, like the ones in London and Geneva.

It wasn't. Not only would the decisions made in Montevideo help save the New Deal, but they would also, by galvanizing the forces that would defeat Nazism, help save the world.

Hull didn't know it, but he was about to capitalize on a convergence in how to think about international law and politics a century in the making.

Hull, from Cumberland to Cuba

Hull's background made him an unlikely founder of global governance. He had been born into a large clan in 1871 in Pickett County, on the Cumberland Ridge in eastern Tennessee. Hull's mountain people spoke what he called King Alfred English, or "the early Anglo-Saxon tongue." Hull was one of those who celebrated, like Thomas Jefferson and Theodore Roosevelt before him, what they believed were the foot soldiers who led the world's march of freedom.

Hull described his people as part of the great Saxon migration. Eight generations back, Reverend Joseph Hull arrived in the Massachusetts Bay Colony in 1634. Hull's great-grandfather fought in the American Revolution, and then moved his family from North Carolina to Tennessee. His grandfather fought in the war with Mexico, and his father, Billy, in the Civil War as a Confederate captain. The end of that war on the Cumberland Ridge was chaotic and unforgiving, with remnant bands of Confederate and Union soldiers raiding and killing long after Appomattox. Billy was shot in the eye by a "Yankee guerrilla," blinded and left for dead. He recovered to live a long life in constant pain, long enough to track his assailant to Kentucky and shoot him in the back. The story became lore in mountain Tennessee, told in different versions by different members of the Hull clan. Cordell often recounted the tale, with the kicker being that nobody thought the worse of Billy for the murder. Captain Hull also tracked down the Yankee murderer of a soldier under his command and shot him dead too.

His retribution obligations fulfilled, Cordell's blind-in-one-eye father, now married, started dirt farming but also earning cash as a moonshiner and a logger. Billy began floating cut poplars down the Obey and Cumberland rivers on a raft to sell the lumber in Nashville.[3] Cordell's family grew prosperous as he grew up, eventually settling in Celina, a new town in the crook of the Obey and Cumberland rivers that thrived with the logging trade.*

It's hard to square the amiable Cordell—the longest-serving secretary of state in United States history—with implacable Billy, or with the people found in photographs of Hull's extended mountain relations. His craggy-faced cousins were suspicious of federal power, including the power to tax distillation. But many of them, after Hull became secretary of state, got federal jobs during the New Deal. The Works Progress Administration and the Tennessee Valley Authority practically had a small subdivision dedicated to the Hulls.

Whatever darkness lay in Billy was suppressed in his son, though Cordell's "sad, gentle eyes" revealed some sorrow. The secretary of state could look mournful and beautiful at the same time, one observer said, which made him a good poker player and a better diplomat. Hull was studious, read voraciously, and, after a ten-month course at Cumberland Law School, became a backwoods lawyer. His political outlook illustrated the evolution of the Democratic Party. His family had worshipped Andrew Jackson. But where the original Jacksonians came together in horror at the

---

* Near Celina there existed an older community, Free Hill, founded by emancipated people of color in the early 1800s. Free Hill was isolated and left alone until the logging boom, after which the white residents of Celina (following the end of Reconstruction and withdrawal of federal troops) started terrorizing the village, burning its school and church. Just four days before the 1878 congressional elections, vigilantes drove out all of Free Hill's African American residents. "Many of the negroes will leave farms," one newspaper reported. Democrats swept most of Tennessee's congressional seats. Shortly after, Billy Hull acquired a "rich river bottom farm" on the outskirts of town.

thought of even sending a representative to Bolívar's Panama Congress, Hull, the son of a one-eyed vengeance dealer, was so open to the world that FDR christened him "father of the United Nations."[4]

At this point in his young life, Hull's experience with Latin America consisted of his involvement in the reconstruction of Cuba after the War of 1898. Hull arrived in Cuba after the fighting was over. With Spain defeated, the U.S. military was carrying out a Jim Crow reconstruction. It dissolved Martí's multiracial Army of Liberation and began to exclude people of color from ranked positions in the military and police. "All officers will be white," one U.S. officer reconstructing Cuba's artillery corps insisted. Soon, U.S. capital would flood the island and take over sugar production, but for now plantations were returned to their old owners, with a United States–organized Rural Guard forcing cane cutters to get back to work.[5]

Hull was put in charge of reforming the city of Santa Clara's property registry. Here was a true clash of culture, the Jacksonian lawyer opening the door to a four-century-old cobwebbed Spanish imperial archive: bundles of deeds, decrees, mortgages, grants, and other legal documents, many with unreadable marginalia, with amendments upon amendments, codicils dangling from codicils dating to the time of Las Casas. Hull was overwhelmed by the complexities of feudal property rules. There were "many practices," he said understatedly, that hindered foreign investment, "which I had to remove."

Hull returned to Tennessee in May 1898 and threw himself into reading John Locke and other English liberals. It must have felt like a philosophical cleanse after months immersed in the swamps of Spanish American land records.

Gruening in Haiti

Hull was lucky to have Ernest Gruening with him on the *American Legion*.

Gruening's parents, Emil Gruening and Phoebe Friedenberg, were secular German Jewish immigrants. Emil, after fighting in the Union Army during the Civil War, became a prominent eye surgeon and held positions at

Mount Sinai and the New York Eye and Ear Infirmary. His children, a boy and four girls, went to the best schools, then just opening their doors to Jews, or at least to a few Jews. Ernest attended Hotchkiss and Harvard and earned a medical degree. But drawn to politics and the peace movement, he never practiced. Later, as Alaska's senator, he'd cast one of only two no votes against Lyndon Baines Johnson's 1964 Gulf of Tonkin Resolution, which escalated United States military involvement in Vietnam. Prior to 1933, Gruening worked as a journalist for several liberal and left magazines, including the Spanish-language *La Prensa* and *The Nation*, where he was also the managing editor.[6]

Gruening and his four sisters, Martha, Mary, Clara, and Rose, became active in left politics, working with unions, the suffrage movement, and the NAACP. The sisters were friends of John Reed and W. E. B. Du Bois, with Martha using her inheritance to open a socialist school in Marlboro, New York. Martha was also a journalist, coauthoring essays with Du Bois and covering the "habitual brutality of white police officers" against African Americans for the NAACP's *The Crisis*. One of Ernest's first assignments was the IWW's Bread and Roses textile strike in Lawrence, Massachusetts. After that, he reported on Nicaragua, the Dominican Republic, and Cuba. He spent five years in Mexico researching its revolution for a book, *Mexico and Its Heritage*, published in 1928. As for Haiti, no other white writer had shown as much sympathy toward the country as Gruening, and as much outrage toward the United States for its military occupation. This was at a time when the U.S. press was publishing the worst slander on Haiti, stories about demon worship and orgiastic quadrilles. "Voodoo Practices Demand Sacrifice of a White Child" ran one headline.[7]

Over the next few years, Gruening was part of a multiracial movement that worked doggedly to end the occupation, which turned especially violent when the United States put into place a system of forced labor to build public roads. In Europe, U.S. soldiers were told they were fighting to make the world safe for democracy. In Haiti, U.S. soldiers were reintroducing a practice indistinguishable from slavery. Haitians were "sometimes manacled like slaves, compelled to work for weeks with little or no pay and inadequate food and shot down if they attempted to escape." Rebellion spread, which

Franklin Delano Roosevelt, then assistant secretary of the navy, described as nothing but lawless banditry infesting the countryside. Haiti, the future president said in 1922, is the "blackest spot in all the Americas."[8]

Gruening's knowledge of French helped build ties between Haitians and activists in the United States. In late 1921, he traveled to Haiti ahead of a Senate delegation, working with the Union Patriotique d'Haiti on the slogans it would use to greet the delegates. Photographers captured the banners: "Shall Haiti be your Ireland?" "Shall Haiti be your Congo?"[9]

Domestic hatreds flowed easily from the United States, where the Klan was resurgent, lynching on the rise, and segregation deepening. Ignored by the mainstream U.S. press, the island was a place of wild racist abandon. Its dark-skinned inhabitants were the victims of unspeakable violence, scenes of terror that could easily be worked into a Cormac McCarthy novel. The U.S. occupation tried to suppress Vodou, outlawing *ouangas*, or talismans: "all dances and other practices calculated to foster fetishism and superstition shall be deemed witchcraft and punished accordingly," read the U.S.-drafted civil code.

But it was the Marines who were truly demonic. Sadism and debasement were their instruments of war. Soldiers tortured—employing a practice known as the "water cure," today called waterboarding—mutilated the living and the dead, razed villages, committed targeted executions, and engaged in arbitrary murder. Soldiers captured women, and girls as young as nine, for concubinage. One report estimated that U.S. Marines had murdered three thousand Haitians by 1922. Much of the terror was executed through the Marine-organized *Garde d'Haiti*, Haitian police under the command of white U.S. officers.[10]

Josephus Daniels, secretary of the navy, ordered an investigation of abuses. As a civilian, though, he found his command essentially ignored by military officers on the island. Records disappeared. Daniels was told that a full report had been completed but was "lost in the mail." Daniels ordered another investigation. That, too, was stymied. The navy's Judge Advocate ruled in favor of the conduct of U.S. soldiers: "Ours is a Christian country; we make war as a Christian country should."[11]

Possibilities for Good

As Hull and his delegates made their way to Montevideo, it was hard to say whether the task at hand was to finish rebuilding a system of law from the ruins of the last war or start preparing the world for the next war.

Early New Deal foreign policy makers were divided into *internationalists* and *Latin Americanists.* The first, led by Hull, thought the United States should pursue a broad global policy, and the second believed that Washington would do better to hunker down in its hemisphere and treat the oceans as trenches. But even the internationalists knew Latin America was important, that they had to get Latin America in order before they could order the world.[12]

Sumner Welles, an assistant secretary of state and FDR's special adviser on Latin America, was exceptionally clear on this point. "If the United States," Welles wrote in 1928, "is to maintain itself as one of the greatest forces in the world of the future," then "the time is at hand when it must reach the conviction that in the Western Hemisphere lies its strength and its support."[13]

Doing so would mean that Washington would finally and forthrightly have to accept the ideal of sovereign equality and reject the right to intervention. Hull was sympathetic to Latin America's complaints. He himself had inserted a "no interference in the internal affairs of other nations" plank in the 1932 Democratic Party platform. But Hull's was a soft anti-interventionism, vaguely in favor of banning interference, but also committed to applying United States power to bring about what he considered stability. It went without saying that the chaotic countries of the Caribbean would be exempt from any nonintervention pledge Washington might make. As for FDR, he had spent his years as Wilson's assistant secretary of the navy cruising the Caribbean looking for investment opportunities. He claimed to have played a role in writing Haiti's new constitution, which repealed a prohibition against foreigners owning property—a repeal that facilitated his efforts to find sugar lands to invest in, including on Île-à-Vache, Cow Island, where Abraham Lincoln had sent emancipated freemen and women. Most people of FDR's status and class simply considered the Caribbean an American lake, by which they meant a United States lake.[14]

Gruening thought differently. He knew that this time there could be no trimming, as there was with Wilson, who promised to forswear intervention and then sent troops into Mexico, Haiti, and the Dominican Republic. After so many broken pledges and worked-up hopes, Latin America's leaders wouldn't be appeased with "words, words, words."

In the crucible of the Great Depression, fascism was mixing hot. Its partisans brought into sharp relief the hypocrisy of liberalism, especially that of the United States. Hitler answered FDR's demand that Germany respect the sovereignty of its neighbors by referring the U.S. president to his nation's own Monroe Doctrine. "We Germans hold exactly the same doctrine for Europe, or at least for the region and the interest of the Großdeutsche Reich."

Already by 1933, some of the more astute members of Hull's delegation—namely Gruening—knew that a new kind of diplomacy would be needed to respond to the growing darkness.* Gruening's left-wing internationalism helped him see how the varieties of authoritarianism were coming into alignment, the convergences between KKK lynch racism in the United States, Marine atrocities in Haiti, and the expansionist militarism in Nazi Germany, Italy, and Japan. If the United States was going to stand for democracy, that alignment would have to be broken, and Washington would have to stake out a higher moral ground. Latin America, Gruening believed, was the place where it could do so.

Gruening knew, after years of writing on Latin America and the Caribbean, that the region had its share of reactionaries. Most countries checked all the boxes indicating the likelihood of militant antiliberalism taking over: vicious manufacturers eager to stomp trade unionism; besieged Catholic traditionalists; patriarchs fearful of losing power over their family in a liberalizing society; masses of rootless, displaced peoples; an established tradition

---

* Gruening's sisters were what J. Edgar Hoover called "pre-mature anti-fascists." In 1935, Clara wrote that fascism was the culmination of the backlash to rationalism and demands for social equality made by women, people of color, and workers. "The reaction," she said, "had long been growing."

of military officers intervening in politics; histories of humiliation, of nations dismembered, be it the North American Southwest from Mexico or Panama from Colombia; and a powerful landed class feudal in its worldview. (On a 1938 swing through Georgia and the lower South, FDR would say "there is little difference between the feudal system and the Fascist system. If you believe in the one, you lean to the other.")

Another factor in determining whether a Latin American nation might turn fascist: parasitical foreign financiers and capitalists—who made the region's nationalists feel as powerless in relation to the United States as Germany felt in relation to Great Britian. Bolívar called them "vultures." "Vampires that suck the blood of the people and drain their vigor," complained a Mexican nationalist of foreign oil companies. "Vampires who haunt our oil fields," wrote the Argentine economist Ricardo Oneto, taking the petroleum "which is essential for the life of the nation and the protection of its sovereignty." In Germany, such imagery was the stuff of anti-Semitism. In Latin America, it referred to Anglo-Saxon capitalists.[15]

The journalist Carleton Beals witnessed the growth of the Italian Fascisti in Italy in 1921. Two years later he witnessed the same in Mexico, noticing similarities between the fascist shock troops organized by the owners of large estates in Italy's Adriatic delta region and Mexican landlords who relied on local paramilitaries for protection. Beals predicted that the success of the Mexican Revolution would stymie the growth of right-wing extremism, but as early as 1923, about 150,000 fascists were operating in Mexico, organized in cells in Tampico, Guadalajara, and Mexico City.[16]

Gruening saw Latin America as a bright spot, its reformers trying to deal with the problems of modern life within a humanist, not a race supremacist, framework. The "possibilities for good are incalculable," he wrote, referring to Mexico's peasant leagues and labor unions. Gruening thought that the Montevideo conference, if handled correctly, could help turn Latin America into an antifascist showcase. He wanted to be there.

Gruening lobbied his friend, Harvard law professor Felix Frankfurter, who was close to FDR, to recommend him to Hull. An outspoken anti-imperialist, he was doubtful that Roosevelt or Hull would agree. Earlier, when he was assistant secretary of the navy, Roosevelt had suggested that critical reporters like Gruening be dropped into the Haitian backlands and left to fend for themselves. But Roosevelt's foreign policy views had evolved since then. And he liked to put people of different ideological positions to work on the same issue. Aside from Hull, the U.S. delegation to the Pan-American Conference already had several conservative members. Hull agreed that a "clash of opinion" would shake "career diplomats out of their ruts." Roosevelt approved Gruening's request.[17]

Frankfurter was thrilled. "There will be at least one man who will convey to the South Americans an informed, deeply sympathetic interest in true 'neighborliness,'" he wrote to Gruening. "I rejoice that you are going."[18]

Hull prepared carefully for Montevideo. Relations were tense between the region's statesmen and his State Department, a result of ongoing U.S. inter-ventionism: Marine occupations of Haiti (1915–1934), the Dominican Republic (1916–1924), and Nicaragua (1927–1932) and shorter interven-tions to protect U.S. property in Cuba, Guatemala, and Honduras. Yet a new thinking had already begun to filter through Washington, an aware-ness that the United States had to find a less inflammatory foreign policy, one that wouldn't constantly draw criticism from Latin America. FDR's pre-decessor, Herbert Hoover, had quietly started withdrawing troops from Haiti. The last Marine had left Nicaragua before FDR's inauguration, in January 1933. So Hull saw a chance. If the Western Hemisphere could pro-duce "a bounteous harvest in our own neighborhood," then it could be a model for "closer cooperation throughout the world." "I always had the hope that what was accomplished in the New World could be achieved in the Old as well."

Latin Americans had plans too. Hull had heard that Mexico's foreign minister, José Manuel Puig, was conspiring to push a resolution defining the Monroe Doctrine explicitly as a doctrine of nonintervention, one that would ban all American nations—including the United States—from inter-fering in the affairs of other nations. Hull asked Josephus Daniels, now his ambassador in Mexico, to find out more about how Mexico meant to apply the ideal of nonintervention within the Western Hemisphere. Daniels raised the matter with Puig, who said he didn't mean to apply it within the Western Hemisphere. He meant to apply it everywhere.

Daniels wired Hull saying that Puig "thinks Monroe Doctrine should include the whole world."

The So-Called Right of Conquest

E ver bookish, Hull used his time aboard the liner to read up on Latin America and hold seminars on the region with Gruening and other advisers and staffers. He courted his fellow diplomats by breaking protocol. Instead of having them call on him, as would be expected since he was the ship's highest-ranking statesmen, Hull spontaneously visited his counterparts, dressed casually, and accompanied only by a translator.

On board were delegations from Haiti, Venezuela, and Honduras. Hull made the rounds. "I'm Hull from the United States" was how he introduced himself, trying to remember what Spanish he had learned stationed in Cuba three decades earlier. Latin Americans were impressed, at least according to news reports. They liked Hull's bad Spanish, spoken with a Southern gentry accent (despite his mountain upbringing) that gently swapped out *r*'s for *w*'s. The secretary of state wore his homespun naturally, and his deference to those on the receiving end of it didn't appear artful. Hull even joined in the boisterous carnival when the *American Legion* crossed the equator, paying homage to King Neptune.

The final terms of the United States' withdrawal from Haiti were still being worked out, but a plebiscite organized by the occupation had brought a slate of nationalists to power. The Haitian diplomats traveling on the *Legion*—of lighter skin and a wealthier class, not the kind likely to be thrown into work gangs by Marines—invited Hull to a state dinner where they served him "much champagne and old liqueur rum" (though Prohibition in the U.S. would still be law for a few more weeks). An aide joked that Hull's Tennessee friends would be surprised to know that he had been "entertained" by "Negroes," to which Hull replied that "when they speak French, that's different."

The secretary went on to offer a "homily" that "inter-American democracy must take no account of racial, linguistic, or cultural differences." A century earlier, Southerners threw a tantrum at the mere thought of having to sit at a table with a Black diplomat. Now here was the Tennessean Hull dining with Haitian statesmen, drinking rum, and preaching racial equality.

If Hull didn't initially understand why Latin Americans feared Washington, he certainly did after days of conversing with Gruening. "Our inheritance of ill will was grim," he later wrote of the United States' history in the hemisphere. Gruening made use of every opportunity to speak with Hull alone, outside of earshot of the "career State Department men." He almost, while still on board the *Legion*, brokered a final plan between Hull and the Haitians for the United States to leave Haiti. But State's career men got hold of what Gruening was up to and quickly had FDR issue a statement declaring that the United States would need to maintain an indefinite supervisory role in the country.[1]

Maybe, Hull thought, the situation in Latin America was ready for a drastic change. It wouldn't be easy. Along with Haiti, Cuba was a sour note. Washington had badly botched a crisis on the island shortly after FDR's inauguration, undercutting a civilian social-democratic reformer favored by most Cubans and urging the army's chief of staff, Fulgencio Batista, to install a government that could impose order. The United States, complained one Cuban diplomat, acts like the "good neighbors who come into your house and never leave."[2]

As the *Legion* entered the great Río de la Plata estuary and the lights of Montevideo came into view, the U.S. delegation learned that the Cuban delegates would push most aggressively for nonintervention. However open Hull might have been to the idea of giving up the right to intervention, he took Cuba's anticipated criticisms personally. "Ah fought in Cuba for the

Cubans. Ah got fever down there," Gruening remembered Hull saying, putting emphasis on the secretary's Southern lisping drawl.

The secretary was also skittish about bad press. "If Ah were to come out against intervention," he said, "the Hearst papers would attack me fwom coast to coast. . . . Wemember, Gwuening, Mr. Woosevelt and Ah have to be weelected."

"Coming out against intervention would help you get reelected," Gruening replied. It would, he insisted, help the New Deal jump off the merry-go-round of invasion, occupation, and insurgency that had badly crippled United States prestige throughout Latin America and much of the world.

"What am ah goin' to do when chaos breaks out in one of those countries and armed bands go woamin' awound, burnin', pillagin', and murdewin' Amewicans?" Hull asked Gruening. "How can I tell mah people that we cain't intervene?"

"Mr. Secretary," Gruening answered, such mayhem "usually happens after we have intervened."

The Hope of America

Bad press and street protests, with unflattering effigies and placards denouncing United States imperialism, greeted Hull upon his arrival. The conference was held in poor, economically stressed Montevideo, which every day received an assortment of newspapers from Buenos Aires, across the estuary. Nearly all were critical of Washington. Hull was accustomed to the Hearst propaganda machine, so he couldn't have felt too bad when "on several occasions, he picked up newspapers whose representatives never had seen him and saw articles putting into quotation marks statements he had not uttered."

Hull had brought along his Kentucky friend, Ulric Bell, a journalist with the Louisville *Courier-Journal*, as press adviser. Bell would go on to work for the Office of War Information, producing anti-isolationist and anti-Nazi film propaganda (much of his work would focus on undermining America Firster Charles Lindbergh's popularity). In Montevideo, he was active getting sympathetic United States delegates, especially the anti-imperialist Gruening, into the Latin America press. A Peruvian newspaper ran an interview with Gruening, in which he hailed the outlawed Alianza Popular Revolucionaria Americana, a socialist internationalist party that claimed to be heir to the spirit of both Bolívar and Marx. Gruening called APRA's founder, the then-exiled Victor Raúl Haya de la Torre, "the hope of America." APRA was one of many left-wing, internationalist, and anti-imperialist parties formed in Latin America in the 1920s. Some supported the Soviet Union, while others opposed Moscow's claim to doctrinal authority. Yet all were breaking new ground. Opening the doors to mass politics, they transformed the diffuse romantic nationalism of intellectuals like Bilbao and Martí into a class-based mobilization centered on workers and peasants.[3]

Their main fight was not yet against what one young member of Chile's Socialist Party, Salvador Allende, later called "the dark threat of fascism." It was against Anglo imperialism, led by Washington and London, especially a financial system that reinforced existing feudal relations.[4]

Bell's strategy was risky. He was using Gruening and others to signal that the United States stood behind radical reform in the hope of winning over public opinion. But he gambled with alienating conservatives, who occupied the presidencies in most of the region's governments—including governments that were curious about how Nazi Germany and Fascist Italy were handling the Great Depression.

Hull, though, carried the day. Conservatives knew he was no radical, and his easygoing style continued to win him friends in the run-up to the start of the conference. He couldn't pronounce most Spanish surnames. With a wide smile, he called the foreign ministers of Argentina and Chile, Carlos Saavedra Lamas and Miguel Cruchaga, respectively, *Mr. Savannah* and *Mr. Chicago*. This came off as self-deprecating. Hull worked Saavedra, pulling South America's leading diplomat into a kind of conspiracy regarding the conference's agenda. Hull whispered that the meeting was Saavedra's to steer, offering the Argentine, the starchiest of starched shirts, who sported dyed red hair, a high collar, and a cigarette holder, the chance to present several of the major resolutions, including the ones Hull had drafted.[5]

There were major issues to tackle. Mexico's José Manuel Puig was going to put forth not just the question of the Monroe Doctrine but a proposal on debt and credit. Hull's flatteries didn't distract from Saavedra's desire to pass a strongly worded nonaggression treaty. And the Cuban delegation had its flash-point resolution demanding that nonintervention become the law of the hemisphere.

Meanwhile, Hull had to negotiate with his own administration before he could begin negotiations with Latin Americans. The first time he wired the White House with his plan to pledge nonintervention in exchange for an agreement to open talks on tariff reductions, he received "a very definite refusal." He telegraphed the next day, and again was told no. Stick to radiating goodwill and promise money for communication and transportation development, the White House said. Nothing else. Hull wired a third time, saying he might as well sail home since he had nothing to bargain with. "Finally I got the president's consent."[6]

Our Sovereign American Life

The program for the conference had been set months earlier, painstakingly designed to avoid a repeat of the chaos that took place at the Pan-American Conference held in Havana five years earlier. Then, the Hoover administration had to beat back a rebellion after El Salvador's envoy, Gustavo Guerrero, "threw the bomb of nonintervention" into the conference's final session, demanding that Washington dock its gunboats and stop intervening in Latin American affairs. The gallery cheered Guerrero on as he recounted old and new grievances and hissed at Charles Hughes, a former secretary of state who headed the U.S. delegation, when he tried to defend Washington's policy.[7]

In Montevideo, Mexico's Puig set off fireworks early by calling for new items to be included for discussion, using a point of order to give a "rousing speech" on the problem of debt. Puig had spent the prior half year building support for a "new legal and philosophical conception of credit."

Hull's strategy on debt was to simply invoke "nonintervention," to say that just as his administration wouldn't interfere in another country's politics, it wouldn't interfere in their economics. No more using the Marines as a collection agency. But as the historian Christy Thornton points out, Puig was arguing *for* intervention—for a conception of debt, credit, and investment as a public good that required planning and regulation to protect poor debtor nations from usurious terms and to ensure that all nations, even those that couldn't make payments, had access to capital to fund social programs and development. After a few days of heated debate, Puig's proposals were deferred to a later meeting.[8]

Hull also had to deal with Saavedra's "South American Anti-War Treaty," which set up mediation protocols to settle disputes and outlawed wars of aggression, armed conquest, and "intervention either diplomatic or armed." Leading up to Montevideo, lawyers in the State Department had objected to the text of Saavedra's treaty since it was clearly a bid to codify doctrines long advocated by American International Law theorists. The word *American* was a sticking point. As United States and European jurists had lectured Latin Americans, "international law" can't have a regional adjective attached to it. *American* International Law, for instance, negates the universalism of law by situating it in a specific location. There can only be an unmodified, unqualified *international law*.[9]

Fine, Saavedra said. Let's drop the prefix "South American" and change the title of the pact to "Anti-War Treaty on Non-Aggression and Conciliation." *America*, Argentina said, was meant to express only the "source" of the treaty's "inspiration" and not to imply any regional specificity. Against all expectations, Hull, on December 15, 1933, signed on to Saavedra's treaty. He called the agreement a blueprint for the Old World, whose trade channels are clogged by armaments, its precious resources wasted "to feed cannon rather than hungry mouths." The world, he said, was "being given another chance to right itself." "The Old World looks hopefully in this direction, and we must not disappoint that hope," Hull said. "We have a belt of sanity on this part of the globe."[10]

It was a remarkable reversal for a nation that had long resisted Latin America's legal reforms. The region's delegates were ecstatic. Still, though, an undercurrent of apprehension ran through the proceedings, an awareness that Saavedra's treaty was just words, one of five similar documents—including the Kellogg-Briand peace pact—making the diplomatic rounds. Things were changing fast in Asia and Europe, and most attending Montevideo knew that something other than a well-crafted preamble and formalistic text outlawing intervention and war would be needed to counter the rise of fascism.

Era of Imperialism Nears Its End

According to a pamphlet published by the State Department, Montevideo was the ninety-eighth official international conference held in the Americas since the Panama Congress of 1826. The United States attended some of these conclaves, and when it did, the script was predictable.

Latin America proposed; the United States opposed. This time was different. Hull did counter Puig's proposal concerning debt, but delicately so. And he endorsed Saavedra's antiwar pact and the conference's Convention of Rights and Duties of States, both of which unambiguously proscribed intervention.

Having dropped the provincializing adjective *American*, Latin Americans were now driving the reformation of universal international law. Hull proposed a resolution calling on the promotion of free trade and lower tariffs. Latin Americans were willing, providing the resolution once again affirmed "the principle of equality" of nations and prohibited the use of tariffs and quotas for political purposes to punish defaulting nations. They also wanted the resolution to ban trade treaties that might benefit some nations while harming "world trade as a whole." This was to mollify Argentina's fears that Washington wanted to build a tariff wall around the hemisphere to create an "economic Monroe Doctrine." Hull accepted all the provisos and his free trade resolution passed.[11]

After the conference, Gruening wrote to a friend that Hull had done a "superb job" sidelining the "career boys" from the State Department who tried to qualify his recognition of the sovereign equality of nations. Hull in Montevideo "rose to the occasion magnificently," Gruening wrote, maneuvering around all the "handicaps imposed" by Washington.

When the secretary announced in one of his speeches that the United

States would henceforth "shun and reject" the "so-called right-of-conquest," Latin American delegates broke out in "thunderous applause and cheers." Hull, however, remained "terribly fearful" that his actions would lead to a public "repudiation" by the president.[12]

On the contrary. FDR knew opportunity when he saw it and understood how Hull's initiatives could provide substance to his earlier pledge that the United States would be a "good neighbor." As president, his first use of that term, in his inaugural address, was not directly related to the Western Hemisphere but to all the nations of the world. Now, though, after Hull's triumph, the Good Neighbor Policy became FDR's Latin American policy. Roosevelt claimed credit for giving up the right of conquest and intervention. The "definite policy of the United States from now on," Roosevelt said as the conference was wrapping up, "is one opposed to armed intervention." "Your Americanism and mine," as Roosevelt put it, signaling the United States' acceptance of hemispheric diversity, "must be a structure built of confidence, cemented by a sympathy which recognizes only equality and fraternity. It finds its source and being in the hearts of men and dwells in the temple of the intellect."

"Our Era of 'Imperialism' Nears Its End," *The New York Times* announced, as though a century of intervention could be left behind with a headline. "'Manifest Destiny' Is Giving Way to the New Policy of 'Equal Dealing' with All Nations."[13]

Hull didn't want to leave. The plan was for him to travel by train and plane to several Latin American capitals, which he eventually did, along with Gruening and a few other advisers. But he stayed in Uruguay a couple of extra days to revel in having won over official Latin America. Plus, after decades in Congress placating Tennessee's Temperance activists, Hull, the son of a moonshiner, celebrated the official end of Prohibition, which had taken place on December 5, 1933. The wine and rum flowed in Montevideo, and Hull announced that when he returned to Washington the first thing he would do would be to reduce tariffs on Latin American liquor. He kept his promise.[14]

Hell Bent for Reelection

H ull sailed back to a New Deal in trouble. After putting forward banking reform, poverty relief, and a jumble of often contradictory economic policies, Roosevelt and his advisers were losing steam. The signature program of the "first New Deal," as historians call FDR's initial run of experimental reform, was the National Recovery Administration, a corporatist boondoggle meant to regulate supply, demand, and wages in the nation's top industries. It wasn't working and anyway would soon be declared unconstitutional by the Supreme Court. The president's counselors wanted to move forward with welfare and labor reform, including the Social Security Act and legislation making it easier for workers to form unions.

But the industrial elites who formed the core of the Republican Party, disoriented by the economic collapse, had begun to regroup and sharpen their hostility to the New Deal. The nationalist, high-tariff-seeking industries that had powered the United States on its global ascent since the Civil War put up the most resistance: agriculture, steel, coal, textiles, mining, furniture, and shoemaking, among others. Along with newer automotive companies, these businesses employed large numbers of workers and were threatened by the upswing in labor organizing and strikes. Unions had been demanding a comprehensive labor law since the Ludlow Massacre, and when Congress started to debate the issue, corporate opposition went into high gear.

Written mostly by New York senator Robert Wagner, what became the National Labor Relations Act, or NLRA, was, according to the legal theorist Karl Klare, "perhaps the most radical piece of legislation ever enacted by the United States Congress." The act, which became law in July 1935, acknowledged that there existed a fundamental antagonism between workers and employers that could only be mediated by the state, via an independent body, the National Labor Relations Board. John Rockefeller swore he would never let it happen, but government arbitration of labor and capital was now law.[1]

What Article 27 was to property relations, the NLRA was to labor relations—a fire bell in the night, awakening the reaction.

The Strong Men

Business responded to the NLRA with a wave of lawlessness. The United States wasn't fascist. But its businesses deployed significantly more private paramilitary armies than their counterparts in other industrializing, democratic nations. "The strange fact appears," wrote one observer at the end of the First World War, that the "least feudal country is today the only country that allows" businesses "to keep in their hands the power to arm their own mercenaries." Pinkerton and Baldwin–Felts detective agencies fielded battalions of "watchmen" to patrol coal fields and cattle lands. In industrial cities, companies like Ford and Republic Steel built up in-house security services. Ford ran the world's largest "quasi-military" organization, armed with the same tear gas and machine guns sold to Chilean fascists. Republic Steel's arsenal was "better stocked with gas weapons and gas munitions than any law enforcement agency, local, state, or federal." General Motors operated, according to a Senate investigation, "the most colossal supersystem of spies." Even as they damned the NLRA in the press and lobbied Congress for revisions, companies terrorized workers as if there were no NLRA.[2]

Old hands from the first Red Scare rallied again. Some joined with the

FBI or patriotic groups like the fast-growing American Legion, founded in Paris in 1919 by soldiers loyal to Theodore Roosevelt Jr., in response to what they saw as the fast-spreading appeal of Bolshevism. In California, Legionnaire veterans were regularly called out to beat and tear-gas Imperial Valley's Mexican farmworkers trying to unionize. Throughout the country, the Klan infiltrated many a Legion Hall, harnessing veteran anger over the way they were treated when they returned from France to an economy wracked by inflation and unemployment.

Roosevelt tried to placate the soldiers. But he opposed militarizing citizenship, the idea that veterans should have extra rights, privileges, or perks denied the general population. "No person, because he wore a uniform," FDR was brave enough to say before an American Legion assembly in late 1933, "must therefore be placed in a special class of beneficiaries." Yet by 1936, "fear of the soldier vote," as Secretary of the Interior Harold Ickes wrote in his diary, forced Roosevelt to back down and sign a few months before the election a bill granting bonus checks to World War I veterans.[3]

The "strong men," Roosevelt said—referring not to rank-and-file strikebreakers but the millionaires who manipulated them—were restless. Powerful people were "used to having their way," and, FDR went on, they believed that "democracy had run its course." It was time for "totalitarians" to take over.[4]

"Anti-Communism" synthesized all the old racial, religious, and sexual bugaboos that had fueled prior backlashes. The anti-Catholic Klan, at first sympathetic to the Protestant Roosevelt, grew antagonistic as the New Deal encouraged cultural pluralism and racial tolerance. Anti-Semitism spread, not least among William F. Buckley Sr. and other Texas oilmen, who said that Jews financed the ongoing Mexican Revolution.[5]

Fascists in the European style marched in a variety of colored shirts and accessories—the White Shirts, the Grey Shirts, the Silver Shirts, the White Bands. The Liberty League brought together some of the wealthiest WASP families, Democrat and Republican alike, including the DuPont siblings, to flirt with fascism and oppose FDR. In 1934, members of the League and commanders from the American Legion approached Major-General Smedley Butler and proposed that he lead a march on Washington to oust

Roosevelt from office. Butler, who embodied both law-and-order and rebelliousness and was unhappy with the direction of the country, nonetheless exposed the conspirators, and their so-called Business Plot against Roosevelt came to naught.

The ties grew thicker, as old-line families, industrialists, (some) New York bankers, local police departments and sheriffs, and organizations like the League and the Legion found unity in action. "The brood of anti–New Deal organizations spawned by the Liberty League are in turn spawning fascism," wrote the *New York Post*. A group named the American Coalition called for a "mass attack" on Roosevelt. "Private property" is freedom, the coalition said, and in the "expropriation of private property lies the fetus of despotism."[6]

The "Americanism" committee of the American Legion demanded increased deportations and urged prison time for anyone circulating left-wing newspapers and "dismissal and punishing for first degree treason" of "any school teacher" who teaches children "in any theory or any practice or any principle that is inimical to the government." The Klan breakaway group, Black Legion, killed and disappeared at least fourteen union activists in Detroit, many of them African American. The German American Bund functioned as a wing of the German Nazi Party, holding parades down Manhattan avenues and running youth camps in the Catskills. Fritz Kuhn headed the Bund and worked for Henry Ford at River Rouge, using the ample time off Ford granted him to organize pro-Nazi cells, including among some Native American groups.* A former member of the German Free Corps, Kuhn had helped "drown in blood" the Bavarian revolution in 1919.[7]

The second half of FDR's first term was a grim, dangerous period. Around this time, other countries were gripped by similar crises and menaced by similar threats, as beleaguered elites looked to mobilize a conservative rank and file to shore up their authority. In the grip of economic

---

* Before coming to the United States in the 1930s, Kuhn had immigrated to Mexico, where he was welcomed by the community of oilmen and ultraconservatives who opposed the Revolution. Kuhn took a job as a chemist with Corona Oil, a subsidiary of Royal Dutch Shell, and worked with local Nazi groups, distributing anti-Semitic literature, including a Spanish translation of the *Protocols of the Elders of Zion*, among the Yaqui and other indigenous groups.

chaos, the institutions of constitutional democracy couldn't simultaneously satisfy the demands of a mobilized citizenry *and* guarantee elites the protection and power they considered their due. The depression had squeezed the middle class, which depending on the political context, could swing right or left.

Italy, Germany, Portugal, and Japan, along with—from a different ideological direction—the Soviet Union, led the revolt against liberalism. Franco was fighting to bring Spain into the authoritarian fold.[8]

Yet most wealthy, industrialized democratic nations, where a large percentage of the population had the vote, managed to keep fascism at bay thanks to mobilized labor unions in alliance with labor or social-democratic parties, which delivered, or pushed for, needed social reform within the confines of democratic institutions. The United Kingdom, France, Norway, Sweden, Denmark, Holland, and Chile are some examples.

In the United States, too, fascism stalled and political liberalism and social welfare advanced. This advance, though, was not led by a social-democratic or labor party but rather took place thanks to the actions Hull took in Montevideo, within the bounds of the nation's historic two-party system.

Realignment

Hull's stubborn push for lower tariffs energized a new corporate coalition that came to the New Deal's rescue. Upon his return from Latin America, Hull found that FDR had devalued the dollar to make exports cheaper. The president also authorized Hull to go put forward his Reciprocal Trade Agreements Act, or RTAA, which passed in Congress and gave the White House, and by extension Hull, flexibility to lower tariffs and enter trade pacts without needing legislative ratification. The industries that supported Roosevelt's reelection tended to be high-tech, export-oriented, and capital- and labor-intensive. They didn't depend on maintaining a large labor force, and therefore weren't so threatened by an increase in union membership.

They may not have been happy about the NLRA, but were, very much so, about the Reciprocal Trade Agreements Act.

The corporate core of the Republican Party was disintegrating, with some stalwart industries, such as oil, chemicals (though not the DuPonts), and banking (though not J. P. Morgan) defecting to the Democrats. Newer financial houses run by Jewish bankers, such as Lehman Brothers, threw in with FDR, in the hope of escaping the hold the Protestant banking establishment had over the financial system. These industries were swayed by Roosevelt's and Hull's promises to open markets and to build the kind of legal and physical infrastructure that would allow their spread overseas.[9]

Hull's trade policies had tied back together Roosevelt's fraying coalition of elite supporters. James Warburg, the German-born banker and early adviser to FDR, had broken with the president over monetary policy and published *Hell Bent for Election*, a scorcher of a book that sold over a million copies and decried the country's drift toward tyranny and socialism. "Almost anyone would be better than Roosevelt," Warburg wrote. His criticisms were unrelenting, and Hearst papers seemed to run them in every edition.

Unrelenting until he relented. In October 1936, Warburg wrote a long trade-policy love letter to Hull, announcing that he was, after all, voting for Roosevelt. Also in October, William Clayton, the world's largest cotton merchant and a former Liberty Leaguer, said he had changed his mind and was voting for Roosevelt because he was afraid that Republican nominee Alf Landon's commitment to protectionism would close markets for cotton. "A vote for President Roosevelt is a vote to keep Secretary Hull in office," Clayton said.[10]

By late 1936, Hull had negotiated fifteen trade treaties, most of them with Latin American countries—Cuba, Brazil, Belgium (and Luxembourg), Haiti, Sweden, Colombia, Canada, Honduras, the Netherlands, Switzerland, Nicaragua, Guatemala, Great Britain, France and its colonies, and Finland, and was working on similar agreements with Costa Rica, El Salvador, Ecuador, and Venezuela. Hull also promised to soon sign a treaty with Canada to begin work on the locks and canals to create a deepwater Saint

Lawrence seaway, which would better connect the Midwest to the Atlantic and supply cheap government-produced electricity to homes and factories. Trade within the hemisphere, which had collapsed with the stock market in 1929, was slowly recovering. It was too soon, by the November election, to know the material effects of Hull's deals, to identify which sectors of the economy they were helping or hurting.[11]

There was no doubt, though, that the promise of more such trade deals excited the new "power bloc of capital-intensive industries, investment banks, and internationally oriented commercial banks." These included Coca-Cola, General Electric, Pan Am, International Telephone and Telegraph, the Radio Corporation of America, Standard Oil, International Harvester, Chase, and National City. Thomas Watson of IBM (a Hoover man in 1932) supported Roosevelt.

Roosevelt gave fire and brimstone at the Democratic National Convention. "Freedom is no half-and-half affair," he said. If the working man has "equal opportunity in the polling place," he must have the same equality "in the market place." "Economic royalists complain that we seek to overthrow the institutions of America. What they really complain of is that we seek to take away their power." But the convention's stage was paid for by those royalists, by banks like Chase and the Manufacturers Trust, which each donated one hundred thousand dollars to his reelection.[12]

Landon could still count on those industries that militantly opposed unions: Pennsylvania steel, Detroit automobiles (though Studebaker went with Roosevelt), Southern textiles, among others. Landon hoped to retain some of the Republican Party's historic labor support, so he couldn't offer a full-on attack of the NLRA. Instead, he went after Hull's tariffs. In attacking Hull's trade treaties, Landon was picking up Hull's sword and using it to commit political suicide. He wouldn't stop doing what one newspaper warned him not to: argue with Cordell Hull about tariffs.

On October 29, four days before the election, two hundred business leaders and former Hoover officials met at 67 Broad Street in Manhattan, two blocks from the Stock Exchange. Most said they were Republicans. All said they were voting for Roosevelt. Hull was hailed, Landon lambasted, and a general agreement reached that if "Secretary Hull's treaties were revoked, there would be a revolution among conservative businessmen."[13]

Hull's success in Montevideo gave him more than a tariff policy to help FDR win over the fat cats. The secretary of state's embrace of nonintervention proved a touchpoint for a new political morality, a code of ethics to help frame the reelection campaign.

The Good Neighbor at Home

On February 23, 1936, FDR gave a radio address to celebrate Brotherhood Day, established by the National Conference of Jews and Christians to promote tolerance in the face of rising global race hatred. "The very state of the world," Roosevelt said, "is a summons to us to stand together." The president ended his remarks with a proposal to set up "Associations of Good Neighbors in every town and city."

Two months later, the Good Neighbor League was established. Led by an official with the National Broadcasting Company and former editor of the *Christian Herald*, Stanley High, the League focused on "applying the principles of the Good Neighbor policy abroad as well as at home." In other words, it sought to expand the moral meaning of a popular diplomatic catchphrase, "good neighbor," to cover much more than foreign policy. The idea of being a good neighbor, both as citizens and as nations, was, Roosevelt said, a "spiritual awakening." New Dealers began to use the phrase to cover FDR's growing multiracial, multidenominational coalition: Catholics, Protestants, Jews; Black, white, and brown. The acceptance of diversity within the hemisphere was equal to the acceptance of diversity within the nation. Your Americanism and mine. Hundreds of Good Neighbor Clubs were organized around the country and charged to "translate the Good Neighbor ideals into reality through votes on November 3rd."[14]

The League self-consciously presented its values as "opposite to those of the Liberty League," to its nativist anti-unionism. One Good Neighbor speaker at a Madison Square Garden rally said the Liberty League might as well change its name to the Bossman and Landlord League, since it is committed to protecting "the liberty of a few men to wring their bread from the sweat of other men's faces," to defend "the right of a private property owner to dictate the amount of rent which he will demand or the wages he will pay." At another Good Neighbor League rally in Columbus, Ohio, broadcast nationally by radio, Secretary of the Interior Harold Ickes linked Landon to the racist and anti-Semitic Father Coughlin. Ickes held up Pan-Americanism, an openness to the world and its refugees, as true Americanism. League staffers published articles in the press hailing "the Americas" as a "haven" for those "fleeing from the countries dominated by the dictators."

The Good Neighbor League also got out the African American vote for FDR, which would expand dramatically between 1932 and 1936. The League was not tagged as a "Black" organization, but organizers did create a National Colored Committee of Good Neighbor clergymen, teachers, small-business owners, and professionals that did party-building groundwork in Black churches in Philadelphia, New York, and Atlanta. It held mass meetings of African Americans on "Emancipation Day" (April 16, the day in 1862 that in Washington, D.C., Lincoln signed the act freeing slaves) in a bid to claim Republican Lincoln for the New Deal and convince African Americans to switch allegiance to the Democratic Party. The League organized an enormous rally in Madison Square Garden featuring Cab Calloway, broadcast, as many of its events were, across the country. A New Mexico chapter of the league tapped into what was then called the "Spanish" vote, pushing back on Southwestern whites who prevented Mexican Americans from voting. Good Neighbor Leaguer Ruth Tuck, an anthropologist and antiracist activist who exposed Klan attacks on indigenous and Latino people in the borderlands, spoke at League rallies, linking FDR's re-election to better, more human "relations with the southern half of this hemisphere."[15]

The magic of the League was that, even as it seeded the New Deal through the grassroots, it helped to consolidate FDR's support among business elites, who associated the phrase Good Neighbor with Hull's free-trade initiatives. Both FDR and Secretary of the Treasury Henry Morgenthau addressed industrialists under the auspices of the Good Neighbor League.

FDR spoke to business leaders, gathered at dinners across the country, by radio hookup: "We seek to guarantee the revival of private enterprise," Roosevelt said, "by guaranteeing conditions in which it can work." Two months before the election, the Good Neighbor League held a rally featuring Cordell Hull, who defined both domestic and foreign policy as based on the ideal of the Good Neighbor. "We have tried to give full meaning to that term."[16]

The League was active in churches, synagogues, and unions. The organization drew on the country's most popular politicians and liberal intellectuals, including Eleanor Roosevelt, to inject a humanitarian, ecumenical ethos into FDR's efforts. It joined Catholics and Protestants as it sold Social Security as if it were preached by Jesus on the Mount. FDR all but said that to be a "Good Neighbor" was a new Golden Rule, using the League to drive home a simple message: "We have preached, and will continue to preach, the gospel of the good neighbor. I hope from the bottom of my heart that as the years go on, in every continent and in every clime, nation will follow nation in proving by deed as well as by word their adherence to the ideal of the Americas—I am a good neighbor."

This is what a coalition rising to dominance sounds like, able to seamlessly unite domestic and foreign interests, to reconcile isolationist and internationalist impulses in a moral vision that offered citizens a new way to think about the world. Roosevelt himself made this point. The Good Neighbor Policy "has the virtue of explaining itself," he told a conference of Anglican and Episcopal clergy.

In San Antonio, Texas, a Good Neighbor bible class, attended by a mix of Anglos and Mexican Americans, was organized with the motto "All Men Are Welcome and There Are No Strangers Among Us." The State Department cited the Good Neighbor Policy to promote cultural exchange programs that directly challenged white supremacy, inviting, for instance, indigenous and Afro Latino American artists and writers, such as the Cuban poet Nicolás Guillén, to spend extended periods of time in the United States. "So the American Negro, under the pleasant Good Neighbor policies," Langston Hughes wrote, "wishes to welcome to our United States all representatives of Latin American cultures whatever their racial strains or complexions may be." Like Langston Hughes, reactionaries recognized the power of the phrase—and they didn't like it: how it encapsulated a tolerant, antiracist, left-liberal humanism. The right-wing radio priest Charles Coughlin devoted many broadcast hours railing against it and FDR's tolerance of economic nationalism in Latin America, especially in Mexico. "Never in the heart of Africa could be found the savagery of Mexico's present government," went one typical complaint, and Washington does nothing "lest the doctrine of neighborliness suffer a setback."[17]

As to Roosevelt, he appreciated the term so much he "wanted the name Good Neighbor League copyrighted," to "keep anyone else from grabbing it." He referenced the Good Neighbor constantly, as a way of conflating nations with families, and continents with neighborhoods, while at the same time conveying a code of conduct that needed no elaboration. "Our closest neighbors are good neighbors," he said in Chautauqua, New York, on the eve of his reelection. But he hinted at coming troubles: "And if there are remoter nations that wish us not good but ill, they know that we are strong; they know that we can and will defend ourselves and defend our neighborhood."[18]

On election day, over twenty-seven million citizens cast their ballot for Roosevelt, who won 523 electoral votes to Landon's 8. FDR floated to a landslide reelection—and held off a protofascist backlash—on the unlikely policy combination of nonintervention, labor rights, social security, good-neighbor humanism, and free trade. And an equally unlikely alliance of foreign-market-oriented corporations and an expanded voting coalition of urban white workers, farmers, poor Southerners, European immigrants, Catholics, Jews, and African Americans. He had won more votes than any other candidate that had ever stood for election in history—not just in the United States but anywhere. That he won them on a program of socialized democracy makes the achievement that much more remarkable.[19]

Like Woodrow Wilson, the last Democratic president before him, FDR campaigned for reelection on domestic reform, only to have the rest of the world get in the way. Unlike Wilson, though, Roosevelt—as he slowly realized that a response to global fascism would be required—didn't, as did

Wilson, unleash domestic repression on his social base, on reformers, social-ists, anarchists, pacifists, and labor activists. On the contrary, his NLRA defended worker militancy, binding organized labor to the Democratic Party.[20]

In 1936, it wasn't yet clear what it meant to prepare for war, or what the country's foreign policy should be—should it be neutrality behind a garri-soned hemisphere or a more proactive defense of liberal Europe. Roosevelt, for much longer than is generally assumed, oscillated between two poles: between wanting to secure a "happy valley" in the Americas made up of good neighbors free from the Old World's trouble, and realizing that no such isolation was possible.

It was Latin America, including the fear of losing Latin America, that pushed him toward internationalism.

38.

The Faith of the Americas

nd what did Roosevelt do after his unprecedented 1936 victory? He went to Latin America.

The confetti and ticker tape had barely been swept from city streets when Roosevelt set sail from Charleston on November 18 on the USS *Indianapolis* bound for Buenos Aires, to preside over an inter-American peace conference.

Over the next five years, from 1936 until the attacks on Pearl Harbor and the Philippines in December 1941, Latin America would help the United States reconcile its isolationist and internationalist tendencies. During this half decade of disequilibrium, no region was more important to the United States. The Standing Liaison Committee, established in 1938 to coordinate the opinion of the departments of State, War, and Navy, held over a hundred meetings in its first two years, and all but six gave top priority not to Europe or Asia but to waging a defensive war in Latin America.[1]

Ever closer political and economic relations made possible by the Good Neighbor Policy broke down the United States' sense of separateness. Internationalists looked to the Americas as a place to gather force for a push outward, to save Europe and extend a greater sphere of hegemony. Isolationists were opposed to a larger involvement in the world, but they agreed that Latin America had to be bound together with Washington in a defensive alliance. But the premise that the Americas had to be defended, and the defense had to be led by the United States, couldn't help but advance the cause of the internationalists.

To commit to defend the entire Western Hemisphere, "half a world," as one New Dealer put it, required a willingness to act in all the world, against potential Japanese expansion into Latin America from the Pacific and German forays from the Atlantic.

Two People Who Invented the New Deal

The United States delegation was bigger than the one that went to Montevideo, reflecting FDR's expanding coalition. Hull was there, as were two key members of Roosevelt's inner circle, Adolf Berle and Sumner Welles. Welles was a family friend of FDR, of old Dutch lineage and with long experience in hemispheric diplomacy. He started his foreign service career under Calvin Coolidge and then worked Woodrow Wilson's Latin American Desk at State. In the years to come, he'd play a large, inside role in Roosevelt's foreign policy, helping to draft some of the president's loftier statements. Both Berle and Welles knew that hemispheric defense entailed more than military strategy. The United States had to help build, or at least not stand in the way of Latin Americans building, something worth defending. Welles, Berle, and others imagined the New Deal being not just a United States initiative but a hemispheric-wide project of transformation: a continental New Deal. They won the election, and now they were ready to export what one Brazilian official called their "peaceful social revolution." On the way down, the president got in some deep-sea fishing.

Invitations to serve on diplomatic delegations were handed out as rewards to FDR supporters. Yet not one corporate contributor accompanied the president. Instead, he sailed with a delightfully diverse cast of characters. Alexander Whitney, of the Brotherhood of Railroad Trainmen, had helped organize labor support for Roosevelt. Philadelphia lawyer and Church layman Michael Francis Doyle had earlier defended Roger Casement, hung by London in 1916 on the charge of smuggling German weapons to Irish revolutionaries. Now he advised FDR on Catholic opinion of the Spanish Civil War.

Elise Musser was a state senator in Utah who spent her younger years in a borderland Mexican Mormon polygamous compound. Refusing to marry, Musser fled to Salt Lake City, where she got involved in social work and politics. "Ninety-nine men and Mrs. Musser," she joked about the composition of the delegation. The local press called her *La Mormona*. The delegation's legal adviser was Emilio del Toro Cuebas, who was born a Spanish subject in 1878 in Puerto Rico and received his law degree from the University of Havana in 1897, a year before the United States invaded the island.[2]

The *Indianapolis* called at Rio de Janeiro, where Roosevelt was greeted by three thousand schoolchildren singing "The Star-Spangled Banner." Brazil's president Getúlio Vargas and FDR rode to the city center on roads covered with rose petals. As the motorcade passed a protest directed at the Brazilian president, Vargas said to Roosevelt, "They call me a dictator." FDR whispered back, "Me too."

Vargas was indeed a dictator. He came to power in 1930 in a revolution and then built a social base, limiting the power of the feudal oligarchy by passing a series of reforms, including labor rights, workers' pensions, insurance—a program many compared to the New Deal.

The Brazilian president straddled left and right, with United States and British intelligence reports concerned that he was too lenient during a wave of strikes that hit industrial centers in 1934 and 1935, too tolerant (at least occasionally) of free speech, and too curious about Mussolini's Italy. Italians funded the green-shirted *Ação Integralista Brasileira*, a Fascist party, while the Germans financed Nazi activity among German nationalists and their Brazilian allies. Brazil's large Jewish population suffered no significant attacks, though conservative Catholics used the fascist opening to give voice to anti-Semitism. As for the radical left, the Soviet Union's Comintern supported a 1935 military revolt that Vargas ruthlessly suppressed. With his crackdowns and flirtations with both Washington and Rome, Vargas was difficult to figure out. One banker described him as "without a doubt the coldest, most rational, and cynical" statesman alive.[3]

But FDR's State Department decided that nothing good would result from pressuring Brazil. The country's size, its strategic location jutting into the Atlantic, and store of important minerals forced Washington to give Vargas room. The hope was that FDR's electoral landslide, his far-reaching social agenda, and Cordell Hull's pledge of nonintervention would cut the legs out from under right-wing Brazilian nationalists who looked to Germany or Italy for leadership. Later, when Vargas seized more power, dissolving congress and extending his time in office, the United States press—certain that Vargas was preparing for an alliance with Portugal's quasi-fascist António de Oliveira Salazar, along with Germany and Italy—went into high dudgeon.

Hitler did have eyes on Brazil, yet the State Department remained calm. Welles responded with a public address delivered at George Washington University titled "On the Need for a Spirit of Tolerance in Inter-American Relations." He chided reporters for writing on things they knew little about. Vargas's move, Welles said, was part of a struggle to overcome "the inheritance from their colonial days," which placed a great deal of the country's wealth in the hands of a "very small percentage of the people." Many New Dealers understood that not just Pan-Americanism, but a social-democratic Pan-Americanism, was required to beat fascism. Nations needed room to fight their internal wars, their class struggles, without worrying about intervention. Formalistic democracy meant nothing if it didn't also entail what Welles called a "more equitable distribution" of wealth and a "higher standard of living." Welles's remarks made a deep impression among the diplomatic corps of Latin American nations.[4]

Hull, for his part, summoned select editors and journalists to his office for an "off-the-record" dressing down for depicting Vargas as a New World Mussolini. Give Brazil time, Hull said. And Vargas did, after his putsch, greatly expand his earlier social and labor reforms.[5]

In Rio, Roosevelt acted as if Brazil were already a fulsome democracy. "It was two people who invented the New Deal," FDR toasted Vargas, "the President of Brazil and the President of the United States."[6]

A More Abundant Life

Onward to Buenos Aires. More cheering crowds at the dock, more roses on the road to the city center. The Chaco War was winding down, and the United States had removed itself from the Caribbean, including from Haiti. Even the skeptical Argentine press hailed the president as the "people's shepherd." A women's peace rally preceded the inauguration of the conference, delivering to Mrs. Musser a petition with more than a million signatures from twenty-one American republics, demanding the abolition of war in "our Western Hemisphere."[7]

The conference's aim was to promote "peace." But Roosevelt was there to begin integrating the hemisphere for defense. The region's statesmen dealt with many issues, but the overarching question that confronted them was how to define regional solidarity in the shadow of the looming European and Asian conflict. Most of the conference's envoys believed that fascism, broadly, was an evil that had to be stopped—especially the German version, which grew more extreme and perverse in its hatreds by the day. Yet not all agreed that Mussolini in Italy, who didn't share Hitler's racial obsessions and wasn't yet closely allied with Germany, was part of this evil. Moreover, nations like Argentina, Chile, and Uruguay had important economic ties with Berlin. Mexico received export tariffs from the oil that Huasteca, Standard, and other companies sold to Germany and Italy. Despite the goodwill that persisted after Hull's visit three years earlier, building consensus was difficult.

Argentina's president, in his welcoming remarks, made clear he didn't know how to move forward: "The general disorientation of the world," he said, makes thing difficult.

Roosevelt, in contrast, gave a rousing, confident opening speech titled "The Faith of the Americas." He celebrated the New World, laying out a grand vision of a consultative, social-democratic hemisphere, where peace reigns because justice has been achieved: "Through democratic processes we can strive to achieve for the Americas the highest possible standard of living conditions for all our people." The formula the president offered was simple: social welfare, freedom of thought, free commerce, mutual defense. "We offer hope for peace and a more abundant life to the peoples of the whole world."[8]

Roosevelt, scheduled to return to the United States, left Hull to wrap up negotiations. Before departing Buenos Aires, however, Roosevelt wheeled unannounced into a meeting of Bolivian and Paraguayan negotiators who were stubbornly haggling over the final terms of a Chaco peace. The president, as the story was told in diplomatic circles, scolded them for wasting time, reminding them that the Nazis would eagerly exploit tensions between the two countries if a deal wasn't immediately reached. A European conflict was inevitable, FDR said, and the Western Hemisphere might very well be drawn in. Whether Roosevelt's intervention helped or not, La Paz and Asunción soon came to a final settlement and a peace treaty was signed.

For the remainder of the conference, the sticking point among delegates was how to define mutual defense. Saavedra stood against building what FDR called a "mighty fortress America," which to the Argentine minister sounded like yet another effort to weaken Argentina's strong trade relations with Europe. Argentina didn't want to go on lockdown. "It would be unwise for us to deepen still more the Atlantic Ocean which separates us from Europe," Uruguay's representative said.[9]

Hull only managed to reach an agreement that nations would quickly "consult" with one another if the hemisphere was attacked. It was weak tea, a promise to talk. To get even this, Hull had to sign yet another pledge renouncing intervention: "directly or indirectly, and for whatever reason, in the internal or external affairs" of any other American nation. Such demands to reaffirm nonintervention weren't pointless rituals. Compared to previous envoys from the United States, who had insisted that intervention was a sacred right, Hull's willingness to sign such repeated pledges without qualification was welcome. The United States even agreed at Buenos Aires to create a commission of legal experts who would "harmonize" American International Law with existing international law as the Great Powers understood it.[10]

The conference boasted some other modest successes. Envoys held sessions on education, communication, transportation, environmental protection, asylum, extradition, postal codes, technological transfers especially related to agriculture, and cultural exchange, laying out the contours of what hemispheric integration would look like. They pledged to expand the Boy Scouts and Girl Scouts and hold Jamborees in "various countries of America."[11]

Delegates also unanimously voted in favor of "moral disarmament." New media technology—radios, films, and newsreels—strained accepted notions of free speech. They could be easily manipulated to promote hate, as they had when radio broadcasts stirred Bolivians to take the Chaco, and as they were doing in Germany, Italy, and now Spain. In the United States, the xenophobic Father Coughlin continued to rouse his many radio listeners. Hearst was then acquiring radio stations to broadcast more persuasive forms of the same propaganda he had been printing for years. The right of "free speech" was fundamental, liberal jurists at the Buenos Aires peace conference affirmed, but they passed a resolution calling for the banning of films that promote "war, disturb good relations between peoples, or incite hatred against foreigners." No mechanisms, though, were put into place to enforce such a prohibition. Conference delegates also pledged to teach less racist, less elitist national histories, to eliminate textbooks engaged in racial or national stereotyping, to downplay the teaching of war and conquest and to write with respect the history of America's original inhabitants.

Brazil worked with Doris Stevens of the National Woman's Party to pass a strongly worded resolution affirming the equality of rights of women. On this, Stevens received no help from Hull, who said that pushing for equal rights for Latin American women would be a form of "intervention." Earlier, on the cruise to Buenos Aires, Adolf Berle went so far as to call the socialist Stevens a "fascist" for pushing equal rights, since such a demand risked, Berle said, alienating potential conservative allies.

The conference's most consequential achievement was to bolster Roosevelt's internationalism. After one full presidential term focused on domestic issues, this was FDR's debut on the world stage, and he was thrilled by his reception. The conference built up his confidence; he'd soon promote Welles to undersecretary of state and ask him to come up with a plan to reimagine world governance. Thus the first whispers of what would become the United Nations.[12]

The Battle for Our Own Continent

Prior to the conference, Mexico's new president Lázaro Cárdenas asked Washington not to let the topic of Spain's civil war, which had broken out in July, "come up for ventilation" at Buenos Aires. Over the next three years, Spanish republicans would have no greater defender in the Western Hemisphere than Cárdenas, but both he and FDR agreed that cultivating American unity took priority, and taking sides in Spain would only sow division.

According to Sumner Welles, the "division of feeling on the continent" over the Spanish Civil War was "extremely bitter and far-reaching." To traditional conservatives, Franco in Spain and Salazar in Portugal seemed like recognizable conservative patriarchs, men committed to defend Iberian Catholic values. Leftists, though, recognized the threat, the growing incidents of paramilitary violence directed at labor activists, the rising voices of conservative ideologues, who understood they were building a global movement. Reformers feared that a Franco victory would give Hitler an entryway into Spanish America. Hermann Göring himself said that a nationalist Spain was key to German domination of the Americas, that if Spain and Latin America could "reunite," then the whole of the Western world would eventually belong to Berlin.[13]

Over the next few years, as Franco advanced toward victory and the fascist nature of his movement became clear, the Spanish conflict sharpened what was at stake in Latin America: the same cleavages that Franco leveraged for his revolt existed in the Americas, but on a continental scale. "Spain has been the first big trench in the battle for our own continent," wrote Carleton Beals.[14]

There was no doubt that Germany, and to a lesser degree Italy and Japan, were competing with the United States for influence in Latin America. Berlin engaged in active economic diplomacy, including offers to finance the construction of steel factories and better terms of trade and credit. Berlin ran a network of spies gathering military and economic intelligence. It took about ninety hours to get from Berlin to Rio on the Luftschiffbau Zeppelin *Hindenburg*, which was making regularly scheduled flights, including one in late November 1936 that carried two agents who went on to Buenos Aires to keep tabs on Roosevelt's peace conference.

The Nazis' overseas outreach operation, the Auslands-Organisation, was active in southern South America, especially Argentina and Brazil—countries with large German populations. Nazi parties were recruiting in Chile—counting twenty thousand members by some estimates—Argentina, and Brazil, and nearly all countries had right-wing shock troops on the march. German economic power was growing, and fascists were making inroads in the region's military and police. Peru's government appointed an Italian general to head the Lima Police Department: General Enriques Cammarota, who had worked with the Opera Vigilanza Repressione Anti-fascismo, Italy's counterpart to the German Gestapo. Cammarota, who had been active in Italy's occupation of Ethiopia, said that his job was to "civilize" the natives of Peru as he had "civilized the Ethiopians." German submarines docked at will at the Peruvian port of Malabrigo.[15]

Colonies of Germans living in Argentina, Uruguay, Paraguay, Chile, and Brazil considered Germany their true government. Their schools taught German racial theory and were filled with children who wore swastika armbands. Berlin, according to the left-wing popular front group, the Committee for Pan-American Democracy, had plans to annex what it called *Antarctica Germanica*, which included the white majority government of South Africa and the Southern Cone governments of Latin America. The phrase *Unser Land Ist ein Stück von Deutschland!* (Our Land Is a Part of Germany!) began appearing on signs in shop windows and graffitied on factory walls in Uruguay and Argentina. In Brazil, German émigrés in the nineteenth century, including writer Thomas Mann's father-in-law, owned slave plantations, and some of their descendants went on to became prominent fascists. One wealthy family of German and Brazilian industrialists owned a backland plantation, adorned with swastikas and photos of Hitler, where they staged pro-Nazi rallies. The land was worked by kidnapped Afro-Brazilian children who were treated as slaves, addressed not by their name but an assigned number, and subject to brutal beatings.[16]

After Hitler's absorption of Austria and invasion of Czechoslovakia in March 1938, Secretary of Commerce Harry Hopkins became convinced that Germany was preparing to invade and annex some part of Latin America. He warned Roosevelt that Berlin had built up a network of technicians working with Latin American airlines, ready for a quick conversion of airfields for military use once German troops landed. Hopkins urged the president to start shoring up the New World's perimeter. Nelson Rockefeller thought that if Washington didn't organize the hemisphere, then "a large portion of Latin America" would go "against us instead of with us."[17]

Many policy and opinion makers in the United States feared that part or all of Latin America would fall to something like the Spanish Falange. Fascists fight "a civil war in each nation of this hemisphere," wrote Nicholas Spykman, a Yale political scientist and prominent foreign policy theorist. If successful, "the New World" will be "conquered from within."[18]

But the antifascist instinct was strong in Latin America. Even in a country like Argentina, with its many Nazis, the feminist Celia de la Serna—Ernesto "Che" Guevara's mother—was already, before FDR's arrival in Buenos Aires, an antifascist activist, helping to settle Spanish republican exiles fleeing Franco's advance. Later, after Germany occupied Paris, de la Serna would organize an extremely active "Free France" movement. Buenos Aires, according to the journalists Diane Vignemont and Phineas Rueckert, "became the beating heart of the French resistance-in-exile," where leaders of the resistance, in contact with Charles de Gaulle, raised funds, published newspapers, and sent volunteers to fight in Europe. "No other part of the world," de Gaulle said in a radio speech, "has shown suffering and fighting France a more ardent sympathy than Latin America. . . . Your souls and ours drink from the same sources of inspiration."

De Gaulle here was stressing the *latine* in *l'Amérique latine*. Both France and Latin America, he said, embody two "living traditions," Catholic humanism and revolutionary equality. "Both traditions are very old," but also, in their ability to defeat fascism, "very young."[19]

Latin America wasn't conquered, either from within or from without. Berlin didn't establish a German Antarctic, nor did it try. Between 1936 and 1941, the United States did begin to build up an extensive defensive perimeter. Yet countering fascism in Latin America had little to do with military strategy. The real work of antifascism took place in the sphere of social struggle for a more just existence, and in the realm of hope, creating trust that the defeat of fascism in all its variations would bring a better world. The key to stymieing fascism's appeal was to fill the forms of democratic proceduralism with content, with what Roosevelt in his Buenos Aires speech called "social justice." The promise of the New Deal couldn't remain confined within the borders of the United States. It had to be continental in scope.

In no place was the need to make it so more critical than Mexico.

Laboratory of the World

Roosevelt's support of the Mexican Revolution complemented Hull's acceptance of the doctrine of nonintervention. A political rival had executed Carranza in 1920, leaving the consolidation of the revolution to his successors, especially to Lázaro Cárdenas. Elected in July 1934 in the depths of the Great Depression, Cárdenas after his December inauguration activated the 1917 constitution. Over his six-year term, he expropriated fifty million acres of land, more than twice the amount taken by his predecessors, and seized British, Dutch, and United States petroleum holdings.

Mexico was a poor, credit-squeezed, war-battered country, with little cash on hand to finance needed social reforms. It paid some compensation to the owners of expropriated property but left most mired in endless negotiations. Roosevelt received a flood of complaints and calls for intervention. The State Department under FDR was a big tent when it came to Mexico. Washington mostly refused to escalate conflicts over property. Sumner Welles managed to keep Congress from taking up Mexican policy, and thus kept the property disputes largely out of the press. More important, FDR had the Treasury Department begin to buy silver. Mine owners in Nevada, Arizona, and Colorado, mostly United States citizens, and many with a property claim against Mexico, were happy to receive a flow of cash from the federal government. As was Mexico—the money helped stabilize its peso and allowed Cárdenas to make at least some payouts to claimants.[1]

Several factors explain such uncharacteristic restraint. Looming wars in Europe and the Pacific convinced Washington that it needed resource-rich Mexico as an ally. New Dealers were too busy trying to reorganize capitalism at home to devote much attention to defending capitalists abroad. Many of them, both in and out of the administration, liked Cárdenas's land reform. They thought that the breakup of large estates and the creation of a population of citizen-farmers might create a bigger market for U.S. exports. It could also, some hoped, slow immigration, which might dilute border xenophobia. Frances Perkins, FDR's secretary of labor, was singled out by anti–New Dealers for being soft on migrants and slow to deport them. "These Communists now have the formal official protection of the Labor Department," complained the National Small Business Men's Association, referring to a group of Mexican migrant labor organizers.

The names of those with love for Mexico are known in New Deal lore: Roosevelt's vice president, Henry Wallace; Rex Tugwell in the Department of Agriculture; Henry Morgenthau and Harry Dexter White at Treasury; Sumner Welles and Laurence Duggan at State; along with scholars and journalists, such as Ernest Gruening, Princeton's Eyler Simpson, Berkeley's Herbert Bolton, Maurice Halperin, and Frank Tannenbaum. Tugwell wished that FDR would break up Southern plantations the way Cárdenas was breaking up Mexico's haciendas.[2]

Josephus the First

By far, the most unlikely conciliator of Mexico and the United States was the North Carolinian Josephus Daniels, as unlikely as Cordell Hull was as a facilitator of nonintervention.

Daniels was seventy-one years old when Roosevelt named him ambassador to Mexico in 1933, older than Hull by nine years. Born at the start of the Civil War to a Wilmington Confederate shipbuilder with Northern sympathies, Josephus had more vivid, resentful memories of federal occupation under Reconstruction than the younger Hull. Hull was a genteel, soft Saxonist. The up-and-coming young Daniels was a hardened white supremacist, worrying that marriages between Blacks and whites would "Mexicanize the South." After purchasing a controlling share in the Raleigh *News & Observer*, Daniels used the influential paper to run boldface hate. His editorials both drove a wedge in the agrarian populist movement between poor Black and white farmers and divided Black and white Republican politicians. In the lurid pages of Daniels's *N&O*, with its tales of rape and mayhem, the "horrors of Negro domination" were boundless. In 1898, Daniels opposed the war on Spain. He feared the annexation of mongrel colonies. Yet that year he drummed up a different kind of war, against Wilmington's Black local government. He used his newspaper to whip white readers into a murderous frenzy. They subsequently massacred hundreds of Wilmington's Black residents and overthrew its mostly Black municipal council.

Appointed by Wilson as secretary of the navy in 1913, Daniels segregated what had been the most integrated branch of the armed forces, as part of Wilson's wider campaign to impose Jim Crow on the federal bureaucracy. He also presided over the invasion of Veracruz and the occupation of Haiti. Wilson's cabinet members referred to him as "Josephus the First, King of Haiti," which Daniels didn't find funny. As Marines destroyed crops and killed livestock, many Haitians experienced starvation. Daniels organized the distribution of food but made sure it was only a temporary program. He didn't want to repeat what he thought was the mistake made during post–Civil War Reconstruction, when the Freedmen's Bureau offered relief. It was "very dangerous," Daniels wrote to Wilson, "to begin to supply provisions because many Haitians are like negroes in the South after the war and would quit work entirely, deserting plantations if our Government undertakes to feed them."[3]

When FDR appointed Daniels ambassador to Mexico, the memory of Woodrow Wilson's occupation of Veracruz was still vivid. As recently as 1928, Mexico had refused to accept the diplomatic credentials of a mere attaché who had served in the incursion. Daniels was behind only Wilson himself in responsibility for landing Marines in Tampico. "The memory of that iniquitous outrage against our sovereignty," wrote a Mexico City daily upon learning of Daniels's appointment, "will cause the new representative to encounter a frigid atmosphere here." Daniels arrived in Mexico City just in time to pick up a newspaper and read a solemn roll call of all the Mexicans who had died during the occupation.

From Joel Poinsett to Henry Lane Wilson, Washington's ambassadors made and broke regimes. Daniels, the demagogue of Wilmington, occupier of Veracruz, and ravisher of Haiti, arrived in Mexico just before the election of Cárdenas, the most militant of Mexico's revolutionary presidents, the man who would finally match deed to word and apply the full force of the revolutionary constitution's Article 27.

Many were quick to point out to FDR that Daniels was hardly an appropriate envoy for the New Deal in Mexico.

World Gone Mad

But Mexico changed Daniels. Maybe witnessing the suffering caused by Mexico's revolutionary wars made him more humane. Or maybe being outside the United States, in a place where racism was expressed differently than it was in North Carolina, directed not at the descendants of chattel slaves but at indigenous peasants, animated his agrarian populism.

Whatever the case, Daniels in Mexico insisted on the need for radical action to destroy "feudalism," which, like Roosevelt, he said was the seedbed of fascism. Roosevelt was too "damn conservative," Daniels complained in jest, his New Deal pale in comparison to Mexico's reforms. Daniels had come to believe that the Good Neighbor Policy, as represented by the pledge of nonintervention, was the key to saving the world. "Your Good Neighbor Policy, which I have tried to incarnate," he wrote FDR, created a bastion of stability and peace in a "world gone mad."

Daniels wasn't an ambassador by trade, and he didn't talk like one. He let it be known that he believed in the sovereign equality of nations and thought the revolution's reforms were not just necessary but wondrous. He also made it clear that his job as a New Deal diplomat was not to defend the status quo but to help in any way he could Mexico's social transformation.

Daniels joked that the United States might "care to copy Mexico's radical Constitution." Mexico, he said, "is a laboratory for new economic and legislative ideas, most of which I regard as very good." Daniels even began to advocate for the distribution of Southern plantations in the United States. He passed over the fact that his earlier vigilante racism was key in upholding planter power.[4]

Daniels liked Mexico's new president, Lázaro Cárdenas, immediately, and the Methodist ambassador supported his efforts to weaken the institutional Catholic Church. Daniels brushed off complaints from U.S. Catholics that the Church was being persecuted. He answered them simply: "The Republic of Mexico belongs to the people of Mexico." Daniels backed Cárdenas's regulation of the national electric system, which had largely been in the hands of British and U.S. corporations, and even sabotaged efforts by Hull at State to set up a commission to try to collect past-due debt, not only from Mexico but from other Latin American countries. "Why should our Government undertake this work and press collections due to those who pressed loans upon South American governments and got big rake-offs?" In this, he was aligned with Mexico's minister of finance José Manuel Puig, who had pushed for a debt moratorium in Montevideo.[5]

Hull asked Daniels to pressure Cárdenas to reconsider a law that enshrined the Calvo Doctrine, which required foreign nationals to submit to Mexican law and prohibited them from asking for the intercession of foreign governments in disputes. Washington didn't accept the legitimacy of that doctrine. As recently as 1927, President Calvin Coolidge had circulated a memo to U.S. ambassadors to Latin America repudiating Calvo: "The person and property of a citizen are a part of the general domain of the nation even when abroad." Coolidge's was an expansive definition of sovereignty, one in which the jurisdiction of the United States didn't stop at its borders but was carried forward to the ends of the earth by its investors.[6]

Daniels backed Cárdenas. He wrote the State Department to say that the law was sound.

Hull pressed the point. Daniels took the matter to Roosevelt, who issued, much to Hull's horror, a full-throated endorsement of the Calvo Doctrine. Hull immediately sent FDR a note reminding him that the laws of a foreign country are by no means uniform in their justness. It would be, Hull said, "extremely dangerous to announce that American property owners in other countries, when their property is expropriated, may expect no better treatment than the nationals of the country taking the property."[7] FDR said no more about the dispute, implicitly backing Daniels.

Cárdenas stepped up his land reform, and Daniels kept up his encouragement. By 1935, Daniels was calling Mexico "the laboratory of the world," a place where people were "not afraid to try new things, even with their small resources." He continued: "Some of the things they are trying, of course, will not work out (that is true also in our own country) but Mexico is not afraid to try."[8]

Hope of a Drifting World

In December 1936, Cárdenas began to distribute land in Sonora's Yaqui Valley. In a way, Article 27 addressed what *uti possidetis* had evaded: the fact that Native Americans were original possessors of the land—and while the stabilizing of national borders may have spared their hurried extermination (the Chaco War notwithstanding, no land grab tied to the expansion of national borders took place in Latin America), it did nothing to secure, much less restore, their farmland. Cárdenas however, under Article 27, distributed nearly forty-five million acres of land to peasants, much of it to indigenous communities, reconstituting peasant commons throughout the entire nation. One of the most spectacular examples of this was in the Yaqui Valley, with its wide and fast river flowing from the Sierra Madre to the Pacific, the historic heartland of one branch of the Yaqui people.

Before the revolution, under Díaz, the Yaqui had been driven off their land by military force, deported to work practically as slaves on Oaxacan sugar and Yucatán henequen plantations. Mexican and United States farmers and ranchers then swooped in, cutting down a stunningly beautiful cacti forest and claiming the land as their own to plant wheat and run cattle. The valley was fecund, its main trunk river and many streams rushing down into the Gulf of California providing easy irrigation to gently sloping land covered in rich soil.

By the end of Cárdenas's term, about 1,198,461 acres had been reclaimed for a reconstituted Yaqui homeland, with its water rights recognized. Thousands of Yaquis returned home. It wasn't what they once had, and their existence now was tied to the fortunes of a bureaucratic state. But the equivalent of such a project in the United States would have been FDR returning sizable portions of the western Carolinas and Georgia to the Cherokees, or the land that Jackson took from the Creeks.

Cárdenas promised to compensate the former owners for their lost land, though he lacked the revenue to do so anytime soon. And anyway, U.S. planters in the Yaqui Valley, he said, had made so much money out of their Mexico holdings that they could easily "have reimbursed themselves." Cárdenas here was putting forward an idea that would later be developed more fully by economic nationalists: that "excess profits" made in the past should be deducted from whatever compensation was due for expropriated property. Mexico, one conservative voice in the State Department said, wanted an "almost unlimited extension of the right of expropriation." Daniels didn't mind.[9]

Back in Washington, Daniels's sometimes ally Sumner Welles, Hull's undersecretary of state, had a direct line to the president. He was able to keep State Department lawyers who were hostile to land reform at bay. In a conversation with his staff, Welles said that the "department was well aware that some American citizens who had gone to Mexico during a previous era and had acquired land for practically nothing, and were now faced with expropriation, were claiming fantastic sums for compensation. The Department had no intention of supporting such claims." Welles wasn't as over the moon for Cárdenas as was Daniels. Like Hull, he believed that international law required Mexico to at least say what steps it would take to compensate for land that was obtained legally.[10]

Negotiations over the Yaqui Valley expropriations went on for years and strained relations between Mexico City and Washington. Forced to choose between compensating expropriated planters and funding social programs, like a credit bank for peasant farmers, Cárdenas let the planters wait. And Roosevelt let him let the planters wait.

Hull grew increasingly frustrated with both Cárdenas and Daniels. The ambassador did due diligence in representing the interests of United States property owners. But nothing more. He refused to engage in threats. By the middle of 1938, Hull had had enough. He issued a belligerent public "note" denouncing Mexico's "astonishing theory" that international law does not make "obligatory the payment of immediate compensation." If Mexico's position was emulated by other countries, he wrote, it would "imperil the very foundations of modern civilization. Human progress would be fatally set back." Daniels responded by posting a letter to Roosevelt saying he was "very glad" that FDR "declined to comment on Cordell's latest note." It was "unduly severe," Daniels said. Referring to Theodore Roosevelt's permission to European nations to "spank" Venezuela, Daniels said that "spanking a nation that is desperately poor in public on account of debts when there is not even a slap on the wrist for great countries that ignore obligations is a severe strain on the Good Neighbor Policy."[11]

Daniels went on, worried about the effect Hull's note would have on "a world on the verge of war."[12]

"Today the Mexican masses as a whole are seeing daylight as never before," Daniels wrote FDR. If the United States could continue to show "devotion" to the principle of nonintervention, "even when it hurts," it would go a long way to "preserve on this hemisphere the hope of a drifting world."[13]

Cárdenas responded angrily to Hull's note, pointing out in a speech to the Mexican congress that there are different forms of "expropriation without compensation," a barb directed at Roosevelt's depreciation of the dollar, which had shrunk the U.S. market for Mexican exports. The heat of the conflict, along with the desperate need to find ways to fund social programs, led leaders like Cárdenas to think more expansively about what "sovereign equality" meant. International debt, denominated in the currency of the powerful, rendered that concept a legal fiction. *Compensation* was a relative term: how much money did United States planters, ranchers, and oilmen make, exactly, with land that was taken from Indians and given to them by a corrupt dictator? Maybe they were owed nothing, Cárdenas suggested. Hull responded with more angry words.

By this point, Daniels was frantic. He wrote note after note to Roosevelt and made public speeches in Mexico that sounded like imperialist confessions, acts of contrition for the harm the United States had done to Mexico, which Daniels listed in detail. He also wrote a remarkable letter to Hull, asking the secretary of state what, exactly, was the alternative to compromise, before then listing the alternatives himself:

> To be sure, we could bring pressure to bear by refusal to buy silver. . . . We could encourage revolution by permitting the importation of arms by those who would wish to oust Cárdenas by force, with the consequent responsibility for the blood that would be shed; we could refuse to buy anything from Mexico, boycott its exports, and thereby reduce the necessities of life to the masses; we could denounce the country as dishonest and do much to strangle her; we could conquer it and put in a man as President who would be beholden to us; we could, after we had conquered it, make it a province or annex it and add Mexican States to the Union.

"We could do any or all of these things," Daniels told Hull. Some might work. Others would backfire. All would be unjust. Daniels's litany of things the United States might do was really nothing more than the summation of all the things the United States *had* done, at some point in the past (and would later, during, and after the Cold War, do again).[14]

Daniels's many letters to Roosevelt are stuffed with historical references, as if all the horrors of the past were lying at the ambassador's feet. "Dear Franklin," went one letter, which started by describing how during the Conquest a "young Indian, Cuauhtémoc, stood up against the invaders when old Moctezuma was taken captive." Daniels then launched into a four-century history before getting to the matter at hand: the agrarian property dispute. Other letters brought up the United States' war on Mexico, annexation of Texas, the creation of Panama, Theodore Roosevelt's Big Stick, and the valuable concessions handed out by Díaz to U.S. investors for pittances.

Many of Daniel's missives narrate the minutia of the revolution itself, all its triumphs and setbacks, failed revolts, and the backstory to alliances made and broken with all its many leaders, from Madero through Carranza to Cárdenas.

Daniels said he saw parallels between Woodrow Wilson's and Roosevelt's sympathy for the revolution and reminded FDR that a conspiracy of oilmen had once put into motion a plan to overthrow Wilson in a coup. "History always repeats itself," he warned.[15]

Daniels began to sound as if he had become possessed with the soul of a Latin American nationalist. His passion was directed toward the service of three things: proving the justness of Cárdenas's policies; demonstrating that New Deal reform in the United States would only be strengthened by accepting reform abroad, by building continental alliances with democrats, socialists, and nationalists; and saving Good Neighbor unity in the face of rising fascism. All Latin America, Daniels wrote, was watching what the United States did with Mexico as a test of the sincerity of its noninterventionist intentions.

Hull still tried to hold Mexico to account. He told Mexico's ambassador to Washington that he didn't like that Mexico was distributing land as *ejidos*—that is, as collectives, which the secretary of state thought was "getting close onto Marxism or the Communistic basis."[16]

This back-and-forth went on for some time. More harsh notes were exchanged. Daniels continued to plead with FDR to shut Hull up. When the United States announced that it would stop buying Mexico's silver, the Cárdenas government took it as warning that more economic sanctions were to come. Daniels interceded and convinced FDR to issue a statement that there was a misunderstanding. Treasury would continue the purchases.[17]

Hungry as Wolves

The advance of Franco's nationalists in Spain strengthened Cárdenas's position. As the conflict over the Yaqui Valley was heating up, some Latin American experts feared that Mexico was primed for a movement like Franco's uprising. We might, Roosevelt's adviser Bernard Baruch said, soon confront "a revolt in Mexico and at our very door a situation similar to that in Spain." Fascists, or as they called themselves in Mexico, *los sinarquistas*, were on the march, setting themselves against the "revolution, liberalism, socialism, class struggle and gringo materialism, offering instead the values of religion, family, private property, hierarchy and social solidarity." They had spread into the United States Southwest and California, with chapters in El Paso, Laredo, McAllen, Los Angeles, and San Francisco, demanding return of Mexican territory taken in 1848.[18]

The fascist threat was one reason Roosevelt continued to purchase Mexican silver, extend loans, and avoid taking Hull's side when it came to compensation. In the spring of 1938, General Saturnino Cedillo launched a German-backed fascist coup against Cárdenas, which failed. FDR then, in a series of radio addresses and speeches, used the failed fascist coup in Mexico to explain to the United States audience why a simple policy of "neutrality" wouldn't be sufficient to protect the United States. "Suppose," he said at one press conference, "certain foreign governments, European governments, were to do in Mexico what they did in Spain. Suppose they would organize a revolution, a fascist revolution in Mexico. Mexico is awfully close to us," and the possibility of fascists getting "control of the whole of Mexico is real."

A United States envoy in London told the British that FDR was seriously "alarmed" at the possibility that "anything like a pitched battle between capital and labour on the Spanish model were to break out in Mexico."

Rumors ran though the officer corps of both the United States and Mexico that Hitler planned to use Franco's expected victory in Spain as a pretext to "make Mexico the keystone of a reconstructed Spanish Empire." Many chapters of Mexico's *Unión Nacional Sinarquista*, were, according to the historian Friedrich Katz, little more than Nazi fronts, maintaining close ties with Berlin. Other militant conservatives, following the lead of the Catholic Church, were followers of Franco.[19]

Workers on both sides of the border already felt they were living under fascism, as ranching and mining companies used an array of shock troops— including local police, the KKK, Texas Rangers, Border Patrol agents, and hired gunmen—to enforce order. In response, Spanish-speaking activists founded the umbrella group El Congreso de Pueblos de Habla Española, or Spanish Speaking People's Congress. Its leaders included the Guatemalan migrant Luisa Moreno, who first arrived in the United States to organize African American and Afro Cuban cigar workers in Florida. The Spanish Speaking People's Congress was allied with the Congress of Industrial Organizations and embraced the social-democratic thrust of the New Deal. Its activists coordinated the work of labor and civil rights groups to fight back against the borderland bosses and the *sinarquistas*. Activists like Moreno understood themselves as part of a global fight against fascism, its front lines not in Berlin and Rome but in Texas, Arizona, and Southern California.

On March 18, 1938, as Spanish fascists launched a major offensive and Mussolini's planes began to bomb Barcelona, Cárdenas nationalized the petroleum industry. Frustrated with oil companies' refusal to negotiate in good faith with strikers, the Mexican government seized fourteen British, Dutch, and U.S. companies, including Standard Oil of New Jersey and Shell. Mexico took their rigs, trucks, storage tanks, maps, and geological surveys. A year earlier, Bolivia had confiscated Standard's extensive but largely untapped fields. Hull shrugged Bolivia off as leftover business from the Chaco War. Mexico's confiscation was different, more threatening to the property rules of the hemispheric order. The industry was valuable— through the 1920s, Mexico had become the world's second-largest producer of petroleum.[20]

The companies responded to Cárdenas from a strong position; without Washington's help, they stopped Mexico's expropriated oil from being sold in the United States and UK market. FDR was under pressure from all sides for not intervening, from Southern Democrats, from corporations (including those that backed him), and from old interventionists from the Taft administration. The White House's refusal to defend "American rights," said one former undersecretary of state, is appalling. "In all this miserable story of despoliation the American Government still continues to turn the other cheek."[21]

Corporations worried that Cárdenas's actions would have a domino effect. Venezuela, where Standard also had extensive holdings, might be next. Already, just two weeks after Cárdenas's action, Venezuela's Supreme Court ordered oil companies to pay back taxes. Tens of thousands of Cubans had gathered in Havana's main plaza to celebrate Mexico's nationalization, calling on their government to nationalize the island's railroads, plantations, and sugar mills. The children of Socialist Party members pledged to raise money to help Mexico cover compensation costs, while the island's leading poet declared that "Mexico at present is the Cuba of tomorrow."[22]

Cárdenas offered to negotiate. But the companies maintained a united front and refused to legitimate the takeover. Daniels was so disgusted by the intransigent attitude of Standard that he made plans to fly to New York and have a sit-down with John Rockefeller. He wanted to "put the matters that were disturbing friendly relations squarely up to him." Hull nixed that idea.[23]

The standoff lasted six months. Hull blinked first. Watching from afar as Franco laid siege to Madrid, and Neville Chamberlain prepared to give Hitler a pass to take Czechoslovakia, the secretary of state, on September 20, 1938, called in Mexico's ambassador and suggested that they put an end to the "hammer and tongs discussions" and settle the matter quietly. They did, eventually, with Daniels siding with Cárdenas against Hull in the ongoing negotiations. "We are strong. Mexico is weak," Daniels said, and Washington should act with generosity if it wants to maintain the goodwill needed in the years ahead.

The first company to break ranks was Sinclair, which entered negotiations with Mexico to decide on a settlement. Other companies, including Standard, followed.

Earlier, when they were in possession of their fields and rigs, foreigner oil companies—Standard, Shell, Gulf, Huasteca, Aguila, Sinclair, Texas Oil Company, or Texaco, and so on—had happily sold the oil it pumped from Mexico (and elsewhere in Latin America) to Germany and Italy and to Franco's forces in Spain. Mexican crude fueled Hitler's Stukas and Mussolini's Sparrowhawks as they dive-bombed Spanish republicans, destroying towns like Guernica and killing thousands. Mexican gas powered the tanks that rolled into Austria.

This, even as Mexico was at the fore in opposing Nazism and anti-Semitism. The note of protest Cárdenas's government sent to the League of Nation's general secretary for allowing Germany to take Austria is scathing.

Hitler once sent a special envoy to Mexico City to suggest strengthening ties
with Berlin. In response, Cárdenas's government helped convene one of the
largest protest marches in Mexican history, with a special emphasis on condemning Germany's persecution of Jews. All told, Cárdenas, even as he
struggled to find revenue for his domestic reform agenda, provided two million dollars in aid to Spanish republicans. When the Spanish republic did
fall, Mexico opened its doors to all refugees. Hundreds of exiles arrived in
Veracruz and were welcomed by crowds on the dock singing popular republican and socialist anthems, the "Himno de Riego," "The Marseillaise," and
"The International." The new arrivals sang the Mexican national anthem in
response.[24]

And yet, for an agonizing six months, with U.S. and British markets
closed and tourism taking a hit due to negative publicity, Mexico had no
choice but to continue to send oil to Germany and Italy. Once the boycott
broke, Cárdenas immediately stopped selling Mexican petroleum to all fascist governments.[25]

The pressure on Roosevelt to intervene in Mexico's agrarian and petroleum
disputes had been tremendous, especially since much of it came from inside
the New Deal coalition. Daniels, FDR's man on the spot, never wavered in
his support for Cárdenas, even when he was going through the motions and
delivering Hull's "notes." "Mexico is looking to do more for the forgotten
man than you have been able to do," Daniels once chided Roosevelt.[26]

"The older I grow the more radically progressive I get," Daniels said.[27]

Daniels's moral progress was good for the United States. Instead of saber-
rattling at the border, instead of threatening to send Marines into Veracruz,
which would have been a boon for Nazi propagandists, there were rose
petals on the streets of Brazil and Buenos Aires, bouquets of tropical flowers thrown from balconies, and a crop of babies named Franklin throughout Latin America. FDR's refusal to escalate the crisis allowed antifascist
activists, like Luisa Moreno, to continue their borderlands work against
the *sinarquistas*. A "love-feast," is how a British diplomat, complaining of

Washington's refusal to support the oil boycott, described the relationship between Roosevelt and Cárdenas.[28]

Aside from the geopolitical importance of good relations with Mexico, the message Roosevelt, Daniels, and all the others who fought to give Mexico time was clear: the global struggle against fascism was not just to eliminate the wicked.

The fight also needed to support the virtuous in creating a social-democratic order in which all could eat, work, and live in health with dignity. Or as Daniels described the holy trinity: work, bread, and a decent home.

40.

Battle for Latin America

With luck, the New World would be the rock on which fascism would crack. "We have created an American system, an American way of life," declared Sumner Welles in 1939, shortly after Germany and the Soviet Union signed a nonaggression pact and both countries invaded Poland. Welles's vision of the "American way of life" was generous, embracing all the Americas, not that narrower jingoism popular later during the Cold War that referred exclusively to the United States. "The twenty-one free nations of the New World," Welles said, as Europe fell into war, "may well constitute the last great hope of the civilization which we have inherited."[1]

Free didn't mean democratic. Of Welles's twenty-one nations, few in Latin America (perhaps Chile, Costa Rica, Colombia, and Mexico) could be said to uphold some sort of electoral democracy, defined by its minima: relatively free, competitive votes between a narrow range of candidates chosen by a small group of enfranchised citizens.

The coming fight against fascism, then, couldn't be framed as one between democracy and dictatorship. There were more dictatorships—governments that had come to power through force or means other than winning a majority of votes in an election—than democracies in the New World.

Diplomats from the United States and Latin America struck on the idea of distinguishing foreign "totalitarian ideologies" from American "republicanism." *Republicanism* was left undefined, yet once a nation was classified as a *republic*, it was a short step to calling it, if not a *democracy*, then "democratically oriented."

Roosevelt was happy to give up the burden of adjudicating what kinds of governments were best for American nations. He wasn't about to get trapped like Wilson got trapped, acting like a schoolmaster teaching Latin Americans how to vote. "The maintenance of constitutional government in other nations is *not* a sacred obligation devolving upon the United States," FDR said. Only when a nation threatens other nations does its behavior become "the joint concern of a whole continent in which we are all neighbors."[2]

Democracy was aspirational. And in Latin America the aspiration was a social definition of democracy: agrarian reform, labor rights, and welfare; or as Daniels put it, work, bread, and a decent home. Suffrage was greatly restricted nearly everywhere, and crisis remained a constant in political life. Latin America swung between extremes in the years after the Buenos Aires peace conference. It was billowed by the hope referred to by Welles, for dignity, solidarity, and equality. And it was buffeted by hope's opposite, by brutalists who held that the "nobodies, the no ones," as the Uruguayan writer Eduardo Galeano described the region's wretched, were not worth the cost of the bullets that killed them.

As Latin America oscillated between democracy and barbarism, the influence of the Mexican Revolution, especially its land reform, helped tip the region toward the first. For instance, land ownership in Chile had been organized since independence around a very Anglo, "absolutist" conception of private property. That ended in 1925, when Article 10 of a new constitution proclaimed that the "exercise of the right of property is subject to the limitations or rules which require the maintenance and progress of the social order." The high countries followed, with mineral-rich Ecuador, Peru, and Bolivia adopting a "social" definition of property rights. Peru's new 1933 constitution held that private property could only exist if it was "in harmony with the social interest." In Bolivia, veterans returned from the Chaco War tired of fighting Paraguay and ready to take on Standard Oil. Soon, nearly all nations, through edicts, legislation, and constitutions, embraced the idea that the right to property carried with it social obligations, that property was not something a person or corporation could possess in isolation but was instead a social relation. Land reform was at the center of most visions of progress. There could be no future without land reform. Nor could there be democracy.[3]

Limiting the right to private property gave this prewar generation of nation builders a weapon with which to tame both local feudal elites and foreign capitalists. It also was the first step in widening the ideal of citizenship to include not only individual rights (of religion, of speech, of protection from arbitrary power) but also social and economic rights. The nationalization of industries and natural resources would help raise revenue that states could then use to distribute a "social" wage, to provide basic human services like health care, education, and pensions. Chile's new constitution expressly stated that the capacity to expand social rights was dependent on the need to limit property rights. "The exercise of the right of property is subject to the limitations" necessary to advance "the health of the citizenry and of the public welfare." In the years to come, in countries such as Guatemala, Colombia, Chile, Peru, and Bolivia, agrarian reforms justified by this social conception of property rights became a mechanism, as it was in Mexico, for indigenous communities to secure their land and to reconstitute their commons.

"To govern is to distribute," said Cuba's Ramón Grau San Martín, who would soon beat dictator Fulgencio Batista in a fair vote. "In my government," he promised during the campaign, "there will be candy for everyone," a sweet slogan on an island that produced much of the world's sugar.[4]

Socialism

No politician more dramatically captures the relationship between electoral democracy and social democracy, and the way the expansion of one contributed to the expansion of the other, than Salvador Allende.

Born to an upper-class family in 1908, Allende graduated from medical school and, in 1933, went on to help found Chile's modern Socialist Party. He won his first congressional seat in 1937 with a total of 2,021 votes, barely 3 percent of his district's population. The franchise was then limited to literate, property-owning men (with literate women having to wait until 1949 to get the vote). Over the next three decades, Allende would run in many more elections. And in each one, his vote margin increased, not just because he was becoming more popular (he was), but because Socialists and reformers were increasing literacy and thus expanding the franchise. In 1937, as many as 350,000 Chilean children had no school to go to. Allende's Socialist Party pushed to build new classrooms and hire new teachers. Allende also supported peasant and worker literacy programs. The goal, he said, was to turn Chile "into one big school"—and at the same time, create more voters. Through the 1940s and '50s, the rate of increase in primary school enrollment greatly outstripped the country's birth rate. It was not until 1957 that Allende and other senators passed legislation establishing a secret ballot (compared with the 1880s in the United States), finally ending the practice by which landowners delivered ballots to their *peones obligados* already filled out with the name of their preferred candidate. And it was not until 1971, a year after Allende was elected president, that all men and women over the age of twenty-one, literate or not, were allowed to vote.[5]

In the years leading up to the Second World War, Allende was key in forming Chile's antifascist Popular Front government, which allied his Socialist Party with the Radical Party, the Democratic Party, the Communist Party, and the Radical Socialist Party. Together, this coalition won the country's presidential elections in 1938 and immediately built over one thousand schools and hired three thousand teachers.

Appointed minister of health in 1939, Allende increased pensions for widows, distributed free lunches for schoolchildren and prenatal care for women, and introduced workplace safety regulations. Allende's antifascism was consistent and unrelenting. He pushed the Socialist Party to prepare for a war "in favor of democracy and against fascism," an ideology of hatred "financed since its first steps by capitalism."[6]

Allende had been tracking what at the time was called Hitlerism since the beginning of his professional career. For his 1933 thesis, a requirement to become a physician, he wrote on crime and mental health, which noted how after the world war demagogues had come to easily manipulate mass democracy. Fascism, he wrote, was an "insidious virus," a "psychopathological phenomenon." The brutality of the fighting touched all sectors of society, not just the tens of millions of surviving veterans. The trauma of the conflict combined with worldwide depression and political instability has, he wrote, given rise to "armed institutions with the characteristics of political parties," filled by alienated, violent men and led by politicians who use "force" in place of argument.[7]

Most Chilean Socialists, attuned to the danger of global fascism, wanted what Allende called "Roosevelt-style social democracy." Allende was part of a broader continental cohort of Socialists, party leaders like Peru's Haya de la Torre, Venezuela's Rómulo Betancourt, and Colombia's Jorge Eliécer Gaitán, who were willing to tone down their complaints about U.S. and British imperialism and focus on fighting *nazifacismo* and *franquismo*. Allende's Socialists vowed to wage "total economic war" against the Axis and put an end to Tokyo's purchasing, on behalf of Germany, Chilean copper, cobalt, and manganese.

Losing the German market was a big hit, leading to a decline in tax revenue available for the ambitious projects carried out by Allende's Ministry of Health. The ministry's studies confirmed that Chile's infant mortality was the highest in the world and its death rate about twice that of the United States. Malnutrition, and even starvation, were common, even though Chile was exporting grain. Chronic, immobilizing illness, Allende wrote, was an everyday part of life for most Chileans. Like defeating fascism, improving the health of the working class required political action. Allende hoped that Roosevelt would make up what was lost by closing the Japanese market with cheap loans, and Washington did allow the Export-Import Bank, which had been chartered by the U.S. Congress to finance commercial projects, to advance credit for public-health programs.[8]

Allende was part of a hemisphere-wide network of health workers who advocated for "social medicine," as distinct from "liberal medicine." Social medicine stressed the economic and political causes of illness and called on the state "to service the collective needs of national populations." Many of the physicians involved, like Brazil's Carlos Chagas and Argentina's Gregorio Aráoz Alfaro, were active in the League of Nations' Health Organization and its various Pan-American spin-offs. More and more Latin American countries went well beyond the U.S. program of Social Security to include health care in their public insurance programs.[9]

Allende, of course, supported Spain's republicans and used his post as minister of health to grant asylum to Spanish exiles after Franco's 1939 victory. Communist Party member Pablo Neruda, already famous for his *Twenty Love Poems and a Song of Despair*, had been serving as Chile's Spanish consul. When Madrid fell, he retreated to France. There, Neruda retrofitted the SS *Winnipeg*, a cargo ship, to carry the maximum number of passengers. Imagine: Neruda bidding bon voyage to twenty-two hundred Spanish evacuees as they departed the French port of Trompeloup-Pauillac, and then Allende, about to be appointed minister of health, greeting those refugees as they disembarked in Valparaíso. Neruda called the help he rendered Spanish refugees his greatest poem. Chile's popular-front government also took in more than thirteen thousand German Jewish refugees, many of them arriving in Buenos Aires and then crossing over the Andes to Chile by mule trains.

Allende trusted Roosevelt, he said, believing that FDR represented "the highest human value" of anticolonial Americanism. He described his own work as the head of the Ministry of Health as turning Chile into a "vast laboratory for experimentation," a working out of policies aimed to end "physical suffering," an answer to FDR's call to create a world where people could "live their lives free from fear and from want." Along with other Chilean Socialists, he began to route his foreign policy concerns through Washington. In late November 1938, a few days after Kristallnacht, Allende signed a telegram to Adolf Hitler in support of FDR's demand that Germany stop persecuting Jews. Later, he asked Roosevelt to intervene with Great Britain to save the life of Mohandas Gandhi, who was then on a hunger strike. Gandhi had been imprisoned in the Aga Khan Palace for demanding, even as the war was under way, India's immediate, absolute independence. Doctors were afraid he would soon die if he didn't break his fast.[10]

Allende believed that capitalism could exist equally well under democracy

or fascism, but it was "absurd" to think there was a moral equivalence between the two forms of government. Fascism had to be defeated before capitalism could be tamed. He also believed that the postwar world would have
to go beyond the New Deal. The fight against fascism was a "people's war,"
he said, a "revolution" that would bring about a new set of expectations and
social relations: "a new way of living." The British and French empires would
have to be broken up. And the riches of the world more evenly shared. The
"masses," he hoped, "will be granted the fullness of rights and the enjoyment of material and cultural welfare."[11]

Allende was well bred and well fed, a member of Santiago's posh Prince
of Wales Country Club. "He loved life, he loved flowers, he loved dogs," as
García Márquez wrote about him, and even the U.S. ambassador who served
during the U.S. coup against him said he possessed "extraordinary and appealing human qualities." He was *simpático*. He took an interest in others,
including those who cooked for him, washed his clothes, and cleaned his
house. His smile radiated goodwill but also some dark knowledge. As much
an existentialist as a Marxist, Allende came of age during the First World
War and its aftermath, when catastrophe was as likely an outcome of political action as progress. He ended his 1933 dissertation by citing Spain's
republican politician, the influential left-wing criminologist Mariano Ruiz-
Funes García, who believed that modern society was driven by irrationality,
by the death drive, as much as by reason.[12]

Every human has within themselves the genius of a great Greek sculptor,
Allende wrote, quoting Ruiz-Funes. They are as capable of carving the most
sublime works of beauty as they are of creating monstrosities. Individuals
conjure their own saints and sinners, their own dreams and nightmares.
Man is his own project, Sartre would soon say, nothing but what he makes
of himself.[13]

Allende would agree, but he would insist that wages—whether people
earned enough to live healthy, dignified lives—determined whether political life was beautiful or monstrous. As minister of health, he compiled research that compared how long it would take a worker in France, the United
States, and Chile to earn enough to buy bread, eggs, and other staples. A
French worker had to work fifteen minutes and a U.S. worker six minutes to

purchase a pound of bread. A Chilean had to work thirty-three minutes. As to a dozen eggs, a laborer in France would have to work two hours and twenty minutes and in the United States fifty-five minutes. In Chile, it took six hours of toil to buy the eggs.[14]

Barbarism

It "smells of communism," complained Colombia's conservative Bishop Miguel Ángel Builes in 1936, of liberalism in general, but especially of the new "heretical" kind that flirted with socialism. Builes was a hard-liner, and he used his pulpit to overdramatize the dangers facing the Catholic family. The Nazis in Germany had a whole class of philosophers and jurists, their Heideggers and Schmitts, to justify will-to-power politics, to turn a century of idealistic and romantic thought into a philosophy of death. Similar intellectuals existed in Latin America, but it was mostly the conservative priesthood that justified the plunge into unreason—in Colombia and elsewhere.

Builes and like-minded clerics blessed the move of ultraconservative hatred from out of the shadows, from the chambers of elites into the streets, the cantinas, military barracks, and police stations, transmitting the anxiety of the middle and upper classes to the general population and readying it for combat. Like Franco in Spain, right-wing priests welded conservative Catholicism to a flexible anticommunism—flexible in that it understood all expressions of democratization and liberalization to be if not communism then "crypto-communism."[15]

Liberalism was a "mortal sin," Builes said, preaching against most manifestations of modern life, including women riding horses. Like a medieval Wordsworth (who complained of the coal smoke from trains sullying England's pastoral glens), the cleric denounced the coming of the railroad into the western interior of Colombia as the chariot of Asmodeus, the king of all demons, who brings ruin. The workers building the line, Builes said, carried all of Bogotá's vices into the innocent countryside: dancing, gambling, drinking, cursing, sloth, fornication, adultery, sinister smiles, and sinful desires. Conservative priests like Builes cheered Franco's victory in 1939, especially when his new fascist state reversed the republican land reform and broke up peasant cooperatives.[16]

As in Europe and the United States, it was at times difficult to say what was and wasn't fascism in Latin America, to distinguish long-held reactionary views, including a diffuse but deeply seated Catholic anti-Semitism, from what seemed like Builes's sharper criticisms of modern life. In El Salvador, the bored sons of the landed oligarchy hunted peasants for sport. Was that fascism?[17]

What about the Dominican Republic? There, in October 1937, President Rafael Trujillo—an admirer of Franco who had been installed in power after the United States withdrew its military in 1924—ordered the execution of some eleven thousand Haitian sugarcane cutters along the Dominican Republic's border with Haiti. "The Dominican people are a white Hispanic nation whose population is weakened by a mixture with the blood of non-white races," said a race ideologue who influenced Trujillo; Haitians living in the country "degenerate the moral and spiritual strength of Dominicans." Was this fascism?[18]

Both the NAACP and leftist journals like *The Nation* said it was fascism. They recognized the link between anti-Black and antilabor terror that took place in Haiti and the Dominican Republic and the rhetoric of racial eliminationism and antisocialism on the rise in Europe. *The Nation* called Trujillo a "little Hitler," part of a pack of "little Hitlers of South and Central America," with their secret paramilitary police. The magazine pointed out the irony of Washington's condemning the persecution of Jews in Europe while saying nothing about the murder of Haitians in the Caribbean. Washington not only downplayed Trujillo's slaughter, but Hull even sent advisers to help him draft new immigration laws that would, as one of Hull's men put it, "facilitate 'neo-white' immigration and at the same time effectively curb the immigration of 'blacks.'"[19]

Right-wing militancy largely spread in reaction to the growth of the Left, in response to peasant and union organizing. The radical peasants of Spain's Aragon looked much like the radical peasants of Mexico's Morelos, both fighting large, landed estates whose owners increasingly turned to paramilitary thugs to shore up their power and the Catholic Church to justify their privilege.

Spanish colonialism's social and intellectual heritage likewise aligned with right-wing extremism. Hitler's will-to-power apocalypticism, his sanctification of conquest, of establishing a larger world Reich—the entire Nazi agenda had already, in a way, been realized in the Spanish Empire, in Sepúlveda's defense of natural slavery, in the expulsion of Jews from Spain in 1492, and in Cortés's "chastisements," the use of exemplary terror, a heritage that conservatives continued to hold dear.

A few Latin American intellectuals did flirt with early fascism's modernist style, to escape not just the domination of the United States but stale and ineffective clericalism. Fascism, for the Brazilian Plínio Salgado, was a "blazing spirit of rebellion" that promised to break "the political rhythm of the country," shatter into pieces the manorialism of the ancients, and create something new. In most countries, though, especially in Mexico, Latin American fascism was theorized by conservative Catholics. As demands for land, bread, and work grew more strident, many men of Christ became defenders of order and private property.

In El Salvador in late January 1932, over a three-day period, local priests helped the military mount a pacification campaign against a rural uprising that murdered tens of thousands of indigenous peasants. The clerics heard the confessions of left-wing peasants and then used the information to draw up death lists to pass on to the military. Accused subversives were lined up in front of church and cemetery walls and executed by firing squad, their blood left on the whitewash for weeks as a warning to other would-be rebels.[20]

This legacy of brutality led Yale's Nicholas Spykman to conclude that if Nazis were able to exploit racism in relatively homogenous Europe, they would run the table in the New World, with its peoples drawn from every corner of the earth. It is true that there exist infamous cases in which Latin American leaders pursued policies of eliminationism of Native Americans and African Americans, along with calls by racist intellectuals for a "whitening" of their nations. Today, the border separating Haiti from the Dominican Republic is perhaps Latin American racism's sharpest edge.

Yet in the 1930s and '40s, the multitude of caste categories left behind by Spanish colonialism made it hard to scale up everyday racism into a full-on *rassenkrieg*, or race war.

The region's fascists looked for scapegoats for their nation's problems, but mostly didn't organize cults of racial purity. In some places, when the status hierarchy was confronted by a mobilized threat, communism could be understood in racial terms, as those U.S. oilmen and their local allies had when they called the Mexican Revolution a revolt against "white" civilization. Yet Catholic theocrats generally looked not to demonize dark-skinned peasants but to recapture them ideologically for the Church. Right-wing nationalism in Latin America continued to fetishize Spanish blood, but it didn't require the elimination of a race of people. Now, though, the category of "communist" began to take on pariah-like qualities, as an evil to be purged from the body politic.[21]

Fascist Europe's opposition to Anglo-Saxonism resonated in Latin America. Berlin's complaints about the pound sterling echoed Latin America's gripes about the dollar. Throughout Latin America, anti-imperialists, at least until Hull's reversal on intervention, described the United States much the way German intellectuals described imperial Great Britain, as grasping, grubbing, materialistic, instrumental. Hitler played on Germans' resentment of the harsh peace terms imposed on them after the First World War. Latin Americans had no end of similar grievances: northern Mexico, Panama, Venezuela, Mexico, Nicaragua, the Dominican Republic, countless gunboat humiliations, and unpayable debt.

Yet by some combination of luck and design, Roosevelt and Hull really had assembled a group of skilled, nimble, and intuitively strategic diplomats who helped contain Latin American fascism. Sumner Welles was one of them. Extremely formal, wealthy, and not particularly radical, Welles used his decades working in Latin America to cultivate the region's conservatives. Yet he identified as a social democrat, believing that Scandinavian socialism offered the best form of governance. So he was at home with Latin American leftists and radicals. Welles was also a patrician racist, though his work with Latin Americans moderated his views, as it did those of Josephus Daniels. Cordell Hull suffered recurrent bouts of tuberculosis, leaving

Welles to run the State Department for long stretches. He was one of the most clear-eyed among FDR's Brain Trust about the hypocrisy of fighting fascism to save British, French, and Dutch colonialism, and thought that at some point Washington was going to have to confront its allies about the need to dismantle their empires. He carried himself as if he were the Viceroy of India, yet Welles thought colonialism an evil as great as chattel slavery. Can the "free world" survive, he asked, echoing Lincoln, "as half slave and half free?"

Allende's existential humanism or Trujillo's genocidal racism? Latin America lurched, and United States diplomats treaded lightly, figuring out how to work with politicians and movements representing a broad spectrum of politics. FDR's chief of staff George Marshall was worried that all South America could fall to right-wing revolutions, leading to the "transformation of Latin American states into dependencies or colonies of Germany or Italy."[22]

But Latin America's antifascists had an ally. They could point to the New Deal United States and call, as Allende did, for "social democracy, Roosevelt-style." More than simply affirming the sovereign equality of nations, or merely asserting the superiority of liberalism over fascism, the New Deal put social-democratic muscle on the bones of political democracy, promising a "more abundant" life—and it didn't (for the most part) stand in the way when Latin Americans tried to do the same.

There was much work to do. Latin American industries desperately needed capital to diversify, to build infrastructure, and to pay better wages. Ruins from the time of colonialism remained scattered across the landscape. They had to be torn down and replaced with new bridges, ports, roads, and railroads. "Everything, everything needs to be remade," said Olavo Egydio de Souza Aranha, a powerful São Paulo industrialist.[23]

And so shortly before Pearl Harbor, FDR preempted German investment, and over the objections of Congress, gave Brazil twenty-five million dollars to build a steel mill at Volta Redonda. Roosevelt also sent the head of the storied Rural Electrification Committee, the engineer Morris Llewellyn Cooke, to Brazil, to help extend the country's electric grid. He gave Mexico a ten-million-dollar loan to replace an out-of-date refinery at Azcapotzalco to process its expropriated oil.[24]

Mexico was grateful. But its congress still passed a law mandating any industry involving foreign investment had to be majority Mexican owned. U.S. capital howled but Roosevelt refused to interfere. There was a war coming.

Rather than simply containing economic nationalists in Latin America, Washington honestly seemed to be trying to tame its own clamorous capitalists.

41.

A People's War

Franco declared victory in April 1939. In September, Germany invaded Poland. By the spring of 1940, Berlin was in control of Holland, France, Denmark, and Norway. In July, the Luftwaffe began bombing Great Britain. Latin America in these months experienced a series of aborted putsches and short-lived coups that almost brought fascists or their sympathizers to power in Bolivia, Brazil, Paraguay, and Argentina, among other places. Nightmare scenarios composed in the councils of war in the United States. A manifesto reportedly circulated by a clique of Nazi officers in Argentina was particularly alarming, laying out a plan by which Buenos Aires would forcefully annex all southern South America and then join the Axis powers.[1]

The manifesto was hyperbole and didn't represent the majority opinion of the Argentine officer class. It did, though, encapsulate the fears of Washington's strategic class, which was convinced that Germany could easily exploit the Western Hemisphere's discontents. If Germany's influence continued to grow in South America, Washington might be reduced to a "quarter-sphere defense" of the New World—that is, securing everything north of the Panama Canal and leaving South America to Hitler.[2]

Secretary of Commerce Harry Hopkins thought such an outcome "dangerous in the extreme." If London fell, Hopkins said the day after Hitler began bombing Britain, he had no doubt that Germany would strike Latin America before it turned its tanks on the Soviet Union. "The danger of delay cannot be overdrawn. Latin America, from Mexico down, is loaded with dynamite."[3]

Hopkins was someone whom FDR listened to. And raising the danger of German encroachment in Latin America helped Roosevelt, who by this point had given up his idea of hunkering down in a hemispheric happy valley, isolate the isolationists and make the case for war preparation. Throughout 1941, up to Japan's attack on Pearl Harbor in December, polls consistently showed that the public, by over 80 percent, would approve of a declaration of war if "any European power" attacked a Latin American country. And so Roosevelt, in order to prepare the public for an inevitable larger, world war, stepped up his insistence that all of the Western Hemisphere had to be defended.

On May 27, 1941, the president broadcast a radio speech just short of a call to war. He addressed his remarks not to the citizens of the United States but to the peoples of "the Americas," announcing an unlimited state of emergency to defend not the United States but the Western Hemisphere. "If we believe in the independence and the integrity of the Americas, we must be willing to fight," he said, "to defend them just as much as we would to fight for the safety of our own homes." The Nazis plan to "treat the Latin American nations as they treat the Balkans today," the president said, and then "they plan to strangle the United States." Later that year, he claimed he had in his possession a "secret map" drafted by German war planners showing all South America reorganized into four German protectorates: *Argentinien*, *Brasilien*, *Chile*, and *Neuspanien*.*

Hitler, FDR said, had "footholds, bridgeheads in the New World."[4]

U.S. military strategists had by this point staked out an expansive definition of the Western Hemisphere, one that roped in the Philippines, Hawai'i,

---

* The "secret map" FDR referred to does exist in his archives, but it was most likely a forgery drafted by British intelligence agents, including Roald Dahl, the children's book author. London hoped to strike fear and hasten the United States' entrance into the war. The British forgery seems to be based on a map that did hang in Argentina's Nazi Party headquarters.

and Guam in the Pacific and the Azores in the Atlantic. All the "island outposts of the New World," as FDR put it in his May speech.

An official policy of neutrality mandated that Washington could only act to defend the Western Hemisphere. So Roosevelt looked for some geographic theory that could stretch the hemisphere as wide as possible, wide enough to include strategically important Iceland. The White House consulted scholars who offered differing opinions, including one who cited the Treaty of Tordesillas. None thought Iceland part of the Americas. Isaiah Bowman, president of Johns Hopkins, came close. He wrote a report placing the Atlantic border of the New World at the 26th meridian, which made Greenland part of America but left Iceland in Europe.[5]

Try again, Roosevelt told Bowman. The professor came back with the "widest channel" theory. Since Bowman considered Greenland part of the New World, a line drawn in the middle of the widest channel separating Europe and Greenland would put Iceland in the Western Hemisphere. That theory gave Roosevelt enough to claim that Iceland was within the "Monroe Doctrine Area." He ordered the naval occupation of the island on July 7, 1941.

When asked by a reporter how far exactly into the Atlantic the Western Hemisphere extended, Roosevelt laughed. It depends, he said, on which geographer you ask. "It is impossible to draw a line and put a buoy on it."

Iron to Make Your Ships

No straight line ran from FDR's 1936 peace conference to a hemisphere united against fascism. There had been more conferences, in Lima, Panama, Rio, Havana, and elsewhere that had fitfully created the architecture of mutual defense. Brazil and Argentina stalled on major commitments, not wanting to give up leverage. The conferences themselves, and the resolutions they produced, mattered less than the work that had already gotten started. The gears had begun to move toward greater integration, taking place under a raft of new agencies. By the time Japan attacked Pearl Harbor and other naval bases in the Philippines on December 7, 1941, Cordell Hull had at his disposal a sprawling continental diplomatic bureaucracy. The hemisphere's nations were not as united as Hull would have liked, but they were at the ready.

Within a month, America's statesmen were gathered in Rio to confirm the principle of mutual hemispheric defense. Hull wanted as strong and bellicose a statement as possible, a collective declaration severing diplomatic relations with all Axis powers. Argentina objected, wanting American nations to retain the right to remain neutral. Sumner Welles, who was at the meeting, negotiated with Buenos Aires a weaker statement, which only *recommended* that American nations sever their ties to Japan, Germany, and Italy. Welles thought it more important to maintain unanimity than issue an overreaching statement with an Argentine dissent.

In Washington, Hull tried to enlist Roosevelt to rebuke Welles. On a three-way call, Hull "quivered with rage" at Welles's compromise. FDR, though, backed Welles, saying that "in this this case I am going to take the judgment of the man on the spot. Sumner, I approve what you have done."[6]

Roosevelt was acting here according to the Department of War's recommendation, which, despite the prewar widening of what counted as the New World, didn't want so big a potential theater of war that it would have to waste resources defending Patagonia.

Stalingrad would eventually break its siege and the Red Army would break the back of the Wehrmacht at Kursk. Tens of millions of Soviet lives were lost holding off Hitler's forces, before finally turning them back in February 1943, a full year before Washington and London opened a front at Normandy. Of the 13.6 million German soldiers killed, wounded, or captured in the war, 10 million were by the Red Army.

But away from the battlefield gore, a unified Western Hemisphere was, in its own way, indispensable to victory. By the time the United States finally entered the war, Washington had built hundreds of military installations on Latin American soil and set up landing fields and outposts across the hemisphere. The Inter-American Defense Board served as a continental war council, made up of the hemisphere's highest military officials. Ad hoc protocols for fast consultation were put into place—any minister of foreign affairs could call a general meeting of his counterparts. Washington beefed up Latin America's militaries, its navies and air forces.[7]

FBI agents were given an open warrant to hunt for Nazi spies. United States engineers lent their expertise to mines and factories. On Washington's request, Latin American nations deported German, Italian, and Japanese residents and citizens, or put them in local concentration camps. Peru sent thousands of Japanese to be interned in the United States. Guatemala seized German-owned plantations. Nearly every nation in the hemisphere opened their doors to agricultural experts, military advisers, and geologists on the lookout for rare minerals sought by the Manhattan Project.

"It really does change the status of the New World," Adolf Berle, an adviser to FDR, said of this buildup, "creating a kind of *pax Americana*."[8]

The security of the Panama Canal alone gave Washington the luxury of running a two-ocean campaign the entire length of the Pacific and Atlantic seaboards. And the United States Air Force used Brazil's bulge into the Atlantic as a staging ground—only sixteen hundred nautical miles separated Natal, Brazil, from Dakar, Senegal. North Atlantic winters could close Icelandic flight routes for months, while a middle route across the Azores was not reliable due to Portuguese neutrality.

Before Pearl Harbor, the U.S. Air Transport Command used the Brazilian route to deliver Lend-Lease planes and other equipment to Great Britain and the Soviet Union. After Pearl Harbor, with Japanese occupation of the Philippines shutting Pacific transport, Brazil became the "air funnel to the battlefields of the world." FDR called Parnamirim airfield in Natal the "trampoline to victory." B-24s, B-25s, B-26s, and other cargo planes landed and took off every three minutes, keeping weapons, matériel, and resources flowing year-round to Europe, Africa, and Asia, and supplying Allied forces in the North African campaign against Field Marshal Erwin Rommel. Ships departing from Brazil likewise shuttled thousands of troops to northern Africa and Southeast Asia. The *Queen Mary*, out of Rio, dodged German U-boats to deliver nine thousand U.S. soldiers to Sydney.[9]

Germany would waste significant energy in trying to secure access to

strategic materials, especially fuel. The United States fought not one battle
for resources. The supply chain from Latin America to northern factories
moved without a snag: zinc, nickel, aluminum, beryl, tungsten, graphite,
iodine, tung oil, sperm oil (from Chile, used as a gun lubricant), manganese
ore, mercury, bauxite, vanadium, platinum from Colombia, copper from
Mexico and Chile, Brazilian mica and quartz crystals for radios, Ecuadoran
cinchona (used to make quinine to fight malaria). And petroleum. When
Malaysia's tin mines and rubber plantations fell to Japan, the United States
still had Bolivia and Brazil. When Japan cut off the supply of Manila hemp
in the Philippines, the United Fruit Company grew the stringy plant in
Panama and elsewhere in Central America, making sure the navy had all
the cordage it needed. Washington purchased Colombia's entire stock of
platinum. Brazilian thorium went into the bombs dropped on Hiroshima
and Nagasaki.

"Nobody knows," recalled one military official after the war, "how much
we relied on the South American and Central American countries for
commodities and things that we simply had to have."[10]

The war was hard on Latin America. U-boats torpedoed ships and damaged food-supply lines, and those cargo vessels ships not sunk by the Germans were converted into war transports. Inflation spiked and shortages of
important foodstuffs were chronic. Politicians of all political stripes pleaded
with Washington to hurry and open a second front, not just to reinforce the
Red Army but because, as Vicente Lombardo Toledano, a Mexican labor
leader and head of the Confederation of Latin American Workers, said, "a
drawn-out war means starvation for our people." Still, every nation save
Argentina, which insisted on neutrality until the very end of the war, stayed
committed to Allied victory.[11]

A precocious Fidel Castro wrote FDR asking for a ten-dollar bill. In exchange, he offered access to Cuban iron mines. "If you want iron to make
your ships," the fourteen-year-old Castro wrote, "I will show to you the biggest mines of iron in all the land."

Writing the Postwar as We Go

It took a sprawling public-private apparatus of procurement, credit and capital, technology, labor management, transportation, production, and warehousing to process Latin American resources for wartime use—an apparatus comprised of an ever-expanding number of committees, boards, bureaus, offices, agencies, and corporations, working under the jurisdiction of competing federal departments, including State, Commerce, Agriculture, and the Interior.

The task set out was enormous and involved both converting the U.S. economy to war production and integrating that conversion with the stepped-up supply of Latin America's resources. Decisions that in the past had been left to the law of market demand, or were made in corporate boardrooms, were now being rationalized by a battery of federal economists and mathematicians, who determined how much, say, rubber or hemp the navy would need, or how much tungsten the army might require, based on models predicting the course of the war. From these determinations, procurement estimates were drawn up, suppliers were identified, and contracts signed.

Roosevelt put potential rivals at the head of these agencies, including several powerful Southern conservatives who were influential in the Democratic Party. These included the Texan Jesse Jones, who ran the Reconstruction Finance Corporation; the Mississippi cotton magnate William Clayton, who oversaw the Federal Loan Administration; and the South Carolinian Jimmy Byrnes, who served as the director of the Office of Economic Mobilization (who later served as President Harry Truman's secretary of state). Their job was to build the supply infrastructure needed to wage total war.

As the world's largest cotton exporter, Clayton, who during World War I served on the War Industries Board, brought vast experience presiding over a transportation network that moved enormous amounts of raw material around the globe, wresting ever-greater efficiency out of a complex human matrix—all, according to his biographer, without having left behind one document that expressed a concern for human welfare. None of these men thought the New Deal needed to be exported to Latin America. They barely tolerated it at home.

But also involved in Latin American resource procurement was Vice President Henry Wallace, who ran the powerful Board of Economic Warfare. Wallace stood apart, even from other progressive New Dealers, in his insistence that winning the war would be meaningless unless Washington also won the peace. For the vice president, this came down to one thing: raising the world's standard of living. If full employment with decent pay wasn't made universal, then fascists, even if they were defeated in war, would regroup. A third world war would be inevitable. According to a British consular report, Wallace felt personally responsible for the pittances foreign workers received in exchange for supplying the United States–led war effort.[12]

Roosevelt told Wallace to concentrate on winning the war first and worry about the future later. But Wallace saw the future in Latin America. "We are writing the postwar world as we go along," he told FDR. "The administrative machinery thus set up to help win the war will be the most effective economic means through which we can win the peace later on."[13]

Since taking charge of the Board of Economic Warfare (BEW) in 1941, Wallace's solution to the problem of poor wages was to insist on including "labor clauses" in procurement contracts. Such clauses would stipulate minimum wages and other worker-rights protections, including a ban on prison labor, a guarantee of decent housing and health care, and no discrimination based on "race, creed, color, or national origin." The first time a State Department official read one of these clauses, he "recoiled in horror," describing the provision as "a complex Frankenstein that will consume us"—raising expectations among foreign workers that couldn't be met, leading to labor strife. But FDR, according to Wallace, supported the clauses. Roosevelt thought they allowed the United States to distinguish itself from the brute methods deployed by colonial Europe to secure resources.

Wallace's board wasn't so far out of the mainstream. Nelson Rockefeller, who presided over his own bureaucratic fiefdom in Latin America with the Office of the Coordinator of Inter-American Affairs, supported the clauses as mechanisms to ensure greater productivity. But Hull at the State Department hated them, and so did Jones and Clayton, who denounced Wallace's board as sheltering dozens of Reds. Jones, a Houston millionaire, called Wallace's work in Latin America "so 'social' as to be practically eleemosynary," a fancy word for *charity*. Business representatives complained of Wallace's Latin American operation as an attack on the "economic system of free enterprise which has prevailed in this country from the time of its birth." Senator William Howard Taft accused Wallace of trying to set up an "international WPA," the Works Progress Administration that was a hallmark of FDR's early New Deal.[14]

Such opposition, which Wallace routinely denounced as fascism, only convinced him that he was right. Wallace had managed, since Pearl Harbor, to have scores of such labor clauses inserted in purchasing agreements, in, among other countries, Mexico, Bolivia, Peru, Guatemala, Haiti, Brazil, and Colombia. He saw the clauses as the lynchpin of a new order that would continue after the war and help create a continental labor code. Soon, the BEW was insisting that employers not only abide by their country's labor code but add new safety and health requirements. Wallace's agents spread out across Latin America inspecting work sites to make sure that "elaborate codes for workers' housing, sanitation, health care, job safety, accident compensation, union representation, and more" were being met. Wallace also used the BEW to send ships filled with tons of food to Latin America's poorest regions, including Central America and the Amazon. His critics called this his "pet food project." Republicans, thinking that FDR would keep Wallace as his running mate in 1944, started calling him "Give Away Henry."[15]

Wallace and his allies ignored such criticism. "We are fighting for the American way which is the way of freedom or liberty," said a board official defending the provisos. "The insertion of labor clauses in our contracts is a down payment guaranteeing fulfillment of our promises." Wallace went further, admitted that what he was doing in Latin America he wanted to do the world over. "Pan-Americanism," he said, "is an ideal which transcends the hemisphere and which can serve as a pattern for an international society where people can live and work in freedom, in friendship, and in peace."

Philosophical Ideal or a Pragmatic Principle?

Wallace met his match in Simón Patiño, one of Bolivia's largest mine owners, a man many thought was as rich as Henry Ford. Patiño became even wealthier meeting the demand for wartime tin but refused to accept the inclusion of Wallace's labor clause in his contracts with the board. One of the mines Patiño owned was called Catavi, sitting two and half miles high in Bolivia's otherworldly, windswept highlands, where labor relations had long been as bleak as the landscape.

Conflict had plagued Catavi for years, as survivors of the Chaco War came back from the battlefield committed to building a militant labor movement. As Christmas approached in 1942, more than ten thousand miners went on strike. Patiño's allies in the army sent in seven hundred soldiers armed with machine guns and trench mortars—weapons supplied to the Bolivian military by the United States. On December 21, the soldiers, stationed on the hills surrounding the mine, opened fire, killing anywhere between dozens and hundreds; the tally is still disputed. Witnesses reported that soldiers threw not just the dead but the wounded into mine pits, and then buried them alive.[16]

Wallace, who had come to see the conflict as a referendum on the morality of U.S. foreign policy, demanded an investigation of the slaughter, an inquiry into the social conditions that contributed to labor unrest. Washington was fighting a war for freedom, he said, and couldn't have its allies gunning down workers demanding a few pennies more a day for lung-destroying labor. Jesse Jones thought Bolivians indolent drunks and suggested sending the FBI in to hunt for agitators. The United States ambassador to Bolivia, Pierre de Lagarde Boal—the son of a union between French aristocracy and U.S. frontier fortune—said the strike had nothing to do with exploitation but was the work of "Nazi saboteurs." La Paz and Washington agreed to an inquiry led by the Congress of Industrial Organizations. The question of fair wages for Bolivian miners, a Wallace ally wrote, captured the "question of whether the Good Neighbor Policy is a philosophical ideal or a pragmatic principle." If the first, the Good Neighbor would endure past war's end. If the second, it was merely a tactic that would be discarded once the war was over.[17]

Patiño continued to buck Wallace, refusing to include labor clauses in his tin contracts. The Bolivian government sent its foreign minister, Tomás Manuel Elio, to Washington to argue that any attempt to interfere with existing salaries, benefits, and working conditions would be an "intervention" in Bolivia's domestic affairs and a violation of national sovereignty (even though Patiño lived in New York's Waldorf Astoria Hotel and his mining empire was incorporated in Delaware). Hull, Jones, Boal, and Clayton sided with Patiño. In response, Wallace sent agents to lobby Bolivia's congress to raise the miners' wages. That didn't go well. Hull was furious.

Wallace's allies in the CIO and in the press issued a damning description of the mine's working conditions, its "appalling poverty, misery, illiteracy, and exploitation of Bolivian tin miners," who rarely live beyond the age of thirty, on the "bleak frigid Andean plateaus." An average of seven thousand miners a year contracted silicosis, only to be let go with no compensation. There was no ventilation in the mines, which were so deep, the dust couldn't escape but accumulated at the bottom of the pit, where the workers breathed it in. Roosevelt himself likened the Bolivian highlands to the Congo under Leopold.

We Are of the New World

In the spring of 1943, Henry Wallace set out on a tour of Latin America. He had already made several to revolutionary Mexico. Now he wanted to see the whole continent firsthand.[18]

At home, the vice president was feeling the reaction setting in. "The forces of Anglo-Saxon fascism are gathering themselves for a mighty effort in the period immediately following the war," he told Rex Tugwell. "Racism, militarism, and extreme nationalism" might yet gain a toehold in the Western Hemisphere—and he didn't mean just in Latin America. Wallace warned Roosevelt that a faction of powerful elites wanted to create a "postwar situation which would eventually bring us into war with Russia."[19]

And so he hoped his tour of Latin America might broaden the New Deal coalition, creating new momentum to hold conservatives in check. All told he traveled eleven thousand miles, visiting factories, mines, and plantations. In Bolivia, he spent three days touring lowland plantations and highland mines, including Patiño's. "The air is so thin, the work is so hard," Wallace said. The vice president spoke Spanish with a warm fluency in what one observer called a "charming" Iowa accent. "We are of the New World, we North and South Americans," Wallace told one crowd. "We are the repositories of the worth of civilizations." Wallace's trip rivaled Roosevelt's to Buenos Aires in 1936, in the enthusiasm and crowds that turned out to greet him. In town after town, thousands of miners and sharecroppers, men and women with creased faces and calloused hands, many waving red flags, listened to Wallace repeat many of the themes of his famous Century of the Common Man speech, telling them that workers were the true "soldiers of democracy." "Never in Chilean history has any foreigner been received with such extravagance and evidently sincere enthusiasm," said Washington's ambassador in Santiago. In Costa Rica, Wallace laid the cornerstone of the new Inter-American Institute of Agricultural Sciences.

Wallace was Martí's sincere man, a man within whom science and spirituality mixed easily, as they did within many Latin Americans. Wallace talked about the war in mythical terms, as a battle of the forces of light against the forces of darkness. But he also talked like a socialist, echoing Allende by calling the fight a "people's revolution," a "people's war," a "long step forward toward the complete emancipation of the common man."

Many of the people he met, not knowing that FDR planned to run for a fourth term, thought they were speaking with a future president, that Wallace would be the Democratic Party nominee in 1944, and that Wallace, not Roosevelt, would, as Wallace put it, lead the world to adopt a "law of decency higher than any single nation." "If a vote were taken in South America now," one columnist speculated, "Henry Wallace would be rated neck-and-neck with Roosevelt as the real leader of the Western Hemisphere."[20]

Wallace was loyal to FDR, and he knew his main job was to secure ongoing support for the war effort, which he did, charming many a conservative politician and industrialist. But he couldn't help talk about the war in any other way than he had been talking about the war: that true victory meant winning the peace through social uplift. And that meant, more than anything else, raising wages and living conditions. In Communist Party strongholds like the Chilean mining town of Lota, Wallace pledged that the Good Neighbor Policy would continue after Allied victory and that Washington would make cheap credit available for nations to industrialize and share farming technology to conserve soil and increase yield. Everywhere he went, Wallace preached the same message: "The working population of the continent is the strongest and the only safeguard of democracy against fascism."*

Neither the FBI, nor the State Department, nor the power brokers who ran the Democratic Party machine were happy about Wallace's Latin American trip. J. Edgar Hoover's men did what they could to keep Wallace from speaking with leftists. In Peru, he sparked a small scandal by trying to meet with Victor Haya de la Torre, the head of the socialist opposition party. In Ecuador, the vice president did manage to break away from a reception and spend "one-and-a-half hours in the house of an Indian couple, discussing with them their way of life, means of livelihood, &c." British diplomats were astonished that Wallace dressed more like a farmer than vice president of the United States.[21]

Wallace's tour was such a success that it backfired on him. Instead of winning a widened base of support, it galvanized his enemies and hastened his marginalization, already under way due to his labor clauses and heavy-handed intervention in Bolivian politics. Senator Harry Truman began red-baiting Wallace.

---

* Not all U.S. ambassadors were as enthusiastic about Wallace's tour as was Washington's envoy to Chile, Claude Bowers. Yet Bowers' rave captures the wild popularity the vice president enjoyed among many Latin Americans: "Never in Chilean history has any foreigner been received with such extravagant and evidently sincere enthusiasm. Great crowds lined the . . . country roads, and great numbers were always standing before any house he entered. The mass meeting at the stadium, with 100,000 people, and 80,000 of them seated, was one of the two greatest popular assemblies I have ever seen anywhere. In the mining town of Lota 40,000 miners, including wives, greeted him at a mass meeting and there Wallace made his best speech. . . . The press publicity is without precedent. . . . His simplicity of manner, his mingling with all sorts of people, his visit to the workers' quarters without notice and his talks there with them and his inspection of the housing projects absolutely amazed the masses who responded almost hysterically." Chile's popular-front government was delighted with Wallace's visit; elsewhere on the vice president's tour, more conservative politicians were less so.

———

The winds were shifting, the war was turning. Friend Wallace was fading.[22]

Dread at the end of 1942, with the Germans on the march and much of Guadalcanal still in the hands of Japan, turned to confidence by the middle of 1943. The Soviets had broken the siege of Stalingrad and the Red Army had driven Axis forces from the Caucasus. By this point, the FBI in Latin America was focusing as much on Socialists and Communists as it was on Nazis and Fascists. Suddenly the need to appease labor unions in Latin America seemed less urgent.

With Japan retreating in the Pacific, Hull, Jones, Clayton, and others opposed to extending the social policies of the New Deal abroad pushed back against Wallace's efforts to increase the wages of foreign workers. At some point Clayton just stopped responding to Wallace's correspondence. Wallace in turn complained that men like Jones and Clayton "all were Texas," by which he meant slave drivers.[23]

By the end of 1943, the Board of Economic Warfare would be defunded, and most of its work passed to the Commerce Department. "We are getting some of these radical boys out of the way and more will go," said another Southerner, Jimmy Byrnes, after Wallace lost control of his board. By September 1943, even Roosevelt had signaled he had grown tired with "Wallace theories" and the idea that, after the war, the U.S. would ensure "a bottle of milk a day for every child in the world." Hull, more than anyone, wanted to draw down some of the high hopes raised by Wallace's "radical boys" and "utopians."[24]

The vice president was on borrowed time, though he still pleaded for Latin America. "It is a rather disturbing thought that we in the United States can maintain a deep interest in Latin America only so long as we think we have something to gain by it," Wallace wrote Rockefeller in December. "I do hope we shall be able so to act during the next few years that Latin America will feel that we are really her friend and not merely a friend for expedient purposes in time of great need."[25]

Within a year, Wallace would be dropped from Roosevelt's reelection ticket, replaced with Senator Truman.

42.

There Would Have Been Nothing

Roosevelt, while meeting with Field Marshal Stalin and Prime Minister Churchill in Tehran in late 1943, held up Latin America as an example of what he had in mind for a cooperative postwar world. The U.S. president mostly directed his remarks at Stalin, giving the Soviet leader a "seminar" on the benefits of the Good Neighbor Policy and how it might serve as a model for the USSR's own sphere of influence. The United States, Roosevelt said, had earned critical goodwill in the Western Hemisphere by giving up the right to intervention without any appreciable loss of influence. Moscow might even have an easier go at establishing a similar benign hegemony, FDR thought, since "the Slavic nations adjoining the Soviet Union" were "nearer in blood to the Russians than Costa Rica or Colombia to us."[1]

At that same summit, FDR presented Sumner Welles's rough draft of what would become the United Nations, a vision that drew heavily from Welles's experience in Latin America: he had in fact been working on a plan to reorganize world governance for years, informally since shortly after FDR's Buenos Aires Peace Conference and officially since early 1942. As an old Wilsonian, he had been thinking about such a project, and why it had failed after the First World War, for even longer.[2]

Welles's draft mirrored the long-standing Latin American insistence that balance-of-power realism was no way to organize the modern world, that it only set the stage for future wars. If the world was to be secure, if it was to be peaceful, it must be just; the gap between the "haves" and "have nots" would have to be narrowed. Welles's vision of a United Nations was Pan-Americanism writ large, a global organization that would maintain security and limit aggression, but would also have offices dedicated to health, social welfare, and nutrition; and departments charged with stabilizing prices, raising wages, protecting workers' rights, and regulating debt—agencies that worked to knit the world together by facilitating not just communication and transportation but culture, art, education, and science. Welles openly said it was modeled on the Western Hemisphere's "inter-American system," based on "sovereign equality, on liberty, on peace, and on joint resistance to aggression."

Latin America, as it did after the previous world war, was providing the processional for postbellum hope. Pan-Americanism, Welles said, "lights the darkness of our anarchic world. It should constitute a cornerstone in the world structure of the future."[3]

To San Francisco

The main lines of the postwar order became clearer over a course of several meetings. Bretton Woods in New Hampshire in July set the rules for the postwar money system. Dumbarton Oaks, outside Washington, D.C., from August to October 1944, sketched out the structure of the United Nations. Participation at Dumbarton was limited to the Big Four, or the "Four Policemen": the United States, the Soviet Union, Great Britain, and China. Latin American nations weren't invited, nor was most of the rest of the world.

The founding meeting, to call into being the United Nations, was to be held in San Francisco in late April 1945.

The question that vexed was how to balance the region and the world. Welles's initial sketch was extremely decentralized, with a weak executive body and power distributed widely across regions. Welles, though, was no longer on the scene by the end of 1944. He had been driven out of office by rumors of a same-sex scandal, rumors that were circulated through Georgetown's social scene by Hull and his wife, Rose Frances Whitney. And Roosevelt would soon be dead.

Sick with tuberculosis, Hull had resigned as secretary of state, but he stayed in Washington and had sway over his replacement, Edward Stettinius, and both men, along with their circle of advisers, wanted to create the opposite of Welles's proposal. They favored a strong organization where power was concentrated, as much as possible, in a Security Council comprised of the United States, the Soviet Union, Great Britain, and China. Regional associations, such as the Pan-American Union, would be marginalized if not eradicated. That was roughly the template that came out of Dumbarton Oaks.

Henry L. Stimson didn't like it. The elder statesman carried weight. He had served as Herbert Hoover's secretary of state, and William Taft's and FDR's secretary of war. And he presided over the Manhattan Project. Stimson thought the Dumbarton proposal would create a too-powerful United Nations, a world body that would put the Monroe Doctrine "at the mercy" of having to obtain "the assent of the security council" for any military action the United States might want to take in the Americas.

"The thing that we are asking for is first a freer hand as a policeman in this hemisphere," Stimson said. "I think it's not asking too much to have our little region over here which has never bothered anybody."[4]

Latin Americans didn't like the idea either. By this point, the region's foreign ministries were deeply invested in the inter-American system, and worried that the Dumbarton plan would lead to its dismantling. In the few weeks he had left, FDR tried to allay such fears. He spoke to Mexico's president personally and gave several addresses assuring that Pan-Americanism would remain the crown jewel of the new order. Nelson Rockefeller, now the assistant secretary of state for Latin-American Affairs, did the same.

Latin America's foreign ministers hurriedly convened yet another meeting, held in Mexico City's Chapultepec Castle, in February 1945. Argentina had remained too close to Germany, and so the question over whether it could join the United Nations had become a flash point. But the conference's main concern was the need to defend the "Western Hemisphere Idea."

Much had changed since the end of the First World War, when the region's politicians and intellectuals thought, rightly, that the League of Nation's affirmation of the Monroe Doctrine ratified their subordination to the United States. Now, Latin Americans *wanted* a regional carve-out—so integrated was the region with the United States. They were worried a too-strong Security Council would run roughshod over small countries. One worrisome scenario was this: "a predatory foreign nation" might "attack the Americas," and then use the veto of an ally on the Security Council to tie the UN's hands. If a Latin American country were to find itself in a standoff with either the United States or the Soviet Union, what would stop Washington or Moscow from using their vetos to prevent other hemispheric countries from coming to their defense?[5]

At Chapultepec, the region's delegates agreed to create a collective self-defense pact "completely free of the world arrangement." Such a pact, they believed, optimistically, would both protect them from too commanding a United Nations, while containing the United States, holding Washington accountable to its hemispheric neighbors.[6]

By the end of March 1945, the U.S. Marine Corps and Navy had control of Iwo Jima and was making ready to land tens of thousands of soldiers on Okinawa. Once that island was secured, it would be a slow grind toward Japan's home islands. On March 27, Argentina finally declared war on the Axis powers. The declaration was a formality; the war was all but over. But Buenos Aires's public repudiation of Berlin muted objections, held by several officials in the Roosevelt administration, to Argentina's joining the United Nations. Now the region's diplomats had a united "Latin bloc" in place for San Francisco.

And they had Nelson Rockefeller. Rockefeller didn't have Wallace's politics. And he didn't have Welles's idealism and vision. But he knew, on an instinctual level, the importance of Latin America to the United States. He also knew the disdain that men like Stettinius and Great Britain's prime minister Anthony Eden had for Latin Americans. And he knew that things in San Francisco could easily go sideways and was determined not to let that happen. Rockefeller wasn't supposed to attend the conference. He had no role. But he showed up anyway, effectively working as the Latin bloc's barrister.

Bald Heads and Gray Hair

Roosevelt died on April 12, 1945, and Harry Truman became president. The Wehrmacht was in retreat to Berlin as Allied forces swept through Europe. Hitler would commit suicide in his bunker at the end of the month.

Then, on April 25, over eight hundred delegates arrived at the War Memorial Opera House in San Francisco to begin the final discussions that would establish the United Nations. Most of Latin America's ambassadors had arrived three days earlier, landing at San Francisco's Municipal Airport on a plane chartered by Rockefeller. "Everything is swell," Rockefeller said exiting the plane. A spokesperson for the Latin American delegates told reporters that the first resolution they wanted passed was a tribute to FDR, "in the name of all delegates from all parts of the world."[7] Cordell Hull sent a letter from his hospital bed to be read at the opening ceremonies. The conference, he said, would be an "acid test of whether mankind had suffered enough and learned enough."

W. E. B. Du Bois attended the opening ceremony. "Naturally I looked for color." He found it, noticing "all types of mankind" in the audience, including what he called token delegates from Europe's colonies. What was missing, Du Bois said, was youth. "Bald heads and gray hair" filled the hall—not, he thought, a good omen for an assembly meant to define the future.

Germany surrendered in the middle of the deliberations, with V-E Day declared on May 8. Costa Rica was the first country in the world to hold a national celebration while residents of Rio filled the streets, dancing the samba through the night.

Rockefeller held his caucus together, making sure that the hemisphere's delegates were active in the conference's main debates, which took place in the city's four-story Veterans Building. Argentina still had its critics, but Rockefeller joined with most of the rest of Latin America to secure membership for Buenos Aires.

Latin Americans advanced proposals that pushed for the prohibition of war, the equality of women, the creation of a court of arbitration, the dismantling of colonialism, the repudiation of racism, and the recognition of economic rights. Brazil's representative was Bertha Lutz, a zoologist and diplomat long active in the Pan-American women's movement. Lutz met resistance from other delegations to some of her proposals meant to advance gender equality. Still, speaking before the General Assembly, she said she was proud to be the first woman to address a "world parliament." She was equally "proud" that she came from a region in the vanguard of social rights. "The first mention of the basic rights of all human beings, regardless of race, creed or sex," Lutz said, was made in a resolution put forth by Brazil, Uruguay, Mexico, and the Dominican Republic—and it was done so at the insistence of "the women on the delegations of these republics." "The status of women in different countries," she went on, "has to be radically improved and their rights extended."[8]

Brazil lost its bid to strengthen the General Assembly's power in relation to the Security Council, and other Latin American efforts to create a more progressive organization failed.

Panama tried to establish an International Office of Migration, both to aid refugees and to help labor find an equilibrium. Panama, a country whose independent existence required the mass migration of West Indian workers to dig its canal, said that laborers should go where needed without stigma or hardship attached. And since social welfare programs were (or so many thought) being adopted by all countries, refugees from now on could migrate without fear of hunger or falling sick. "Mobility," Octavio Méndez Pereira, the head of Panama's delegation believed, "was essential to the maximum development of the world's resources." The proposal was shelved, though, since the convening members had agreed that no specialized agency would be mentioned in the charter.[9]

Latin America had better luck in the arena of human rights. At Chapultepec, Mexican delegates had drafted a "statement on basic human rights" that put forth a unitary vision of the "political, social, and economic rights of man having universal moral validity." Other Latin American nations arrived in San Francisco with similar proposals to affirm the right to work; to organize labor unions; to enjoy rest, leisure time, and adequate pay; and to have access to food, clothing, housing, health care, and education. Panama emphasized the importance of individual freedom, social security, and non-discrimination. The Dominican Republic insisted on treating men and women as equals, and Mexico advocated for the right to marry, regardless of race, nationality, or gender. Nearly all these proposals made it into the final draft of what became the Universal Declaration of Human Rights.[10] Nearly all of the declaration's wording and ideas related to social rights came, according to one legal scholar, from "the tradition of Latin American Socialism." Hernán Santa Cruz, Chile's representative on the drafting committee, however, said that "Roman Catholics" had a far greater influence than Communists on the final declaration.[11]

Regional Arrangements

Rockefeller kept assuring Latin Americans that regional alliances such as the Pan-American Union would find a place within the final version of the United Nations. Yet the issue almost broke up the conference. A balance was hard to strike. The White House promised not to forsake Pan-Americanism but didn't want to "invite a general break-up of the world." If the Security Council didn't have the power to veto the actions of regional alliances, then the new global order might fragment into competing spheres of interest. There were bitter arguments within the Truman administration over these questions. The United Kingdom's Anthony Eden threatened to give up, showing an "intense dislike" for the kind of regionalism being proposed. "Clearly," he said, such proposals were "of Latin American origin."[12] "Either we have a world organization or we don't," Eden said. Michigan senator Arthur Vandenberg said he was sick of Latin Americans "pushing us around."

Rockefeller, among others, helped broker a compromise. If the United States would publicly, before the conference ended, announce it would join

Latin America's hemispheric self-defense pact, then the region's nations would be willing to place that pact within the loose jurisdiction of the United Nations. The Soviet Union, Great Britain, and China agreed to the deal.

The Department of State made its promised announcement on May 16. And drafters of the UN Charter worked out the language to capture the compromise: in the event of an attack, Article 51 guaranteed member nations the right to act individually or collectively in matters of self-defense, without having to wait to obtain permission from the UN. Article 52 not only allowed for "regional arrangements" but encouraged such arrangements to settle local disputes.[13]

Latin America's insistence on a local variance would prove a boon for the United States, as it began, slowly, to reorient its policy toward the containment of the Soviet Union. The term *Cold War* to describe the growing antagonism between the United States and the Soviet Union wouldn't be coined until April 1947, but relations between Washington and Moscow would fast unravel after the San Francisco conferences. Truman, in January 1946, told his secretary of state that it was "time to stop babying the Soviets."

And as initial rivalry hardened into a more rigid antagonism between the United States and the Soviet Union, Washington wouldn't have to choose between the region and the world. It could, thanks to Latin America, have both.

Winston Churchill himself appreciated how Pan-Americanism let Washington play a nimble "Great Game" against Moscow. On the one hand, if Latin America could be organized as a caucus behind its leadership, Washington would enjoy a disproportionate influence in steering the course of the United Nations toward isolating the Soviet Union. "We," Rockefeller said, by which he meant the United States, "could not do what we wanted on the world front unless Western Hemisphere solidarity was guaranteed." On the other hand, if the United Nations ever stood in the way of Washington's designs, the U.S. had the option of acting through its Pan-American alliance.[14]

In 1947, the United States, as promised, joined what became known as the Rio Pact, a hemispheric mutual defense treaty. Two years later, in 1949, as tensions with Moscow worsened, NATO was established, which was modeled on the Rio Pact. In 1954, the Southeast Asia Treaty Organization, or SEATO, was created, also based on the Rio Pact. Without Latin America, John Foster Dulles, an architect of the early Cold War, told Rockefeller, "there would have been no NATO, no SEATO, no Rio Pact." "There would have been nothing," said Churchill, but for Latin America.[15]

What the nations of the New World had created was unprecedented. Great Britain, Holland, and France emerged from the war either with their colonies intact or restored (even if they wouldn't keep them for long). Soviet Russia had secured its hinterlands and extended its rule over eastern Europe. Yet no power anywhere, at any time, had enjoyed authority over such a vast territory as the United States did over Latin America. And, for the moment, without much coercion. The Americas were so cemented together that it was Latin Americans themselves who demanded that their hemispheric associations remain independent, free from the meddling of the United Nations. It's hard to think of another empire, formal or informal, that ever enjoyed such a luxury: an entire resource-rich hemisphere eager to work with Washington to create a new order.

The compromise saved the United Nations. Fifty countries, twenty of them from Latin America and the Caribbean, signed the Charter of the United Nations on June 26, 1945, bringing the organization into existence.

By some estimates, the war claimed as many as eighty million lives. Such a sacrifice had to be honored by creating a better world. "The revolutionary desire to realize the kingdom of God on earth," Friedrich Schlegel wrote centuries earlier, "is the elastic point of progressive civilization and the beginning of modern history." The vision of God's Kingdom proposed by Latin Americans in their many declarations of human rights was modest: bread, a warm coat, and a decent home, as both Josephus Daniels and Allende's Socialist Party put it. Also, neonatal and maternity care, work at livable pay, land, health, equal rights, education, a good life, and dignified death, with burial insurance to cover the cost. A more "abundant world," as Roosevelt had said in Buenos Aires.

"Let us take such good things as we have put together," said the Brazilian Bertha Lutz, of the resolutions calling for health care and other social rights, "and see if we can make them grow."

Such a humble vision was not to be realized. Latin America did remain important to the United States—but increasingly more as an abstraction, or illustration of what could be accomplished on a broader global stage, than a geopolitical region that had to be accommodated.

Gone, by 1944, were the New Dealers who treated Latin America tenderly, who thought struggle against the fascist defenders of the oligarchy, and the raising of wages and provision of welfare, the best way to advance democracy. Came to power a new generation of serious men—among others, George Marshall, Dean Acheson, James Forrestal, George Kennan. To them, the four-year, many-fronted conflict proved that technology, logistics, scale, science, industry, and planning were the safeguards of democracy. The experience of global war led to a revaluation of pure power and force, of the will needed to bring the hammer down on the anvil.

In a June 1945 report to the Department of War just weeks after the fall of Berlin, Army Chief of Staff George Marshall wrote that only strength could keep the peace: "The world does not seriously regard the desires of the weak. Weakness presents too great a temptation to the strong, particularly to the bully who schemes for wealth and power. We must, if we are to realize the hopes we may now dare have for lasting peace, enforce our will for peace with strength."[16] The "gangsters of the world" must know our wrath. Marshall wasn't referring to a potential postwar conflict with the Soviet Union. He was offering a general principle no matter the gangster.

Two months later, the U.S. Army dropped atomic bombs on Hiroshima and Nagasaki. The war was over—and so seemingly was the era of modern imperialist conquest, from Cortés to Hitler.

PART VIII

THE KILLING
OF JORGE ELIÉCER GAITÁN

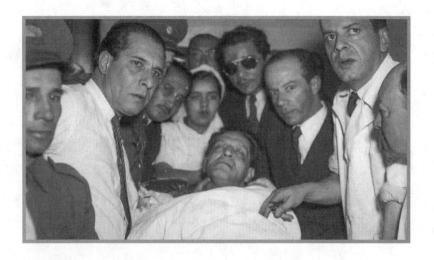

The corpse of Jorge Eliécer Gaitán in the city morgue

43.

Underdeveloped Economists

S ocial democracy seemed ascendant. In early 1944, only five Latin American countries could have been considered some kind of democracy: Mexico, Costa Rica, Colombia, Uruguay, and Chile. Two years later, in 1946, only five couldn't: Paraguay, El Salvador, Honduras, Nicaragua, and the Dominican Republic. In the mining heartland of Ecuador, Peru, Bolivia, and Chile, in oil-pumping Venezuela, in Argentina, Brazil, and Guatemala, governments either turned democratic or became more democratic, with the meaning of citizenship broadening—coming to include social welfare and a vibrant working-class mobilization, a sense that those who had long been kept on the backstreets were now filling the boulevards, taking control of the direction of history.

"We are socialists," said Juan José Arévalo, who led Guatemala's democratic revolution, "because we live in the twentieth century."

Reality was catching up to the promise. One government after another passed laws that extended social rights. Even countries still ruled by dictators saw an expansion of labor rights and the welfare state. Nicaragua's Anastasio Somoza García—installed by Washington as the repressive head of the U.S.-created National Guard after the Marines withdrew in 1933—felt the new winds blowing and adjusted accordingly. Pressured by unions, he adopted a labor code in 1944 that legalized strikes, provided workers compensation for injuries, and mandated a one-month paid vacation. Somoza called socialists the "best sons" of the nation, and in a speech that could have been delivered by Henry Wallace hailed peasants who labor from "dawn to dusk sowing the earth, and the workers in the shops and factories, and in the mines, who give their sweat and blood working through nights without stars to add to the national wealth." By the end of the war, more than four million Latin Americans belonged to a union and strike waves in Mexico, Peru, Brazil, Chile, and Argentina had wrested better pay from industries.[1]

Reformers understood their advances as part of a worldwide awakening. In "Old Europe," Salvador Allende wrote, voters have made clear they were "finished with outdated economic concepts." Even "Churchill's England" has witnessed the raising of the red flag, with the "categorical, overwhelming, resounding" victory of its Labour Party.[2]

The region's young democrats were confident, and they were ambitious. Rómulo Betancourt, the president of Venezuela, Guatemala's Arévalo, and Cuba's Ramón Grau San Martín thought the war against fascism wasn't yet over, and that a new front should be opened in the Americas to complete the "people's revolution." They financed a vanguard military group called the Caribbean Legion whose first objectives were to topple the dictators Trujillo in the Dominican Republic and Somoza in Nicaragua. The Dominican Republic was a nest for plotting right-wing Venezuelan reactionaries, so Betancourt especially was intent on getting rid of Trujillo.

The twenty-one-year-old Fidel Castro was among the twelve hundred Cubans and Dominicans who had gathered on a Cuban beach in late summer 1947 in the hope of restaging Normandy in the Caribbean. The plan was to use a couple dozen rickety fishing boats and small yachts to launch an "American D-Day" to liberate the Dominican Republic. It was their bad luck that the United States had begun, as part of its broader strategy to contain the Soviet Union, its shift away from encouraging democracy to seeking anticommunist stability. The State Department pressured Cuba's president Grau San Martín to give Trujillo a break and squash the invasion. Grau San Martín didn't have the standing to countermand Washington, so he had local police break up the flotilla. Castro jumped ship before he could be detained and swam back to shore.[3]

The Caribbean Legion's major success was siding with José Figueres in Costa Rica's civil war, on the promise that Figueres would then take the lead in overthrowing Somoza. Figueres won that war, and though he didn't oust Somoza he did push through suffrage for both women and Afro-Caribbeans, provide citizenship to the children of Black Caribbean migrants, nationalize banks, reform the tax code, and expand the welfare state. Figueres also abolished Costa Rica's military, having gotten the idea for the need for universal disarmament while a student at MIT, from reading H. G. Wells's *The Salvaging of Civilization*, which had been published in 1921.

Some socialists, including Salvador Allende, were slow to give up the idea that the United States was an agent of progress in the world. "Happily," Allende said in late 1945, "the United States of today isn't the United States of yesterday." Yet a younger generation—Fidel Castro's generation—had begun to worry about Washington's anti-Communist turn. They started demonstrating against symbols of U.S. power, calling, for example, for an end to Jim Crow segregation of Panama Canal Zone workers and for the independence of Puerto Rico. In March 1947, university students in Bogotá stoned the U.S. embassy, protesting Washington's demand that Colombia's coffee exporters stop using government-owned merchant marine ships and instead contract with United Fruit Company's private cargo ships.[4]

Still, the period immediately after the end of World War II was mostly a time of optimism. Reformers still felt that the headwinds from the Allied victory would sweep away America's last "little Hitlers."

The Dollar Curtain

Forward-looking manufacturers who wanted to move beyond exporting raw materials had expected Washington to assist in their industrialization. Vice President Henry Wallace, in 1943, had repeatedly promised that the United States would, when the Axis powers were defeated, provide capital to increase productivity and, more important, raise wages. George Messersmith, who replaced the elderly Daniels as ambassador to Mexico and was as tenacious in advancing the ideals of the Good Neighbor as his predecessor, seconded this pledge. "Mexico," Ambassador Messersmith said, "will never be a completely satisfactory neighbor" until "the present wide gap between our standards of living is reduced."

Behind closed doors in the State Department, early discussions of what eventually became the Marshall Plan—named after Truman's secretary of state, George Marshall—were focused on Europe. Officials who had visited the devastated continent returned to Washington alarmed, warning that the misery they had witnessed would surely spread Bolshevism.[5]

Yet when U.S. politicians and intellectuals talked about postwar reconstruction, they often weren't specific about details. The war had made the United States rich, with a many-billion-dollar trade surplus. It had to do something with all that money. "The United States couldn't be the world's only wealthy nation," as Truman officials liked to say. "The welfare of one country is dependent upon and derived from the welfare of other countries," said the State Department.[6] Recalling Wallace's and even FDR's pledge, Latin American politicians and industrialists could easily have gotten the impression that Washington policymakers were talking about a recovery for the whole world—or at least that part of the world that Washington had been holding up as a model for the rest of the world.

Then Secretary of State Marshall gave his June 1947 speech at Harvard announcing the plan that would bear his name. The "whole world of the future" might be hanging in the balance, and the threat of hunger-induced revolution might be worldwide, but, Marshall said, only Europe would get a vast infusion of billions of U.S. dollars to rebuild its industrial base.

Latin America not getting free public capital did not mean that the region was left out of the Marshall Plan. The denial of such capital was the plan, or at least a key part of it.

Western Europe would be reindustrialized, while "underdeveloped countries" would continue, as one report to the president put it, to export "raw materials." As early as 1945, Washington's economists expressed concern that "ways and means must be found to keep some twenty" essential Latin American commodities—that whole long list of minerals, metals, fuels, grains, and other materials that had fed the war machine—available "in sufficient volume and price to prevent economic depression." This meant discouraging Latin America from industrializing, lest investment be sucked away from resource extraction, from providing a "dependable flow of materials at the lowest cost." Washington, writes the economist Jon Kofas, was "unambiguous about subordinating Latin America's economic development to Europe's reconstruction needs." Europe, then, not only got billions of free dollars, it also benefited from a secondary subsidy, in the form of cheap Latin American resources.[7]

Learning that the Marshall Plan would not include Latin America jolted the continent's policymakers and businessmen. Several of Brazil's most prominent manufacturers convened a meeting in Petrópolis, Brazil, in October 1947, where they condemned the proposed U.S. policy as little but a continuation of the wartime economy, when most available capital (apart from some notable industrial initiatives associated with FDR) was used to meet wartime demand to extract natural resources—with nothing left to help industries develop and diversify. Now, the Marshall Plan would continue the same dynamic.[8]

Europe with its billions of free dollars to spend would, said Roberto Simonsen, a wealthy Brazilian industrialist and state senator, prompt an expected 30 to 50 percent spike in demand for raw materials. This demand would spur Latin America to expand mining, agriculture, and oil production at the expense of industry and manufacturing. Investment would be channeled to "backward" industries, while efforts to create value-added commodities would be starved for capital. Studies carried out by industrial groups in Brazil came to the same conclusion.

The region would become drunk on the dollars spent on coffee, rubber, jute, oil, bauxite, and copper. Yet once Marshall Plan funds dried up, demand would collapse and Latin America would be left with built-out mines and abandoned plantations, but no new factories.[9]

Senator Simonsen was no leftist. He won his Senate seat in a close race against Candido Portinari, Brazil's renowned modernist painter, a Communist Party member whose enormous *War* and *Peace* murals would soon adorn the entrance to the United Nation's General Assembly meeting hall.

Simonsen was committed to building a modern, capitalist, and prosperous Brazil. As did more liberal and radical economists, he warned that under the terms proposed by Washington, Latin America's "desperate poverty" would continue unabated.

Simonsen met with the country's generals and colonels at Rio de Janeiro's Clube Militar to discuss the conclusions reached at Petrópolis. He said that Latin America wasn't asking for "handouts." It was owed "compensation." Brazil, as did all Latin America, had made "wartime sacrifices." Its buildings, machinery, and tools had depreciated, worn down by relentless use. The continent had waited patiently while Washington and London delayed and delayed again opening a second European front, which many felt unnecessarily prolonged the agony of food shortages.

That Washington had refused to invite Brazil to the 1945–1946 Paris conference on war reparations was another insult Simonsen aired at the Clube Militar. In June 1942, Hitler had begun a major U-boat campaign off the coast of Latin America, with German torpedoes sinking forty-eight ships in May and June alone, many of them Brazilian. By August, the U-boats were taking out ten ships every few days. In a memo sent to the State Department, Brazil's foreign ministry enumerated the many ways Brazil's resources helped defeat fascism, all of which "caused a considerable disequilibrium of its means of productions and distribution, of daily aggravation caused by the constant drain on its transportation system and its industrial equipment."[10]

Simonsen complained that Washington, London, Paris, and Moscow had divvied up Europe's war booty. Now, the United States was refusing to help Latin America industrialize. The result would be that the "rich countries would get richer and the underdeveloped ones would continue along with an illusionary progress, becoming centers of social unrest." Simonsen's politics were not Henry Wallace's. But the two men understood the need to raise wages and improve living standards to prevent political extremism. And Simonsen's notes of aggrievement and warnings of unrest resonated among the generals in his Clube Militar audience of generals and colonels.

Such criticisms were not confined to the political class, or to industrialists like Simonsen. They quickly entered public discourse.

Brazil's powerful General Gomes echoed Simonsen, saying that "we cannot accept the colonial or semicolonial status of exporters of raw materials that later come back to our country in the form of manufactured goods with their value increased tenfold or a hundredfold." Gomes continued: "The Marshall Plan, for Europe alone, will represent the continuation, if not the aggravation, of Brazil's subordinate situation." Next door in Argentina, Juan Perón, elected president in June 1946, had his critics in the rest of Latin America, left, liberal, and right. Yet many shared his opinion that, while Moscow might have lowered an Iron Curtain across Europe, Washington was trying to lock Latin America behind a "Dollar Curtain."[11]

The Great Heresiarch

Sociologists and economists began to methodize the complaints of industrialists and politicians. The reams of statistics produced by wartime planning made it easier for researchers to study the economy and to produce a critical theory of economic underdevelopment. "Agricultural prices have fallen more profoundly than those of manufactured articles," wrote Raúl Prebisch. Why?

Prebisch, founder of Argentina's Central Bank, made his name answering that question, with what would become known as the Prebisch-Singer thesis. The thesis's coauthor, Hans Singer, was a German-born United Nations economist who came to the same conclusion as Prebisch independently: that over time, the terms of trade between a resource-exporting country and a value-adding manufacturing country would worsen at the expense of the first.

The price of raw materials was more vulnerable to competition from other countries than were manufactured goods. Many countries grew wheat. Few made state-of-the-art threshers. And there were no steps any single resource-exporting country could take on its own to counter the trend and its dire consequences. A government might depreciate its currency to make its exports cheaper. Yet that would lead to punishing domestic inflation, reducing the value of wages. And the benefits of technological advances tended to accrue to those nations that already were technologically advanced, deepening the rift.

In the past, observers talked about Great and Small Powers, or divided the world between creditor and debtor nations. Now Prebisch described, in 1946, the world as comprised of a "core" of industrial nations and a "periphery" of resource-exporting nations. It was an idea that had been intuited by many, but Prebisch popularized the imagery. There was a "structural rift" in the world's political economy between manufacturing and raw-material-exporting nations, a fundamental inequality that "free trade" made worse.[12]

A hemispheric system divided between a mass of countries whose laborers earned a dollar a day in mining and one country producing jackhammers and drill bits for wages of three dollars or more an hour was untenable. According to the Prebisch-Singer thesis, that wage gap would inevitably widen as the terms of trade deteriorated, leading the world back to the kinds of depressions and recessions that breed extremism and war.

Later, a leading Colombian economist explained how Prebisch's theory played out in a world of unequal power relations, using an example from 1954: With Colombian coffee selling at eighty cents a pound that year, it took fourteen sacks of the crop to buy, for $1,377.00, one Willys Jeep. But U.S. coffee importers thought eighty cents a pound an exorbitant price and so they launched an extensive PR campaign to reduce the amount of Colombian coffee the United States imported, including advertisements designed to convince the "American housewife" to water down her husband's morning brew. Banks stepped in and made loans to nations on "other continents" to expand coffee production. The point of the campaign was to teach coffee-exporting nations a lesson: if you try to raise prices, we have a range of options to break you. As world coffee prices fell, so did the wages of those who picked the beans. Colombian growers increased exports to try to make up the difference, but the country's foreign exchange earnings on coffee still dropped by 42 percent.[13]

Within a year, the number of coffee sacks needed to buy one jeep jumped from fourteen to forty-three.

In the mid-1940s, around the time Prebisch and Singer's work was becoming known, economists in top-tier research universities in the United States were elaborating elegant mathematical models "proving" the opposite: that trade, left unencumbered, would transfer wealth and power from prosperous to poor countries. In the United States, these models—part of what is now called neoclassical economics—became creedal. But in Latin America, Prebisch's less formalistic, more muscular arguments, grounded in history and attuned to political power, caught on. They were expanded by other scholars to show how "free trade" had locked in underdevelopment. Politicians picked them up to justify policies promoting import substitution, including the imposition of high tariffs on imports to nurture local industries.

Late in life, Prebisch complained about the way economists at places like Harvard and Chicago radiated "arrogance toward those poor underdeveloped economists of the periphery." They treated Latin American scholars as "second-class economists, or even third class," as though underdeveloped economies could only produce "underdeveloped economists."

Prebisch thought the rich world's orthodox economists "scholastic," working from a false first premise: that a free market funded by private capital would lead to an equitable balance of supply and demand, prices and wages. That first erroneous idea, accepted as writ, gave rise to ever more fantastical follow-up assertions bearing little relationship to the way the world works. They were used to justify, not explain, inequality, thus becoming "ideological weapons." Prebisch's followers called him *El Gran Heresiarca*, or the Great Heresiarch. More than a heretic, Prebisch was the founder of a heresy.[14]

Look around, Prebisch said. It's not like in your textbooks. The only way out of the trap was to provide poorer, peripheral nations with low-cost or free credit, letting them control their exchange rates and direct investment. Government intervention was needed to steer capital away from mines and fields toward factories. The continent faced two alternatives, Prebisch said: remain an impoverished supplier of raw material to the United States and Europe, or *"crecer hacia adentro"*—"grow inward"—and industralize. *Crecer hacia adentro* would become a battle cry for postwar Latin American economists.[15]

Soon, various strands of critical economics would take the name *dependency theory*. Less a unified body of thought than an ethical impulse, dependency theory held that the development of the first world *depended* on the underdevelopment of the third. Latin America, wrote the Uruguayan Eduardo Galeano, has been since the Conquest force-fitted into "the universal gearbox of capitalism," its history "an endless chain of dependency endlessly extended."[16]

To break the chain of dependence, Latin Americans like Simonsen and Prebisch believed that their region needed its own comprehensive Marshall Plan. Without access to public credit and capital, the region's nations would never get out of debt, never have a sustainable balance of trade and thus a stable currency. They'd never be able to pay wages high enough for its citizens to enjoy a decent life.

And they'd never be able to build stable, durable political institutions to back a sustained program of reform and modernization, as FDR was able to do with the New Deal in the United States. Political turmoil in Latin America was nothing new. Bolívar at the end of his life saw no exit from the chaos. Allied victory had seemed to promise a way out of the labyrinth, as the region's politics coalesced around a deeply popular social-democratic consensus.

Yet no stable coalition (like the New Deal) would emerge to transform that consensus into an enduring program, and critical economists now had an explanation: crisis was systemic, a feature of a global economy in which the prosperity—and the good, strong coffee that started a workingman's day—of the core depended on the poverty of the periphery.

As the details of the Marshall Plan were coming into view, the State Department, along with Latin America's foreign ministries, were putting together the agenda of what would be the ninth—and last—Pan-American Conference, to be held in Bogotá, Colombia, in March and April 1948.

Expectations ran high. Conference delegates were to lay to rest the sixty-eight-year-old Pan-American Union, which had shepherded the hemisphere through the world wars, and call into existence the Organization of American States, a body meant to represent the ambitions of a postwar world. Latin Americans saw the OAS—with its own American Declaration of the Rights and Duties of Man—as a complement to the United Nations, a key part of the worldwide assemblage of the new multilateral order. They also saw the Bogotá meeting as a chance to press their economic demands on the United States.

To that end, Chile's ambassador to the United Nations, Hernán Santa Cruz, had proposed in July 1947 that the UN create a permanent task force: the Economic Commission for Latin America and the Caribbean, or CEPAL, as it was called in Spanish and Portuguese, a body to support the work of critical economists. Santa Cruz imagined CEPAL playing a role not just in Latin American but in "world economic reconstruction"—repairing the ravages not of war but of unequal terms of trade and interest rates.[17]

Santa Cruz, a former Jesuit student and close friend of Salvador Allende, was at that moment also helping Eleanor Roosevelt draft the United Nation's Declaration of Human Rights. He knew that liberalism would have to take up questions of political economy if it was to be more than a slogan. "Democracy—political as well as social and economic—comprises, in my mind," he said, "an inseparable whole." And so he hoped that a working group like CEPAL that focused on economics would help make the ideals embodied in the declaration a reality.[18] In the coming decades, some of Latin America's most influential heterodox economists would begin their careers at CEPAL.

The United States tried but failed to block CEPAL's creation, and then it did all it could to hamstring its work once it was established in February 1948. State and Commerce were then not only designing the Marshall Plan but also organizing the General Agreement on Tariffs and Trade—to rebuild the world's economy around the terms of free trade. The last thing Washington wanted was a permanent grievance bureau—a radical department of economics, chaired by Raúl Prebisch himself.[19]

A Chapter on Latin America

This, then, was the setup for the 1948 Bogotá conference: A continent mobilized. Citizens asking for an expansion of the welfare state; workers demanding higher pay; scholars putting forth new, compelling explanations to account for poverty and instability; and politicians and industrialists looking for cheap credit.

The region's envoys arrived in Colombia ready to cash in their chits, to get from Washington what it was owed—for Latin America's sacrifices, for its resources, for its good faith, for its usefulness as a model Washington touted elsewhere as an ideal of postwar reconstruction. Mexico expected massive United States aid and investment, something like the Tennessee Valley Authority, but for the whole hemisphere. The people of the Americas were "no longer moved by pamphlets filled with high-sounding principles," Mexico's foreign minister had said. "The way to the heart of the masses is through raising the standard of living."[1]

They were greeted by a secretary of state, George Marshall, who would offer them trifles.

As if to intentionally mock expectations and exacerbate resentment, President Harry Truman signed the Marshall Plan into law on April 3, shortly after talks in Colombia had gotten under way. No funds were included for Latin American reconstruction. As the plan's formal name made clear, it was exclusively a European Recovery Program. Earlier in the year, after the government of Brazil had asked Washington to fund a modest program of industrial development, the White House sent down a commission headed by the economist John Abbink, chairman of McGraw-Hill, to study the request. The commission's response: try "self-help," and "do it yourself." Adding to such insults, Truman, when pressed on whether Latin America would receive a recovery plan, answered: "There has been a Latin American Marshall plan for the Western Hemisphere for a century and a half and known as the Monroe Doctrine."[2]

Those Who Love the Region Are Few

Marshall had little to give because Washington had, by this point, moved on from the region.

The train of global events hurtled forward, as fighting a Cold War against Moscow became official policy. Early skirmishes took place in northern Iran and Turkey. In March 1947, Truman delivered what the *Chicago Tribune* called his "Cold War Against Russia" speech, giving "notice that Russian communism is regarded as an enemy force which will be resisted where it is encountered." One such encounter was in Greece's civil war, where Truman announced he was sending millions of dollars and military advisers to help a collaborationist government made up of pro-Hitler fascists and monarchists against popular-front partisan rebels who had fought against Nazi occupation. Also in March, Truman instituted a loyalty program for federal employees. In June, the Taft-Hartley Act watered down the National Labor Relations Act. In July, Truman signed the National Security Act, creating the National Security Agency and the Central Intelligence Agency, which immediately began delivering "bags of money" to allies in Italy and France, hoping to prevent popular Communists who fought the Nazi rule from becoming a viable political force.[3]

In February 1948, Czechoslovakia's Communist Party seized power. A month later, the U.S. began to expand its peacetime military budget. "Every department of the government now has gone warlike," Truman said. By this, he meant that an aggressive bipartisan policy against the Soviet Union would justify all-around spending, that the United States could have guns and butter, that it could fund the New Deal at home and fight the Cold War abroad.[4]

The world's war was over yet nothing seemed settled. British colonialism was winding down, leaving, in many places, political and racial schism in its wake. The end of London's rule in South Asia resulted in the partition of India and Pakistan, with millions killed and millions more displaced. In early 1947, the paramilitary Stern Gang began attacking Palestinian villages, as Israeli forces drove hundreds of thousands of Palestinians from their homes. Elsewhere, the territories that made up the French and Dutch empires demanded an end to colonialism. In China, Mao Zedong's Communist army was marching toward victory.

Nothing seemed settled, except in Latin America. At the start of 1948, there existed no significant conflicts among the hemisphere's nations, no threat of interstate war. There were protests, strikes, and riots, yet nothing on the scale of violence elsewhere. The region was not only within the United States' sphere of influence, it was uncomplicatedly and willingly within that sphere.

Washington's new Cold War national security apparatus was mostly in place. It included not just the CIA and the NSA but the Policy Planning Staff at State, headed by George Kennan, along with nongovernmental policy shops, such as the Council on Foreign Relations, in Cambridge and New York. Their mimeographs rolled out memos, directives, and analyses at a rapid clip, on topics related to Europe, Asia, the Middle East, and Africa.

As the mountains of policy papers piled up on staffers' desks, there remained a studied incuriosity about Latin America. The war had produced a new cohort of geostrategic thinkers who shunted the region into the shadows. Yale's Nicholas Spykman feared that Washington would lose the postwar peace if it concentrated its power solely in the Western Hemisphere. Control of Latin America, Spykman said, could not compensate for loss of influence in Europe and Asia. If Washington intended to continue its ascendence in a postwar world, it had to, in effect, forget about Latin America and start thinking about the world as a whole.

The region fell out of mind. What mattered was a renewed Washington–London alliance, with a focus on a rebuilt Western Europe and, now that Mao was in Peking, a Japan-centered Asia.[5]

Some of these planners were militantly hostile to the idea of the Monroe Doctrine. A more than century-long obsession with geography—"the Western Hemisphere Idea"—had constrained the imagination, they argued; the Atlantic would provide no more protection to the United States than did the Maginot Line for France. It was time to shake off the shackles of Pan-Americanism. United States interests had to be projected and protected globally. Others thought the Monroe Doctrine tied U.S. fortunes to racially suspect nations. "Great Britain, Canada, Australia, and even Germany have closer racial ties with the United States than does Latin America," read one Council on Foreign Relations study.[6]

"Schemes" to bind the Americas together were foolhardy, the council maintained. Latin Americans were "nearly always" falling into crisis, forcing the United States to intervene and then complaining about intervention.

Even the CIA at first treated Latin America with contempt, as an "old Hoover fiefdom," where the Bureau's agents, now that the war was over, did little more than gossip and frequent brothels. "Men who know the hemisphere and love it are few," lamented Adolf Berle. Those few who did know it had other kinds of feelings. Truman continued to fill Latin American posts with Southerners, with Texans in particular, the ideological kin of William Buckley and others who, financially and emotionally invested in Mexico, hated economic nationalism.[7]

In mid-February 1948, George Kennan's Policy Planning Staff produced a paper meant to "trace the lines of development of our foreign policy as they emerged from our actions in the past, and to project them into the future, so that we could see where we were going." Sending the paper on to Marshall, Kennan apologized for not including Latin America. "The document should properly have included a chapter on Latin America," Kennan said. But, he confessed, "I am not familiar with the problems of the area, and the Staff has not yet studied them."[8]

The irony: Good-Neighbor Pan-Americanism was such a spectacular diplomatic and strategic success that, after Allied victory, not much diplomacy or strategy was needed to administer the region. Latin America fell back to being a place to make money and rehearse new strategies of global policing. By 1948, the White House and the State Department had largely ceded responsibility for Latin America to the Pentagon and the private sector.[9]

A Vast, Untapped Market

Roosevelt was barely in his grave when in April 1945 the State Department made clear it wanted, as quickly as possible, to move toward fewer exchange controls, and to lower tariffs, end subsidies, and, above all, protect investment and private property. Washington even began using the Export-Import Bank—originally established to help Latin America industrialize—to provide loans to U.S. companies to purchase nationalized industries in Mexico and elsewhere.[10]

The corporate bloc that had come together during FDR's first term still supported the New Deal, yet its industries began to take an aggressive stance in foreign policy. Export-oriented companies were ably represented by the National Foreign Trade Council (and its hemispheric affiliate, the Council for Inter-American Cooperation). In December 1947—just before Kennan told Marshall he had nothing to say on Latin America—the council presented the Truman administration a twenty-two-page detailed report, *Economic Proposals for Consideration*: a wish list of policies businesses wanted Marshall to push for at the Bogotá conference. Latin American nations, the report said, should give up on demanding Marshall Plan–like grants or cheap loans. They should, instead, create a "healthy investment climate" by forswearing nationalization and guaranteeing private property, low tax rates, and profit repatriation.

In effect, the proposals called for the continuation of every aspect of hemispheric trade that critics like Simonsen and Prebisch said were part of a system of structural, and worsening, inequality.[11]

Latin America was to be a trial run: if the United States could overcome the objections of nationalists and liberalize capital and sanctify property rights in the Western Hemisphere, it would "furnish an example to the rest of the world."

Economic Proposals conveyed urgency. The United States had "emerged from the war as the greatest creditor nation in the world with a capacity for production unequaled in the history of the world. The government, the report said, must find outlets for private capital and credit to sustain the demand. The "present level of prosperity" depended on ensuring that Latin America would soak up private surplus capital, which in turn would both expand the export of commodities back to the United States and expand the market for U.S.-made goods.

The industries that made up the National Foreign Trade Council fully supported Truman's Cold War push. Businessmen overwhelmingly (70 percent according to a *Fortune* poll) backed the Marshall Plan. They clapped when the president said he was sending Curtiss Helldivers to the fascists and monarchists in Greece, to bomb and strafe partisan holdouts in the Pindus Mountains, driving the last of the rebels into Albania. They supported the creation of both the United Nations and NATO. They didn't complain when Congress passed a peacetime arms buildup budget, despite fears of inflation.

In exchange for such support, they wanted Latin America. They wanted their views not just represented but put into operation. Bogotá was a chance to sweep away the claptrap that FDR had indulged and reestablish the authority of investors. No more of Wallace's "labor clauses."

And no more Calvo clauses, the contractual provisions that forced foreign investors to agree that they were protected only by the laws of the countries they invested in and couldn't appeal to Washington or London to back them up in their disputes. Major industries, including General Electric, Kennecott Copper, Standard Oil, United Fruit, General Foods, Goodrich, International Harvester, and General Motors would soon tell Truman officials to sign no treaty that affirmed the legality of the Calvo Doctrine. These industries hired Dean Acheson's old law firm to press the issue. Don't even mention Calvo as a "procedural point," the attorneys said. To do so "might enhance the doctrine as a principle of international law." At stake was control. In a decolonizing world comprised of sovereign nations, the protection of property rights was one of the few legal mechanisms great powers had left to vouchsafe their greatness.

Economic Proposals urged Washington "to go to Bogotá with a complete program of economic cooperation, consistent with the principles of the private enterprise system." To make available Latin America's "vast, untapped market" for "American exporters of machinery, construction materials, hardware and electrical equipment." For radios, refrigerators, power generators, motion-picture projectors, textile and mill machinery, and dairy equipment, for trucks, trains, ships, planes, cars, and Willys Jeeps. Pharmaceutical executives believed the Latin American market was worth $150 million. Madison Avenue advertising agents too were eager to expand in Latin America. The United States Chamber of Commerce told Truman and Marshall that it wanted "a suitable climate" for investment in all the "American Republics."[12]

These were the corporations that provided the economic foundation for the twin goals of Cold War liberalism: a gradual expansion of political rights at home and a hard-line against Soviet Communism in defense of open markets abroad. Truman, up for election in November in a close race against Thomas Dewey, would not buck this bloc.[13]

The Reaction

Back in Latin America, the postwar social-democratic spring had come under assault. Already before the Bogotá Conference, violence against union and peasant activists was on the rise. True, the defeat of fascism had animated democrats and socialists, reformers who thought social rights were as much a part of democracy as the right to vote. More quietly, it fortified what the U.S. Army, in one of its reports on the region, called "the reaction."

The expanded security and intelligence agencies used to root out Nazis were now targeting not just Communists but all labor and peasant activists. The wartime buildup of Latin American militaries created a powerful "Pan-American" class of ranked officials with shared worldviews. Military officers approved of Truman's anti-Soviet "Arms Plan" since it meant they'd continue to receive weapons and training. Cuban army officers who traveled to the United States for training, wrote one reporter, "have returned home enthusiasts for the Norteamericano way." Since there were no interstate wars on the horizon, the weaponry was for domestic use.[14]

The destruction of Latin America's social-democratic interlude began in earnest as countries were preparing to attend the Bogotá conference. Chile is illustrative.

In September 1946, Chileans elected Gabriel González Videla president, continuing the antifascist popular-front coalition. Pablo Neruda, then a senator representing the Communist Party, served as one of Videla's campaign managers and even wrote him a poem. On campaign stops, Videla recited Neruda's "The People Call You Gabriel" with tears in his eyes as he promised to end the suffering of Chile's people. Videla wasn't even in office a month when, in November, the State Department sent word it was unhappy with his pro-union policies and, acting on behalf of New York banks, cut Chile off from credit and loans.

Caught between rising inflation (due to cut-off credit) and demands for better pay, Videla broke his alliance with the left, cracking down hard on unions. When eighteen thousand miners walked off their jobs demanding better pay, Videla attacked. He sent in the Good Neighbor–fortified armed forces who, writes historian Jody Pavilack, took "total control of the mines, towns, and surrounding countryside" and "sent hundreds of people to military prison camps and banished thousands more from the region." Just four years earlier, many of these strikers had heard Henry Wallace tell them they were democracy's front line. Now, they were being hunted down by a young army captain, Augusto Pinochet, who rounded up coal and nitrate miners and detained them in the Pisagua penal colony in the Atacama Desert, which during the war held Germans, Japanese, and Italians who had been living in Chile as residents and citizens. (During his dictatorship, Pinochet would use Pisagua again, as a detention and torture center and site of mass graves for victims of his regime.)[15]

Massacres had occurred before in Chilean history. Never, though, says Pavilack, had a president ordered a "full military assault on an entire region of the nation." Likewise in Ecuador around this time, the government used tanks and planes it received from the U.S.'s wartime Lend-Lease program to lay siege to a student protest led by what the *New York Herald Tribune* called the "anti-communist and moderate-minded Socialist Party." Bolivia and Paraguay also used United States–supplied tanks to break up strikes. Back in Chile, Videla followed up by passing the "Permanent Defense of Democracy" law, which stripped the right to vote from thousands of Communists, a law so draconian that even the Falangist leader, Eduardo Frei, condemned the legislation as unconstitutional. Videla used it to crush the Communist Party, sending Neruda into exile.*

Throughout Latin America—as Bogotá's municipal authorities readied their city for the Pan-American Conference, building new hotels and restaurants, cleaning the streets, whitewashing downtown buildings—Washington had begun pressuring countries to adopt similar laws that banned Communists and Communist parties from political life.[16]

Starting at the end of March 1948, representatives from twenty-one American states began to arrive in Bogotá, where they would establish the Organization of American States. The New World finally had its preamble: "The historic mission of America is to offer to man a land of liberty."

Secretary of State General George Marshall officiated. During the war, as FDR's army chief of staff, Marshall had presided over the fastest and largest military expansion in history. He had a half a world at his command. Now, though, he had limited room for maneuver and worked with considerably fewer resources. Think back to Hull in Montevideo. Then, world crisis, the informality of the Roosevelt administration, the sudden impotence of economic elites, and the fact that since no one really knew what to do even dissidents like Gruening got a hearing, gave Secretary of State Hull remark-

---

* That this crackdown took place at the *exact* moment Hernán Santa Cruz was serving as Chile's representative to the United Nations, helping to found CEPAL and pushing for the inclusion of economic rights in the Universal Declaration of Human Rights, highlights the disjuncture between repression at home and high ideals abroad—not as hypocrisy but desperation, the idea held by many Latin Americans that domestic politics couldn't be stabilized until the interstate system that destabilized them was reformed.

able latitude to both satisfy Latin American demands and set up his own free-trade agenda.

Marshall, in contradistinction, was one cog in an ever more complex machine, a multipart imperial engine comprised of an array of powerful interests. And he had little to offer. Washington wanted to run its "showcase for the world" on the cheap. Between 1946 and 1950, Latin America received a paltry $446 million in aid (about a quarter from grants and the rest Export-Import Bank loans). During this same period, the United States gave Europe $23 billion. Between 1945 and 1951, Washington gave Belgium and Luxembourg more direct aid than it did *all* Latin America.

In Bogotá, Marshall admitted that Europe "comes first on our priorities list" and stuck to the script provided by the National Foreign Trade Council. Standing in front of a portrait of Simón Bolívar, he delivered a long speech on April 1 instructing delegates to return to their home countries and "remove barriers to private capital investment." The United States, Marshall said, had prospered with "private capital from abroad" after it won its independence, and there was no reason Latin America couldn't as well.[17]

Latin Americans in the audience responded to Marshall's speech with dismay, followed by a week of intense criticism. On April 8, Marshall said he had an announcement to make. Some hoped that the complaints had hit home, that Truman had rethought the United States' postwar economic program for Latin America. He hadn't. Marshall told the gathered delegates that Washington would free up a few million dollars in loans to be used for development. But Marshall reiterated that there would be no major program of economic assistance. "Capital required during the coming years," the secretary of state said, "must come from private sources."[18]

"You could see people literally going down like a pricked balloon," said one person in the audience.[19]

The next day, Bogotá went up in flames.

45.

The Killing of Gaitán

At 1:00 p.m. on April 9, the man thought to be Colombia's president-in-waiting, Jorge Eliécer Gaitán, was shot to death on Seventh Avenue, one of downtown Bogotá's busiest streets.

Dressed neatly in a midnight-blue suit, Gaitán had stepped out of his law office for lunch. He was standing in front of a popular nightclub, El Gato Negro, surrounded by several associates. A young man named Juan Roa Sierra, later said to be unstable, pushed through the lunchtime crowd and approached Gaitán from behind. As he stepped closer to the circle of men, Roa raised a small, nickel-plated pistol and fired three times, putting one bullet in Gaitán's head and two in his back.

Gaitán's death was nearly instantaneous. The uprising that followed was so powerful, so violent, it can't but be read as a metaphor: all the energy compressed in the postwar, all the passions and repressed expectations, had reached combustion point—so intense that, in retrospect, it could be read as a preview of the Cold War horror to come.

Earlier, in 1944, the Guatemalan Juan José Arévalo had said that he believed that the spread of social democracy marked the arrival of the twentieth century in Latin America. The Colombian Gabriel García Márquez, who was on the scene, thought otherwise, thought that with Gaitán's death it wasn't hope but anguish that marked modern times. "In the full light of day," he wrote in his memoirs, "I think I became aware that on April 9, 1948, the twentieth century had begun in Colombia."[1]

The city exploded. Bootblacks used their shine boxes to beat Roa to death. By morning, much of Bogotá was reduced to ruin. Protesters had set buildings aflame. The large, dry beams that held up its impressive colonial adobe facades burned like tinder as the conference delegates scattered, some going into hiding, others taking shelter on military bases or behind barricaded embassy residences.

The New Ones

El Negro Gaitán, as the Liberal Party leader was called, was born in 1898 into a poor mestizo family, his mother a teacher and father a bookseller. He worked hard and earned a law degree from the national university. Some thought cold, coffee-dependent Bogotá the "Athens of South America," and in its many cafés, especially Café Windsor, student factions argued the world, as they say.

Politicians had long grouped together in two parties, Conservative and Liberal. Both were elite parties, though in the early decades of the twentieth century the left wing of the Liberal Party began to push for higher wages, better housing conditions, and land reform, building a base in the countryside and among unions.

A younger generation added to the ferment. One student group called itself *los nuevos*—the new ones, the moderns. They rejected a stultifying political order run by and for elites who, in addition to losing Panama in 1903, had practically given away Colombia's Caribbean coast to the United Fruit Company. Most were attracted to socialism, introduced to Marxist and other radical literature by Silvestre Savitsky, a Russian émigré who ran a print shop in downtown Bogotá. Some would go on to found socialist and communist parties or work to further radicalize the Liberal Party. Others took the name *los Leopardos*—the Leopards—and planted fascism in Colombia. The line between the two groups was blurry, at least until Hitler seized power and clarified matters.[2]

Young Gaitán, at first, straddled the middle. Both movements were contemptuous of their country's languid ruling elders. Both were concerned with national sovereignty. All were Bolivarian: they wanted the world made whole, to stem the disaggregation caused by the pursuit of individual interests and private corruptions. Gaitán moved leftward. His law thesis, "Socialist Ideas in Colombia," focused on the possibility of using the state and the law as bulwarks against the "absurd" power elites held in the country.

He traveled to Rome in 1926 to study under Enrico Ferri in the Royal University, shortly after Benito Mussolini, already prime minister, had declared Italy a Fascist state. Ferri was of Mussolini's generation, a liberal socialist who helped modernize the legal code to treat crime as a social problem. Gaitán arrived in Italy just as Ferri was throwing himself into Fascist service and repudiating his earlier progressive scholarship.[3]

While in Rome, Gaitán attended Fascist rallies and saw firsthand the power of Fascist theatrics, particularly Mussolini's emotional oratory, whose tonal modulations and spontaneous bodily gestures created a bond with and among the crowd. Gaitán graduated with honors yet did so without sipping from Ferri's Fascist cup—or not deeply. Unlike, say, Chile's Francisco Bilbao, his vision of a just society didn't entail abolishing but rather shoring up the patriarchal family. He emphasized social order, organized around traditional roles for men and women.[4]

Gaitán left Italy as Mussolini was stepping up his repression of socialist-aligned unions—returning to Colombia where the Conservative Party–led government was doing the same.

The banana-growing Caribbean slopes were gripped by a series of wildcat strikes that crippled the operations of the United Fruit Company. The local U.S. consul described the region as in a state of "revolt" with strikers waging "guerrilla warfare." United States warships patrolled the coast to support the company, providing an opportunity for opposition leaders to remind the public that similar vessels had been used to take Panama a few decades earlier. Would the Caribbean be the next region to be dismembered? Washington backed the Colombian government crackdown on the banana workers' union, which included the mass arrest of strikers and their transport to a remote prison. Such actions "would give adequate protection to American interests," the U.S. ambassador wrote to the secretary of state. On December 6, 1928, the Colombian army placed machine guns on a roof overlooking a public square packed with workers and their families assembled to listen to the state governor's address. Soldiers opened fire, killing over a thousand people.* According to witnesses, soldiers fired their machine guns and then used company equipment to dig mass graves. Buried were not just the dead but the wounded, still alive when the dirt was pushed back into the pit.[5]

Revolution on the March

Gaitán, soon a rising star in the Liberal Party and member of congress, toured the banana zone and was shocked by the poverty. He returned to Bogotá and commandeered Congress for a fifteen-day filibuster, giving speech after speech describing the violent humiliation families endured at the hands of the military and fruit company thugs. Gaitán used the moment to rehearse the oratory style he had heard in Italy, mixing political theory, facts, personal stories, outrage, and sentimentalism. Thanks to the new technology of radio, nearly the whole nation listened to his performance, often from speakers set up in town plazas. Gaitán identified Colombia's "oligarchy" as an obstacle to peace and democracy during one of his speeches, and he charged the United Fruit Company with bribing soldiers with money and prostitutes. The Conservative government acted as the handmaid of the banana company, he said, and compared Colombia to Nicaragua, which was then convulsed by an insurgent opposition to U.S. occupation.[6]

Gaitán may have been influenced by Fascist theatrics, but he was opposed to authoritarianism. Violence was a sign of weakness, he thought, restraint an indicator of power. He denounced Colombian democracy as a "simulacrum" enjoyed exclusively by the well-off. He didn't want to shatter the illusion but rather call the substance of democracy into being, by using

---

* Later, García Márquez would use this killing as the climax of *One Hundred Years of Solitude*.

government institutions and laws to provide Colombians a decent, just existence.

Liberals began winning national elections in 1930, in large part thanks to Gaitán's forceful public advocacy. In 1934, Alfonso López Pumarejo became president and launched what he called a *revolución en marcha*, a revolution on the march, on the move—an early expression of the social-democratic politics that would take hold elsewhere in Latin America in 1944. López adopted a labor code, increased taxes on oil exports, expanded welfare services, and implemented a land distribution program.

Conservatives fought back. Traditionalist priests seeded the countryside with allied peasant settlers, building bulwark villages tied to the extreme right. "Only by means of the kind of terror demonstrated majestically by Hitler," said Silvio Villegas, a founder of the Leopards and now, in 1937, a fascist leader of the Conservative Party, "will the threat of the proletariat be silenced." The Conservative Party returned to power in 1946—not because of a coup or repression but due to a split between moderates and radicals in the Liberal Party, which allowed the Conservative Party to win a presidential election with only 41 percent of the vote. Still, the coming to power of a party that was ever more openly fascist was experienced by many Colombians as part of a wider backlash to the idea of a hemispheric New Deal. Violence against rank-and-file peasants aligned with the Liberal or Communist parties spiked in the countryside. Thousands fled to Venezuela, hundreds were killed. *La revolución en marcha* was in retreat.[7]

During this moment of Conservative pushback, Gaitán became a national focal point, a figurehead public defender, a clear, forceful tribune standing up in Bogotá and denouncing the killing of peasants and workers. His popularity by 1947 was messianic. One labor leader noted that in the rural department of Bolívar, "all campesinos have a portrait of Gaitán in their homes, and daily they tend it with a *mística* that approaches adoration." Gaitán's magnetism drew young activists into his circle, not just Colombians but from all the Americas. Fidel Castro, fresh from participation in the failed effort to invade the Dominican Republic and overthrow Trujillo, was in Bogotá at the time of his death, as part of a larger contingent of activist students. Gaitán, with his long history of fighting against the United

Fruit Company, shared this younger generation's sense that the United States had turned. That it wasn't a vanguard of global democracy but the patron of reaction. In speeches and editorials, Gaitán accused the U.S. military attachés of arranging for weapons, bombs, and tear gas to be flown into the country from the Canal Zone on U.S. planes and distributed to Colombian fascists.[8]

The Conservative Party's main ideologue was the aged Laureano Gómez, who was close to Franco. Gómez was a xenophobic racist, believing that the nation's rot could be found in the "black element," that is, Colombians of African descent. Fanatically opposed to land reform and the idea that the right to property ownership should be subordinated to the larger common welfare, Colombia's Falangists had become some hybridized spawn of Sepúlveda and Locke: theocratic racists committed to an absolutist theory of property rights. "Imbecile Indians" didn't know the worth of property, Gómez said, and therefore could claim no right of possession.[9]

When Gómez talked of the "black element" and the "imbecile Indian" he was talking about Gaitán. El Negro Gaitán had something of the field hand about him, something of the corn plot. Colombia's political discourse, apart from occasional remarks like the kind just cited by Gómez, wasn't explicitly racialized. But Gaitán, and his movement, were considered "dark," not just *dark* meaning skin tone but *dark* meaning sinister. Or both. The historian Herb Braun writes that campaign photos of him "show a dark-complected Gaitán, his eyes half closed in the culturally recognized sign of suspicion and distrust held to be characteristic of *malicia indígena*." Yet these weren't images disseminated by his detractors; Gaitán himself deployed them. His followers draped Bogotá with banners showing Gaitán baring white teeth, projecting authority and menace. After being vilified for so long as El Negro Gaitán, Braun writes, he was now "forcing his image" on the nation's subconscious. Yet he never talked about race or racism. Just *el pueblo*.[10]

In preparation for the next presidential election in 1950, Gaitán had pledged the Liberal Party to "struggle against the forces of regression that are trying to impose fascism or falangism on our countries." He also promised to nationalize all fundamental public services, to implement a fair tax system, to expand labor and land reform, and, despite his earlier misogyny, to guarantee equal rights for men and women.[11]

Gaitán used the markers of race to signal power, pride, and danger. He also used similar earthy images to project accessibility.

"I have invited the pueblo to participate in politics," Gaitán said in 1947, and "I believe that the salvation of our country resides in all of us participating in politics."[12]

Beyond the Spanish Country

Gabriel García Márquez's memoir captures Gaitán's attraction. As a university student, García Márquez had resisted the Liberal Party politician. The young reporter and future novelist ran in Communist circles, and Communists viewed Gaitán with suspicion, believing that his talk of *el pueblo* obscured rather than clarified class relations, while his popularity in the countryside was undermining Communist support.

But then on one chilly Andean night, García Márquez was walking home to his Bogotá boardinghouse when he was suddenly startled by a crisp, metallic voice that bounced off the walls of the old city's narrow streets. He had stumbled upon one of Gaitán's regular Friday rallies. Gaitán's speech, he said, sounded liked the "lashes of a whip." The rally's venue was the city's municipal theater, which held no more than a thousand people. But the speech was broadcast "in concentric waves," first by loudspeakers and then "radios played at top volume."

García Márquez called his encounter a "revelation." Most politicians in Colombia still gave speeches in a stilted Spanish formalism incomprehensible to most citizens. But hearing Gaitán, he understood "all at once" his rhetorical power. Not only did Gaitán redefine the conflict gripping Colombia: the nation wasn't divided between Liberals and Conservatives, he said, but exploiters and the exploited, and he called for a union of the "liberal-conservative commoners" against the "liberal-conservative oligarchy." But he did so in understandable language. Gaitán "had gone beyond the Spanish country"—that is, beyond the heavy use of legal abstractions and hollow formulae, of tortured, passive syntax—to invent a democratic "lingua franca for everyone."

Gaitán's subject that night was "an unadorned recounting of the devastation caused by official violence," the killing of peasants and the growing population of starving refugees who had fled to the cities. After completing his mournful tally, Gaitán's voice began to rise and the "tension in the audience increased to the rhythm of his speech, until a final outburst exploded within the confines of the city and reverberated on the radio into the most remote corners of the country."[13]

Gaitán, as did Allende in Chile, rejected the use of force to achieve political ends. He valued procedural democracy. He didn't explicitly preach a politics of nonviolence, as Gandhi had in South Asia and Martin Luther King would soon do in the United States. But he did politicize silence. Since the Liberal Party lost power in 1946, many rural Colombians lived in such silence, subordinated to landlords and their armed security.[14]

A month before his death, he held a silent march through Bogotá's newly cobbled streets and spruced-up facades, made nice at a high cost to welcome General Marshall—even as Bogotá's slums were filling up with starving, wounded, and traumatized refugees from the countryside. García Márquez joined the estimated hundred thousand protesters. Gaitán again astonished the writer, this time with his ability to choreograph such self-control. When one old man started muttering a prayer under his breath, a group of women gently asked him to pray in silence. The quiet was a mourning for fallen citizens. It was also an exercise in discipline, a message to elites who believed that common people were incapable of self-governance.

"There was only one rallying cry: absolute silence," García Márquez recalled, "maintained with inconceivable dramatic effect, even on the balconies of residences and offices where people watched us walk." The "supernatural silence" was overwhelming. The careful steps and quiet breathing brought García Márquez to the "verge of tears." The crowd filed into the Plaza Bolívar, pressed in against the National Congress building. Gaitán had delivered the kind of social suffering usually hidden from public life to the doorstep of Colombia's leaders.

From the balcony of the municipal comptroller's office, kitty-corner to

Congress, Gaitán spoke in muted tones, a funeral oratory for the victims of state and capitalist violence. Colombians helped defeat Nazi tyranny in the 1940s, he implored: stop killing them. García Márquez wrote that Gaitán and his followers communicated intuitively: "In his epic speeches he himself would advise his listeners in a guileful paternal tone to return in peace to their houses, and they would translate that in the correct fashion as a coded order to express their repudiation of everything that represented social inequalities and the power of a brutal government."

So it was on this silent march, when Gaitán asked that no one clap when he finished speaking. No one did. The nation's rulers, wrote another Colombian writer Carlos Arturo Ruiz (who published under the name Arturo Alape) understood the power behind the silence to be a threat.[15]

Gaitán's death order was signed that day, Ruiz said.

Things Not Spoken Of

It was the shooter himself, Juan Roa Sierra, who first suggested conspiracy. After he emptied his revolver into Gaitán, a group of police officers grabbed the assassin and pulled him into a drugstore, La Nueva Grenada, and shut the door. It was bedlam inside and out, but one officer asked Roa: *"Por qué ha cometido este crimen?"* Roa stayed silent. As the crowd pressed against the storefront's window, the officer asked again: Why did you kill Gaitán? This time Roa answered, paraphrasing a book of esoterica he had been reading, *Los Dioses Atómicos* (or, *The Atomic Gods*, published in 1931): *"¡Ay, señor, cosas poderosas que no le puedo decir!"* "Oh, sir, there are powerful things that can't be spoken of!" The officer asked again: Who ordered you to kill? Again, Roa said some things are too powerful to name.

Before he could say whether he was referring to earthly or astral power, the owner of the drugstore, hoping to save his windows, opened the door and the crowd rushed in. Roa was dragged outside. Fidel Castro, who had an appointment to meet with Gaitán later in the afternoon, was having lunch on the same street where the killing took place. He and his friends ran out and joined the protests. Having commandeered a rifle from a local police station, Castro jumped up on a bench and tried to rouse a group of soldiers to join the uprising.

"Everyone listened," he recalls, "no one did anything, and there I was with my rifle making my speech."

García Márquez had heard about Gaitán's murder on his dorm room's radio. He hurried to El Gato Negro in time to witness the bootblacks beat Roa to death.[16]

As he made his way through the crowd, the future magical realist was stunned by "the speed with which accounts of witnesses were changing in form and substance until they lost all resemblance to reality." Everyone already had a different story as to who they saw doing what. Roa's beaten body was still warm when rumors started running that he wasn't the only killer, or if he was, he must have been acting on someone's behalf. Who was that thin man with green eyes that witnesses say they saw directing the assassin? And who was the man in the expensive suit with alabaster skin, seen only by García Márquez in front of the pharmacy inciting the crowd? "I have not found him in any of the countless testimonies I have read to this day," García Márquez admitted. There was also a fat man, as described by a Liberal Party associate of Gaitán, Plinio Mendoza Neira, seen coming out of Café Asturias wearing a black hat and jacket. Mendoza watched him, only seconds after the killing took place, calmly take the pistol out of Roa's hand and turn both the gun and the killer over to police officers. The heavyset man was later identified as Pablo Emilio Potes, an agent with Colombia's national security services, who also ran a rural anti-Gaitanista paramilitary squad.

Men and women wept. Those near Gaitán's corpse dipped their handkerchiefs into the blood flowing from his wounds, to keep as relics. One woman, already dressed in black as if in premonition, waved her memento mori screaming, "Sons of bitches, they went and killed him."

Who killed him? Colombians have spent decades trying to answer that question. The accused have included the Conservative Party, rivals in the Liberal Party, Communists, Fascists, the Catholic Church, the landed oligarchy, the United Fruit Company, a jilted suitor of Gaitán's mistress, an angry relative of a man Gaitán had defeated in court, assassins from the

Ancient and Mystical Order Rosæ Crucis, and the CIA. Maybe one of those new "attachés" recently arrived at the U.S. embassy—agents from the newly created CIA that was just then taking over the FBI's Latin American work.

After the 1959 triumph of the Cuban Revolution, William Pawley, a diplomat who worked with the CIA and was in Bogotá as Marshall's main adviser, said that the twenty-two-year-old Castro choreographed events, along with another "Cuban" who Pawley thought might have been Che Guevara. (Guevara, of course, wasn't Cuban but Argentine, and he wouldn't be introduced to Castro until 1955, in Mexico. By most accounts he had spent April 1948 in Buenos Aires studying medicine.)

Over the years, individuals have claimed responsibility, including a CIA operative captured by the Cuban government. The Cubans made a documentary that included a filmed confession, yet Havana decided the agent was spinning disinformation and didn't release the film. Scotland Yard said Roa acted alone. Decades after the killing, Emilio Potes, the undercover security agent on the scene identified by Plinio Mendoza, gave a deathbed confession saying that he had organized Gaitán's execution. The official legal investigation of the murder went on for over twenty years and proved inconclusive.[17]

Meanwhile, the tall man with green eyes was picked up two weeks after the murder. Police identified him as César Bernal Cordovez, employed in the print shop of Bogotá's leading conservative newspaper, El Siglo. Many in Colombia's middle class who didn't have access to materialist or political-economic explanations to make sense of the early twentieth-century's epic world conflicts were drawn to conspiracism, to a fascist occultism that mixed Christian eschatology with racial mythologies and Hindu or Nordic symbology. Bernal, like Roa, was a mystic who deliriously rambled on about thought-transference wheels. A judge ruled him insane, suffering from a "persecuted-persecutor" complex, confining him for the rest of his life in a "phrenopathic" sanatorium on the outskirts of Bogotá. He was, according to the institution's director, afflicted with a "paraphrenic dementia that reduced his thoughts to a few litigious and vengeful ideas." Doctors diagnosed him as "incurable."[18]

Roa's past was hard to pin down. His motives and associates are as difficult to piece together as any of the century's more famous assassins to come, including Lee Harvey Oswald. Where did he get the seventy-five pesos to buy the gun? Some spread rumors that they had seen, hours before the assassination took place, Venezuelan newspapers with headlines of Gaitán's death.[19]

An unemployed bricklayer, Roa had worked as a doorman for the German embassy (where his brother was employed as a chauffeur) until it was shuttered in 1943. After Hitler's suicide, Roa had fallen in with a crowd of esoteric Nazis who mythologized Hitler's defeat by giving him a Hydra-headed afterlife. A Greek English writer, Savitri Devi, popularized the movement, which was then elaborated by disciples all over the world. The Chilean Nazi Miguel Serrano, a reader of Jung, mashed together various premodern epics. He turned Hitlerism into a celestial origin story, a myth as dense and convoluted as the Old Testament prophesies that Spanish priests pored over to make sense of the New World. According to Serrano, Hitler, like Christ, an avatar of the Gods Vishnu and Shiva, was a redeemer, an embodiment of ancient racial memory. And like Christ, he would return, not in his old form but as the Goddess Kali, the bringer of death. Serrano wouldn't popularize his völkisch mythology until later, in a series of books including *Adolf Hitler: The Last Avatar*. But such ideas were floating around before the fall of Berlin. Roa picked them up in occult magazines he found at the German embassy.[20]

Roa had become a member of the Ancient and Mystical Order Rosæ Crucis, based in San Jose, California—Diego Rivera was also a member—and regularly consulted a German-émigré astrologer named Johan Umland Gert. The Mystical Order had ties to both the fascist and intelligence community, and some have searched for explanations for Gaitán's murder in that foggy place where Nazi occultism and covert activity intersect.

Some say Roa was a Fascist. Others, a Communist. Whatever the case, Roa was obsessed with Gaitán. He regularly showed up at Gaitán's law office seeking an audience. Roa told Gert, shortly before shooting Gaitán, that he was coming into money, a statement some have taken to mean that Colombia's elite paid him to rid themselves of Gaitán. Maybe. Though it could also have meant that, inspired by *The Atomic Gods*, Roa thought he could visualize good fortune. Another rumor circulated that Gaitán and Roa shared the same father and that the illegitimate Roa was avenging his pariahdom.

The coming of the Cold War to the Americas, as announced by Gaitán's killing, was no less conspiratorial, no less haunted by prophesies than was the coming of the conquering Spanish.

Like London After the Blitz

George Marshall was having lunch in his residence, the Payana House, when he heard news of Gaitán's killing, followed shortly by gunfire sounding through the city. Radio stations commandeered by insurgents blamed Gaitán's death on the secretary of state and urged rioters to take revenge. Marshall waited out the night protected by a small contingent of Colombian soldiers. Across Bogotá, hardware stores were ransacked for weapons and machetes used to slash car tires and shatter windows. Radio stations were taken over, with protesters calling on Colombians to revolt. Rioters passed through the conference's first-floor meeting rooms like locusts destroying everything in sight, while a handful of delegates hid in closets on the upper floors.

Fidel couldn't get anyone to pay attention to him, and most investigations concluded that the uprising was spontaneous. Still, Harry Truman's ambassador to Colombia, Willard Beaulac, believed the "looting was organized and systematic." Thomas Dewey, Truman's Republican opponent in 1948's presidential race, said on April 10 that the rioting was following a "classic Communist pattern."[21]

The worst of the destruction took place over the course of two days. Most police supported Gaitán and joined the protesters. But Marshall could count on the Colombian military. The wartime Good Neighbor Policy had left its generals well paid, well trained, and well armed. Bogotá's battalions had been outside the city on maneuvers, so it took a few long hours before the first soldiers began to arrive to put down the riot.

General Matthew Ridgway rounded up stray Colombian infantrymen to stage an operation that transferred diplomats and staff from their hotels to more secure locations. Protesters set the United States embassy on fire. The night's steady rain, combined with the low oxygen of the high Andean air, kept the flames contained. Other buildings burned bright no matter the oxygen levels, including the ministries of justice, communication, and foreign affairs. "The flames set the heavens aglow," wrote one witness, sending up "strange sulphuric colors, interspersed with great billows of black smoke." A fancy restaurant, The Golden Deer, built especially for the conference's delegates, was demolished. Buildings associated with clerical and secular authority were targeted, including the archbishop's residence. The house where Simón Bolívar had lived was left undisturbed.[22]

Rioting continued through the night, with soldiers arriving the next day to establish order. On the second day, the devastation was visible to all. One conference staffer reported driving up Séptima Avenida and seeing "block after block of gutted shops and smoking skeletons of buildings. Here and there corpses were visible." The streets were filled with shattered glass and debris. Bodies were being hauled away on carts and buried in ditches. Estimates placed the number of dead at three thousand. No individual associated with the conference was harmed. One delegate said there were fewer machetes visible than on the first day, but he still jumped every time someone shouted *Viva la revolución*. "Churches were in ruins, burnt motor cars, burnt trucks, burnt trolley cars littered the way. It was like a ghastly nightmare." It was, he said, a "disaster proportionately comparable to London after the Blitz." The city's main plaza was strung with barbed wire.[23]

One United States general thought the devastation was worse than anything he had witnessed in Europe. Another noted the "nihilistic, anarchic" quality of the violence. The dead were taken to the general cemetery, where first they were laid respectfully in a line, but as corpses continued to arrive, bodies were piled one on top of the other, waiting for excavators to dig a mass grave.[24]

Marshall rigged a command center, using walkie-talkies and the embassy's still-functioning radio to communicate with Washington and to organize food runs from Panama. The Canal Zone's Transport Command organized an airlift home of all nonessential personnel and family members. Convoys of military cargo trucks shuttled evacuees to the airport, where they were flown first to Panama before being put on connecting flights.[25]

Marshall's aide-de-camp William Pawley arranged for one of the Panama planes to deliver pots of caviar and foie gras and bottles of champagne. Having survived days on army rations, Pawley thought the "luxuries of life" would get delegates in the mood to return to contemplating the higher order of international politics.[26]

Juan Roa Sierra's brutalized, naked body was left lying in front of the National Palace for days.

Mario Vargas Llosa opens his novel *Conversation in the Cathedral* with the question: "At what precise moment had Peru fucked itself up?" Colombians ask themselves the same question: *¿En qué momento se jodió Colombia?* They have an answer: at 1:00 p.m. on April 9, 1948. Plinio Apuleyo Mendoza, sixteen years old that spring, was running to meet his father, who was with Gaitán on their way to lunch. Plinio arrived at the scene a moment after the shooting took place. He looked at his father, and then he looked down at Gaitán's corpse. A lifeless face returned the gaze. There was "great sadness in its open, staring eyes." "Nothing after was ever the same again," Plinio, who like his friend García Márquez would go on to be a journalist and novelist, later wrote.

Gaitán's murder was an event so dense, so compacted with unanswered desire that standard observational metrics offer no insights into its factual meaning. Historians have largely given up on trying to figure out the particulars of Gaitán's killing, leaving it to fiction writers and playwrights to ponder its significance.

April 9, 1948, is a "void in Colombian history," writes Juan Gabriel Vásquez in his novel *The Shape of the Ruins*, an act unknowable in its essence that sent a "whole nation into a bloody war." Vásquez's narrator talks about growing up in the shadow not of Gaitán's murder but of obsessions with Gaitán's murder, with the endless speculation as to who was behind the killing and counterfactuals of what Colombia might have been like if Gaitán had lived and been elected president. The novel's protagonist points out that Colombia's "collective neurosis" is shared with many other nations, especially those that have experienced the execution of leaders who are remembered as promising a different path than the one taken. Frustrated hope, unrequited dreams. Fantasies of what a country might have been.[27]

A Red Masterpiece

Gaitán's murder turned out to be a godsend for George Marshall. The revolt that followed creating a besieged camaraderie among the delegates, giving the secretary of state a chance to move the discussion away from what Latin Americans said they wanted—capital—to what he said the world needed: security and solidarity against the growing menace of world Communism.

Marshall met with what delegates he could find, telling them the uprising was a deliberate effort to sabotage the European Recovery Program. Staffers were confused and nervous. An envoy from Argentina asked the U.S. Air Force to secure Bogotá's airport. Marshall thought that a bad idea, but he ordered the United States' base in Panama to remain on high alert. Rumors circulated of simultaneous uprisings in Bolivia and Paraguay, that Somoza had sent Nicaraguan troops across the border into Costa Rica to unseat José Figueres. Some columnists and congressmen in the U.S. thought the conference should be canceled, that with the world spinning out of control, Marshall should be in Washington "doing something about it." Marshall insisted, and Truman agreed, that the conference finish its business. "We must at all costs continue our work," the secretary of state said.[1]

Several Latin American delegates had already started conversations in the barracked Honduran embassy, but soon the meeting was reconvened in the library of a local high school, outfitted with banks of telephones for delegates to communicate with their foreign ministries. In the days to come, delegates, alarmed by the force of the uprising, adopted security resolutions that aligned Latin America behind the United States in the Cold War, much like an earlier set of resolutions united them in the war against fascism. Communism was defined as a threat originating outside of the Americas, a "foreign" doctrine. Even if the Communists were born and raised in, say, Guatemala or Chile, they would be considered agents of "European powers."

Many didn't need much arm twisting to sign on to Marshall's security proposals, their governments having already taken cues from Washington to gird for a new war. Nicaragua's delegation, the Somoza family, welcomed the shift in emphasis from democracy to security. "Anti-Communist resolution cinched," Marshall reported to Washington on April 20. He returned to Washington on April 24, and the conference adjourned a week later.

Others worried—correctly, as it turned out—that going on a war footing against Communism would allow conservatives to attack all reformers, not just members of Communist parties aligned with the Soviet Union. As the proceedings advanced, Guatemala's foreign minister Enrique Muñoz Meany posted a note to Guatemala's president Arévalo saying he feared the saber-rattling. "Democratic action and not police persecution," Meany wrote, was the best way of fighting "all forms of totalitarianism," not just Stalinism but *franquismo* as well.[2]

Entertaining Negros

Meanwhile, back in the United States, the Second Red Scare was well under way by the time Roa shot Gaitán, with an early focus on public employees who worked on matters related to Latin America. Under Roosevelt, the FBI and its allies in government considered State's entire Latin American desk—if not Latin America itself—a Communist-front organization. The Bogotazo, as the riot that followed Gaitán's killing is known, would only confirm such an opinion.

As early as March 1942, with the outcome of the war by no means certain, Martin Dies, the chair of the House Un-American Activities Committee, felt no need to maintain antifascist unity. He announced that he had evidence that thirty-five staffers in Henry Wallace's Board of Economic Warfare were Reds, including one who was also a nudist.* Dies was especially concerned that the board, which already in 1942 was planning for the postwar world, would have so many officials who "reject the American way of life in favor of this or that scheme for revolution."[3]

The left-wing Council for Pan American Democracy, founded by scholars such as Franz Boas and activists with a focus on exposing fascism in Latin America and defending republicanism in Spain, was also targeted in 1942, referred by the FBI to Dies's committee. The council's secretary Marion Bachrach was later brought up on treason charges.

This was around the time that conservatives were beginning to isolate Henry Wallace and smear Sumner Welles—a campaign that Rex Tugwell understood as an internal coup. The goal was to get rid of progressives close to FDR who weren't hard-liners when it came to prospective postwar relations with Moscow: "The game was to pick off all those who were really loyal to Franklin. The conservatives who were now gathering about Hull succeeded with Welles who was too proud and too reserved to fight back."[4]

When in late 1944 Nelson Rockefeller became assistant secretary of state for American Republic Affairs, he purged what he said were "a hell of a lot" of "fairies" from the division. Most were undoubtedly also social democrats. The FBI accused several high-level Latin America policymakers of being Soviet agents, including the head of State's Mexico desk, Laurence Duggan, who lost his position and apparently committed suicide. The Spanish Civil War–veteran Gustavo Durán, a classical music composer and friend of the martyred Spanish poet Federico García Lorca, worked with Ernest Hemingway to set up a private antifascist spy network in Cuba made up of Spanish

---

* The nudist in question was the board's chief economist, Maurice Parmelee, who authored several books Dies found suspect, including *Farewell to Poverty, Bolshevism, Fascism, and the Liberal-Democratic State*, and the illustrated *Nudism in Modern Life*, which Dies quoted as evidence of what the board had planned for the postwar: Nudist "colonies furnish excellent opportunities for experiments along communistic lines, some of which may be successful. To say the least, these colonies would be democratic in their character." Parmelee was made to resign.

loyalists. J. Edgar Hoover had the network shut down. Hemingway, in turn, complained that FBI agents were more sympathetic to fascists then they were to antifascists. Durán then entered the State Department, working his way up to become an adviser to Rockefeller, only to resign when anticommunists began accusing him of working as a Stalinist enforcer while in Spain.[5]

Most accusations were leveled against lower-level staffers or scholars, with the intention of squashing what was left of the early, experimental spirit of the Good Neighbor Policy. The National Labor Relations Board's Edwin Smith, who, standing next to Cárdenas, had given a few fiery speeches in Mexico comparing Article 27 to the NLRA, drew the attention of Congress's "Special Committee." Smith was "very zealous" in defense of union rights. "Maybe too zealous." He was let go.[6]

It was a witch hunt, and many of the witches were feminists and antiracists. The anthropologist Ruth Landes, a student of Ruth Benedict, came under surveillance because of her "ideas and dress," which suggested to a colleague-informant that she was a Communist. While doing fieldwork on race, male homosexuality, and matriarchy in Brazil in the late 1930s, Landes associated with scholars in or close to the Communist Party, including an Afro-Brazilian party member whom she took as a lover. Upon her return to the United States, the FBI prevented Landes from obtaining a decent university position. Caroline Ware, a professor of history who worked in several New Deal bureaus, came under investigation by the FBI due to her "socialistic teaching," her fondness for "entertaining negroes," and "tendency to empathize with downtrodden of other nations," a reference to the courses she taught on social work in Puerto Rico, Bogotá, Medellín, and San Salvador. Luisa Moreno, the Guatemalan-born migrant who did cross-border antifascist work with Spanish-speaking unions, was deported.[7]

By 1948, the U.S. public was primed to slot events in Bogotá seamlessly into an emerging Cold War narrative. The details of the killing or uprising didn't matter—whether Communists killed Gaitán, whether Gaitán was a Communist, or whether Communists were merely taking advantage of the pandemonium that followed his murder. It was of no import that Latin American Communists were far removed from the USSR, that their relations with Moscow were, as George Kennan said, "tenuous and indirect." What mattered was the political benefit that could be gained by laying the chaos on Moscow.

"International communism" was to blame, Marshall told reporters. The press printed rumors of a (nonexistent) Communist coup in Paraguay and "waves of revolt" sweeping across Latin America.

A "red masterpiece" was the *Los Angeles Times* description of the crisis, the "crowning achievement of the master craftsmen of discord," designed to sabotage the Pan-American conference. Within weeks of the riot, Colombia expelled Soviet diplomats and broke relations with the USSR, citing fundamental spiritual differences.[8]

Donald Jackson, a Republican representative from California who fled Bogotá for Washington, provided breathless testimony at a hastily called House hearing. After describing his dramatic escape from a burning building and fighting "surging mobs armed with clubs and machetes," Jackson told his colleagues that "this is war as truly as if we were opposed by armed might and a physical enemy." The Bogotazo proved there were no borders in this new, ideological war, and the United States needed to go on the offensive abroad and at home. Republicans and Democrats alike gave Jackson a standing ovation. Radio broadcasts and newspapers excitedly reported on the riot. Paramount titled its newsreel "Colombia's Reign of Terror."

Gaitán's killing allowed newspapers and politicians to reinforce the idea that the enemy wasn't a nation but an ideology. Henry Wallace, for instance, had already broken with the Democratic Party over Truman's foreign policy and was running for president on the Progressive Party line with Communist Party backing. Events in Colombia allowed cold warriors to fit his insurgent campaign into a larger global picture.

"Henry Wallace in this country" is just like the murdered Gaitán, the CIA's first director Admiral Roscoe Hillenkoetter told Congress, a politician who allied with the "extreme left and communists." Wallace was in fact worse than Gaitán, read one report. At least Gaitán had continued to work within Colombia's Liberal Party, whereas Wallace had broken with the Democrats. *The Christian Science Monitor* blamed the violence that followed Gaitán's murder on Gaitán himself, on his having "constantly and vehemently told the masses that 16 years of Liberal administrations had not brought them what they could rightfully expect."

The point was obvious: by 1948, the New Deal coalition in the United States had been in power exactly sixteen years, and Wallace was telling his followers that Democrats had not brought them what they rightfully should expect. They could have more. More jobs, better wages, higher prices for farm goods, decent houses.

For years, Wallace and FDR had stirred up the left in Latin America, a reader wrote in a letter to the editor of the *Chicago Daily Tribune*, and now we are seeing the results. The correspondent noted that the name *Henry* in Spanish is *Enrique*, and *Wallace*, if pronounced in Spanish, would sound like *Váyase*, which translates as "go away," or "get lost": "Get Lost, Henry."[9]

Perpetual Bondage

Pan-Americanism, for United States conservatives, was little but a front for all the threats to the American way of life: attacks on private property, social rights, political radicalism, class struggle, sexual perversion, and racial subversion, including all those visas the State Department was handing out to Latin America's "negro" artists and intellectuals under the patronage of the Good Neighbor Policy.

And health care. Several Latin American jurists had by this point made the argument that the liberal right to life was indistinguishable from the social right to health care. "The right to exist, the right to live," the Cuban legislator Pedro Albarrán Domínguez had affirmed earlier in the century, "necessarily comes before all other rights." Cuba's 1940 constitution, drafted by an assembly that included almost as many doctors as lawyers, explicitly guaranteed health care as a right of citizenship.

Conservatives in the United States mobilized to ensure that this idea did not spread north. Marjorie Shearon is an unsung hero of the U.S. New Right (as the conservative movement that flowered after the war is known) and should be considered a precursor to Phyllis Schlafly. Historians debate the origins of this movement, whether it was motivated by racist opposition to desegregation or Christian patriarchal opposition to feminism. Shearon's underappreciated activism suggests an obsession with stopping socialized medicine should also be considered as an accelerant of modern conservatism.[10]

Throughout 1947 and 1948, Shearon relentlessly fought against national health care. Like Schlafly later in the 1970s, Shearon wrote, mimeographed, collated, stuffed envelopes, compiled a mailing list, petitioned, testified, and organized. She ran the Shearon Legislative Service out of her home in Chevy Chase, Maryland, putting out a newsletter "no less than 30 times per year" warning of the different ways socialism was stealthily entering the United States. And like Schlafly, she was on guard against the possibility that liberal internationalism would be used to advance domestic reform. The "nationalization of medicine," she testified to Congress, was being forced on the United States by the State Department via its associated hemispheric organizations, among them the Pan-American Union and the Inter-American Conference on Social Security. Shearon called her organization Individuals for Freedom and juxtaposed the sanctity of individual rights with what she saw as the perversion of social rights.

While cold warriors celebrated the national security measures passed in Bogotá at the Pan-American Conference, Shearon alerted the American Medical Association to other resolutions passed in the days after Gaitán's killing, including one affirming that health care was a basic right. Shearon condemned the State Department for "blindly" following the "the health directives of socialists."

"America is being led into socialism and its doctors into perpetual bondage by the Pan-American Union," she said.[11]

Communist or Otherwise

In Latin America, the backlash against the social democratic opening—from 1944 to 1946—accelerated after Bogotá. The new OAS charter encouraged the quick recognition of governments no matter how they came to power, a wink at the right-wing and crypto-fascists, letting them know that if they overthrew a government drifting to the left, their actions would be rewarded by fast recognition.

In the months after Gaitán's murder, military men in Peru and Venezuela were the first to test this new protocol, staging two sequential coups, on October 27 and November 24, respectively. In both cases, the soldiers overthrew anticommunist social-democratic parties. The Venezuela putsch, which brought General Marcos Pérez Jiménez to power, had direct U.S. support, in the form of a U.S. military attaché, Colonel Edward Adams, and U.S. oilmen like William F. Buckley (who had transferred his operations from Mexico to Venezuela). In Peru, General Manuel Odría took control. Truman, citing the new OAS guidelines, quickly recognized both coup governments, which reciprocated by passing investor-friendly laws.[12]

Most of the region's mainstream politicians, desperate for capital, had made their peace with Washington's switch from an aggressive antifascism to an equally aggressive anticommunism. But the about-face disoriented rank-and-file activists. Socialists in Chile, now under attack, organized protests where they carried placards with images of Franklin Delano Roosevelt. It was touching, really, the idea that a photograph of the three-years-gone FDR would move the hearts of the men in Washington laying the foundation of the Cold War national security state.

U.S. Socialist Michael Harrington quipped that 1948 was "the last year of the thirties," referring to the conservative turn within the United States. A similar turn took place in Latin America, where the raucous, working-class democracy that had come to the fore after the war had been beaten back. By the end of 1948, nearly every government in the region had fallen to dictators or had taken a sharp right turn. Maybe six could still be considered democratic: Costa Rica, Chile, Uruguay, Guatemala, Mexico, and Colombia. But that's a stretch. Mexico held regular elections but had tamped down on union autonomy as the ruling party became more authoritarian. Citizens could continue to vote in Colombia, even as, in the years after Gaitán's murder, the country went to hell.[13]

Kennan's Policy Planning Staff did get around to writing that long promised "chapter on Latin America," and its analysis was bracingly clear-eyed. The report, known as PPS-26, downplayed the danger of Communism as "not immediately serious," and instead rightly predicted a fascist upsurge. An even earlier CIA study, written a month after Gaitán's killing, acknowledged that faraway Moscow exerted little influence in the region: in "no Latin American country" is "the Communist Party capable of seizing and holding office, nor have the Communists any apparent intention of making such an attempt." Rather, the Policy Planning Staff identified the threats to democracy as Catholic reactionaries, military officers, and large landowners who were using "totalitarian police state methods" to quash dissent.[14]

However spot-on its analysis, the Policy Planning Staff's policy recommendations were pure fantasy. The report urged Washington to cultivate "liberal and Socialist elements" that, though on the left, were opposed to Soviet Communism. The goal was to build up a "democratic left" while isolating a "communist left." That proved impossible, for the people and security forces the U.S. relied upon to do the isolating were, as the report itself notes, targeting "all political opposition, Communist or otherwise."

The Truman administration insisted that "business and private capital could easily flow more freely into countries to the south of us if obstacles which now stand in the way were removed."

Those "obstacles" were human beings. They were trade unionists, peasant activists, students, intellectuals, voters, economic nationalists, dissenting priests—they were the "democratic leftists" who were then being eliminated across the region, anyone who might scare off investment or increase a nation's loan risk, which in turn would raise the rate on interest payments, already hard to cover due to the tendency of terms of trade to deteriorate, as Prebisch taught. The exclusion of Latin America from Marshall Plan–like funds ensured that there was no space for a third-way force, no chance that a "democratic left"—like the governments that ran Peru and Venezuela before their military coups—could take shape. Politicians and businessmen who wanted to modernize their economies had to eliminate dissent, since, as George Marshall told them in Bogotá, and Washington constantly reiterated, they needed to attract private capital. For that, they had to show they had matters in hand.[15]

Europe in the postwar years was different. There, with the power of reactionary elites weakened, a massive infusion of no-strings-attached dollars meant reindustrialization could proceed without the suppression of unions. Industrialists didn't have to promise investors a pacified labor movement to attract investment. Non-Communist unions and reform parties such as social-democratic and Christian-democratic parties could be both tactical anti-Soviet bulwarks and advocates for an expansion of social benefits. In France, the Marshall Plan, according to the CIA, had rapidly raised the standard of living and weakened support for Communist parties, while letting anti-Communist socialist parties and their "restive" unions demand a greater percentage of national income for workers. Great Britain could let the Labour Party use its "categorical, overwhelming, resounding" victory to establish a National Health Service.

In Western Europe, access to public capital and cheap credit allowed liberalism to reestablish itself, to expand social welfare. In Latin America, the need to placate foreign capital allowed no such outcome. For instance, in Germany, the founding document of the Christian Democratic Union called for the creation of a "socialist economic order." When Christian Democrats in El Salvador and Guatemala said they wanted the same thing, they were executed.[16]

Peace, Peace, Don't Kill Us

B ogotá was largely pacified within a week of Gaitán's death. The Colombian countryside not so. Peasants and oil workers up and down the Magdalena River seized power in local villages. Workers declared the sweltering Standard Oil town of Barrancabermeja a liberated "commune." Rebels forged cannons out of oil pipes and placed improvised mines around the town, holding the army at bay for more than a week. Leaders of the Liberal Party, hoping to avoid a bloodbath, negotiated the commune's surrender. The Colombian military retook control of the river.[1]

Mariano Ospina Pérez, the Conservative Party president, declared martial law and began replacing departmental governors with right-wing extremists. These new governors restructured local police precincts and set loose paramilitary shock troops, goons who worked security for landowners. As in the United States South and Southwest, Colombian planters and ranchers had long operated their own private security forces. Now, though, after Gaitán's killing, vigilantism took on a sharper political profile, used not just to defend any single *patrón* but to fight a larger, national war against subversion. Los Párajos, or the Birds, was one of Latin America's first modern death squads. The group, along with Los Chulavitas, another paramilitary organization, operated as an adjunct of the Conservative Party, responsible for killing thousands of Liberal Party members.[2]

In Bogotá, the military was in control. Scotland Yard had sent Sir Douglas Gordon and a team of twelve advisers to reorganize the city's police, many of whom had been loyal to Gaitán. Having served as a police commander in colonial India for thirty-nine years, Gordon knew how to create a constabulary that supported the forces of order. "The Conservatives were building up a terror machine," *The Atlantic* reported.[3]

In Those Extremes

The situation deteriorated quickly. *Paz*—peace—was chanted everywhere. But it was a backward incantation, bringing about a state of being opposite to the one desired. Citizens placed a large electric sign bearing the word in front of the National Congress in a plea for civility and order. But the crimson neon bathed the square a menacing red, which couldn't have helped settle nerves.

Shortly thereafter, on September 8, 1949, a Conservative representative stood up in Congress, took out a revolver, and started shooting at Liberals. Other Conservative representatives drew their weapons and began firing too. Liberals took cover behind their desks. By the time the police arrived, many were wounded, and Liberal representative Gustavo Jiménez was dead. That congressional session was being broadcast over the radio, so many Colombians got to hear not just the gunshots but Liberals pleading, "Peace, peace, don't kill us."

The Liberal Party had another martyr, and more public processions protesting violence wound through the streets. On October 22, a little over a month before a presidential election, Conservative cadres killed nearly two dozen Liberals at their party convention in the city of Cali. In retaliation, Liberals dynamited the town hall of Yacopí, killing eleven, including the town's Conservative mayor. Order broke down quickly in the countryside.

Conservatives turned to a man of the past to run for president—Laureano Gómez, leader of the Falange in the 1930s who fretted about the influence of the "black element" in Colombia society. Gómez won easily, unopposed since the Liberal Party boycotted the election. Truman immediately sent Gómez a telegram congratulating him on his victory. Many former Black Shirts, who a decade earlier had operated from the office of Gómez's newspaper *El Siglo*, now entered the government as ministers and diplomats. Scotland Yard's training of the police had turned the institution into Gómez's personal gendarmerie.

The 1950s in Colombia looked a lot like the 1930s in Germany, with Nazis holding public assemblies in Medellín: smiling men sporting swastika armbands gathered to mourn the fourth anniversary of the Nuremberg hanging of Hitler's minister of foreign affairs, Joachim von Ribbentrop. Just two years after Gaitán's killing, the country was being ruled by the "extreme fringe of Falangistas," *The New York Times* reported, with most of the violence originating "in those extremes." Washington kept quiet, refusing to take up the opposition's complaints that Gómez was a fascist who would create a Bogotá-Madrid axis. Colombian Liberals overestimated how much the Truman administration would be bothered by such an alliance: Washington would soon fully recognize Franco and include Spain in the Marshall Plan.[4]

Gómez wasn't the only fascist-like leader in Latin America. By 1950, nearly the entire region was ruled by brutal men: Batista in Cuba, Trujillo in the Dominican Republic, Duvalier in Haiti, Stroessner in Paraguay, Odría in Peru, Pérez Jiménez in Venezuela, Somoza in Nicaragua, among others. All were faithful to the United States. All modeled themselves on Franco (though Venezuela's Marcos Pérez Jiménez earned the nickname "Himmler of the hemisphere" for his repression of trade unionists). In El Salvador, one death squad chose a drawn-out name—the Fuerzas Armadas de Liberación Anti-Comunista Nacional Guerra de Exterminación—just so it could use the acronym FALANGE.[5]

Stroessner's secret police were trained by former Gestapo agents. A significant number of Nazi fugitives, such as Adolf Eichmann and Josef Mengele, had made their way to Latin America. Many of them, along with local fascist allies, hoped Latin America might be a place to regroup to continue their struggle. The CIA had other plans, folding many of them into the new intelligence apparatus being built in the hemisphere to fight Communism. Klaus Barbie, former head of the Gestapo in Lyons, France, was, with the help of the Agency, set up in Bolivia, where he taught death squads and military men how to torture.[6]

The Catholic Church, Israel's secret services, and the CIA joined forces to get the SS officer Walter Rauff, who during the war killed tens of thousands with his mobile gassing vans, first to Ecuador and then Chile. There, he started building a network of refugee Nazis that he put at the service of the region's militaries and intelligence agencies. When Pinochet overthrew Allende in 1973, Rauff began working with Chile's secret police, the DINA, Pinochet's notorious gestapo. Rauff also helped the government construct a concentration camp on Dawson Island in remote Patagonia and had close ties to the cultish Colonia Dignidad in the low Andes, a guarded community of German immigrants that served Pinochet as a torture center.*

United States investment soared during this decade of jackboot stability, with a "great surge" of capital flowing into Latin America. The State Department, now led by John Foster Dulles, turned away appeals for intercession on behalf of "the political prisoners rotting in the dungeons of Pérez Jiménez." "We must concede," wrote Kennan in 1950, "that harsh government measures of repression" are necessary to establish stability.[7]

No Seed Left to Sprout

A cadaverous Laureano Gómez gave interviews to the foreign press about the peace that reigned in Colombia even as his minister of defense was

---

* Argentina has a reputation as being a haven for fleeing Nazi war criminals, yet records indicate that more came to the United States, perhaps ten thousand in total. In all Latin America, an estimated nine thousand Nazis took refuge: five thousand in Argentina, fifteen hundred to two thousand in Brazil; five hundred to one thousand in Chile, with most of the remainder in Paraguay and Uruguay.

promising a war of extermination and *Life* magazine described a "reign of terror in the interior." The violence was extraordinary.[8]

The military, police, and death squads engaged in beatings and torture, starving prisoners, hanging them in pressure positions, administrating electric shocks to their genitals and tongues. "No seed was to be left to sprout" was a common slogan that some conservative cadres understood to be an order issued directly by President Gómez to execute the children of Liberals and Communists. Soldiers raped wives and murdered and eviscerated pregnant women. Some conservatives encouraged their own children to participate in the torture, letting them make shallow cuts in their victims' bodies, so that they would slowly bleed to death.[9]

Colombia's Air Force provided backup as death squads and government troops obliterated Liberal and Communist strongholds. Planes bombed redoubts of hunkered-down peasants, obstinate rebels who refused to surrender. Thousands abandoned their homes and fields. Thousands were killed.

The building block of the post–World War II order was to be a sovereign nation, administering to the needs of its citizens, protecting their rights, and promising them social and physical security. Mexico, with its land reform, was able to find a place for many who had been tossed around by the revolution. But in rural Colombia, in the decade following Gaitán's murder, two million people fled their homes, part of a great global upheaval that the Colombian writer Gonzalo Canal Ramírez in 1966 called "the century of the exile." The dispossession has continued. Today, Colombia, with millions uprooted, competes with Syria and Sudan for the distinction of being the nation with the world's most internally displaced people.[10]

Terror took on a mystical cast under Gómez, a cultlike figure who combined a ghastly visage with a fierce intellect. Politics draped in a death shroud. Castrations, vivisections, mutilations, and "rough cesareans" became commonplace. No more "shouts of *vivas* to the Liberal Party," one victim was told after having his tongue cut out.[11]

One repentant conservative Catholic activist, writing under a pseudonym out of fear of reprisal, accused Gómez of working with the bloodiest sectors of the Church to create a "religious-political sect" where it is "better to damn than save, curse than bless, expel than welcome." Gómez was the kind of right-wing intellectual who understood fascism to be but an update of sixteenth-century Spanish ecclesiasticism, which allowed for no separation between civil and clerical authority. In political campaigns, he lashed out at atheists, Communists, and Protestants and understood politics to be war, a fight for the soul of Christianity. During his presidential term, he turned the violence that flowed out of Gaitán's execution into a religious crusade, a means to vivify the Church's most Sepulvedian impulses.[12]

One parish priest in a poor Bogotá neighborhood gave a sermon urging congregants to shoot to kill. "If you kill a looter don't come to me to confess it. It's not a sin." Churches were used as command centers for Conservative field forces, their bell towers turned into sniper blinds. Priests who continued to preach charity, who sheltered their peasant parishioners, were executed in the most gruesome way, their bodies mutilated.[13]

Prior to Gaitán's death, rural violence was often anarchic, difficult to understand in simple class or political terms. After Gaitán's murder, increasing United States involvement imposed the Cold War's either/or polarity on rural politics.

Peasants in the grasslands and foothills of the Andes, in Antioquia, Tolima, and Cundinamarca, had begun by late 1949 to organize guerrilla bands to protect themselves—armed self-defense groups that mobilized in a coordinated fashion. For inspiration, they drew on the storied history of Colombia's nineteenth-century's fighting Liberal generals, who launched one revolt after another against Conservative Party rule. Rebel folk songs and hymns sang of the exploits of Liberals like General Rafael Uribe Uribe, who in 1902 predicted that Colombia had seen its "last civil war." "Our grandchildren," he said, "will find it hard to understand what kind of insanity led to such bloodshed among brothers." He was wrong, needless to say.

By 1953, peasant defense organizations were fielding thousands of militants and launching coordinated offensives on military installations. That year, in response to the failure of Gómez's shock troops to suppress the rebels, the military began a more intensive scorched-earth campaign, massacring villagers within an expanding perimeter. And still the government couldn't pacify the countryside.[14]

Washington knew the Colombian military and their paramilitary allies were killing reformers of all kinds in the countryside. Gómez couldn't "tell a communist from a Liberal," said a State Department report, "and sees Reds hiding behind every coffee bush." The White House knew that Communists, as the CIA wrote in 1952, had "played little part in the guerrilla disturbances." And it knew that leftover fascists, Falangists, and Nazis had embedded themselves in the military, and that Gómez was undermining democratic institutions, shutting presses, and extending states of exception.[15]

Throughout the 1950s and early 1960s, U.S. military aid to Southeast Asia and Colombia was intertwined. In November 1959, Eisenhower's State Department sent a team with experience fighting the Vietcong in Vietnam and defeating the Hukbalahap Rebellion in the Philippines to Colombia to assess the situation. Included in the group were Philippine Colonel Napoleon Valeriano and Charles Bohannon, apprentices of Edward Lansdale, one of the most storied names in the dark arts of special-forces counterterror. The group's mission was to import the "Lansdale approach" to Colombia, that is, organizing local forces into paramilitaries to conduct a campaign of terror against the enemy. Conservatives already had their own rural death squads, so the job of these advisers was to turn them into more efficient units. Another infamous counterinsurgent, William Yarborough, helped Colombia create "intelligence hunter-killer teams," special forces modeled on the U.S. Green Berets, trained to carry out "paramilitary, sabotage and/or terrorist activities."[16]

By the 1950s, Colombia had become part of a far-flung covert-ops campus, which including Laos, Cambodia, Vietnam, Indonesia, and the Philippines, with U.S. counterinsurgents applying methods they worked out in Asia in Latin America, and vice versa.

Gómez was astute. He saw the opportunity created by the Cold War and let Washington know that he may represent a clique of violent fascists, but they were fascists who had made their peace with a liberal capitalist world order led by Anglos. The move won him favor in Washington. "Colombia's record of participation in the affairs of the Inter-American system has been excellent," wrote a CIA analyst. Its statesmen backed up U.S. diplomats at international conferences, cooperated at the United Nations, and supported the United States, policy in Europe during the Berlin crisis and in the Middle East. "Excellent and effective," Colombia was.

As such, it was rewarded with loans and increased military assistance. Throughout the 1950s, Colombia received more military aid from Washington than any other Latin American nation, and purchased, at subsidized prices on low-interest credit, a formidable arsenal. Washington placed "no restrictions" on the use of the weapons it gave or sold to Bogotá. Conservative generals could use them on whomever they liked. The Colombian military doubled in size during the first half of the 1950s, fielding new ranger and marine units trained in-country by United States personnel. The Department of State drew the line at providing Colombian troops with napalm. There was a "reluctance to be charged with having made possible the use of this horror weapon in the Colombian civil strife," an official at Foggy Bottom wrote.[17]

Colombia responded by simply acquiring the equipment and material to make the gel, which sticks on skin as the fuel burns, on the open market.* So Washington dropped its objection and began supplying Bogotá with the gelatinous incendiary.

Gómez's successors continued the counterinsurgency, racking up short-run wins but creating a long-run catastrophe: a sense felt by many that the only way to end the terror and break conservative rule was to fight fire with fire. The war escalated. At least one British counterinsurgent adviser lent security forces a hand, offering lessons from the pacification of Malaysia and Northern Ireland—"emergency measures," according to one British intelligence report. This time, those Irish tactics didn't pacify the rebels.[18]

The historian Eric Hobsbawm wrote that Colombia in the late 1950s and

---

* Japan didn't get Marshall Plan funds, but the U.S. funded the creation of factories to make weapons, including napalm, to be used in Korea.

early '60s was—apart from the Mexican Revolution—the scene of "probably the greatest armed mobilization of peasants" in "the recent history of the western hemisphere." In May 1964, a campaign of massive air bombing, followed by on-the-ground massacres, broke up one rebel redoubt, but the war went on.[19]

48.

The Perpetual
Rhythm of Struggle

mong the many extraordinary and consequential things that took
place soon after Gaitán's execution was George Kennan writing a
top secret memo calling on the United States to wage a permanent,
global "psychological war."

Events in Bogotá influenced Kennan's decision to make the recommendation, both the shock of the city's uprising and the bitter feud that broke
out between the CIA, the FBI, Defense, and State, with each blaming the
other for not seeing the uprising coming. Kennan painted an image of a
United States handicapped by its innocence, by its childlike faith that war
was war, and that once it was over, business went back to normal. Both
Lenin and London, Kennan wrote, knew differently. The Soviet Union and
the British Empire were skilled in waging psychological war after the guns
were put down, for they knew that the struggle for influence—for ideological hegemony—was never over.[1]

There was no stasis in international politics, Kennan wrote. Power,
legitimacy, and authority were always accumulating or dissipating. And, he
continued, "we cannot afford to leave immobilized our resources for covert
political warfare." Kennan here was recommending a full-on, unending effort to ensure that journalists, opinion makers, and scholars aligned with

the worldview of the State Department. The United States needed to synchronize itself to "the perpetual rhythm of struggle, in and out of war."

According to his biographer John Lewis Gaddis, Kennan believed that the Marshall Plan needed such a robust covert operation to be successful, to prevent European Communists—popular due to their underground work against Fascist occupation—from being elected to office. It would be difficult for Washington to say it was fighting a war against world communism if it was at the same time providing Marshall Plan dollars to, say, a Communist-led coalition government in Italy.

Kennan imagined his proposed office doing "things that very much needed to be done, but for which the government couldn't take official responsibility." Marshall himself worried that a permanent covert war would degrade democratic life, in and out of the United States. But like Kennan, the Bogotazo scared him, adding to growing concern about events in Europe and Asia, including the Prague coup, tensions over Berlin, and Mao's triumph in China. He came to agree with Kennan that covert action was a "necessary evil that had to be used on a much larger scale." Truman accepted Kennan's recommendation, and the work of the Office of Policy Coordination, as the psych-war shop was first called, grew rapidly. Its remit was the entire world, but the devastation it caused in Latin America is notable.[2]

The front-office analysts at State might talk about working with a "Democratic Left," but it was hard to control the clandestine demons Kennan conjured: a permanently mobilized action unit designed to shape the ideological terrain through all (disavowable) means necessary: assassination, torture, and psychological destabilization.

Frank Wisner, a former OSS agent and the first head of the OPC, called his operation "my mighty Wurlitzer." Tap one key to buy and sell politicians and political parties. Tap another to infiltrate labor unions. Another, and a smear campaign was mounted in one of the many papers Wisner influenced or subsidized, in both friendly and unfriendly countries, or bombs would be exploded to unsettle a population, planes would dive-bomb and drop leaflets spreading rumors alleging this or that prominent labor leader or politician was corrupt. Pump the pedals and antagonists would be eliminated and governments overthrown.

Distrust, Division, Suspicion, and Doubt

Kennan and Wisner went about weaponizing the kind of confusion, speculation, and conspiracy that swirled around Gaitán's execution. The routine bewilderments of daily life, and the muddle that came with rapid social and technological change, were hypercharged whenever groups of men in the White House, at Langley, or at Foggy Bottom decided that there were things that needed doing.

Washington was concerned about the Middle East, and various agencies were coming up with "psychological warfare" strategies, especially to keep Iran an ally. Secretary of State Dean Acheson, in 1951, worried that "the Persians might be crazy enough to do the same thing the Mexicans did," and nationalize their oil. When Iran tried to do just that, the CIA helped London's MI6 bring down Iran's elected prime minister Mohammad Mossadegh in 1953. But the operation in Iran was fast: a quick maneuver of Mossadegh's enemies, and he was gone.

Latin America was where the techniques of psychological warfare would get a full rehearsal.[3]

Wisner's first comprehensive operation, and the CIA's first real regime change, took place in Guatemala in 1954. The campaign lasted nearly a year and served as an opportunity to apply psych-war techniques to oust a government—the best government that one of the poorest countries in the world had ever had, one simply trying to extend a modest program of social reform, including the distribution to peasants of fallow land owned by the United Fruit Company. The story has been told in detail in many places. Here it is useful to emphasize the prolonged and diverse application of disinformation, of lies and rumors, to manipulate not political elites or rebels but ordinary citizens. Wisner's Wurlitzer in quadraphonic.

Washington used every instrument at its disposal to destabilize the elected presidency of Jacobo Arbenz. The new Organization of American States, arising out of the ashes of Bogotá, isolated Guatemala diplomatically, justified by the lie that Arbenz was controlled by Communists, and Communism was a threat foreign to the New World. United States businesses applied pressure, creating an economic crisis. The CIA, coordinating its work with Edward Bernays (Sigmund Freud's nephew, and an expert in mass marketing who worked for the United Fruit Company), applied insights from social psychology to produce a sense of disorientation. Madison Avenue at this moment was perfecting the art of creating new wants, selling "not only goods," the economist John Kenneth Galbraith wrote, "but the desire for the goods."

The same techniques were used to manufacture apprehension. Radio broadcasts incited government officials and soldiers to treason and attempted to convince Guatemalans that a widespread underground resistance movement existed. Borrowing from Orson Welles's "War of the Worlds" broadcast, the Agency produced a radio show that claimed to be transmitted from "deep in the jungle" by rebel forces but was in fact taped in Miami and beamed into Guatemala from Nicaragua.

The goal of the operation was to create the illusion that a significant anti-Arbenz insurgency existed within the country. Operatives mined books such as David Maurer's *The Big Con*, a 1940 ethnography of the disappearing world of Depression-era grifters, who perfected the art of running complicated scams. The Agency planted stories in the Guatemalan and U.S. press. When Arbenz presented evidence to reporters that the "Government of the North" was working with conservative regimes in Honduras and Nicaragua to overthrow him, the CIA recommended planting distracting stories in newspapers. "If possible, fabricate big human interest story, like flying saucers, birth sextuplets in remote area to take play away."[4]

Psychological operations of the kind the CIA rehearsed in Guatemala weren't meant to win hearts and minds. Contra Galbraith, agents didn't apply Madison Avenue methods to convince Guatemalans that the United States was a better buy than the Soviet Union. Rather, as CIA field officers made clear, the point was to create "dissension, confusion, and fear." Propaganda designed to "attack the theoretical foundations of the enemy" was misplaced. The point, one agent wrote in March 1954, was to nullify trust and intensify "anti-government sentiment." Psychological efforts should be directed at the "heart, the stomach and the liver (fear)." "Distrust, division, suspicion, and doubt" were the goals. Fake funeral notices were posted on the doors of government and union officials, and signs reading A COMMU-

NIST LIVES HERE appeared on the doors of Arbenz supporters. The Agency posted "black letters" from a fake "Organization of the Militant Godless" to arouse Catholic fears and spread rumors that the government was about to seize bank accounts, collectivize all plantations, and ban Holy Week.

It was a yearlong escalating campaign of sabotage, political agitation, rumors, and propaganda designed to destabilize and demoralize government supporters and create schisms in the military. Events built to a crescendo as the Agency deployed bombers to drive home the point. "What we wanted to do was to have a terror campaign," said one of the CIA operatives, Howard Hunt, "much as the German Stuka bombers terrified the population of Holland, Belgium, and Poland at the onset of World War II and just rendered everybody paralyzed."[5]

The campaign succeeded and Arbenz fell. The CIA installed Carlos Castillo Armas as president, who with his hollow cheeks and toothbrush moustache modeled himself on Hitler. As might be expected, no "left democracy" emerged from this chicanery. Pure murder followed: the reversal of the land reform, the execution of a generation of activists, the mass imprisonment of peasants, and the beginning of a four-decade civil war that would climax in acts of genocide committed against the country's majority Mayan population.

The fallout from this catastrophic intervention seemed manageable. Latin America was Latin America, sequestered, as far as Washington was concerned, from the world's debate. At home, the bipartisan Cold War consensus still held.

Then came the Cuban Revolution.

A New Force

When the insurgent army led by Fidel Castro took power in Cuba on January 1, 1959, the RAND Corporation calculated that the "book value" of United States investment in Cuba was greater than in any other Latin American country, apart from Venezuela.[6]

More than money was at stake. Cuba had been a part of the United

States in sentimental terms at least since Benjamin Franklin and Thomas Jefferson thought its incorporation into the union inevitable. The island was the "apple" of John Quincy Adam's eye, the Spanish damsel in distress. That its inevitable absorption was constantly deferred only added to the island's appeal. When the U.S. finally did take Cuba, circumstances led Washington to sacrifice formal possession in exchange for informal control. As a site of massive investment in sugar production, the island was a rum-runner's paradise during Prohibition. Prohibition ended, but smuggling continued, including opium and heroin made from Mexican-grown poppies and Andean cocaine. Cuba didn't become a state, as many had predicted it would. But with organized crime established on the island since at least the 1930s, Cuba was incorporated into the union in a different kind of way, as a shadow state of offshore desire, for drugs, gambling, and sex.

It matters when in time a revolution takes place. Notably, Cuba's social program, at first, was no more radical than was the Mexican Revolution's during its day. The CIA called Castro's agenda "the common stock of Latin American reformist ideas": land reform, housing, health care, education, control over natural resources, and national sovereignty. Mexico, though, was lucky to have the most radical phase of its revolution unfold during a recessional, with Washington's power handicapped by the Great Depression and military threats on the horizon. If Cuba's had occurred in the 1930s, say, it might have progressed at the pace of the Mexican Revolution, with cycles of reform, radicalization, reaction, and consolidation, and fights over property rights playing out over decades.[7]

Yet Cuba's rebel army drove Fulgencio Batista out of Havana not in 1939 but in 1959, at the end of a decade of unparalleled U.S. investment in Latin America, with its foreign policy planners sure, after their win in Guatemala in 1954, that they could change regimes at will. The Cold War required not compromise and conciliation but a pliant Latin America.[8]

Washington pressed fast and hard on Cuba, and much earlier than is generally acknowledged. On January 29, 1959, Castro, yet to be sworn in as Cuba's prime minister, visited Venezuela. The CIA's Caracas operative, Jake Esterline, knew the United States had a problem. Esterline, who had helped run the Agency's coup in Guatemala four years earlier, was in awe. Castro's charisma, he said, was "something different, something more impressive" and definitely "harder to handle than anyone had ever seen." The United States by now had the hydrogen bomb, and Esterline described Castro's popularity in Venezuela as a similar force: "A chain reaction was occurring all over Latin America after Castro came to power. I saw—hell, anybody with eyes could see it—that a new and powerful force was at work in the hemisphere." Esterline here is describing Castro the way García Márquez did Gaitán, as a phenomenon whose moral energy radiated across the Americas.[9]

Venezuela's dictator, Pérez Jiménez, had just fallen. Castro said he felt as emotional arriving in Caracas as he had felt "when he entered Havana" after Batista's exit: that both Cuba and Venezuela were liberated territory, he said. Pablo Neruda, in exile from Chile, was there and read a poem, "Un canto para Bolívar," dedicated to Fidel. Half a million Venezuelans arrived in the city's main plaza to hear Castro muse on the "unitary thought" of Bolívar and Martí and of Latin America's common destiny. He was welcomed by a joint session of congress, university rectors, students, and politicians.

Frank Wisner passed through Caracas not long after Castro's visit. Like Esterline, Wisner knew Cuba had to be contained. He asked Esterline if he would be "interested in getting back into harness" to lead an operation against Cuba. Esterline said yes. He transferred back to Washington to begin working with Cuban exiles on a plan of attack, an invasion from the south side of the island on a beach called Girón near a village called Bahía de Cochinos, or the Bay of Pigs. The CIA put mafia hit men on its payroll to establish kill teams on the island, which would be activated as soon as the invasion got under way.

All this was organized anticipating that relations would deteriorate. Castro was sworn in as prime minister on February 16, 1959. A year of worsening relations between Havana and Washington followed. Revolutionaries made good on their promise to distribute land to those who needed it, and began to expropriate property from large farms, including those owned by U.S. interests. When Esso, Shell, and Texaco refused to process oil sent to

Cuba by the Soviet Union, Castro nationalized their refineries. In response, Eisenhower cut Cuba's sugar quota. The revolutionary government confiscated more U.S. property.

So it went, back and forth. The White House accused Cuba of supporting insurgencies in other Latin American countries. Havana, no doubt, eventually would do so. But in the first years of the revolution, the activity that buzzed around the island was more a hearkening back to the Caribbean Legion, as activists from the Dominican Republic, Haiti, and Nicaragua hoped to follow Cuba's lead and dislodge their dictators. It wouldn't be until June 6, 1961—two months after the United States tried to overthrow Castro at the Bay of Pigs—that Cuba would establish a Ministry of the Interior in charge of training recruits from other countries to spread the revolution in a more coordinated fashion.[10]

Well before that happened, Eisenhower, in late October 1959, had approved a plan to cultivate opposition leaders within Cuba and allow Cuban exiles to stage sea raids from United States territory. On March 17, 1960, he authorized "a program of covert action against the Castro regime." The U.S. president also ordered Castro's assassination, saying he wanted him "sawed off." On April 6, Eisenhower's assistant secretary of state for Latin America wrote that the economic sanctions put in place by the White House were meant to decrease "real wages, to bring about hunger, desperation and overthrow of government."

The revolution had the support of a vast majority of Cubans, the official wrote, and the "only foreseeable means of alienating internal support is through disenchantment and disaffection based on economic dissatisfaction and hardship." This was around the same time that the White House directed the Agency to eliminate Patrice Lumumba, prime minister of the newly independent Congo republic. Lumumba was killed on January 17, 1961.[11]

Closer to home, Washington had less luck. Kennedy had taken over from Eisenhower and green-lit the CIA's proxy invasion, a battle that started on April 17, 1961. Cuba's revolutionary army easily beat back the Cuban exiles, a triumph that turned Castro into a continental hero. Cuba did what Guatemala couldn't: hold off the United States.

Cuba, Arthur Schlesinger wrote, "was high" on Kennedy's "list of emotions." He wanted, Schlesinger said, to unleash "the terrors of the earth" on the island.

JFK followed up the fiasco at the Bay of Pigs with Operation Mongoose, putting his brother Robert, the nation's attorney general, in charge, alongside the legendary Edward Lansdale, pioneer of death-squad covert ops in the Philippines and Southeast Asia. "My idea is to stir things up on island with espionage, sabotage, general disorder," JFK wrote in his diary. Taking out Castro, Robert Kennedy said in a January 19, 1962, meeting of the Mongoose group, was "top priority" and "no time, money, effort—or manpower is to be spared." The operation discussed using chemicals to debilitate sugar workers and unleashing "gangster elements" who had been shut down by the revolution. "It's got to be done and it will be done," said JFK.[12]

Pause for a moment and think back to how nuanced and gentle FDR's response was to the Mexican Revolution, and to economic nationalism more broadly, and that will provide a good contrast to how hard, unbending, and remorseless the United States' Cold War national security state had become by the time Castro marched into Havana.

Lansdale set up operations in a Miami office, in a campaign worked by nearly four hundred people. The CIA had quickly established relations with anti-Castro groups throughout Latin America, drawing up "extensive plans for the formation of goon squads throughout much of Latin America in an attempt to counter the pro-Castro elements of various nations." The CIA's deputy director of plans, Richard Bissell, took "considerable interest" in this "goon squad program," and soon pro-U.S. gangs were breaking up Cuban solidarity rallies in Mexico City, Lima, and San José, Costa Rica.[13]

Lansdale and other covert operators worked up ever more outlandish schemes to end Castro. None of them worked—many, though proposed, weren't ever actually tried. In a way, the psychological warriors became their own marks, having conned themselves into overestimating their talents and intelligence. Lansdale's proposal to spark a messianic counterrevolution brings us full circle, back to Cotton Mather's and Samuel Sewall's hope that "bombing" Havana with the gospels would presage the Second Coming. Lansdale's plan entailed spreading rumors that Castro was the Antichrist and the return of the true Christ was imminent. At a critical point, a U.S. submarine stationed off Cuba would fire star-shell flares to illuminate the sky, the effect amplified by broadcasts announcing Jesus's arrival.

More effective were mundane covert operations, paramilitary violence, and more credible psyops, reinforced by payoffs, press propaganda, and manipulation of allied unions and political parties. In the wake of the Cuban Revolution, the United States backed a quick round of coups: El Salvador in 1961; the Dominican Republic, Guatemala (again), and Honduras in 1963; Brazil and British Guiana in 1964. All told, Washington had a hand in sixteen regime changes between 1961 and 1969.[14]

Washington kept its mighty Wurlitzer tuned, directing psychological warfare across the continent, keeping time to the "perpetual rhythm of struggle, in and out of war."*

---

* Psychological war didn't end with the Cold War. In 2014, Washington funded the creation of the Twitter-clone ZunZuneo, which is Cuban slang for a songbird's tweet. The goal, according to government documents, was to first build users through mundane content, on popular topics such as soccer and music. Later, when ZunZuneo reached a critical level of users, the network's managers would begin to introduce more political content with the goal of sparking "smart mobs." The point, according to one document, was to encourage a Cuban revolutionary "spring" that would "renegotiate the balance of power between the state and society." The Wurlitzer is still pumping.

War of the Gods, or,
A Second Enlightenment

Camilo Torres was nineteen years old when Gaitán was assassinated. He watched the fire engulf Bogotá's downtown from his leafy diocesan seminary in the Andean foothills north of the city. No newspapers or radios were allowed within the seminary walls, as the space was meant to inspire timelessness. Time broke in that day.

Torres was from a wealthy, Liberal family. He was born in the historic center of the city, not far from where Simón Bolívar lived his last years. The area housed the public buildings, including the ministry of justice, which were in flames. Camilo attended Bogotá's best city schools and was kicked out of more than one for troublemaking. Handsome and charismatic, he knew everyone, just as his parents knew everyone, including Jorge Eliécer Gaitán. His father, Calixto, was a well-traveled pediatrician and diplomat who had represented Colombia at the League of Nations before being appointed rector of Colombia's medical school. His mother, Isabel, was a Restrepo Gaviria—two surnames that carried status. Isabel's wealthy merchant grandfather was an *aguerrido*—one of those warring Liberals mentioned earlier—who funded endless nineteenth-century revolts against Conservative governments. Isabel's father had died in one of those wars. And they inspired Camilo's university friend Gabriel García Márquez, who in *One*

Hundred Years of Solitude depicted one such Liberal, Colonel Aureliano Buendía, and his thirty-two failed revolutions.

The Conservative father of Camilo's girlfriend, Teresa Montalvo, had earlier introduced the boy to two French Dominican priests, Gabriel-Marie Blanchet and Jean-Baptiste Nielly, who were part of an exchange program meant to revitalize Colombia's moribund Dominican order. Blanchet had been there since the late 1930s. Father Nielly had arrived in early 1947 after fighting in the French resistance. In the great struggle within the Catholic Church between tradition and modernity, Gabriel-Marie and Jean-Baptiste were with the moderns, those who were horrified that many of their brethren had turned themselves into servants of Nazi totalitarianism. The two clerics believed Catholicism should shed its pretense of immutable transcendence. Along with other French Dominicans in Colombia, they were members of a Catholic renewal group called Economy and Humanism, founded in Marseille in 1941 and dedicated to the belief that the economy should serve humans, not humans the economy.[1]

Torres was attracted to Blanchet and Nielly's vision of a "simple Catholicism," unaligned in Colombia's eternal war between Liberals and Conservatives, and to their idea that Catholicism could reclaim its organic unity—not by restoring the ecclesiastic power of the Church but by recentering it on the dignity of individual human beings. Torres appreciated their efforts to solve problems in a "more rational, more humane way." By early 1948, a movement for Catholic lay reflection had spread throughout Colombia, through study groups organized as if they were revolutionary cells. After the Bogotazo and during the war that followed, many of these groups became political, more interested in addressing humans as "social beings." Good intentions and well-formed philosophies weren't enough, as Father León José Moreau, another French Dominican in Colombia, wrote, to understand the "apocalyptic nature of current events."[2]

Camilo's decision to become a priest had unnerved his Liberal parents. To them, the Dominicans, despite their French resistance bona fides, seemed more fascist than socialist, their talk of Catholic renewal stalking for falangism. Isabel refused to let her son enter the Dominican order's Our Lady of Chiquinquirá convent, which was located eighty miles outside of Bogotá.

She raced to the city's railroad station to pull Camilo off a train just before it was set to depart. Calixto, then attending a medical convention in Washington, flew home to help with the crisis. In the end, the family compromised, and Camilo entered the nearby archdiocese seminary.

Camilo Torres would go on to be one of the founders of modern Latin American sociology. He had already spent time in Bogotá's sprawling shanty towns and imagined he knew some of the people setting the fires in the city below. What he remembered most about that night, hours after Gaitán's murder, was an acrid, sulphury smell.[3]

Not Going to Be Good and Is Liable to Be Bad

In Colombia, the first priests to radicalize were the conservative ones. During times of calm, Catholicism functioned as a unifier, of the sprawling Spanish Empire and then of independent nations. During times of social stress, however, Catholicism could transform into a field of bloody struggle.

There was the loving Christ, accepting of the world he made and saved. Then there was the implacable Christ, who sided with the *encomenderos* as they murdered Bartolomé de las Casas's allies. Over the years, Christ the Punisher appeared, say his followers, to avenge specific grievances—the New Laws, independence, abolition, secular marriage and divorce, and land reform, for example. Now, in Colombia, starting with Gómez's reign, the fight was against "crypto-Liberals" and "crypto-Communists."

What became known as liberation theology wasn't a vanguard, but a rear guard, a reaction to a reaction that left no breathing room, no space for Catholics who wanted to find remedies for the suffocating servility of everyday life.

It's worth quoting two descriptions of such servility, given years after Allied victory promised political equality. The first is by a U.S. aid worker, David Lazar, who when asked to give his opinion of Peru answered: "Feudal would describe it." Well into the 1960s, haciendas were still being sold "with their Indians," as if they were chattel. When approached by strangers, peasants would immediately look downward. Lazar said you could almost hear them thinking: "Please just go away. If you do anything it is not going to be good and is liable to be bad, so please just go away." The other account is by Salomon Isacovici, a Romanian Jew who survived the Nazi death camps before emigrating to Ecuador. Isacovici couldn't forget the horrors he witnessed, not because of traumatic repetition but because labor relations in Ecuador reminded him of the relations between prisoners and guards: "No matter how hard I would try to erase the Holocaust from my mind, the expressionless faces of the Indians constantly reminded me of those times of interminable torture." There was nothing but "pain and suffering" for Indians working the mines and plantations of the high Andes. "The magnitude of their physical and mental suffering made me wonder if I were not once again trapped in the camps at Auschwitz and Jaworzno."[4]

Conservative Catholics in Colombia, as elsewhere, wanted to keep the world the way Lazar and Isacovici described it. "New Catholics," as reformers were called before the term *liberation theology* entered circulation, believed such servility, the way feelings of inferiority and helplessness were internalized, was an insult to God.

Many priests and nuns, even before Gaitán's murder but accelerating quickly thereafter, began to advance Catholic social doctrine. Colombia's Jesuits in the 1950s worked as "moral advisers" to trade unionists, and before long the Jesuit-allied Union of Colombian Workers was the nation's largest federation. In the shantytowns that ringed cities and in the countryside, priests, nuns, and Church laypeople built Christian Base Communities—rural and urban collectives dedicated both to improving their members' lives and to democratizing national politics. These communities helped organize literacy campaigns, cooperatives, and community radio stations. This work inevitably became politicized.

Most Protestant missionaries in Colombia hailed from mainline churches back home, and upon arriving in country, thought of themselves as not just preachers of the word of God but defenders of what they called an American way of life. Yet ministering to the poor, in witness to their daily struggles, created more than a few "inflammatory radicals." President Gómez let loose against the missionaries, encouraging his followers to dynamite their churches and break up their congregations. They killed hundreds of Protestants, mostly Colombians but also several United States citizens.[5]

The violence affected Reverand Richard Shaull, a Presbyterian minister who had arrived in Colombia prior to the events of 1948. Shaull lived and preached in a working-class neighborhood in Barranquilla, and over time became entranced by Gaitán's humanism. The people are living in "black despair," he wrote his church superior after Gaitán's killing. Shaull transferred to Brazil, which brought him into contact with more progressive Catholics, and he eventually carried his Gaitanismo with him back to the United States, joining with activists like Martin Luther King Jr. to push the National Council of Churches and the World Council of Churches to take stands on civil rights and the Vietnam War and toward a reckoning with decolonization and structural domination.* Shaull dedicated himself to connecting Catholic liberation in Latin America with Protestant dissent in the United States. He came to believe that if Protestants threw themselves into the struggle of the poor, they would rediscover the lost radicalism of their Reformation.[6]

A New Sociology, a New Clampdown

Camilo Torres was out of the country for most of the 1950s. He took his vows and then traveled to Belgium, studying at Université Catholique de Louvain, where he was influenced by a cohort of young Belgian Catholic Marxist professors and fellow students. Torres had come to believe in the Church's capacity to change, to become the only worldwide institution that could make real "a life centered totally on the love of others." Theological debates attempting to find points of unity between Christianity and Marxism, then starting to take place in Latin America, held little interest for

---

* Once settled in Princeton Theological Seminary, Shaull directed the dissertations of several Latin American Catholics, including the Brazilian Rubem Azevedo Alves, an influential advocate of liberation theology.

Torres. "What mattered," writes the historian John Womack, was that Catholic activists were saying that "God now revealed Himself not for men to depend on, but for them to answer to. This Torres took as a commandment."[7]

Torres returned to Colombia in 1959. The war in the countryside was ongoing, though it was largely removed from public discussion in Bogotá. Liberal and Conservative elites had brokered a so-called National Front, in which their parties would alternate power and Liberals would urge their peasant supporters to stand down and disarm. The "chain reaction" of the Cuban Revolution, combined with the general revolt of the 1960s, had jump-started intellectual life. Peace among political elites thanks to the National Front made it possible to do political work in cities, and in some places in the countryside.

Father Torres was appointed chaplain of the National University. His real objective, which he quickly achieved, was to establish the school's first department of sociology and the nation's first sociological association. C. Wright Mills's work in the early 1960s on the "power elite" in the United States was part of a renewal of sociology, linked to a broader New Left and to decolonization struggles. In Brazil, the Instituto Superior de Estudos Brasileiros, founded in 1955, became a focal point of critical thought, key in the education of Paulo Freire, author of the influential *Pedagogy of the Oppressed*. Torres and other social scientists dedicated themselves to using applied sociology to study the sources of Colombian misery, investigating the living and working conditions of the country's marginalized population. In 1959, Torres and his associates, both Christian and secular, established a Communal Action Commission within the Ministry of National Education, a vehicle to use literacy programs to increase grassroots political participation.[8]

Within a short time, Juntas de Acción Comunal were established in nearly every municipality in the country. The project reflected efforts to build social movements beyond the traditional vehicles of unions and peasant leagues. Torres's Juntas echoed community-organizing initiatives elsewhere, including, in the United States, Saul Alinksy's Industrial Areas Foundation and King's Southern Christian Leadership Conference.

Latin America's political opening of the 1960s was not unmarred by repression. In response to the Cuban Revolution, the Pentagon and CIA loaded the national-security forces of allied nations with fearsome repressive power, providing a greater capacity to terrorize than the little Hitlers, Himmlers, and Francos possessed a decade earlier.* These were the years when the region became most associated with forced disappearances, torture, and massacres.[9]

Fear wouldn't settle over all the continent all at once. There existed enclaves in which writers, artists, and activists could work in relative safety. Mexico, and then Cuba, offered secure refuge for exiles of all kinds, not just from Spanish or Latin American dictators. Racism existed, no doubt, yet many exiles from the United States said hatred based on skin color felt less totalitarian, less all-pervasive in Latin America. The African American artist Elizabeth Catlett gave up her U.S. citizenship and moved to Mexico, calling it the "the nearest place without racism and segregation." Chile until its 1973 coup, and then Argentina until the military took over in 1976, were also places of intellectual and cultural vibrancy. Nicaragua after the triumph of the 1979 Sandinista Revolution was a whirlwind of scholarly and artistic creation.[10]

The experience of unevenness added to the ferment, of living in countries that were modern but not quite modern, where the countryside felt like Europe in the sixteenth century and city streets were jammed with big Detroit cars. Washington touted freedom and democracy, even as it was destabilizing democratic institutions, subverting the press, buying politicians and trade unionists, spreading disinformation, and funding cultural magazines to slander intellectuals committed to change. The raw material of irony there was aplenty, and it was mined by artists, writers, poets, and musicians.

---

* One example: Navy veteran Dan Mitrione arrived in Brazil in the early 1960s as part of a team whose job it was to systematize torture, to apply a "scientific method." Mitrione took beggars off the streets and tortured them in classrooms filled with Brazilian police. According to the Brazilian Church, the pain inflicted was designed to create "an absolute schism between body and the spirit," to render asunder that which makes us mortal humans: the unity of flesh and soul. Mitrione then transferred to Uruguay, where he taught the same lessons and invented unique torture instruments. If they had electricity, Spanish Inquisitors might have found Mitrone's devices, including something called "the dragon's chair," useful.

Feminist novelists probed realms of experience that their male counterparts ignored. "My style, as you know," wrote Mexico's Rosario Castellanos, "consists of taking an insignificant fact and turning it into a transcendent truth."

A Second Enlightenment

The biggest irony is that the institution the philosopher Sidney Hook once called the "oldest and greatest totalitarian movement in history"—the Catholic Church—supplied exploited communities with the tools for critical thinking. The region's critical intellectuals, including teachers, agronomists, health-care workers, economists, psychologists, novelists, artists, poets, playwrights, and musicians, probed what had become a key phrase for Latin America's emerging New Left: *realidad social*. The term comes from phenomenological philosophy, having to do with one's perception of the external world. Latin Americans used it in a more politicized way, meaning to peel back the layers of mystification, to break through the commonplaceness of exploitation, to not just see the kinds of scenes described by Lazar and Isacovici but understand how such misery is maintained across the generations and how it could be transcended.[11]

Much of this new critical thinking was run through Catholic organizations called Centros de Capacitación Social, or Centers of Social Empowerment. A Basque-born Jesuit, Father Manuel Aguirre Elorriaga, started the first such center in Venezuela, with others soon sprouting throughout the hemisphere. The Centros offered short courses, or *cursillos*, on political and economic problems. They were meant to channel concerned Catholics away from Marxism and into Christian Democratic parties.

In many places, the opposite occurred. It was difficult to find instructors who weren't working within a broad Marxist perspective. And as it turned out, it was hard to analyze any given country's social structure, its *realidad social*, in a way that didn't lead to greater militancy. In Guatemala in the middle of the 1960s, a mix of middle- and upper-class boys and girls from the Jesuit's Liceo Javier and Maryknoll's Monte María attended seminars in Guatemala City's Centro. They went on, in the early 1970s, to organize what they called the Guerrilla Army of the Poor, a rebel group that led a formidable insurgency that nearly brought down Guatemala's military government.

Father Torres was ahead of his time. The theorists of the new Catholicism hadn't yet written their foundational books. Peru's Father Gustavo Gutiérrez wouldn't give his influential lecture, "Hacia una teología de la liberación," until 1968, which gave the movement its name: Liberation Theology.

Yet before that, Torres's "new sociology" spread throughout a hemisphere alive with art, song, poetry, fiction, criticism, and social science. The darkness would soon come. But before it did, Latin America in the 1960s was a period of such intense intellectual vitality it should be considered equal to Europe's Enlightenment.[12]

New Catholics pursued advanced degrees in Europe and the United States, becoming doctors, anthropologists, psychologists, economists, and philosophers. In the late 1950s, a group of Central American–based Jesuits made a collective decision to enter doctoral programs abroad to gain knowledge that they then would use to aid in their country's emancipation from neocolonialism. Father Segundo Montes became an anthropologist; Father Ignacio Ellacuría, a philosopher; and Father Martín-Baró, a social psychologist. Martín-Baró founded what became known as Liberation Psychology, or the *Psicología de Liberación*, which developed methods to treat the kind of social trauma associated with Latin America's high levels of exploitation and political repression. A radical psychology, Martín-Baró thought, could also help "deideologize reality," puncturing the myths that internalize feelings of inferiority. Martín-Baró and his students wanted to help peasants look their *patrones* in the eye.[13]

As a young boy, Father Ellacuría and his family had barely survived Franco's savage bombing of Guernica by taking shelter in the city's metro. Ignacio joined the Jesuits in 1947 and was sent to El Salvador a year later. Considered among the most philosophically rigorous of Latin America's liberation theologians, Ellacuría wrote that Christ's Crucifixion wasn't meant to enforce abnegation but, like that disemboweled Indian who died in Las Casas's arms, to show that all humans are equal: we all die. It's time, Ellacuría wrote just before his own execution, "to bring the crucified down from their crosses." Wood can be used for more useful things than martyrdom.[14]

Scholars tend to study Latin America's various contributions to the humanities and social sciences in silos. Literary theorists study the "boom" novels of García Márquez, Mario Vargas Llosa, and others. Economists and sociologists focus on dependency theory. Intellectual historians have recently noticed the importance of American International Law, along with the efforts of the region's jurists to shape the global order. And scholars of religion have written a great deal on liberation theology.

But these strains of knowledge were intertwined. The Latin America challenge was of a piece.

By the end of World War II, Latin America had done the unthinkable: it had forced the great powers to recognize the sovereign equality of all nations, abrogated the doctrine of conquest, and provided a model for a world system organized around the presumption of mutual interests rather than inherent antagonisms. But a reform of diplomacy wasn't enough to strike at the domestic sources of exploitation. Just as eighteenth-century philosophers wrote against royal absolutism in all its stultifying effects, Latin Americans wrote and worked against all the various manifestations of dependency: economic, psychological, cultural, political, and moral.

The spread of liberation theology, dependency theory, and artistic critique went hand in hand. "Dependence and liberation are correlative terms," Father Gutiérrez wrote. "An analysis of the situation of dependence leads one to attempt to escape from it."[15]

Correlative Terms

Just as the conservative clergy were the principal popularizers of fascist philosophy, egalitarian ecclesiastics transmitted theoretical critiques of empire, capitalism, and militarism to the Catholic grassroots. They did so through workshops, meetings, sermons, and conferences. By late 1960s, the Protestant minister Julio de Santa Ana, affiliated with the Ecumenical Centre of Services for Evangelization and Popular Education in São Paulo, Brazil, was organizing seminars with students on "the theory of dependency." Phillip Berryman was a Roman Catholic priest based, in the 1960s, in Panama City's poor Afro Panamanian neighborhood of El Chorrillo. He recalls being thunderstruck when he first heard a critical economist making the case that the overdevelopment of Europe and the United States depended on the underdevelopment of the poorer regions of the globe. It "clicked right away, once you see it, it clicks," Berryman said.

Nicaragua's Ernesto Cardenal had spent two years as a novice monk at Thomas Merton's Cistercian Abbey of Gethsemani in rural Kentucky before returning to Central America to establish a commune of peasant poets, painters, and sculptors on Mancarrón Island in Lake Nicaragua's Solentiname Archipelago. Every Sunday, Cardenal held Mass. But in lieu of a traditional sermon, he encouraged political discussion on economics and world affairs. Folk songs filled the rustic church, singing of Christ Worker, or Christ Peasant.

"The campesinos' discussions were often more profound than those of many theologians," remembered Cardenal, translating concepts associated with dependency theory into an emancipationist folk theology. An everyday egalitarianism governed this and similar Christian Base Communities spreading throughout Latin America. Priests, nuns, professors, and professionals dropped their titles. Everyone was *compañero* or *compañera*. A quiet feminism began to sprout, with women taking more of a role in pastoral work.*

Critical economics infused the region's postwar cultural ferment. Gabriel García Márquez's *One Hundred Years of Solitude* reads like a literary corollary to dependency theory, where even the memories of banana plantation workers are captured by foreign capital. Socialist realism, in art and literature, tends to focus on the outward manifestations of injustice. Latin America's magic realism, in contrast, used fantastical imagery to capture what Gaitán's executioner, Juan Roa Sierra, called the things you can't see. All

---

* After Somoza's national guard, in 1977, broke up the collective, burned down its buildings, and killed several congregants, Father Cardenal and many of his congregation joined Nicaragua's Sandinista insurgency.

sorts of impossibilities happened in the stories of, among others, Cuba's Alejo Carpentier, Guatemala's Miguel Ángel Asturias, and Colombia's García Márquez, as they sought to reveal the less visible metaphysics of power, the intangible ways patriarchs, dictators, landlords, and foreign capitalists maintained their rule. Magic realism as a genre would capture the imagination of the decolonizing nations, where the unevenness—the incongruities and hypocrisies—of the postwar world were especially sharp.

In Buenos Aires, artists associated with the Centro de Arte y Comunicación pioneered a world movement they called *Arte de Sistemas*, or systems art, whose objective was to reveal structures of economic underdevelopment. Repression in Argentina increased, and as it did the work of these artists, at first abstract, became more explicit. After the Argentine army summarily executed sixteen political prisoners on a remote Patagonia naval base in 1972, the artists Roberto Duarte, Eduardo Leonetti, and Luis Pazos turned a public restroom in Buenos Aires into a protest memorial. First, they wrote *La realidad subterránea* above the bathroom's door, over which they painted sixteen white crosses. Inside the building, they installed graphic photographs of Holocaust victims. The point was clear. Under the simulacra of everyday Argentine politics there existed a "subterranean reality," a fascism that could be traced back to Nazi Germany.[16]

Liberation theology and dependency theory were "correlative" from their inception. It was a potent mix. Faith and moral fire plus theorems and data added up to a belief that capitalism was a system void of virtue, and that God's children deserved a life of dignity, not one subject to the punishments, plunders, and prizes of the so-called free market. It was not commerce that made one a more benevolent human, as some of the West's moral philosophers would have it. Rather, insisted the theologians, psychologists, playwrights, and pedagogues of liberation, it was through politics—and especially through political dissent and struggle—that one became a more defined and empathetic individual, that one cultivated sympathies and solidarities, that one got a sense of one's self in time and space, in history and the world.[17]

The Vatican had coordinated with the National Security Agency against Moscow since the start of the Cold War. Yet as early as 1962, the CIA was warning Kennedy that the papacy couldn't be counted on to backstop Communism, due to the "left-wing drift" of the Church in Latin America. In many countries, Christian Democrats were splitting between conservatives and militants, with the militants breaking with their CIA handlers. Father Thomas Melville and Sister Marian Peter, members of the Maryknoll Order, had arrived in Guatemala after the coup against Arbenz as part of an effort to consolidate conservative Church authority in the countryside. By the late 1960s, they had grown so horrified at the abuse endured by the rural poor that they shut down their mission and joined a guerrilla front, to give the rebel movement a "Christian presence."

Such a rapid turnaround in political allegiance led Lyndon Johnson's national security adviser Walt Rostow to write the president in astonishment: "Just look at what our Maryknolls are up to."[18]

Richard Nixon, too, complained. In a March 1971 meeting with Henry Kissinger and other members of his staff, he said that in the "old days" one could "count on the Catholic Church for many things." Not anymore.[19]

The radicalization of Catholicism amused Fidel Castro, who shared the generational anticlericalism of Torres's Liberal parents. Ever annoyed at the Soviet Union for turning socialism into a rigid orthodoxy, Castro asked an interviewer how it was possible that the Soviet Politburo was becoming ever more "ecclesiastic" just as "sectors of the clergy are becoming revolutionary."

The United States found none of it funny. "A growing despair," a CIA analyst wrote of the situation in Guatemala, "is indicated by the defections" of priests and nuns to the left, who now believe that "no solution" exists "to the miserable poverty of most Guatemalans" except the "violent destruction of the prevailing order." According to *The New York Times*, some 340 Brazilian bishops, out of a total of 358, supported liberation theology. Priests calling for "revolutionary change," noted a CIA report, were more absolute in their beliefs than "Moscow-aligned Communists in Latin America."[20]

The Catholic Church was bursting open, no longer able to reconcile its Sepúlvedas and its Vitorias, nor contain Las Casas's indignant force, pent up for centuries, within shady cloisters mewed. The prophetic promise of deliverance could no longer be deferred, no longer remediated by individual acts of charity and decency. Gutiérrez described it as an "irruption of the poor into history."

Back in Colombia, Father Camilo Torres tried to work within the narrow confines of Colombia's Liberal-Conservative pact. By the early 1960s, he'd become known throughout the Americas, even in the United States, for his sociology and for his essays on faith and justice. At home, Torres was a national figure, not unlike Gaitán.

In March 1965, he organized the Frente Unido del Pueblo, or United Front of the People. His goal was to merge all the dissident parts of Colombian society: disaffected Liberals, trade unionists, peasants, new Catholics, critical Protestants, socialists, the fledgling Christian Democratic Party, the historic Communist Party, and Cuba-inspired radicals. Torres hoped to gather those he called *los no-alineados*, citizens nonaligned with either the Liberal or Conservative parties. They comprised, Torres said, most of the nation's population. He referred to their politics as *anti-nada*, against nothing—since nothing is all they ever got. The phrase was also used to mean that while the United Front was not Communist, it was not anti-Communist either.[21]

Anti-nada but pro-everything—everything that brought dignity to people's lives. The United Front's platform was familiar: land reform; nationalization; planned, decent housing; better wages; and a more expansive welfare state.[22]

But how to take power? Torres said he wanted to find a new path, a mass movement based on participatory democracy that could break the two-party monopoly yet somehow try to maintain, as Gaitán hoped to do, the rule of law and political pluralism. But much had changed since Gaitán's time. The state capacity to repress had grown exponentially, and it was inconceivable that political elites would have allowed the return of the kind of mass movement Gaitán had led. Torres spoke vaguely of a general strike, or a popular coup. He called himself a revolutionary and his movement a revolution, long before he joined the insurgency. "The revolutionary struggle is a priestly and Christian struggle," he said in a speech at a union rally.

Torres took Cuba as an inspiration but not a model to emulate. He wanted a peaceful transition to a more just, more democratic society. Yet in Colombia, the line between unarmed and armed politics was fluid. Rebel groups popped up, and then faded away. Jorge Eliécer Gaitán's daughter, Gloria, organized, with the help of Cuba, a handful of intellectuals into a guerrilla front, which conducted a few hit-and-run actions before dissolving.[23]

There existed, by the mid-1960s, three insurgent groups in Colombia. One was the small Ejército Popular de Liberación and another the larger Fuerzas Armadas Revolucionarias de Colombia, or FARC, which had grown out of the peasant self-defense leagues of the 1940s. The third was the newly formed Ejército de Liberación Nacional, or ELN. The FARC was part of an older left, and tended to be secular, led by radicalized Liberals and Communists; its cadre were the survivors of the wrath unleashed by Conservatives in the years since Gaitán's killing. The ELN, in contrast, flowed out of the currents that gave rise to liberation theology. Torres was close to the ELN, since it had several priests and nuns in its ranks—men and women who understood themselves to be less fighting a war than creating a new kind of Christian community. They imagined the ELN to be an expression of "the true Church," Christ the "first guerilla."

Torres had come a long way in the two decades since he looked down from his seminary and saw Bogotá burning. He was a prolific writer, and he agonized in his essays over the question of violence. Revolution was "inevitable," Torres wrote, considering the intolerable circumstances in which people lived. He returned again and again to Saint Paul and the Christian ideal of love, but added that for love to mean anything it had to be effective, it had to alleviate suffering. "I understood that in Colombia one could not achieve this love solely by means of charity. There was an urgency to make a change in political, economic, and social structures. This called for a revolution that was inextricably linked with love."[24]

The United Front of Popular Movements splintered. Torres had hoped that the urgency of the moment might be enough to overcome the suffocating politics of the Cold War. It couldn't. Christian Democrats and Socialists wouldn't work with Communists. By 1966, after years of Washington's blank-check funding of the country's security forces, Torres felt he was left with two unacceptable choices. He could continue doing what he was doing and, as he put it, be "murdered on Septima Avenida like Gaitán." Or he could go into exile. The CIA had by this point decided that Torres was a problem, describing him as a "rallying point" for student extremists, Communists, and other radicals.[25]

Torres refused both options. He instead joined the Ejército de Liberación Nacional. "I say, a little bit in jest but also quite seriously," he told an interviewer before going underground, "that the Catholic who is not revolutionary, who is not with the revolution, is living in mortal sin."[26]

Like José Martí, Camilo Torres was killed in his first military operation, on February 15, 1966. He was thirty-seven years old. An obituary in *Commonweal* magazine wondered if it were essentially a suicide—if his true death hadn't come earlier, if, seeing no political solution for his country's intolerable social reality, he had given up and joined the guerrillas to die.

The war continued for another half century, soon to fuse with the violence associated with cocaine trafficking, and as it did, Colombia remained a steadfast Washington ally.

50.

Restoring the Magisterium

A merican International Law, dependency theory, liberation theology. It would be crude, but not wrong, to say that Washington responded with blunt force, with the goon-squad program, to defeat these three political and ethical traditions. By 1976, a decade after Father Torres's death, nearly all of South and Central America were run by radical anti-Communist military regimes aligned with Washington. The repression they unleashed was epic. Yet while violence was necessary to defeat Latin America's challenge to the United States, it wasn't sufficient to declare victory. The Americas have been, since the Conquest, an arena of ideological struggle, a battle over how to justify dominion. And so as Washington gained ground and Moscow faltered, a moral adjustment began to get under way, a rearrangement of premises and principles to legitimate what would soon be a new, unipolar global order.

The General Domain of the Nation

In Nicaragua, the governing Sandinistas, who had won their revolution and toppled the Somoza dynasty in 1979, were eclectic leftists, allied with Cuba but considerably more democratic, filled with Socialists, Marxists, doctors, lawyers, engineers, economists, peasants, workers, writers, feminists, and Christians, like the poet-priest Ernesto Cardenal. Their agenda was, as the CIA put it for Cuba, the "common stock" of Latin American reform: land, food, housing, health. They wore their humanism on their sleeves, and for a time after their victory all of Managua felt like Cardenal's Christian Base Community at Solentiname, full of music, open-air masses, and murals.[1]

A year later, Ronald Reagan won the U.S. presidency, promising to restore his nation's power and purpose after the grim 1970s, after Vietnam and Watergate. And with the Soviet Union fading, the United States was indeed resurgent, gathering new powers, building new momentum. The Sandinistas in Nicaragua in the 1980s were as unacceptable as Castro's coalition in Cuba in the 1960s, leading the White House to begin to finance the Contras, a counterrevolutionary force made up mostly, at first, of Somoza's former national guard. The Contras soon developed a reputation for brutality, known for cutting the throats of their captives with the large Kabar knives, burning down schools and health clinics, and blowing up rural hydroelectric plants.[2]

In 1986, the International Court of Justice found Washington guilty of waging an illegal war of aggression against Nicaragua. The ICJ ruled that the United States' patronage of the Contras was illegal, as was the CIA's mining of Nicaragua's harbors and distribution of "how-to" torture manuals to anti-Sandinistas. These actions, the court said, all violated Nicaragua's sovereignty and the prohibition against intervention. The court ordered Washington to pay reparations. Nicaragua asked for seventeen billion dollars.

The court constituted the legal arm of the United Nations, founded in 1945 with significant input from Latin American jurists. Washington had brought numerous cases to it over the years, including most recently a boundary dispute with Canada. Yet as decolonization advanced, as London, Paris, and Amsterdam gave up their African and Asian possessions, many of the court's judges now came from the new nations of the Third World. In the case Nicaragua took to the court, judges from Great Britain, Japan, and the United States voted mostly in favor of Washington. Judges from Poland, Nigeria, Senegal, Italy, France, India, and China ruled for Nicaragua.

In response, the Reagan administration announced it was withdrawing from the ICJ's compulsory jurisdiction. Nicaragua then went to the United Nations to seek redress, but Washington used its Security Council veto to squash the complaint. All that talking in San Francisco in 1945 trying to find a way to balance the world and the region, the endless hours of debates and committee meetings, and finally the compromises—and four decades later all that mattered was that the United States had an absolute Security Council veto.

Nicaragua was "politicizing" international law, Reagan's State Department complained. The White House justified its exit from the court's authority by invoking the "basic issue of sovereignty." The right of a nation "to defend itself," the Reagan administration said, "is an inherent sovereign right that cannot be compromised."[3]

Washington's nervy citations of sovereignty and self-defense to justify its aggression discredited international law. And if the United States, once the ICJ rejected that defense, could simply withdraw from its jurisdiction, then it was clear that law was not law at all. The thing is legal because I wish it, France's Louis XIV is reported to have said. And Washington didn't wish it legal that others could judge its right to lay siege to a small nation. The Soviet Union made no pretense that international law represented anything other than power, marshaled to serve the interests of the powerful. But the United States fought the Cold War in defense of the liberal order, supposedly founded on human rights and the rule of law. The legal scholar Eric Posner called Reagan's withdrawal from the court a "watershed moment" in the unraveling of multilateralism.[4]

Another watershed moment was George H. W. Bush's 1989 invasion of Panama, launched just days after the fall of the Berlin Wall, to capture a former CIA asset, the dictator Manuel Noriega. Noriega had been a helpful Washington ally in the past but had become a liability. The UN and even the OAS (which for decades rubber-stamped Washington's actions as if Nelson Rockefeller were still caucusing its member states) refused to sanction the operation. It didn't matter. The Soviet Union was soon to collapse. Who was left to argue?

It was the first such military action since the start of the Cold War not justified by the need to contain Communism. Rather, Bush cited Noriega's violation of human rights, his trafficking in narcotics, and the need to re-store democracy to Panama. And, like Reagan earlier with Nicaragua, self-defense: Noriega was reported to have encouraged the harassment of U.S. soldiers and U.S. employees of the Panama Canal Zone. To that end, the White House invoked Article 51 of the United Nations' charter. That article recognized the right of *nations*, not *individuals*, to defend themselves. But the Bush team took an expansive view of self-defense, extending the article to cover U.S. citizens abroad. Thus echoed Calvin Coolidge's boundless definition of sovereignty, in which "the person and property of a citizen are part of the general domain of the nation even when abroad."[5]

A Lower International Plane

It had been exhausting for Cold War policymakers and intellectuals to wage an ideological struggle against Socialists, Communists, and left-wing Christians who claimed to represent a higher stage of humanism, of Western reason, than did property-grubbing, profit-worshipping capitalists. Noriega, though, was clownishly brutal, indifferent to human life. That brutality was useful to Washington when he was a friend. And useful when he became a foe.[6]

Back in the early 1900s, in that conflict with Venezuela over tar and debt, a Hague judge ruled that even countries that were "revolutionary, nerveless, and of ill report" were covered by international law. Noriega let Washington revisit that opinion. The Panamanian was unquestionably nerveless and of ill report, with journalists inevitably commenting on his squat stature and pockmarked face. Elliott Abrams, the secretary of state for Inter-American Affairs, was, upon first meeting him, "taken aback by his ugliness." *Newsweek* described Noriega as a "mean-streets Mestizo, the bastard son of his father's domestic," who shook hands with a "damp" palm and a "limp" grip. "A prima facie thug" said one military officer, as the press reported on his sexual depravity and "voodoo" practices.[7]

Washington called the Sandinistas many things, but never devil worshippers.

Noriega, though, conjured a new—or old—demonology, going back not just to when Theodore Roosevelt called Venezuela's Cipriano Castro a vile ape but to Spanish conquerors who justified the Conquest by describing Native Americans as something other than fully human: half men, half monkeys. After his capture, the military happily gave reporters tours of his "lair," or, as the press called it, his "witch house." Vats of blood and animal entrails among other totemic items were reportedly found in his home. Noriega was literally an idolator, and the invasion of Panama was the most high-tech and expensive witch hunt yet.[8]

Now that the United States was no longer locked in a world-historical contest over the nature of justice, Noriega was the kind of animalistic enemy it needed, one whose unpleasantness confirmed the perversity of Third World sovereignty. "Pause long and hard," Bush's ambassador to the OAS warned his fellow delegates, before arguing that no ruler as wicked as Noriega deserved the protection of sovereignty. In fact, the founders of American International Law most committed to the ideal of "absolute sovereignty" wouldn't have disagreed that Noriega had forfeited his legitimacy. They just would be opposed to granting Washington the unilateral authority to sort the deserving from the undeserving.

Without consulting Congress, Bush sent more than twenty thousand Marines into Panama. Overkill would be an understatement. For no tactical reason, the U.S. firebombed the shanty neighborhood of El Chorrillo, whose wooden houses went up in flames like tinder, killing many hundreds, though nobody has an exact count, of its residents.[9]

The Bush administration and the Pentagon had put a good deal of thought into how to contain independent journalism on the ground (to roll back the critical on-the-ground reporting that took hold in Vietnam) while still taking advantage of the new medium of cable TV to stage the invasion. After all had been made ready, with the choppers gassed and bombs laid in the holds of the planes, the final thing Bush wanted to know before he gave the order to proceed was the temperature of the press and public. Only after the White House press secretary reported that he was sure the reaction would be favorable, did Bush turn to his secretary of defense, Colin Powell, and say, "Okay, let's go."[10]

Latin American observers described the slaughter in El Chorrillo as a "little Hiroshima" and a "little Guernica," suggesting that the invasion of Panama had hurled the world back to dark days. The Pentagon saw a bright future: "A bold new era in American military force projection: speed, mass, and precision, coupled with immediate public visibility" was how General John Brown described the pyrotechnics that lit up Panama's night sky. CNN and other TV networks ran the invasion nonstop: Pentagon briefings; punditry from retired generals; and reports from a tightly controlled pool of reporters who were flown in by the army but kept on the tarmac for hours and so missed the beginning of the assault. It was a good show, and a model for how the Pentagon would handle the press in wars to come, with reporters kept on a short leash, unable to see the destruction.

Five days of the military blasting Guns N' Roses and other hard rock outside the Vatican's embassy, where Noriega had taken asylum until he surrendered on January 3, made good TV. *Cops* had just aired on Fox in March, the first reality show dedicated to domestic law enforcement. The Panama invasion was the first, but not last, reality TV war, a distraction from the New Year's Day 1990 killing of two nuns, one of them a U.S. citizen, in northeastern Nicaragua by the Contras—murders that the U.S. press, focused on the hunt for Noriega, ignored.[11]

The Bush administration knew it had violated the charter of the OAS. "They were operating very near the line," said one inside source. The line had in fact been crossed; the era of sovereignty, inaugurated in 1933 with Hull's forswearing the right of intervention, was over.

From this point forward, Washington would barely bother to find a multilateral justification for militarism. Rather, the United States would take unilateral, preemptive action when it thought necessary, justified after the fact by either a very broad definition of self-defense or very lofty humanitarian ideals.

The attack on Panama was meant to allow the United States to kick the Vietnam syndrome. In place of the incremental military escalation held responsible for defeat in Southeast Asia, the Pentagon in Panama rehearsed a new "doctrine of invincible force." A follow-up war, launched a year later to liberate Kuwait from an Iraqi occupation, was sold as a "mature version" of the Panama operation. "Suddenly, massively, and decisively," the United States military assaulted Baghdad and Iraqi forces, this time with network news broadcasting the bombing. "A marvel," CBS's Charles Osgood said about the first bombs. "Two days of almost picture-perfect assaults," said Jim Stewart, also on CBS.

Another quick and seemingly painless win that put a said-to-be invincible United States on the road to ruin in Afghanistan and Iraq.[12]

The Blessed Soldier

It would be unkind, at near the end of a long book, to drag readers through the weeds of neoliberalism. I'll keep it short. The phrase is associated with Milton Friedman, Friedrich von Hayek, and other economists, who, in a world seduced by the welfare state, held true to a pure vision of capitalism. "Necessitous men are not free," FDR liked to say. "People who are hungry, people who are out of a job are the stuff of which dictatorships are made." Libertarians disagreed. Only necessitous men are free, for their struggle to survive creates value and expands the realm of liberty and wealth. The too-easy provision of social welfare, Hayek would say in his writings, put the world on the road to serfdom. Social security is the stuff of dictatorships.[13]

The 1973 coup that ended Chile's democracy and Salvador Allende's life can be taken as neoliberalism's mythogenesis. After the putsch and under the protection of the dictator Augusto Pinochet, Chilean students trained by University of Chicago professors launched a now famous punishing program of economic shock therapy: deregulation, liberalization, privatization, and austerity.

In truth, this program was not all that different from the one the U.S. business lobby wanted Truman to press on Latin America in 1948. But economic nationalism, in Latin America and elsewhere in the decolonizing world, had too strong a hold on policymakers. Latin American politicians might have gone along with the security protocols set out in Bogotá in 1948. Anti-Communism, fine. But they scoffed at Secretary of State Marshall's toasts to the wonders of free enterprise. Venezuela, Colombia, Argentina, Brazil, and

Mexico, along with poorer nations elsewhere, such as India, Indonesia, Egypt, Ghana, Ivory Coast, Iran, Turkey, and Tunisia, enacted state-directed industrialization policies, which were, for the most part, successful—not spectacularly so but enough to provide a degree of economic security to significant portions of their populations. In the three decades between 1950 and 1980, Latin America's economy grew at an impressive annual rate of 5.5 percent.[14]

The overthrow of Allende proved a turning point for this growth model, a chance for the Chicago libertarians to dismantle Chile's welfare state and discredit its theoretical underpinnings: dependency theory, as well as more mainstream Keynesian developmentalism. More than anything, the Chicago Boys wanted to destroy the belief, consecrated in the war against fascism, that social democracy completed political democracy, that one enabled and strengthened the other. This idea was common sense throughout most of Latin America and much of the world, but nowhere truer or more radiant than in Allende's Chile.

Chile's coup set out the ideological stakes: economic liberalism was the essence of true democracy. If voters thought otherwise, if they thought that, say, democracy required social welfare, then Chile's dictatorship would change their thinking. Hayek saw no problem with Pinochet using the state's "coercive powers" to provide moral instruction, to force freedom and teach citizens that true liberty was not to be found in the voting booth, casting ballots for politicians promising national health care. Rather, liberty was found in universal rules that protected the sanctity of the market and private property. There are moments, Hayek said, when "democracy needs 'a good cleaning' by strong governments."

The problem wasn't any one policy, but the seemingly intractable sociality of Latin America's worldview. That's what had to be dissolved. Pinochet justified its terror as needed not to prevent Chile from turning into a Stalinist gulag but to sweep away five decades of labor legislation and social welfare provisions—a "half century of errors," said Chile's finance minister Sergio de Castro.

Many of these Chicago Boys were theocratic Catholics, some were members of Opus Dei. As it did on the left, economics and religion converged; conservative Christians took inequality—the fact that some people, as some nations, were rich and others poor—not as evidence of structural dependency and injustice, as the liberation theologians would have it, but proof of sanctification, evidence of God's grace. Politics trumped theology, as conservative Protestants sang hymns to the Catholic Pinochet, who, for many, symbolized the restoration to power of the *pater familias*. Soon after his coup, thirty-two evangelical pastors, including Lutherans, Baptists, and Pentecostals, wrote a letter announcing their unconditional support for the general—for "the blessed soldier."[15]

Libertarian ideas might not have spread so quickly had it not been for the global economic turmoil of the early 1970s, marked by inflation, recession, growing debt, and rising energy prices. "Free trade" also got an assist from U.S.-based multinational corporations, which since the early 1960s had started working closely with the CIA to destabilize nationalist governments. For its part, the International Monetary Fund pushed structural adjustment, which was also a kind of moral adjustment. In exchange for new loans to cover unpayable debt, the IMF required borrowing nations to cut social spending, weaken their labor law, deregulate finance, lower tariffs and subsidies, and remove other trade barriers. And privatize. Governments were to sell what they could and give up the idea of nurturing a national manufacturing sector that couldn't compete in a free global market.[16]

Neoliberalism wasn't called neoliberalism in Washington. *Globalization*, with its notes of one-world harmony, was the preferred term of art. Globalization's proponents said that a return to the rule of law, including the protection of property rights, would build "trust" and stimulate investment, which in turn would lead to development. But the destruction of state economies and their reorientation to serve the interests of already wealthy nations brought suffering on a massive scale, first in Latin America, then in much of the rest of the world, including the United States.

The selling of government holdings in Latin America built the opposite of "trust" and "transparency." The sale was run like a criminal racket. "Dollars and decadence, and unprecedented corruption," was how a *Frontline* documentary described the atmosphere in Mexico, as the extended family of President Carlos Salinas dismantled the reforms of the Mexican Revolution. The country had one billionaire in 1987 when Salinas was elected and began the process of economic liberalization. Six years later, there were twenty-four, all of whom had made their money scooping up the nation's banks, mines, toll roads, sugar plantations, TV stations, and telephone services. Citigroup's vice president gave the Salinas family concierge service, personally helping transfer hundreds of millions of dollars out of Mexico, to Switzerland and Ireland.

The sale of Mexico's railroads, telecommunications, industrial plants, mines, airlines, community swimming pools, cemeteries, pension funds, schools, municipal water companies, and roads was riddled by graft. Between 1985 and 1992, over two thousand government industries were privatized, passing into the hands of multinational corporations or a new class of "super billionaires." In Chile, Pinochet's son-in-law took possession of the country's lithium reserve. Pinochet himself, whom many thought a model of martial rectitude, squirreled away more than fifteen million dollars in over 125 different accounts in banks that included Riggs and Citigroup.

Argentina, by the end of Carlos Menem's presidency in 1999, looked like late Sunday afternoon at a weekend estate sale. There was nothing left to buy. Hundreds of public enterprises had been sold, many of them at greatly undervalued prices under suspicious circumstances. In Peru, the family of dictator Alberto Fujimori siphoned donations from a state-owned philanthropy. Then they sold the government charity and pocketed the profits. In Bolivia, Cochabamba privatized its municipal water system and told residents they were prohibited from collecting rainwater for their personal use.

Grotius, who held that some elements of the earth were so plentiful that they couldn't be held as private property—"water free to all," he said—would have been horrified.

United States banks, law firms, and consultants all had their hands in this giveaway, racking up billable hours. The scale of the pillage made Pizarro look like a piker.

Become Pinochet

As Communism collapsed in Europe and Central Asia, Latin America was once again held up as a "visionary blueprint"—of how to implement a radical program of economic restructuring, even if it contradicted the wishes of most citizens. Argentina, Mexico, and, above all, Chile provided templates for Russia, Armenia, Georgia, Moldavia, Ukraine, Yugoslavia, East Germany, Hungary, and other countries. *The Economist*, Citibank, and the U.S. Treasury Department urged Russian reformers to follow Pinochet's "pragmatic" model. Wayne Merry, chief political analyst for the U.S. embassy in Moscow from 1990 to 1994, described how the U.S.-led IMF and the Treasury Department "played an enormous role" in driving an "unfettered, unregulated capitalism" forward. Washington advisers, according to Merry, saw their mission as cultivating "greed" to offset the "egalitarian leveling" culture of the Soviet Union. "We pushed" forward, Merry recalls, "with an almost religious zeal," with the same zeal with which their policy predecessors fought the Cold War itself.[17]

A cult of Pinochet had already existed in the USSR. As the country disintegrated in the last decade of Soviet rule, the Chilean strongman had become a symbol of order and austere probity (even though he and his family were stealing millions). In April 1991, about seven months before the Soviet Union would come to an end, libertarian economists associated with Hayek's Mont Pelerin Society and the Atlas Foundation organized a pilgrimage of Russian economists to Chile, to provide inspiration on how to build a build a freer market in Russia. Not all the delegates sent to Chile came away bewitched, but many marveled at meeting Pinochet and his legendary Chicago Boys. They especially appreciated the Chilean economists' freedom to act, with little in the way of apparatchiks or democratic concerns to bother them. Pinochet's economists had the country to themselves like a "laboratory," where they could "work like engineers," one of the Soviet visitors remarked enviously. "I developed a lot of my mentality in Chile," said Alfred Kokh, who'd soon oversee the selling off of Soviet state assets.[18]

Economic restructuring devastated Russia the way it had devastated Latin America. Both Mikhail Gorbachev, in his desperate last days, and Boris Yeltsin, during the hopeful beginning of his presidency, asked—like Latin American asked half a century earlier—for large-scale financial aid, something like a new Marshall Plan. Both were brusquely turned down by the victorious cold warriors in the White House. Yeltsin begged for help servicing Russia's debt, through a restructuring of terms if not a pause in payments. A stern "No" was again the answer. Yeltsin's representatives were told that if they didn't pay "every last dollar as it came due," NATO, G7, and the U.S. would immediately turn around ships carrying much needed emergency food destined for Russia's hungry poor.[19]

By 1993, inflation was running twenty-five hundred times higher than the year before, and Russia entered a near decade-long period of intense economic pain. "More shock," as the journalist Janine Wedel wrote, "than therapy." Life expectancy went into free fall. Birth rates took a nosedive. By the end of the 1990s, there were nearly four million fewer children than there were at the start of the decade. Unemployment skyrocketed as basic state services collapsed. Infectious disease, including tuberculosis, spread, as rural hospitals were being shuttered. Public elementary education was gutted. *The New York Times* called this a "costly and painful, if good, progressive and necessary" turn toward liberal capitalism.[20]

The historian Vladislav Zubok recently offered a different opinion: "Russia experienced the worst of Latin American capitalism of the 1980s and 1990s." In the 1980s, 30 percent of Russians lived in poverty. After economic restructuring, the number was close to 80 percent.[21]

Through the 1990s, one strong man after another auditioned for the role of a Russian Pinochet, someone who would end the corruption and restore a sense of order. Vladimir Putin got the job, after prosecuting a ruthless war to keep Chechnya part of Russia. The journalist David Remnick writes that early in the 1990s, public support for Pinochet by Russian reformers who called themselves "liberal" or "democratic" would have been unthinkable. By 1996, it was "common currency." After Putin came to power, newspapers, bankers, and Treasury Department officials all urged him to "use the Pinochet stick," to "become Pinochet"—to shock harder to achieve "fast liberal reforms."[22]

To this day, both Pinochet and Allende remain icons of two very different ways to imagine how the world should be organized.

Bloody Instructions

In El Salvador on the night of November 16, 1989, the Atlácatl Battalion—an elite rapid-response unit created in 1980 by the Salvadoran military under the direction of United States advisers—entered the campus of the Central American University. The battalion was infamous for an earlier massacre of 811 residents of El Mozote and surrounding villages. Soldiers raped the women and killed with ferocity, sometimes with their U.S.-supplied M16s and other times with their machetes. Casings left behind indicate the bullets were manufactured in Missouri, in the U.S. Army's Lake City Army Ammunition Plant.

Now, Atlácatl was on the hunt for Father Ignacio Ellacuría, who had been trying to broker a truce between the government and the insurgency. They found him sleeping at the Jesuits' dormitory, along with his Jesuit colleagues Ignacio Martín-Baró, Segundo Montes, Juan Ramón Moreno, Amando López, and Joaquín López y López. Atlácatl murdered them all. Soldiers also killed the priests' housekeeper, Julia Elba Ramos, and her daughter, Celina Ramos.

Between the deaths of Father Torres in 1966 and Father Ellacuría and his comrades in 1989, the terror campaign supported by Washington had caused ruin on a massive scale. Teachers, trade unionists, peasant activists, Christian Democrats, Socialists, liberation theologians, intellectuals, doctors, teachers, engineers, economists, Communists, psychologists, artists, writers, feminists, priests, and nuns were killed, tortured, disappeared, and forced into exile.

Since its founding, the CIA had used religion as a weapon in its various psychological operations. Over the years, the Agency worked with Buddhists in Southeast Asia; Christians in Communist China; Pentecostal, Baptist, and Methodist ministers in Bulgaria; and Jewish émigrés from the Soviet Union. In 1953, Agency operatives worked with conservative Islamists, including members of Fadaiyan-e Eslam, or Devotees of Islam, to unseat Prime Minister Mossadegh.[23]

In Latin America, operatives funneled a large amount of money to Catholic priests, some of whom worked as Agency assets, and financed caucuses within the Vatican such as Opus Dei. In the 1960s, the CIA spent tens of millions of dollars shoring up Chile's Christian Democratic Party as a bulwark against Allende's Socialists.[24]

Yet starting in the late 1970s, the CIA's covert manipulation of religion took a step toward the apocalyptic. In 1975, the Agency began work with Bolivia's Interior Ministry, including the fugitive Klaus Barbie, then living under the name Klaus Altmann, to draw up a strategy to contain liberation theology through a combination of violence, psyops, and expulsion of foreign missionaries.*

The CIA also stepped up its effort to exploit the split between the liberationist and traditionalist wings of the Catholic Church and encourage the Agency's anti-Communist allies to target progressive priests and nuns. The Agency funded Christian militants to "sharpen internal divisions within the church, to smear and harass progressive church leaders, and cause the arrest or expulsion of foreign priests or nuns who supported social change." The Wurlitzer was playing hymns.[25]

Starting with the 1980 murder of El Salvador's Archbishop Oscar Romero—shot in the heart while saying Mass—Central America took on an intense end-time cast, with evangelicals holding masses with politicized liturgies and giving sermons explaining why killing for Christ was just. A powerful Christian conspiratorialism took over the right, with rank-and-file death squad members seeing themselves as purifiers, charged with cleansing evil from the nation.[26]

Afghanistan's mujahideen, backed by the CIA to fight against the Soviet occupation, knew themselves to be in a holy war. So did the Contras, along with the Guatemalan and Salvadoran militaries. Evangelicals worked with Israeli and Argentine military trainers, participating in torture sessions. Victims reported being interrogated about their views of liberation theology

---

* Barbie, under the name Altmann, operated freely in Bolivia, interrogating and torturing leftist prisoners, and running his own eight-hundred-man-strong Nazi paramilitary group, the Novios de la Muerte, or the Grooms of Death. Barbie/Altmann helped start Bolivia's fledgling cocaine industry and imported Austrian rifles to sell to Colombian cocaine cartels and paramilitaries, all the while continuing to provide intelligence to the CIA. After multiple requests, Bolivia finally extradited Barbie in 1983 to France, where, having been convicted of crimes against humanity, he died in prison in 1991.

and their understanding of Christ. Their torturers sang Christian hymns as they did their work, with verses describing Christ's own torments, his hands nailed to the cross, his pierced side and bound feet. In Guatemala, scores of priests and nuns were killed. Soldiers rampaged through the highlands, seizing villages thought to be liberation theology strongholds, murdering Mayan catechists and turning simple, white-adobe churches or rectories—some of them built around the time Las Casas was serving as bishop in nearby Chiapas—into torture and rape chambers.

"The army doesn't massacre Indians," said one evangelical supporter of the killing, "it massacres demons." By the early 1980s, the army's scorched-earth campaign had driven 70 percent of the country's highland Maya— more than a million people, the majority Catholics aligned with liberation theology—from their homes. Many fled into the mountains and lowland jungles, where they lived in hiding for about a decade. Parents faced choices of Abrahamic anguish: smother their infant to stop its crying or risk alerting patrolling soldiers to their location. The Conquest was over. The Conquest continued.[27]

Some analysts in both the State Department and the CIA were alarmed at the enthusiasm with which CIA director Casey and Reagan were willing to harness right-wing Christianity and radical Islam in the service of U.S. foreign policy. But Casey, a member of the Knights of Malta who attended Catholic Mass daily, liked the idea of former crusading enemies coming together to fight socialism.

The consequences of this mobilization—the spread of radical Islam abroad and the rise of theocratic Christianity at home—continue.[28]

"We but teach bloody instructions," Macbeth says, "which, being taught, return."

No Double Magisterium

More than torture and murder contained liberation theology. The Vatican, headed by Pope John Paul II, refuted its core beliefs. To portray Christ as "a political figure, a revolutionary," the pope said, violates Church catechism.

There are "social sins" that "cry to heaven," John Paul said, but to preach to only the poor denies the rich God's Word and adds to society's cruelty. To focus only on the people's nonmetaphorical hunger leaves "their hunger for God unsatisfied."

The Vatican either removed from office or reassigned to less influential positions priests thought to be liberationists. The pope imposed "penitential silence" on others, including the Brazilian friar Leonardo Boff, who was ordered not to edit, write, or speak in public. John Paul condemned the idea of a parallel hierarchy, with its own interpretation of Christ's teachings embedded within the Church. That Christian Base Communities looked to Boff or Gutiérrez for doctrinal guidance rather than the Vatican was unacceptable. "There will be no double magisterium," he said.

Cardinal Joseph Ratzinger, head of the Congregation for the Doctrine of the Faith (which until 1965 had been known as the Office of the Inquisition), believed that assigning Christ's Crucifixion political meaning denied the mystery of the Christian divine. The grandeur of the Church should be shrouded in the mist of ages, not turned into an office to do social work. Ratzinger judged liberation theology to be a "singular heresy."

In 1984, Ratzinger released a sharp denunciation, in a paper titled "Instruction on Certain Aspects of the 'Theology of Liberation.'" The simplicity and egalitarian culture of the "people's church," Ratzinger wrote, intentionally mocked "the sacramental and hierarchical structure" of the Roman Church—the splendor of which "was willed by the Lord Himself." On its own, the phrase "liberation theology" is unobjectionable, but it is the Church's "first and foremost" duty to liberate people from "the radical slavery of sin." Not from poverty. Marxism is pathos, a fundamentally false way of positing human relations as irreparably divided by class. The Church in contrast strives for wholeness. Ratzinger, who later became pope himself, directed Peruvian bishops to investigate Father Gustavo Gutiérrez, to read Gutiérrez's liberationist writings closely for evidence of doctrinal deviation, for ways in which he used modern ideas drawn from Marxism and dependency theory to corrupt Church teaching. Ratzinger wanted proof that

Gutiérrez had selectively read the Gospels to overemphasize the virtues of the poor. At one point, Gutiérrez was summoned to defend his ideas before a jury of eight inquisitors. The investigation stumbled due to division among the Peruvians, and Gutiérrez was left uncensored.[29]

No matter. There would be no double magisterium. The people's church was decimated by the death squads.

Still, the spirit of liberation theology, or, as it is sometimes called in tamer terms now, *teología del pueblo*, or theology of the people, would not be easily dispelled. The archbishop of Buenos Aires, Jorge Mario Bergoglio, who followed Ratzinger as Pope Francis, was not a member of the radical Church in Argentina. But he was born in Peronist Argentina, as the poor were beginning to demand entrance into the political arena, living through his country's industrial expansion, its dictatorship, then neoliberalism's corrupt sell-off of industries, and the country's economic collapse at the start of the new millennium. "No one can accept the premises of neoliberalism and consider themselves Christian," Bergoglio wrote. Neoliberalism corrupts democracy by denying the fullness and interdependency of humans, he said, by splitting what is whole asunder. Later, he'd describe hyper-capitalism as a system that "devours everything that stands in the way of increased profits, all that is fragile, like the environment, is defenseless before the interests of a deified market."[30]

Francis's tenure as pope has been marked by disputes whose terms were set in the sixteenth century. In 2019, he hosted indigenous Latin Americans at the Vatican in what critics decried was an "Amazon Synod." Dozens of delegations made up of over a hundred representatives—all dark-skinned, many in traditional dress, some with their faces painted—debated a range of issues related to capitalism, natural resources, and sustainability. Just prior to the gathering, on the feast day of Saint Francis, the pope joined a couple dozen delegates to plant a tree in the Vatican Gardens. Francis watched as the Indians sang and danced around a "mandala of Amazonian symbols" that included a photograph of Sister Dorothy Stang, from Dayton, Ohio, who was murdered in Brazil by hit men contracted by loggers and ranchers. The Church, the pope said, should have an "indigenous face"—should find a way to reconcile the world's diversity with universal values.[31]

Traditionalists responded as if they were Sepúlveda, and Las Casas had floated a ship filled with Aztec priests, Ayacucho caciques, and Mapuche warriors to Seville to give their opinion on Christian doctrine and global economics, to sit with Vitoria and debate questions of sovereignty and dominion. The "counterrevolution" to this Native American summit, one critic said, was sharp. Ultraconservatives accused the pope of twisting Christ's Church into a pagan cult of tribal chaos. A high-ranking Vatican monsignor called the delegates idolators and demon worshippers and charged Francis with trying to create a "Pachamama Church."

The conflict over the First Peoples' visit to the Vatican marked an uptick in talk about a Catholic "schism," a polarization within the Church between Francis-led modernizers and ultraconservatives that has continued. As Pope Francis turned eighty-seven in 2023, he stepped up his criticisms of powerful conservative bishops in the United States, who are buoyed by a broader right-wing confrontational culture. "The situation in the United States is not easy," he said. "There is a very strong, reactionary attitude." Here, Francis seems to be speaking more as an Argentine than the head of the Catholic Church, carrying on his country's tradition of being among Latin America's most persistent magpies. "Backwardism is useless," Francis said.[32]

Meanwhile, Father Gutiérrez, though acquitted, felt he needed to provide a fuller answer to the charges against liberation theology. He began work on a multivolume biography of Bartolomé de las Casas. The point of the study was clear: Liberation theologians didn't need Marxism or dependency theory to justify their politics or analysis of structural exploitation. They could draw from arguments made centuries ago, at the height of the Church's ecclesiastical power. Father Las Casas taught, Gutiérrez wrote, that if one confronted a situation that was justified by Church doctrine but violated Christ's love, then Church doctrine had to change.[33]

Las Casas's greatest insight, wrote Gutiérrez—who passed away as I was finishing this book, in late 2024, at the age of ninety-six—was that Christ speaks through the persecuted. The Conquest was the Crucifixion, wrote Las Casas, and Indians were Christ suffering.

"I saw Jesus Christ, our God, scourged and afflicted, and buffeted and crucified," Las Casas said of his time in America, "not once but a thousand times."

EPILOGUE

America, América

America

I t is a maxim in both electrical engineering and international relations theory that power needs a ground. For a long many years, Latin America was that to the lightning-like United States: its persistent opposition to intervention and conquest, and its unwavering demand for the recognition of absolute national sovereignty, obliged Washington to learn how to discipline itself, to control its energies, letting its power flow more efficiently and evenly.

This restraining function generally served the United States well, especially so in the lead-up to World War II. Working with Latin America's economic nationalists allowed FDR to breathe new life into a moribund liberalism and assume the authority to rally for the fight against fascism—to speak on behalf of the world and have the world think him sincere.

Hitler was not yet defeated when, in the United States, a new generation of battle-hardened leaders chafed at the restraint. They sensed, starting around 1943, the enormity of the world that would lay open to them once they won the war. It took a few decades, but in the terminal years of the Cold War the United States finally did break free of Latin America. The pivot from the Panama Invasion to the first Persian Gulf War captures this move: one can either say that the Monroe Doctrine, as a regional shackle, was cast off—or that the doctrine was implicitly extended, with the U.S. assuming world policing functions.

Going global—shaking off Latin America as a restraint and returning the region to the status of an informal dependency—had the effect of unleashing Washington's worst policy instincts. On others, but also on itself.

As early as 1975, Idaho's senator Frank Church warned of the "Latin Americanization of the United States." Church didn't mean the phrase in a reactionary way, to suggest that the country was losing its WASP identity and becoming mongrelized, or that plebeians were falling for strongman populism. Rather, Senator Church, writing two years after the overthrow of Salvador Allende in Chile, was worried about the power that corporations exercised over domestic institutions. A regressive upward distribution of income, the emergence of "mammoth corporations operating on a global scale that transcends political boundaries" and function "beyond the effective control of the nation-state," and the abandonment of the idea that it is the obligation of politicians to close the gap between rich and poor threatened, he worried, to do great damage to the nation. The senator was right to be worried, and the situation only grew worse in the decades that followed.[1]

Every industrial, high-GDP country in the last decades of the last century took steps to restructure their economies in response to inflation, unemployment, rising energy prices, and global competition. Yet no other wealthy nation did so as gleefully as did the United States. It's leaders facilitated deindustrialization and the outsourcing of decent-paying jobs; deregulated finance and other industries; pushed for the elimination of small farms and the massive upscaling of agribusiness; gave up their ability to discipline and tax corporations; and revised laws to allow first Walmart's and then Amazon's destruction of Main Street. No other comparable nation, not even Thatcher's, presided over such an enormous redistribution of wealth upward, creating a superclass of billionaires immune to democratic control. None so happily let its political class and institutions fall captive to money, while at the same time gutting the institutions—welfare, unions, housing, farm communities, hospitals, mental health care, the media—that might have softened the blow.[2]

During a period of unheralded economic expansion, with no contending challenger on the horizon of near comparable might, the United States ramped up police and prison spending—treating itself as it would an occupied nation and its citizenry as belligerents.[3]

Then came the many-trillion-dollar wars in Afghanistan, Iraq, and elsewhere.

In the past, wars helped tie the United States together. Soldiers came home—from Mexico, from Florida's swamps, from Virginia, from the frontier, from the Caribbean and the Pacific, from Europe—to a country expanding its capacity, building out physical and social infrastructure. Capital invested in factories. The government built schools, hospitals, and highways as unions and social movements fought to extend, however fitfully and incompletely, the liberal promise of equality for all. That changed with the end of the Cold War. As companies dismantled factories and shipped the machinery to Mexico, China, and Southeast Asia, veterans returned from the First Gulf War—and every war since—to a country taking itself apart: its industrial base, its safety net, its unions, its farm communities, and its social compact.

War-bred militancy was brought home, and so was the psychological warfare that the United States has been waging on large parts of the world, especially Latin America, since George Kennan wrote his 1948 memo.* The nation's social breakdown has been worsened by an epistemic fog, a sense that nothing can be trusted, that all news was fake, and that manipulation and surveillance was all pervasive. Meanwhile, a small cult of tech billionaires flush on government contracts was left free to tinker with the way people experience daily life, with what it means to be human.[4]

The unraveling has been quick. Sociologists call what is happening to the United States the "de-pacification of everyday life": a coarsening of sentiment, an upward spiral of nihilistic aggression, impulsive and orchestrated

---

* Much of the spadework on how to use social media to "hack" elections was done in Latin America, before the technique's big rollout in the 2016 presidential vote in the United States.

violence, a citizenry on edge, and a general distrust of institutions that in the past had guided and instructed. What scholars define as hegemony— the ability of political leaders to acquire legitimacy and govern by consent— has given way to an all-enveloping conspiricism, a sense that nothing and no one is legitimate. Like most aspects of our current crisis, this informational morass is the result of specific government policies, in this case Reagan's 1987 revocation of the Fairness Doctrine (which limited uncontested misinformation on the airwaves) and Clinton's 1996 Telecommunications Act, which, political scientists have shown, intensified ideological polarization. What's dangerous about the kind of culture war that has gripped the United States is that its stakes and endgame aren't clear, so the only logic the war follows is the logic of escalation.[5]

The United States is now a two-tier nation, where about 30 or so percent of the population benefits from globalization and the rest struggle to make their bills. Infant mortality is up. Life expectancy down. And every year breaks a new record for suicides, which are significantly higher in rural areas.

Easy and cost-free, for a time, resorting to military action in response to international crises has led to a near total abandonment of diplomacy. The answer to every problem, the response to every provocation, is to strike, or to send bombs so others can strike. There's a new scramble for Africa, a proxy war for the continent's resources fought between Russia, China, the United States, and France. Washington funds and arms dangerous, potentially escalatory wars, in Ukraine and Gaza, in Lebanon, Yemen, Syria, and the Gulf of Aden, wherever. Yet politicians are clueless about what comes after the guns go silent, or if they ever will go silent.

Wilson imagined a world without war. FDR imagined a world without fear or want. Today's political class imagines nothing. Its grand strategists do no better than offer perilous talk of a new cold war, of restarting nuclear testing, abrogating disarmament treaties, rearming Germany and Japan, expanding NATO, and garrisoning Africa. Wars are seen not as things to be ended but chances to leverage strategic tension to advantage, create new realms of influence. If the past teaches anything it is that opening a belligerent multifront balance of power—with the United States pushing against

China, pushing against Russia, with all countries, everywhere, angling for advantage—will lead to more confrontation, more brinkmanship, more war. As with the United States' shapeshifting, amorphous domestic culture war, the lack of any clear objective to this new era of militarized economic competition, of war by proxy and privateer, increases the chance of conflict spinning out of control.

The international institutions and rules that Latin America helped create or inspire in the years after World War II, long enfeebled, are today nearly worthless. NATO, modeled on the Inter-American Treaty of Reciprocal Assistance, is now a blunt instrument of United States power in Europe. The world's many wars proceed as if there never was a thing called international law. Considering the growing dependence on private mercenaries, corporate intelligence firms, and the accelerating power of out-of-control technologies, the head of Amnesty International, Agnès Callamard, says that the world stands on the brink of a "descent into hell." Private firms like Palantir Technologies and Israel's Elbit Systems have teamed up to turn Ukraine, the U.S.-Mexico borderlands, and Gaza into their testing grounds, integrating high-tech, AI-driven intelligence gathering into what the CEO of Palantir calls "digital kill chains."[6]

In 1945, Panamanian representatives to the United Nations thought that victory in the world would facilitate the expansion of a global welfare state, which, in turn, would make migration a less fraught experience, and that the United Nations should create an office to help resettle those displaced by the war—a simple, humane idea from a time when the world had hope, when it thought it had a future. Now, the handful of wealthy countries do everything they can to keep the hordes created by Washington's wars and economic policies out, including building walls and hatching plans to ship them to Rwanda the way Lincoln wanted to send emancipated people to Central America and Haiti. With the results of the 2024 presidential elections, mass deportation, of millions of undocumented laborers, is back on the agenda. So is a revived doctrine of territorial conquest, in Ukraine, Gaza, Syria, Lebanon, Yemen, Sudan, and Somalia. In the United States, the president threatens to seize the Panama Canal (which the U.S. had ceded to Panama in 1999) and jokes, sort of, about filling out the New

World by annexing Canada and Greenland, as if he knows intuitively that, in a nation as hollowed out as the United States, political vitality can only be maintained through the promise of expansion.

The United States is still the most powerful nation on earth, and its financial system dominates the world economy. Yet the country is sparking in all directions at once. At home, its power is self-devouring. Abroad, it is unfocused, as scattered as Washington's diplomats, who fly here and there to say this and that, with no larger vision to offer apart from the most immediately transactional, usually involving a transfer of weapons and an infusion of cash. The threats are existential, and include a fast-warming world. Yet governing elites offer nothing but tepid solutions. The promise of a better future—or of any future at all—is like a weight from the past, hard to bear, easy to toss aside.[7]

Chaos, chaos, chaos, as Cordell Hull described the scene after World War I.[8]

América

Latin Americans tried to warn the United States. By the time al-Qaeda operatives in September 2001 hijacked planes and flew them into the World Trade Center buildings and the Pentagon, Latin America's anti-Communist dictatorships had largely given up power and its nations had returned to constitutional rule. Not in every country, and not all at the same time, but in many places, voters began to elect independent-minded policymakers to office, politicians who represented the region's historic social movements: trade unionists, liberation theologians, feminists, critical economists, populists, medical doctors, and student, peasant, and indigenous activists. American International Law, liberation theology, and dependency theory might have been broken up as holistic schools of criticism, but their ethical spirit still infused politics.

So when the administration of George W. Bush made moves to enlist Latin America in its Global War on Terror, arguing that radical Islam was a variant of fascism, Latin Americans balked. The region, with the Cold War over and dictatorships having given way to democracies, had returned to its

magpie role. Presidents and ambassadors cautioned against sidelining diplomacy and international institutions to wage reckless unilateral war. They
knew the invasions of both Afghanistan and Iraq were folly and criticized related policies, including the ongoing sanctions against Cuba, the isolation of
Iran, and the continued occupation of Gaza and the West Bank. They spoke
out forcefully against the CIA's global torture program and told Washington
that its predatory economic policies would bring ruin to the world.[9]

Luiz Inácio Lula da Silva, president of Brazil from 2003 to 2010, took the
lead in putting forth an alternative vision of global governance. A former
metalworker and labor organizer, Lula had stocked his chancellery with jurists, such as Celso Amorim, who would have been at home debating Secretary of State James Blaine over the doctrine of conquest. Brazil, along with
other countries, insisted that the world had to return to thinking about war as
an option of last resort, that the art of diplomacy had to be relearned. "Brazil
has no enemies," Lula's defense minister, Nelson Jobim, declared in 2009.[10]

"The cause of terrorism," Brazil's vice president, José Alencar, told the
White House, is not "just fundamentalism, but misery and hunger." "The
remedy is much worse than the illness," Uruguay's then president, José Mujica, said, referring to the NATO assault on Libya. "This business of saving
lives by bombing is an inexplicable contradiction."

The world would be in a better place if, after 9/11, Washington had listened to Latin America, on any number of issues. There wouldn't have been
so many millions of desperate war refugees hoping to get into Europe, fueling
the return of right-wing xenophobia there. But Washington didn't listen. Instead, the United States went forward with its catastrophic wars in Afghanistan, Iraq, and Libya, among other places, while in the Americas it returned
to interventionism, subverting elections, backing coups, and imposing economic sanctions on governments it doesn't like, in Venezuela and Nicaragua.
The now more than six-decades-old embargo against Cuba continues.[11]

The situation is dire in many Latin American countries, the ongoing
fallout of neoliberal austerity. Low wages, corruption, hollowed-out social
services, and weakened labor protections have combined to make the region
the most economically unequal in the world, with high rates of child malnutrition. Deep-seated corruption—much of it linked to narcotic production

and distribution to feed the U.S.'s insatiable demand—erodes faith in government institutions and legal systems. The region's murder rate is high, with historically safe cities and nations experiencing sharp spikes in crime. Mirroring the United States, amphetamine and fentanyl use is up in Latin America, a marked change in the region's traditional drug-use culture. The Moloch of consumerism and numbing mass corporate culture does its job, eating into the region's long tradition of critical historical thinking and artistic dissent. Apathy—and even more corrosively, cynicism—weakens civic engagement. School shootings, once unheard of in Latin America, are on the rise, with the shooters inspired by rampages in the United States.[12]

Paramilitaries, drug cartels, and gangs stalk the countryside and, at times, rampage through cities, armed with guns and assault rifles that in the majority come from the United States. Hundreds of trade unionists, students, journalists, environmentalists, feminists, sexual-rights advocates, and peasant activists are assassinated every year.

The wolves are at work; the right is on the rise. In some countries, such as Bolivia, Brazil, and Argentina, right-wing militants are possessed by the same demons, the same obsessions, that afflict their counterparts to the north. No border wall can stop the escalation of the U.S. cultural wars into Latin America, as libertarians, Christian nationalists, gun rights activists, patriarchal avengers, and white supremacists open fronts in southern nations. *No es posible poner puertas al campo.* In the United States, new alliances are coming together in Miami, long the headquarters of the anti–Cuban Revolution right. You can't understand the radicalization of Florida—itself an incubator for the radicalization of much of the United States—without understanding its role as a sanctuary state for those leaving countries governed by leftists: Venezuela, Bolivia, Brazil, Mexico, Nicaragua, are some. There they bank their wealth. There they plot, as they have since the days of JFK and Nixon, their return to power. And there they deepen ties with U.S. conservative comrades, understanding their struggle as hemispheric in scope.[13]

In any given election, agitated conservatives might tap into misogyny, gender panic, Christian supremacy, or racism to win, sometimes spectacularly so, such as when Jair Bolsonaro took power in Brazil in 2018, or in 2023, when the Hayekian Javier Milei won in Argentina. El Salvador's president, Nayib Bukele, has, in the name of fighting gang violence, done away with due process to line up thousands of young men, stripping them naked and displaying them to the world with shaved heads. Octavio Paz died before he could witness such a Dantesque display of fascist dehumanization, or otherwise he might have revised his assertation that Latin America's Catholic culture produced no pariahs.

A strong hand to deal with the region's very real problems, including gang crime that afflicts mostly the vulnerable poor, is undeniably appealing. Bukele, as Pinochet before him, has found admirers throughout the Americas. He wants to build mega prisons the way Vargas wanted to build steel mills. Republicans want to help him, and in Donald Trump he, along with Argentina's Milei and Brazil's Bolsonaro, will have a powerful ally. Democrats, for their part, have few critical words for what is shaping up to be a long-lasting dictatorship.[14]

It feels like the 1930s all over again, as Latin America teeters between the dark and the light. Only this time its reformers are on their own in the fight against reaction—there's no equivalent of Gruening, Daniels, or Welles to work with.

Yet despite the best efforts of reactionaries to consolidate their forces—to build their own brand of neofascist Pan-Americanism—they haven't been able to escalate episodic victories into a full-on continental *Kulturkampf.* And so far, the left has held the authoritarian right at bay as it always has, by putting forth a coherent social-democratic agenda.

One would think that, after all the region has suffered, from the tortures and terrors of the Spanish Inquisition to the death squads and disappearances of the Cold War, Latin Americans would have given up on the idea that history is redeemable. Yet centuries of violence seemed to have seared into activists an irrepressible ability both to recognize the dialectic lurking behind the brutality and to answer every bloody body with ever more adamant affirmations of humanity.

One reason for the persistence of a humanist, social-democratic left, one absorbent enough to take in demands related to gender, race, and sexuality, has to do with, I think, the fact that Spanish colonialism's moral crisis came early with the Conquest. The critique launched by dissenters was frontal and all encompassing, and when independence from Spain finally came, many of those who led that movement understood "emancipation" (even if they didn't always act on that understanding) in its fullest sense, to include, potentially at least, all forms of oppression. This, I think, helps explain Latin America's commitment to a panoramic conception of citizenship, one that includes social rights.

The Anglo experience was different. Evasion and denial were English settlement's hallmarks. And remained so for centuries. No ethical dilemma accompanied the destruction of the continent's indigenous people. When a moral crisis over chattel slavery did finally come, in the 1800s, it abstracted Black-skin bondage as a singular, exceptional sin. This, as the historian David Brion Davis wrote fifty years ago, had the "great virtue" of providing an "ideal" and "clear-cut" model of evil, which was useful for abolitionists when it came to fighting it but a hindrance to later historians and activists when they tried to relate it to the persistence of "other species of barbarity and oppression." This, I think, helps explain the United States' inability to overcome a narrow conception of individual rights.[15]

As of this writing, more than 480 million Latin Americans, out of a total of 625 million, live under some kind of social-democratic government. These governments operate with greater and lesser degrees of efficiency, greater and lesser infighting, greater and lesser virtue. Cuba is still authoritarian Cuba, and though the social achievements that justified that authoritarianism haven't been completely gutted, they are wisps of what they once were. Venezuela and Nicaragua are hard to defend, except historically, as the legacies of a long siege imposed by the most powerful country in human history. Still, combined, there is no area in the world where the left maintains such fidelity to universal humanism—no area where its leaders (again, not all, but an impressive many) are committed to repair the "rupture in the moral history of the world"—a rupture separating the hopes of 1945 from current distempers.[16]

Latin American nations do not always agree on the best way forward to calm international problems, including, for example, Venezuela's 2024 electoral crisis. Yet despite their differences, most of their leaders all start with the founding premises of American International Law: persistent diplomacy, arbitration, de-escalation, respect of sovereignty, and, as Sumner Welles put it when Vargas made his power grab, "patience." Washington, be it led by Republicans or Democrats, has forgotten Welles's call for forbearance—for letting countries work out their own internal class struggles—and rampages through Venezuela like that bull in that china shop, making matters considerably worse.

Uti possidetis has mostly held. Not just Brazil, but no Latin American nation has a serious enemy (setting aside Washington's sanctions on regimes it doesn't like). Interstate conflicts among Latin America's league-of-amity nations are rare: Bolivia still wants access to the sea, and Bogotá and Managua jockey over the archipelago of San Andrés. Yet there's no nuclear competition—thanks to one of the most successful arms control treaties in history, the 1967 Treaty for the Prohibition of Nuclear Weapons in Latin America and the Caribbean.

Other countries have retreated into a nasty, authoritarian nationalism, among them the Philippines; India; Turkey; Israel; Hungary; China, especially under Xi; and, most dangerously, Russia. Latin American nations mostly haven't. Their reaction to corporate globalization is rarely expressed in xenophobic, anti-Semitic, or conspiratorial tropes, as a struggle against "globalists." Though U.S. economic sanctions on governments it doesn't like, as well as Washington's other destructive financial and drug interdiction policies, have led to a sharp rise in refugees looking for work. Venezuelans in Brazil and Colombia, Haitians in the Dominican Republic, for example, have been met with hostility and suspicion, part of the new demonology of the desperate millions on the move.

Still, Latin America remains among the most peaceful continents in the world, in terms of state-to-state relations. For many, nationalism is still a gateway not toward rivalry but universalism. Native Americans have entered mass politics in countries like Bolivia, Ecuador, Peru, Guatemala, and Mexico not under the banner of ethnonationalism or separatism. Rather, indigenous-led social movements and political parties are often the primary carriers of the region's social-democratic heritage.[17]

Notwithstanding the efforts of the Chicago Boys and their allies, most Latin Americans (based on a tally of elections over the last few decades) still believe democracy means social democracy. They don't think that government-run health care leads to enslavement. Compared with the middling numbers in the United States who think that global warming is a serious threat, a staggering 88 percent of Latin Americans—according to a large-sample, thirteen-country poll conducted by the European Investment Bank—want stricter government measures to curb climate change.

Not everywhere but in many places, rights related to gender identity are advancing, so much so that the political scientist Omar Encarnación describes Latin America as the "undisputed champion of gay rights in the global south," a remarkable occurrence considering the "region's historic reputation as a bastion of Catholicism and machismo." Same-sex marriages are recognized in Brazil, Chile, Colombia, Costa Rica, Cuba, Mexico, Uruguay, and Argentina, and civil unions are legal in Bolivia. As abortion rights in the United States are being rolled back, momentum in Latin America moves in the other direction. Three of the most populous countries in Latin America—Argentina, Mexico, and Colombia—have either decriminalized or legalized abortion. Exceptions to this trend include Ecuador, the Dominican Republic, Nicaragua, and El Salvador, which have put into place some of the world's most punitive laws. Scores of Salvadoran women are currently imprisoned, convicted on charges of "attempted murder" for having miscarriages or stillborn births. Yet even in a country as repressive as El Salvador, they are fighting back. The organization Mujeres Libres El Salvador, founded by Teodora Vásquez, who spent ten years in jail for a miscarriage, are pushing to change the country's laws.[18]

Mexico has ended its string of Harvard- and Yale-educated neoliberal technocratic presidents and has begun electing leaders who at least say they want to return to the ideals of the Revolution. They've legalized abortion, lifted millions out of poverty, and doubled the minimum wage.

In 2024, over thirty-three million Mexicans cast their ballots for a female, Jewish, leftist climate scientist, Claudia Sheinbaum, to lead them as president, a remarkable 60 percent of the total vote. Sheinbaum's paternal grandparents were Lithuanian Communist militants who arrived in Mexico in the 1920s. Her grandfather, Jonas Sheinbaum Abramovitz, joined Mexico's Communist Party and stayed a member until his death in 1962. Her mother's grandparents came from Bulgaria in the 1940s, fleeing fascism and the Holocaust. Sheinbaum is a true granddaughter of the revolution—testament to insurgent Mexico's welcoming of the world's outcasts.

Latin America's social democrats have imagination. They have policy ideas. And like their forebears, they believe that the key to solving their own considerable domestic problems lies in their ability to revamp the global order. Most of Latin America's leaders want the drug war wound down and narcotics treated like a social problem. They think that property rights shouldn't be so inviolable that they prevent poor countries from manufacturing affordable generic versions of lifesaving drugs. They want fair and equitable trade, of the kind that will raise wages across the board, and they want migrants to be treated humanely. The flood of assault rifles that enter Mexico, and the rest of the region, from the United States must end.[19]

In 2022, Colombia, long a proxy for Washington's interests, elected a former rebel leader, Gustavo Petro, to its presidency. Petro is limited in what he can do: the country's power structure is even more intractable than it was when Father Torres was alive. In 2023, assassins murdered at least seventy-nine environmental activists, making the country the world's deadliest for those defending forests, water, and land. Still, Petro has aligned Colombia with a group of countries that want to set up an international organization to manage the world's transition away from fossil fuels. "Why would the president of a country that relies on fossil fuels want to commit economic suicide?" Petro said some would ask. Because, he answered, "We are trying to halt a suicide, the death of everything that is alive, everything that exists. This is not economic suicide. We are trying to avoid the omnicide of the world, of planet Earth." He continued, "There is no other path. Everything else is an illusion."

There's a lot to learn from Latin America in terms of progressive policy, but also politically—namely, how to go on the offensive against right-wing extremism.

If liberalism is to be something more than a heraldic device, it must confront entrenched power. "Democracy has," FDR said over the radio in 1938, "disappeared in several other great nations, not because the people of those nations disliked democracy, but because they had grown tired of unemployment and insecurity, of seeing their children hungry while they sat helpless in the face of government confusion and government weakness through lack of leadership." Latin Americans know that the way to beat fascism now is the same as it was then: by welding liberalism to a forceful agenda of social rights, by promising to better the material conditions of people's lives. Nearly every Latin American nation has the "right to health care" enshrined in their constitutions—a simple, clear popular objective liberals and leftists in the United States should consider fighting for.[20]

It's probably too late to recreate the protocols by which Latin America, in criticizing U.S. power, helped focus that power and socialize liberalism. That bird has flown.

In the 1930s, the best of the Americas converged. Now, the worst, despite efforts by good people on both sides of the border to hold off the eclipse. If the Conquest inaugurated the "slow creation of humanity," we, America, América, seem to be living through its dismantling.

Aspirant reformers in the United States—hamstrung by an antiquated, antimajoritarian political system, constantly upended by the volatility of deregulated capital; beholden to consultants, lobbyists, and donors; and unable to challenge the country's entrenched militarism—have little room to maneuver, making a continental realignment to push for humane change unlikely. It's difficult to imagine any politician or coalition in the United States, from any party, rising above the country's cresting anger or its vertiginous politics of fear to become a stable ally, the way the politicians of the New Deal were to Cárdenas's Mexico, Vargas's Brazil, or Popular Front Chile. One can hope.

In any case, the way things are now are not the way they will always be, as Brazil's Ruy Barbosa said in 1907, looking to shake Europe's statesmen out of their Belle Époque complacency. If those who today rule won't allow for reform, if they won't allow for a world where citizens live in dignity, then catastrophe awaits. The future comes fast at the present, Barbosa said, and when it does, it brings the unexpected.

ACKNOWLEDGMENTS

America, América is the culmination of many obsessions, and its length, along with the more than half a millennium it covers, demands as short an acknowledgment as possible. Here are some whose work and friendship contributed in different ways: Sinclair Thomson; Ada Ferrer; Barbara Weinstein; Alejandro Velasco; Christy Thornton; Nikhil Singh; Josh Frens-String; Marcial Godoy; Lloyd Gardner; the late Marilyn Young and Walt LaFeber, both now gone, both dearly missed; Corey Robin; Dan Denvir; Noam Chomsky; Kirsten Weld; Carlota McAllister; Colette Perold; Tony Wood; Gil Joseph; Anne Eller; Marcela Echeverri; Di Paton; Jen Adair; Rachel Nolan; Miriam Pensack; Stuart Schwartz; Matt Hausmann; Amy Hausmann; Bob Wheeler; Thea Riofrancos; Javier Porras; Steven Cohen; Polly Lauer; Mark Healey; Ernesto Semán; Chase Madar; Jen Turner; Mark Weisbrot; Susan Rabiner; Elizabeth Oglesby; Naomi Klein; Avi Lewis; José Miguel Martínez; Edwina Unrath; Tom Unrath; Adam Eaglin; DeeDee Halleck; Marc Becker; Jess Cruz; Rick Rowley; Jacque Soohen; Hilary Goodfriend; and everybody at the North American Congress on Latin America, especially its editors Bret Gustafson and Michelle Chase. I encourage readers to subscribe to its indispensable *Report on the Americas*. The list goes on. I owe much to Mariana Díaz Chalela, who helped with research and fact-checking.

All love and gratitude to family—to Tannia Goswami, Toshi Goswami, and, for everything, Manu and Eleanor, to whom this book is dedicated, along with the forever beloved Diane Nelson.

The folks at Penguin Press have been wonderful to work with, especially Natalie Coleman and Kiara Barrow. This is the sixth book I've done with Sara Bershtel. How many times can I thank her? Many more, I hope. It is impossible to describe how much better she makes each one, and how her mix of patience, intelligence, and intensity makes each turnaround a joyful adventure in synthesis. You, dear reader, however, must thank her for the book's length: Early in the process, I suggested that I begin with the Monroe Doctrine. "No," she said, "I think you need to start with the Conquest." "Really?" I asked. "I'm afraid so," she answered. Okay then.

NOTES

Introduction: On the Utility of Magpies

1. The diary is part of a large collection of documents Miranda acquired during his life that have remained remarkably intact (organized in sixty-three volumes by London's Public Record Office and acquired by Venezuela in the 1920s), published at different points throughout the twentieth century, including twenty-four volumes between 1929 and 1950 under the title *Archivo del General Miranda* by a private Venezuela publisher, and then again in twenty volumes in the 1970s by the Venezuelan government under the title *Colombeia*. In 1982, Fundación Biblioteca Ayacucha, based in Venezuela, published *América espera,* a condensed volume of these papers. Abridged versions of the diary have appeared in English. I've used, for references here and elsewhere in the book, the original Spanish, mostly either from *Archivo del General Miranda* (for example, the description of Washington, which is dated December 8, 1783, and found on p. 232 of *Archivo*) or *América espera* (for the Wheatley reference below, found in an undated entry from 1794, on p. 64). Karen Racine's *Francisco de Miranda* (2002) is the indispensable biography.

2. Juan Carlos Chirinos, *Francisco de Miranda, el Nómada Sentimental* (2006), p. 23. For Miranda in New England: Roy Peterson, "A South American's Impressions of New England after Yorktown," *The New England Quarterly*, v. 4, n. 4 (1931).

3. In the years after Miranda's visit, some theorists began to credit the United States' democratic equality to a historic lack of feudalism. Miranda thought the opposite when it came to gender equality, that the absence of an aristocratic court with its full social calendar made it easier for men to dominate women, to keep them isolated. Mónica Bolufer, "A Latin American Casanova? Sex, Gender, Enlightenment and Revolution in the Life and Writings of Francisco de Miranda," *Gender and History*, v. 34, n. 1 (2022).

4. Racine, *Miranda*, p. 53.

5. Daniel Walker Howe, "The Evangelical Movement and Political Culture," *Journal of American History*, v. 77 (1991); Jackson Lears, *Animal Spirits: The American Pursuit of Vitality from Camp Meeting to Wall Street* (2003).

6. In a review of Gregorio Funes, *Ensayo de la Historia Civil del Paraguay, Buenos-Ayres, y Tucuman* (1816), in *North American Review*, v. 12 (1921), p. 435.

7. P. N. Furbank, *E. M. Forster: A Life*, v. 2 (1978), p. 89; *A Passage to India* (1924), pp. 284–85.

8. *Family Letters of John Adams and His Wife Abigail Adams* (1875), p. 45.

9. *The Works of John Adams*, v. 10, (1856), p. 142.

10. Mier's letter: "Servando Teresa de Mier a Pedro Gual," September 12, 1821, in the Mier Papers of the Benson Latin American Library, University of Texas, Austin.

11. Washington Irving, writing under the pseudonym Geoffrey Crayon, "National Nomenclature," *Knickerbocker*, v. 14 (August 1839), pp. 158–62.

12. According to one poll, Canadians use public health care and other examples of social rights to distinguish themselves from the more individualistic United States; "What Does It Mean to Be Canadian," *BBC*, May 17, 2012; https://www.bbc.com/news/world-radio-and-tv-18086952; John Lynch, *The Spanish American Revolutions 1808–1826* (1986), p. 34; Instituto Histórico e Geográfico Brasileiro, *Contribuições para a biographia de D. Pedro II* (1925), p. 563.

13. Bemis, *The Latin American Policy of the United States* (1943), p. x; Galeano, *Las Venas Abiertas de América Latina* (1971), p. 14.

14. In the last few decades, ever more extensive archival work has produced a "New Conquest History," one that departs from older views which downplayed indigenous resistance and opposition. Some of these works now consider what was called the Spanish Conquest a prolonged civil war among multiple peoples, or, over the long run, a "revolution," whereby indigenous and African peoples carved out considerable independence, preventing the creation of a truly empowered feudal class. Gone are the histories of Cortés and his few hundred men defeating a sprawling empire. Also challenged in this new history are depictions of the Spanish Empire as dogmatic, as allowing no space for individualism—in comparison to the liberty-loving English, whose later takeover of North America is presented as, as Woodrow Wilson once put it, simply "methodizing" Anglo-Saxon freedom. Among the leaders in this revision is University of Texas's Jorge Cañizares-Esguerra, whose forthcoming *The Radical Spanish Empire*, coauthored with Adrian Masters, will be a defining work. See also Matthew Restall, "The New Conquest History," *History Compass* (2012).

15. The influences on this book are many and will be cited throughout. One can be mentioned here: Andrew Fitzmaurice's work on how Spanish criticisms of the Conquest associated with the Dominicans and the Salamanca School led later English-speaking philosophers to find work-arounds to justify dominion and dispossession. See Fitzmaurice's *Humanism and America* (2003) and *Sovereignty, Property and Empire* (2014).

16. The best work (such as Susan Pederson's *The Guardians* [2015] and Mark Mazower's *No Enchanted Palace* [2009]) on either the League of Nations or the United Nations place the organizations within a broader "crisis of empire" (Pederson's subtitle) which largely ignores Latin America. Mazower examines how the United Nations emerged out of the contradictions of European empire, with the League of Nations an important antecedent allowing white settlers to retain their prerogatives in a world of nations. Here, the British Commonwealth, and not the experience of Latin American's community of republics, gestates the postwar order. Other works, including John Ikenberry, *A World Safe for Democracy* (2020); Erez Manala, *The Wilsonian Moment* (2007), and Paul Kennedy, *The Parliament of Man* (2006), mention Latin America in passing. Patrick Cohrs in *The New Atlantic Order* (2022) details the importance of the Monroe Doctrine in debates over the League of Nations but downplays, in an otherwise encompassing work, Latin America's challenge to and model for U.S. aspirations to world leadership. Recognition of Latin America threads in and out of scholarship concerned with various facets of the post-WWII global order. But a broader, comprehensive picture has so far been lacking. Some historians, including Warren Kimball in his *The Juggler: Franklin Roosevelt as Wartime Statesman* (1991), have stressed the importance of Latin America. Also: Mark

Gilderhus, *Pan American Visions* (1986). Recently, intellectual historians have started to consider the influence of Latin American jurisprudence. See my discussion of American International Law in "Your Americanism and Mine: Americanism and Anti-Americanism in the Americas," *The American Historical Review*, v. 111 (2006) and of the Chilean jurist Alejandro Alvarez in "The Liberal Traditions in the Americas: Rights, Sovereignty, and the Origins of Liberal Multilateralism," *The American Historical Review*, v. 117 (2012). Historians of law and ideas are now building a larger body of scholarship from the perspective of the Americas. For example: Juan Pablo Scarfi, *The Hidden History of International Law in the Americas* (2022). Also: Arnulf Becker Lorca, *Mestizo International Law* (2014) and Liliana Obregon, "Between Civilization and Barbarism: Creole Interventions in International Law," *Third World Quarterly*, v. 27 (2006). Felipe Fernández-Armesto has written two excellent New World surveys: *The Americas: A Hemispheric History* (2003) and *Our America: A Hispanic History of the United States* (2014), the latter arguing, prior to the ascension of Donald Trump, that the history of the United States should be understood within the larger global context of greater Spanish-speaking history.

Chapter 1: Leaves of Grass

1. According to Plato, in *The Dialogues of Plato*, v. 4 (1892), p. 210. Also attributed to Aristotle. For Hegel, "*Geschichte als Schlachtbank*," or "*History as a slaughter-bench*," in Hegel's lectures on the philosophy of world history. Discussion in Glenn Alexander Magee, *The Hegel Dictionary* (2010), p. 210.

2. "*Rarezas*" in Edmundo O'Gorman's introduction, p. lxxvii, to Las Casas's *Apologética Historia Sumaria* (1967).

3. The statement *Así que todo linaje de los hombres es uno* is found in *Apologética Historia* and is usually translated as: All mankind is one (see Hanke below). The quote here, as well as the paraphrase of Las Casas, is found in volume 1 of the 1967 Spanish-language edition, p. 258. The original manuscript is housed in Spain's Real Academia de la Historia. Lewis Hanke and Edmundo O'Gorman agree that Las Casas finished this work around 1552. Hanke believes it reflects a consistency in thought going back some time, while O'Gorman suggests it represents a radicalization of Lascasian humanism, a result of his disappointment that his 1550 debate with Sepúlveda (see below in the text) led to little change. See the discussion in Hanke, *All Mankind Is One: A Study of the Disputation Between Bartolomé de Las Casas and Juan Ginéz de Sepúlveda in 1550 on the Intellectual and Religious Capacity of the American Indians* (1974), pp. 173–76. Las Casas likely started writing *Apologética* in 1527, as part of a ceaseless production of pages that resulted—in addition to many other theses, petitions, and doctrinal guidebooks—in three major works: *Brevísima Relación de la Destrucción de las Indias*; *Apologética Historia*; and *Historia de las Indias*. Of these three, only *Brevísima* was published in Las Casas's lifetime. *Apologética Historia* was a work of theoretical abstraction that argued that Native Americans were part of the ontological unity of humanity. *Historia* was a documentation of Spanish crimes and includes a history of Christopher Columbus's voyages. And *Brevísima* was a polemical broadside meant to draw attention to New World horrors. All have been published in multiple editions, both complete and abridged.

4. These quotations are from a series of letters the Dominicans of Hispaniola wrote protesting Spanish abuse of Indians, cited only in a few places. "*Carta Latina de Los Dominicos y Franciscanos de las Indias Sobre los Grandes Males de las Terra Nuevas y Sus Posibles Remedios*," May 27, 1517, found in José María Chacón y Calvo, *Cartas censorias de la conquista* (1938). Also see the annexes in Beatríz Charria Angulo, *Primera Comunidad Dominicana en América* (1987) and Gustavo Gutiérrez, *Dios o el Oro en las Indias* (1989), p. 44.

5. Dave Davis, "The Strategy of Early Spanish Ecosystem Management on Cuba," *Journal of Anthropological Research*, v. 30 (1974); Bartolomé de las Casas, *Brevísima Relación de la Destrucción de las Indias* (1552; 1991), p. 7.

6. *The Dispatches of Hernando Cortés* (1843), p. 76. The term *Aztecs* is a simplification of the diversity of the indigenous empire that ruled much of modern-day Mexico. The early pages of Matthew Restall's *When Montezuma Met Cortés* (2018) provide details on the proper nomenclature. Also James Lockhart, *The Nahuas After the Conquest* (1992), p. 1.

7. Alexander Koch, Chris Brierley, Mark Maslin, Simon Lewis, "European Colonisation of the Americas Killed 10% of World Population and Caused Global Cooling," *The Conversation*, January 31, 2019, https://theconversation.com/european-colonisation-of-the-americas-killed-10-of-world-population-and-caused-global-cooling-110549; Tzvetan Todorov, *The Conquest of America* (1984; 1999).

8. For questions regarding Las Casas's involvement: Lawrence Clayton, *Bartolomé de las Casas* (2012), pp. 36–39.

9. Arthur Helps, *The Spanish Conquest in America*, v. 4 (1868), p. 334.

10. Louis Pérez, *Cuba: Between Reform and Revolution* (2015), p. 19.

11. Las Casas, *Historia de las Indias*, v. 4 (1876), pp. 23, 39. The literature on Las Casas is enormous, including exegeses of the many books, reports, treatises, and letters he left behind. Hanke and O'Gorman are touchstone scholars, but there are many more. A good place to begin is Hanke's *All Mankind Is One*, with its useful bibliography. Also Hanke, *The Spanish Struggle for Justice in the Conquest of America* (1949). Other work: Juan Friede and Benjamin Keen, eds., *Bartolomé de Las Casas in History* (1971); Marcel Bataillon, *Etudes sur Bartolomé de las Casas* (1965), emphasizes Las Casas's humanist universalism as influenced by Erasmus and More. José de Freitas Neto Alves, *Bartolomé de Las Casas* (2002). The larger context: Luis Rivera Pagán, *A Violent Evangelism: The Political and Religious Conquest of the Americas* (1992). Some, both his contemporaries and subsequent scholars, thought Las Casas clinically manic: "La Locura de Fray Bartolomé de Las Casas," *Revista hispanoamericana de ciencias, letras y artes*, v. 6 (1927). Ramón Menéndez Pidal, *El Padre Las Casas: Su Doble Personalidad* (1963), judges him a paranoid schizophrenic. Most scholars are understandably overwhelmed by the enormity of Las Casas's life, historical significance, and writings. Recent works include Daniel Castro's skeptical *Another Face of Empire: Bartolomé de Las Casas, Indigenous Rights, and Ecclesiastical Imperialism* (2007); David Orique provides a mercifully short and chronological summary of Las Casas's life and works in "Bartolomé de Las Casas (1484–1566)," *Revista de literatura hispánica* (2017). Manuel M. Martínez, "Las Casas on the Conquest of America," in Friede and Keen, eds., *Bartolomé de las Casas in History*, p. 340. For an accessible narrative of his life: Clayton, *Bartolomé de las Casas*.

12. In 1977, shortly after the Argentine military took power in a coup and carried out a very violent defense of traditional Spanish Catholicism, the Argentine philosopher Enrique Dussel argued that Cortés's *Ego conquiero*, the New World's "conquering self," served as an antecedent to Descartes' *Ego cogito*. Colonial wealth raised the standard of living of enough Europeans that their intellectuals could begin to philosophize, could begin to imagine, that their private thoughts were the world itself.

13. Alicia Mayer, "Controversial Cases on Humanitarian Doctrines: Bartolomé de las Casas's Intellectual Legacy among New England Puritans," in David Thomas Orique and Rady Roldán-Figueroa, eds., *Bartolomé de las Casa* (2019).

14. Franco Cardini, *La culture de la guerre: Xe-XVIIIe siècle* (1992), cited in Jean Jacques Frésard, *The Roots of Behaviour in War* (2004), p. 34.

15. Paul Vickery, *Bartolome de las Casas* (2006), chapter 2; Juan Friede, "Las Casas and Indigenism," pp. 208–9; "Many Indians," wrote one of the first chroniclers of the Conquest, Pietro Martire, an acquaintance of Columbus, "perish because of their great fatigue in the mines; so great is their despair that many take their own lives"; Pedro Mártir de Anglería, *Décadas del Nuevo Mundo* (1989), p. 285.

16. Example: Girolamo Benzoni's *La Historia del Mondo Nuovo* (1572) contains woodcuts, based on Benzoni's visit to Hispaniola, of collective suicide subsequently reproduced by Theodore de Bry and used to illustrate several books, including English translations of *Brevísima Relación*.

17. The colonial gold rush did lead to the desertification and waste-ification of forestland. See Daviken Studnicki-Gizbert and David Schechter, "The Environmental Dynamics of a Colonial Fuel-Rush: Silver Mining and Deforestation in New Spain, 1520 to 1810," *Environmental History*, v. 15 (2010).

18. "500 Years Later, Scientists Discover What Probably Killed the Aztecs," *The Guardian*, January 15, 2018. https://www.theguardian.com/world/2018/jan/16/mexico-500-years-later-scientists-discover -what-killed-the-aztecs; Rodolfo Acuna-Soto, David Stahle, Matthew Therrell, Richard Griffin, "When Half of the Population Died: The Epidemic of Hemorrhagic Fevers of 1576 in Mexico," *FEMS Microbiology Letters*, v. 240 (2004).

Chapter 2: There Is Only One World

1. Jacques Cartier, *Voyages de découverte au Canada entre les années 1534 et 1542* (1843; 1968), p. 196.

2. In 1970, John Elliott, in *The Old World and the New: 1492–1650* (1970), argues against the idea that the New World was so radically novel it shocked Europe's intellectual foundation. I believe evidence suggests that the degree of violence and the extent of population collapse did shatter governing moralities and force the creation of new ones. Also: Anthony Pagden, *European Encounters with the New World* (1993), p. 58.

3. Louis-André Vigneras, "Saint Thomas, Apostle of America," *Hispanic American Historical Review*, v. 57, n. 1 (1977); Count B. G. de Montgomery, *Ancient Migrations and Royal Houses* (1968); David Lupher, *Romans in a New World: Classical Models in Sixteenth-Century Spanish America* (2006); Barbara Fuchs, *Mimesis and Empire: The New World, Islam, and European Identities* (2004), p. 74.

4. Jorge Cañizares Esguerra, "New World, New Stars: Patriotic Astrology and the Invention of Indian and Creole Bodies in Colonial Spanish America, 1600–1650," *The American Historical Review*, v. 104 (1999).

5. Sabine Hyland, "Biblical Prophecy and the Conquest of Peru: Fernando de Montesinos' *Memorias historials*," *Colonial Latin American Historical Review*, v. 11 (2002).

6. Historians have pointed out that phrases such as a "new world" and "another world" were, at the time, common and could be used to refer to unknown areas of a familiar region, as if, say, Columbus landed on a part of Asia that Europeans hadn't yet known. Las Casas and Gómara mean *new* and *other* as radically so. Las Casas, *Historia de las Indias*, v. 1 (1875), p. 43. Francisco López de Gómara, *Historia General de las Indias*, v. 1 (1922), p. 4. Edward Bourne, *Spain in America, 1450–1580* (1904), p. 94, for a discussion of "otro mundo."

7. Tzvetan Todorov, *The Conquest of America* (1999), p. 47, for Columbus's "subtle distinctions" to justify slavery.

8. Luis Weckmann, *The Medieval Heritage of Mexico*, v. 1 (1992), p. 53; Juan José de la Cruz y Moya, *Historia de la Santa y Apostólica Provincia de Santiago de Predicadores de México en la Nueva España*, v. 2 (1954), pp. 45–48. Cruz y Moya was describing ideas that took shape during the early years of the Conquest, but he lived later than did Las Casas, in the 1700s. His defense of "America" was a Catholic complement to the writings of Puritans like Samuel Sewall and Cotton Mather, who argued against theologians who saw the New World as rotten, as where Satan would muster his army to wage war against the soldiers of Christ. Jorge Cañizares Esguerra has written of this multigenerational cohort that, while defending the New World from negative stereotypes, laid the foundation for colonial forms of scientific racism.

9. Louis-André Vigneras, "Saint Thomas, Apostle of America," *Hispanic American Historical Review*, v. 57 (1977), p. 83.

10. Antonio Tello, *Libro Segundo de la Crónica Miscelanea en que se Trata de la Conquista Espiritual y Temporal de la Santa Provincia de Xalisco* (1891), p. 34.

11. Andrés Reséndez, *The Other Slavery: The Uncovered Story of Indian Enslavement in America* (2016), p. 25.

12. Carlos Deive, *La Española y la esclavitud del indio* (1995), pp. 70–80. Las Casas participated in some way in this expedition and received an enslaved captive as compensation for his services. *Historia de las Indias*, v. 2 (1877), p. 30.

Chapter 3: Ego Vox

1. The *encomienda* system was an emergency response to the free-for-all crisis unleashed by the arrival of thousands of Spanish settlers in the years immediately after Columbus's arrival.

2. Reséndez in *The Other Slavery* summarizes the existing scholarly consensus: 200,000 to 300,000 Taino in 1492; by 1508, the population had fallen to 60,000; by 1514, to 26,000. Recently, a group of scholars led by geneticist David Reich and sociologist Orlando Patterson put the pre-contact number lower. Based on DNA sampling they say they "can confidently conclude that the pre-contact population size of Hispaniola was no more than a few tens of thousands of people." See, David Reich and Orlando Patterson, "Ancient DNA Is Changing How We Think About the Caribbean," *New York Times*, December 23, 2020, https://www.nytimes.com/2020/12/23/opinion/dna-caribbean-genocide.html. Whatever the case, by 1540, a Spanish census listed a total of 250 Indians in all of Hispaniola. If we take Reich and Patterson's upper number to be 30,000 Taino at the time of Columbus's arrival, dropping to 250 forty-eight years later, we have a mortality rate well higher than the 90 percent figure given in chapter 1. A "few tens of thousands of people" supports an argument that Reséndez makes: high pre-contact population obscure how much death was dealt directly and quickly by European killers, as opposed to the slow work of invisible germs. As Reséndez puts it, "It is hard to fathom each Spaniard killing one thousand Indians with anything other than germs" (p. 17). The revised numbers, though, make it easier to imagine more immediate and direct forms of terror, with "each conquistador, possessing superior technology and motivated by greed, subduing thirty Indians, who ultimately perished through a combination of warfare, exploitation, famine and exposure to new diseases." Las Casas's estimate of a million inhabitants on Hispaniola when the Spanish arrived was wrong. He was right, though, that conquerors and settlers murdered on "a vast scale."

3. Bartolomé de las Casas, *Historia de las Indias*, v. 3 (1986) pp. 10–20.

4. Cited in Daniel Macmillen Voskoboynik, *The Memory We Could Be: Overcoming Fear to Create Our Ecological Future* (2018).

5. For complaints about Spanish refusing to work: Juan Friede, *Bartolomé de las Casas: Precursor del Anticolonialismo* (1974), p. 23, especially the June 9, 1545, letter by the Bishop of New Granada Martín de Calatayud to the Consejo de Indias.

6. The Requirement ritual drew on Islamic rules of war, which stipulated that before a battle began a "messenger" be dispatched to enemy Catholic camps to offer an opportunity for conversion. Patricia Seed, *Ceremonies of Possession in Europe's Conquest of the New World, 1492–1640* (1995), p. 75.

7. Lewis Hanke, *The Spanish Struggle for Justice*, p. 34.

8. Martín Fernández de Enciso, *Suma de Geographia* (1987), pp. 224–27; James Parsons, "The Settlement of the Sinu Valley of Colombia," *Geographical Review*, v. 42 (1952), p. 67.

9. Hanke, "The Development of Regulations for Conquistadores," in *Selected Writings of Lewis Hanke on the History of Latin America* (1979), p. 9.

10. Luis Torres De Mendoza, ed., *Colección de documentos inéditos: Relativos al descubrimiento, conquista y organización de las antiguas posesiones españolas de América y Oceanía*, v. 7 (1867), p. 423. Gustavo Gutiérrez, *Dios o el Oro en las Indias* (1989), p. 44, cites many of these letters. Also: P. M. A. Medina, "Cartas de Pedro de Córdoba y de La Comunidad Dominica," *Guaraguao*, v. 21 (2017), p. 167. Su-

sanne Zantop, *Colonial Fantasies: Conquest, Family, and Nation* in *Precolonial Germany, 1770–1870* (1997), p. 22. For the death of Montesinos: Mirtha A. Hernández, "Fray Antonio de Montesinos and the Laws of Burgos," MA thesis, Louisiana State University (1977); Julia Roth, "Sugar and Slaves: The Augsburg Welser as Conquerors of America and Colonial Foundational Myths," *Atlantic Studies*, v. 14 (1917); Demetrio Ramos Pérez, "El Negocio Negrero de Los Welser y Sus Habilidades Monopolistas," *Revista de Historia de América*, v. 81 (1976); Giovanna Montenegro, *German Conquistadors in Venezuela* (2022); Juan Friede, *Los Welser en la conquista de América* (1961); Manuel Giménez Fernández, *Bartolomé de las Casas: Delegado de Cisneros para la reformación de las indias*, v. 1 (1953), p. 44; Las Casas's German pun is in the 1552 edition of *Brevísima Relación*, p. 33.

11. The letter from thirteen Dominican friars, including Montesinos, sent on December 4, 1519, to Cardinal Chievres, in Mendoza, ed., *Colección de documentos inéditos*, v. 35 (1880). Las Casas most likely read of the corpses floating as buoy markers in this letter, which he repeats in *Brevísima Relación*, p. 266.

12. For context of Las Casas's conversion: Clayton, *Bartolomé de Las Casas*, pp. 70–81.

Chapter 4: Goodbye Aristotle

1. Anthony Pagden, *The Fall of Natural Man* (1982), p. 17; Las Casas, *Apologia* (1988), p. 101.

2. Fray Toribio de Benavente Motolinía, *Historia De Los Indios De La Nueva España* (1985), p. 318.

3. Miguel Martínez, *Front Lines: Soldiers' Writing in the Early Modern Hispanic World* (2016); Diego Muñoz Camargo and Alfredo Chavero, *Historia De Tlaxcala* (1892), p. 141; Bernal Díaz del Castillo, *Historia Verdadera de la Conquista de la Nueva España*, v. 2 (1837), p. 35; Luna Nájera, "Contesting the Word: The Crown and the Printing Press in Colonial Spanish America," *Bulletin of Spanish Studies*, v. 89 (2012); E. Shaskan Bumas, "The Cannibal Butcher Shop: Protestant Uses of Las Casas's 'Brevísima Relación' in Europe and the American Colonies," *Early American Literature*, v. 35 (2000).

4. Diego Barros Arana, *Historia Jeneral de Chile*, v. 3 (2000), p. 104; Alonso González de Nájera, *Desengaño y reparo de la guerra del reino de Chile* (2017).

5. Pagden, *European Encounters*, p. 76; Matthew Restall, *Seven Myths of the Spanish Conquest* (2003).

6. "Carta de Bartolomé de las Casas al Padre Carranza de Miranda," August 1555, in Martín Fernández de Navarrete, ed., *Colección de documentos inéditos para la historia de España*, v. 71 (1879), p. 389.

7. Joshua Weiner, "'Discoveries Are Not to be Called Conquests': Narrative, Empire, and the Ambiguity of Conquest in Spain's American Empire," PhD dissertation, Northeastern University (2009), p. 225; Victor M. Maurtua, *Antecedentes de la recopilación de Yndias: Documentos sobre la visita del consejo de Indias por el licenciado Juan de Ovando* (1906), pp. 22–23.

8. Juan Ginés Sepúlveda, *Tratado Sobre las Justas Causas de la Guerra contra los Indios* (1941), p. 155.

9. Venancio Carro, *La teología y los teólogos-juristas españoles ante la conquista de América* (1951), p. 595; Sepúlveda's apocalyptism is discussed in Luna Nájera, "Myth and Prophecy in Juan Ginés de Sepúlveda's Crusading 'Exhortación,'" *Bulletin for Spanish and Portuguese Historical Studies*, v. 35 (2011).

10. Matthew Restall, "'There Was a Time We Were Friends': Las Casas and Cortés as Monstrous Doubles of the Conquest Era," in David Thomas Orique and Rady Roldán Figueroa, eds., *Bartolomé de las Casas* (2019), p. 66. My quotation is translated from the Spanish Restall provided in footnote 5.

11. For Sepúlveda and others like him, it would be ludicrous, and potentially anarchic, to think of human units of the earth's enormous diversity as sovereign equals. Look no further than the chaos caused by

the profane individualism of Luther and Calvin in Mitteleuropa. There, mobs were running into churches and smashing icons and priceless works of art. There was only one alternative to such bedlam: affirm that the source of all authority was divine revelation, papal infallibility, and faith in Jesus Christ, and sort the world's diversity on a spectrum ranging from savage to civilized, heathen to Christian.

12. In addition to the problem of applying European notions of rights to New World Native Americans, Vitoria's legal scholarship raises three broad concerns. The first has to do with whether his legal arguments ultimately undermined or upheld Catholic Spain's claim to title in the New World. The second relates to how Protestant colonialists and jurists, many associated with England, understood the implications of Vitoria's arguments: Did they delegitimate Spanish title to the New World? Or, more troubling for would-be colonists, did they delegitimate all forms of conquest, war, dispossession, and settlement? The third is Vitoria's role in the broader history of international law. Early advocates of liberal multilateralism, such as James Brown Scott, claimed Vitoria as a founder of international law. See his *The Spanish Origin of International Law* (1934). For an early assessment of Vitoria in the years immediately after the founding of the United Nations: José Manuel de Aguilar, "The Law of Nations and the Salamanca School of Theology," *The Thomist*, v. 9 (1946); Paolo Amorosa, *Rewriting the History of the Law of Nations: How James Brown Scott Made Francisco de Vitoria the Founder of International Law* (2019), provides the context for when and why Vitoria is incorporated into histories of law. In no implied order, the following works are essential: Santiago Piñón, *The Ivory Tower and the Sword: Francisco Vitoria Confronts the Emperor* (2017); Annabel S. Brett, *Changes of State: Nature and the Limits of the City in Early Modern Natural Law* (2011); Anthony Pagden, "Dispossessing the Barbarian: The Language of Spanish Thomism and the Debate over the Property Rights of the Americas," in *Theories of Empire: 1450–1800* (1998); Brian Tierney, *The Idea of Natural Rights* (2001); Rolena Adorno, *The Polemics of Possession in Spanish American Narrative* (2007); Antony Anghie, *Imperialism, Sovereignty, and the Making of International Law* (2004); Robert Williams, *The American Indian in Western Legal Thought* (1990); Ignacio de la Rasilla del Moral, *In the Shadow of Vitoria: A History of International Law in Spain: 1770–1953* (2018); José María Beneyto, Justo Corti Varela, eds., *At the Origins of Modernity: Francisco de Vitoria and the Discovery of International Law* (2017); Rubén Vargas, "Fray Francisco de Vitoria y el derecho a la conquista de América," *Boletín del Instituto de Investigaciones Históricas*, v. 11 (1930), p. 34; among others, including some cited above.

13. Daragh Grant, "Francisco de Vitoria and Alberico Gentili on the Juridical Status of Native American Polities," *Renaissance Quarterly*, v. 72 (2019). Antony Anghie, "Francisco De Vitoria and the Colonial Origins of International Law," *Social & Legal Studies*, v. 5 (1996) for a cogent critique of Vitoria.

14. Anghie, in *Imperialism* and subsequent essays, has a more critical interpretation of Vitoria.

15. Alonso de Valle, "Colección de Historiadores de Chile y de documentos relativos a la história nacional," *Histórica Relación del Reino de Chile*, v. 13 (1888), p. 81.

16. Alonso de Ercilla y Zúñiga, *La Araucana*, v. 1 (1776), p. 143.

17. Charles's letter is in Maía del Carmen Rovira, *Francisco De Vitoria: España y América* (2004), pp. 116–18.

Chapter 5: New Laws

1. David Brion Davis, *The Problem of Slavery in Western Culture* (1988), p. 170.

2. Fray Tomás de la Torre, *Diario de viaje de Salamanca a Ciudad Real de Chiapa, 1544–1545* (1985), pp. 59–60.

3. Henry Raup Wagner and Helen Rand Parish, *The Life and Writings of Bartolomé de las Casas* (1967), pp. 131–32; Carol Damian, "Guatemala Churches: The Mayan Legacy in Organic Facades," *Oxford Research Encyclopedias* (2021).

4. Lesley Byrd Simpson, *The Encomienda in New Spain* (1950), p. 230.

5. "Carta de D. Fr. Juan de Zumárraga, Obispo de México, Fr. Martin de Hojacastro y Fr. Francisco de Soto, al Emperador" (October 4, 1543), in Joaquin Garcia Icazbalceta, *Don Fray Juan de Zumárraga* (1881), pp. 146–50; Enrique Dussel, *Historia General de la Iglesia en América Latina* (1983), for persecution of Lascasian clerics. For repression of clergy: Carlos Sempat Assadourian, "Fray Bartolomé de Las Casas Obispo," *Historia Mexicana*, v. 40 (1991). For a summation of what Las Casas hoped to achieve in Chiapas, and how his failure there shaped his subsequent life: José Cárdenas Bunsen, "The Legal Foundations of Las Casas's Warnings on the Destruction of Spain," *Revista de Literatura Hispánica*, v. 85/86 (2017).

6. Alan Gallay, "Introduction: Indian Slavery in Historical Context," in Alan Gallay, ed., *Indian Slavery in Colonial America* (2010), p. 17; Richard Flint, *Great Cruelties Have Been Reported: The 1544 Investigation of the Coronado Expedition* (2002), p. xvii. The conquest of the Philippines and Florida, and the campaigns through North America, mostly took place after Las Casas's death in 1566 and after Charles abdicated the Spanish throne to his son Philip.

7. In Hanke, *All Mankind Is One*, p. 10.

8. Alvaro Huerga, *Historia de los Alumbrados*, v. 2 (1986) p. 273. Reference to the nicknames of Las Casas and Andrada come from an unpublished manuscript, written while Las Casas was still alive, by Fray Juan de la Cruz, "*Crónica de la Orden de Predicadores*" (1567), cited in Helen Rand Paris and Harold E. Weidman, "The Correct Birthdate of Bartolomé de Las Casas," *The Hispanic American Historical Review*, v. 56 (1976), p. 387.

9. Las Casas, *Brevísima Relación* (2011), p. 67; Las Casas, *Aqui se co[n]tiene[n] vnos auisos y reglas para los confessores q[ue] oyeren confessiones delos españoles que son, o han sido en cargo a los indios de las Indias del mar oceano* (1552), np.

10. Two studies describe Las Casas's confessional strategy: Regina Harrison, *Sin and Confession in Colonial Peru* (2014), especially chapter 1, and David Orique, *To Heaven or to Hell: Bartolomé de las Casas's Confesionario* (2018). Las Casas wrote his first instructional as Bishop of Chiapas, revising, expanding, and reprinting it over the years. Orique, *To Heaven or to Hell*, offers both context and an English translation of the guide's most complete edition. For a sense of how exceptional Las Casas's strategy was: Patrick J. O'Banion, *The Sacrament of Penance and Religious Life in Golden Age Spain* (2012). Earlier, Las Casas used the tactic in 1532, barging into a room where another priest was hearing the confession of a dying *encomendero* to tell the would-be penitent he would not receive last rites unless he paid for all the "extortions he had committed" and freed his Indians. Hispaniola society was scandalized, and Las Casas was forced to spend a year secluded in Santo Domingo's monastery.

11. Martti Koskenniemi, *To the Uttermost Parts of the Earth: Legal Imagination and International Power, 1300–1870* (2021), p. 113.

12. John Bossy, "The Social History of Confession in the Age of the Reformation," *Transactions of the Royal Historical Society*, v. 25 (1975); Stephen Haliczer, *Sexuality in the Confessional* (1996).

13. Orique, *To Heaven or to Hell*, pp. 77–78; Aliocha Maldavsky, "Teología moral, restitución y sociedad colonial en los Andes en el siglo XVI," *Revista Portuguesa de Filosofía*, v. 75 (2019), p. 1130.

14. Harrison, *Sin and Confession*, p. 27; Orique, *To Heaven or to Hell*, pp. 51–70.

15. From a January 2, 1555, letter from Fray Toribio de Motolinía to Charles V, a strident polemic against Las Casas that gives a sense of how threatening his confessionary strategy was to Church and royal officials. See Toribio de Motolinía, *Carta de fray Toribio de Motolinía al emperador Carlos V* (2010).

16. Guillermo Lohmann Villena, "La restitución Por Conquistadores y Encomenderos: Un Aspecto de la Incidencia Lascasiana en el Perú," *Anuario de Estudios Americanos*, v. 23 (1966).

17. José de la Riva-Agüero, *El Primer alcalde de Lima Nicolás de Ribera el Viejo* (1952), p. 28.

18. Eugenio Alarco, *El hombre peruano en su historia*; *El encuentro de dos podres: Españoles contra Inkas*, v. 6 (1971), p. 833.

19. Bermart Hernández, *Bartolome de las Casas*; Raúl Porras Barrenechea, "El Testamento de Mancio Serra," *Revista De Indias*, v. 1; Stuart Stirling, *The Last Conquistador: Mansio Serra de Leguizamon and the Conquest of the Inkas* (1999).

20. De la Riva-Agüero, *El Primer alcalde*, pp. 28–33.

21. Anthony Pagden and Jeremy Lawrence, eds., *Vitoria: Political Writings* (1991), p. 333.

22. Juan Antonio Llorente, *Colección de las obras del venerable obispo de Chiapa, don Bartolomé de las Casas, defensor de la libertad de los Americanos*, v. 2 (1822), p. 327.

23. Sam McFarland, "The Slow Creation of Humanity," *Political Psychology*, v. 32 (2011), pp. 1–20; Las Casas's multivolume *Historia de las Indias*, v. 3 (1986), contains numerous references condemning the enslavement of Africans, and condemning his own short-lived proposal in favor of African slavery. Clara Camplani writes that behind Las Casas's florid expressions you find a "coherent," absolutist rejection of African slavery. Clara Camplani, "La defensa de los Negros en Bartolomé de Las Casas" in Victorien Lavou Zoungbo, ed., *Bartolomé de Las Casas: Face à l'esclavage des Noires en Amériques* (2017).

24. David Orique, *The Unheard Voice of Law in Bartolomé de Las Casas's Brevísima Relación de la Destrucción de las Indias* (2021); José Cárdenas Bunsen, "The Legal Foundations of Las Casas's Warnings on the Destruction of Spain," *Revista de Literatura Hispánica*, v. 85/86 (2017).

Chapter 6: Bartolomé's Many Ghosts

1. Manuel Giménez Fernández, *Últimos días de Bartolomé de Las Casas* (1958), p. 715.

2. Parish and Weidman, "The Correct Birthdate of Bartolomé de Las Casas," *The Hispanic American Historical Review*; James Lockhart, "Encomienda and Hacienda: The Evolution of the Great Estate in the Spanish Indies, *Hispanic American Historical Review*, v. 49 (1969); Lesley B. Simpson, *The Encomienda in New Spain: The Beginning of Spanish Mexico* (1966); Silvio Zavala, *La encomienda indiana* (1935), and *De encomiendas y propiedad territorial en algunas regiones de la América española* (1940), for more on the legal relationship of land and labor, and the circuitous evolution from *encomiendas* to haciendas.

3. Thomas A. Abercrombie, "La perpetuidad traducida: del 'debate' al Taki Onqoy y una rebelión comunera peruana," in Jean-Jacques Decoster, ed., *Inkase indios cristianos: Elites indígenas e identidades cristianas en los Andes coloniales* (2002).

4. Rolena Adorno, *Polemics of Possession in Spanish Narrative* (2007), p. 51. Eugenio Alarco, *El hombre peruano en su historia*, pp. 696–99, provides a good account.

5. Adorno, *Polemics of Possession*, p. 86.

6. Steve Stern, *Peru's Indian Peoples and the Challenge of Spanish Conquest* (1982), p. 52; Juan Carlos Estenssoro Fuchs, "Las Bailes de los indios y el proyecto colonial," *Revistia Andina*, v. 10 (1992); Jeremy Mumford, "The Taki Onqoy and the Andean Nation: Sources and Interpretations," *Latin American Research Review*, v. 33 (1998), p. 162.

7. For Toledo's centralization of the provision of forced labor as a function of the colonial state: Stern, *Peru's Indian Peoples*.

8. Gustavo Gutiérrez, *En busca de los pobres de Jesucristo* (1993), p. 578, footnote 45. For a good description of this crackdown see pp. 561–93. Wagner and Parish, *Life and Writings*, pp. 188–89.

9. Anonymous letter dated March 16, 1571, in Martín Fernández de Navarrete, *Colección de Documentos Inéditos para la Historia de España*, v. 13 (1848), p. 4; Eugenio Alarco, *El hombre peruano en su historia*, p. 834.

10. David Brading, *The First America: The Spanish Monarchy, Creole Patriots and the Liberal State, 1492–1866* (1991), p. 189; Jorge Cañizares-Esguerra, *How to Write the History of the New World* (2001), p. 83. Also: Antonio Benítez-Rojo, *The Repeating Island: The Caribbean and the Postmodern Perspective* (1997), p. 85.

11. Rolena Adorno discusses the link between Las Casas and Poma, in *Polemics of Possession*. As time passed, Spanish authorities assumed that all Las Casas's writings had been suppressed. In 1660, though, officials in Seville came across two volumes, in Latin, of *Brevísima Relación de la Destrucción de las Indias*. The Crown's prosecutor searched the archives but couldn't find an official decree banning the book. There must be one, he said, considering the damage it had done to Spain. The prosecutor remitted the book to the Inquisition, which judged it "pernicious" and issued an edict that finally had it banned. In Lewis Hanke, "Bartolomé de Las Casas, historiador," in *Historia de las Indias*, ed., Agustín Miyares Carlo (1965), p. xl. For Las Casas's followers' turn toward prophesizing retribution: José Cárdenas Bunsen, "Manuscript Circulation, Christian Eschatology, and Political Reform," in Rolena Adorno and Ivan Boserup, eds., *Unlocking the Doors to the World Guaman Poma* (2015). Las Casas himself, in his very last essays, warned Spain that the consequences of its inequities would bring divine wrath. See José Cárdenas Bunsen, "The Legal Foundations."

12. For the intersection of Las Casas and de la Cruz, Alvaro Huerga, *Historia de los Alumbrados*, pp. 274–75. Catholic Spain established the Inquisition in 1478 as its long war against Islam was ending, a prosecutorial body infamous for torturing and burning alive apostates. The idea that women fared better under the liberalizing ethos of Protestantism is a myth. In Europe, Protestants burned accused witches, those sexualized adjuncts of the devil, with a frenzy that far outpaced Catholics. Allison Courdert, "The Myth of the Improved Status of Protestant Women: The Case of the Witchcraze," in *Witches of the Atlantic World: An Historical Reader and Primary Sourcebook*, ed., Elaine Breslaw (2000), p. 311.

13. Marcelino Menéndez y Pelayo, *Historia de los heterodoxos españoles* (1880).

14. Vidal Abril Castelló, *Francisco de la Cruz, Inquisición*, v. 2, pt. 1 (1996), p. 50; Vidal Abril Castelló, "Francisco de la Cruz, la utopía lascasista y la Contrarreforma virreinal-inquisitorial, Lima 1572–1573," *Cuadernos para la historia de la evangelización en América Latina*, v. 3 (1988); Regina Harrison, *Sin and Confession in Colonial Peru* (2014), p. 39.

15. Luis Martin, *Daughters of the Conquistadores* (1983), pp. 297–98.

16. Huerga, *Alumbrados*, v. 3, p. 304.

17. Fuchs, "Las Bailes de los indios y el proyecto colonial"; Vidal Abril Castelló, *Francisco de la Cruz, Inquisición*, v. 2, p. 503; Huerga, *Alumbrados*, p. 274, says that de la Cruz "radicalized Las Casas' hypothesis to unthinkable levels." Also: Alvaro Huerga, "Sobre una Teoría del Padre Las Casas: La Emigración de la Iglesia a Indias," Escritos del VEDAT, v. 11 (1981).

18. López kept notebooks that were filled with Las Casas–like political arguments. Martín Fernández de Navarrete, *Colección de Documentos Inéditos para la Historia de España*, v. 94 (1889), p. 473; Information on Pizarro, de la Cruz, and López: Isacio Pérez Fernández, *Bartolomé de Las Casas en el Peru* (1988); José Toribio Medina, *Historia del Tribunal de la Inquisición de Lima, 1569–1820* (1956); Andrés Prieto, "The Visitor and the Viceroy: Juan de la Plaza and the First Visitation to Jesuit Peru, 1575–79," in Robert Maryks, ed., *With Eyes and Ears Open: The Role of Visitors in the Society of Jesus* (2019). For the trial's proceedings: Vidal Abril Castelló, *Francisco de la Cruz, Inquisición*, 3 vols.

(1992–97); Andrew Redden, *Diabolism*; Marcel Bataillon "La herejía de Fray Francisco de la Cruz y la Reacción Antilascasiana," in *Miscelánea de Estudios Dedicados a Fernando Ortiz* (1955).

19. Ricardo Palma, *Tradiciones Peruanas*, v. 2 (1924), p. 211.

20. Deborah Poole, *Vision, Race, and Modernity: A Visual Economy of the Andean World* (1997) chapter 4, "A One-Eyed Gaze"; Henry Willis Baxley, *What I Saw on the West Coast of South and North America, and at the Hawaiian Islands* (1865), pp. 111–13. Henry Willis Baxley, Washington's envoy to Lima in the early 1860s in the middle of the U.S. Civil War, likened the *sayo y manta* to "Mokanna's veil." The reference is to Thomas Moore's "The Veiled Prophet of Khorassan," a 1817 satire that mashed together Islam and Jacobinism, telling of a revolution led by al-Muqanna—Mokanna— that promised "freedom to the world" and "man's enfranchisement."

21. Antonio de León Pinelo, *Velos Antiquos y Modernos en los Rostros de las Mujeres: Sus Conveniencias y Daños*, v. 2 (1966); Andres Mille, *Itinerario de la Orden Dominicana en la conquista del Peru, Chile y el Tucuman: Y su Convento del Antiguo Buenos Aires, 1612–1807* (1964), p. 90; Liliana Pérez Miguel, "Encomenderas, Legislación y Estrategias en El Perú en el Siglo XVI" in Claudia Rosas, ed., *Género y Mujeres en la Historia del Perú* (2019); Martín Fernández de Navarrete, *Colección de Documentos Ineditos para la Historia de España*, v. 94 (1889), p. 328; Rocío Quispe-Agnoli, "Taking Possession of the New World: Powerful Female Agency of Early Colonial Accounts of Perú," *Legacy*, v. 28 (2011).

22. John Leddy Phelan, *The Millennial Kingdom of the Franciscans in the New World* (1970); José Antonio Maravall, "La utopia politico-religiosa de los Franciscanos en Nueva España," *Estudios Americanos*, v. 2 (1949).

23. Huston Smith, *The Soul of Christianity: Restoring the Great Tradition* (2005), p. 14; Elsa Cecilia Frost, *Este Nuevo Orbe* (1996), pp. 31–42; 75–103; 155–64; For more on Mendieta: Jaime Cuadriello, "Winged and Imagined Indians," in *Angels, Demons and the New World*, Fernando Cervantes and Andrew Redden, eds., (2013).

24. Phelan, *The Millennial Kingdom*, p, 150; Juan Burke, "Civitas Angelorum: The Symbolic Urbanism of Puebla de Los Ángeles in the Early Modern Era," McGill University, PhD dissertation (2017).

25. Bernardino de Sahagún, *Historia general de las cosas de Nueva España* (1938), p. 282; Segundo Alailea, *Ascenso a la Libertad* (1990), pp. 81–83; Mendieta, *Historia eclesiástica indiana,* p. 63. Las Casas and other critics of the Conquest said that the settlements themselves were Satan's work; the *encomienda* system "bred satanic tyranny." Jorge Cañizares-Esguerra, *Puritan Conquistadores: Iberianizing the Atlantic, 1550–1700* (2006), p. 74.

26. Silvio Zavala, *El servicio personal de los indios en la Nueva España: 1521–1550* (1984), p. 165; Letter to Padre Fray Francisco de Bustamante, Comisario General de las Indias, January 1, 1562, in Joaquin García Icazbalceta, *Colección de documentos para la historia de México*, v. II (1866), p. 524.

27. Claudio Lomnitz, *Death and the Idea of Mexico* (2005), p. 75. Also: Sahagún, *Historia general de las cosas de Nueva España*, v. 2, pp. 308–9; Mendieta, *Historia eclesiástica indiana*, v. 3, pp. 184–85.

28. Coerced Indian labor helped accelerate the spread of mercantile capitalism. The Catholic Spanish Empire was the largest currency union in history, its Indian-mined silver pesos and dollars flooding the world's economies and sparking an expansionary boom.

29. Virginia Tilley, *Seeing Indians: A Study of Race, Nation, and Power in El Salvador* (2005), p. 108.

30. Magnus Mörner, *Race Mixing in the History of Latin America* (1967), p. 58.

Chapter 7: Empty Houses

1. Neal Salisbury, *Manitou and Providence: Indians, Europeans, and the Making of New England: 1500–1643* (1982), p. 103.

2. John Smith, *A Description of New England* (1616), p. 37.

3. Thomas Dermer, *Letter Describing His Passage from Main to Virginia* (1619), p. 10.

4. Fred Wilson, *Some Annals of Nahant, Massachusetts* (1928), p. 12.

5. William Bradford, *Of Plymouth Plantation* (1856), p. 325.

6. Arlene Hirschfelder and Martha Kreipe de Montaño, *Native American Almanac* (1993), p. 2.

7. J. S. Marr and J. T. Cathey, "New Hypothesis for Cause of Epidemic among Native Americans, New England, 1616–1619," *Emerging Infectious Diseases*, v. 16 (2010), pp. 281–86; Roger Williams, *A Key into the Language of America* (1643), p. 72.

8. Cited in Elijah Middlebrook Haines, *The American Indian* (1888), p. 315. For Jamestown cannibalism, see the firsthand account of George Percy, discussed in Dale Hutchinson's *Disease and Discrimination: Poverty and Pestilence in Colonial Atlantic America* (2019), chapter 7.

9. Thomas Morton, *Manners and Customs of the Indians* (1637).

10. A "Golgotha of Unburied Carcasses," Cotton Mather wrote later.

11. Frank Moody Gregg, *The Founding of a Nation* (1915); George Nutting, *Massachusetts* (1937), p. 324. The story of the corpse-sentinels comes from a voyager on the *Mayflower*, Phineas Pratt, and is cited in many subsequent histories, including Joseph Felt, *Ecclesiastical History of New England*, v. 1 (1853), p. 68.

12. Alexander Young, *Chronicles of the Pilgrim Fathers of the Colony of Plymouth* (1844), p. 292.

13. John Winthrop to John Endecott (1634), *Papers of the Winthrop Family*, v. 3; Edward Winslow, *Mourt's Relation* (1622); John Winthrop, *General Observations*, v. 2 (1629); Johnson quote in John Gorham Palfrey, *History of New England during the Stuart Dynasty*, v. 1 (1859), p. 177; George quote in David S. Jones, *Rationalizing Epidemics* (2004), p. 37; Bradford, *Of Plymouth Plantation*, p. 270; Nathaniel Morton, *New England's Memorial* (1826), p. 37. For the footnote discussing using disease as a weapon: Elizabeth Finn, "Biological Warfare in Eighteenth-Century North America: Beyond Jeffery Amherst," *The Journal American History*, v. 86 (2000).

14. J. Franklin Jameson, *Johnson's Wonder-Working Providence, 1628–1651* (1910), p. 80.

15. Williams, *A Key into the Language*, pp. 57–62. For the footnote: John U. Nef, "An Early Energy Crisis and Its Consequences," *Scientific American*, v. 237 (1977); Isaac Weld, *Travels Through the States of North America* (1799), pp. 232–41.

16. *Collections of the Massachusetts Historical Society, Winthrop Papers*, v. 1 (1871), p. 147. For nonproperty-related uses of the term: Leonard Hoar and Josiah Flint, *The Sting of Death . . .* , (1680).

17. Paul Corcoran, "John Locke on Native Right, Colonial Possession, and the Concept of *Vacuum domicilium*," *The European Legacy*, v. 23 (2017), for the early use of the term.

18. James Savage, Richard Dunn, and Laetitia Yeandle, eds., *The Journal of John Winthrop, 1630–1639* (1996). Also: David Grayson Allen, "Vacuum Domicilium: The Social and Cultural Landscape of Seventeenth-Century New England," in Jonathan Fairbanks and Robert Trent, eds., *New England Begins* (1982); Christopher Tomlins, *Freedom Bound: Law, Labor and Civic Identity in Colonizing English America* (2010), pp. 148–49; Egbert Benson, *Memoir, on Names, Read Before the Historical*

Society of the State of New-York, December 31, 1816 (1825); George Edward Ellis, *Puritan Age and Rule in the Colony of the Massachusetts Bay, 1629–1685* (1888; 1970), p. 220; "John Cotton's Answer to Roger Williams," in *Proceedings of the Massachusetts Historical Society, 1871–1873*, v. 12 (1873), p. 352.

19. Robert Cushman, *Reasons and Considerations Touching the Lawfulness of Removing out of England into the Parts of America* (1622), cited in Alan Heimert and Andrew Delbanco, *Puritans in America* (2005), p. 44.

20. Christopher Tomlins and Bruce Mann, eds., *The Many Legalities of Early America* (2001), p. 42; Nathaniel B. Shurtleff, ed., *Records of the Governor and Company of the Massachusetts Bay in New England* (1853–1854), p. 247; Robert Ludlow Fowler, *History of the Law of Real Property in New York* (1895), p. 3.

21. John Cotton, *God's Promise to His Plantations* (1630).

22. John Winthrop to John Endecott (1634).

Chapter 8: Irish Tactics

1. David Edwards, "Tudor Ireland: Anglicisation, Mass Killing and Security," in *The Routledge History of Genocide* (2015); Gosling, William Gilbert, *The Life of Sir Humphrey Gilbert, England's First Empire Builder* (1911), pp. 49–50.

2. Colm Lennon, *Sixteenth-Century Ireland: The Incomplete Conquest*, p. 227; Catherine Canino "Reconstructing Lord Grey's Reputation," *Sixteenth Century Journal*, v. 29 (1998), p. 6.

3. Thomas Wright, *The History of Ireland*, v. 1 (1849), p. 494. For Marx in footnote: Lawrence Krader, ed. and comp., *The Ethnological Notebooks of Karl Marx* (1972), p. 305.

4. Thomas Addis Emmet, *Ireland Under English Rule: Or, A Plea for the Plaintiff*, v. 1 (1903), p. 68.

5. Loren Pennington, "The Amerindian in English Promotional Literature, 1575–1625," in K. R. Andrews, N. P. Canny, and P. E. H. Hair, eds., *The Westward Enterprise* (1978), p. 183; George Peckham, *A True Reporte, of the Late Discoveries, and Possessions, Taken in the Right of the Crowne of England of the New-Found Landes* (1583).

6. Nicholas Canny, "The Ideology of English Colonization from Ireland to America," in David Armitage, ed., *Theories of Empire, 1450–1800* (1991).

7. Alva Curtis Wilgus, *The Development of Spanish America* (1941), p. 178; *Annual Report of the Director, U.S. Coast and Geodetic Survey* (1885), p. 533; K. R. Andrews, "The English in the Caribbean, 1560–1620," in *The Westward Enterprise*, p. 109; Frank Craven, "The Earl of Warwick, a Speculator in Piracy," *The Hispanic American Historical Review*, v. 10 (1930); Paul-Dubois, Louis François Alphonse, *Contemporary Ireland* (1908); Jane Ohlmeyer, "A Laboratory for Empire?: Early Modern Ireland and English Imperialism," in Kevin Kenny, ed., *Ireland and the British Empire* (2004); Eamon Darcy, *The Irish Rebellion of 1641 and the Wars of the Three Kingdoms* (2015), p. 29.

8. Richard Hakluyt, *Discourse of Western Planting* (1584).

9. Walter Raleigh, *History of the World* (1614).

10. Walter Raleigh, *The Discovery of Guiana* (1848).

11. April Lee Hatfield, "Spanish Colonization Literature, Powhatan Geographies, and English Perceptions of Tsenacommacah/Virginia," *The Journal of Southern History*, v. 69 (2003); John Elliott, *Spain, Europe and the Wider World, 1500–1800* (2009), p. 38, discusses the grudging admiration the English had for the Spanish, and the comparison of the Irish and American Conquests.

12. John M. Thompson, ed., *The Journals of Captain John Smith* (2007), p. 217; Edmund Morgan, *American Slavery, American Freedom* (1975), p. 77; Mather, *Magnalia Christi Americana* (1855), p. 557. I changed "salvages" in the John Smith quote to "savages."

13. David Harding, "Objects of English Colonial Discourse: The Irish and Native Americans," *Nordic Irish Studies*, v. 4 (2005), p. 54; E. M. Rose, "Lord Delaware, First Governor of Virginia: 'The Poorest Baron of This Kingdom,'" *The Virginia Magazine of History and Biography*, v. 128 (2020); William Fitzhugh, *Cultures in Contact: The Impact of European Contacts on Native American Cultural Institutions, A.D. 1000–1800* (1985), p. 241. For more on the connection of Ireland and America: A. L. Rowse, *The Expansion of Elizabethan England* (1955), pp. 126–57.

14. Armstrong Starkey, "European-Native Warfare in North America 1513–1815," in Jeremy Black, ed., *War in the Early Modern World* (2005); William Shea, *The Virginia Militia in the Seventeenth Century* (1983), p. 140; Nicholas Canny, "The Ideology of English Colonization: From Ireland to America," *William and Mary Quarterly* (1973).

15. Cromwell, speaking of his massacre at Drogheda: "I am persuaded that this is a righteous judgement of God upon these barbarous wretches." Antonia Fraser, *Cromwell* (1975), p. 338.

16. Crawford Gibben, *The Irish Puritans* (2014), p. 77. For Ireland's influence on Penn: Andrew R. Murphy, John Smolenski, eds., *The Worlds of William Penn* (2019). For Quaker pacifism: John Howard Yoder, *Chapters in the History of Religiously Rooted Nonviolence* (1994), chapter 6. Professor Ian McBride, in an electronic communication, speculates that Protestantism was still too besieged a movement in Europe to engage in the kind of criticism conducted by Las Casas, and might have been reluctant to criticize London, their most powerful patron.

17. Gerald of Wales, *The History and Topography of Ireland* (1982), pp. 101–2.

18. Rhodri Lewis, "William Petty's Anthropology: Religion, Colonialism, and the Problem of Human Diversity," *Huntington Library Quarterly*, v. 74 (2011).

19. On these points: David N. Livingstone's essays, "Preadamites: The History of an Idea from Heresy to Orthodoxy," *Scottish Journal of Theology*, v. 40 (1987), and "The Preadamite Theory and the Marriage of Science and Religion," *Transactions of the American Philosophical Society*, v. 82 (1992); David Livingstone, *Adam's Ancestors: Race, Religion, and the Politics of Human Origins* (2008), p. 41; Thomas Herbert, *Some Years Travel. . . .* (1677), p. 18.

20. Reginald Horsman, "Origins of Racial Anglo-Saxonism in Great Britain Before 1850," *Journal of the History of Ideas*, v. 37 (1976). For footnote see Cristián Andrés Roa de la Carrera, *Histories of Infamy* (2005), pp. 106–7.

21. Cited in Patrick O'Malley, "Irish Whiteness and the Nineteenth-Century Construction of Race," *Victorian Literature and Culture*, v. 51 (2023).

Chapter 9: Lost in the World's Debate

1. This is Hanke's summation of the collective position of the dissident generation of the 1530s and their successors. Las Casas himself wasn't a pacificist. In addition to believing that Indians had the right to fight back, he continued to hold to the idea that the doctrine of just war could be applied to Muslims, Jews, and heretics. Alicia Mayer, "Controversial Cases on Humanitarian Doctrines: Bartolomé de las Casas's Intellectual Legacy among New England Puritans," in David Orique and Rady Roldán-Figueroa, eds., *Bartolomé de las Casas, O.P.* (2019); Robert Fastiggi, "Suárez, the Natural Law, and the Limits of Religious Freedom," *Filosofia Unisinos*, v. 23 (2022), p. 7.

2. "A Justification for Planting Virginia Before 1609," from *The Records of the Virginia Company*. Original is found in the Tanner manuscripts, XCIII, folio 200 (old folio 352). Document in the Bodleian

Library, Oxford University, but available online through the University of Virginia Library at https://xtf.lib.virginia.edu/xtf/view?docId=2005_Q3_2/uvaGenText/tei/b002245360.xml; brand=default;;query=defend%20our%20title.

3. Cited in Matthew Page Andres, *The Soul of a Nation: The Founding of Virginia and the Projection of New England* (1943), p. 175.

4. Harry Culverwell Porter, *The Inconstant Savage* (1979), p. 372; Fitzmaurice, *Sovereignty, Property and Empire*, p. 68.

5. Edward Waterhouse, "A Declaration of the State of the Colony and . . . A Relation of the Barbarous Massacre . . ." 1622, in *The Records of the Virginia Company*, https://xtf.lib.virginia.edu/xtf/view?docId=2005_Q3_2/uvaGenText/tei/b002245360.xml;chunk.id=d226;toc.depth=100;toc.id=;brand=default;query=drudgery#1.

6. *Hakluytus Posthumus, Or, Purchas His Pilgrimes: Contayning a History of the World in Sea Voyages and Lande Travells by Englishmen and Others*, v. 19 (1906), p. 228.

7. Anthony Pagden, "Conquest and the Just War," in Sankar Muthu, ed., *Empire and Modern Political Thought* (2012).

8. C. V. Wedgewood, *The Thirty Years War* (1939), p. 538.

9. James Brown Scott in his *The Spanish Origin of International Law*, (1934) sees a progressive movement from Vitoria to Grotius onward. Richard Tuck argues that northern European protoliberal theorists were not an evolution of Vitoria but deviators. Grotius, according to Tuck, granted states "the most far-reaching set of rights to wage war." For more on Vitoria's influence on Grotius: Peter Borschberg, *Hugo Grotius, the Portuguese and Free Trade in the East Indies* (2011).

10. Benedict Kingsbury and Benjamin Straumann, eds., *The Roman Foundations of the Law of Nations: Alberico Gentili and the Justice of Empire* (2010), p. 253. Richard Tuck, *The Rights of War and Peace: Political Thought and the International Order From Grotius to Kant* (2001), p. 95.

11. Locke spent a good deal of time organizing and promoting colonial settlements in Virginia and Carolina to a skeptical public. Locke handwrote some of Carolina's laws, helping to draft the colony's first constitution in 1669, which read: "Every freeman of Carolina shall have absolute power and authority over his negro slaves." Locke also invested in the Royal African Company, which helped expand the Atlantic's chattel slave trade. Historians continue to debate the degree to which Locke's original writings justified or questioned empire, as well as to the degree they influenced Thomas Jefferson and the American Revolution. Barbara Arneil, *John Locke and America: The Defense of English Colonialism* (1996), provides an indispensable summation of subsequent differing positions up to the time of its publication. As to Locke's influence on the American Revolution, in 1937, Merle Curti called Locke "America's philosopher" ("The Great Mr. Locke: America's Philosopher, 1783–1861," in *The Huntington Library Bulletin*, v. 11 [1937]). In the 1950s and early 1960s, scholars such as Carl Becker and Maurice Cranston emphasized a similarly influential relationship. C. B. Macpherson's *The Political Theory of Possessive Individualism* (1962) was a key work, against which revisionists, starting in the late 1960s, pushed back on. Bernard Bailyn, John Dunn, and Garry Wills highlighted influences other than Locke on Jefferson and downplayed the "individualism" of U.S. revolutionary culture. Martyn Thompson argued that Locke was *too* conservative to have been much of an influence on the Revolution, since, as a partisan of the well-to-do, Locke's vision of expansion was not an every-man-free-for-all. Locke was a philosopher not just of freedom but of limits and constraints. David Armitage, "John Locke: Theorist of Empire?" in Sankar Muthu, ed., *Empire and Modern Political Thought* (2012), stresses Locke's ambiguity. To raise the topic of the "great Mr. Locke" is to raise the great debates within intellectual history over the last half century regarding the meanings of *republicanism* and *liberalism*, as well as the relationship of modern to classical republicanism, associated with J. G. A. Pocock, Bernard Bailyn, and

Quentin Skinner. The so-called Republican Synthesis argued that the colonists drew more heavily on debates related to commercial mercantilism, themselves reaching back to an earlier version of civic republicanism. In the 1980s, with Reaganism and New Right libertarianism ascendant, a revision of the revisionists began with scholars again stressing Lockean possessivism as a powerful element in justifying unlimited property accumulation through coercion. For example: James Tully, *An Approach to Political Philosophy: Locke in Contexts* (1993). Tully concludes, as Barbara Arneil writes in *John Locke and America* (1995), p. 9, "that Locke is implicitly supporting the practice of 'wars that . . . may become ethnocidal or genocidal because they are fought outside the domain of jus gentium.'"

12. Ángel Manuel Fernández Álvarez, "Juan de Mariana: Heredero de la Escuela de Salamanca y Precursor del Liberalismo," PhD dissertation, Universidad Complutense de Madrid (2015), contains an appendix that lists the similarities between arguments made by Mariana and those made by Locke. For the quotations in the footnote, see Johannes Laures, *The Political Economy of Juan de Mariana* (1928). Today, Father Mariana is celebrated by economic libertarians as an early proponent of the idea that individuals possess the right of property before the existence of government, that the consent of individuals is needed to constitute government, and that the only legitimate government is one that protects property rights. This is a wishful reading of Mariana, who made clear that he believed that individuals could not exist absent the existence of society and government. "Society is the natural state for man," Mariana wrote, "rather than the state of nature."

13. It is impossible to overstate the influence of Acosta on Europeans. Felipe Castañeda in *El Indio, Entre el Bárbaro y el Cristiano* (2002) argues that Acosta broke the impasse created by Vitoria, with his ethnography providing a way that colonialism could be justified in modern terms. See also Ivonne del Valle, "From José De Acosta to the Enlightenment: Barbarians, Climate Change, and (Colonial) Technology as the End of History," *The Eighteenth Century*, v. 54 (2013).

14. David Harding, "Objects of English Colonial Discourse: The Irish and Native Americans," *Nordic Irish Studies*, v. 4 (2005).

15. Peter Gowan, "The Origins of Atlantic Liberalism," *New Left Review*, v. 8 (2001).

16. Emer de Vattel, *The Law of Nations* (1883), p. 104.

17. Enrique Dussel, "Origen de la Filosofía Política Moderna: Las Casas, Vitoria y Suárez (1514–1617)," *Caribbean Studies*, v. 33 (2005).

18. Johnson's *Wonder-Working Providence, 1628–1651*, v. 10 (1910), p. 210.

19. An example: The town of Dedham set aside their claim of *vacuum domicilium* to grant a group of "sitting" or "praying" Indians land under the auspices of John Eliot. In *The Early Records of the Town of Dedham, Massachusetts, 1659–1673*, v. 4 (1894).

Chapter 10: The Western Design

1. C. H. Firth, ed., *The Clarke Papers*, v. 3 (1899), pp. 207–8.

2. Tom Feiling, *The Island That Disappeared: The Lost History of the Mayflower's Sister Ship* (2018).

3. James Morone, *Hellfire Nation: The Politics of Sin in American History* (2003), p. 57.

4. Eve LaPlante, *American Jezebel* (2010), for Hutchinson and her relationship to Cotton. Andrew Delbanco, *The Puritan Ordeal* (2009), for Cotton as a Puritan bishop.

5. William Bradford, *Of Plymouth Plantation* (1901), pp. 425–26.

6. Jameson, *Johnson's Wonder-Working Providence*, p. 45. Scattered: James Duncan Phillips, *Salem in the Seventeenth Century* (1933), p. 45. Also: William Davis, *Bradford's History of Plymouth Plantation, 1606–1646* (1908), pp. 221 and 142.

7. Delbanco, *The Puritan Ordeal*, p. 89.

8. Joy Gilsdorf, *The Puritan Apocalypse* (1989), p. 71. Historical time did feel like it was speeding up. The rise of Oliver Cromwell certainly seemed an accelerant. "The neerer these things come unto their accomplishment," Cotton preached in 1645, "the swifter their motion will be, as it is with all natural motions," in Cotton, *The Pouring Out of the Seven Vials: Or an Exposition of the 16th Chapter of the Revelation, with an Application of It to Our Times . . .* (1645), p. 11.

9. Charles Andres, *The Rise and Fall of New Haven Colony* (1936), p. 33.

10. Cotton, *The Pouring Out of the Seven Vials*. Other prominent Puritans cited Revelations's passages concerning the Seven Vials and the drying up of the Euphrates, including Samuel Sewall, who will be discussed in the next chapter. Ola Elizabeth Winslow, in her biography *Samuel Sewall of Boston* (1964), traces Sewall's interest in this passage from Revelation to his "schoolboy tutelage" by Cotton's contemporary, Newbury's Reverend Thomas Parker. Parker made "the book of Revelation a lifelong puzzle" for Sewall. Sewall knew about Cotton's role in urging Cromwell to attack Hispaniola, and of the importance Cotton placed in the image of a dried-up Euphrates. See *Diary of Samuel Sewall, 1674–1729*, v. 1, p. 437.

11. *The Harleian Miscellany* (1809), p. 513.

12. Thomas Birch and John Thurloe, eds., *A Collection of the State Papers of John Thurloe . . . : December 1654 to September 1655* (1742).

13. On Robert Venables: C. H. Firth, *The Narrative of General Venables* (1900), p. 156.

14. George Frederick Zook, "The Company of Royal Adventurers Trading into Africa," *The Journal of Negro History*, v. 4 (1919), p. 194.

15. Adam Smith, *Lectures on Jurisprudence* (1896), p. 96. Onur Ulas Ince writes that Smith, while condemning the treatment of Native Americans, refused to consider that there might be a relationship between indigenous dispossession and the growing wealth of the Atlantic's commercial economy. He tended to see (as did those philosophers, like Locke, influenced by Acosta) "American land as res nullius." When Smith criticized New World plunder he mostly focused on the brutalities of Cortés in Mexico and Pizarro in Peru. Acosta's typologies were dynamic and relatively nuanced when presented in the sixteenth century. By the late eighteenth century, they (as reflected in Smith's *Wealth of Nations*) had ossified: "There were but two nations in America, in any respect superior to savages, and these were destroyed almost as soon as discovered. The rest were mere savages." Onur Ulas Ince, "Adam Smith, Settler Colonialism, and Limits of Liberal Anti-Imperialism," *The Journal of Politics*, v. 83 (2021).

16. Felix Waldmann, "David Hume Was a Brilliant Philosopher but also a Racist Involved in Slavery," *The Scotsman*, July 17, 2020. Waldmann, a scholar of Hume, recounts his recent discovery of new letters documenting Hume's involvement in facilitating the purchase of slave plantations. Polygenism wasn't the only form of racism in early modern England: another kind held that all races are indeed humans but that some—Amerindians and Africans especially—had "degenerated." In response to criticism by a fellow Scottish philosopher, James Beattie, Hume revised some of his writings in a way that distanced himself from polygenism while still holding to the idea that some races were inferior, if not degenerated, compared to the pinnacle of whiteness. Also: John Immerwahr, "Hume's Revised Racism," *Journal of the History of Ideas*, v. 53 (1992).

17. William Lytle Schurz, "The Spanish Lake," *The Hispanic American Historical Review*, v. 5 (1922).

18. Hugh Thomas, *The Slave Trade* (1997), p. 236; Kenneth Morgan, *Slavery and the British Empire* (2007), p. 14.

19. Karen Kupperman, *Providence Island, 1630–1641: The Other Puritan Colony* (1993), p. 178; James Ballagh, *A History of Slavery in Virginia* (1902), p. 31; Almon Wheeler Lauber, *Indian Slavery in Colonial Times Within the Present Limits of the United States* (1913); Ethel Boissevain, "Whatever Became of the New England Indians Shipped to Bermuda to Be Sold as Slaves," *Man in the Northwest*, v. 11 (1981); Lion Gardiner, "Relation of the Pequot Warres," in *History of the Pequot War: The Contemporary Accounts of Mason, Underhill, Vincent, and Gardiner* (1897), p. 138; Laura Murray, "Joining Signs with Words: Missionaries, Metaphors, and the Massachusetts Language," *The New England Quarterly*, v. 74 (2001), pp. 62–93.

20. All cited in Lauber, *Indian Slavery*; for Winthrop quote: Amicus (pseud.), "Slavery Among the Puritans: A Letter to the Rev. Moses Stuart" (1850), found in *Nineteenth Century Collections Online: Religion, Society, Spirituality, and Reform*.

21. Wendy Warren, *New England Bound* (2014), p. 37. See Warren also for the exceptional 1845 story of the *Rainbow*, pp. 37–40.

22. See *The New England Historical and Genealogical Register*, v. 23 (1869), p. 485, for the enslavement of white indentured servants for committing crimes, albeit for a limited period.

23. Margaret Ellen Newell, *Brethren by Nature: New England Indians, Colonists, and the Origins of American Slavery* (2015), p. 52. I standardized the spelling of the quotation.

24. Jill Lepore, *The Name of War* (1998), p. 154.

25. Winthrop Jordan, "The Influence of the West Indies on the Origins of New England Slavery," *William and Mary Quarterly*, v. 18 (1961).

26. Benjamin Church, *Entertaining Passages Relating to Philip's War* (1716), p. 45; Increase Mather, *An Earnest Exhortation to the Inhabitants of New England* (1676).

27. From the 1611 King James Version, which Harry Stout ("Word and Order in Colonial New England," in *The Bible in America: Essays in Cultural History*, Nathan Hatch and Mark Noll, eds., [1982]) suggests was by this time becoming the dominant text, displacing the Geneva Bible.

Chapter 11: Opening the Mexican Fountain

1. In 1623, the colony's military commander Myles Standish, who like John Smith modeled himself on Cortés, led his men into a village and slaughtered all its inhabitants. Standish reportedly held a Bible with one hand and cut the head of the village leader with his other, after which the head, like Metacom's, was placed on a Plymouth pike. Later, a Leiden preacher named John Robinson wrote to ask if Standish had to kill them all. "How happy a thing had it been if you had converted some before you had killed any." For Underhill quotes: John Underhill, *Newes from America* (1638), p. 36.

2. Philip Vincent, *A True Relation of the Late Battell* (1637), p. 3.

3. For ambition straddling the line between vice and virtue: Robert Cushman, *The Sin and Danger of Self-Love Described in a Sermon Preached at Plymouth* (1822), p. 18.

4. For Acosta and Mede see John Kuhn, "Left Behind: George Herbert, Eschatology, and the Stuart Atlantic, 1606–1634," in *Prophecy and Eschatology in the TransAtlantic World, 1550–1800*, ed., Andrew Chrome (2016).

5. Cotton Mather, *The Wonders of the Invisible World* (1862).

6. Samuel Sewall, *Phaenomena Quaedam Apocalyptica* (1697); Bernard Bailyn, *The New England Merchants in the Seventeenth* Century (1955); Vernon Louis Parrington, *Liberalism, Puritanism and the Colonial Mind* (2011), p. 97.

7. *Letter-Book of Samuel Sewall*, v. 1 (1886), p. 326. *Letter-Book of Samuel Sewall*, v. 2 (1792), p. 156. Sidney Kaplan, "'The Selling of Joseph': Samuel Sewall and the Iniquity of Slavery," in Allan Austin, ed., *American Studies in Black and White* (1991). Sewall, objecting to a proposal which would have weakened the autonomy of one of Eliot's praying towns, reminded a Boston magistrate that the conversion of the Indians was indispensable to the Second Coming. We cannot, he said, "extirpate them as the Spaniards did." Kevin Sharpe, *Reading Authority and Representing Rule in Early Modern England* (2013), p. 101.

8. David Hall, *Worlds of Wonder, Days of Judgment: Popular Religious Belief in Early New England* (1990), p. 221.

9. Agnès Delahaye, *Settling the Good Land: Governance and Promotion in John Winthrop's New England* (2020), p. 236.

10. The Quaker George Keith published *An Exhortation & Caution to Friends Concerning the Buying or Keeping of Negroes* in 1693; Elizabeth Winslow, *Samuel Sewall of Boston* (1954); Zachary McLeod Hutchins, *Before Equiano* (2022), p. 33.

11. *Diary of Samuel Sewall* (1878), p. 152.

12. Thomas Gage, *A New Survey of the West Indies* (1677), p. 120.

13. Miller, *Errand into the Wilderness*, p. 74; "America was not a place of damnation" is in Bernstein, *Origins of Inter-American Interest, 1700–1812* (1945), p. 67.

14. Richard Cogley, "Millenarianism in Puritan New England, 1630–1730," *Harvard Theological Review*, v. 115 (2022).

15. *Letter Book of Samuel Sewall*, v. 1, pp. 171–79.

16. Kirsten Silva Gruesz, *Cotton Mather's Spanish Lessons: A Story of Language, Race, and Belonging in the Early Americas* (2022).

17. Sewall, *Letter-Book*, v. 1, p. 297; *Collections of the Massachusetts Historical Society*, v. 2, 6th series (1888), p. 181.

18. The War of Spanish Succession, or Queen Anne's War, between Spain, France, and Protestant England, began in the middle of 1702 and lasted for a decade, involving battles for territorial control in North America that pulled Native Americans into the fighting. Some thought the war a fulfillment of the New England Almanac's prophecy that the February comet would bring: "Wars, clashing of Armies, Bloodshed, evil to Great men, Death of some mighty prince, Droughts, terrible Diseases among men, etc."

19. Gary Kronk, *Cometograpy*, v. 1 (1999), p. 387; Luis Gómez Solano, *Phoenomeno examinado discurso del aparecido metheiro, a viente y seis de Febrero de este presente año de 1702* (1702). For the palm tree, see Antonio de Robles and Antonio Castro Leal, *Diario de sucesos notables (1665–1703)*, v. 3 (1946), p. 208.

Chapter 12: Three Kings

1. Worthington Chauncey Ford, ed., *The Writings of George Washington*, v. 7 (1890), p. 209.

2. Thomas Chávez, *Spain and the Independence of the United States* (2002); Thomson Buchanan Parker, "Spain: Forgotten Ally of the American Revolution," *The Journal of American History*, v. 64 (1977); José Yániz, *Role of Spain in the American Revolution* (2009); Washington quote in Otis Ham-

mond, ed., *Letters and Papers of Major-General John Sullivan*, v. 3 (1939), p. 104, Washington to Sullivan, August 24, 1779.

3. R. W. Gibbes ed., *Documentary History of the American Revolution: 1776–1782* (1857), p. 101.

4. Brian DeLay, "The Arms Trade and American Revolutions," *The American Historical Review*, v. 128 (2023).

5. John William Fortescue, *A History of the British Army*, v. 3 (1902), p. 395.

6. James A. Lewis, "Las Damas de la Havana, el Precursor, and Francisco de Saavedra: A Note on Spanish Participation in the Battle of Yorktown," *The Americas*, v. 37 (July 1980).

7. Saavedra's phrase, *linaje humano*, is often translated into English as *human race*. My sense is that *lineage* better captures movement, the flow of history, of generations moving down generations, avoiding the charged implications of the word *race*. In Francisco Saavedra de Sangronis, *Diario de don Francisco de Saavedra* (2004), p. 84.

8. D. H. Robinson, *The Idea of Europe and the Origins of the American Revolution* (2020), p. 344.

9. The original Spanish for "truly oriental pomp" is *fausto verdaderamente oriental*. Marrero quotes are found in Jorge Luján Muñoz and Marcos Marrero Valenzuela, "Consideraciones Sobre la Independencia de los Estados Unidos en un Documento de Época en el Archivo General De Indias," *Revista de Historia de América*, v. 82 (1976).

10. Varela Marcos, "Aranda y su Sueño de la Independencia SurAmericana," *Anuario de Estudios Americanos*, n. 37 (1980), p. 351. There is some basis for believing that this document was not written by Aranda but by Prince Godoy. In any case, the analysis, fears, and proposed remedies are well founded. See Richard Konetzke, *Die Politik des Grafen Aranda* (1939), pp. 182–85, and José Antonio Escudero, *El Supuesto Memorial del Conde Aranda Sobre la Independencia de América* (2020).

11. An example of one such alliance: Alejandro O'Reilly, Spain's Louisiana governor, had affirmed the autonomy of the Mississippi's multitudinous indigenous nations and outlawed the enslavement of Indians. "No Indian slaves shall be allowed in the King's realm," O'Reilly told his ministers, "not even those of hostile tribes." O'Reilly's goal was to win loyalty and build up quasi-sovereign indigenous realms that could block Anglo expansion. "General Instructions of O'Reilly to the Lieutenant Governor of the Villages of Ste. Genevieve, St. Louis, etc., dated February 17, 1770," in Louis Houck, ed. *The Spanish Regime in Missouri*, v. 1 (1909), pp. 44–45. For O'Reilly: David Ker Texada, "The Administration of Alejandro O'Reilly as Governor of Louisiana, 1769–1770," Louisiana State University, PhD dissertation (1968); Gilbert Din, *Spaniards, Planters, and Slaves: The Spanish Regulation of Slavery in Louisiana, 1763–1803* (1999), p. 259; Gwendolyn Midlo Hall, *Africans in Colonial Louisiana* (1992), p. 320.

12. Jay to Livingston, November 17, 1782, in *The Revolutionary Diplomatic Correspondence of the United States*, v. 6 (1889), p. 24; Carroll Smith-Rosenberg, *This Violent Empire* (2012), p. 5.

13. Quotations in this section come from Doyce Blackman Nunis, "The Diplomatic Defense of the Old Northwest, 1701–1789: America's Quest for Empire," University of Southern California, PhD dissertation (1958), which provides a detailed account of the negotiations.

14. Escudero, *El Supuesto Memorial*, p. 229.

15. Carlos E. Muñoz Oraá, "Pronóstico de la Independencia de América, y un proyecto de Monarquías en 1781," *Revista de Historia de América*, v. 50 (1960).

16. Quotations in this section come from Escudero, *El Supuesto Memorial*, pp. 241–46.

17. Cañizares Esguerra, *How to Write a History of the New World*, pp. 204–5.

18. Francisco Javier Clavijero, *Historia Antigua de Mexico*, v. 1 (1917).

19. Francisco Morales Padrón, *Diario de Don Francisco de Saavedra* (2004), pp. 29–30, 247–48.

20. *The Miscellaneous Works of Edward Gibbon: With Memoirs of His Life and Writings*, v. 2 (1814), p. 480; David Brading, *Miners and Merchants in Bourbon Mexico* (1971), p. 27.

21. On Puglia and his book: José Toribio Medina, *Historia del tribunal del Santo oficio de la inquisición en México* (1903), p. 436; Rodrigo Lazo, *Letters from Filadelfia: Early Latino Literature and the Trans-American Elite* (2020), chapter 1; Antonio Saborit's introduction to *El desengaño del hombre* (2014); Merle Edwin Simmons, *La Revolución Norteamericana: En La Independencia De Hispanoa-mérica* (1922), p. 350; Merle Edwin Simmons, "Santiago F. Puglia de Filadelfia (y de Caracas)," *Montalbán*, v. 19 (1987), pp. 205–55.

22. Original Spanish: *De tantos monstruos como ha producido este siglo.*

Chapter 13: Come the Crows

1. David Weber, "Conflicts and Accommodations: Hispanic and Anglo-American Borders in Historical Perspective, 1670–1853," *Journal of the Southwest*, v. 39 (1997); Gilbert C. Din, "The Immigration Policy of Governor Esteban Miró in Spanish Louisiana," *Southwestern Historical Quarterly*, v. 73 (1969–70); and "Spain's Immigration Policy in Louisiana and the American Penetration, 1792–1803," *Southwestern Historical Quarterly*, v. 76 (1972–73). For context: James David Nichols, *The Limits of Liberty: Mobility and the Making of the Eastern U.S.-Mexico Border* (2018).

2. For Hamilton's eagerness to take Spanish Louisiana and Florida in 1798: Arthur Whitaker, *The Mississippi Question, 1795–1803* (1934), pp. 118–25. For Spanish response, p. 180.

3. Barry Jean Ancelet, Jay Edward, Glen Pitre, *Cajun Country* (1991), p. 12; Houck, *The Spanish Regime*, p. 156; on the Irish priests, Gilbert C. Din, "The Irish Mission to West Florida," *Louisiana History*, v. 12 (1971), pp. 318, 324.

4. Adam Rothman, *Slave Country* (2005). Quote found in Houck, *The Spanish Regime*, p. 275.

5. Robert Remini, "Andrew Jackson Takes an Oath of Allegiance to Spain," *Tennessee Historical Quarterly*, v. 54 (Spring 1995), p. 7; William Shepherd, "Wilkinson and the Beginnings of the Spanish Conspiracy," *The American Historical Review*, v. 9 (1904); Clarence Edwin Carter, ed., *The Territorial Papers of the United States*, v. 9 (1940), p. 702; Charles Gayarré, *The Spanish Domination* (1903), pp. 97, 95; Ray Allen Billington and Martin Ridge, eds., *America's Frontier Story: A Documentary History of Westward Expansion* (1969), p. 220.

6. Austin Hatcher, *The Opening of Texas to Foreign Settlement, 1801–1821* (1927).

7. James Lewis, "Cracker: Spanish Florida Style," *The Florida Historical Quarterly*, v. 63 (1984), pp. 191, 199.

8. James Lewis, *The American Union and the Problem of Neighborhood* (1998), p. 16.

9. John Bassett, ed., *Correspondence of Andrew Jackson*, v. 1 (1926), p. 13; Kristofer Ray, "Land Speculation, Popular Democracy, and Political Transformation on the Tennessee Frontier, 1789–1800," *Tennessee Historical Quarterly*, v. 61 (2002), pp. 169–70.

10. Pearl Vivian Guyston, *Our Mississippi* (1952), p. 84; Cormac O'Riordan, "The 1795 Rebellion in East Florida," MA thesis, University of North Florida (1995).

11. Robert May, *Manifest Destiny's Underworld: Filibustering in Antebellum America* (2003); Lewis, *The American Union and the Problem of Neighborhood*, p. 92.

12. Irene A. Wright, "Dispatches of Spanish Officials Bearing on the Free Negro Settlement of Grace Real de Santa Teresa de Mose, Florida," *Journal of Negro History*, v. 9 (April 1924); Jane Landers,

"Spanish Sanctuary: Fugitives in Florida, 1687–1790," *The Florida Historical Quarterly*, v. 62 (1984). According to Mabel Manning, "The East Florida Papers in the Library of Congress," *The Hispanic Historical Review*, v. 10 (1930), Spain ended the sanctuary policy in east Florida in 1790 and signed a treaty with the U.S. pledging to return slaves in 1797.

13. Ada Ferrer, "Haiti, Free Soil, and Antislavery in the Revolutionary Atlantic," *The American Historical Review*, v. 117 (2012), p. 49.

14. Herbert Klein, *Slavery in the Americas* (1967), pp. 59–66; *Recopilación de las Leyes del Gobierno Español*, v. 4 (1851), pp. 46–48; Eric Herschthal, "Slaves, Spaniards, and Subversion in Early Louisiana: The Persistent Fears of Black Revolt and Spanish Collusion in Territorial Louisiana, 1803–1812," *Journal of the Early Republic*, v. 36 (2016), p. 289; Hernán Venegas Delgado, Bárbara Venegas Arbolaez, and Israel García Moreno, "Rebeliones de Indios Apaches y Chichimecos en Cuba: Historiografía y Realidades," *Caravelle*, v. 108 (2017).

15. Washington to Jefferson, August 23, 1789, found here: https://founders.archives.gov/documents /Washington/05-11-02-0009.

16. Arthur Preston Whitaker, *The Spanish-American Frontier, 1783–1795* (1969); Charles Gayarré, *The Spanish Domination*, p. 95; Abraham Nasatir, *Spanish War Vessels on the Mississippi, 1792–1796* (1968); Gilbert Din, "Mississippi River Gunboats on the Gulf Coast: The Spanish Naval Fight against William Augustus Bowles, 1799–1803," *Louisiana History: The Journal of the Louisiana Historical Association*, v. 47 (2006). Gilbert Dinn, "Father Jean Delvaux and the Natchitoches Revolt of 1795," *Louisiana History*, v. 40 (Winter 1999); Raphael Hoermann, "Figures of Terror: The 'Zombie' and the Haitian Revolution," *Atlantic Studies*, v. 14 (2017).

17. Jefferson to the Secretary of State, *The Writings of Thomas Jefferson*, v. 5 (1871), p. 164.

18. De Salcedo, "Plan de Oposición de las Empresas de la República de los Estados Unidos de América," in Miguel Artola, *La Guerra de Independencia* (2011). Martha Menchaca, *The Mexican American Experience in Texas* (2022), covers much of the history of Salcedo. Also: J. C. Harrison, "The Failure of Spain in East Texas: The Occupation and Abandonment of Nacogdoches, 1779–1821," PhD dissertation (1980), pp. 207–8.

19. Scholars have long compared U.S. to Latin American slavery. Recent examples include Alejandro de la Fuente and Ariela Gross, "Comparative Studies of Law, Slavery, and Race in the Americas," *Annual Review of Law and Social Science* (2010), and Enrico Dal Lago "Comparative Slavery," in Mark Smith and Robert Paquette, eds., *Oxford Handbook of Slavery in the Americas* (2010).

20. Alice Baumgartner, *South to Freedom: Runaway Slaves to Mexico and the Road to the Civil War* (2020), chapter 1; James Christopher Harrison, "The Failure of Spain in East Texas: The Occupation and Abandonment of Nacogdoches, 1779–1821," PhD thesis, University of Nebraska, Lincoln (1980), pp. 207–8; Claiborne to Salcedo, November 22, 1808, *Official Letter Books of W. C. C. Claiborne*, v. 4 (1917), pp. 254–57; Thomas Mareite, *Conditional Freedom: Free Soil and Fugitive Slaves from the U.S. South to Mexico's Northeast, 1803–1861* (2022).

21. Carter, *The Territorial Papers of the United States*, v. 9, pp. 62–66; Dianna Everett, *The Texas Cherokees: A People between Two Fires, 1819–1840* (1995).

22. Ira Berlin, *Many Thousands Gone: The First Two Centuries of Slavery in North America* (1998); Jefferson quote cited in John Craig Hammond, "'They Are Very Much Interested in Obtaining an Unlimited Slavery': Rethinking the Expansion of Slavery in the Louisiana Purchase Territories, 1803–1805," *Journal of the Early Republic*, v. 3 (2003), p. 359.

23. Billington and Ridge, *America's Frontier Story*, p. 297. The example they give is from a few decades later than the period discussed in this chapter. The relationship of western expansion to the growth of slavery is well established by scholars. See my *The End of the Myth* for a more detailed discussion and citations. Not cited in that book are these two important studies: John Craig Hammond,

Slavery, Freedom, and Expansion in the Early American West (2007) and Stephen Hyslop, *A House Divided: Slavery, Westward Expansion, and the Roots of the Civil War* (2023).

24. For *Comancheria*: Pekka Hämäläinen, *The Comanche Empire* (2006); Brian Delay, *The War of a Thousand Deserts* (2008); David Weber, *The Mexican Frontier* (1982).

Chapter 14: Grand Strategies

1. Miranda to Hamilton, February 7, 1798, with a note attached by Hamilton, *The Papers of Alexander Hamilton Digital Edition* (2011), https://rotunda-upress-virginia-edu.yale.idm.oclc.org/founders/ARHN-01-21-02-0203.

2. John Trumbull to George Washington, March 24, 1799, in Trumbull, *Autobiography, Reminiscences and Letters . . .* (1841), p. 382.

3. Miranda to Adams, March 24, 1798, University of Virginia, Founders Early Access, https://rotunda.upress.virginia.edu/founders/default.xqy?keys=FOEA-print-03-02-02-2390.

4. Adams is referencing a satiric anti-Spanish poem "The Journal of Don Gonzalez from the Moon," written by the pseudonymous Antilunaticus; the poem imagined the moon run by despots, priests, and courtiers, burdened by bureaucrats ("laws they have many, ten thousand or more") where no one could be trusted and nothing was as it seemed—in other words, like Spain. *The Tickler Magazine*, n. 7 (July 1, 1821), p. 137.

5. Adams quotes found in Adams to James Lloyd, March 27, 1815, *The Works of John Adams*, v. 10 (1856), pp. 140–49.

6. Lewis, "Las Damas de la Havana."

7. Wesley Campbell, "The Origin of Citizen Genet's Projected Attack on Spanish Louisiana: A Case Study in Girondin Politics," *French Historical Studies*, v. 33 (2010).

8. For Miranda's trial and military role, including charges his actions led to a key defeat: Patricia Chastain Howe, *Foreign Policy and the French Revolution* (2008); Freeman Hawke, *Paine* (1974), p. 285. Paine's testimony: *Archivo de General Miranda*, v. 12 (1931), pp. 170–72.

9. For quotes on the two revolutions: *Archivo de General Miranda*, v. 15 (1931), pp. 232–33.

10. Thanks to William Hogland for helping make sense of Miranda's opinion of Monroe.

11. *The Papers of Alexander Hamilton*, v. 21 (1974), p. 2.

12. Francisco de Miranda, *South American Emancipation: Documents, historical and explanatory, showing the designs which have been in progress . . .* (1810).

13. Carlos Pi Sunyer, *Patriotas Americanos en Londres* (1978), p. 211; "Notas Acerca de Una Pretendida Conspiración de Mexicanos," *Boletín del Archivo General de la Nación* (1938), pp. 768–86.

14. Lewis Hanke, *Bartolomé de Las Casas: Bookman, Scholar, and Propagandist* (1952), pp. 70–75.

15. Servando Teresa de Mier a Pedro Gual, September 12, 1821, in the Mier Papers of the Benson Latin American Library, University of Texas, Austin; Ernesto Mejía Sánchez, "Mier, defensor de Las Casas," *Boletín de la Biblioteca Nacional*, v. 14 (1963), p. 72; Begoña Pulido Herráz, "Fray Bartolomé de las Casas en la Obra y el Pensamiento de Fray Servando Teresa de Mier," *Historia Mexicana*, v. 61 (2011); Lewis Hanke, *Bartolomé de las Casas: letrado y propagandista* (1965), p. 122. One of the first efforts to clarify Las Casas's position on African slavery took place around this time: Henri Grégoire, "Apología de don Bartolomé de Las Casas, obispo de Chiapa, por el ciudadano Gregoire," written in 1801 and published in Paris in the two-volume anthology: *Colección de las ob-*

ras del venerable obispo de Chiapas don Bartolomé de las Casas, defensor de la libertad de los americanos (1922).

16. Chernow, *Alexander Hamilton* (2004), p. 720. For Bentham quotes: David Armitage, "Globalizing Jeremy Bentham," *History of Political Thought*, v. 23 (2011). Simón Bolívar, who beginning in 1810 would take charge of Spanish America's liberation movement, said that the function of a moral state was to "make men good, and consequently happy." The goal of constituted societies was, he wrote, to produce "the greatest possible sum of happiness, the greatest social security, and the highest degree of political stability." Later, in Chile, Salvador Allende, in the 1970s, would say that there existed a "human right to happiness" that was distinct from the pursuit of individual interests.

17. Chernow, *Alexander Hamilton*, pp. 567–68.

18. *The Works of Alexander Hamilton*, v. 6 (1850), p. 347.

19. William Spence Robertson, *The Life of Miranda* (1929), pp. 180–81.

20. Thomas Jefferson to A. Stewart, January 25, 1786, in *Memoir, Correspondence and Miscellanies from the Papers of Thomas Jefferson*, v. 1–2 (1829), p. 432.

21. Thomas Jefferson to James Bowdoin, April 2, 1807, *Memoir, Correspondence and Miscellanies*, v. 3–4 (1829), p. 71.

22. *The Writings of Thomas Jefferson*, v. 5 (1861), p. 435; Sowerby, *Catalogue of the Library of Thomas Jefferson*, v. 4, pp. 251–93; Robert Stewart Castlereagh, ed., *Correspondence, Dispatches, and Other Papers: Military and Diplomatic*, v. 11 (1853), p. 326.

23. Thomas Jefferson to Alexander von Humboldt, December 6, 1813, Founders Online, National Archives, https://founders.archives.gov/documents/Jefferson/03-07-02-0011.

24. José Nucete Sardi, *Aventura y tragedia de Don Francisco de Miranda* (1935), p. 309.

25. Mexico quote in James Ripley Jacobs, *Tarnished Warrior* (1938), p. 214; Robertson, *The Life of Miranda*, p. 294.

26. Racine, *Francisco de Miranda*, p. 157; Arthur Scheer, *John Adams, Slavery and Race: Ideas, Politics, and Diplomacy in an Age of Crisis* (2018), p. 62.

27. Kenneth Wiggins Porter, *John Jacob Astor* (1931), p. 126.

28. Alan Taylor, "James Fenimore Cooper Goes to Sea," *Studies in the American Renaissance* (1993), pp. 43–54. A detailed account of this 1806 expedition, along with Miranda's activity up until his return to Caracas in 1811, is found in William Robertson, "Francisco de Miranda and the Revolutionizing of Spanish America," in *Annual Report of the American Historical Association*, v. 1 (1907). A few months after Miranda set sail, in June, British troops, in a campaign unrelated to Miranda, occupied Buenos Aires for over forty days. This and other skirmishes were part of the Napoleonic Wars, in which the British Navy maintained an aggressive presence off the Spanish Main, as popularized in Patrick O'Brian's Master and Commander novels. British forces were eventually driven out of Buenos Aires, but the occupation, which had some local support, precipitated the beginning of Argentina's independence movement.

29. Details used to narrate this event come from Lindsay Schakenbach, "Schemers, Dreamers, and a Revolutionary Foreign Policy," *New York History*, v. 94 (2013).

Chapter 15: The Ambiguity in Which We Live

1. Kirsten Schultz, *Tropical Versailles: Empire, Monarchy, and the Portuguese Royal Court in Rio de Janeiro, 1808–1821* (2001).

2. Rebels in the city of Quito were the first, deposing Spanish officials and establishing a "sovereign" junta on August 10, 1809. Venezuela, though, was the first to declare complete independence from Spain.

3. Racine, *Francisco de Miranda*, pp. 183–84, 284. Reports of the Caracas revolution reached London on June 1810. For Miranda spreading the news: Mario Rodríguez, *"William Burke" and Francisco de Miranda: The Word and the Deed in Spanish America's Emancipation* (1994), p. 276. Also: Juan Goytisolo, *El Español y la independencia de Hispanoamérica* (2010), p. 111.

4. Juan Vicente González, *El Primer Congreso de Venezuela y la Sociedad Patriótica* (1959), p. 4; Juan Vicente González, *Biografía del General José Félix Ribas* (1917), pp. 41–42.

5. Narciso Coll y Prat, "Discurso pronunciado en el Supremo Congreso de Venezuela," printed in *Gaceta de Caracas*, August 3, 1811.

6. Narciso Coll y Prat, *Memoriales Sobre la Independencia de Venezuela* (1960), p. 143.

7. Racine, *Miranda*, p. 218; Manuel Palacio Fajardo, *Bosquejo de la Revolución en la América Española* (1953), pp. 70–71.

8. Cristina Soriano, *Tides of Revolution: Information, Insurgencies, and the Crisis of Colonial Rule in Venezuela* (2018), p. 177.

9. "Universal joy" in Manuel Palacio Fajardo, *Bosquejo de la Revolución en la América Española* (1953), pp. 70–71; "French abyss" in Rómulo A. García, *Juan Vicente González* (1901), p. 36; Rafael Sánchez, *Dancing Jacobins: A Venezuelan Genealogy of Latin American Populism* (2016).

10. "Discurso del Coronel Simón Bolívar en la Sociedad Patriótica, July 3, 1811," in José de Austri, *Bosquejo de la Historia Militar de Venezuela* (1857), p. 42.

11. Narciso Coll y Prat, *Memoriales*, pp. 167–68.

12. The phrase "insurgentes de otra especie" comes from José Francisco Heredia, *Memorias sobre las Revoluciones de Venezuela* (1895), p. 30, to describe the rural, racialized Boves rebellion that took place after Venezuela's first republic fell. Otra especie was occasionally used to signify vestigial belief in polygenesis, as noted by an early twentieth-century Venezuelan criminologist: "Blacks and Indians were seen to be individuals of another species, inferior to much of humanity," in Alejandro Urbaneja, "Curso de Derecho Penal," in Anales de la Universidad Central de Venezuela, v. 7 (1911). For enslaved peoples fighting to maintain Spanish rule: Jane Landers, *Atlantic Creoles in the Age of Revolutions* (2010); Marcela Echeverri, *Indian and Slave Royalists in the Age of Revolution: Reform, Revolution, and Royalism in the Northern Andes, 1780–1825* (2016). For rebel slaves: Peter Blanchard, *Under the Flags of Freedom: Slave Soldiers and the Wars of Independence in Spanish South America* (2008). For slavery throughout Latin America in general during the last decades of the empire: Jeremy Adelman, *Sovereignty and Revolution in the Iberian Atlantic* (2006), chapter 2.

13. González, *José Félix Ribas*, p. 225.

14. José Manuel Villavicencio, *Constitución de los Estados Unidos de América. Traducida del inglés al español* (1810); also: Puglia, *El Desengaño del Hombre*; Merle Simmons, *La Revolución Norteamericana en la Independencia de Hispanoamérica* (1992). For years, Caracas and Philadelphia were sister cities, with Venezuelans working with local printers, publishing key republican texts translated into Spanish, for distribution throughout the Americas, including the Federalist Papers, Thomas Paine, and, in 1810, the U.S. Constitution. For the constituent assembly, Juan Garrido Rovira, *El Congreso Constituyente de Venezuela*, (2010).

15. Robert Wilberforce, *The Life of William Wilberforce by his Sons*, v. 3 (1838), p. 435.

16. Quotes cited in George Dawson Flinter, *A History of the Revolution of Caracas* (1819), p. 22.

17. Racine, *Francisco de Miranda*, p. 223.

18. Rafael Rojas, *Las repúblicas de aire. Utopía y desencanto en la Revolución de Hispanoamérica* (2009).

19. The emphasis Spanish American republicans placed on sociability is clear in a question Miranda had earlier asked an aging Samuel Adams during his first tour of the United States: How can the United States, founded in the name of republican virtue, be governed by laws that do nothing other than protect private property? The unrestricted right to property, when not tempered by laws or morals concerned with the common good, is "the poison of republics," a corruptor of virtue, Miranda said. Adams couldn't easily come up with an answer because perhaps Miranda's premise confused him. For Adams and others who made their revolution, the expansion of the realm of individual freedom wasn't virtue's venom but its nourishment. Adams said he would think the question over and get back to Miranda. He might have. Miranda recorded no response in his travel diary. The distinction drawn here between Anglo and Spanish republicanism is not absolute but of degree. John Locke, in chapter 2 of his *Second Treatise*, was clear that that there existed a difference between *liberty* and *license*.

20. Quintard Taylor, *In Search of the Racial Frontier: African Americans in the American West 1528–1990* (1999), p. 36. Also: Ann Twinam, *Purchasing Whiteness* (2015); John Lombardi, *The Decline and Abolition of Negro Slavery in Venezuela, 1820–1854* (1971), p. 44.

21. René Saavedra, ed., *De Bolívar a Bolivia* (1989), p. 108.

22. Peter Guardino, *Peasants, Politics, and the Formation of Mexico's National State* (1995), p. 65; Diego A. von Vacano, *The Color of Citizenship: Race, Modernity and Latin American/Hispanic Political Thought* (2012).

23. Also, this 1825 decree issued by Bolívar in Cuzco: "Se proclaman los derechos del indio como ciudadano y se prohíben las practicas de explotación a que se les tenia sometidos desde siglos atrás," in Iván Duque Escobar, *Simón Bolívar, Una Visión Dispersa* (2000), p. 212.

24. For Bolívar as more republican than liberal: Jeremy Adelman, "What's in a Revolution?" *Latin American Research Review*, v. 47 (2012), pp. 187–95.

25. John Williamson, *Caracas Diary* (1954), p. 126.

26. Simon, *The Ideology of Creole Revolution* (2017), p. 2.

27. Orlando Bentancor, "Decolonizing Material Culture: Colonialism and Will to Technology," *Hofstra Hispanic Review*, v. 3 (2006). Roscio and Isnardi's opinion of the Conquest reflected French Enlightenment thought at the time, as expressed by Joseph Mandrillon and Abbé Guillaume Raynal; Mandrillon described the Conquest as an "evil."

28. Joshua Simon, *The Ideology of Creole Revolution* (2017), p. 2; John Lynch, *Simón Bolívar: A Life* (2006), p. 151, writes that when Bolívar, in 1814, offered his slaves emancipation in exchange for military service, only fifteen accepted. Bolívar offered unconditional emancipation to all in 1821.

Chapter 16: War to the Death

1. José Domingo Díaz, *Recuerdos sobre la Rebelión de Caracas* (1829).

2. Myles Cooper, *Poems on Several Occasions* (1761), p. 159.

3. Felipe Larrazábal, *The Life of Simon Bolívar*, v. 1 (1866), p. 69. Some sources report that the earthquake hit at 4:05 and others at 4:35.

4. Rogelio Altez, *El desastre de 1812 en Venezuela* (2006), p. 213.

5. Flinter, *A History of the Revolution of Caracas*, p. 33.

6. Mary Watters, *A History of the Church in Venezuela* (1933), p. 61.

7. Watters, *A History of the Church*, p. 6; Coll y Pratt, *Memoriales*, p. 56.

8. Robertson, *The Life of Miranda*, v. 2 (1930), p. 148.

9. Alexander von Humboldt, *Personal Narrative of Travels to the Equinoctial Regions of the New Continent During the Years 1799–1804*, v. 4 (1824), p. 2; Felipe Larrazábal, The Life of Simón Bolívar (1866), p. 71.

10. Robert Lowry to James Madison, June 5, 1812, in *Diplomatic Correspondence of the United States Concerning the Independence of Latin-American Nations*, v. 2 (1925), p. 566.

11. Stephen Stoan, *Pablo Morillo and Venezuela* (1974).

12. Coll y Pratt, *Memoriales*, p. 59.

13. Robertson, *Miranda*, p. 162.

14. Felipe Larrazábal, *Vida y correspondencia general del libertador*, v. 1 (1875), p. 138; Giovanni Meza Dorta, *Miranda y Bolívar, Dos Visiones* (2011), pp. 143, 153; Stoan, *Pablo Morillo and Venezuela*, p. 48.

15. Robertson, *The Life of Miranda*, v. 2, p. 190.

16. Karen Racine, "Message by Massacre: Venezuela's War to the Death, 1810–1814," *Journal of Genocide Research*, v. 15 (2013), p. 207.

17. Felipe Larrazábal, *Correspondencia General del Libertador Simon Bolívar* (1865), p. 353.

18. Juan Uslar Pietri, *Historia de la Rebelión Popular de 1814* (1962), pp. 118–19.

19. Lynch, *Bolívar*, p. 80.

20. Stoan, *Pablo Morillo and Venezuela*, pp. 50–59 for Boves.

21. Pietri, *Historia de la Rebelión Popular de 1814*, p. 177.

22. Rufino Blanco-Fombona, *Bolívar y la Guerra a Muerte* (1984), p. 44.

23. For Bolívar's "dilemma" on slavery see Lester Langley, *Simón Bolívar: Venezuelan Rebel, American Revolutionary* (2009), pp. 177–180; Alexander Allen, "U.S. Owes Haitians Gratitude, Not Abuse," *The Crisis*, v. 89 (1982), p. 47.

24. Daniel F. O'Leary, *Bolívar y la emancipación de Sur América*, v. 1 (1915), p. 598; Lynch, *Bolívar*, p. 97. For the lessons John Quincy Adams drew from wartime slave emancipation in Spanish America: Isaac Arnold, *The History of Abraham Lincoln and the Overthrow of Slavery* (1866), p. 711.

25. As the war for independence generalized across the hemisphere, Republicans proved more effective at attracting enslaved peoples to their cause than royalists. The historian Thomas Blanchard, in *Under the Flags of Freedom*, writes that "Bolívar's military advances made his offer of freedom in return for military service more than just a recruiting ploy."

26. Rufino Blanco-Fombona, ed., *Cartas de Bolívar* (1921), p. 141.

Chapter 17: A Kind of International Law for America

1. "Notes for a Conversation with George Hammond," December 10, 1792, in John Catanzariti, ed., *The Papers of Thomas Jefferson*, v. 24 (1990), pp. 717–21. Quotation is from editor's exegesis.

2. Note to George Hammond from Thomas Jefferson, June 2, 1792, *The Papers of Thomas Jefferson*, v. 24, 1 June–31 December 1792 (2018), p. 19.

3. Emily Millicent Sowerby, *Catalogue of the Library of Thomas Jefferson*, v. 4 (1955), pp. 251–93. Jefferson lent four volumes of Las Casas to Madison. He didn't, it seems, own any editions of Vitoria's lectures, but his library did contain Bernardo de Vargas Machuca's history of the conquest of the Mapuche, *Milicia y descripción de las Indias*, described by a prominent military historian as "the first manual of guerrilla warfare ever published." For background on relating Native American history to diplomatic history: Brian DeLay, "Indian Polities, Empire, and the History of American Foreign Relations, *Diplomatic History*, v. 39 (2015); Alexandra Harmon, "American Indians, American Law, and Modern American Foreign Relations," *Diplomatic History*, v. 39 (2015); Francis Paul Prucha, *The Great Father: The United States Government and the American Indians*, v. 1 (1995), p. 60.

4. Caitlan Fitz, "The Hemispheric Dimensions of Early U.S. Nationalism: The War of 1812, Its Aftermath, and Spanish American Independence," *Journal of American History*, v. 102 (2015).

5. Gene Allen Smith, *The Slaves Gamble: Choosing Sides in the War of 1812* (2013), pp. 164, 170.

6. Adams in his memoirs called the British proposal a "species of game law," a curious analogy that equates Native Americans to Norman and Saxon aristocrats, in control of vast estates, and white settlers to commoners, prohibited by "game laws" from hunting and poaching on those estates. Such a prohibition, Adams said, would be "as incompatible with the moral as with the physical nature of things." Massachusetts Historical Society, *John Quincy Adams Digital Diary*, September 1, 1814, p. 143.

7. *Writings of John Quincy Adams*, v. 5 (1915), p. 116.

8. "Thomas Jefferson to Secretary of War General Henry Dearborn, 1807," Thomas Jefferson Papers, Library of Congress, Manuscript Division.

9. John T. Fierst. "Rationalizing Removal: Anti-Indianism in Lewis Cass's *North American Review* Essays," *Michigan Historical Review*, v. 36 (2010); Kyle Massey Stephens, "To the Indian Removal Act, 1814–1830," PhD dissertation, University of Tennessee (2013); Claudio Saunt, *Unworthy Republic: The Dispossession of Native Americans and the Road to Indian Territory* (2020).

10. Gary Nash, *Race and Revolution* (1990), p. 49. In his last essay, published posthumously with the aid of Paul Spickard, Winthrop Jordan explored the history of the one-drop rule: "Historical Origins of the One-Drop Racial Rule in the United States," *Journal of Critical Mixed Race Studies*, v. 1 (2014). Also: Daniel Sharfstein, "Crossing the Color Line: Racial Migration and the One-Drop Rule, 1600–1860," *Minnesota Law Review*, v. 91 (2007), and Scott Leon Washington, "Hypodescent: A History of the Crystallization of the One-Drop Rule in the United States, 1880–1940," PhD dissertation, Princeton (2011).

11. Larry Tise, *Proslavery: A History of the Defense of Slavery in America, 1701–1840* (1990), p. 143; Theodore Clapp, *Slavery: A Sermon* (1838), p. 13.

12. Adams cited in George Baker, ed., *The Life of William H. Seward* (1855), p. 154.

13. J. Leitch Wright, "A Note on the First Seminole War as Seen by the Indians, Negroes, and Their British Advisers," *The Journal of Southern History*, v. 34 (1968).

14. Richard Stenberg, "Jackson's 'Rhea Letter' Hoax," *The Journal of Southern History*, v. 2 (1936); Deborah Rosen, *Border Law: The First Seminole War and American Nationhood* (2015), p. 185.

15. Gordon Chappell, "Some Patterns of Land Speculation in the Old Southwest," *The Journal of Southern History*, v. 15 (1949); Steve Inskeep, "How Jackson Made a Killing in Real Estate," *Politico* (July 4, 2015). For the land "mania" that accompanied the Revolutionary War: Michael Blaakman, *Speculation Nation: Land Mania in the Revolutionary American Republic* (2023).

16. Steve Inskeep, *Jacksonland* (2016), p. 103; Robert Remini, *Andrew Jackson: The Course of America Empire, 1767–1821* (1998), p. 345, says that his associations and family "enjoyed a small financial killing on account of their Pensacola speculation," but that Jackson himself didn't profit.

17. Jean-Guillaume Hyde de Neuville, *Mémoires et Souvenirs du Baron Hyde de Neuville* (1893), p. 389; Coolidge Brooks, *Diplomacy and the Borderlands* (1939), p. 42. According to Adams, it was the French statesman Jean-Guillaume Hyde de Neuville who called Jackson a "Napoléon des bois."

18. Brian Loveman, *No Higher Law* (2010), pp. 33–44.

19. United States Department of State, *Message from the President of the United States . . . transmitting, in pursuance of a resolution of the House of representatives, such further information, in relation to our affairs with Spain . . .* (1819).

20. Henry Wise, *Seven Decades of the Union* (1881), p. 151.

21. Thomas Marshall, *A History of the Western Boundary of the Louisiana Purchase, 1819–1841* (1914).

22. Luis de Onís, *Memoria sobre las negociaciones entre España y los Estados Unidos de América, que dieron motivo al tratado de 1819* (1826).

Chapter 18: The Balancing Power:
Monroe's Doctrine

1. James Hopkins, ed., *The Papers of Henry Clay: The Rising Statesman 1815–1820*, v. 2. (1961), p. 857.

2. John Gallagher, Ronald Robinson, and William Roger Louis, *Imperialism: The Robinson and Gallagher Controversy* (1976), p. 62.

3. Bolívar to Guillermo White, May, 1, 1820, in Lecuna, ed., *Cartas del Libertador*, v. 2 (1929), p. 157; Brian DeLay, "How Not to Arm a State: American Guns and the Crisis of Governance in Mexico, Nineteenth and Twenty-First Centuries," *Southern California Quarterly*, v. 95 (2013).

4. Albert Bushnell Hart, *The Foundations of American Foreign Policy* (1901), p. 119.

5. John Burgess, "The Recent Pseudo-Monroeism," *Political Science Quarterly*, v. 11 (1896).

6. N. Andrew, N. Cleven, and William Thornton, "Thornton's Outlines of a Constitution for United North and South Columbia," *The Hispanic American Historical Review*, v. 12 (1932).

7. Edward Everett, "Review of *Ensayo de la historia civil del Paraguay, Buenos-Ayres, y Tucuman*," *North American Review*, v. 12 (1821), p. 436.

8. For Vitoria as prelude to Monroe Doctrine: Max Savelle, "Colonial Origins of American Diplomatic Principles," *Pacific Historical Review*, v. 3 (1934), p. 338. Camilo Barcia Trelles, "La Doctrine de Monroe dans son Développement Historique Particulièrement en ce qui Concerne les Relations Interamericaines," in *Collected Courses of the Hague Academy of International Law*, v. 32 (1930) and *Doctrina de Monroe y Cooperación Internacional* (1931). Another notable antecedent to Monroe's statement: In 1750, Madrid and Lisbon had ended a war with a treaty barring future war from spilling over into the New World. The "vassals of both crowns in all of America meridional will remain in peace, living one with the other as if there were no war being fought among their sovereigns." Thus "perpetual peace and good neighborliness will continue." Two centuries before FDR would pledge the United States to be a "Good Neighbor," the idea that the Americas were a sanctuary, exempt from European conflicts, was signed into colonial treaty law; *Tratado firmado en Madrid a 13 de enero de 1750 . . .* (1836), p. 11.

9. Johnson & Graham's *Lesee v. McIntosh*, 21 U.S. 543 (1823).

10. Anthony Trollope, the British writer, would later take note of the swagger: "He has told the world of his increasing millions," Trollope wrote of the New World's Anglo-Saxon Man, "he has pawed in the valley, and rejoiced in his strength"; Anthony Trollope, *North America*, v. 2 (1999), p. 393.

11. Office of the Governor of Indiana, *Messages and Papers* (1922), pp. 163–64.

12. For Argentina: Bartolomé Mitre, *Historia de Belgrano y de la Independencia Argentina*, v. 3 (1902), discusses the underlying political theory behind the "Inka Plan." Also: the Brazilian legal historian Manuel de Oliveira Lima, *La Evolución Histórica de la América Latina* (1915), p. 127.

13. Alejandro Alvarez, *The Monroe Doctrine: Its Importance in the International Life of the States of the New World* (1924), p. 21.

14. Bolívar to Martín Jorge Guise, April 28, 1824, found in José Félix Blanco, *Documents para la historia de la vida pública del libertador de Colombia, Perú y Bolivia . . .* , v. 9 (1876), p. 265.

Chapter 19: As You Possess

1. For contrast between European balance-of-power system and U.S. federalism: Peter Onuf and Nicholas Onuf, *Federal Union, Modern World* (1993). Also: Peter Onuf, *Statehood and Union* (1987); Cathy Matson and Peter Onuf, *Union of Interests* (1990).

2. Octavio Méndez Pereira, *Bolívar y Las Relaciones Interamericanas* (1960), p. 30.

3. Madison, *The Federalist*, n. 10 (22 November 1787); *Transaction of the Illinois State Historical Society*, v. 13 (1909), p. 54.

4. The text of these treaties, in English, signed between a Gran Colombia and several other countries, including Mexico and Central America, are found in *Register of Debates in Congress: Comprising the Leading Debates . . . Session of the . . . Congress*, v. 2, part 2 (1825), pp. 50–53.

5. *Uti possidetis* had been used earlier by insurgents during Venezuela's first republic, when its ministers signed a treaty with Colombia.

6. Vicente Santamaría de Paredes, *A Study of the Question of Boundaries between Ecuador and Peru* (1910), p. 270; Gual: "*Que nuestros derechos están fuera de toda duda fundados en la pactacion y en el Utti Possidetis al tiempo de la fundación de la república*," in July 1822 (exact date unknown), letter from Gual to Bolívar, in Daniel O'Leary, *Memorias del General O'Leary*, v. 19 (1883), p. 319.

7. Julio Londoño, *La Visión geopolítica de Bolívar* (1950), p. 83.

8. Vicente Gregorio Quesada, *La Patagonia y las Tierras Australes del Continente Americano* (1875); Paulo Cavaleri, *La Restauración Del Virreinato: Orígenes Del Nacionalismo Territorial Argentino* (2004).

9. Brazil, in contrast, tended to define *uti possidetis* as effective possession, the ability to administer and defend territory. One can trace the idealist and realist threads within *uti possidetis* from an earlier, colonial application, related to an ongoing border conflict between Spain and Portugal concerning the Tupí-Guaraní peoples. In 1769, Madrid and Lisbon both appealed to *uti possidetis* as a doctrine that bestowed the right to keep conquered land *and* required the protection of the people on the land. The Tupí-Guaraní, who lived on Jesuit missions on the borderlands between the two empires, were targeted for capture by Portuguese slave raiders, and Spain and Portugal each claimed that they could better defend the missions if *uti possidetis* was applied and the boundary line made clear.

10. José Macedonio Urquidi, *El Uti Possidetis Juris y el de Facto* (1946); *Exposición de los títulos que consagran el derecho territorial de Bolivia, sobre la zona comprendida entre los ríos Pilcomayo y Paraguay* (1914), p. 15. The Colombian Florentino González, "Los Limites de las Repúblicas

hispanoamericanas y el Principio del uti possidetis," *La Revista de Buenos Aires*, v. 18 (1869), argued against utility of making *uti possidetis* the foundation of a new kind of international law, since to take the borders of the old empire as legitimate was to legitimate the empire—which in turn legitimated the conquest that made the empire. It also denied that large parts of America—in southern Chile, for example, Mexico's Yucatán, or the Amazon—were effectively controlled not by the Spanish Empire but by Native Americans. For González, the affirmation of *uti possidetis* was a retroactive affirmation of an imperial sovereignty that never fully existed.

11. Nicola Miller, *Republic of Knowledge: Nations of the Future in Latin America* (2020), chapter 7; Nancy Appelbaum, *Mapping the Country of Regions* (2016).

12. Guillermo Feliú Cruz, *Historiografía colonial de Chili* (1958), pp. 118–220; José Miguel Yrarrázaval Larraín, *La Patagonia: Errores geográficos y diplomáticos* (1996), p. 85. Also: Allen Woll, *A Functional Past: The Uses of History in Nineteenth-Century Chile* (1982), chapter 6. By 1907, Peru had published seventeen volumes of *Arbitraje de limites entre el Peru y el Ecuador*. For application of *uti possidetis* in Africa: Dirdeiry Ahmed, "The Frontier Dispute Case and Applying Uti Possidetis to Africa," in *Boundaries and Secession in Africa and International Law* (2015).

13. M. A. Raeder, *L'arbitrage international chez les Hellenes* (1912), pp. 14–16, 144; Marcus Niebuhr Tod, *International Arbitration among the Greeks* (1913), p. 174; A. Burn, "The So-Called 'Trade-Leagues' in Early Greek History," *The Journal of Hellenic Studies*, v. 49 (1929). Both Grotius and Pufendorf endorse the practice of third-party mediation, which grew more common as secular international law replaced Christianity as Europe's organizing principle. Harry Fraser, "Sketch of the History of International Arbitration," *Cornell Law Review*, v. 11, n. 2 (1926), pp. 179–208.

14. Alvarez, *The Monroe Doctrine*, p. 13. In 1847, Colombia, Ecuador, Peru, Chile, and Bolivia mutually adopted the doctrine as international law. Valentín Abecia Baldivieso, *Historiografía Boliviana* (1965), p. 347. For *uti possidetis* more generally: Mikulas Fabry, *Recognizing States: International Society and the Establishment of New States since 1776* (2010). For the importance of Latin America in reviving *uti possidetis*: Fabry, *Recognizing States*, pp. 66–77; Suzanne Lalonde, *Determining Boundaries in a Conflicted World: The Role of "Uti Possidetis"* (2002); Sharon Korman, *The Right of Conquest: The Acquisition of Territory by Force in International Law and Practice* (1996); *British and Foreign State Papers*, v. 11 (2015), p. 803. The account of Alvear's meeting with Monroe comes from Alvear's official report of the session and the recollections of Thomás de Iriarte, the Argentine delegation's secretary, as recounted in Thomas Davis, *Carlos De Alvear, Man of Revolution: The Diplomatic Career of Argentina's First Minister to the United States* (1955). Also: Harold Peterson, *Argentina and the United States: 1810–1960* (1964), p. 78.

Chapter 20: This American Party

1. William R. Manning, *Early Diplomatic Correspondence Between the United States and Mexico* (1916), p. 242.

2. Joel Poinsett, *An Inquiry into the Received Opinions of Philosophers And Historians: On the Natural Progress of the Human Race from Barbarism to Civilization* (1834). For "faithful negro Sam": Charles Lyon and R. Smith, "The Life of Joel Roberts Poinsett," *The Pennsylvania Magazine of History and Biography*, v. 59 (1935), p. 25.

3. When President James Madison sent Alexander Scott as an agent on a "secret mission" to Caracas in 1811, Scott took his enslaved house servant Fanny Tarlton with him. Upon the end of Scott's mission, abolitionist lawyers took up the cause of Tarlton's emancipation, arguing that her return to the United States as a slave was a violation of federal and Maryland laws prohibiting the importation of enslaved people. At some point after 1813, Scott sold Tarlton and her children to Cartwright Tippett. In 1823, lawyers petitioned for Tarlton's freedom, arguing that she should not be considered the property of Tippett. The court ruled against Tarlton on the grounds that since Scott, as an agent

of the United States government, had not decided to live permanently in Venezuela, his return with Tarlton did not violate the prohibition against "importation."

4. Joel Poinsett, *Notes on Mexico* (1825), p. 252.

5. For Alamán: Simon, *The Ideology of Creole Revolution.*

6. *Historia de las relaciones internacionales de México, 1821–2010: América del Norte,* vol. 1 (2011), p. 68.

7. William Manning, "Texas and the Boundary Issue, 1822–1929," *The Southwestern Historical Quarterly,* v. 17 (1918); William Manning, "Poinsett's Mission to Mexico," *American Journal of International Law,* v. 7 (1913); Andrés Reséndez, "Masonic Connections, Pecuniary Interests, and Institutional Development along Mexico's Far North," in Jaime E. Rodriguez, ed., *The Divine Charter: Constitutionalism and Liberalism in Nineteenth-Century Mexico* (2005), p. 190.

8. Charles R. Salit, "Anglo American Rivalry in Mexico, 1823–1830," *Revista de Historia de América,* v. 16 (1943), p. 73.

9. Manning, *Diplomatic Correspondence,* document 916, pp. 1662–67; José María Tornel, *Breve reseña histórica de los acontecimientos mas notables de la nación Mexicana* (1852), p. 46.

10. Poinsett to Joseph Johnson, November 10, 1826, in *Calendar,* p. 17; Henry George Ward, *Mexico,* v. 2 (1829), p. 546.

11. Thomas Mareite, "Abolitionists, Smugglers and Scapegoats: Assistance Networks for Fugitive Slaves in the Texas-Mexico Borderlands, 1836–1861" in *Cahiers du Mémoire(s), identité(s), marginalité(s) dans le monde occidental contemporain,* v. 19 (2018). Alice Baumgartner, quoted in Taryn White, "Just Across the Border, this Mexican Community Also Celebrates Juneteenth," *National Geographic,* June 17, 2021, notes the Mexican policy of providing escaped slaves land and tools; James Winston, "Kentucky and the Independence of Texas," *The Southwestern Historical Quarterly,* v. 16 (1912), p. 31.

12. John Ficklen, "The Louisiana Purchase vs. Texas," *Publications of the Southern History Association* (1910), goes into some detail to prove that Texas was *not* part of the original Louisiana Purchase; Fred J. Rippy, *Rivalry of the United States and Great Britain over Latin America,* p. 99.

13. American Historical Association, *The Austin Papers,* v. 2, pt. 2 (1924), p. 1539.

14. Ohland Morton, "The Life of General Don Manuel de Mier y Terán: As It Affected Texas-Mexican Relations," *The Southwestern Historical Quarterly,* v. 48 (1945).

15. Andrés Reséndez, *Changing National Identities at the Frontier: Texas and New Mexico, 1800–1850* (2005), p. 69, writes, "All told, more than half of all land grants in Mexican Texas were awarded to Anglo-American, Mexican, and Native American Masons, while the proportions of Masons within the population of Texas at large was less than 10 percent."

16. Richard Drinnon, *White Savage: The Case of John Dunn Hunter* (1972).

17. Leland Hamilton Jenks, *The Migration of British Capital* (1927), p. 109.

18. Sarah Cornell, "Citizens of Nowhere: Fugitive Slaves and Free African Americans in Mexico, 1833–1857," *The Journal of American History,* v. 100 (2013).

19. Manning, *Diplomatic Correspondence,* v. 3, p. 1663.

Chapter 21: Sister Nations

1. Demetrio Castro, "Razones Serviles: Ideas y Argumentos del Absolutismo," Pedro Rújula and Jorge Canal, eds., *Guerra de Ideas: Política y Cultura en la España de la Guerra de la Independencia* (2012),

p. 107. For Bolívar's diplomatic ambition: Judith Ewell, "Bolívar's Atlantic World Diplomacy" in Langley and Bushnell, eds., *Simón Bolívar; Cartas del Libertador*, v. 4 (1967), pp. 272–75.

2. A May 26, 1821, essay in the popular Spanish journal *El Censor*, "El equilibrio Européo," used ancient Greece to criticize the Congress of Vienna, in which the aristocrats of Great Britain, France, Austria, and Russia built a post-Napoleonic order around "balances of power"—a concept where, ideally, each imperial nation pushes their interests and reacts to their fears just enough to create counterpoise. *Censor's* anonymous author wrote that unless the international community was founded on some higher value other than power, no such equilibrium would last. An "ambitious usurper" would always find it easy to upset the order, to create a new era of chaos, to kick off a new rotation between feudal anarchy and centralized despotism. For the Panama Congress as the beginning of Pan-Americanism: Joseph Byrne Lockey, *Orígenes del panamericanismo* (1927); Daniel Guerra Iñiguez, *Bolívar, Creador del Panamericanismo Actual* (1946); Arthur Whitaker, *The Western Hemisphere Idea* (1954); Jesús María Yepes, *Del Congreso de Panamá a la Conferencia de Caracas 1826–1954* (1955); José Caicedo Castilla, *El panamericanismo* (1961); Henry Bernstein, *Formación de una conciencia interamericana* (1961); Antonio del Castillo Martínez, *El Congreso de Panamá de 1826 convocado por el Libertador, iniciación del panamericanismo* (1972).

3. Both quotations from W. S. Robertson, "South America and the Monroe Doctrine," *Political Science Quarterly*, v. 20 (1915), p. 84; Alejandro Alvarez, *The Monroe Doctrine* (1924), p. 143.

4. The idea for the kind of gathering Bolívar was proposing went back decades. Independence leaders were influenced by several authors who had reimagined the international order as forming a single commonwealth, among them Maximilien de Béthune, the Abbé de Saint-Pierre, and Chile's Juan Egaña. The Central American José Cecilio del Valle, a correspondent friend of Jeremy Bentham, proposed the creation of a League of American Nations to counter what he derided as Europe's "League of Kings and Tyrants." (Bentham so appreciated Valle's brilliance he sent him a lock of his hair and a gold ring.) Ramón Rosa, *Biografía de José Cecilio del Valle* (1971), p. 100.

5. Simón Bolívar, *Convocatoria del Congreso de Panamá* (1824).

6. Harold Alfred Bierck, *Vida Pública de Don Pedro Gual* (1983).

7. Bierck, *Vida Pública*, p. 200; Germán Latorre, *El panamericanismo y el porvenir de la América Española* (1924).

8. Frank Griffith Dawson, *The First Latin American Debt Crisis: The City of London and the 1822–25 Loan Bubble* (1990), pp. 25–26. Also for background: Éric Toussaint, *The Debt System: A History of Sovereign Debts and Their Repudiation* (2019); Miguel Centeno, "Blood and Debt: War and Taxation in Nineteenth-Century Latin America," *American Journal of Sociology*, v. 102 (1997).

9. Miguel Centeno, *Blood and Debt: War and the Nation-State in Latin America* (2003), p. 138; Enrique Márquez, *La Nación en Armas: Venezuela y la Defensa de su Soberanía, 1810–1812* (2015), p. 141.

10. Michael Blaakman, *Speculation Nation: Land Mania in the Revolutionary American Republic* (2023). Earlier works that emphasize the importance of dispossession of and speculation in Native American land are Clarence Walworth Alvord, *Mississippi Valley in British Politics: A Study of the Trade, Land Speculation, and Experiments in Imperialism Culminating in the American Revolution*, two volumes (1917); and Thomas Perkins Abernathy, *Western Lands and the American Revolution* (1937).

11. *Memorias del General O'Leary*, v. 18 (1882), p. 393.

12. Lynch, *Bolívar*, p. 218.

13. The phrase *Fuera de México todo es Cuautitlán* goes back to the early 1800s and is attributed to María Ignacia Rodríguez de Velasco, a Mexico City *criolla* who was one of Simon Bolívar's lovers. Cuautitlán was an autonomous Nahuatl village in the early 1800s, just north of Mexico City, now incorporated into the greater capital region.

14. Bolívar, *Un pensamiento sobre el Congreso de Panamá* (1916).

Chapter 22: Torments

1. *Writings of Levi Woodbury* (1852), p. 82; *The Works of James Buchanan*, v. 1 (1908), p. 194.

2. *Speech of Mr. Van Buren of New York, Delivered in the Senate of the United States, on the Mission to Panama* (1826), p. 41.

3. Andrew Cleven, "The First Panama Mission and the Congress of the United States," *Journal of Negro History*, v. 8 (1928), p. 233. Lockey, *Pan-Americanism*, argues that opposition to attending the Panama Congress was not related to support for slavery but rather concern about entering "entangling alliances."

4. Thomas Hart Benton, *Thirty Years' View; Or a History of the Working of the American Government* (1857), p. 69.

5. For an example of abolitionist coverage: "Congress of Panama," *Genius of Universal Emancipation*, November 19, 1825; Josiah Stoddard Johnston, *Speech of Johnston in the Senate* (1826), pp. 16–18; *Niles' Weekly Register*, v. 30 (March 4, 1828), p. 13.

6. Calhoun to Joseph Swift, December 11, 1825, in *The Papers of John C. Calhoun* (1959), p. 56; Robert Elder, *Calhoun: American Heretic* (2021), p. 226; Jay Sexton, *The Monroe Doctrine: Empire and Nation in Nineteenth-Century America* (2011), p. 78.

7. *Gales and Seaton's Register of Debates in Congress*, 19th Congress, 1st Session, pp. 112–14; Elder, *Calhoun*, p. 224.

8. *Register of Debates in Congress*, v. 2 (1826), pp. 113, 119.

9. *The End of the Myth*, chapter 11, discusses how, after WWII, the conservatives mobilized against foreign policy initiatives—treaties and alliances—that they felt would mandate domestic integration and an expansion of economic rights; "Speech of Mr. Hayne, Delivered in the Senate of the United States, on the Mission to Panama, March 1826," in Benjamin Abney, comps, *Miscellaneous Speeches*, no date, no page.

10. *Correspondence of Andrew Jackson: 1833–1838* (1928), p. 301; Joseph Wheelan, *Mr. Adams's Last Crusade* (2008), p. 46; *The Papers of Andrew Jackson: 1825–1828* (1980), p. 166.

11. Henry Adams, *John Randolph* (1899), pp. 285–89.

12. Robert Remini, *Andrew Jackson and the Course of American Empire, 1822–1832*, v. 2 (1981), pp. 111–15.

13. Remini, *Course of American Empire*, p. 410.

14. Vanessa Spadafora Galvez, Eduardo Tejeira Davis, *El Casco Antiguo de la Ciudad de Panamá* (2001).

15. José Manuel Restrepo, *Historia de la Revolución de la República de Colombia*, v. 6 (1827), pp. 232–33; Germán de la Reza, "El traslado del Congreso anfictiónico de Panamá al poblado de Tacubaya (1826–1828)," *Revista brasileira de política internacional*, v. 4 (2006); E. Taylor Parks, Alfred Tischendorf, "Cartagena to Bogotá, 1825–1826: The Diary of Richard Clough Anderson, Jr.," *Hispanic American Historical Review*, v. 42 (1962), p. 225.

16. Tudor's report to Clay, November 20, 1827, in Manning, *Diplomatic Correspondence*, document 1005, pp. 1840–43. See p. 1843, for where Tudor forwards a secret communication from the head of the Peruvian military to Mexico's president Victoria, so to further pull Mexico away from Gran Colombia. Gregorio Selser, *Cronología de las intervenciones extranjeras en América Latina*, v. 1 (1994), provides a detailed chronology of these early machinations. Also: Florencio O'Leary, *Memorias del General O'Leary*, v. 29 (1917), p. 373; Fred J. Rippy, "Bolívar as Viewed by Contemporary Diplomats of the United States," *The Hispanic American Historical Review*, v. 15 (1935).

17. *Cartas del Libertador corregidas conforme a los originales*, v. 9 (1929), p. 267; Alejandro Próspero Révérend, *La Última Enfermedad, los Últimos Momentos y los Funerales de Simón Bolívar, Libertador de Colombia y del Peru* (1866), p. 35.

Chapter 23: The March of God

1. Marie G. Kimball, "Unpublished Correspondence of Mme. De Staël with Thomas Jefferson," *North American Review*, v. 208 (1918), p. 71.

2. Margaret Fuller, *Summer on the Lakes* (1843), chapter 6.

3. F. O. Matthiessen, *American Renaissance* (1941); Edward Widmar, *Young America* (2000); Mark Lause, *Young America: Land, Labor, and the Republican Community* (2010); Yonatan Eyal, *The Young America Movement and the Transformation of the Democratic Party* (2007).

4. Ralph Waldo Emerson, *The Young American* (1844).

5. In Chile, neither conservatives nor radicals were eager to expand suffrage. Conservatives because they distrusted mass politics. Radicals because they feared that an expanded vote could be manipulated by elites, who had the power to order how their peons voted. To expand suffrage would only expand that power.

6. This is an argument with many qualifications. See Robin Archer, *Why Is There No Labor Party in the United States?* (2010), and Eric Foner, "Why Is There No Socialism in the United States?," *History Workshop*, v. 17 (1984), pp. 57–80; Mark Lause, *Young America: Land, Labor, and the Republican Community* (2010), pp. 79, 39.

7. Roy Robbins, "Pre-Emption—A Frontier Triumph," *Mississippi Valley Historical Review*, v. 18 (1931).

8. Anthony Gronowicz, *Race and Class Politics in New York City Before the Civil War* (1999), p. 139.

9. Brendan Lindsay, *Murder State: California's Native American Genocide 1846–1873* (2012); Lause, *Young America*; Paul Foos, *A Short, Offhand, Killing Affair* (2003), p. 162.

10. Eyal, *The Young America Movement*, p. 135; Robert Sampson, *John L. O'Sullivan and His Times* (2003), p. 227; "Eighteen Fifty-Two, and the 'Coming Man,'" *The Democratic Review*, n. 168, (June 1852), p. 492.

11. William H. Goetzmann, ed., *The American Hegelians* (1973), p. 4. Thanks to Peter Wirzbicki for pointing out Bancroft's impression of Hegel's lecture style. See his *Fighting for the Higher Law: Black and White Transcendentalists Against Slavery* (2021) for Bancroft's broader intellectual and political moment, and for Hegel's influence on New England's transcendentalist abolitionists. The writer Robert Kaufman, who helped Richard Nixon work on a book titled *Beyond Peace*, reports that Nixon "originally contemplated grounding the domestic section of that book in the philosophy of Nietzsche and Hegel, whom he claimed to be reading with great sympathy and interest." In the end, though, "Nixon decided to abandon Nietzsche and Hegel in favor of the arguments of Hamilton and Tocqueville." Useful: Fred Burwick, "The Göttingen Influence on George Bancroft's Idea of Humanity," *Jahrbuch Für Amerikastudien*, v. 11 (1966).

12. Walt Whitman, "More Stars for the Spangled Banner," *Brooklyn Daily Eagle* (June 29, 1846), p. 2.

13. Julius Pratt, "John L. O'Sullivan and Manifest Destiny, *New York History*, v. 14 (1933).

14. Esteban Echeverría, *Dogma Socialista y otras páginas políticas* (1837).

15. Benjamín Vicuña, *Los Girondinos Chilenos* (1989), p. 23.

16. Manuel Blanco Cuartín, "Francisco Bilbao, su vida y sus doctrinas," in *Revista La Cañada: pensamiento filosófico chileno*, v. 5 (2015), originally published in *El Mercurio*, August 31, 1872.

17. Francisco Bilbao, *Obras Completas*, v. 1 (1897), pp. 114–15.

18. David Sobrevilla Alcázar, "Francisco Bilbao y el Perú: El inicio del radicalismo en el Perú y su aporte a la abolición de la esclavitud," in *Repensando la tradición de Nuestra América* (1999), pp. 123–24; Natalia Sobrevilla Perea, "The Influence of the European 1848 Revolutions in Peru," in Guy Thompson, ed., *The European Revolutions of 1848 and The Americas* (2002).

19. Unless otherwise cited, for this section: the essays by Cara Lida, David Rock, Eduardo Posada-Carbó, and Natalie Sobrevilla Perea in Thompson, ed., *The European Revolutions of 1848 and the Americas*; Jay Robert Grusin, "The Revolution of 1848 in Colombia," PhD dissertation, University of Arizona (1978).

20. Allen Woll, "A Functional Past: The Politics of History in Nineteenth-Century Chile," PhD dissertation, University of Wisconsin, Madison (1975), p. 55.

21. Victorino Lastarria, *Investigaciones sobre la influencia social de la conquista y del sistema colonial de los españoles en Chile* (1844).

22. Alamiro de Ávila Martel, *Estudios sobre José Victorino Lastarria* (1988), p. 208.

23. Allen Woll, "The Philosophy of History in Nineteenth-Century Chile: The Lastarria-Bello Controversy," *History and Theory*, v. 13 (1974), p. 281.

24. For *Krausismo* as a synthesis of liberalism, metaphysics, utilitarianism, and positivism: Michela Coletta, *Decadent Modernity: Civilization and 'Latinidad' in Spanish America, 1880–1920* (2018), pp. 16–19.

25. Juan López-Morillas, *The Krausist Movement and Ideological Change in Spain, 1854–1874* (1981), pp. 27–28; José Victorino Lastarria, *Recuerdos literarios* (1885), pp. 252–53. Also: Cristina Hurtado, "Lastarria y el krausismo, siglo XIX en Chile," in M. Muñoz and P. Vermeren, eds., *Repensando el siglo XIX desde América Latina y Francia* (2009); Carlos Beorlegui, *Historia del pensamiento filosófico latinoamericano* (2006), pp. 245–49; Jaime Suchlicki, "The Political Ideology of José Martí," *Caribbean Studies*, v. 6, n. 1 (1966), pp. 25–36; Hugo Biagini, ed., *Origines de la democracia Argentina: El trasfondo Krausista* (1989); Arturo Andrés Roig, *Los Krausistas Argentinos* (1969); Manuel de Rivacoba y Rivacoba, *Krausismo y derecho* (1963); Susana Monreal, *Krausismo en el Uruguay* (1993); Richard Gott, *Karl Krause and the Ideological Origins of the Cuban Revolution* (2002). Jens Hentschke, "José Victorino Lastarria's Libertarian Krauso-Positivism and the Discourse on State- and Nation-Building in Nineteenth-Century Chile," *Intellectual History Review*, v. 22 (2012), pp. 241–60.

26. Allen Woll, "A Functional Past," p. 52.

27. Bilbao, *Obras*, v. 1, p. 373.

28. James Wood, *The Society of Equality* (2011), p. 113. Not all young intellectuals were Socialists. Socialism, wrote Félix Frías, was "plebeian philosophy of sensual arrogance," the "science of envy." Alberdi, mentioned above, would go on to be an influential liberal legal theorist. He came to see 1848 as unleashing "democratic fanaticism and idolatry," and remained hostile to Socialism for his entire life.

29. Chilean republicans tried to achieve dispossession passively through the law: All Mapuche were technically citizens, which gave them the right to sell their land and move wherever they wanted in the republic. Letting the market break up Mapuche autonomy was slow work. Other colonial restrictions on alienating land, including the ongoing traditions of primogeniture and entailment, which preserved large hacienda estates intact, were drags on the transformation of land into capitalist

real estate. The assault on Mapuche land picked up in the 1850s: Jorge Pinto Rodríguez, "Del anti-indigenismo al proindigenismo en Chile en el siglo XIX," in Leticia Reina, ed., *La reindianización de América* (1997), pp. 137–57.

30. Andrew Daitsman, *The People Shall Be All* (1995); Santiago Arcos, *Carta a Francisco Bilbao y otros escritos* (1989), p. 107.

31. Gabriel Sanhueza, *Santiago Arcos* (1956), p. 195.

32. Álvaro Kaempfer, "Lastarria, Bello y Sarmiento En 1844: Genocidio, Historiografía y Proyecto Nacional," *Revista de Crítica Literaria Latinoamericana*, v. 32 (2006); Lastarria, *Investigaciones*.

Chapter 24: Two Americas

1. Matthew Karp, *This Vast Southern Empire: Slaveholders at the Helm of American Foreign Policy* (2016).

2. "Eighteen Fifty-Two, and the 'Coming Man,'" *The Democratic Review* (June 1852), p. 491.

3. John Burgess, "The Recent Pseudo-Monroeism," *Political Science Quarterly*, v. 11, n. 1 (1896).

4. Robert May, *Slavery, Race, and Conquest in the Tropics: Lincoln, Douglas, and the Future of Latin America* (2013), p. 60; Karp's *This Vast Southern Empire* and Walter Johnson's *River of Dark Dreams: Slavery and Empire in the Cotton Kingdom* (2013) for Jacksonian foreign policy more broadly. Susanna Hecht, *The Scramble for the Amazon and the 'Lost Paradise' of Euclides da Cunha* (2013).

5. "Situation of the Kansas Question," *New York Times*, April 5, 1858.

6. Will Soper, *Greytown Is No More!* (2022); Alan McPherson, *A Short History of U.S. Interventions in Latin America and the Caribbean* (2016), p. 30.

7. Lord Palmerston to British Foreign Secretary Lord Clarendon, December 31, 1857, reprinted as appendix to *Journal of Modern History*, v. 3 (1961).

8. Alanson Ellsworth, *One Hundred Eighty Landings of United States Marines, 1800–1934* (1934); Harris Gaylord Warren, *Paraguay: An Informal History* (1949), p. 194; Thomas Jefferson Page to José Falcón, October 16, 1854, U.S. Congress, *Executive Documents, Senate Documents*, 35th Congress, 1st Session, No. 11, 40; William L. Marcy to Thomas J. Page, June 2, 1854 and Page to Marcy, October 17, 1854, in William Manning, ed., *Diplomatic Correspondence of the United States: Inter-American Affairs, 1831–1860*, v. 10 (1935).

9. Gustave A. Nuermberger, "The Continental Treaties of 1856: An American Union 'Exclusive of the United States,'" *Hispanic American Historical Review*, v. 20 (1940).

10. Manning, *Diplomatic Correspondence*, v. 5, *Chile and Colombia* (1935), p. 847.

11. Bilbao, "Iniciativa de la América. Idea de un Congreso Federal de las Repúblicas" and José María Samper, "La Confederación Colombiana," in José Victorino Lastarria y otros, comps., *Colección de ensayos y documentos* (1976), pp. 281, 290, and 364.

12. Michel Gobat, "The Invention of Latin America: A Transnational History of Anti-Imperialism, Democracy, and Race," *The American Historical Review*, v. 118 (2013). Also: Aims McGuinness, "Searching for 'Latin America,'" in Nancy P. Appelbaum, Anne S. Macpherson, and Karin Alejandra Rosemblatt, eds., *Race and Nation in Modern Latin America* (2003); Miguel Rojas Mix, "Bilbao y el Hallazgo de América Latina: Unión Continental, Socialista y Libertaria," *Cahiers du Monde Hispanique et Luso-Brésilien*, v. 46 (1986); Mauricio Tenorio-Trillo, *Latin America: The Allure and Power of an Idea* (2017); Arturo Ardao, *Génesis de la idea y el nombre de América latina* (1980).

13. "Felipe José Pereira Leal a la cancillería del Brasil" (December 21, 1856), in "Correspondência Recebida (Oficios) 1856–1857," *Cuadernos do Centro de História e Documentação Diplomática*, v. 2 (2003), p. 377.

14. Gobat, "The Invention of Latin America."

15. Francisco Bilbao, "Prefacio a los evangelios (inedito): El Libro en América," in *Obras Completas*, v. 1 (1866), pp. 77–78.

16. José María Torres Caicedo, "Las dos Américas," *El Correo de Ultramar* (1857).

17. Reginald Horsman, *Race and Manifest Destiny: The Origins of American Racial Anglo-Saxonism* (1981).

18. Bilbao, "Prefacio a los evangelios," p. 72.

19. Sexton, *The Monroe Doctrine*, p. 79, for quotations and comment on 1828 *Webster's Dictionary*. Noah Webster, *An American Dictionary of the English language* (1830); Noah Webster, Chauncey Allen Goodrich, *An American Dictionary of the English language . . .* (1847). Less than a decade later, Stephen Douglas, the leader of the Democratic Party who would lose to Abraham Lincoln in the 1860 presidential election, defended Walker's invasion of Nicaragua because Walker was an "American by birth" who enjoyed the "sacred" right of being able to migrate to any country that would have him. And if Nicaraguans wanted him as their president, who was to argue? Under Walker, Nicaragua would be, Douglas said, so "thoroughly Americanized" it could be admitted into the union as a state. "Senator Douglas on Nicaragua Affairs," *St. Paul Daily Pioneer*, May 20, 1856.

Chapter 25: Lincoln Belongs to Us

1. Sharon Hartman Strom, "Labor, Race, and Colonization," in Steven Mintz and John Stauffer, eds., *The Problem of Evil: Slavery, Freedom, and the Ambiguities of American Reform* (2007). Also: Robert May, *Slavery, Race, and Conquest*.

2. Frank Blair, *The Destiny of the Races of This Continent* (1859).

3. For the various efforts to remove people of color: Frederic Bancroft, "The Colonization of American Negroes, 1801–1865" in chapter 2, "Schemes to Colonize Negros in Central America," found in Jacob Cook, *Frederic Bancroft, Historian* (1957).

4. Henry Louis Gates and Donald Yacovone, eds., *Lincoln on Race and Slavery* (2009), pp. 235–41.

5. *Diary and Correspondence of Salmon P. Chase* (1903), pp. 59, 93; Ousmane K. Power-Greene, *Against Wind and Tide: The African American Struggle Against the Colonization Movement* (2014), p. 185.

6. Willis Boyd, "The Île a Vache Colonization Venture, 1862–1864," *The Americas*, vol. 16 (1959), pp. 45–62; the Seward quotation is on p. 57. Also: James D. Lockett, "Abraham Lincoln and Colonization: An Episode That Ends in Tragedy at L'Ile a Vache, Haiti, 1863–1864," *Journal of Black Studies*, v. 21 (1991).

7. Phillip Magness, "James Mitchell and the Mystery of the Emigration Office Papers," *Journal of the Abraham Lincoln Association*, v. 32 (2002). For "safety-valve" quotation: *Memoirs and Letters of Charles Sumner* (1893), p. 254.

8. Dionisio Poey Baro, "'Race' and Anti-Racism in José Martí's 'Mi Raza,'" *Contributions in Black Studies*, v. 12 (1994).

9. Paul Kennedy, *The Rise and Fall of the Great Powers* (1987), p. 242.

10. The quotation is from Sarmiento's interpretation of the importance of Lincoln and the Civil War, as discussed in Nicola Miller's "'That Great and Gentle Soul': Images of Lincoln in Latin America," in Richard Carwardine and Jay Sexton, eds., *The Global Lincoln* (2011).

11. Example: Miguel González Saravia, *Compendio de la historia de Centro-América* (1879). José Martí and Luis Baralt, trans., *Martí on the U.S.A.* (1966), p. 66.

12. For Martí's "The Poet Walt Whitman": Gay Wilson Allen, ed., *Walt Whitman Abroad: Critical Essays from Germany, France, Scandinavia, Russia, Italy, Spain and Latin America, Israel, Japan, and India* (1955), pp. 201–13. Gilberto Freyre, "Camerado Whitman," in Allen, *Walt Whitman Abroad*, quote from p. 231. The Whitman cult in Latin America deepened through the Good Neighbor Policy and Popular Front period of the 1930s until the years immediately following World War II. His influence on poets such as Pablo Neruda and Gabriela Mistral is apparent. See Luis Franco, *Walt Whitman: El mayor demócrata que el mundo ha visto* (1940), and José Gabriel, *Walt Whitman: La Voz Democrática de América* (1944).

13. The Cuban nationalist weekly *Patria* was among the first to use the term *imperialismo*, in 1898 (October 15); in Peru, Luis de las Casas wrote a doctoral thesis titled "Imperialismo" (1901). Lenin's analysis of the determining causes of imperialism has been available in Latin America since 1917. The Peruvian Francisco García Calderón in 1914 ("El imperialismo yanquí en la América Central," *Cuba Contemporánea*) identified Panama as a line marking two forms of U.S. imperialism: South of the canal, informal "financial, industrial, and commercial penetration" reigned. North of the canal, "absolute and indisputable political hegemony."

14. José Enrique Rodó, *Ariel* (1900), pp. 98–135; Victoria Quintana, "Heirs of Martí: The Story of Cuban Lawyers," *University of Miami International and Comparative Law Review*, v. 17 (2010).

15. Lester Langley, *The Banana Wars* (1983).

16. Quintana, "Heirs of Martí."

Chapter 26: Twilight

1. "José Martí to Juan Bonillo," August 8, 1890, in José Martí, *Obras Completas*, v. 1 (1963), p. 260; Carlos Márquez Sterling, *Martí: Ciudadano de América* (1965), p. 282.

2. Julio Le Riverend, "*Teoria martiana*," in Emilio Roig de Leuchsenring, et al., eds., *Vida y pensamiento de Martí*, v. 1 (1942), p. 88.

3. José Martí, *Martí y la identidad Latinoamericano* (1995), p. 28.

4. Anne Fountain, "Martí and Emerson," in Ryan Anthony Spangler and George Michal Schwarzmann, eds., *Syncing the Americas: José Martí and the Shaping of National Identity* (2017).

5. José Martí, "Fragmentos del Discurso Pronunciado en el Club de Comercio," Caracas, Venezuela, March 21, 1881, in *Obras Completas*, v. 7 (1963), p. 284. Rodolfo Sarracino, "Martí en el Club Crepusculo: En Busca de Nuevos Equilibrios," *Revisa Casa de las Americas*, v. 251 (2008); William Isacson, "Jose Martí en el Club Crepusculo," *Archivo Jose Martí*, v. 15 (1950).

6. For Mexicanization: Gregory Downs, "The Mexicanization of American Politics: The United States' Transnational Path from Civil War to Stabilization," *The American Historical Review*, v. 117 (2012).

7. Robert Waters, *Career and Conversation of John Swinton* (1902), p. 81.

8. Emerson, like Martí, was apparently influenced by Krause. Martí, condemned by a Spanish colonial judge to hard labor, no doubt appreciated Emerson's notion that any law imposed from afar was

"laughable." Both Emerson and Martí were nationalists, and Martí must have enjoyed Emerson's dismissal of the "courtly muses of Europe." "We will walk on our own feet; we will work with our own hands; we shall speak our own minds" said Emerson in his famous lecture "The American Scholar." That is what Martí wanted for Cuba. Both were abolitionists, yet Emerson was more conflicted about burdens of race than Martí.

9. John Bassett Moore, ed., *A Digest of International Law*, v. 6 (1906), p. 72.

10. "The United States, Cuba, and Spain," *Chicago Daily Tribune*, June 27, 1889; for example: Blaine to Comly, December 1, 1881, in Ruhl Jacob Bartlett, *The Record of American Diplomacy* (1964), p. 360.

11. Laura Lomas, "El Negro es Tan Capaz Como El Blanco," in Rodrigo Lazo, Jesse Alemán, eds., *The Latino Nineteenth Century* (2016), p. 307.

12. Sarracino, "Martí en el Club Crepusculo."

13. On the conference: James Vivian, "The Pan American Conference Act of May 10, 1888: President Cleveland and the Historians," *The Americas*, v. 27 (1970). For Blaine and Pan-Americanism: Edward Crapol, *James G. Blaine: Architect of Empire* (2000); David Healy, *James G. Blaine and Latin America* (2001); David Pletcher, "Reciprocity and Latin America in the Early 1890s: A Foretaste of Dollar Diplomacy," *Pacific Historical Review*, v. 47 (1978); Lester Langley, "James Gillespie Blaine: The Ideologue as Diplomat," in Frank Merli, Theodore Wilson, eds., *Makers of American Diplomacy* (1974); Allan Peskin, "Blaine, Garfield and Latin America," in *Americas: A Quarterly Review of Inter-American Cultural History*, v. 36 (1979).

14. "Delegates See the Sun; They Also Hear Warm Words of Welcome Reception," *New-York Tribune*, December 20, 1889; "The Evening's Banquet," *New York Times*, December 21, 1889; "Pan-American Delegates: The Aldermen Appropriate $5000 to Entertain Them," *New York Times*, December 4, 1889.

15. José Martí, *Argentina i La Primera Conferencia Panamericana* (1955).

16. For Alberdi: Jeremy Adelman, "Between Order and Liberty: Juan Bautista Alberdi and the Intellectual Origins of Argentine Constitutionalism," *Latin American Research Review*, v. 42 (2007).

17. Juan Bautista Alberdi, "Memoria Sobre la Conveniencia y Objetos de un Congreso Jeneral americano," in *Obras completas de J. B. Alberdi*, v. 2 (1840), p. 402.

18. Edgar Turlington, *Mexico and Her Foreign Creditors* (1930). Grotius did say that the Dutch East India Company had the right to intervene in the affairs of other nations to retaliate against violations of international law, including the right to use military force to collect unpaid debt.

19. Calvo extended the arguments of the Salamanca School, especially those of the Jesuit Luis de Molina, who held that *only* the authorities of the state where a violation of law occurred had the power to punish. A decade before Calvo codified his ideas, the attorney general of the United States, Caleb Cushing, agreed with the principle that "a foreigner sojourning in a country" should only be protected by "the general laws of that country." Cushing noted that "Great Britain, France, and the United States" had often assumed "rights of interference" on behalf of its citizens that they would not "tolerate at home." He suggested that the United States might adopt something like a Golden Rule, in which Washington would try "abstaining" from taking any action it wouldn't want took on itself. For Cushing: John Bassett Moore, *History and Digest of the International Arbitrations to which the United States has Been a Party . . .* , v. 2 (1898), p. 1632.

20. Juan Bautista Alberdi, *El Crimen de la Guerra* (1920), p. 46.

21. Mariano H. Cornejo and Felipe de Osma, *Memoria del Peru en el arbitraje sobre sus límites con el Ecuador*, v. 7 (1906), p. 121. The influential Chilean jurist Manuel Alejandro Alvarez thought the Monroe Doctrine might be salvaged, that its essence was defensive and anticolonial. Alvarez argued that the Monroe Doctrine had evolved in two distinct but related realms: *politics*, where Washington's

preponderant power allowed it to interpret the doctrine according to its own interests; and *law*, which, while initially dependent on United States unilateralism, would eventually transcend that dependence and become the keystone of a true universal multilateralism. See Alvarez, "Latin America and International Law," *American Journal of International Law*, v. 3 (April 1909), pp. 311–12.

22. Leslie Bethell, "The Decline and Fall of Slavery in Nineteenth Century Brazil," *Transactions of the Royal Historical Society*, v. 1 (1991), pp. 79–81.

23. V. G. Kiernan, "Foreign Interests in the War of the Pacific," *The Hispanic American Historical Review*, v. 35 (1955), for the Blaine quotations. For W. R. Grace in Peru: Lawrence Clayton, *Grace: W. R. Grace & Co* (1985). Also: Perry Belmont, *An American Democrat: The Recollections of Perry Belmont* (1940), p. 260.

24. For Poland: Andrés Bello, *Principios de Derecho de Jentes* (1840), p. 25; José Silva Santisteban, *Curso de Derecho Internacional o de Gentes* (1864), p. xii.

Chapter 27: America for Humanity

1. Unless otherwise cited, the following descriptions come from Bill Karras, "Jose Martí and the Pan American Conference, 1889–1891," *Revista de Historia de América*, v. 77/78 (1974).

2. For the quote in the footnote: Nancy Mitchell, *The Danger of Dreams: German and American Imperialism in Latin America* (1999).

3. Roque Sáenz Peña, *El Zollverein Americano* (1890).

4. Gail Hamilton, *Biography of James G. Blaine* (1895), p. 716. For Mexico-U.S. arbitration commission: Allison Powers Useche, "The Specter of Compensation: Mexican Claims Against the United States, 1868–1938," in Pablo Mitchell and Katrina Jagondinsky, eds., *Beyond the Borders of the Law: Critical Legal Histories of the North American West* (2018).

5. Santiago Guzmán, *El derecho de conquista y la teoría del equilibrio en la América latina* (1881), pp. 152–53.

6. José Manuel Estrada, *El Doctor Manuel Quintana* (1904), p. 109.

7. Carolyne Larson, ed., *The Conquest of the Desert* (2020).

8. James Kent, *Commentaries on American Law* (1832), pp. 258–59; Robert Phillimore, *Commentaries Upon International Law*, v. 3 (1857), p. 741.

9. The account of this conflict, and Carnegie's compromise, is in Martí, *Obras Completas*, v. 6 (1963), pp. 111–13, and Carlos Márquez Sterling, "The First International Conference of American States," *Américas*, v. 22, n. 4 (1970).

10. "Conference Finished," *New York Times*, April 19, 1890.

11. Lawrence Sanders Rowland, Alexander Moore, George C. Rogers, *The History of Beaufort County, South Carolina: 1541–1861* (1996), p. 436; William Howard Russell, *My Diary North and South*, v. 1 (1863), chapter 10, provides a description of Barnwell, including of its slave quarters, church, and the work-hymns of enslaved peoples; Karp, *This Vast Southern Empire*, pp. 179–82. Also: Adrian Brettle, *Colossal Ambitions: Confederate Planning for a Post–Civil War World* (2020); for Mrs. Trescot's quotations: William Howard Russell, *My Diary*, v. 1 (2023), p. 214. I would like to thank Cynthia Nicoletti, a professor of law and history at the University of Viriginia, who shared her thoughts on Trescot as well as an early draft of her essay "William Henry Trescot, Pardon Broker," which was published in *The Journal of the Civil War Era* in 2021.

12. "Minority Report on Claims and Diplomatic Intervention from the Delegate from the United States," in *International American Conference, Reports and Recommendations Concerning a Uniform Code of International Law* (1890), p. 26.

13. President Herbert Hoover, for instance, helped broker a partial solution to the conflict between Chile and Peru over territory seized by Chile during the War of the Pacific.

14. For Kasson: Henry Wellington Wack, *The Story of the Congo Free State* (1905), pp. 107–8; G. Spiller, ed., *Papers on Inter-Racial Problems Communicated to the First Universal Races Congress* (1911), p. 407; R. J. Gavin and J. A. Betley, *Scramble for Africa: Documents on the Berlin West African Conference and Related Subjects* (1973), p. 22. For Kasson and free trade: Matthew Craven, "Between Law and History: The Berlin Conference of 1884–1885 and the Logic of Free Trade," *London Review of International Law*, v. 3, n. 1 (2015), pp. 31–59; Robert Ellsworth Elder, *The United States and the Berlin Congo Conference of 1884–85*, MA thesis, University of Chicago (1937), p. 28; G. Macharia Munene, "The United States and the Berlin Conference on the Partition of Africa," *Transafrican Journal of History*, v. 19 (1990), pp. 73–79. Also: Lysle E. Meyer, "Sanford and the Congo: A Reassessment," *African Historical Studies*, v. 4, n. 1 (1971), pp. 19–39; Joseph Baylen, "Senator John Tyler Morgan, E. D. Morel, and the Congo Reform Association," *The Alabama Review*, v. 15 (1962).

15. The Hearst-Remington telegram story comes from a few sources. The first being a September 1906 *Pearson's Magazine* article, "The Real Mr. Hearst," by a Hearst loyalist and former employee, James Creelman. Jimmy Breslin claims an old Hearst archivist showed him the actual cable when he worked as a sports journalist for the Hearst-run *Journal-American*. Breslin recounted the story on February 20, 1983, for the *New York Daily News* as tensions between the Reagan administration and Iran were worsening, with Reagan sending the USS *Nimitz* into Iranian waters. "Breslin Remembers the Maine and Hopes He Won't Have to Remember the Nimitz," ran the front-page lead for the story. Another source is Charles Michelson, *The Ghost Talks* (1944). See the discussion in Ken Lawrence, "You Furnish the Pictures, and I'll Furnish the War," published online in 2019 and found at https://www.rfrajola.com/2k19/Hearst_telegram_2019.pdf. W. Joseph Campbell, in *Getting It Wrong* (2016), says the story of the telegram is apocryphal.

Chapter 28: Tar Wars

1. Benjamin Coates, "Securing Hegemony Through Law: Venezuela, the U.S. Asphalt Trust, and the Uses of International Law, 1904–1909," *Journal of American History*, v. 102 (2015).

2. Paolo Amorosa, "The American Project and the Politics of History: James Brown Scott and the Origins of International Law," PhD thesis, University of Helsinki (2018), chapters 1 and 2.

3. Beveridge cited in Willard L. Beaulac, *The Fractured Continent: Latin America in Close-Up* (1980), p. 58.

4. Albert Weinstein's *Manifest Destiny* (1935) remains among the best studies of its topic, especially the way expansionists used the contours of nature to make their case.

5. Benjamin Wetzel, *American Crusade* (2022), p. 84; Mitchell, *The Danger of Dreams*, p. 41.

6. "Our Correspondence," *American Asphalt Journal*, May 1902.

7. Peter McCaffery, *When Bosses Ruled Philadelphia* (2010); Peter McCaffery, "The Evolution of an Urban Political Machine: Republican Philadelphia, 1867–1933," PhD thesis, University of London (1989), p. 164.

8. "Asphalt Receivers Sued," *New York Times*, December 19, 1902.

9. See the entry for John M. Mack in *Harper's Weekly*, November 15, 1902, p. 1713. For the web of corruption surrounding Jaurett and other U.S. citizens and diplomats: U.S. Department of State, *In the Matter of the Charges of Mr. Herbert W. Bowen, United States Minister to Venezuela: against Mr. Francis B. Loomis, first assistant Secretary of State, and the counter charges of Mr. Loomis against Mr. Bowen* (1905). For other aspects of the scandal: Richard Harding Davis, "The Asphalt Scandal," *Collier's*, May 13, 1905; Brian Stuart McBeth, *Gunboats, Corruption and Claims: Foreign Intervention in Venezuela, 1899–1908* (2001).

10. Nikita Harwich Vallenilla, *Asfalto y Revolución: La New York & Bermúdez Company* (1992); Kenneth O'Reilly, *Asphalt: A History* (2021); McBeth, *Gunboats, Corruption, and Claims*, p. 46. Also: "Admits Aid to Matos," *New-York Tribune*, October 18, 1905.

11. "Du Bois Takes Issue with Roosevelt," *New York Times*, July 2, 1914.

12. Philip Jessup, *Elihu Root*, v. 1 (1938), p. 494.

13. Castro promptly (according to McBeth, *Gunboats, Corruption, and Claims*, p. 166) paid off loans he took out to defeat the National Asphalt Trust–backed revolution.

14. Jessup, *Root*, v. 1, p. 496.

15. "Possibility of a War with German Empire," *New York Times*, December 29, 1901.

16. Referring to his earlier dispatch of Marines to Cuba, Panama, and the Dominican Republic, Roosevelt said, "I would have interfered in some similar fashion in Venezuela," Jessup, *Root*, v. 1, p. 497.

17. United Nations, "Reports of International Arbitral Awards," v. 10 (1962).

18. Christina Duffy Burnett, "Contingent Constitutions: Empire and Law in the Americas," PhD thesis, Princeton (2010), p. 300. Chapters 4 and 5 detail the codification of American International Law.

19. "The Asphalt Trust Behind Revolution," *Arizona Republican*, December 35, 1908; "Clash over Asphalt Dispute Cause a Halt in Negotiations with Venezuelan Regime," *Cincinnati Enquirer*, January 29, 1909; "Agreement Made with Venezuela, *Atlantic Constitution*, February 14, 1909.

20. Jessup, *Root*, v. 2, p. 74; Cyrus Veeser, *A World Safe for Capitalism: Dollar Diplomacy and America's Rise to Global Power* (2002), discusses a similar crisis in the Dominican Republic caused by reckless financiers. Also: Benjamin Coates, *Legalist Empire: International Law and American Foreign Relations in the Early Twentieth Century* (2016), pp. 122–23.

21. Martha Finnemore and Michelle Jurkovich, "Getting a Seat at the Table: The Origins of Universal Participation and Modern Multilateral Conferences," *Global Governance*, v. 20 (2014), pp. 361–73.

22. Robert Klein, *Sovereign Equality Among States: The History of an Idea* (1974), pp. 52–62.

23. Jessop, *Root*, v. 2, p. 78; James Brown Scott, ed., *Instructions to the American Delegates to the Hague Peace Conference and Their Official Reports* (1916), pp. 79–80; James Brown Scott, *The Hague Peace Conferences of 1899 and 1907*, 2 vols.

24. Root to Elbert Baldwin, November 1, 1907, Elihu Root Papers, Library of Congress, Box 188, Part 2.

25. Ruy Barbosa, *The Equality of Sovereign States* (1907); Barbosa, *Actas e discursos* (1917); J. R. Dos Santos, *O Brazil em Haya, Seguida de dez discursos de Ruy Barbosa na segunda Conferencia da Paz* (1925).

Chapter 29: Mexico's Revolution

1. "Not in Danger," *Nashville Tennessean*, February 25, 1912; "Splendid Lark," *Evening Journal* (Adelaide), April 6, 1912.

2. John Sloan, "United States Policy Responses to the Mexican Revolution: A Partial Application of the Bureaucratic Politics Model," *Journal of Latin American Studies*, v. 10 (1978), p. 285; Mark Wasserman, "Foreign Investment in Mexico, 1876–1910: A Case Study of the Role of Regional Elites," *The Americas*, v. 36 (1979), pp. 3–21.

3. Lorenzo Meyer, *Mexico and the United States in the Oil Controversy* (2014), p. 14; "Joint Commission to Consider Yankee's Claims is Not Favored by Mexicans," *Cincinnati Enquirer,* November 28, 1912.

4. "Wilson Pleases Mexico: Madero Ministers Expect Him to Continue Policy of Non-Intervention," *New York Times*, November 8, 1912.

5. Lowell Blaisdell, "Henry Lane Wilson and the Overthrow of Madero," *The Southwestern Social Science Quarterly*, v. 43, n. 2 (1962).

6. Robert Murray, "Huerta and the Two Wilsons," *Harper's Weekly*, v. 62, in six installments, January to May 1916.

7. Gene Hanrahan, *Documents on the Mexican Revolution* (1976), p. 147; Committee on Foreign Relations, United States Senate, *Investigation of Mexican Affairs: Preliminary Report and Hearings of the Committee on Foreign Relations*, pt. 2, v. 2 (1920), p. 2258; Richard Challener, *Admirals, Generals, and American Foreign Policy, 1898–1914* (2015), p. 358.

8. Buckley summoned a dozen Texas strongmen to deal with a squatter problem. Reid Buckley, *An American Family: The Buckleys* (2008), p. 122.

9. According to Eugene Frank, "The Diplomatic Career of Henry Lane Wilson in Latin America," PhD thesis, Louisiana State University (1957), the State Department, if Taft had been reelected, was preparing for a military intervention in June 1913. "Seeress Forecasts Roosevelt as Next White House Occupant and Predicts U.S. Will War on Mexico," *Washington Post*, October 17, 1915.

10. For Pettegrew: Gene Hanrahan, *Documents on the Mexican Revolution* (1976), p. 151.

11. Alan Knight, *The Mexican Revolution* (1990), p. 487.

12. A June 18, 1913, report by William Bayard Hale, in Arthur Link, *Papers of Woodrow Wilson*, v. 27 (1978). Friedrich Katz, *La Guerra Secreta en Mexico* (1983), p. 136, discusses the implications of this long, private, and curiously timed discussion between Ambassador Wilson and Huerta. Evidence is strong, Katz writes, that Huerta ordered Madero's murder that night. Montgomery Schuyler, secretary of the U.S. embassy, told General Leonard Wood that Wilson was "largely responsible" for the death of Madero. A few days later, one Major Bryan told Wood that the ambassador was "morally responsible" for the killing. Library of Congress, Leonard Wood Papers, Diary Box 7, January 1, 1913–December 31, 1913, entries: April 7, 1913; April 10, 1913.

13. John Womack, *Zapata and the Mexican Revolution* (2011), p. 160; Robert McCaa, "Missing Millions: The Demographic Costs of the Mexican Revolution," *Mexican Studies/Estudios Mexicanos*, v. 19, n. 2 (2003), pp. 367–400.

14. Lars Schoultz, *Beneath the United States: A History of U.S. Policy Toward Latin America* (1998), p. 244.

15. Carey Walsh, *Building the Borderlands: A Transnational History of Irrigated Cotton along the Mexico Texas Border* (2008).

16. John Mason Heart, *Revolutionary Mexico* (1987), p. 362. Later, in the 1930s, when President Lázaro Cárdenas accelerated the revolution's land reform, Hearst's lawyers saved the ranch from expropriation. According to Frank Dobie, who had visited Hearst's ranch, Babicora, in the 1930s, Hearst's fearsome security forces killed as many as seventy-five peasant activists during this period (Cormac McCarthy's *The Crossing* is partly based on Dobie's *Babicora*). Hearst died in 1951, and Babicora was sold to the Mexican state in exchange for government-issued bonds.

17. Randolph Greenfield Adams, *A History of the Foreign Policy of the United States* (1924), p. 207.

18. See Benjamin Allen Coates, *Legalist Empire*, chapter 5, for the legal issues involved in nonrecognition.

19. Arthur Link, *Woodrow Wilson and the Progressive Era, 1910–1917* (1954), p. 109.

20. Louis Teitelbaum, *Woodrow Wilson and the Mexican Revolution, 1913–1916* (1967), pp. 44–45.

21. Lloyd Gardner, in "Woodrow Wilson and the Mexican Revolution," in Arthur Link, ed., *Woodrow Wilson and a Revolutionary World* (1982), p. 19, offers a compelling account of Wilson's Mexican policy, which has greatly influenced this work.

22. John Mason Hart, *Empire and Revolution*, p. 206.

23. *The Letters and Friendships of Sir Cecil Spring Rice*, v. 2 (1929), p. 196.

24. Larry Hill, "Woodrow Wilson's Executive Agents in Mexico: From the Beginning of His Administration to the Recognition of Venustiano Carranza," PhD thesis, Louisiana State University and Agricultural & Mechanical College (1971); William Weber Johnson, *Heroic Mexico* (1968), p. 146.

25. John Mason Hart, in *Revolutionary Mexico* and *Revolution and Empire*, writes that business backers of Wilson, short of recognizing Huerta, were willing to back Carranza.

26. "The Reminiscences of Walter Lippmann," Columbia University Oral History Collection, pt. 2, n. 118, p. 89.

27. Edward Haley, *Revolution and Intervention: The Diplomacy of Taft and Wilson with Mexico, 1910– 1917* (1970).

28. John Judis, *William F. Buckley, Jr.* (2001), p. 185; Delbert Haff to Wilson, May 12, 1913, in *The Papers of Woodrow Wilson*, v. 27 (1978), p. 421.

29. Committee on Foreign Relations, *Investigation of Mexican Affairs*, pt. 2, v. 3 (1920), p. 2255.

Chapter 30: Wilson's Dilemma

1. John M. Mulder, "Joseph Ruggles Wilson: Southern Presbyterian Patriarch," *Journal of Presbyterian History (1962–1985)*, v. 52 (1974); Mark Benbow, *Leading Them to the Promised Land* (2010), p. 9.

2. Wilson said he now understood that intervention wasn't a *response* to chronic unrest but its *cause*. As Secretary of State Bryan explained the dynamic, "The financiers charge excessive rates" because they insist on being "paid for the risk that they take." Bryan was referring not to interest rates but up-front fees just to secure the loan. "And as soon as they collect their pay for the risk they then proceed to demand" that Washington ensure "the risk shall be eliminated by governmental coercion. No wonder," Bryan continued, "the people of these little republics are aroused to revolution by what they regard as a sacrifice of their interests." Notwithstanding such sharp criticism of his predecessors' "financial imperialism," Wilson signed the Federal Reserve Act into law early in his first term. A complicated piece of legislation, the act did many things to rationalize the financial system, one of which was removing restrictions that limited the kind of businesses national banks could do in foreign countries. As was the case with many other expressions of United States global power, the Ca-

ribbean and Latin America were the act's launching pad. National City Bank was already the dominant financial house in Haiti and Cuba. Now, the Reserve Act allowed it to move against London banks in South America, first opening an office in Argentina, the historic domain of British capital, followed by scores of branches throughout Latin America. National City would soon become the world's largest bank. The Federal Reserve Act laid the foundation for a new kind of financial imperialism, much more sophisticated and all-encompassing than the gunboat-dollar diplomacy that both Theodore Roosevelt and Woodrow Wilson complained about. See Peter James Hudson, *Bankers and Empire: How Wall Street Colonized the Caribbean* (2017).

3. Enrique Krauze, "The April Invasion of Veracruz," *New York Times*, April 20, 2014; James McCaffrey, *Army of Manifest Destiny: The American Soldier in the Mexican War, 1846–1848* (1994), p. 170.

4. "Daniels Answers Angry Refugees," *Chicago Daily Tribune*, May 8, 1914.

5. Robert Vitalis, *America's Kingdom: Mythmaking on the Saudi Oil Frontier* (2006)

6. Ray Stannard Barker, *Woodrow Wilson: Life and Letters*, v. 6 (1927), pp. 57–60.

7. *Congressional Record*, vol. li, pt. xvii (1914), pp. 522–23, 9096.

8. "The Key to President Wilson's Mexican Policy," *The Literary Digest*, May 30, 1914.

9. "T. R. Flays Wilson as Traitor to U.S.," *New-York Tribune*, January 25, 1914.

10. Edward Haley, *Revolution and Intervention: The Diplomacy of Taft and Wilson With Mexico, 1910–1917* (1970), p. 122.

11. For Ludlow: Adjutant-General's Office, Colorado, *The Military Occupation of the Coal Strike Zone of Colorado* (1914). For massacre as the culmination of a cycle of Western militancy: Howard Zinn, *The Politics of History* (1970), pp. 79–101. A more recent account is Scott Martelle, *Blood Passion: The Ludlow Massacre and the Class War in the American West* (2008).

12. *Congressional Record*, vol. li, pt. xvii (1914), p. 7454.

13. Wilson's most generous contributor and longtime patron was the patrician Cleveland Hoadley Dodge, the second-generation heir to the copper mining and smelting company, Phelps Dodge, with interests throughout the Western states and in Mexico. Cleveland had some early influence in Wilson's tilt toward Carranza, but his lobbying was gentle, and by late 1913, Wilson was making his own decisions on Mexico. Robert Daniel, "The Friendship of Woodrow Wilson and Cleveland H. Dodge," *Mid-America: An Historical Quarterly*, v. 18 (1961).

14. *Congressional Record*, vol. li, pt. ix (1914), p. 9097.

15. Domicio de Gama, Romulo Sebastian Naón, and Eduardo Suarez-Mujica to William Jennings Bryan, April 25, 1914, *Wilson Papers*, v. 29, pp. 505–6.

16. Rafael Alducin, *La revolución constitucionalista, los Estados Unidos y el "ABC"* (1916), p. 145; Alexander Waller Knott, "The Pan-American Policy of Woodrow Wilson," PhD thesis, University of Colorado (1968), chapter 2, details the negotiations leading to Chile's offer to mediate; Berta Ulloa, *La Revolución Intervenida: Relaciones Diplomáticas Entre México Y Estados Unidos (1910–1914)*, (1971), p. 188.

17. Germany offered to bankroll a new revolt to restore Huerta to power, but Huerta would soon die of cirrhosis. George Rausch, "The Exile and Death of Victoriano Huerta," *The Hispanic American Historical Review*, v. 42 (1962).

18. *The Public Papers of Woodrow Wilson*, v. 3, p. 409. The quote is from *The Intimate Papers of Colonel House*, v. 4 (1928), p. 2, an interpretive paraphrasing of House's diaries, "arranged as a narrative" by Charles Seymour. Also: Lester Woolsey, "The Personal Diplomacy of Colonel House," *The American Journal of International Law*, v. 21 (1927), pp. 706–15.

19. James Slayden, "The A.B.C. Mediation," *The American Journal of International Law*, v. 9 (1915); Carnegie to Wilson, received at the White House, September 26, 1914, Wilson Papers, Library of Congress.

20. For a sympathetic account of Wilson's transformation: Arthur S. Link, *Woodrow Wilson and the Progressive Era, 1910–1917* (1954). More critical accounts are found in Gabriel Kolko, *The Triumph of Conservatism* (1963); James Weinstein, *The Corporate Ideal in the Liberal State, 1900–1918* (1968).

21. A detailed summary of the compensation: "Haiti's 'Double Debt,'" *New York Times*, May 24, 2022.

22. Kendrick Clements, "Woodrow Wilson and World War I," *Presidential Studies Quarterly*, v. 34 (2004).

23. For a summary of Carranza's position: "The Secretary of Foreign Relations of the de facto Government of Mexico to the Secretary of State," May 22, 1966, *Foreign Relations of the United States*, https://history.state.gov/historicaldocuments/frus1916/d714.

24. Linda Hall and Don Coerver, "Woodrow Wilson, Public Opinion, and the Punitive Expedition," *New Mexico Historical Review*, v. 72 (1997); Charles Harris and Louis Sadler, *The Great Call-Up: The Guard, the Border, and the Mexican Revolution* (2015); Friedrich Katz, "Pancho Villa and the Attack on Columbus, New Mexico," *American Historical Review*, v. 83 (1978).

25. In early 1917, the British government intercepted and decrypted a telegram sent by the German Foreign Office to Carranza's government suggesting an alliance. "Make war together, make peace together," and Berlin will help you "reconquer the lost territory in Texas, New Mexico, and Arizona." London passed the intercept on to Wilson, who made the cable available to the press. "Zimmermann Telegram," 1917, National Archives, Record Group 59; Harris and Sadler, *The Great Call-Up*, p. 315.

26. Charles W. Hackett, "How Plans for a Pan-American League of Nations Miscarried," *Current History*, v. 27, n. 4 (1928).

27. Ruy Barbosa, "*Discursos na assembléia provincial da Bahia*," in *Obras Completas*, v. 5 (1983) pp. 31–32; Ruy Barbosa, "A Grande Guerra," in *Obras Completas*, v. 44 (1988). On Latin America and World War I: Percy Alvin Martin, *Latin America and the War* (1925); Emily Rosenberg, "World War I and 'Continental Solidarity,'" *The Americas*, v. 31 (1975); Stepfan Rinke, *Latin America and the First World War* (2017).

28. *Information Annual* (1917), p. 128.

29. "The Secretary of State to the Ambassador in Mexico," April 21, 1917, and "The Ambassador in Mexico to the Secretary of State," April 27, 1917, *Papers Related to the Foreign Relations of the United States, 1917*, supplement 1, "The World War" (1931), pp. 261, 265.

30. This quotation comes not from Wilson but from a Republican speaker of the house, Frederick Huntington Gillett, during a period when Carranza was trying to influence the postwar peace talks, a topic addressed below. In *The Independent*, June 28, 1919. Also: Christy Thornton, *Revolution in Development*, p. 22, for a British Foreign Office staffer also calling Mexico a "plague spot."

Chapter 31: Monroe Doctrine of the Future

1. "The Reminiscences of Walter Lippmann," Columbia University Oral History Collection, pt. 2, n. 118, p. 89. For renewed interest in the League of Nations: Susan Pedersen, "Back to the League of Nations," *American Historical Review*, v. 112 (2007), pp. 1091–117; Adam Tooze, *Wages of Destruction* (2006); Margaret MacMillan, *Peacemakers* (2001); Erez Manela, *The Wilsonian Moment* (2007).

2. Examples of calls for reform of U.S. Latin American policy: Hiram Bingham, *The Monroe Doctrine, An Obsolete Shibboleth* (1915); Leo Rowe, "Misconceptions and Limitations of the Monroe Doctrine," *Proceedings of the American Society of International Law* (1914); Charles Sherrill, *Modernizing the Monroe Doctrine* (1916); John Barrett, "A Pan-American Policy: The Monroe Doctrine Modernized," *The Annals of the American Academy of Political and Social Science* (1914). Herbert Croly, an influential progressive intellectual, wanted a renewed foreign policy built around "a stable American international system."

3. Alejandro Alvarez, *The Monroe Doctrine* (1924), p. 8; Alberto del Solar, *La doctrina de Monroe y la América Latina* (1898), p. 13.

4. Cristián Guerrero Yoacham, *Las Conferencias del Niágara Falls* (1966), p. 24; Pérez Triana, "A Manifest to the Peoples of America," in *The Pan-American Financial Conference of 1915* (1915), p. 132.

5. For "belittle": *Papers Relating to the Foreign Relations of the United States, With the Annual Message of the President Transmitted to Congress December 3, 1912* (1919), pp. 1–2. For Pérez Triana: Jane Rausch, "Santiago Pérez Triana and the Pan-Americanization of the Monroe Doctrine," *Historia y Sociedad* v. 35 (2018), pp. 223–40.

6. "Noted South American Diplomat on Monroe Doctrine of the Future," *New York Times*, December 13, 1914.

7. Charles Seymour, *The Intimate Papers of Colonel House*, v. 1 (1926), p. 206.

8. "Latin America and the War," *The Financial Review of Reviews*, March 1915, p. 4.

9. *Official Proceedings of the Twenty-First Annual Session of the Trans-Mississippi Commercial Congress* (1910), pp. 114–16; Arthur Link, *The Papers of Woodrow Wilson*, v. 28 (1913), p. 491; Samuel Flagg Bemis, *The Latin American Policy of the United States* (1943).

10. Percy Alvin Martin, *Latin America and the War* (1925), p. 22; Fredrick Pike, *Freedom or Reform in Latin America* (1963); W. R. Sater, *Chile and the United States* (1990); Fredrick Pike, *Chile and the United States* (1963); Gilderhus, *Pan-American Visions: Woodrow Wilson in the Western Hemisphere* (1986).

11. Martin, *Latin America and the War*, p. 22; Link, *The Papers of Woodrow Wilson*, v. 62, p. 403.

12. Gilderhus, *Pan American Visions*, pp. 134–36.

13. The idea that the Monroe Doctrine had evolved from unilateral edict to universal law, from a principle of domination to one defending sovereign equality, was shared by Latin American and U.S. jurists. For example: James Garner, "The Monroe Doctrine," *The Women Citizen*, September 18, 1920, pp. 430–31.

14. "Wilson Praised and Condemned in Senate Views," *New-York Tribune*, January 23, 1917; John Milton Cooper, *The Warrior and the Priest* (1985), p. 327.

15. There is a relationship between constitutional and Monroe-Doctrine originalism, and Christian nationalists were especially fond of the doctrine. Mary Baker Eddy, the leader of the increasingly popular First Church of Christ, Scientist, didn't believe in the Trinity. But she did, as she told *The Boston Globe* when asked in 1905 to comment on Theodore Roosevelt's role in arbitrating peace between Russia and Japan, "believe strictly in the Monroe doctrine, in our Constitution, and in the laws of God."

Chapter 32: Subsoil Socialism

1. John Tutino, *Making a New World: Founding Capitalism in the Bajío and Spanish North America* (2011).

2. For context: Hilarion Noel Branch, *The Mexican Constitution of 1917 Compared with the Constitution of 1857* (1917); Eberhardt Victor Niemeyer, *Revolution at Querétaro: The Mexican Constitutional Convention of 1916–1917* (1974).

3. Alfonso Sánchez Arteche, *Molina Enríquez: La Herencia de un Reformador* (1990). For Colombia's 1913 petroleum law: Fred J. Rippy, *The Capitalists and Colombia* (1931).

4. I'm thankful to Mariana Díaz Chalela for pointing out that the expansion of social rights in Latin America was less an emulation of Mexico than it was a dialogue with Mexico, and that other countries in turn influenced how Mexico came to interpret Article 27.

5. Andrés Molina Enríquez, "El Artículo 27 de la Constitución Federal," *Boletín de la Secretaria de Gobernación* (September 1922). Lorenzo Meyer Cosio, *Mexico y los Estados Unidos en el Conflicto Petrolero, 1917–1942* (1968), for the international context of article 27. Charles Johnson, "Two Mexicos," *Atlantic Monthly*, v. 126 (1920), wrote: "The old legal doctrine of the Crown's title to all the land has been rephrased in Article 27, to meet modern Republican conditions." For Díaz's efforts to create a "modern" property-rights regime: Stephen Haber, Armando Razo, and Noel Maurer, *The Politics of Property Rights* (2003).

6. Lansing to Parker, January 22, 1917, Albert Fall Papers, The Huntington Library.

7. Raoul E. Desvernine, *Claims against Mexico* (1921), pp. 51–53; Ira Jewell Williams, "Confiscation of Private Property of Foreigners under Color of a Changed Constitution," *American Bar Association Journal*, v. 5 (1919), pp. 152–62.

8. Coates, *Legalist Empire*, p. 119.

9. Secretaría de Relaciones Exteriores (Mexico) and Department of State (United States), *The Mexican Oil Controversy as Told in Diplomatic Correspondence Between United States and Mexico* (1920).

10. Donald Carl Baldridge, "Mexican Petroleum and United States–Mexican Relations, 1919–1923," PhD thesis, University of Arizona (1971); Philip Lowry, "The Mexican Policy of Woodrow Wilson," PhD thesis, Yale University (1949), pp. 187–88; Bernard Baruch, "A Few Kind Words for Uncle Sam," *Saturday Evening Post*, June 12, 1948. See also Linda Hall, *Oil, Banks, and Politics: The United States and Postrevolutionary Mexico* (2010).

11. For Buckley's role as liaison between the Catholic right in Mexico and its counterpart in the United States: David Bailey, *Vivo Cristo Rey! The Cristero Rebellion and the Church-State Conflict in Mexico* (1974), pp. 120–34. Buckley lobbied and fundraised on behalf of the Liga Nacional Defensora de la Libertad Religiosa, a proto-Falangist Catholic effort to install a Catholic conservative government that would restore the power of the landed class and foreign investors. The oil companies also founded an "independent" University of California think tank, housed on the Berkeley campus and stocked with political scientists and lawyers handpicked by the petroleum industry. The Doheny Research Foundation was chaired by a professor of international law, George Winfield Scott, a descendent of General Winfield Scott, who had helped carry out Indian Removal and led the war against Mexico in 1846. Oil interests also founded an action group called the Association for the Protection of American Rights in Mexico, headed by none other than William F. Buckley Sr. The foundation's scholars confirmed that Article 27 was heresy. The association disseminated that opinion, beating the drum for a more aggressive Mexican policy. *The University of California Chronicle*, v. 20 (1918), p. 271. United States Congress, Senate Committee on Foreign Relations, Investigation of Mexican Affairs (1920) provides examples of business opinion that Article 27 stood in violation of U.S. law.

12. Investigation of Mexican Affairs: Hearings before a Subcommittee of the Committee on Foreign Relations, United States Senate, Sixty-sixth Congress (1919), p. 829.

13. Buckley remark on Bolshevism coming from Mexico is summation of intelligence he received from a Mexican source. "Report from: No. 16," "Source: Pedro del Villar," November 4, 1919, Folder 177, William Buckley Sr. Papers, University of Texas; Juan Gómez-Quiñones, "Plan de San Diego Re-

viewed," *Aztlán*, v. 1 (1970), pp. 124–32; Benjamin Johnson, "The Plan de San Diego Uprising and the Making of the Modern Texas-Mexican Borderlands," in Samuel Truett and Elliott Young, eds., *Continental Crossroads: Remapping U.S.-Mexico Borderlands History* (2004); James Sandos, *Rebellion in the Borderlands: Anarchism and the Plan of San Diego 1904–1923* (1992). For Hanson and Johnson: Alfredo Aguilar, "Uprooted: African Americans in Mexico," in Toyin Falola and Cacee Hoyer, eds., *Human Rights, Race, and Resistance in Africa and the African Diaspora* (2017). Also on Johnson, the indispensable Gerald Horne, *Black and Brown: African Americans and the Mexican Revolution, 1910–1920* (2005); William Hanson to Judge Kearful, October 11, 1919, Folder 177, William Buckley Sr. Papers; Claudio Lomnitz, *The Return of Comrade Ricardo Flores Magón* (2014), p. 450. Private police working for the mining company Phelps Dodge in the Arizona borderland towns of Bisbee and Jerome rounded up thousands of strikers and shipped them to the middle of the desert in cattle cars. Scores of others were killed. Rumors circulated that Woodrow Wilson himself had approved of the deportations—or "kidnappings," as labor leaders called them—since Cleveland Dodge was his good friend and most generous patron. In a letter begging Wilson for help in stopping the deportations, workers made mention of this relationship. "Are we to assume that Phelps Dodge interests," they asked, "are superior to the principles of democracy?" An indignant Wilson thought such a question "unjust and offensive" but did nothing to help the deportees. For Wilson's relationship with Dodge: James Byrkit, *Forging the Copper Collar* (2016), p. 227; *Woodrow Wilson: Life and Letters*, v. 7 (1939), p. 208. Buckley's Texas Ranger ally was William Hanson: John Weber, *William Hanson and the Texas–Mexico Border* (2024), details Buckley's relationship with Hanson and their ongoing efforts to spark a counterrevolution in Mexico.

14. Theressa Runstedtler, *Jake Johnson, Rebel Sojourner* (2012), p. 229; *Woodrow Wilson: Life and Letters*, v. 6 (1937), p. 447; Hanson to Kearful, October 11, 1919, folder 177, William Buckley Sr. Papers, University of Texas, Austin.

Chapter 33: Bolívar Dreamt

1. Christy Thornton, "'Our Balkan Peninsula': The Mexican Question in the League of Nations Debate," *Diplomatic History*, v. 46 (2022).

2. Thornton, "'Our Balkan Peninsula,'" p. 249; "GOP Gropes in Alarm for Wilson's Aims," *Chicago Daily Tribune*, February 3, 1919.

3. "Monroe Doctrine Guarded," *Cincinnati Enquirer*, February 5, 1919.

4. Thornton, *Revolution in Development* (2021), p. 23. For Colonel House's influence in this, see his Diaries, v. 7, ser. II, pp. 113–14, 394, House Papers, Yale University.

5. The National Archives, Kew, UK, "The Monroe Doctrine and the League of Nations," Foreign Office 608/174.

6. David Hunter Miller, *The Drafting of the Covenant*, v. 2 (1928), p. 369.

7. Thomas W. Burkman, *Japan and the League of Nations* (2008), p 32.

8. Just as medieval Spain was interested in knowing the varieties of humans it came to rule over in the New World, the United States, on the threshold of global power, convened the Inquiry in 1918. Reporting to Colonel House, the staff of the Inquiry was to do a thorough racial profile of every area of the globe. In Latin America, researchers were to document "the distribution of the Indian tribes at the time of the Conquest and to put into synoptical statements an account of their civilization and characteristics." They would also "trace out the subsequent immigration and the mingling of races with a view to ascertaining the present complexion of the inhabitants of the country. . . . This ethnographic study is to serve as a basis for the interpretation of the history of the peoples on racial lines." The information was to be cross-referenced with other regions and recorded on "card stock of different color" for easy reference. To think that "race" could be frozen in time and its deduced

political importance summarized on index cards resembled earlier efforts by Spanish scribes to compile lists of names used to describe myriad forms of miscegenation. Yet the work of the Inquiry was of a rising power about to inherit the earth, wanting to know what it was getting, what kind of people came with it. For the classification scheme: National Archives, RG 256, Records of the American Commission to Negotiate; Peace Special Reports and Studies Inquiry Document #978 "Appendix to Vital Issues in Relation to the Peace Conference, n.d." Same citation for the ethnographic instructions, in a document titled "General Statement Regarding Instructions Concerning Political Boundaries, Population, Ethnography, and History of Exploration." For the other quotations by Stabler regarding the difficulty of organizing Latin Americans, see the various memos in Frank Lyon Papers in the Manuscripts and Archives Collection at Yale University, MS 656, serial number 1, box 12, folder 445. Also: Gilderhus, *Pan American Visions*, v. 146, pp. 152–53.

9. "To Oppose Alien Rights in Mexico," *New York Times*, January 23, 1919. A British diplomat summed up the Mexican mission as to argue "(1) that no nation shall interfere with another country, even where property rights of its own citizens are concerned. (2) That a Govt. by altering its constitution can legally take over any properties of which it has need"; FO 9479/127, Folio 163: February 24, 1919, The National Archives, Kew, UK.

10. For Mexico's active, though unofficial involvement in the Paris talks, see Thornton, "Our Balkan Peninsula." Also: Michael Streeter, *Central America and the Treaty of Versailles* (2010), pp. 133.

11. *The Intimate Papers of Colonel House* (1928), p. 25.

12. Alan McPherson, Yannick Wehrli, eds., *Beyond Geopolitics: New Histories of Latin America at the League of Nations* (2015); Edwards, Don Agustin, "Latin America and the League of Nations," *Journal of the Royal Institute of International Affairs*, v. 8 (1929); Warren Kelchner, *Latin American Relations with the League of Nations* (1929).

13. Schmitt rejected Latin America's more idealistic interpretation of Monroe, believing that efforts to turn the territorial doctrine into an abstract "world doctrine"—what Schmitt called a *weltmonroedoktrin*—would transform a stabilizing legal framework that recognized the reality of political sovereignty rooted in territory into a destabilizing "pan interventionist" crusade with "humanist pretensions." George Schwab, "Contextualizing Carl Schmitt's Concept of Grossraum," *History of European Ideas*, v. 19 (1994); Hjalmar Falk, "Carl Schmitt and the Challenges of Interwar Internationalism," *Global Intellectual History*, v. 7 (2022); Fred J. Rippy, *The Capitalists and Colombia* (1931); Marcelo Bucheli, "Negotiating under the Monroe Doctrine: Weetman Pearson and the Origins of U.S. Control of Colombian Oil," *The Business History Review*, v. 82 (2008).

14. J. W. Garner, "The Monroe Doctrine," *The Women Citizen*, September 18, 1920. Other critics feared the wording of Article 21 relegated the Monroe Doctrine to just another "regional understanding" and diluted what was exceptional about the United States. Other critics linked "pan-Latinism" to Bolshevism and the IWW. Carranza wanted to "put the Saxon in his place," said William Gates; in *United States Congressional Serial Set*, "Investigation of Mexican Affairs, Preliminary Report and Hearings of the Committee on Foreign Relations United States Senate," v. 2 (1920), p. 2844.

15. The prominent role the "Monroe Doctrine" had in the United States Senate's refusal to approve the League of Nations, see Thornton, "Our Balkan Peninsula."

16. M. de Oliveira Lima, "Pan Americanism and the League of Nations," *Hispanic American Historical Review*, v. 4 (1921), p. 242; Enrique Gil, *Evolución del Panamericanismo* (1933).

Chapter 34: Death and the Salesmen

1. League of Nations, *Committee on the Composition of the Council . . .* (1926), p. 156; "Suggests Entente by US with League: Mello-Franco Urges Cooperation for Arms Parley," *New York Times*, December 11, 1925.

2. Percy Alvin Martin, *Latin America and the War* (1925). Then, in 1926, at the centenary anniversary of the Congress of Panama (which also served as a continental memorial for Woodrow Wilson, who had died three years earlier), Latin American delegates put forth yet another tender for an American League of Nations, "which shall conform to the Pan-American concepts of the Congress of Bolívar." Again, the United States scotched the idea, saying that the gathering was called to celebrate Bolívar, and its delegates had no power to vote on such motions.

3. For the politics of arms sales in the immediate run up to World War II: John Knape, "Anglo-American Rivalry in Post-War Latin America," *Ibero-Amerikanisches Archiv*, v. 15 (1989), pp. 319–50.

4. Chuck Acree, "Waco Warplanes of Latin America," *The Latin American Aviation Historical Society*, March 6, 2019; Raymond Brandly, *WACO: "Ask Any Pilot"* (1979), pp. 119, 125.

5. Herbert Von Rauch, "A South American Air War," *Air Enthusiast*, v. 26 (December 1984–March 1985), pp. 3–4.

6. H. C. Engelbrecht, *One Hell of a Business* (1934); Philip Noel Baker, *The Private Manufacture of Armaments* (1936); and W. H. Williams, *Who's Who in Arms* (1935).

7. For the Colombian figure, see the dispatch sent by Consul Jefferson Caffery to the Secretary of State on January 16, 1929, https://web.archive.org/web/20070301194908/http://www.icdc.com/~paulwolf /colombia/caffery16jan1929.jpg. For more information, see the collection of documents and photographs compiled by of Kevin Coleman on the 1928 massacre: https://kevincoleman.org/the-1928 -massacre-of-banana-workers/. A fictionalized account of the Guayaquil massacre that draws on historical sources: Joaquín Gallegos Lara, *Las cruces sobre el agua* (1946).

8. "Fascism on Parade," *Newsweek*, May 27, 1933; "Bitter Fight in Chilean Politics," *Cincinnati Enquirer*, November 5, 1933; *The Atlantic Constitution*, May 22, 1937. "Chile Nabs 10 Nazis for Hurling Tear Gas Bombs," *Chicago Daily Tribune*, May 23, 1937. For details on the split between the Falangists and the "Nacistas": Sandra McGee Deutsch, *Las Derechas: The Extreme Right in Argentina, Brazil, and Chile, 1890–1939* (1999), p. 183.

9. Jayne Spencer, "Oil, Politics, and Economic Nationalism in Bolivia, 1899– 1942," PhD thesis, University of California Los Angeles (1996), p. 67. Spencer cites U.S. diplomat Jesse Cottrell writing to Secretary of State Frank Kellogg on January 2, 1925.

10. The League of Nations, *Report of the League of Nations Commission on the Chaco Dispute* (1934), pp. 16–17.

11. Agnes S. Waddell, "Unsettled Boundary Disputes in Latin America," *Foreign Policy Association, Information Service*, v. 5 (1930), pp. 483–90. Another account of the boundary issue: Cecilio Báez, *Historia diplomática del Paraguay*, 2 vols. (1931–1932).

12. Leslie Rout, *Politics of the Chaco Peace Conference* (1966).

13. Georg von Rauch, "The Green Hell Air War," *Air Enthusiast Quarterly*, v. 2 (1976); Antonio Luis Sapienza, *The Chaco Air War 1932–35: The First Modern Air War in Latin America* (2018); Thomas Wewege-Smith, *Gran Chaco Adventures: The Thrilling and Amazing Adventures of a Bolivian Air Caballero* (1937).

14. "Paraguay Will Recruit Cossacks for Chaco War," *New York Herald Tribune*, September 28, 1933.

15. Trifonio Delgado Gonzales, *Carne de cañón ¡ahora arde kollitas!: diario de guerra 1932–1933*, cited in Bret Gustafson, *Bolivia in the Age of Gas*. In the United States, Louisiana senator Huey Long denounced Standard Oil on the floor of the Senate, accusing the company of forcing Bolivia to fight Paraguay to take the Chaco. Oil, or the desire for oil, was one of the causes of the war, though in a more complicated way than partisans like Long understood it to be. For the war and its context: Gustafson, *Bolivia in the Age of Gas* (2020); Spencer, "Oil, Politics, and Economic Nationalism in Bolivia"; Rout, *Politics of the Chaco Peace Conference*; Christine Mathias, "South America's Final

Frontier: Indigenous Leadership and the Long Conquest of the Gran Chaco, 1870–1955," PhD thesis, Yale University (2015); Bruce Farcau, *The Chaco War* (1991); Michel Gillette, "Huey Long and the Chaco War," *Louisiana History: The Journal of the Louisiana Historical Association*, v. 11, (1970); David Zook, *The Conduct of the Chaco War* (1960); William Garner, *The Chaco Dispute: A Study in Prestige Diplomacy* (1966). For the relationship of debt, weapons, and oil: Margaret Marsh, *The Bankers in Bolivia* (1928); Kendall Foss, "Horrible Chaco War Rages," *Washington Post*, May 27, 1932.

16. Dominic Tierney, *FDR and the Spanish Civil War* (2007); "Monroe Doctrine for the Orient," *New York Herald Tribune*, January 21, 1933.

17. "Fall Witnesses from Mexico," *New York Times*, March 15, 1924. For the footnote regarding Calles's call to Coolidge: Camile Nick Buford, "A Biography of Luis N. Morones, Mexican Labor and Political Leader," PhD thesis, Louisiana State University (1971), chapter 6, has a good account of the leaked documents and their use as leverage. Jürgen Buchenau, *Plutarco Elías Calles and the Mexican Revolution* (2006), p. 13.

18. United States Senate, Hearings Before a Subcommittee of the Committee on Foreign Relations, p. 19 (1935). The quotation is from Hull's questioner, Senator Hiram Johnson, paraphrasing Hull's position.

19. One can always hope: "Drilling in Search of Oil in Paraguay to Continue," *MercoPress*, September 16, 2022.

Chapter 35: To Montevideo

1. "Memorandum on Hull," April 12, 1934, Part I, General Correspondence (1915–1946), Box I:15, George Fort Milton Papers, Library of Congress.

2. Katherine Marino, *Feminism for the Americas* (2018).

3. Fred Hixon, "'Cord' Hull: Tennessee Statesman," *Current History*, v. 51 (1940), pp. 24–27. Steven Schulman, "The Lumber Industry of the Upper Cumberland River Valley," *Tennessee Historical Quarterly*, v. 32 (1973), pp. 255–64. For Free Hill in the footnote: The Klan was mostly suppressed between 1870 and 1873 in Tennessee but reemerged in 1874 for another wave of race terror, including the Trenton massacre and the Celina expulsion. For context: Everette Swinney, *Suppressing the Ku Klux Klan: The Enforcement of the Reconstruction Amendments, 1870–1874* (1966); Philip Hamer, *Tennessee, A History: 1675–1032*, v. 2 (1933); "Exodus of Blacks," *Daily True American*, November 2, 1878; "Tennessee Negroes Frightened from their Homes," November 2, 1878. Thanks to Carroll West and David Blight for context on this period and region.

4. "The Hulls of Tennessee," *Life*, March 18, 1940, provides a photo essay of the Hull clan; "Hull's Office Is Tendered to Stettinius," *Arizona Republic*, November 28, 1944.

5. Louis Pérez, *Army Politics in Cuba, 1898–1958* (1976), p. 15; Pérez, "Insurrection, Intervention, and the Transformation of Land Tenure Systems in Cuba, 1895–1902," *Hispanic American Historical Review*, v. 65 (1985), pp. 229–54; John Brooke, *Civil Report of Major-General John R. Brooke, U.S. Army, Military Governor, Island of Cuba* (1899), p. 7.

6. Ernest Kolowrat, *Hotchkiss: A Chronicle of an American School* (1998), p. 267.

7. Elsie Clews Parsons, "Injustice to Haitians," Letter to the Editor, *New York Times*, January 7, 1917.

8. Letter to the Editor, "Americans in Haiti," *New York Times*, October 18, 1920; Franklin Delano Roosevelt Library, hereafter FDRL, Family Business and Personal Papers, Box 14, Folder 35, "Memorandum on Haiti," 1922.

9. U.S. Senate, *Inquiry into Occupation and Administration of Haiti and Santo Domingo: Hearings Before a Select Committee on Haiti and Santo Domingo* . . . , v. 2 (1922).

10. Ernest Gruening, "Conquest of Haiti and Santo Domingo," *Current History*, v. 15 (1922); "U.S. Troops Attack Haitian Girls," *Chicago Defender*, May 15, 1920. Emily Greene Balch, *Occupied Haiti* (1927); "Anti-Haytien Immigration Meeting," *The Christian Recorder*, May 25, 1861; Laurent Du-Bois, *Haiti: The Aftershocks of History* (2012) has more on Marine sadism.

11. Hans Schmidt, *The United States Occupation of Haiti* (1922), p. 1667. Also: James Weldon Johnson, *Self-Determining Haiti: Four Articles Reprinted from "The Nation" Embodying a Report of an Investigation Made for the National Association for the Advancement of Colored People* (2015).

12. "Instructions to the Delegates to the Seventh International Conference of American States, November 10, 1933, *Foreign Relations of the United States*" (hereafter *FRUS*), 1933 "The American Republics," v. 4, available online. *FRUS* is the principle method the Office of the Historian of the State Department makes its documents public. Citation information entails the year the documents were issued, the title of the volume, and the volume number, in this case: "*FRUS*, 1933 'The American Republics,' v. 4." Most of the previously printed volumes are now online, found at the website of State's Office of the Historian. Except for one instance, where I cited documents from a volume not yet digitized, I will not include page numbers or the date the original volume was published (since this information is not available on State's website) but merely note that the document is available online. Also: Randall Bennett Woods, *The Roosevelt Foreign Policy Establishment and the 'Good Neighbor'* (1979), pp. 193–202, and *Nazis and Good Neighbors: The United States Campaign Against the Germans of Latin America in World War II* (2003), p. 78. For regionalism, see the chapter "'Baffled Virtue . . . Injured Innocence': The Western Hemisphere as Regional Role Model," in Kimball, *The Juggler*, pp. 107–25.

13. Sumner Welles, *Naboth's Vineyard: The Dominican Republic, 1844–1924*, v. 2 (1928), p. 937.

14. Already, under Herbert Hoover, business and political leaders began to recommend that the United States wind down its Caribbean militarism. For Roosevelt's efforts to acquire agricultural land in Haiti: Hans Schmidt, *The United States Occupation of Haiti, 1915–1934* (1971), pp. 111–13. The new U.S.-imposed constitution did allow foreigners to buy property, but FDR had little hand in drafting it, which was the work of the Office of the Solicitor of the State Department.

15. Joaquín Santaella, "Estudio del Proyecto del Ley," *Boletin del petróleo* (1919), p. 241; Ricardo Oneto, *El petroleo argentino y la soberania nacional* (1929), p. iv.

16. Carleton Beals, *Mexico: An Interpretation* (1923), pp. 142–44; Beals, "The Mexican Fascisti," *Current History*, v. 19 (1923).

17. *The Daily Washington Merry-Go-Round*, September 27, 1933; Frank Freidel, *Franklin D. Roosevelt: The Ordeal* (1952), p. 136.

18. Felix Frankfurter to Ernest Gruening, November 7, 1933, Ernest Gruening Collections, Series 1, Box 13, folder 182, University of Alaska, Fairbanks.

Chapter 36: The So-Called Right of Conquest

1. Earnest Gruening to Martha Gruening, May 17, 1934, Ernest Gruening Collections, Series 1, Box 13, folder 182, University of Alaska, Fairbanks.

2. For concerns on the Monroe Doctrine, see Hull to Daniels, September 28, 1933, and Daniels to Hull, September 29, 1933, *FRUS*, 1933, "The American Republics," v. 4, documents 20 and 21, available online. Ministry of Foreign Affairs of Cuba, Directorate of Information, *Guantanamo, Base Naval Yanqui de Crimenes y Provocaciones* (1970), p. 10. The remark concerning the "good

neighbors" comes from Cuban lawyer and diplomat Manuel Márquez Sterling, who fought in the Cuban liberation army and was part of a delegation that traveled to Washington to protest the imposition of the Platt Amendment.

3. *La Tribuna*, January 7, 1934.

4. Cited in Oren Schweitzer, "Revolutionary Socialism in Capitalist Democracy: The Socialist Party of Chile and Its Democratic Road to Socialism," BA Honors Thesis, Yale University (2023).

5. *The Daily Washington Merry-Go-Round*, January 30, 1934.

6. "Memorandum on Hull," April 12, 1934, General Correspondence (1915–1946), Box I:15, George Fort Milton Papers, Library of Congress.

7. "Tormentosa sesión en la Conferencia Panamericana," *La Prensa*, February 19, 1928.

8. For Puig's proposals: Christy Thornton's *Revolution in Development*, chapter 1.

9. Several treaties proposing to outlaw war were traveling around the world's diplomatic circuits, including the celebrated Kellogg-Briand Pact. Saavedra reminded the other delegates that the Uruguayan Juan Alberdi was the first to seriously propose the abolition of war in his 1870 book, *El Crimen de la Guerra*.

10. Philip Jessup, "The Saavedra Lamas Anti-War Draft Treaty," *American Journal of International Law*, v. 21 (January 1933), provides a good description of the relationship of Saavedra Lamas' treaty to Kellogg-Briand and the League of Nations preamble. The treaty is found in *Supplement to American Journal of International Law: Official Documents*, v. 28 (1934). Samuel Flagg Bemis, in *The Latin American Policy of the United States* (1967), p. 270, thought that FDR was trying to steal Saavedra Lamas's "thunder" by issuing a precocious appeal for all the nations of the world to sign a "nonaggression pact." Roosevelt thought that he, and not the Argentine, should be the "champion of non-intervention."

11. Cordell Hull Papers, Box 85, Folder 384, Manuscripts Division, Library of Congress, Washington, D.C., for Hull's understanding of the resolution.

12. Gruening to unnamed recipient, January 31, 1934, Ernest Gruening Collections, Series 1, Box 13, folder 182, University of Alaska, Fairbanks.

13. Ernest Gruening, "Our Era of 'Imperialism' Nears Its End," *New York Times*, June 10, 1934.

14. As to Gruening, Roosevelt put him in charge of an unwieldly office within the Department of the Interior called the Division of Territories and Island Possessions. What better place to put an anti-imperialist critic of the administration but in an office that administered the empire?

Chapter 37: Hell Bent for Reelection

1. Thomas Ferguson, "From Normalcy to New Deal," *International Organization*, v. 38 (1984); Karl Klare, in "Juridical Deradicalization of the Wagner Act and the Origins of Modern Legal Consciousness," *Minnesota Law Review*, v. 62 (1978), argues that the NLRA had the potential to radically restructure the labor market and with it "the premises and institutions of capitalist society." Instead, the Supreme Court and Congress targeted the act's most effective provisions, leaving it largely gutted.

2. Robert Hunter, *Violence and the Labor Movement* (1919), p. 280.

3. On the American Legion and G.I. bonus legislation: Taylor Branch, "Justice of Warriors," *New York Review of Books*, April 12, 2007.

4. Cited in Jonathan Katz, *Gangsters of Capitalism* (2022), p. 317, which also provides a good summation of the "Business Plot" coup attempt against FDR.

5. Pedro del Villar's November 1919 report on "Bolshevism," found in the William F. Buckley Sr. Papers at the University of Texas, notes the popularity of *The Protocols of the Elders of Zion* among U.S. businessmen in Mexico and Texas, and the general belief that the Warburg banking family was financing world Bolshevism.

6. Roger Shaw, "Fascism and the New Deal," *The North American Review*, v. 238 (1934); Katz, *Gangsters of Capitalism*, provides a good summation of the "Business Plot" coup attempt against FDR.

7. "Veterans Ask Miss Perkins Be Censured," *Washington Post*, August 13, 1934; Alan Taylor, "American Nazis in the 1930s—The German American Bund," *The Atlantic*, June 5, 2017; Arnie Bernstein, *Swastika Nation: Fritz Kuhn and the Rise and Fall of the German-American Bund* (2013), p. 98.

8. Shaw, "Fascism and the New Deal."

9. Thomas Ferguson, "From Normalcy to New Deal: Industrial Structure, Party Competition, and American Public Policy in the Great Depression" *International Organization*, v. 38 (1984).

10. "Hull Wins Warburg to Roosevelt," *New York Herald*, October 18, 1936; "William L. Clayton Backs Roosevelt," *New York Times*, October 12, 1936.

11. Frank Niess, *A Hemisphere to Itself* (1990); Hull, *Memoirs*, v. 1, p. 308; Hull estimated exports to "trade agreement countries" growing 41 percent, compared to 28.6 percent to "non-agreement countries," State Department, Foreign Trade of the United States, 1937, Roosevelt Papers, President's Secretary File (hereafter PSF), Departmental File, State, Box 70, FDRL. Judith Goldstein and Robert Gulotty, "America and Trade Liberalization: The Limits of Institutional Reform," *International Organization*, v. 68 (2014), pp. 263–95, argue against the importance of Hull's reciprocity treaties.

12. Thomas Ferguson and Joel Rogers, *Right Turn* (1987), p. 46. In 1938, according to Joan Raushenbush, *Look at Latin America* (1940), pp. 109–32, the lion's share of the nearly four billion dollars of U.S. investment in Latin America was found in Cuba, Mexico, Brazil, Colombia, Argentina, and Venezuela. For more on the treaty countries, see Nystrom, "Free Trade and the New Deal," p. 181. Also: Thomas Ferguson, "Industrial Conflict and the Coming of the New Deal: The Triumph of Multinational Liberalism in America," in *The Rise and Fall of the New Deal Order, 1930–1980*, eds., Steve Fraser and Gary Gerstle (1989), pp. 3–31; Louise Overacker, "Campaign Funds in the Presidential Election of 1936," *The American Political Science Review*, v. 31 (1936).

13. "Two Hundred Trade Leaders Back New Deal Aims," *New York Times*, October 29, 1936, cited in Ferguson, *Golden Rule: The Investment Theory of Party Competition and the Logic of Money-Driven Political Systems* (2011), p. 156.

14. Assorted undated files in PSF, Series 2: Confidential File, Box 136; "Good Neighbor League," PSF, FDRL.

15. "Negro Rallies Back Roosevelt," *New York Times*, September 22, 1936; There had existed an independent network of mutual aid "Good Neighbor Leagues" created by the Church of God's African American preacher Lightfoot Solomon Michaux. Michaux's league provided meat and potatoes to the Bonus Army March, a multiracial protest that had laid siege to Washington, D.C. After Hoover cracked down on the March, the Republican Michaux threw his support to Roosevelt and facilitated the fusion of Stanley High's reelection-focused Good Neighbor League with Michaux's preexisting organization rooted in Black churches and communities. Later, Michaux would ally with J. Edgar Hoover against Martin Luther King Jr. See: Lillian Ashcraft-Eason, "Elder Lightfoot Solomon Michaux: His Social and Political Interests and Influence," PhD dissertation, College of William and Mary (1975); Thomas T. Spencer, "The Good Neighbor League Colored Committee and the 1936 Democratic Presidential Campaign," *Journal of Negro History*, v. 63 (1978), pp. 307–8; Donald McCoy, "The Good Neighbor League and the Presidential Campaign of 1936," *Western Political Quarterly*, v. 13 (1960).

16. Cordell Hull, *Our Foreign Relations* (1936).

17. *The Collected Works of Langston Hughes* (2001), p. 252. In August 1936, Coughlin approached General Butler again, trying to recruit him to command a 260,000-man army to overthrow the Mexican government. It was bluster, and Butler once again reported the plot to the FBI.

18. Amy Lynn Spellacy, "Neighbors North and South: Literary Culture, Political Rhetoric and Inter-American Relations in the Era of the Good Neighbor Policy, 1928–1948," PhD thesis, University of Iowa (2006), pp. 41–49. For Roosevelt wanting to patent the phrase: "Memorandum for Files," from March 23, 1939; Folder: President's Personal File 3435, Good Neighbor League, Inc.; Good Neighbor League Memorandum (1936), Manifestoes and Publicity, Box #9, Correspondence File, Good Neighbor League Papers, Roosevelt Presidential Library.

19. For contrast, a total of twenty million people voted in the 1935 general election in the United Kingdom, with Conservatives handily beating Labour.

20. Roosevelt asked Hoover to have the Justice Department investigate "subversive activities in the United States" yet he made clear he didn't want a Wilson-type crusade against the left. Athan Theoharis, "The FBI's Stretching of Presidential Directives, 1936–1953," *Political Science Quarterly*, v. 91 (1976).

Chapter 38: The Faith of the Americas

1. Ernest May, "The Alliance for Progress in Historical Perspective," *Foreign Affairs*, v. 41 (1963).

2. Thomas Mathews, "Puerto Rican Politics and the New Deal," PhD dissertation, Columbia University (1957).

3. Robert Levine, *Father of the Poor: Vargas and His Era* (1998), p. 149.

4. When Vargas, on June 12, 1940, gave a fiery speech that the U.S. press interpreted as anti-U.S., Welles sent a note to FDR saying that aside from a few strong phrases meant for a domestic audience, the speech was unexceptional. He followed up by asking FDR to send a friendly telegram, with wording that would include the phrase "complete respect for the sovereignty of one another." Roosevelt did, writing Vargas that he was sure that the United States and Brazil would continue to cooperate "to further the ideals of our New World." Welles to Roosevelt, June 12, 1940 (document 732); Welles to Roosevelt, June 25, 1940 (document 738), which includes Draft of Telegram from President Roosevelt to the President of Brazil, in *FRUS*, 1940 "The American Republics," v. 5, and The Chargé in Chile (Frost) to the Secretary of State, March 2, 1938, *FRUS*, 1938 "The American Republics," v. 5, all available online.

5. The Secretary of State to the ambassador in Brazil (Caffery), November 12, 1937, *FRUS*, 1937 "The American Republics," v. 5, available online.

6. Cited in Kiran Klaus Patel, *The New Deal: A Global History* (2017), p. 240.

7. "Women Stage Buenos Aires Anti-War Rally," *Herald Tribune*, December 5, 1936.

8. FDR, *The Faith of the Americas* (1936).

9. The Ambassador in Argentina (Weddell) to the Secretary of State, May 8, 1936, *FRUS*, 1936, "The American Republics," v. 5, available online.

10. Arthur Nussbaum, *A Concise History of the Law of Nations* (1947), pp. 194, 274, 183.

11. Keri Lewis, "Negotiating for Nature: Conservation Diplomacy and the Convention on Nature Protection and Wildlife Preservation in the Western Hemisphere, 1929–1976," PhD dissertation, University of New Hampshire, Durham (2008). For more on how migrant birds figured into

international law and states' rights, see *The End of the Myth*. For Stevens: Doris Stevens Papers, Inter-American Commission of Women, Correspondence and office files. Buenos Aires conference: "Record of Main Events," 1937, MC 546, folder 63.6, Schlesinger Library, Radcliffe Institute, Harvard University. Also from Marino, *Feminism for the Americas*, p. 137. For Hull and Berle: "Record of Main Events," p. 5 for Hull and p. 3 for Berle.

12. Sumner Welles, *Seven Decisions That Shaped History* (1950), pp. 70–73; Welles to Roosevelt, October 6, 1937; Welles to Roosevelt, October 9, 1937; Welles to Roosevelt, October 26, 1937, all in President's Secretary File, Box 76, FDRL; "Draft Proposal for Concerted International Effort to Reach Common Agreement on the Principles of International Conduct Necessary to Maintain Peace," October 26, 1937, *Foreign Relations of the United States* Diplomatic Papers: 1937, v. 1; General (1954): pp. 668–70.

13. Daniels to Welles, October 26, 1936; Welles to Daniels, November 2, 1936, Special Correspondence (Sumner Welles, 1927–1936), both in Josephus Daniels Papers, Library of Congress. The historian Kirsten Weld's forthcoming book on the Spanish Civil War in Latin America is previewed here: "A Holy War: Latin America's Far Right," *Dissent* (Spring 2020), and "The Spanish Civil War and the Construction of a Reactionary Historical Consciousness in Augusto Pinochet's Chile," *Hispanic American Historical Review*, v. 98 (2018).

14. Carleton Beals, *The Coming Struggle for Latin America* (1940), pp. 159–60.

15. "Progress of 'Isms' in S. America," *The Philadelphia Inquirer*, April 1, 1939.

16. David Efron, "Latin America and the Fascist 'Holy Alliance,'" *The Annals of the American Academy of Political and Social Science*, v. 209 (1939); "The Brazilian Ranch Where Nazis Kept Slaves," BBC, January 21, 2014.

17. FDR paraphrased in Lourival Coutinho, *O General Góes Depõe* (1955), p. 363.

18. Nicholas Spykman, *America's Strategy in World Politics* (1942), p. 209.

19. Diane Vignemont and Phineas Rueckert, "How Exiles in Argentina Shaped France's Resistance to Nazi Occupation," *New Lines Magazine*, June 7, 2024; Michel Anfrol, "Les discours et messages du général de Gaulle, chef de la France Libre, à l'Amérique latine," in Maurice Vaïsse, ed., *De Gaulle et l'Amérique latine* (2017).

Chapter 39: Laboratory of the World

1. John Dwyer, *The Agrarian Dispute: The Expropriation of American-Owned Rural and in Postrevolutionary Mexico* (2006), p. 163.

2. "Miss Perkins' Aid to Aliens Is Censured: Small Businessmen Charge She Saved 700 'Deportables,'" *Washington Post*, July 29, 1940. Dwyer, *The Agrarian Dispute*, p. 181. Because the Department of Labor was in charge of border enforcement and immigration, a campaign against migrants was also a campaign against labor unions—and against women, or at least one particular woman deemed subversive: Frances Perkins, who bore the brunt of much anti–New Deal animus. Perkins constantly had the "inefficiency" of her department contrasted with the Department of Justice, and especially J. Edgar Hoover's FBI. "Veterans Ask Miss Perkins Be Censured," *Washington Post*, August 13, 1934.

3. Diary, July 24, 1917, Diaries, Roll 1; and Daniels to Wilson, August 2, 1915, Container No. 2; Correspondence Daniels to Wilson, 1911–1923, both in Josephus Daniels Papers, Library of Congress.

4. Tore Olsson writes that Daniels used what he learned in Mexico to later push agrarian reform in North Carolina. In *Agrarian Crossings: Reformers and the Remaking of the US and Mexican Countryside* (2020), p. 93; Lee Allan Craig, *Josephus Daniels: His Life & Times* (2013).

5. David Cronon, "American Catholics and Mexican Anticlericalism, 1933–1936," *The Mississippi Valley Historical Review*, v. 5 (1958).

6. "Address of President Coolidge at the Dinner of the United Press," April 25, 1927.

7. Memo for the President, March 26, 1937, President's Secretary Files, Departmental File, State, Box 70, FDRL.

8. Joseph Morrison, "Josephus Daniels—*Sympatico*," *Journal of Inter-American Studies*, v. 5 (1963), pp. 277–89.

9. "The Acting Secretary of State to the Ambassador in Mexico (Daniels)," December 12, 1936, and "The Ambassador in Mexico (Daniels) to the Secretary of State," December 16, 1936, *FRUS*, 1936 "The American Republics," v. 5, available online.

10. "Memorandum of Conversation, by the Chief of the Division of the American Republics (Duggan)," December 14, 1937, *FRUS*, 1937 "The American Republics," v. 5, available online.

11. "The Secretary of State to the Mexican Ambassador (Castillo Nájera)," August 22, 1938, *FRUS*, 1938 "The American Republics," v. 5, available online.

12. Morrison, "Josephus Daniels—*Sympatico*."

13. Edmund Cronon, *Good Neighbor Ambassador* (1953), p. 373.

14. Address by Ambassador Daniels at the Conference of American Consuls in Mexico City, October 9, 1937, Box 44, Series 3: Diplomatic Correspondence, PSF, FDRL; Daniels to Hull, September 3, 1938, folder six, Box 44, PSF, FDRL.

15. Numerous letters from Daniels to FDR on these matters in file 6, Box 44, Series 3, Diplomatic Correspondences. Also: Box 44, Series 3: Diplomatic Correspondence, PSF, FDRL.

16. "Memorandum of Conversation, by the Secretary of State," September 10, 1938, *FRUS*, 1938 "The American Republics," v. 5, available online.

17. Daniels to Roosevelt, March 39, 1938, along with addendum "Suggested Morgenthau Statement," in file 6, Box 44, Series 3, Diplomatic Correspondences, PSF, FDRL.

18. Bernard Baruch to Hull, March 29, 1938, Selected Correspondence, 1912–1945, v. 42, Bernard Baruch Papers, Seeley G. Mudd Library, Princeton University; Alan Knight, "The Rise and Fall of Cardenismo," in Leslie Bethell, ed., *Mexico Since Independence* (1991), p. 292. Also: Jean Meyer, *Le sinarnuisme: un fascisme mexicain?* (1977).

19. David Haglund, *Latin America and the Transformation of U.S. Strategic Thought, 1936–1940* (1984), p. 140; Henry Wallace, *The Price of Vision: The Diary of Henry Wallace* (1971), p. 188; Friedrich Katz et al., *Hitler sobre América Latina* (1968), p. 47.

20. Herbert S. Klein, "American Oil Companies in Latin America: The Bolivian Experience," *International Economic Affairs*, v. 18 (1964); "The Undersecretary of State (Welles) to the Representative of the Standard Oil Company of New Jersey (T. R. Armstrong)," November 15, 1937, *FRUS*, 1937 "The American Republics," v. 5, available online. Also: "Memorandum of Conversation, Secretary of State," April 11, 1939, cited above.

21. Josephus Daniels, *Shirt-Sleeve Diplomat* (1947), p. 231; "The Day in Washington," *Detroit Free Press*, December 8, 1938.

22. "Mexico Is Hailed by Cuban Throng," *New York Times*, June 13, 1938.

23. Daniels, *Shirt-Sleeve Diplomat*, p. 241.

24. Katz, et al., *Hitler sobre América Latina*, p. 46; Gabriel Jackson, *The Spanish Republic and the Civil War* (1967), p. 260; *The Daily Worker*, April 26, 1939.

25. Adam Hochschild, *Spain in Our Hearts* (2016), for Texaco selling Colombian oil directly to Franco.

26. Cronon, *Josephus Daniels in Mexico* (1960), p. 135.

27. Olsson, *Agrarian Crossings*, p. 96.

28. Shigeru Sugiyama, "Reluctant Neighbors: United States–Mexican Relations and the Failure of Cardenista Reforms, 1934–1948," PhD dissertation, University of California, Santa Barbara (1996), p. 93. Morgenthau at Treasury had concerns about the stepping up of nationalizations and land reform yet worked with his counterparts in Latin America to stabilize Latin American currency, and mitigate debt, in the hope of eventually cutting out Germany and Italy. Henry Morgenthau Jr. Papers. Series 3; Morgenthau Diaries, Conditions: Latin America: Mexico, FDRL.

Chapter 40: Battle for Latin America

1. "On the Margin of War," September 25, 1939, by Sumner Welles, Panama, Speech Files, Box 194, folder 13, Welles papers, FDRL. Also: "The Victory of Peace," by Sumner Welles, February 26, 1943, Speech Files, Box 196, folder 1, Welles papers, FDRL.

2. Gerald Haines, "Under the Eagle's Wing: The Franklin Roosevelt Administration Forges an American Hemisphere," *Diplomatic History*, v. 4 (1977); Burton Hendrick, *The Life and Letters of Walter H. Page*, v. 1 (1922), p. 204.

3. Some Latin American politicians liked to quote the French theorist Léon Duguit: "Property is not an untouchable and sacred right, but rather a right that is constantly evolving and that ought to adapt itself to the social necessities to which it responds." "Landed, capitalist, and inheritable property," Arturo Alessandri, president of Chile in the 1930s, said, quoting Duguit, is impossible to justify except by its "social use," unless it serves a "social function." Weimer Germany's 1919 Constitution was the second in the world, after Mexico's, to recognize the social function of private property. The third paragraph of Article 153 read: *Eigentum verpflichtet. Sein Gebrauch soll zugleich Dienst sein für das Gemeine Beste*: "Property obligates. Its use should at the same time be at the service of the common good." For Duguit: Matthew Mirow, "Origins of the Social Function of Property in Chile," *Fordham Law Review*, v. 80, (2011). For Duguit in Colombia: Helena Alviar García, "Leon Duguit's Influence in Colombia," in Günter Frankenberg, ed., *Order from Transfer: Comparative Constitutional Design and Legal Culture* (2013), p. 316.

4. Mary Elizabeth Speck, "Let There be Candy for Everyone: The Politics of Sugar in Cuba, 1902–1952," PhD dissertation, Stanford (2008); *El automóvil de Cuba*, v. 34 (1950), p. 45.

5. Thomas Weil, *Area Handbook for Chile* (1969), p. 129.

6. Some Latin American Communist parties got turned around by the Soviet Union's geopolitical pirouettes, especially after Moscow, desperate to buy time, signed a "nonaggression" pact with Hitler in August 1939. For the most part, these European diplomatic maneuvers mattered little for the region's oppositional politics, as Communists continued to focus their struggle against local Fascists. For Chile's Communist Party during this period: Richard Walter, *Politics and Urban Growth in Santiago, Chile* (2005), p. 230.

7. In 2005, a Berlin-based Chilean scholar, Victor Farías, published *Salvador Allende: antisemitismo y euthanasia*, arguing that his medical school 1933 thesis ("Higiene mental y delincuencia") reveals Allende to be a eugenicist. It is clear, though, that Allende, in his thesis, was summarizing the racist views of the Italian criminologist Cesare Lombroso, so to move beyond them. For a discussion of the controversy, see the prolegomena to the 2005 published version of Allende's thesis, by Joan Garcés, Juan Carlos Carbonell Mateu, and Pablo Oyarzun.

8. "Chile's Trade Need Utilized by Japan; Tokyo Buying Up, Apparently for Reich, Increased Supply of War Materials," *New York Times*, June 2, 1941.

9. Eric Carter, "Social Medicine and the International Expert Networks in Latin America, 1930–1945," *Global Public Health*, v. 14 (2019).

10. Joshua Frens-String, *Hungry for Revolution* (2021), p. 86.

11. Salvador Allende, *Obras Escogidas, 1933–1948* (1988), p. 273.

12. Nathaniel Davis, *The Last Two Years of Salvador Allende* (1985), p. 49.

13. Allende, in "Higiene mental y delincuencia," p. 115, quotes Mariano Ruiz-Funes García, *Endocrinología y criminalidad* (1929), p. 6. In turn, Ruiz-Funes is citing the French writer Hippolyte Taine, an influential historian and philosophical conservative who wrote in the wake of the Paris Commune.

14. Salvador Allende, *La Realidad Medico-Social Chilena* (1939), p. 42.

15. For comparison: Lukács, *The Destruction of Reason*, p. 730.

16. Jorge Mario Betancur Gómez, *Moscas de todos los colores* (2006), p. 84; Hernando Figueroa Salamanca, "Monseñor Miguel Ángel Builes, un político intransigente y escatológico (1925–1950)," *Anuario de Historia Regional y de las Fronteras*, v. 21 (2016).

17. Benjamin Schwartz, *American Counterinsurgent Doctrine* (1991), p. 71.

18. Cited in Bridget Wooding, *Needed but Unwanted* (2004), p. 21.

19. Eric Rooda, *The Dictator Next Door*, chapter 5 (1998). Allen Wells, *Tropical Zion: General Trujillo, FDR, and the Jews of Sosúa* (2009), p. 25.

20. Jeffrey Gould and Aldo Lauria-Santiago, *To Rise in Darkness* (2008), p. 230. For Argentina's 1919 pogrom against trade unionists, anarchists, and Jews: Victor Mirelman, "The Semana Trágica of 1919 and the Jews in Argentina," *Jewish Social Studies*, v. 37 (1975), p. 63; Federico Finchelstein, *The Ideological Origins of the Dirty War* (2014). Also: Sandra McGee Deutsch, *Las Derechas: The Extreme Right in Argentina, Brazil, and Chile, 1890–1939* (1999); Luis María Caterina, *La Liga Patriótica Argentina. Un grupo de presión frente a las convulsiones sociales de la década del '20* (1995).

21. Brazilian Integralists represented a less apocalyptic variety of antiliberal Catholicism; Daniel Silver, *Anti-Empire: Decolonial Interventions in Lusophone Literatures* (2018), p. 99.

22. John Ellis van Courtland, *Confines of Concept: American Strategy in World War II* (1988), p. 150.

23. Edward Fertik, "Steel and Sovereignty: The United States, Nationalism, and the Transformation of World Order, 1898–1941," PhD dissertation, Yale University (2018), p. 402.

24. Fertik, "Steel and Sovereignty." For how Berlin's aggressive trade offensive was bound up in U.S. efforts to blacklist German firms: Max Paul Friedman, "There Goes the Neighborhood: Blacklisting Germans in Latin America and the Evanescence of the Good Neighbor Policy," *Diplomatic History*, v. 27 (2003); John Mason Hart, *Empire and Revolution* (2006), p. 415.

Chapter 41: A People's War

1. The manifesto in original Spanish can be found in Gontran de Güemes, *Así se gestó la dictadura* (1956), pp. 125–27.

2. Graeme K. Howard, *America and a New World Order* (1940), pp. 80, 87–90.

3. Commerce Department memorandum on hemisphere defense, June 11, 1940, Harry Hopkins Papers, container 311, Latin American Affairs folder, FDRL.

4. John Bratzel and Leslie B. Rout, "FDR and the 'Secret Map,'" *The Wilson Quarterly*, v. 9 (1985); Fireside Chat, September 11, 1941, available at the UC Santa Barbara American Presidency Project, https://www.presidency.ucsb.edu/documents/fireside-chat-11. A short border war fought between Ecuador and Peru broke out in July 1941, along the Zarumilla River deep in the roadless Amazon, threatening, at this critical moment, to break Pan-American unity—except that both sides, Ecuador and Peru, appealed to Pan-Americanism to denounce the other side as would-be "conquerors." The fighting lasted only a few days, as provincial grievances withered in the heat of the world's looming horrors. A truce brokered by the United States and Brazil established a demilitarized zone over the disputed area.

5. FDRL, Isaiah Bowman to FDR, May 19, 1941, with attachment, "The Western Hemisphere: A Note on Atlantic Limits," PSF, Box 80. For more on Bowman: Neil Smith, *American Empire: Roosevelt's Geographer and the Prelude to Globalization* (2004); "Lesson in Geography," *Time*, July 17, 1941; Stimson diary, April 10, 1941, Henry L. Stimpson Papers, Yale University. For Bowman's importance in founding the field of International Relations: Smith, *Roosevelt's Geographer*. For "widest channel" theory: Vilhjalmur Stefansson, "What Is the Western Hemisphere?" *Foreign Affairs*, v. 19, n. 2 (1941). Also: Byron Fairchild, *Decision to Land United States Forces in Iceland* (1941).

6. Julius William Pratt, *Cordell Hull, 1933–44*, v. 13 (1964), p. 707.

7. Rebecca Herman, *Cooperating with the Colossus* (2022), p. 1.

8. Berle Diary, August 26, 1939, Box 210, Berle Papers, FDRL.

9. Stetson Conn and Byron Fairchild, *The Framework of Hemispheric Defense* (1989).

10. Stephen Rabe, *The Road to OPEC* (2011), p. 73.

11. Martin Brown, "Duel Below the Rio Grande," *New Masses*, October 12, 1943.

12. For what follows on Wallace, the Board of Economic Warfare, and the labor clauses: David Ernst and Victor Jew, eds., *Total War and the Law: The American Home Front in World War II* (2002), p. 166; Wallace and Blum, *The Price of Vision* (1973), p. 156; Document 5 of Folder 13 (258-272), Date: July 22 1943, "File on our Labor Clause Policy," Memo from RE Mathews, Office of the General Counsel to Morris Rosenthal, in US Board of Economic Warfare (BEW) Collection, 1942–1944, Columbia University, Rare Books and Manuscript Library; Document 2 of Folder 13, "Reasons for Labor Clauses," Memo from Ted (Kreps) to Morris Rosenthal, US Board of Economic Warfare (BEW) Collection, 1942–1944, Columbia University, Rare Books and Manuscript Library. Thanks to Josh Friends-String for sharing these files. Wallace's remarks on the postwar are reprinted in *Army and Navy Journal*, August 29, 1942. For a comprehensive account of the workings of the BEW: Torbjon Sirevag, *The Eclipse of the New Deal* (1985).

13. Henry Wallace and John Morton Blum, *The Price of Vision: The Diary of Henry A. Wallace, 1942–1946* (1973), p. 55. For the central role Latin America played in Wallace's politics: Edward and Frederick Schapsmeier, *Prophet in Politics* (1970).

14. "An Open Letter to Mr. Wallace," published in several newspapers, including the *New York Journal of Commerce*, *The Washington Post*, and the *Washington Times Herald*, paid for by the New York Coffee & Sugar Exchange, Inc., found in Folder 3: Coffee, US Board of Economic Warfare (BEW) Collection, 1942–1944, Columbia University, Rare Books and Manuscript Library. For complaints of Communist influence on the Board: Harvey J. Gunderson to W. L. Clayton, December 5, 1942, and W. L. Pierson to Jones, February 11, 1943, both in Jesse Jones Papers, Box 176, Library of Congress; Jesse Jones, *Fifty Billion Dollars: My Thirteen Years with the Reconstruction Finance Corporation* (1951), p. 425; Edward Schapsmeier, *Prophet in Politics* (1971), p. 45.

15. Jesse Stiller, *George Messersmith: Diplomat of Democracy* (1987), p. 193; Jones, *Fifty Billion Dollars*. For "Give Away Henry," *Ironwood Daily Globe*, March 13, 1943.

16. For the Cativi Massacre and its fallout: June Nash, *We Eat the Mines and the Mines Eat Us: Dependency and Exploitation in Bolivian Tin Mines* (1993); Herbert Klein, "Prelude to the Revolution," in J. Malloy and R. Thorn, eds., *Beyond the Revolution: Bolivia Since 1952* (1971); J. Knudson, "The Impact of the Catavi Mine Massacre of 1942," *The Americas*, v. 26 (1970); Martin Kyne's report was published as *Report to the Congress of Industrial Organizations on Labor Conditions in Bolivia* (1943); *British Documents on Foreign Affairs—Reports and Papers from the Foreign Office Confidential Print: From 1940 through 1945, Latin America*, Part III, Series D (1998), p. 114; "Trouble in Bolivia: The Truth about the Tin Workers," *Commonweal*, June 11, 1943; Henry Wallace, *The Price of Vision: The Diary of Henry A. Wallace* (1971), p. 156; Sergio Almaraz Paz, *El Poder Y la Caída: El Estaño en la Historia de Bolivia* (1967), p. 135. Wallace asked Paul Nitze, who for a time worked at the Board, to be part of the inquiry commission. Nitze at first agreed, but when he learned that Wallace wanted him to provide evidence that would help with the Board's fight against conservatives, he refused to participate. Paul H. Nitze Oral History Interviews, June 11 and June 17, 1975, Harry S. Truman Library, https://www.trumanlibrary.gov/library/oral-histories/nitzeph1.

17. S. Sándor John, *Bolivia's Radical Tradition* (2009), p. 91.

18. Wallace's Latin American tour: Culver and Hyde, *American Dreamer* (2001), pp. 297–300. For Wallace in Chile, Pavilack, p. 23; "Chilean Says Wallace Did Much for U.S.," *Baltimore Sun*, April 6, 1943. For the State Department's account of Wallace's tour, see the documents, starting with "Visit of the Vice President Henry A. Wallace to Some of the American Republics," in *FRUS*, 1943 "Diplomatic Papers," v. 5 pp. 55–75. For the footnote: "The Ambassador in Chile (Bowers) to the Acting Secretary of State," April 3, 1943, pp. 66–67.

19. J. Samuel Walker, *Henry A. Wallace and American Foreign Policy* (1976), p. 103; Wallace to Josephus Daniels, January 28, 1944; Wallace to Nelson Rockefeller, February 2, 1944, Henry Wallace Papers, University of Iowa.

20. Wallace to Nelson Rockefeller, February 2, 1944, Henry Wallace Papers, University of Iowa; Drew Pearson, "South America Sends Back Word Wallace Is Top Man There," *Washington Post*, May 16, 1943.

21. Becker, *The FBI in Latin America*, p. 114.

22. Walter Winchell reported that while Wallace was away in Latin America, the forces who wanted to "jilt" the vice president and drop him from the 1944 ticket began to organize against him. "Unlikely FDR Won't Run in '44," *The Knoxville Journal*, March 5, 1943.

23. Theodore Stallone, *The Political Economy of William L. Clayton* (1997).

24. Selected Papers of Will Clayton (1971), p. 67; Sirevag, *Eclipse of the New Deal*, pp. 298, 329; George Rothwell Brown, "Political Parade," *San Francisco Examiner*, March 3, 1943.

25. Wallace to Rockefeller, December 15, 1943, Henry Wallace Papers, Box 87, folder: Rockefeller, Nelson A. 1943–1945, FDRL.

Chapter 42: There Would Have Been Nothing

1. Forrest Davis, "What Really Happened at Tehran," *Saturday Evening Post*, May 13, 1944.

2. Christopher O'Sullivan, *Sumner Welles, Postwar Planning, and the Quest for a New World Order, 1937–1943* (2008) is indispensable on this issue. For Welles's early attention to Latin America, be-

fore even Hull's triumph at Montevideo, see in the Franklin Delano Roosevelt Library and Archives: "Welles to Roosevelt," April 6, 1933, and "Welles to Hull," April 7, 1933, both in Welles Papers, Box 149, Folder 1. For Welles's belief that the Western Hemisphere model could be exported elsewhere: "On the Margin of War," September 25, 1939, Welles Address to Foreign Ministers of the American Republics, Box 194, Folder 13; "An Association of Nations," July 22, 1941, Box 195, Folder 2, both in Welles papers, speech files. Also Sumner Welles, *The Time for Decision* (1944), pp. 374–83; "Draft Constitution of International Organization," July 14, 1943, FDRL.

3. Sumner Welles, Address at Arlington National Amphitheater, Memorial Day, 1942, in U.S. Office of War Information, "Toward New Horizons: The World Beyond the War" (1942).

4. Stimson's diary entries for March 29, April 27, and May 2, 1945, and transcript of Stimson's telephone conversation with John McCloy, May 8, 1945, in Stimson Papers, Yale University.

5. Stephen Schlesinger, *Act of Creation: The Founding of the United Nations* (2003), chapter 11.

6. Thomas Campbell, *Masquerade Peace: America's UN Policy, 1944–1945* (1973), pp. 165–75. Also: Cabot to Rockefeller, Memorandum on Unfavorable Factors in our Inter-American Relations, December 13, 1944, Lot Files, Box 9, RG 59, National Archives.

7. "San Francisco Greets Latins," *Atlanta Constitution*, April 22, 1945.

8. *Documents de la conférence des nations unies sur l'organisation internationale, San Francisco, 1945, Tome VII, Commission II Assemblée Générale* (1945), p. 58 for Lutz and p. 97 for Panama.

9. Alfred Edward Volpe, "Latin America at San Francisco," PhD dissertation, Stanford University (1950); *The United Nations Conference on International Organization, San Francisco, California, April 25 to June 26, 1945: Selected Documents* (1946), p. 645; John Houston, *The Role of the Latin American States in the Establishment and Practice of the United Nations* (1951).

10. "Conversation between Lic. Alfonso Garcia Robles, Assistant Director of Political Affairs and of the Diplomatic Service of the Ministry for Foreign Affairs, and Messrs. Bohan and Sanders," February 6, 1945, in *Foreign Relations of the United States: Diplomatic Papers*, v. 9, The American Republics, 1945 (1969), p. 92. Susan Waltz, "Universalizing Human Rights: The Role of Small States in the Construction of the Universal Declaration of Human Rights," *Human Rights Quarterly*, vol. 23 (2001). In 1948, the same year Mexico pushed to add this clause to the "right to marry" section of the Universal Declaration, the California Supreme Court struck down an antimiscegenation law that had prevented Andrea Pérez, the U.S.-born daughter of Mexican migrants, considered white, and Sylvester Davis, an African American man, from marrying. See Mark Brilliant, *The Color of America Has Changed* (2010), pp. 106–14. For how the Universal Declaration was shaped by a triangular consensus among Catholics, Marxists, and Liberals: Samuel Moyn, *Not Enough: Human Rights in an Unequal World* (2018).

11. Johannes Morsink, *The Universal Declaration of Human Rights* (1999), p. 131; John Humphrey, *Human Rights & the United Nations* (1984), p. 66. Daniel Ricardo Quiroga-Villamarín, "'An Atmosphere of Genuine Solidarity and Brotherhood': Hernán Santa-Cruz and a Forgotten Latin American Contribution to Social Rights," *Journal of the History of International Law*, v. 21 (2019), provides an excellent survey of the various ethical threads that came together in Santa Cruz's vision. Also, of course: Samuel Moyn, *Christian Human Rights* (2015) and *Not Enough: Human Rights in an Unequal World* (2019).

12. J. Tillapaugh, "Closed Hemisphere and Open World? The Dispute over Regional Security at the U.N. Conference, 1945," *Diplomatic History*, v. 2 (1978).

13. "U.S. to Invite Latins to Sign Defense Pact," *New York Herald Tribune*, May 16, 1945. For Article 52: Geoff Simons, *The United Nations: A Chronology of Conflict* (2016), p. 85.

14. The disproportionate influence of Latin America as a bloc was already on display at the 1944 Bretton Woods conference, where John Maynard Keynes complained that more than fourteen Latin

American nations had been invited to participate, a "pack of countries which know nothing of international finance." "The most monstrous monkey-house," he said, "ever assembled." For Keynes's remarks within their complex context: Eric Helleiner, *Forgotten Foundations of Bretton Woods* (2016). One of the first uses of the United Nations by the United States took place during the vote to create the state of Israel—a move not against the Soviet Union but against Great Britain, to make clear that Washington, not London, would be the senior partner in their Anglo "special relationship." The Truman administration overcame its initial reluctance to support calls to quickly create a Jewish state, breaking with London when it voted, on November 29, 1947, in favor of the partition of Palestine. (Great Britain abstained.) To ensure the vote went the way it wanted, the State Department relied on the Guatemalan diplomat Jorge García Granados to rally Latin America. García Granados, a defender of the doomed Spanish republic and advocate for the ostracization of Franco's Spain from the United Nations, thought that the Jewish kibbutzim might provide a model for how to justly organize the distribution of land in Guatemala. The CIA thought him a Communist and London believed him a Soviet "stooge," but García Granados did his work with alacrity. He helped deliver thirteen Latin American votes to pass the partition resolution. Five Latin American countries abstained, an outcome that some scholars believe Washington wanted so as to not appear to the world that it was rigging the count. No Latin American nation voted against moving forward with the founding of Israel. Jorge García Granados, *Así nació Israel* (1949); Ignacio Klich, "Latin America, the United States and the Birth of Israel: The Case of Somoza's Nicaragua," *Journal of Latin American Studies*, v. 20 (1988).

15. Richard Norton Smith, *On His Own Terms: A Life of Nelson Rockefeller* (2014).

16. *Biennial Report of the Chief of Staff of the United States Army to the Secretary of War* (1945), p. 6.

Chapter 43: Underdeveloped Economists

1. Jeffrey Gould, "'For an Organized Nicaragua': Somoza and the Labour Movement, 1944–1948," *Journal of Latin American Studies*, v. 19 (1987). Indispensable on this conjuncture: Leslie Bethell and Ian Roxborough, "Latin America between the Second World War and the Cold War: Some Reflections on the 1945–8 Conjuncture," *Journal of Latin American Studies*, v. 20 (1988), pp. 167–89.

2. Salvador Allende, "El socialismo chileno y su finalidad Americanista," in *Obras Escogidos, 1933–1948* (1988), p. 389.

3. "The Ambassador in the Dominican Republic (Butler) to the Secretary of State," October 4, 1946, *FRUS*, 1946, "The American Republics," v. 11, available online.

4. "Politica Internacional: Estatuto internacional de las Naciones Unidas," September 12, 1948, https://www.archivochile.com/S_Allende_UP/doc_de_sallende/SAde0065.pdf. For how the CIA's 1954 coup in Latin America radicalized Allende: Mark Hove, "The Arbenz Factor: Salvador Allende, U.S.-Chilean Relations, and the 1954 U.S. Intervention in Guatemala," *Diplomatic History*, v. 31 (2007).

5. "Memorandum by the Under Secretary of State for Economic Affairs," May 27, 1947, *FRUS*, 1947, "The British Commonwealth," Europe, v. 3, available online.

6. See interview in Bogotá's *El Tiempo* with U.S. Ambassador Beaulac, January 25, 1948. In general: Charles Maier, "The Politics of Productivity: Foundations of American International Economic Policy After World War II," *International Organization*, v. 31, n. 4 (1977), pp. 607–33.

7. Washington offered aid to all of Europe, including Soviet-occupied nations. Yet according to Scott Parrish and Mikhail Narinksy, "New Evidence on the Soviet Rejection of the Marshall Plan, 1947: Two Reports," Woodrow Wilson International Center for Scholars (1994), Moscow was damned if it participated in the Marshall Plan and damned if it didn't. If all of Europe, including the USSR and its

Eastern European allies, participated, Russia would be pulled into a global economy dominated by the United States. But if Moscow and the Eastern Bloc refused, then the Marshall Plan would bind Western Europe in an alliance apart from, and inevitably opposed to, Eastern Europe. After much internal debate, Moscow declined Marshall Plan funds. Gordon Gray, *Report to the President on Foreign Economic Policies* (1950), p. 60; Bohan to McClintock, January 29, 1945, *FRUS*, 1945, "The American Republics," v. 9, available online; United States, President's Materials Policy Commission, *Resources for Freedom*, v. 1 (1952), pp. 1–3, 171. Kofas specifically discussed an idea floated by the Truman White House called the "Clayton Plan" for Latin America, named after Assistant Secretary of State William Clayton. Clayton, who played a central role in designing the Marshall Plan, proposed nothing more than private investment in mining and agriculture. Jon Kofas, *Foreign Debt and Underdevelopment* (1996), p. 26.

8. *Conferência pronunciada no Clube Militar, no Rio de Janeiro, a 28 de abril de 1948* (1949).

9. For Simonsen as one of Brazil's most important industrial modernizers: Barbara Weinstein, *For Social Peace in Brazil: Industrialists and the Remaking of the Working Class in São Paulo, 1920–1964* (2000).

10. The ministry's statement is found among the documents under the heading "Interest of the United States in Brazilian Problems Involving Former Enemy Property and Persons," including the secretary of state to the embassy in Brazil, January 28, 1947, in *FRUS*, 1947, "The American Republics," v. 8, available online.

11. For Gomes: Stanley Hinton, "Brazil's International Economic Strategy, 1954–1960: Revival of the German Option," *Hispanic American Historical Review*, v. 66 (1986). Perón's brand of populism helped Cold War social scientists collapse Red Marxism and Brown Fascism into the single threat of illiberal "totalitarianism." Ernesto Semán, *Breve historia del antipopulismo: Los intentos por domesticar a la Argentina plebeya, de 1810 a Macri* (2021). Glenn Dorn, *The Truman Administration and Bolivia* (2015), details the increasing use the word *totalitarian*, often in relation to Peronist influence, to describe populism in general.

12. Prebisch wasn't the first to use the concepts "core," or, as Prebisch first put it, "cyclical center" and "periphery." Joseph Love, "Raul Prebisch and the Origins of the Doctrine of Unequal Exchange," *Latin American Economic Review*, v. 15 (1980); J. F. J. Toye and Richard Toye, "The Origins and Interpretation of the Prebisch-Singer Thesis," *History of Political Economy*, v. 35 (2003); Edgar Dosman, *The Life and Times of Raúl Prebisch, 1901–1986* (2008), p. 241. Also: Claudio Katz, *Dependency Theory After Fifty Years: The Continuing Relevance of Latin American Critical Thought* (2023).

13. Carlos Lleras Restrepo remarks at the National Press Club, June 13, 1969, found in U.S. Congress, House Committee on Foreign Affairs, *Hearings*, v. 3 (1969), pp. 123–24. Also: "Carlos Lleras Restrepo relata la jornada del nueve de abril," *El Tiempo*, April 8, 1973

14. Celso Furtado, "Raúl Prebisch, el gran heresiarca," *Revista de la CEPAL* (1978), p. 375.

15. Another Argentine economist, Rómulo Bogliolo, offered one of the first detailed refutations of Friedrich Hayek's influential 1944 *The Road to Serfdom*. See Bogliolo's *Socialismo, Libertad, Dirección: Réplica al Profesor Hayek* (1946).

16. Dependency theory: Sixteenth-century Catholic theologians anticipated dissident anticolonial arguments. If the empire *made* Spain—cobbled out of Iberia's multilingual Christian kingdoms—where did Spain, the imperial core, end and the imperial periphery begin? Did the Indies fulfill Spain, complete it with its blood-soaked gold and silver? Or did the flood of mineral wealth corrupt Spain, only to flow, after wrecking the peninsula's economy with inflation, into the hands of its Protestant enemies? "Conquered by you, the New World in its turn has conquered you," wrote Justus Lipsius, a Flemish Catholic philosopher, less than a century after the Conquest of Mexico.

17. Margarita Fajardo, *The World That Latin America Created: The United Nations Economic Commission for Latin America in the Development Era* (2022), p. 27.

18. Hernán Santa Cruz, *Cooperate or Perish*, v. 1 (1984), pp. 42, 319; Comisión Económica para América Latina, *Antecedentes sobre la creación de la CEPAL, 1948–1988* (1949).

19. In 1950, CEPAL published in English a "manifesto" written by Prebisch, "The Economic Development of Latin America and Some of its Principal Problems," which had an enormous influence on Latin American thought. The original Spanish version was passed around in mimeographed copies, and finally published as "El Desarrollo Económico de La América Latina y Algunos de Sus Principales Problemas," *Desarrollo Económico*, v. 26, n. 103 (1986).

Chapter 44: A Chapter on Latin America

1. "Memorandum of Conversation by Merwin Bohan," January 29, 1945, *FRUS*, 1945, "The American Republics," v. 9, available online.

2. "Peace Attainable, Says Truman," *New York Times*, August 15, 1947; "Brazil by the Bootstraps," *Time*, March 21, 1949; "The United States Co-Chairman of the Joint Brazil-United States Technical Commission (Abbink) to the Secretary of State," March 17, 1949, *FRUS*, 1949, "The United Nations; The Western Hemisphere," v. 2, available online. The proposal was made prior to Bogotá; the rude response was given after.

3. Mario Del Pero, "The United States and 'Psychological Warfare' in Italy, 1948–1955," *The Journal of American History*, v. 87 (2001).

4. Michael Lacey, *The Truman Presidency* (1991), p. 215.

5. Spykman, *America's Strategy in World Politics* (1942), p. 448.

6. Stephen Wertheim, *Tomorrow, the World: The Birth of U.S. Global Supremacy* (2020), p. 60.

7. Evan Thomas, *The Very Best Men: Four Who Dared: The Early Years of the CIA* (1996), p. 323.

8. "Memorandum by the Director of the Policy Planning Staff (Kennan) to the Secretary of State and the Under Secretary of State (Lovett), February 24, 1948," *FRUS*, 1948, "General; The United Nations," v. 1, pt. 2, https://www.history.state.gov/historicaldocuments/frus1948v01 p2/d3.

9. Already by 1946, Lewis Hanke, a respected intellectual authority who did extensive scholarly research on Las Casas, sensed a change in attitude toward Latin America. Hanke, "Friendship Now with Latin America," *The Virginia Quarterly Review*, v. 22 (1946).

10. Wallace, *Price of Vision*, pp. 460–61.

11. The minutes of an October 19, 1945, meeting (found in the Hagley Museum and Library Archives) held by the Council for Inter-American Cooperation, attended by Nelson Rockefeller, gives a sense both of how quickly Latin America (now that the war was won) was falling off the State Department agenda and the degree the Truman administration was ceding policy to the private sector. Also: "Trade Council Offers Proposals to Get Private Capital to Latin America," *Wall Street Journal*, February 2, 1948; "Plan Seeks Bar on Double Tax in Hemisphere: Trade Council also Offers Proposals to Lure U.S. Funds to Latin America," *New York Herald Tribune*, February 2, 1948. The proposal is published as *National Foreign Trade Council, Economic Proposals for Consideration of the Ninth International Conference of American States* (1947).

12. "Free Enterprise Sought at Bogotá," *New York Times*, March 22, 1948; "Vast Market Seen in Latin America," *New York Times*, February 23, 1947; "Huge Markets Seen in France, Latin America," *New York Herald Tribune,* February 7, 1946; "Report of the Committee on Foreign Investments on the Foreign Investment Chapter on the Draft Basic Agreement of Inter-American Cooperation," cited in

Stephen Rabe, "The Elusive Conference: United States' Economic Relations with Latin America, 1945–1952," *Diplomatic History*, v. 2 (1978), p. 289.

13. Thomas Ferguson and Joel Rogers, *Right Turn* (1987), p. 46.

14. Ray Josephs, *Latin America* (1948), p. 37.

15. Jody Pavilack, *Mining for the Nation: The Politics of Chile's Coal Communities from the Popular Front to the Cold War* (2011).

16. Pavilack, *Mining for the Nation*, p. 1; "US Arms Used in Disputes in South America: Tanks, Guns Employed to Settle Local Uprisings," *Herald Tribune*, June 28, 1946.

17. U.S. Department of Commerce, *Foreign Aid by the United States Government, 1940–1951* (1952), p. 5; Stephen Rabe, "The Elusive Conference," provides good overview of the thinking of Truman's diplomats as to the exclusion of Latin America from economic policy. Also: "How Little we Know the Southern Nations," *The Courier-Journal*, April 11, 1948.

18. Special Message of the President to the Congress on Economic Aid to Latin America, April 8, 1948, Public Papers: Truman, 1948, pp. 207–8.

19. "Marshall Urges Latins to Put Need of Our Help After ERP," *New York Times*, April 2, 1948; "Marshall's Bogotá Difficulties," *Washington Post*, April 6, 1948; "No Big Applause," *New York Times*, April 9, 1948. For more on Latin American demand for a Marshall Plan, as well as Clayton's response: Ellen Clayton Garwood, *Will Clayton* (2011), p. 125. Later, in the 1960s, some of the veterans involved in the original Marshall Plan worked on John F. Kennedy's Alliance for Progress, which was billed as an "Economic Recovery" plan for Latin America. The money on offer, however, was insufficient to what would be needed to bring about good-paying jobs, and the Alliance was too directly tied to Kennedy's counterinsurgency policies: Michael Latham, *Modernization as Ideology* (2003), p. 79.

Chapter 45: The Killing of Gaitán

1. Gabriel García Márquez, *Vivir para Contarla* (2002), p. 357.

2. For details on this period, and the consolidation and radicalization of the Liberal Party: Richard Sharpless, *Gaitán of Colombia: A Political Biography* (1978), p. 24; Ricardo Arias, *Los Leopardos: Una historia intelectual de los años 1920* (2007).

3. Paul Garfinkel, "Criminal Law and Juridical Culture in Liberal and Fascist Italy," PhD dissertation, Brandeis University (2004), p. 329.

4. W. John Green, "'Vibrations of the Collective': The Popular Ideology of Gaitanismo on Colombia's Atlantic Coast, 1944–1948," *Hispanic American Historical Review*, v. 96 (1976).

5. The late human rights lawyer Paul Wolf did dogged work tracking down U.S. documents related to this period of Colombian history, including the execution of Gaitán. Quotations related to the 1928 massacre are in U.S. consulate and embassy cables, https://web.archive.org/web/20060822120928/www.icdc.com/~paulwolf/colombia/colombiawar.html/. The estimate of the numbers killed comes from the United Fruit Company, as reported to the U.S. embassy in Bogotá. See embassy cable to State Department, December 29, 1928. Also: Jorge Eliécer Gaitán, *La Masacre en las bananeras: Documentos, testimonios* (1965).

6. *El Espectador*, July 19, 1929; Sharpless, *Gaitán of Colombia*, p. 58.

7. José Ángel Hernández, "Los Leopardos y el fascismo en Colombia," *History y comunicación Social*, v. 5 (2000), pp. 221–27. Two "novels" based heavily on historical facts and firsthand eyewitness, Fidel

Blandon Berro's *Lo que el cielo no perdona* (1996) and Eduardo Caballero Calderón's *El Cristo de Espaldas* (1952), capture this radicalization of the Catholic Church.

8. Green, "Vibrations of the Collective," p. 283; Sharpless, *Gaitán of Colombia*, p. 165.

9. Laureano Gómez, *Interrogantes Sobre el Progreso de Colombia* (1928). For Gómez as a Falangist and patron of Colombia's Black Shirts: Germán Arciniegas, *The State of Latin America* (1952), pp. 163–66.

10. Herbert Braun, *The Assassination of Gaitán* (2003), p. 82.

11. Luis Emiro Valencia, *La Plataforma del Colón* (1968), pp. 329–47.

12. Braun, *The Assassination of Gaitán*, p. 200.

13. García Márquez, *Vivir para Contarla* (2002).

14. Arturo Alape, "El 9 de Abril: Muerte y Desesperanza," in *Versions del Bogotázo* (2018).

15. Arturo Alape, *El Bogotazo: Memorias del Olvido* (2016).

16. Or so he says in his memoir *Living to Tell the Tale*. His biographer, Gerald Martin, in *Gabriel García Márquez: A Life* (2010), p. 115, writes that García Márquez arrived at the scene after the crowd dragged Roa's body to the gates of the National Palace.

17. Nicholson Baker, in *Baseless: My Search for Secrets in the Ruins of the Freedom of Information Act* (2020), p. 259, tells of the efforts by the now deceased human rights lawyer Paul Wolf, mentioned in a note above, to petition access to U.S. government documents on Gaitán. Wolf was told by the CIA that records from the post–World War II era "are on microfilm, and that their microfilms are indexed by an old IBM-type punch card computer which is no longer operational," and that he would have to pay $147,000 to read the film. *"The Scotland Yard Report"* by Sir Norman Smith, the original found in the British Public Record Office, is cited in Anthony Carrozza, *William D. Pawley* (2012). For more on Gaitán: *Alberto Figueredo Salcedo Colección, Jorge Eliécer Gaitán: Documentos para una biografía* (1949); José Álvarez Osorio Lizarazo, *Gaitán: Vida, Muerte y Permanente Presencia* (1952); Arturo Alape, *El Cadáver Insepulto* (2005); *El Saqueo De Una Ilusión: El 9 de Abril, 50 Anos Después* (1997). Also the CIA's history, declassified in 1996, based on its own archives, "The Bogotazo," https://www.cia.gov/resources/csi/studies-in-intelligence/archives/vol-13-no-4/the -bogotazo/. For Potes's confession: Luis Arturo Mera Castro, "¿Quién mató a Gaitán?," *Primicia*, April 11, 2012.

18. Guillermo Uribe Cualla, "Estudio retrospectivo de la personalidad de Roa Sierra, y concepto psiquiátrico sobre Bernal Cordovez," *Revista de medicina legal de Colombia*, v. 15 (1958), pp. 31–43; Susana Bianchi, *Los espiritistas argentinos, in Ocultismo y espiritismo en Argentina* (1992); Eric Kurlander, *Hitler's Monsters: A Supernatural History of the Third Reich* (2017).

19. José Vicente Pepper, *La gran emboscada* (1948), pp. 60–61; and Vernon Fluharty, *Dance of the Millions: Military Rule and Social Revolution in Colombia, 1930–1956* (1957), p. 106.

20. *Adolf Hitler: El Último Avatara*, first published in Chile in 1984, was widely popular, translated into many languages, including German.

21. Carrozza, *William D. Pawley*, chapter 11; Braun, *The Assassination of Gaitán*, p. 188.

22. The buildings targeted for arson were selected for their complicity. "Bogotá Is Semi-Destroyed," was *El Tiempo*'s first headline once it started, on April 12, printing again. Felipe Arias Escobar, "Bogotazo: El Mito de la Ciudad Destruida," March 24, 2018, https://feloarias.com/2018/03/24 /Bogotazo-el-mito-de-la-ciudad-destruida/.

23. Paul Oquist, *Violence, Conflict, and Politics in Colombia* (1980), p. 119.

24. Cecil Lyon, "Bogotá, April 9," *The American Foreign Service Journal*, v. 25 (May 1948); Vernon Walters, *Silent Missions* (1978), p. 168.

25. Washington had kept many of its wartime military bases in operation, including the U.S. Caribbean Defense Command in Panama. "D.C. Evacuees Tell of Revolt," *Washington Post*, April 14, 1948.

26. Carrozza, *William D. Pawley*, p. 160.

27. In addition to *The Shape of the Ruins*, other novelistic accounts of Gaitán's murder are *Ignacio Gómez Dávila, El Monstruo* (1954) and Miguel Torres's trilogy, *El crimen del siglo* (2006), *El incendio de abril* (2012), and *La invención del pasado* (2016); Plinio Apuleyo Mendoza, et al., *En qué momento se jodió Colombia* (1990).

Chapter 46: A Red Masterpiece

1. "The Ambassador in Colombia (Beaulac) to the Acting Secretary of State," April 12, 1948, *FRUS*, 1948, "The Western Hemisphere," v. 9, available online.

2. Enrique Muñoz Meany Papers; Muñoz Meany to Arévalo, April 23, 1948, found in the historical archive run by *El Centro de Investigaciones Regionales de Mesoamérica*, in Antigua, Guatemala.

3. "Dies Hits 35 U.S. Officials as Reds; Finds Nudist Is Planner for Post-War Era," *Chicago Daily Tribune*, March 30, 1942. John Earl Haynes, Harvey Klehr, and Alexander Vassiliev in *Spies* (2010) argue that the various agencies in charge of Latin American affairs, including the State Department, Wallace's Board of Economic Warfare, and Rockefeller's Office of the Coordinator of Inter-American Affairs, were penetrated by members of the United States Communist Party, many of whom worked as Soviet agents, including Maurice Halperin, who had been chief of the Latin American Division of the Research and Analysis Section of the OSS. Also: Christopher O'Sullivan, *Summer Welles, Postwar Planning, and the Quest for a New Order* (2008), p. 226.

4. "Subversion Laid to 32 More Groups in a Supplemental List by Clark," *New York Times*, May 29 1948. For Rockefeller: Irwin Gellman Interview with Nelson A. Rockefeller, August 11 and 12, 1976, in Nelson A. Rockefeller personal papers, Oral Histories, Series I (FA344), Box 4, Folder 27, Rockefeller Archive Center.

5. Allen Weinstein and Alexander Vassiliev, *The Haunted Wood: Soviet Espionage in America* (2000), pp. 3–21. Durán was born in Barcelona and a defender of the Spanish Republic during its civil war, where he fought with a socialist railroad worker militia. After he fled Spain, and following his stint with Hemingway, political connections led him to a position as adviser to Spruille Braden, Truman's assistant secretary of state for Latin America. Like many purged from government positions, he found a job in the United Nations, which had become a sanctuary for the blacklisted. There, Durán worked the with the Chilean Hernán Santa Cruz to establish CEPAL.

6. "NLRB Is Defended by Smith in Mexico," *New York Times*, September 4, 1938; James Gross, *Making of the National Labor Relations Board* (1974), p. 171.

7. Jamie Lee Anderson, "In the City of Women: The Life and Work of Ruth Landes," in *Bérose—Encyclopédie internationale des histoires de l'anthropologie* (2021). For Ware: Landon Storrs, *The Second Red Scare and the Un-Making of the New Deal Left* (2013), p. 84.

8. "Red Masterpiece," *Los Angeles Times*, April 14, 1948.

9. "Bogotá Warning Relayed by U.S. Agency," *Christian Science Monitor*, April 14, 1948, "Congress Told Bloody Revolt Could Happen Here," *Los Angeles Times*, April 16, 1948; "New Dealers Planted the Seed," *Chicago Daily Tribune*, June 11, 1948; "What Really Went On at Bogotá," *Christian Science Monitor*, May 3, 1948.

10. For Albarrán Domínguez: Daniel A. Rodríguez, *The Right to Live in Health* (2020). "Statement of Marjorie Shearon," *National Health Plan Hearings* (1949), p. 178. On Shearon, Sarah D. Kim, in her Honors' Thesis, provides the most detailed account: "Of a Healthy Constitution: Socialized Medicine Between the Triumphs of Social Security and Medicare" (2017), https://elischolar.library.yale .edu/applebaum_award/12.

11. "Says Socializers Use Health as a Weapon," *Medical Economics*, v. 25 (1948), p. 200.

12. William Buckley to George Marshall, December 9, 1948, original in National Archives, cited in Steven Schwartzberg, "Romulo Betancourt: From a Communist Anti-Imperialist to a Social Democrat with US Support," *Journal of Latin American Studies*, v. 29 (1997), pp. 613–65. For the U.S. role in the coup, and the different opinions of State and Defense: Bethany Aram, "Exporting Rhetoric, Importing Oil: United States Relations with Venezuela, 1945–1948," *World Affairs*, v. 154 (1992), pp. 94–106; "Venezuela Reds Accused by U. S. Business Men," *New York Herald Tribune*, August 13, 1946; Linda Wills Qaim-Maqami, "Max Thornburg and the Quest for a Corporate Foreign Oil Policy," PhD dissertation, Texas A&M University (1986); "Gallegos Lists U.S. Officer as Adviser in Coup," *New York Herald*, December 10, 1948. On the Pentagon pushing for fast recognition of Venezuelan coup: "Memorandum by Mr. George H. Butler of the Policy Planning Staff, to the Acting Secretary of State, December 15, 1948, *FRUS*, 1948, "The Western Hemisphere," v. 9, available online.

13. Harrington, *Fragments of the Century* (1973), p. 64.

14. Kennan was on leave due to ill health when the report was being prepared, leaving George Butler to take the lead in writing PPS-26, released in March 1948, on the cusp of Bogotá's uprising. "Paper Prepared by the Policy Planning Staff; Problem: To Establish U.S. Policy Regarding Anti-Communist Measures Which Could Be Planned and Carried Out Within the Inter-American System," March 22, 1948, in *FRUS*, 1948, "Western Hemisphere," v. 9, available online; National Security Council, Central Intelligence Agency, "The World Situation as It Relates to the Security of the United States . . ." CIA 5-48, May 12, 1948, Truman Library, Papers of Harry S. Truman, PSF.

15. For this shift in policy, from understanding democracy and development being mutually dependent to seeing them as mutually exclusive: Margarita López-Maya, "The Change in the Discourse of US-Latin American Relations from the End of the Second World War to the Beginning of the Cold War," *Review of International Political Economy*, v. 2 (1995); David Schmitz, *Thank God They're on Our Side* (1999); Roger Trask, "The Impact of the Cold War on United States–Latin American Relations, 1945–1949," *Diplomatic History*, v. 1 (1977); Leslie Bethell and Ian Roxborough, "Latin America Between the Second World War and the Cold War," *Journal of Latin American Studies*, v. 20 (1988). Early in the Cold War, the Stanford economist Paul Baran condemned what he called the "prodigious waste" involved in keeping poor countries on a war footing. Baran: "In Hitler's extermination camps the victims were forced to dig their own graves before being massacred by their Nazi torturers. In the undeveloped countries of the 'free world,' people are forced to use a large share of what would enable them to emerge from their present state of squalor and disease" to pay for repressive security forces "to support regimes perpetuating this very state of squalor and disease," *The Political Economy of Growth* (1957), p. 259.

16. "France, Postwar Industrial Recovery . . . ," Office of Reports and Estimates, November 14, 1949, Truman Library, Papers of Harry S. Truman, PSF, Central Intelligence Agency, U.S. Declassified Documents Online.

Chapter 47: Peace, Peace, Don't Kill Us

1. Lesley Gill, *A Century of Violence in a Red City* (2016), pp. 56–57.

2. Mateo Rodríguez Machado, "'Los Pájaros' y La Violencia en Colombia," PhD dissertation, University of Antioquia (2018); Charles Bergquist, *Violence in Colombia* (1992), pp. 87–91.

3. Reprinted in "Dictatorship Has Control of Land," *The Windsor Daily Star*, January 10, 1950.

4. *Life*, November 20, 1950, pp. 56–57; "South American Tensions Mount," *New York Times*, November 29, 1949. For more on Gómez, who wound up splitting the Conservative Party and not finishing his term: Helwar Figueroa Salamanca and Carlos Tuta Alarcón, "El Estado corporativo colombiano: una propuesta de derechas, 1930–1953," *Anuario Colombiano de Historia Social y de la Cultura*, v. 32 (2005).

5. Ronald Hilston, *Hispanic American Report*, v. 3 (1950), p. 24; previews of Weld's forthcoming book on the Spanish Civil War in Latin America, "A Holy War: Latin America's Far Right," *Dissent* (Spring 2020), and "The Spanish Civil War and the Construction of a Reactionary Historical Consciousness in Augusto Pinochet's Chile," *Hispanic American Historical Review*, v. 98 (2018).

6. Raphaël Ramos, "An Unfinished Battle: George C. Marshall and Intelligence in the Early Cold War," *War in History*, v. 29 (2022); "French Nazi Hunters Says CIA 'Protected' Barbie," *New York Times*, April 10, 1983; "Operation Ratline was Barbie's Ticket Out," *Washington Post*, August 21, 1983; "Secret Files Reveal 9000 Nazi War Criminals Fled to South America," March 19, 2012. For the United States, most entered either through Operation Paperclip or the Displaced Persons Act, which was focused on the Baltic states and Ukraine, regions that were well represented by Nazi collaborators. The ten thousand number comes from Allan Ryan, who was the director and prosecutor of the Department of Justice's Office of Special Investigation, cited in Peter Gorner, "Our Good Neighbors," *Chicago Tribune*, February 17, 1985. Others have cast doubt on Ryan's estimate. On this: Judy Feigin, *The Office of Special Investigations: Striving for Accountability in the Aftermath of the Holocaust* (2008), p. ix, note 3.

7. Tad Szulc, "U.S. Investing Up in Latin America: Area Drawing Capital Again after Retrenchment," *New York Times*, October 19, 1964; Stephen Rabe, *Eisenhower and Latin America* (2017), p. 39.

8. "How to Win an Election in Colombia," *Life*, December 12, 1949.

9. Germán Guzmán Campos, *La Violencia en Colombia* (1968), p. 330.

10. Robert Pineda Giraldo, *El Impacto de la Violencia en el Tolima: el Caso de Libano* (1960). I thank Robert Karl for pointing me to his essay "Century of the Exile: Colombia's Displacement and Land Restitution in Historical Perspective, 1940s–1960s" (2017), *Canadian Journal of Latin American and Caribbean Studies*, which discusses Gonzalo Canal Ramírez.

11. Eric Hobsbawm, "The Anatomy of Violence," *New Society*, April 11, 1963, p. 18; Karl, "Century of the Exile." These descriptions are found in volume 1 of Germán Guzmán Campos, Orlando Fals Borda, and Eduardo Umaña Luna, *La violencia en Colombia* (1962). Also: David Mauricio Figueroa Melo, "A La Sombra del Monstruo: Cultura Política, ideología y Literatura Testimonial en Colombia y Antioquia, 1930–1954," MA thesis, University of the Andes (2007). See also Lina Britto and Ricardo López-Pedreros's two edited collections highlighting the work of more than forty scholars on politics, social relations, and political violence in Colombia: *Histories of Solitude: Colombia, 1820s–1970s* and *Histories of Perplexity: Colombia, 1970s–2010s*. Both were published in spring 2024.

12. Ernesto León Herrera, *Lo que el cielo no perdona* (1954), p. 291; Abelardo Patino, "The Political Ideas of the Liberal and Conservative Parties in Colombia during the 1946–1953 Crisis," PhD dissertation, American University (1954), p. 154.

13. "The Ambassador in Colombia (Beaulac) to Acting Secretary of State," April 11, 1948, *FRUS*, 1948, "The Western Hemisphere," v. 9, available online. I edited the priest's quotation on killing looters to correct syntax. Edwin Gorr, *The Political Process in Colombia* (1972), p. 65; *New York Times*, April 12, 1948, p. 11; Francisco González, "Persecución religiosa en Colombia en el golpe del 9 de abril de 1948," *Revista Javeriana*, v. 30 (1948); Gustavo Zola y Ponce, *Raza de Cain* (1978), p. 141.

14. The most comprehensive study of violence during this period is by the Socialist Catholic priest Germán Guzmán Campos and his coauthors, the two-volume *La Violencia en Colombia* (1962 and 1964).

Timothy P. Wickham-Crowley uses the data in this study to correlate rural political violence to the structure of sharecropping, in *Guerrillas and Revolution in Latin America* (1992), p. 360. Other important works: Mary Roldán, *Blood and Fire: La Violencia in Antioquia, Colombia, 1946–1953* (2002); Catherine LeGrande, *Frontier Expansion and Peasant Protest in Colombia, 1850–1936* (1986); Gill, *A Century of Violence in a Red City*; Gonzalo J. Sánchez, et al., *Violence in Colombia: The Contemporary Crisis in Historical Perspective* (1992).

15. Sheldon Mills to Albert Gerberich, November 17, 1949, Department of State, Decimal Files, 1945–1949, Box 5243, RG 59, National Archives. Also available at U.S. Declassified Documents Online: Central Intelligence Agency, "Increased instability of several Latin American governments outlined," April 28, 1952.

16. Dennis Rempe, *The Past as Prologue?: A History of U.S. Counterinsurgency Policy in Colombia, 1958–66* (2002), p. 25. Yarborough is quoted in McClintock, *Instruments of Statecraft*, p. 222, original in Headquarters, U.S. Army Special Warfare School, "Subject: Visit to Colombia, South America, by a team from Special Warfare Center, Fort Bragg, North Carolina, 26 February 1962," Box 319, National Security Files, Special Group, Fort Bragg Team, Visit to Colombia, 3/62, Kennedy Library.

17. "Memo on Colombia," May 8, 1950, *FRUS*, 1950, "The United Nations; The Western Hemisphere," v. 2, available online. Also: National Security Council, "Implementation of U.S. policy toward inter-American military collaboration," March 18, 1952; White House, "Progress report on NSC 5432/1: U.S. Objectives and Courses of Action with Respect to Latin America," December 27, 1954; and Department of Defense, "DOD report on status of military assistance programs as of 6/30/55—Section I: Area and Country Report," October 1, 1955. These three documents are accessible online at U.S. Declassified Documents Online.

18. Robert Karl, "Sovereignty Beyond Decolonization," *Humanity*, v. 14 (2023), p. 56.

19. Both the numbers of dead and Hobsbawm quote are from Robert Karl, "Sovereignty Beyond Decolonization."

Chapter 48: The Perpetual Rhythm of Struggle

1. Raphaël Ramos, "An Unfinished Battle."

2. John Lewis Gaddis, *George F. Kennan: An American Life* (2012), p. 317. The OPC was formally under the jurisdiction of the CIA but was controlled, in its early years, by State. By the early 1950s, it had passed fully to the CIA, and had undergone various name changes; John Prados, *Safe for Democracy: The Secret Wars of the CIA* (2006). Gregory Mitrovich, *Undermining the Kremlin* (2000), calls the OPC the "intelligence apparatus for the departments of state and defense."

3. Secretary Acheson meets with Paul Nitze and Sir Oliver Franks, Department of State, April 27, 1951, U.S. Declassified Documents Online.

4. "Telegram from Operation PBSUCCESS Headquarters in Florida to the Central Intelligence Agency," *FRUS*, 1952–1954, "Guatemala," available online. The *FRUS* volume indicates that its original source was Central Intelligence Agency, Job 79_ 01025A, Box 1, Folder 3. Secret; Routine; PBSUCCESS; RYBAT.

5. Interview with E. Howard Hunt, transcript available at the National Security Archive web page, https://nsarchive2.gwu.edu/coldwar/interviews/episode-18/hunt1.html.

6. Leland Johnson, "U.S. Business Interests in Cuba and the Rise of Castro," RAND Corporation paper (1964), https://www.rand.org/content/dam/rand/pubs/papers/2008/P2923.pdf.

7. Central Intelligence Agency, "The Situation in the Caribbean Through 1959," June 30, 1959, · https://www.cia.gov/readingroom/docs/DOC_0000132410.pdf.

8. Compare Sumner Welles's "On the Need for a Spirit of Tolerance" to State Department planner Louis Halle's 1950 "On a Certain Impatience with Latin America." Halle styled himself a Latin Americanist George Kennan, publishing his policy essay under the byline "Y" in *Foreign Affairs*.

9. Servando Gonzalez, *The Secret Fidel Castro* (2001), p. 33.

10. Thanks to Piero Gleijeses for helping with this chronology.

11. "Memorandum from the Deputy Assistant Secretary of State for Inter-American Affairs (Mallory) to the Assistant Secretary of State for Inter-American Affairs (Rubottom)," April 6, 1960, *FRUS, 1958–1960*, "Cuba," v. 6, available online. Lumumba was killed by Belgian agents working with Congolese allies with the support of the Agency. Stuart Reid, *The Lumumba Plot* (2023).

12. United States Senate, 94th Congress, *Alleged Assassination Plots Involving Foreign Leaders* (1975), p. 141; "Priority Operations Schedule for Operation Mongoose," May 17, 1962. *FRUS, 1961–1963*, "Cuba," v. 10, available online. Even Thomas, *Robert Kennedy: His Life* (2013), pp. 145–52, for a good discussion of how the Kennedys' obsession with Castro ran into bureaucratic obstacles and rivalries, and how a fascination with "psych-ops," especially when it came to Cuba, was often just that, a fascination rather than applicable policy.

13. For the CIA's list of anti-Castro groups: CIA, "Major Cuban Exile Organizations," attached to "John McCone to Maxwell D. Taylor," May 3, 1962, Folder: Cuba; Subject: Exiles, Box 48, National Security Files, Presidential Papers, Papers of John F. Kennedy, John F. Kennedy Presidential Library.

14. The 1963 coup in the Dominican Republic against Orlando Bosch, an anti-Communist social-democrat who won the post-Trujillo election with 58 percent of the vote, was supported by the U.S. labor attaché Fred Somerford, who thought the Dominican president a stalking horse for Castro. Somerford mobilized the U.S.-created and -funded labor federation, CONATRAL, against him, demanding the military oust Bosch. CONATRAL was part of what planners hoped was a "democratic left," a middle-way union. And so here was a variation on the dynamic described earlier, not the reactionary right eliminating the democratic left, but rather the "democratic left" eliminating the "democratic left," a "free labor" union movement mobilized to overthrow an anti-Communist social-democratic president. Piero Gleijeses, *The Dominican Crisis* (1978), pp. 98–99, for Somerford working "overtly to overthrow Bosch." During this decade, blue-chip corporations began to coordinate their activities in Latin America more closely with the CIA.

Chapter 49: War of the Gods, or, A Second Enlightenment

1. For Economy and Humanism in Colombia: Julián Alberto Gómez Delgado, "El Trabajo de la Misión de Economía y Humanismo en Colombia," BA thesis, Universidad Javeriana (2015). Juan Correa, "Les Dominicains lyonnais dans la province de Colombie entre 1938 et 1950," master's thesis, Sorbonne (2017–18). Colombia's French Dominicans were part of a larger transnational Catholic movement, which included Jacques Maritain, author of the 1936 *Integral Humanism*, a "manifesto for a democratic, Catholic modernity"; Madoc Cairns, "The Red Christian," *New Statesman*, May 3, 2023. Maritain in turn influenced Peter Maurin and Dorothy Day's Catholic Worker Movement in the United States.

2. León José Moreau, "Economia y Humanismo," *Política y espíritu*, v. 7 (1951), p. 248.

3. Joe Broderick, *Camilo Torres* (1975), p. 57.

4. Salomon Isacovici and Juan Manuel Rodriguez, *Man of Ashes* (2001), p. 36.

5. James Ernest Goff, "The Persecution of Protestant Christians in Colombia 1948–1958," PhD dissertation, San Francisco Theological Seminary (1965).

6. Richard Shaull, *Encounter with Revolution* (1955); for "Black Despair": Report from Bogotá, December 1948, Presbyterian Historical Society, Richard Shaull, Folder 1, RG360s.

7. Jean Pierre Sargent, "Entrevista A Camilo Torres," p. 64, unpublished, available online at https://bibliotecadigital.univalle.edu.co/server/api/core/bitstreams/34f22de4-977a-4396-8423-031 24fb59fd3/content; John Womack, "Priest of Revolution," *New York Review of Books*, October 23, 1969.

8. In 1964, a United States–organized scorched-earth campaign targeted the insurgents' high Andean redoubts, which the rebels had taken to calling "independent republics." Charles Brisco, "Plan Lazo: Evaluation and Execution," *Veritas: Journal of Army Special Operations History*, v. 2 (2006). The Cuban Revolution influenced C. W. Mills and his understanding of sociology: A. Javier Treviño, *C. Wright Mills and the Cuban Revolution* (2017); Orlando Fals Borda, "Acción Comunal: En una Vereda Colombiana," *Monografías Sociológicas*, v. 4 (1961); Camilo Torres Restrepo, "El espíritu de la acción comunal," Facultad de Sociología de la Universidad Nacional (1959).

9. The "dragon's chair" was made from conductive metal, with articulating bars that pressed on limbs of the naked prisoner every time shock was applied, creating deep gashes in the skin. Hundreds of Brazilians and Uruguayans were thus trained in the "theory and practice" of torture. Washington sent many men like Mitrione to Latin America. Stuart Schrader, *Badges without Borders: How Global Counterinsurgency Transformed American Policing* (2019).

10. Gerald Horne, *Black and Brown* (2005); Rebecca Schreiber, *Cold War Exiles in Mexico: U.S. Dissidents and the Culture* (2008).

11. Hook's remark comes in an essay on the French Catholic integralist Jacques Maritain, one of the antecedents of liberation theology. Hook was suspicious; for every St. Francis of Assisi there's a Torquemada, and for every Maritain, a Coughlin. The original was published in 1940 but can be found in *Reason, Social Myths and Democracy* (2009), p. 76.

12. Eduardo Umaña Luna, *Camilo Torres, el nuevo humanismo* (1978).

13. See Charles Beirne, *Jesuit Education and Social Change in El Salvador* (2012), pp. 82–83.

14. Ellacuría, *Filosofía de la realidad histórica* (1990), p. 21.

15. Ecumenical research centers sprang up in many nations, bringing together scholars, religious activists, and movement leaders to discuss vital issues. The Evanelização e Capacitação e Assessoria in São Leopoldo, Brazil, for one example, or the Instituto Bartolomé de las Casas in Lima in 1974. One of the first workshops held by Costa Rica's Departamento Ecuménico de Investigaciones critiqued Jimmy Carter's use of "human rights," producing the two-volume *Carter y la Lógica del Imperialismo*.

16. Jorge Gusberg, *Hacia un perfil del arte latinoamericano: presentación del grupo de los treces* (1972).

17. Father Louis-Joseph Lebret, Economy and Humanism's founder, became interested in political economy in the 1930s, while ministering in Breton fishing villages on France's north coast, impoverished because they were unable to compete with a consolidating, technologically advanced fishing industry. Lebret extrapolated a larger global economics from his experiences, one very similar to Prebisch's. Alfredo Bosi, "Economy and Humanism," *Estudos avançados*, v. 26 (2012).

18. This Rostow quotation is a paraphrase, based on a declassified document I once read (during my work with the Guatemalan truth commission) but can no longer locate. It was a one-line memo to the president, too good to just let slip away. For Thomas Melville and Sister Marian, who now goes by Margarita Melville: Susan Fitzpatrick Berhens, *Confronting Colonialism: Maryknoll Catholic Missionaries in Peru and Guatemala, 1943–1968* (2007).

19. The WASPS who ran the early Cold War were leery of the Catholic Church, despite its impeccable anti-Communist credentials. Be careful joining with the Vatican in waging a Holy War against

Moscow, *The Christian Century* warned, for the Church "is out to extend its own spiritual authority and ecclesiastical power over all the earth." Also: William Inboden, *Religion and American Foreign Policy* (2008), p. 59. For the Nixon quotation: National Archives, Nixon Presidential Materials, White House Tapes, Oval Office, Conversation No. 462–5, Oval Office. March 5, 1971.

20. Central Intelligence Agency, "Intelligence memorandum regarding background and updated information on the political situation in Guatemala following that country's military shake-up," May 13, 1968, U.S. Declassified Documents Online; "Vatican Lifting 'Silence' Order on Brazilian Friar," *New York Times*, April 1, 1986; Central Intelligence Agency, "The Committed Church and Change in Latin America," September 10, 1969, U.S. Declassified Documents Online.

21. Torres, *"Cristianismo y revolución,"* p. 483.

22. Lopera Sánchez, "Ciencia, revolución y creencia en Camilo Torres," *Revista Nórmadas*, v. 25 (2006).

23. Alfredo Molano Bravo, *Ahi Les Dejo esos Fierros* (2009).

24. Camilo Torres and John Gerassi, *Revolutionary Priest* (1971), p. 350; Camilo Torres, *Cristianismo y revolución* (1970), p. 407.

25. Rick Edwards, "Religion and the Revolution? . . . A Look at Golconda," *NACLA Newsletter*, v. 2, n. 10 (1970), p. 2; CIA weekly summary, September 3, 1965, online at CIA.gov.

26. Adolfo Gilly, "El programa del cura Camilo," *Marcha*, June 4, 1965.

Chapter 50: Restoring the Magisterium

1. Mateo Jarquín, *The Sandinista Revolution: A Global Latin American History* (2024).

2. The Contras were first run as a joint CIA-Argentine operation, an extension of Operation Condor. But after the Argentine junta fell following its disastrous effort to take the Malvinas Islands from Great Britain, the Agency took over. See my *Empire's Workshop* for details on Iran-Contra.

3. Withdrawal from Proceedings in the Nicaragua Case: Statement Issued by the Department of State, 1985, reprinted in Michela Pomerance, *The United States and the World Court as a Supreme Court of the Nations: Dreams, Illusions, and Disillusion* (1996).

4. Eric Posner, "All Justice, Too, Is Local," *New York Times*, December 30, 2004.

5. Reagan had already set precedent for this expansion of Article 51's meaning in his 1983 invasion of Grenada and his 1986 bombing of Libya. See Grandin, *Kissinger's Shadow* (2015), chapter 10. Bush's citation of Article 51 to justify invading Panama: "Letter to the Speaker of the House of Representatives and the President Pro Tempore of the Senate on United States Military Action in Panama," the American Presidency Project, https://www.presidency.ucsb.edu/node/264386.

6. For a fuller account of Operation Just Cause and its consequences: Grandin, *Empire's Workshop*. The Oliver North Files available online at the National Security Archive webpage provides information on Noriega's role in Iran-Contra. "Bush and Noriega: Examination of Their Ties," *New York Times*, September 28, 1988.

7. Frederick Kempe, "The Noriega Files," *Newsweek*, January 15, 1990.

8. Kevin Buckley, *Panama* (1991), p. 45.

9. Mike Gonzalez, "12 Years Later, Scars of the U.S. Invasion Remain," *New York Times*, November 3, 2001.

10. Bob Woodward, *The Commanders* (1991).

11. Mark Cook and Jeff Cohen, "How the Media Sold the Panama Invasion," *Extra!*, February 1990, https://msuweb.montclair.edu/~furrg/panamainv.html.

12. "Vietnam, Panama, and Iraq," *Boston Globe*, December 24, 1990; Jim Naureckas, "Gulf War Coverage," FAIR, *Extra!* "Special Gulf War Issue" (1991), https://fair.org/topic/extra-special-gulf-war-issue-1991/.

13. In 1944, Friedrich von Hayek's *Road to Serfdom* distinguished between command-economy socialism and the welfare state, even allowing that it was a government's responsibility to guarantee "food, shelter, and clothing, sufficient to preserve health and the capacity to work." Yet Hayek in his later writings, including those composed around the time of the overthrow of Allende, did put the "welfare state" on his target list, saying that in a way it was more insidious and dangerous than command-economics since it seemed benign. Henry Farrell sums up this evolution in "Hayak and the Welfare State," May 13, 2012, *Crooked Timber*, https://crookedtimber.org/2012/05/13/hayek-and-the-welfare-state/.

14. For the 1950 to 1980 stats: Eliana Cardoso and Albert Fishlow, "Latin American Economic Development: 1950–1980," *Journal of Latin American Studies*, v. 24 (1992).

15. Kenneth Aman, "Fighting for God: The Military and Religion in Chile," *CrossCurrents* (1986); "Amplio respaldo brindaron las Iglesias evangélicas al general Augusto Pinochet," *La Tercera de la Hora*, December 13, 1974. Neoliberalism failed as a growth model. Per capita GDP fell throughout the 1980s by 8 percent. By 1989, the GDP of most Latin American nations stood below their 1980 levels—Venezuela, Nicaragua, and El Salvador below their 1960 mark. Eliana Cardoso and Albert Fishlow, "Latin American Economic Development," *Journal of Latin American Studies*, v. 24 (1992), pp. 197–218; "Clinton Drawing Visionary Blueprint of Global Economy," *Los Angeles Times*, December 5, 1994; Glen Biglaiser, "Military Regimes, Neoliberal Restructuring, and Economic Development: Reassessing the Chilean Case," in *Studies in Comparative International Development*, v. 34 (1999); Jeffery Sachs, *Understanding Shock Therapy* (1994); "Shock Therapy for Sick Economies," *Washington Post*, January 5, 1992. Experts and consultants who had worked in Latin America during the first phase of neoliberal restructuring could claim first dibs on the billions USAID had to hand out to promote the transition to capitalism in Eastern Europe.

16. In 1963, President Kennedy asked David Rockefeller to organize what became known as the Business Group for Latin America. Within two years, 175 U.S. blue-chip corporations had joined the group, including Pepsi, ITT, U.S. Steel, and Pan Am. Apart from its PR work, the organization created an "action unit" that coordinate activity with the CIA. Enno Reimar Hobbing became the group's liaison with Latin American business and military elites. Hobbing was an Agency veteran, having started his intelligence career helping to get useful Nazis into the United States and then, using his cover as the head of *Times*'s Paris Bureau, working to oust Arbenz in Guatemala and to ensure that his social policies, especially his land reform, was dismantled. With the Business Group, Hobbing advanced a destabilization campaign to topple Brazilian president João Goulart, who was deemed to be too committed an economic nationalist. By April 1964, Goulart was out and a military junta installed. United States investment rushed back into Brazil. Nine years later, Hobbing and various businesses, most famously International Telephone and Telegraph, would do similar work in Chile, in the coup that ended Allende's presidency in 1973. By 1965, the organization had changed its name to the Council for Latin America. "Bankers Announce the Merge of 3 Latin American Aid Units," *New York Times*, February 6, 1965. Information on the Business Group for Latin America isn't as extensive as one might imagine, considering that it marked a change in the relationship of U.S. industry and foreign policy. Two of the most interesting sources are Ambassador Edward Korry's congressional testimony (given during hearings to confirm Cyrus Vance as Jimmy Carter's secretary of state), and a privately published book, written by Enno Reimar Hobbing, *More than Profits: The Story of Business Civil Action*, an "eyes only" account written for the internal use of the Council for Latin America (the successor organization to the Business Group, which in turn now functions under the joint partnership Council of the Americas and Americas Society). Hobbing, a

longtime CIA agent, claimed to have retired from the Agency by the time he began work with the Business Group. Amy Offner, *Sorting Out the Mixed Economy* (2021), pp. 153– 55, has more details on the Business Group/ Council for Latin America, and 1963 as a turning point in elevating private investment over development aid. Also: A. J. Langguth, in *Hidden Terrors: The Truth About U.S. Police Operations in Latin America* (1978).

17. Janine Wedel, *Collision and Collusion* (2015); "Bleak and Bloody Russia," *The Economist,* December 1999; Michael Schrage, "Pinochet's Chile: A Pragmatic Model for Soviet Economy," *Washington Post*, August 22, 1991; William Rhodes, "Latin Lessons for the Russian Economy," *Wall Street Journal*, September 21, 1992. The economist Jeffrey Sachs, who shocked Bolivia in 1985 before shocking Poland in 1989 and Russia in 1991, said that shock therapy wasn't "just an economic strategy" but a "political strategy" used to clear the field, to remove the entrenched statist order and overcome democratic opposition to liberalization; in "Life in the Economic Emergency Room," John Williamson ed., *The Political Economy of Policy Reform* (1994), p. 510. For Merry: PBS *Frontline*, interview with E. Wayne Merry, https://www.pbs.org/wgbh/pages/frontline/shows/yeltsin/interviews/merry.html; Janine R. Wedel, "The Harvard Boys Do Russia," *The Nation*, May 14, 1998; NPR *Planet Money*, Greg Rosalsky, "How 'Shock Therapy' Created Russian Oligarchs and Paved the Path for Putin," March 22, 2022. Social scientists in the United States believed that Latin America had to overcome its Thomistic inheritance, to make peace with the flux of modern life and accept that politics was not a venue for the creation of the common good but a means to satisfy "interests in the style of Locke." Donald E. Worcester, "The Spanish American Past—Enemy of Change," *Journal of Inter-American Studies*, v. 11 (1969), pp. 66–75. More recently, legal theorists have appreciated Latin America's influence on the development of both human rights and social rights. Example: Paolo G. Carozza, "From Conquest to Constitutions: Retrieving a Latin American Tradition of the Idea of Human Rights," *Human Rights Quarterly*, v. 25, n. 2 (May 2003), pp. 281–313.

18. Along with Naomi Klein, in her 2007 *Shock Doctrine*, Tobias Rupprecht is one of the few scholars who convincingly highlights the influence of Pinochet's 1975 Chilean shock theory on Russia (it is more common to point out the influence of market experiments in Poland before the fall of the Berlin Wall and elsewhere in the Eastern bloc, or in Western European democracies led by Socialists like Spain's Felipe González). "Formula Pinochet: Chilean Lessons for Russian Liberal Reformers during the Soviet Collapse, 1970–2000," *Journal of Contemporary History*, v. 51 (2016); "Entrevistaron con General Augusto Pinochet: Soviéticos Elogiaron Plan Económico de Gobierno Militar," *El Mercurio*, April 20, 1991. The trip was paid for with funds from the Tinker Foundation. I thank Professor Rupprecht for sharing these details with me, from his forthcoming book project, in an email correspondence.

19. Jeffry Sachs, "How the Neocons Chose Hegemony over Peace Beginning in the Early 1990s," *In-DepthNews*, September 5, 2024.

20. Janine Wedel, "The Harvard Boys Do Russia," *The Nation*, June 1, 1998.

21. Janine Wedel, *Collision and Collusion: The Strange Case of Western Aid to Eastern Europe* (2015); Vladislav Zubok, *Collapse: The Fall of the Soviet Union* (2021), p. 33.

22. David Remnick, *Resurrection: The Struggle for a New Russia* (1998), p. 205; Alan Cullison, "Santiago East: Prominent Russians Love General Pinochet," *Wall Street Journal*, February 6, 2001; "Putin Urged to Use the Pinochet Stick," *The Guardian*, March 31, 2000; "Banker/Oligarch Calls on Putin to Become Pinochet," *RFE/RL Newsline*, April 3, 2000.

23. Jean-Philippe Platteau, *Islam Instrumentalized* (1917), p. 319.

24. Michael Graziano, *Errand into the Wilderness of Mirrors: Religion and the History of the CIA* (2021). Following the February 1979 Iranian Revolution, Jimmy Carter, worried about the spread of religious extremism, asked, in a memo that equated Islamic fundamentalism with liberation theology, the CIA to infiltrate the "liberal Church" in Latin America. Fausto Fernandez-Ponte, "Pide Carter

espiar a religiosos liberales," *El Excelsior*, February 3, 1979; Penny Lernoux, "CIA Ordered to Survey Latin American Church," *National Catholic Reporter*, February 16, 1979. It was around this time that the CIA began to cultivate radical Islam to fight the Soviet occupation of Afghanistan the same way it was cultivating conservative Christianity to fight the left in Latin America.

25. Martin Lee, "Their Will Be Done," *Mother Jones*, July/August 1983, https://www.motherjones.com /politics/1983/07/their-will-be-done/. An example of Reagan courting the religious right and de- monizing the religious left: "Summary of French news media reports on the following issues: De- partment of State, East-West relations; dismissal of French Army Chief of Staff General Jean Delaunay; *New York Times* report on visits to the U.S. in 1969 and 1970 by Nazi war criminal Klaus Barbie; U.S. military aid to El Salvador," March 10, 1983, accessed through the database U.S. De- classified Documents Online; Penny Lernoux, *Cry of the People* (1980), p. 143. Kevin Kruse, *One Nation Under God* (2015), discusses the anti–New Deal roots of Christian libertarianism. Bethany Moreton, *To Serve God and Wal-Mart: The Making of Christian Free Enterprise* (2009), describes Christian libertarianism's links to dynastic capitalism. Grandin, *Empire's Workshop*, chapter 5, fo- cuses on how free-market Christians took to the field in Central America, and how liberation theol- ogy sparked a convergence among evangelical and secular economists. Also: Melinda Cooper, *Family Values: Between Neoliberalism and the New Social Conservatism* (2017).

26. For a good sense of how apocalyptically violent Latin American anti-Communists had become: Scott Anderson and Jon Lee Anderson, *Inside the League: The Shocking Expose of How Terrorists, Nazis, and Latin American Death Squads Have Infiltrated the World Anti-Communist League* (1986); Theresa Keeley, *Reagan's Gun-Toting Nuns: The Catholic Conflict over Cold War Human Rights Policy in Central America* (2020); Sara Diamond, *Spiritual Warfare: The Politics of the Christian Right* (1990); "The Contras' Chaplains," NACLA's *Report on the Americas*, September 25, 2007; Virginia Garrard-Burnett, *Terror in the Land of the Holy Spirit* (2010); Robert Dreyfuss, *Devil's Game: How the United States Helped Unleash Fundamentalist Islam* (2006), p. 283; Operation Cyclone, as the CIA's support between 1979 and 1992 of the Afghan mujahideen was called, was one of the Agen- cy's longest and most expensive operations.

27. For evangelicals participating in torture sessions of liberation theologians: *Instituto Latinoamericano de Estudios Transnacionales, Sectas y religiosidad en America Latina* (1984); Sara Diamond, *Spiritual Warfare*; Ecumenical Program for Inter-American Communication and Action, "Out of the Shad- ows: The Communities of Population in Resistance in Guatemala," *Social Justice*, v. 20 (1993), p. 147.

28. Dreyfuss, *Devil's Game*, p. 283.

29. John Allen, *Pope Benedict XVI: A Biography* (2001), p. 153; Christine Gudorf, "Ratzinger, Gutierrez, and the Bishops of Peru," *Commonweal*, February 8, 1985.

30. Jorge Mario Bergoglio, *Diálogos entre Juan Pablo II y Fidel Castro* (1998), pp. 48–49.

31. "On Feast of St. Francis, Pope Joins Amazonians to Plant Tree at Vatican," *National Catholic Re- porter*, October 4, 2019.

32. Fr. Thomas Weinandy, "Pope Francis and Schism," *The Catholic Thing*, October 8, 2019.

33. Gutiérrez, *Dios o el oro en las indias* (1989); *En busca de los pobres de Jesucristo. El pensamiento de Bartolomé de Las Casas* (1992). This point is made by Christian Smith, in "Las Casas as Theological Counteroffensive: An Interpretation of Gustavo Gutiérrez's 'Las Casas: In Search of the Poor of Je- sus Christ,'" *Journal for the Scientific Study of Religion*, v. 41 (2002), pp. 69–73.

Epilogue: America, América

1. Frank Church, "Profits of Doom," *Washington Post*, January 19, 1975; Maxwell Cameron and David Cameron, "The Harsh Impact of Economic Liberalism," *Ottawa Citizen*, June 16, 1992. Mehrsa

Baradaran, *The Quiet Coup: Neoliberalism and the Looting of America* (2024). As this book neared completion, following the 2024 election of Donald Trump to the presidency, elected leaders in both the Republican and Democratic parties suddenly began to regularly declare that "neoliberalism" is over, using a term that until this point had mostly been confined to scholarly and activist circles. "The Left," Connecticut Senator Chris Murphy said shortly after Trump's victory, "has never fully grappled with the wreckage of fifty years of neoliberalism." "The Left" of course has been drawing attention to that wreckage for decades now. Senator Murphy would have been more accurate were he to have referenced the leadership of the Democratic Party.

2. For restructuring and austerity, among others: Ferguson and Rogers, *Right Turn*, pp. 44–111; Armin Schäfer and Wolfgang Streeck, eds., *Politics in the Age of Austerity* (2013); Frances Ryan, *Crippled: Austerity and the Demonization of Disabled People* (2019); Theodoros Rakopoulos, *The Global Life of Austerity: Comparing Beyond Europe* (2018); Clara Mattei, *The Capital Order: How Economists Invented Austerity* (2022); Randolph Hohle, *Race and the Origins of American Neoliberalism* (2015); Jason Hackworth, *Manufacturing Decline: How Racism and the Conservative Movement Crush the Rust Belt* (2019); Kim Phillips-Fein, *Fear City: New York's Fiscal Crisis and the Rise of Austerity Politics* (2017).

3. Elizabeth Hinton, *From the War on Poverty to the War on Crime* (2016).

4. Robert McAlexander, M. A. Rubin, and R. Williams, "They're Still There, He's All Gone: American Fatalities in Foreign Wars and Right-Wing Radicalization at Home," *American Political Science Review*, October 19, 2023; Kathleen Belew, *Bring the War Home* (2018); Grandin, *The End of the Myth*, chapter 15. Pre-2016 trial runs of hacking elections are discussed in Jordan Robertson, "How to Hack an Election," *Bloomberg*, April 8, 1916. For ZunZuneo, "US Secretly Created 'Cuban Twitter' to Stir Unrest and Undermine Government," *The Guardian*, April 3, 2014. For the "two economies," see the panel discussion held by the Institute for New Economic Thinking on October 21, 2023, on the "Growth of a Dual Economy," moderated by Thomas Ferguson, https://www .ineteconomics.org/conference-session/growth-of-dual-economy. Dagmar Herzog, in *Cold War Freud* (2017), draws on the work of German-born, Chilean-based psychologist David Becker to suggest that the clinical diagnosis of PTSD, an effect of the political terror of the Cold War—directed at Latin Americans and citizens in the decolonizing world—served as the basis for a new type of aggrieved late imperial masculinity. Extending this point to the arguments made in this book, it could be argued that the highly atomizing psychological language, which stripped trauma of its political context, contained moral qualms, preventing the kind of reckoning and social analysis that went hand-in-hand with the Spanish Conquest. Also: Alex Colston, "This War Is Causing Mass Trauma," *The Nation*, n. 10 (2023).

5. Jay Hmielowski, Michael Beam, Myiah Hutchens, "Structural Changes in Media and Attitude Polarization: Examining the Contributions of TV News Before and After the Telecommunications Act of 1996," *International Journal of Public Opinion Research*, v. 28 (2016).

6. Anais Raiss, "'Digital Kill Chains': The Dark Side of Tech in Warfare," *The Cradle*, June 6, 2024.

7. Alex Little, "The 'Adults' Are Not Back in Charge," *American Conservative*, January 31, 2024; Steve Fraser, "The End of the Future," *Jacobin*, March 2, 2023. The last sentence paraphrases Irving Howe, *Socialism and America* (1985), p. 55, on the Socialists who folded themselves into the New Deal.

8. Edwar Prasad, "Enduring Preeminence," International Monetary Fund (June 2022).

9. Greg Grandin, "The Latin American Exception," *Le Monde Diplomatique*, February 19, 2013, examines how Latin America refused to participate in the CIA's global rendition program; *Empire's Workshop* likewise deals with Latin America's ongoing dissent to many of Washington's policies.

10. Nelson Jobim: "Una buena defensa es tener la capacidad de decir que no," *El País*, October 28, 2009.

11. *Empire's Workshop*, the 2022 edition, for this post–Cold War turn, including the escalation of the War on Drugs and Plan Colombia. For sanctions: Nicholas Mulder, *The Economic Weapon: Rise of Sanctions as a Tool of War* (2002). Since the end of the Cold War, Washington has supported, in degrees of varying involvement, destabilizing or lawfare campaigns in Haiti, Venezuela, Paraguay, Honduras, Brazil, Ecuador, and Bolivia. Mark Weisbrot, "A Note About 'Our Backyard': Advice Thomas Shannon Might Give to Mike Pompeo," Center for Economic and Policy Research, July 25, 2018, describes the quiet way Obama's State Department undermined the Latin American left. Since then, more evidence has appeared that Washington took an active role in the campaign to drive Dilma Rousseff out of office and Lula into jail (which barred him from running against Bolsonaro in 2018) on trumped-up charges of corruption. For one example: Andrew Fishman, Natalia Viana, and Maryam Saleh, "'Keep it Confidential': The Secret History of U.S. Involvement in Brazil's Scandal-Wracked Car Wash," *The Intercept*, March 12, 2020.

12. "American School Shooters Inspire Teen Killers Abroad," *Washington Post*, April 12, 2023.

13. Oliver Wiseman, "The Least Woke City in America," *City Journal*, Winter 2022; Paola Ramos, *Defectors: The Rise of the Latino Far Right and What It Means for America* (2024).

14. Zack Beauchamp, "Meet the MAGA Movement's Favorite New Autocrat," April 8, 2023.

15. *The Problem of Slavery in the Age of Revolution* (1975), p. 564.

16. Pankaj Mishra, "The Shoah after Gaza," *London Review of Books*, March 21, 2024.

17. Regarding border conflicts: An important exception is Venezuela's long-standing conflict with Guyana. The British had a toehold in the area around the Essequibo River since even before the founding of Jamestown, vying with the Dutch and Spanish to establish colonies. Spain never surveyed a clear boundary line that could be used as the *uti possidetis* basis of the eastern border of Gran Colombia; still, by custom, the new country's leaders understood that border was the Essequibo River. Great Britain, though, claimed territory further to the river's west, starting a dispute that has lasted to this day. In the 1960s, Venezuela issued another formal complaint that a good part of what was called British Guiana rightly was Venezuelan territory. Then, Fidel Castro advised Caracas to drop the matter. Now, with reportedly a large deposit of oil existing under the rich jungle soil, Venezuela is once again insisting that the 1899 arbitration was a sham imposed by Great Britain and the United States and that Great Britain had, in fact, in 1824, recognized the Essequibo River as the eastern border of Gran Colombia. For the de-escalation of a potential nuclear arms race between Brazil and Argentina: Nicholas John Wheeler and Matias Spektor, "How Brazil and Argentina Defused Their Nuclear Rivalry," *The Conversation*, July 30, 2015.

18. EIB Climate Survey, "Large Majority of Latin Americans Demand Stricter Climate Policies, EIB Survey Reveals," EIB.org, https://www.eib.org/en/surveys/climate-survey/6th-climate-survey /latam. Omar Encarnación, "Latin America's Gay Rights Revolution," *Revista*, November 23, 2023.

19. Ieva Jusionyte, *Exit Wounds: How America's Guns Fuel Violence Across the Border* (2024).

20. Some poorer countries can't turn this right into a reality, but Latin America has a few excellent national health care and health insurance programs, including in Costa Rica, Colombia, Argentina, Mexico, and Chile. "Universal Health Care on the Rise in Latin America," World Bank, February 14, 2013.

ILLUSTRATION CREDITS

Part 1: No portrait of Las Casas in his lifetime is known to exist. This image is derived from a widely circulated 1788 engraving by the Spanish brothers José, Vicente, and Tomás López Enguídanos.

Part 2: Enrico Della Pietra / Alamy Stock Photo

Part 3: Glasshouse Images / Alamy Stock Photo

Part 4: IllustratedHistory / Alamy Stock Photo (*left*) / Via Wikimedia Commons, Colección de Arte del Banco Central de Venezuela (*right*)

Part 5: Courtesy of Yale University Beinecke Rare Book and Manuscript Library

Part 6: Via the Estelle Doheny Collection, courtesy of the Archive of the Archdiocese of Los Angeles, Mission Hills, California

Part 7: Everett Collection Historical / Alamy Stock Photo

Part 8: Associated Press

Endpaper map: Courtesy of Yale University Beinecke Rare Book and Manuscript Library

INDEX

Page numbers in italics indicate photos or pictures.